D0537176

For Reference

Not to be taken from this room

American River College Library
4700 College Oak Drive
Sacramento, California 95841

AMERICAN RIVER COLLEGE

3 3204 01438 8150

ABC-CLIO LITERARY COMPANION

Encyclopedia of
Literary
Epics

ABC-CLIO LITERARY COMPANION

Encyclopedia of
Literary
Epics

Guida M. Jackson

ABC-CLIO
Santa Barbara, California
Denver, Colorado
Oxford, England

Copyright © 1996 by Guida M. Jackson

All rights reserved. No part of this publication may be reproduced, stored in a retrieval system, or transmitted, in any form or by any means, electronic, mechanical, photocopying, recording, or otherwise, except for the inclusion of brief quotations in a review, without prior permission in writing from the publishers.

Library of Congress Cataloging-in-Publication Data

Jackson-Laufer, Guida M. (Guida Myrl)
    Encyclopedia of literary epics   /   Guida M. Jackson.
      p. cm.—(ABC-CLIO literary companion)
    Includes bibliographical references and index.
    1. Epic literature—Encyclopedias.   2. Epic literature—History and criticism.   I. Title.   II. Series
    PN56.E65J33   1966b   809.1'32'03—dc21   96-36995

ISBN 0-87436-773-5 (alk. paper)

02   01   00   99   98   97   96   10 9 8 7 6 5 4 3 2 1

ABC-CLIO, Inc.
130 Cremona Drive, P.O. Box 1911
Santa Barbara, California 93116-1911

This book is printed on acid-free paper ∞.
Manufactured in the United States of America.

To Daniel, Ashley, Mikie, Mattie, Gregory, Elizabeth,
and Eleanor

"No writer, however skillful, can say anything important for his
own time, or for any future time, in a style, however good, that
belongs to a past age."
—T. S. Eliot

CONTENTS

PREFACE

This book is designed as an aid to the student of world literature, who faces an increasingly bewildering variety of works as more of the world's poetry is translated into English. The *Encyclopedia of Literary Epics* is meant to be a companion to the *Encyclopedia of Traditional Epics*—as if the two terms were mutually exclusive; as if there were only two distinct categories into which all epics could clearly be divided; and as if the term *epic* itself were so cogently defined as to make rendering any arbitrary judgment unnecessary. In fact, about some—even many—works there is no consensus as to their status as "true" epics. It is not the purview of the compiler to pronounce judgments. Generally, I have followed the guideline that if any scholar has considered a work an epic, it is included, disregarding my personal opinion. An old saying goes, "One is never really impartial until she has voted against her better judgment."

Broadly, we think of traditional epics as those meant to be recited, or sung, to an audience, while literary epics are written by one person to be read by another. But what about those that straddle the marsh, like the Persian *Shāh-Nāmah* by Firdausi, who borrowed from oral tradition for the first part of his 4,000-year historical epic and composed the rest himself? Where to put it? My solution is to include it in both volumes, with altered emphasis.

A large number of poets draw on traditional or other literary epics in the composition of their own epics. If a poem is a new treatment of an existing epic listed in either volume, rather than repeat the story, I have referred the reader to the original plot—unless there is a substantial variation in the two versions. For example, many epics have been written on material from the great Sanskrit epics *Mahābhārata* and *Rāmāyaṇa*. This book would be impossibly long if their summaries were repeated.

For those epics that I consider of most interest to the contemporary reader, I have attempted to offer much more than the brief sketch that might be found in a study guide. The epic is summarized by cantos or "books" or chapters, and a sampling of the text is often quoted, so that the reader can consult the original version and find the complete passage. In some cases the text samplings also serve to give the reader a flavor of the original style and, perhaps, bring the summary to life. It must be remembered, however, that if the epic was composed in a language other than English, we must contend with what

W. P. Ker terms the "curse of Babel," which does not plague the other arts. The gist of a plot may be communicated across cultures, though some of the nuances of behavior may not be understood; but even mastery of a foreign language does not give one access to thought, sentiment, ethnic idiom, and the deep sense of national identity present in the original. Poetic melody, Ker tells us, is not the same at all as music, and each nation hears only its own tune. Nor can poetic image be conveyed as can a painter's.

This volume also includes biographical data about the epics' authors, as well as definitions of some literary movements that influenced their writing, and definitions of certain poetical forms used frequently in specific regions of the world. In the interest of brevity, biographical entries in most cases focus on the composition of epics rather than the author's entire oeuvre, and on the relation of the poet to the common fashion of the times, it being understood that, in Ker's words, "a mighty Providence subdues the mightiest minds to the service of the time being." It is hoped that the inclusion of these entries will shed additional light on the entries themselves, particularly since this is not a work of literary criticism and consequently interpretative comment is kept to a minimum.

Also included is the category of the mock-epic—for truly these satirical gems represent some of our most entertaining writing, very often offering bardic insights into the culture of the poet—and beast epics, a subcategory.

Finally, this encyclopedia contains the synopses of some romances that were either the bases of later epics or closely tied to the epic tradition. Occasionally, one of these has been labeled "epic romance," a term possibly meant to convey the scope of its influence on later works.

A good argument could be made for the inclusion of the epic drama, except that again space dictates that this collection be limited to the epic poem— and to the one or two prose works clearly considered poetic: Fenelon's *Telemaque* comes to mind. This means the exclusion even of such masterpieces as Kālidāsa's Sanskrit drama *Sakuntala* to avoid opening the floodgate. However, a brief discussion of these other works usually appears in the poets' biographical entries.

Some attempt has been made to standardize the spelling of names of characters appearing in more than one epic, unless in my judgment the difference helps the reader to keep similar epics straight. Thus, "Ranaldo" in *Orlando Innamorato* is "Rinaldo" in *Orlando Furioso*. Alternate spellings are noted in parentheses following the names.

Diacritical marks, particularly those in Indian, Slavic, Persian, Turkish, and North African entries, have been standardized to conform to those appearing in the translation used for the synopsis.

In the preparation of this volume, I received invaluable aid from Dr. Thomas Amherst Perry, Professor Emeritus at Texas A&M University–Commerce, who is responsible for some of the epic entries and subsidiaries. These have been marked with his initials (TAP) at the end of the entries.

I am deeply indebted to William Laufer for his assistance in translation and for his many thousand supportive labors large and small; to Tucker

Jackson and Mary Winzig for their help in locating materials; to Dr. Bill Norwood and Ruby Tolliver; to my editors Henry Rasof, Mary Kay Kozyra, and Martha Whitt; to Sallie Greenwood, who procured illustrations for both this and its companion volume; and to that loyal band of family, friends, colleagues, and students whose interest, support, and patience allowed for this volume's compilation.

INTRODUCTION

For centuries we have claimed the luxury of affixing certain categories to literary works with some exactitude, and nowhere has that practice left us in more of a muddle than in the genre of narrative poetry. We have conscientiously labeled certain works "epic," in that most—but not all—of the old epics follow certain conventions. There is also the "epyllion," which pops up later under another name or two.

Along came some oral epics written down during the Middle Ages, and we had to decide whether these vernacular poems were to be considered oral or written. The same was true of another group of narrative poems called "metrical romances," some of which entertained many of the epic conventions. From that same period were religious poems written in vernacular style that became known as "religious epics" and other poems, not exactly religious, that we labeled "didactic epics."

At the end of the Middle Ages, a new kind of narrative poem appeared in England that was quickly labeled neither epic nor romance, but allegory. But then we conceded that Dante's allegory was epic and that even a couple of the *Canterbury Tales* bordered on the epic tradition. While not yet awash in overlap, we were at least wading.

We reached firmer ground during the Renaissance, when the great epic tradition flowered in the works of Boiardo and Ariosto. Then along came Tasso, who combined the heroic epic with the romance. The power and harmony of the Italian measures and modes inspired poets in many countries—although Germany and France were not among them. Before long, the Italian model had spread to the Spain of Garcilaso, the Portugal of Camões and from Ercilla y Zuñiga, even to the New World.

Meanwhile, poets in Dubrovnik (Ragusa), warmed by the Italian fire, produced a prodigious number of epics. However, some had to be given hyphenated names, such as the philosophical-allegorical epic of Mavro Vetranić. Ivan Gundulić modified Tasso's model, combining Romantic with classical heroic by writing his epic on contemporary Balkan history.

But Slavic poets would not be content with those small deviations. The large epic works often offered mixtures of various genres. Pushkin produced a work called a "Byronic epic," or "verse novel." In fact, the most significant verse epics of Slavic Romantic literature belonged to this "Byronic epic," also known as "free-epic" or "humoristic epic," genre. Lermontov's and Ševčenko's narrative poems are examples of "tragic epics," in which the ballad endings of Erben or Michiewicz (whose *Pan Tadeusz* has been labeled both "humoristic epic" and "antiprophetic epic") become laments for the tragic demise of the heroes. "Free form" is associated with the Romantic conception of the poet as creator bound by no laws or rules, a style eminently attractive to the Slavic temperament of the time.

Despite this Slavic revolt from convention, only minor adjustments had to be made in terminology. The epic rocked along in its new altered, hyphenated state until the time of Whitman, who shocked the world of letters so thoroughly that it was a while before many noticed that he had also pointed the way to a new bardic model. Then Pound perplexed us by reminding the world that the epic is a poem including history, proclaiming at the same time his *Cantos* as an epic.

And therein we were presented a conundrum. Until recent times, we have not often, in our thoughtful enumeration of characteristics of the epic, noted "accessibility" as a requirement, although Whitman said that a great poem (which surely must include the epic) is for "all degrees and complexions and all departments and sects."

Bob Perelman, writing in *The Trouble with Genius*, does not regard accessibility as vital: "Works of literature are presumed to have social value, but they must be inaccessible to some degree or there would be no need to study them and no need for the structures of authority that study produces." But here we must wonder what is the purpose of writing but for communication? The duty of genius is to make itself understood, something Pound admitted he had failed to do. For that matter, Whitman, who actively tried to find some ground upon which polemic bard and unconscious reader could meet, was not wholly successful, but at least he tried rather manfully.

In the matter of communication in the western hemisphere, while *Cantos* gave way to the "American modern epic" or the so-called "personal epic," such as *Paterson,* the *Maximus Poems,* and *"A,"* the Nobel Prizes were picked up south of our borders: Neruda gave us the personal lyrical epic *Canto general,* and in the Caribbean, *Omeros,* a pearl of great price, reached back to our worship of classical Greek to level an ironic finger at man's inhumanity to man rooted in that ancient past. Walcott also brought to the epic an economy of dialogue Pound's symbolists could have envied, substituting telling snippets for the long sonorous passages characterizing past epics. In a letter to his mother, Pound once defined the epic as "the speech of a nation through the mouth of one man." Walcott's new Helen speaks volumes about culture, tradition, and the human condition when she says merely, "I pregnant,/but I don't know for who."

Walcott indicts more than the rapers of his island in Plunkett's musings: "We helped ourselves/to these green islands like olives from a saucer,/munched on the pith, then spat their sucked stones on a plate. . . ." He and Nigerian poet Chi Chi Layor may fall into the category that Northrop Frye labels the "contrast epic" poet: one who excoriates—or views with ironic contempt—the sins of society "from an ethical perspective already recognized by that society as authoritative." In Africa, while men recorded the rich traditional matter of Liyongo, Shaka, Mwindo, Sundiata, and the like, feminist poet Layor expanded the epic's horizons by producing the first epic of the old kingdom of Benin, in which women take the primary roles in many of the episodes. This is the first feminist literary epic on the continent, although a rich oral tradition exists about female rulers, particularly Queen Nzinga.

We recall that Elizabeth Barrett Browning and Owen Meredith composed works with feminist overtones, labeled "verse novels," and in this category one is not likely to forget Vikram Seth's brilliant California work *The Golden Gate*, which could as easily be termed a "free-epic" if one is not rigid about denying the organic nature of the epic.

Just as *Song of Roland* introduced a different kind of hero totally unlike Achilles or Odysseus, *"A"* and *Omeros* also introduced personal heroes. Blake said that great ideal figures are not abstract, but no longer does the epic figure have to be either great or ideal. As the nature—sometimes even the gender—of the hero has evolved, so have the conventions of this literature. In Nazim Hikmet's contemporary Turkish epic, the epic hero has many faces—farmer, worker, doctor, poet. The multifaceted epic hero corresponds to the varieties of style, techniques, genres, and points of view that render his *Human Landscapes* a cultural whole.

Calling the epic the "great matrix of all poetic genres," Suzanne Langer names a few of the elements in this contemporary work: "There are lyric verses, romantic quests, descriptions of ordinary life, self-contained incidents that read like a ballad." In our complex world, narrative structure, like metrical prosody, has become dispensable and may not even be possible. Poets can no more escape the influence of their times than they can deny that they shape that influence. But poets have, since the time the first singer stepped into the circle of campfire, a supreme duty. Matthew Arnold expressed it well enough: ". . . their business is not to praise their age, but to afford to the men who live in it the highest pleasure which they are capable of feeling."

Now it appears to boil down to scope. The height, depth, and breadth of a work, and the lengths to which it reaches into the common human psyche, may be the new ethos by which we judge whether a work is an epic—if what it is called matters at all anymore.

ABC-CLIO LITERARY COMPANION

Encyclopedia of
Literary
Epics

 "A"

American epic poem-cycle (1974) by Louis Zukofsky (1904–1978). The poet called the epic, begun in 1928 and completed in 1974, the "poem of a life." Written in 24 parts, or movements, and containing 147 poems, it follows the poet from his boyhood in the teeming Jewish quarter of New York's Lower East Side to his college days at Columbia University, through the Depression era, the World War II years, and on into the space age, ending only four years before the poet's death.

Throughout the poem, the poet's personal experiences come to light. Movements 1–7 are concerned with the poet's breaking away from the family unit and traditions of the old culture. Movements 8–12 make connections between past and present, particularly with regard to relating poem and poet to history and the literary tradition. Movements 13–20 pertain to both life's calamities and its victories, particularly the withdrawal of the poet's son Paul from home and the poet's lack of recognition for his work. Movements 21–24 are an overview of the poet's life in the context of human history, in which the poet catalogs those things he loves best and values most. (Zukofsky 1978)

See also Zukofsky, Louis.

 ABBO

French scholar and monk of St. Germaine, Abbo is the author of *The Siege of Paris* (ca. 897). Written in Latin, the poem is a scholarly imitation of Roman epics. It describes the Norman attack on Paris and contains moral reflections on the state of France. (Brogan 1996; Preminger 1974)

 ABSALOM AND ACHITOPHEL

English Baroque mock-epic (1681) by John Dryden (1631–1700). Part I appeared in 1681; part II, written mostly by Nahum Tate, appeared a year later, with identifiable persons as heroes. The poem is both satire and allegory on the unsuccessful attempt by the earl of Shaftesbury to place the duke of Monmouth, illegitimate son of Charles II and Lucy Walter, on the throne as Charles II's successor.

The poet was inspired by Alessandro Tassoni's *Rape of the Bucket* (*q.v.*) and Boileau's *Lectern* (*q.v.*), but the poet used an episode from Hebrew history for his plot: the story of King David (Charles II), his favorite son Absalom (Monmouth), and the duplicitous Achitophel (Shaftesbury), who persuades Absalom to revolt against his father. Very early in the poem the poet has the audacity "upon the desire of King Charles the Second" to describe the king's exploits: "His vigorous warmth did variously impart/To wives and slaves; and, wide as his command,/Scattered his Maker's image though the land." (1:8–10)

The poem is written from the point of view of the king and his Tory ministers, depicting the Whig leaders as simpletons. The poem, whose character Absalom is a political criminal, uses the "stopped couplet": "From hence began that Plot, the nation's curse,/Bad in itself, but represented worse." (1:108–109)

Part II, written primarily by Nahum Tate, contains one long section by Dryden. With scathing brilliance Dryden aims barbs at "Doeg and Og" (dramatists Elkanah Settle and Thomas Shadwell). Dryden calls Og "a monstrous mass of foul corrupted matter,/As all the devils had spewed to make the batter." (2:464–465) (Grebanier 1949; Kingsley 1958)

 # ACHILLEID

Post-Augustan Latin epic, unfinished, by Publius Papinius Statius (ca. 45–ca. 96). The poem was to be a scholarly reworking of Greek legend on the life of Achilles, including his early education, and his death in the Trojan War. The poet planned 12 books, but because of the poet's death, the epic ends abruptly at the point where Odysseus takes him off to Troy (Book II:167). (Statius 1928)

 # ACHILLEIS

Uncompleted German epic poem (1799) by Johann Wolfgang Goethe (1749–1832). Written in hexameters, the poem was projected to have eight cantos, but only the first, containing 651 lines, was completed. The poem's intent was to fill the temporal gap between the *Iliad* and the *Odyssey*; its subject is the death of Achilles. The canto opens outside Troy as the flames of Hector's funeral pyre die down. (Garland and Garland 1986)

 # ADAM HOMO

Danish epic (1841–1848) by Frederik Paludan-Müller (1809–1876). The three-volume epic, written after the manner and form of Byron, portrays a gifted but opportunistic protagonist who strives for and achieves his goals of worldly success, but in the process abandons the woman who loves him and loses his soul. The woman, a devout Christian, continues to love him even after his death, and her love brings about his ultimate salvation. The epic is a biting satirical portrayal of Danish culture of the mid-nineteenth century. (Brogan 1996)

ADENET LE ROI
(Adenet of Brabant)

Flemish poet and musician, author of the chanson de geste *Berthe aux grands pieds* (*Berta aus grandes pies*, Bertha of the big feet, ca. 1270), referring to Berta of Hungary (d. 782), mother of Charlemagne. Adenet was born about 1240 in Brabant and received his education in the court of Henry III, duke of Brabant at Louvain. After Henry's death in 1261, Adenet's future was in question until 1268 or 1269, when he secured a position in the service of Guy de Dampierre, count of Flanders, as a *ménestrel*, or paid entertainer. In 1270–1271 he accompanied the count to Naples on the Tunisian campaign as a poet and musician. He was made principal *ménestrel*, hence his title *Roi* ("king"). He called himself Roi Adam or Li Rois Adenet. His poems contain many references to parts of their return through Sicily and Italy.

He was also the author of *Les Enfances Ogier* (The youth exploits of Ogier the Dane), *Beuve de Comarchis*, and a fantastic romance, *Cléomadès*, or *Le Cheval de Fust*, written in octosyllabic couplets for Queen Marie de Brabant, daughter of his old patron and wife of Philip III of France.

He died about 1300 in Brabant. (Harvey and Heseltine 1959)

ADHYĀTMA RĀMĀYAṆAM

Late medieval Indian Malayalam epic (ca. 16th c.) by Tuñchattu Ezhuttacchan (ca. late 15th–early 16th c.), the most outstanding Malayalam poet. Based on the old Sanskrit epic *Rāmāyaṇa*, the poem differs from it in making the hero Rāmā both the ideal man and the ideal god. A synopsis of the *Rāmāyaṇa* can be found in the *Encyclopedia of Traditional Epics*. (Dudley and Lang 1969)

ĀDIPURĀṆA
(First or original scriptures)

South Indian religious epic (10th c.) by Jaina poet Pampa (fl. 940). Written in the Kannada language rather than Sanskrit, the epic was the greatest work of Pampa, who is called *ādikavi*, or first poet of the Kannada language. The poem was written to espouse Jaina doctrine. It relates the past lives of the Jaina hero-saint Purudēva, as well as his life on earth, including his birth, deeds, marriage, and death. It also tells the stories of the lives of two of his 100 sons: Bharata, the first universal ruler (ca. 100–200) and Bāhubali (Strong of Arm). (Dudley and Lang 1969; Embree 1988)

 # *ADONE*

Italian epic (1623) by Giambattista Marino (1569–1625), published in Paris in 1623. A lascivious work of 20 years' labor, the poem contains 45,000 lines in ottava rima arranged in 20 cantos. It tells, with many digressions, the love story of Venus and Adonis. Some passages are brilliant, with clever plays on words, but others are filled with exaggerated rhetoric about far-fetched situations, illustrating why the *marinismo* school of poetry became a pejorative term. (Preminger 1974)

 # *THE ADVENTURES OF KHUN CHANG AND KHUN PHEN*
(Also *Khun Chang, Khun Phaen,* or *Pen*)

Popular Thai epic poem (18th c.) by several authors, including Sunthọn Phu (ca. 1786–ca. 1855), partially transcribed by Phuttaleutla, Rama II (r. 1809–1824). Its 20,000 lines are written in a lively and amusing style, relating the story of two noblemen attached to the royal court who are rivals for the hand of the beautiful heroine, Phim. Scholars relate the epic to historical events occurring in the sixteenth century. (Dudley and Lang 1969)

 # *THE ADVENTURES OF TRISTRAM*
(Variously spelled Tristan, Tristam, and Tristrant)

Medieval Czech epic, an adaptation of the Middle High German epic by Gottfried von Strassburg. (Dvornik 1962)
See also Gottfried von Strassburg; *Tristan; Tristrant und Isalde.*

 # AENEAS

Hero of Vergil's *Aeneid*, he is the son of the goddess Venus and Anchises, husband of Creüsa, father of Ascanius, and leader of the Trojan quest for their

Italian homeland. Aeneas is a Trojan prince allied to, but not descended from, Priam. With his bride Lavinia, he is the legendary founder of Lavinium, forerunner of Alba Longa and Rome. (Vergil/Dickinson trans. 1961)

 # *AENEID*

Roman epic (30 or 29–19 B.C.) by Vergil (Publius Vergilius Maro, 70–19 B.C.), who began the great Roman national epic a year or two after the sea battle of Actium at the request of Octavius, the new master of the Roman world. Vergil died in 19 B.C. without completing this poem celebrating the glory and valor of the Roman race, but it was published two years after his death by decree of Octavius, now Emperor Augustus. The poem, consisting of 12 books, is almost complete, with only some 60 lines unfinished and certain passages in draft form only. Vergil combined historical figures with ancient Greek legends that Rome was founded by fleeing Trojans and that the family of Augustus was founded by Aeneas. The *Aeneid* is the first of the great literary epics of Europe, the greatest book of the Western world for 2,000 years, as a matter of fact, and Vergil was the greatest poet Rome ever produced.

In Book I, after announcing his theme and invoking the Muse, the poet relates how Aeneas, his family, and his men flee Troy after their defeat by the Greeks. Juno is determined to prevent their arrival in Latium. Instead, after a great storm, they land in Africa. Jupiter foretells the course of Roman history to Venus, who guides Aeneas to Carthage, where Dido welcomes him: "For I have had ill fortune and sufferings/Like yours before I found this place to rest in. I am no stranger to sorrows and they have taught me/To succor those in misery and distress."

In Book II, Aeneas tells Dido and her court the story of the sack of Troy after protesting, "Great Queen, the tale you bid me tell again/Recalls a throe too terrible for speech." He describes the trick of the wooden horse, the destruction of the city, and his escape with the survivors, including his father, Anchises, and his son Ascanius.

In Book III, Aeneas continues his tale, recounting the seven years of wandering when "We were driven on by the auguries from the gods/To scour the empty regions of the world/For a home of exile. . . ." He tells of landing in Thrace and building a city. He relates the advice by the Oracle of Apollo at Delos to continue westward. They stop for a while in Crete, then go on to Strophades, Epirus, Italy, and Sicily, where Anchises dies. Aeneas calls his father "my prop and stay who had lightened my every care."

In Book IV the queen, manipulated by Venus, falls in love with Aeneas: "Her chastity melted/In a furnace of desire. . . ." Aeneas returns her feelings, and their love is consummated in a cave while "The skies shudder;/The vault of heaven feels that mortal surge." The love-struck couple neglects all duty until Jupiter orders Aeneas to sail on. When Dido discovers he is leaving, she cries, "You traitor! Did you hope to mask such treachery/And silently slink

Roman poet Vergil's *Aeneid*, begun in about 30 B.C. to celebrate the glory of Roman history, mixes Greek myth with legends about Rome's founding. A fifteenth-century French illustration shows Dido, queen of Carthage, committing suicide as Aeneas, hero of the epic *Aeneid,* sails away, eventually to found Rome.

from my land?" When he leaves, she places a curse on him: "Let him die before his time and lie/Unburied upon the field!" She turns to her people and admonishes them to "For ever persecute them . . ./Let them fight each other in every generation!" She makes a pyre of their marriage bed and commits suicide.

Book V describes Aeneas's voyage to Italy by way of Sicily, where Aeneas visits Anchises's tomb and attends funeral games in his father's honor. Tired of wandering, the Trojan women burn the ships, but Jupiter sends a rainstorm to save them. Aeneas leaves behind a colony of Trojans and sails on toward Italy, but on the way he loses his pilot, Palinurus.

In Book VI, they stop at Cumae, where the Cumae Sibyl guides Aeneas down to the Underworld to hear from Anchises the story of the future of Rome. His father tells him that the special skill of the Romans will be "to impose upon the nations/The code of peace; to be clement to the conquered,/But utterly to crush the intransigent!"

In Book VII the Trojan fleet reaches the Tiber. Aeneas sends a mission to King Latinus, who offers the hand of his daughter Lavinia in marriage. Rutulian chief Turnus, whom Lavinia has spurned, and his ally, the famous warrior maid Camilla, prepare to lead an attack against the Trojans, urged on by Juno and the Fury Allecto. Camilla is described as "a maiden ready to take/The hard knocks of a battle, and to outpace/The winds in speed of foot."

Book VIII recounts the war preparations. Divinely inspired, Aeneas sails up the river to Pallanteum, the future site of Rome, to seek an alliance with Greek king Evander. He spends his first night ashore in Evander's humble abode, on the very spot where Emperor Augustus's palace will stand. Evander sends his son Pallas with an army to assist Aeneas, and advises him to seek Etruscan aid. Vulcan forges for him a magic shield decorated with scenes of the future of Rome. In the center is a picture of the battle of Actium.

In Book IX, meanwhile, Turnus attacks the Trojans' ship and camp. Two of Aeneas's men, Nisus and Euryalus, attempt to spy on the Rutuli camp, but they are captured and slain.

War breaks out in Book X, in which Aeneas succeeds in breaking the Latin siege, but Pallus is killed by Turnus. In turn Aeneas kills several Latin chiefs, including Mezentius and his son Lausas.

In Book XI a 12-day truce is called for burial of the dead, then fighting resumes. Turnus's men suffer severe setbacks and panic in disarray.

In Book XII a confrontation between Aeneas and Turnus results in Turnus's death: "And his soul flew, resentful of its fate,/Down to the Shades, with many a sigh and groan." Aeneas marries Lavinia and they found Lavinium, forefunner of Alba Longa and Rome. (Vergil/Dickinson 1961)

 # *AFRICA*

Unfinished Latin epic (ca. 1338) by Italian humanist, scholar, and poet laureate Francesco Petrarca (1304–1374). Written in hexameters, the poem was intended to cover the Second Punic War, but even after many revisions it was never completed. The poet began in 1338 or 1339 with a vision of producing an epic on a par with Vergil's *Aeneid*. He worked on it for the next three decades, but was not satisfied with it. It was published posthumously in 1396, more than two decades after his death. The epic's hero is Scipio Africanus (236–184/183 B.C.), notable for liberating Italy by defeating the Carthaginian leader Hannibal at the Battle of Zaza (202 B.C.), bringing the Second Punic War to an end. The story revolves around the romance of Massinissa and Sophonisba. (Durant 1953)

ALAIN DE LILLE
(Alan of Lille, also Alanus de Insailis)

French theologian and poet, author of the Latin epic *Anticlaudianus* (1182–1183) and the allegory *De Planctu naturae* (ca. 1170). He was born about 1128, probably in Lille, France. In addition to his considerable theological writings, his poetry was well received. His earlier work, *De Planctu naturae,* is a clever philosophical satire in the tradition of Boethius's *Consolation of Philosophy* (ca. 524) and Martianus Capella's *De nuptus Mercurii et Philologiae* (on the marriage of Mercury and Philologia (ca. 410–439) on vices. It is written in the form of a dialogue with Nature on sodomy. Alain's *Anticlaudianus,* composed a decade later, concerns the nature and powers of man and the soul's growth to perfection through nature, religion, philosophy, and the practice of the virtues and the arts. He died at Cîteaux in 1202. (Highet 1976; Howatson and Chilvers 1993)

ALAMANNI, LUIGI

Italian poet, author of the epic *Avarchide,* an imitation of Homer's *Iliad; Girone il cortese* (Girone the courteous), a poem focused on the single character Girone; and *La Coltivazione,* a poem about agriculture on the order of Vergil's *Georgics.* Alamanni was born in 1495, and for a while he was a part of the tradition of the great Platonic Academy at Florence, founded for classical scholarship. However, to escape the academy mold he moved to France, where he wrote *La Coltivazione,* which was considered almost as fine as its model. He was among the first Italians to employ versi sciolti (blank verse), and his *Avarchide* was considered a great epic feat in his day. He died in 1556. (Durant 1953)

ALAUDDIN
(Also Allah-ud-din)

The reign of Alauddin Khalji, Muslim sultan of Delhi (1296–1316), was marked by an ambitious conquest or authority over the whole of the Indian peninsula. Even this did not satisfy the ambitious sultan, who tried to emulate Alexander the Great as conqueror of the world and even considered himself competent to

Alexander the Great rides Bucephalus into battle against Persians in a portion of a dramatic mosaic from Pompeii, Italy. Alexander's reign lasted only seven years, but his conquests encompassed lands from the Mediterranean to the Indus and provided grist for many literary epics.

establish a new religion and creed. Although persuaded against his project, he continued to describe himself on coins as the second Alexander.

Among his operations was the conquest of Mewar, land of the Rajputs. Tradition has it that this venture was inspired by reports of a beautiful queen, but the true reason was his desire to subdue a strong principality near Delhi, and he proceeded to lay a long siege on its principal city, Chitor, which fell on 26 August 1303. History records that its fall was followed by the women performing the rite of *Jauhar* (self-immolation) and the slaughter of the men, 30,000 in one day. (Arshad 1967; Srivastava 1964).

 # ALEXANDER

Middle High German epic poem fragment (between 1220–1250) by Rudolf von Ems (13th c.). The extant fragment suggests that the poem was to have been of great length, because the fragment contains more than 21,000 lines. The poem relates the deeds of Alexander the Great, whom the poet portrays in idealistic terms as brave, just, and humane. The action reaches to Alexander's expedition to the Oxus, which was to be the halfway point in the unfinished work. As in another of Rudolf's works, *Willehalm von Orlens,* the poem contains a review of his contemporaries' works. (Garland and Garland 1986)

See also Rudolf von Ems; *Willehalm von Orlens.*

 # *ALEXANDREIS*

The name of several epics based on the life of Alexander the Great of Macedon, among them:

(1) A Latin epic (ca. 1182) by Gautier de Châtillon (Gaultherus de Castellion), who based his epic on two histories by Curtius and Jostinius.

(2) A German epic (ca. 1287) by Ulrich von Etzenbach (fl. 13th c.), based on the poem by Gautier de Châtillon. The poem consists of 30,000 lines in 11 books, the last of which is thought to have been written by someone else. The poet began the work about 1271 as a glorification of King Ottokar (r. 1253–1278), but the poem was not completed until about 1287, long after Ottokar's death in 1278. This historical epic portrays Alexander of Macedon in idealistic terms. It includes elaborate depictions of courtly and military life, as well as a number of digressions into Greek legend.

(3) A Czech epic (ca. 13th or 14th c.), the earliest secular work in Czech, by an unknown author who based his model on the work of Gautier de Châtillon. The epic is thought to have originally contained over 8,000 verses, of which only half are extant. Although the poet follows the Gautier version, he brings in his own contemporary Czech concerns. For example, Přemysl Otakar II (r. 1253–1278) is lauded for offering aid to the duke of Cracow and other Polish dukes in driving out the Mongol infidels. The poet expresses the wish for a Czech leader with the strength of Alexander who would bring into the Christian fold such people as the Prussians (he takes some biting satirical jibes at the Germans), Russians, Lithuanians, and Tatars. The poet, a devout Christian and Czech patriot, evinces a wide knowledge and wisdom. (Raby 1934)

See also Ulrich von Etzenbach.

 # ALEXANDRINE

A line of iambic hexameter verse (six iambs totaling 12 syllables) with a caesura after the sixth. There is no enjambment (runover line in either sentence structure or thought). A French alexandrine often adds a thirteenth syllable and is usually phrased with four stresses. The name derives from a twelfth-century chanson de geste about Alexander the Great, *Le Roman d'Alexandre,* which uses this form. The Spenserian stanza ends with an alexandrine. (Deutsch 1974)

AL-ḤADĪQAT AL-ḤAQĪAH WA SHARĪ'AT AṬ-ṬARĪQAH
(The garden of truth and the law of practice)

Persian Islamic mystical epic (ca. 12th c.) by Sanā'ī (d. ca. 1131). The poem, consisting of 10,000 couplets in ten graduated sections or cantos, is dedicated to Ghaznavid sultan Bahrām Shāh (r. 1117–1157). It is the Ṣūfī poet's philosophical creed on God, life, mysticism, ethics, and reason, interspersed with illustrative anecdotes. The poem is in effect a verse adaptation of the Ṣūfī prose treatises of Qoahairi and Hojwiri. (Attar/Arberry trans. 1966)

See also Sanā'ī.

AL-INKISHAFI

Swahili *utendi* (epic, ca. 1800) by Sayyid (also Seyyid) Abdalla bin Ali Nasir (1725–1820). He wrote the poem with black ink made by grinding burned rice into a powder that was mixed with water, gum, lemon juice, and lamp black. "Al-Inkishafi" means "self-examination," but the epic title has been translated as "catechism of a soul" and "the soul's awakening." It is an extremely popular epic that describes the passing of the Arab citadels (city-states) along the East African coast, and additionally offers a soliloquy on the inevitability of death. In this context the poem is an attempt to interpret Swahili society through poetry. The *utendi* verse form consists of four short hemistichs (four-line stanzas, each line having eight syllables), of which the first three rhyme together and the fourth carries a rhyme repeated as the terminal rhyme of every stanza. (Dudley and Lang 1969)

See also Sayyid Abdallah bin Ali bin Nasir.

ALLEGORY

A technique of narrative in which an extended metaphor is used to speak of one subject in terms of another, in which the fictional events and characters of a text actually refer to literal events or actual people. Examples of allegory are *Piers Plowman, Divine Comedy, Faerie Queene, Jerusalem Delivered,* and beast epics. (Hornstein 1973)

ALMEIDA GARRETT, JOÃO BATISTA DA SILVA LEITÃO DE

Portuguese dramatist poet, author of the epics *Dona Branca* and *Camões* (1825), concerning the epic poet of that name. Almeida Garrett has been called the father of Portuguese Romanticism. He was born in 1799 in Porto, Portugal, and educated in law at the University of Coimbra. By the time of his graduation in 1820 he had already distinguished himself as a playwright, and would in time become Portugal's foremost dramatist. However, his liberal political views forced him into exile in England in 1823. He became a disciple of the school of neoclassicist Francisco Manuel do Nascimento (called Filinto Elísio), considered the greatest poet of his time, who died in exile in Paris in 1819.

Almeida Garrett studied French and English literature and, from England, introduced the Romantic movement to Portugal with two patriotic epics, *Camões* and *Dona Branca*. In 1832 he was able to return to Portugal, where he became active in political affairs. He was sent to Brussels for one year as consul general (1834), and in 1837 he entered Parliament. When the government assigned him the task of creating a national theater, he rose to the occasion by writing a series of plays: *Un Auto de Cil Vicente* (1838), *O Alfageme de Santarém* (1841), and *Frei Luís de Sousa* (1843). The latter is considered one of the finest Portuguese plays of the nineteenth century.

In 1851 he was made Visconde de Almeida Garrett. The following year he served briefly as minister of foreign affairs. A love affair late in life inspired his love poems, collected as *Fôlhas Caídas* (Fallen leaves) and published in 1853, shortly before his death a year later in Lisbon. His position in Portuguese literature has been compared to that of Goethe in German literature. (Preminger 1974)

See also Camões, Luís Vaz de.

 # ÁLVAREZ DE TOLEDO, HERNANDO

Spanish poet, author of *Purén indómito* (Purén untamed). He was born in Spain in 1550. His epic has a New World theme, one of many sequels inspired by Alonso de Ercilla y Zuñiga's great epic *La Araucana* (1569, 1578, 1589). (Anderson-Imbert 1969)

 # AMADIGI

Italian epic (1560) by Bernardo Tasso (1493–1569). Of 100 cantos of "heavy seriousness," the epic is a versified version of the Spanish chivalrous romance *Amadís de Gaula* (1508) by Garci-Ordóñez Montalvo. The poem contains several subplots, but the main plot concerns Amadís, the illegitimate son of King Perión, who is abandoned in the sea by his mother Elisena, princess of Brittany, and rescued by the knight Gandalés. He is reared in the court, where at the age of 12 he meets and falls in love with Oriana, daughter of English king Lisuarte. Amadís performs a number of fantastic feats, eventually winning his true love. The poem was labeled "tedious" by one critic. It lacked the humor of

Ariosto's work and was given a cool reception by the public. However, the poet used a short—usually five-line—stanza employed extensively by later poets. Torquato Tasso, his son, reworked one unfinished episode that Bernardo had been amplifying, and published it as *Floridante* (1857). (Durant 1953; Siepmann 1987)

See also Tasso, Bernardo.

 # AMUKTAMĀLYADĀ

Indian epic poem (1520) written in Telegu by Vijayanagar king Kṛṣṇa Deva Rāya (r. 1509–1529). He wrote the poem possibly as advice for his young son, in whose favor he abdicated the throne in 1524.

The poem covers various duties of the ruler, offering the reader a vivid picture of courtly life and customs. It refers to the potential wealth that overseas trade provided the empire. For example, in Book IV the poet says, "A king should improve the harbors of his country and so encourage its commerce that horses, elephants, precious gems, sandalwood, pearls, and other articles are freely imported into his country." (IV:245)

The poet-king was also a great diplomat, but he did not limit his diplomacy to matters of statecraft. He extended his interest to every level of commerce, discussing the treatment of common seamen as well as their captains: "He [the king] should arrange that the foreign sailors who land in his country on account of storm, illness, and exhaustion are looked after in a matter suitable to their nationality. . . ." (IV:248)

In Book V the poet reveals the secret of his trading success: "Make the merchants of distant foreign countries who import elephants and good horses be attached to yourself by providing them with daily audience and presents and by allowing decent profits. Then those articles will never go to your enemies. . . ." (V:258)

Unfortunately, the king's young son did not live to profit from the poetic advice that took his father so long to compose: The son was poisoned soon after he assumed the title of king, and Rāya had to resume the throne about 1525. (Thapar 1966)

 # ANGELICA

In *Orlando Innamorato* and *Orlando Furioso*, Angelica is the daughter of Galafrone, the king of Cathay, sent by the king to France to so stupefy Charlemagne's paladins that they would be easily defeated. As the love interest of both Orlando and Rinaldo, as well as many other knights both Christian and Saracen, Angelica is the pivotal character around whom much of the action revolves.

ANTOKOLSKY, PAVEL

Russian poet, author of several epic poems, among them *The Commune of 1871* (1933), *Eighteen-Hundred and Forty Eight (1948)*, and *The Strength of Vietnam* (1960). He was born in 1896 in St. Petersburg, the son of a lawyer. He first became an actor, then a director in Evgeny Vakhtangov's experimental theater.

His first collection was called *The West* (1926), reflecting his affinity for Europe. During World War II he wrote patriotic lyrics. His best work is *The Son* (1943), a poem lamenting the death of his own son. After the war he wrote more epics, including *Eighteen-Hundred and Forty Eight*, written 100 years after the fact, with a setting in Europe. Later, during the Vietnam crisis, he wrote an epic in praise of the common people, *The Strength of Vietnam*. The latter is an experimental work combining verse, prose, social commentary, and descriptions. Antokolsky died in 1978. (Bristol 1991)

 # *ANUSH*

Armenian short epic poem (late 19th c.) by Hovhannes Thumanian (1869–1922/1923), called "the poet of all Armenians" and also "Armenia's best epic poet." The epic, considered the poet's masterpiece, is full of songs that the Armenian people have taken as traditional, and is full of nationalistic themes; it was adapted as an opera. (Brogan 1996; Preminger 1974)

 # APOLLO
(Also known as Phoebus, or the Far-Darter)

Greek god of the sun. Angered when Agamemnon, a Greek in the Trojan War, kidnapped the daughter of one of his priests, Apollo sided with the Trojans. He later became the protector of the Trojan Aeneas, son of his sister Aphrodite.

 # APOLLONIUS RHODIUS
(Apollonius of Rhodes)

Greek poet, author of *Argonautica*. He was born in Egypt near the beginning of the third century B.C. Two conflicting accounts of his life exist. He was a pupil and friend of Callimachus, one of the most influential poets and scholars of the Hellenistic Age and an official in the library at the museum in Alexandria maintained by the Ptolemies about 260 B.C. Apollonius became the librarian, thus outranking Callimachus, who was making the first catalog. A dispute arose between the two. It was once believed that the dispute concerned the differences in their views of epic poetry: Callimachus contended that it was obsolete in the Hellenistic world, while Apollonius attempted to prove him wrong by writing the *Argonautica*. However, scholars now think the dispute had to do with a problem at the library. Apollonius was forced to resign his position, and he retired to the island of Rhodes. In composing his epic, he imitated the verse forms of Homer. At Rome, his work influenced Vergil, who based the story of Dido in the *Aeneid* (Book IV) on Apollonius's description of Medea's love in *Argonautica* (Book III). (Clauss 1993; Dudley and Lang 1969; Hornstein 1973)

See also Argonautica.

 # ARANY, JÁNOS

Hungarian epic and lyric poet, author of the *Toldi* trilogy (1847–1879), *Bolond Istók* (Steven the fool, 1850), and *Buda halála* (Death of King Buda, 1864). Arany was born in 1817 in Nagyszalonta, Hungary, into a poor farming family. He managed to study in Debrecen, but soon left to join a band of strolling players. At length he returned home and worked as a teaching assistant until he could become a notary. He married an orphan, Judith Ercsey, and the couple had two children.

In 1847 he published the epic *Toldi* to immediate popular acclaim. But political unrest drew him into participating in the Hungarian revolution in 1848 and editing a government-sponsored newspaper. That same year the first version of his second *Toldi* epic appeared: *Toldi szerelme* (Toldi's love), again to popular acclaim. After the revolution was quelled, Arany taught school and wrote the fragmentary epic *Bolond Istók* (1850), a humorous if acerbic work of introspection. The third *Toldi* book appeared in 1854: *Toldi estéje* (Toldi's evening). In 1858 he was named to the Hungarian Academy. He moved to Pest, where he edited a literary journal and began work on a Hungarian epic. He envisioned the work as a trilogy, but he completed only the first volume, *Buda halála* (The death of King Buda), published in 1864.

In 1870 he was elected secretary-general of the academy. He resigned nine years later due to poor health. At his death in 1882 in Budapest, he was considered the greatest Hungarian epic poet. (Encyclopedia Britannica 1983)

 # ARAUCANA, LA

Spanish-American epic poem (1569–1590) by Alonso de Ercilla y Zuñiga (1533–1594). The poem, consisting of 21,072 lines, is the first epic poem about the New World. Its theme is the stubborn and heroic resistance of the Araucanian Indians against Spanish rule in Chile, and particularly the courage and nobility of their leaders Lautaro (d. 1557) and Caupolicán (d. 1558). Originally having 37 cantos, the poem appeared in three separate installments in 1569, 1578,

Janos Arany, Hungarian epic and lyric poet, 1817–1882

and 1589. In 1590, the next printing, two more cantos were added for a total of 39. It was the first epic on the founding of a nation written while the events were still in progress.

According to tradition, Lautauro, a northern Chilean Indian, was required in boyhood to work as a stable groom for Spanish conquistador Pedro de Valdivia. When Valdivia invaded Araucanian territory to the south (1550), Lautauro escaped and joined the Araucana tribe. Along with Araucanian chief Caupolicán, Lautauro led the tribe in their battles of resistance. In 1553, during a battle at Tucapel, the Indians captured and executed Valdivia, although Caupolicán attempted to prevent his torture. In 1557, Lautauro was defeated at the Battle of Peteroa, captured, and executed by Francisco de Villagrán. Caupolicán continued the battle, but was badly beaten in three encounters with Don García Hurtado de Mendoza, and lost more than 6,000 warriors in one encounter. He fled to the mountains near Cañete, where he was apprehended by Captain Alonso de Reinoso and brutally murdered in 1558. The poet, a Spanish soldier, apparently witnessed some of these episodes himself and calls Caupolicán a "noble savage."

The poet devotes a great deal of space to relating his own experiences. His is the first epic in which the author appears as an actor in the action. Partly poetry, partly doggerel, the epic has no individual hero. The poet developed an original form of epic, singing of the birth of a nation, exalting the people of both Spain and South America, in a blend of direct realism, primitive epic, classical (particularly Lucan), and touches of the Italian *Romanzi*. He uses the meter of Ariosto, although the narrative style is at times prosaic. Much space is devoted to the colorful description of battles. The epic is enhanced by prophecies, love scenes, supernatural occurrences, mythological tales, dreams, and imaginary voyages.

In Canto I he speaks of those "who far on surge-ensundered shore,/Bent the proud neck of Araucania's race/To Spain's stern yoke, by war's arbitrament." He describes the Chilean Indians as "Robust and strong, hairless of lip and chin/Well-grown and tall above the run of men. . . ."

In Canto II the wise old patriarch Colocolo tells the Indians, "I am not sad to see this warlike flame/That fires your hearts; instead it gives me joy." However, he does not foresee victory: ". . . I fear this valor may defame/Your honored past. . . ." To choose as their leader one who will be "obeyed by all, that all may win renown," they should choose the man "who longest bears this great tree's heavy bole/Upon his back—him shall we captain crown." By this method Caupolicán is chosen: he holds up a huge log for 24 hours. The feat is timed by the appearance of Tithonus's lady, Aurora, and the sun-god Apollo.

In Canto III the valorous Indians are depicted as being braver than the self-devoted Decii and many other Greek and Roman heroes.

In Canto VII the sack of Concepción is labeled worse than the sack of Troy.

In Canto IX, of the events leading up to the war, the poet admits, "I gleaned this information/From the lips of many authors," then goes on with happenings in 1550 at the onset of the invasion.

Canto X depicts a particularly colorful crowd scene in which, after an early victory, the victorious Indians hold elaborate games, with prizes formally awarded.

In Canto XXIII, the Indian sorcerer Fiton, who lives in a cave copied from the witch's cave in Lucan's *Pharsalia* (Book 6), conjures up a vision of the Battle of Lepanto for Ercilla to view, although he is on duty in Chile, on the opposite side of the globe. Fiton invokes such classical demons as Cerberus, Orcus, and Pluto.

Canto XXXIV, about Caupolicán's execution, is the most powerful. In the beginning, he is "Shoeless, unkempt, with warbonnet forgot,/Bent by the weight of long and heavy chain," But when he sees the "eager executioner,/An ill-clad negro slave from overseas," his fighting spirit returns. He cannot endure being executed by someone he considers "a cur." There is a change in his gait: "There with his usual energetic stride,/Unhesitatingly and without retort,/He climbed the narrow steps as carelessly/As though from prison he had been set free." His voice is "shot through with rage" as he says, "It shall not be that hand of baseborn man/Shall touch the noble chief, Caupolicán." He kicks the man aside and throws himself upon the sharpened stake, cheating the executioner.

Instead of ending with the noble chieftain's death, the poet rambles on about his own adventures and lapses into a political discussion on Spain's attempt to conquer Portugal. Nevertheless, the poem was so well thought of, by Cervantes, for example, that in *Don Quixote* (1.6), when the curate and the barber are culling through Don Quixote's books, discarding most, they keep *La Araucana*, declaring it one of the best three heroic poems in the Spanish language. (Ercilla 1945)

See also Ercilla y Zuñiga, Alonso de.

 # ARAUCO DOMADO
(Arauco tamed)

Unfinished Spanish-American epic (1596) by Pedro de Oña (1570–ca. 1643), intended to restore to Don García Hurtado de Mendoza the valor and glory denied him by Ercilla's epic *La Araucana*. As it stands, Oña's epic consists of 19 cantos of 16,000 lines in eight-line stanzas, but at the end of the poem the warrior-chief Caupolicán is still alive, and the Araucanians remain "untamed." Oña, a lyric poet, uses more striking metaphors, and his images are more sensitive and personal than Ercilla's.

The poem is a mixture of European and New World culture. In his version, the Araucanians know Greek mythology. For example, Canto V describes an interlude with the warrior Caupolicán and his wife Fresia at rest in the forest: "The sinuous brooklet plashed in rippled pleats,/And formed into a chain of purest glass./. . ./'Twas here Caupolicán siesta took,/Impassioned, with his Fresia hand in hand. . . ."

The emphasis in Oña's poem is on the bravery of the Spaniards. Although there is not the attention to battle detail afforded by Ercillo, Oña describes the ferocious attack by 20,000 Araucanian warriors on the Spanish fort of Penco, of whose victims, "little Gracolano was the first,/A lad courageous, strong, robust, and bold." Another of the victims of the attack is "that bravest lion magnanimous,/The dauntless Don García preeminent. . . ." (Jones 1966)

See also *Araucana, La*; Pedro de Oña.

ARCHIL III

Georgian poet, author of *Archiliani* (ca. 17th c.). He was born in 1647, the son of the *vali* (viceroy) of Kartli, Vakhtang V (Shahnevaz I, r. 1658–1676). At the time, Georgia had fallen under Safavid overlordship, while Ottoman Turks and Iran warred for the right to Georgian land. Archil was restless and energetic, so his father tried to find a throne for him. He was installed briefly in the Georgian kingdom of Imereti (1661) and later in the eastern Georgian kingdom of Kakheti, where he ruled from 1664 to 1675. Ultimately Archil was driven into exile in Russia to escape the encroaching Iranians. As Iran threatened the Georgian kingdoms with extinction, Archil attempted to preserve his country's history with his epic. (Preminger 1974; Suny 1988)

See also *Archiliani*.

ARCHILIANI

Georgian historical epic (ca. 17th c.) written by Kakheti king Archil III (1647–1712, r. 1664–1675). The poem, containing more than 12,000 verses, is an encyclopedic depiction of Georgian life and history, written as Iran threatened to wipe out all vestiges of the Georgian kingdoms and culture. (Preminger 1974; Suny 1988)

See also Archil III.

ARCHITRENIUS
(The man of many sorrows)

Latin satirical/didactic epic (1184) by Jean de Hauteville (John of Hanville, fl. 1184). The poem, consisting of about 4,500 lines of eloquent Latin hexameters in nine books on the order of Juvenal, tells of the sufferings and quest of Architrenius. Dissatisfied with his purposeless life, in which he is a victim of vicious cruelty, he sets out in searth of Nature, to ask her why she has made him so helpless. He passes by the abode of Gluttony, the mountain of Ambition, the

University of Paris; he watches a rousing drinking bout. He passes the palace of Venus, finally reaching Thule, where he hears speeches of wisdom from Cato, Plato, and Archytas. At length he finds Nature, who admonishes him, then gives him a beautiful wife named Moderation. (Highet 1962)

 # *ARGENTINA*

Spanish-American epic poem (1602 or 1612) by Spaniard Martín del Barco Centenera (1544–1605). The mediocre poem relates the poet's adversities and failures endured while he was in the Río de la Plata region. The archaic tone of his verse is due to his adherence to models of medieval didactic poetry. Although the violent incidents he recollects are based on reality, they are told in scathing hyperbole. The poem is forgettable, but the poet's repeated use of "argentine" as adjective and "the Argentine" as the name of the river and country became the origin of the modern name of the Republic of Argentina. (Jones 1966)

 # ARGIVES

Argives, derived from Argos in Greece, was a synonym for the Greeks, especially in the Trojan War.

 # *ARGONAUTICA*

Argonautica is the name of at least three epic poems:

(1) The Hellenistic Greek epic (ca. 260 B.C.) by Apollonius Rhōdius (ca. 295–215 B.C.) about Jason and the Argonauts. Apollonius's version contains nearly 6,000 lines in four books. In the Proemium (Chapter 1) of Book I, the poet relates the topic of his epic: how King Pelias of Iolcos convinces his nephew Jason to undertake an expedition (as a means of getting rid of the one fated to kill him) to sail on the *Argo* to the Black Sea on a quest for the Golden Fleece of the ram, which once belonged to Jason's cousin Phrixus. Now the Fleece hangs on a sacred oak in the barbarous land of Colchis. In the Catalogue (Chapter II), Jason's crew originally consists of Minyans like himself, but other well-known Greek heroes are included, notably Heracles, Orpheus, Polydeuces, Peleus, Castor, Meleager, and the winged sons of Boreas and Orithyia, Calais and Zetes. They are organized into two groups, one led by a man of skill—Orpheus; the other, by a man of strength—Heracles. The narra-

tive proper begins at the home of Aeson, with a glimpse of the hero and his family. On the beach at the Gulf of Pagasae, Jason calls for an election to name a captain; meanwhile, Heracles kills an ox with one blow of his club. The description of their departure is considered one of the most vivid in the epic, with the thunderous noise of both ship and harbor; the ship's foamy wake; Orpheus's music, which calls schools of fish; and the festive arrival of divine spectators, including the babe Achilles. The *Argo* sets sail and stops at the island of Lemnos, inhabited only by women. Having killed off their husbands the previous year, the lustful women entice the heroes to stay for several months to enjoy a life of sensuality, which threatens to scuttle the entire mission. While Jason is entertained by Hypsipyle, Heracles grows weary and calls the men to depart. Eventually they row to Samothrace, where Orpheus initiates the men in the rites of the four Great Gods, the Cabiri, whose worship is a safeguard against misfortune. They journey to Oros Arkton by way of Mount Ida. Oros Arkton is the land of the Doliones, and King Cyzicus offers them hospitality. But after they sail away, they are blown back by a storm; mistaking them for intruders, the Doliones attack. In the ensuing battle Jason inadvertently kills King Cyzicus. Heracles, stirred to anger by the gods, is subdued after Jason receives a sign while sleeping and performs rites of expiation. When the wind fails, the others exhaust themselves in a rowing contest, and Heracles uses his strength to row the *Argo* to Mysia by himself. He breaks an oar and goes off to look for wood to make another one. When the Argonauts sail from Mysia, they accidentally leave behind Heracles, his boyfriend Hylas, and Polyphemus. Telamon accuses Jason of purposely abandoning Heracles. They try to return to look for Heracles, but the Boreads prevent it. Glaugus appears and explains that Zeus has ordained Heracles's departure from the group. He also describes the fates of the three.

In Book II, in another episode on the way to Colchis, they sail to Bebryces, where King Amycus, a famous boxer, challenges them to a match. After he refuses to give the Argonauts food or water, Polydeuces fights and kills him. Farther along, they meet the blind king Phineus, who deprived his children of their sight and was punished by the gods by losing his own sight. Zetes and Calais run off the Harpies, who have been stealing and contaminating his food. Amycus tells the Argonauts how to pass the Clashing Rocks (Symplegades) safely, and as a reward the gods restore his sight. Jason sends a dove ahead, and after the rocks have moved together and rebounded, they quickly pass through the Clashing Rocks without being crushed. They enter the Black Sea, where they rescue the four sons of Phrixus from shipwreck. Phrixus and his sister Helle had ridden the golden-fleeced ram from Thebes to Colchis, where Phrixus married Chalciope, daughter of King Aeëtes of Colchis. In gratitude for rescuing them from shipwreck, the four sons of Phrixus lead the Argonauts to Colchis. Aeëtes promises to give Jason the Golden

Fleece if he will plow the field of the war god Ares with two fire-breathing bulls, sow the field with dragons' teeth, and, when giants spring up from the seed, slay them. Jason succeeds in the tasks with the help of the king's sorceress daughter Medea, who has fallen in love with him. A famous passage in Book III describes Medea's look. When Aeëtes refuses to honor his promise and instead plots to kill Jason, Medea puts to sleep the dragon guarding the fleece so that Jason can steal it. Medea flees Colchis with Jason on the *Argo,* with the Colchians in pursuit.

Book IV tells of the return voyage to Iolcus in Thessaly out of the Black Sea, up the Danube River, across inland central European waterways without portages to the Adriatic Sea, the Po, Rhône, and even the North African coast, enduring many hardships and perils along the way. Just before the Argonauts meet with Heracles in North Africa, Heracles has slain Ladon, the dragon guarding the golden apples of the Hesperides. (Clauss 1993; Gillis 1928)

(2) *Argonautica* is also a post-Augustan Latin epic by Gaius Valerius Flaccus (d. A.D. 92 or 93), based on Apollonius's epic.

Valerius Flaccus (full name Gaius Valerius Flaccus Setinus Balbus) began his epic about A.D. 72, 15 or 20 years before his death. Written in hexameters in seven books and a partial eighth, the poem obviously owes much to Apollonius's version, but Book 1 adds an underworld scene reminiscent of both Homer's *Odyssey* and (especially) Vergil's *Aeneid.* However, the poet adds new episodes in the seventh and eighth books concerning Medea, who is torn between loyalty to her father and her love for Jason. The poem breaks off abruptly, leaving Jason contemplating betraying his bride, despite the fact that his success depends upon her. Valerius's poem is of mediocre quality and was not particularly well received. A contemporary writer on education, Marcus Fabius Quintilian (A.D. 33/35–d. before A.D. 100), commented: "In Valerius we have lately lost much." (Bowder 1980; Howatson and Chilvers 1993)

(3) *Argonautica* is the name of a Latin free translation of Apollonius's epic by Varro Atacinus (Publius Terentius Varro, b. 82 B.C.). His work exists in fragments only. (Howatson and Chilvers 1993)

See also Apollonius Rhodius.

 # ARIOSTO, LUDOVICO

Italian poet and dramatist, author of *Orlando Furioso.* He was born in 1474 at Reggio Emilia, the firstborn of a noble family of five sons and five daughters. His father, Niccolo Ariosto, or Ferrara, was governor of the citadel of Reggia under Duke Ereole I. His mother, Doria Malaguzzi Valera, was the daughter of a physician who was also a minor poet. Niccolo Ariosto was appointed to other posts, and eventually the family settled in Ferrera, where Niccolo became chief administrator of the state.

To oblige his father, Ludovico Ariosto studied law for five years, but after that time his father agreed that he should pursue a literary career. He studied under the humanist Gregorio of Spoleto and perfected his command of Latin. When Gregorio left to become the tutor of Francesco Sforza in Milan, Ariosto attended the university and studied classical literature.

When his father died in 1550, Ludovico was forced to take responsibility of the large family, so he sought employment under the Estensi, rulers of Ferrara and Modena. He became governor of the citadel of Canossa in 1502, and the following year he became confidential secretary to Cardinal Ippolito d'Este, brother to Alfred, who became duke of Ferrera in 1505. As early as 1505, Ariosto began his masterpiece *Orlando Furioso,* which he continued to revise for the next 30 years. In 1525, after seeing active service in the ongoing war between Ferrara and Venice, Ariosto became the duke's director of theatrical entertainment. He wrote several verse comedies, one of which was finished by his crippled brother Gabriele, who lived with him. He also wrote a number of satires not far behind *Orlando Furioso* in literary merit.

From 1522 to 1525 he served as governor of Garfagnana, and when he returned to Ferrara he could afford to buy his own house and garden where he, his brother, and his illegitimate son Virginio lived. Virginio's mother was Orsolina Catinelli de Sassomarino, who married someone else. He also had an older, sickly son by a family servant named Maria, who brought him up. In ca. 1528 he secretly married Alessandra Benucci. Ariosto died of tuberculosis in 1533 at the age of 59. (Ariosto [Vol. 1] 1973)

See also Cinque Canti; Orlando Furioso.

ARJUNAVIVĀHA
(Also *ardjunawiwāhā;* Arjuna's wedding)

Javanese epic by Mpu Kanwa (fl. 11th c.) This eleventh-century poem is an allegorical epic based on the great Indian Sanskrit epic *Mahābhārata,* but casting the Indonesian ruler Airlangga (991–1049) as hero. Employing Sanskrit meters and poetic style, the poem is written in a mixture of courtly Javanese and Sanskrit. For a synopsis of the *Mahābhārata,* see the *Encyclopedia of Traditional Epics.* (Preminger 1974)

ARMAS ANTÁRTICAS
(Antarctic wars)

Spanish-American epic (1608–1615) by Juan de Miramontes y Zuázola (fl. 1615), a Spanish soldier who participated in the struggles against the English pirate

Thomas Cavendish (1560–1592). After passing through the Straits of Magellan, Cavendish, a navigator and freebooter, attacked the Spanish settlements on the coast of South America and intercepted shipments from South America to Mexico. Miramontes y Zuázola describes the New World with the skill and imagination of one trained in the epic tradition. He was one of many who described the depredations of the "Lutheran" pirates. (Anderson-Imbert 1969)

See also Miramontes y Zuázola, Juan de.

 # ARNOLD, SIR EDWIN

English poet, author of *The Light of Asia* (1879) and *The Light of the World* (1891). He was born in 1832 in Gravesend, Kent, England, the son of Robert Coles Arnold. He was educated at King's School, King's College in London, and Oxford University, from which he received both his B.A. and, in 1856, his M.A. degrees. In 1852, while still an undergraduate, he received the Newdigate Prize for his poem *Belshazzar's Feast.* He taught at King Edward's School in Birmingham before receiving appointment as principal at Deccan College in Poona, India. Winning a fellowship to the University of Bombay, he studied Indian, Persian, and Turkish languages. He was there during the infamous mutiny and won a commendation for his conduct as principal.

In 1861, Arnold returned to England, where he served as journalist for the London *Daily Telegraph,* becoming chief editor in 1873. Under his editorship the journal sponsored the expedition of George Smith to Assyria in 1874 and, along with the New York *Herald,* the expedition of Stanley in Africa. Arnold defended the role of Turkey in the Russo-Turkish War of 1877 and was decorated by the sultan. He was made C.S.I. (Companion of the Order of the Star of India) in 1877, and knight commander of the Indian Empire in 1888. In that same year he traveled to Japan and the Pacific.

He married Katharine Bidulph in 1854, and after her death in 1864 he married Fannie Channing of Boston, Massachusetts, who died in 1889. His third wife, Tana Kuro Kawa, was Japanese.

After his initial venture into poetry he wrote several works of verse, most of it exotic. The most popular was the epic *The Light of Asia* (1879), which capitalized on the current popularity of poetry with Eastern themes. It is a poetic interpretation of the life and teachings of Buddha, then virtually unknown in Europe. The poem caught the public's fancy, and it was immediately so popular that Arnold was invited to make lecture tours, including a very successful one in the United States in 1891. The epic's success encouraged him to use Eastern themes in other works and to make translations of Sanskrit poetry. He also attempted another (but less successful) epic, *The Light of the World,* on the life and works of Jesus.

Alfred Lord Tennyson died in 1892, but by 1894 a new poet laureate had still not been chosen, although Arnold was one of those considered. In the last ten years of his life he was troubled by failing eyesight, but he continued to

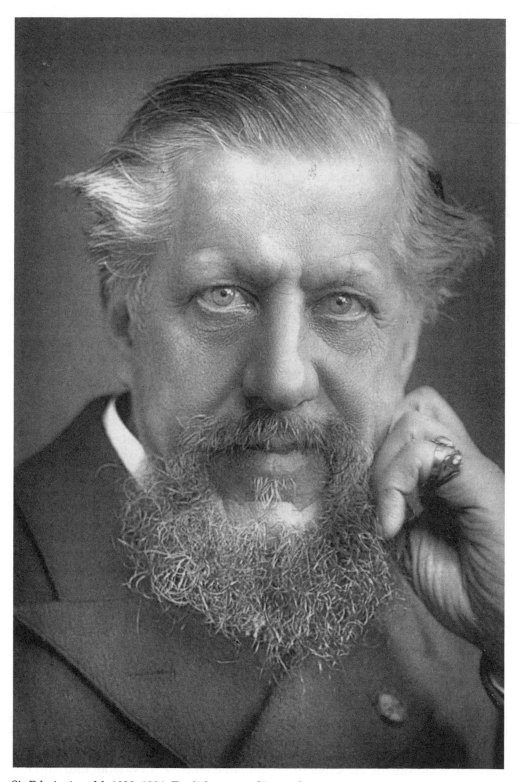
Sir Edwin Arnold, 1832–1904, English poet and journalist

write. His last work, *Ithobal,* was published in 1901, three years before his death on 24 March 1904 in London. (TAP) (Kunitz and Haycroft 1936; Walker 1931)

 # ARNOLD, MATTHEW

English poet and literary and social critic, author of the epic episode *Sorhab and Rustum* (1853), based on the Persian epic *Shāh-Nāmah* by Firdausi, and of the dramatic poem *Empedocles on Etna* (1852). He was born in Laleham, Middlesex, Endland, in 1822, the first son of Dr. Thomas Arnold, Requia Professor of Modern History at Oxford. He attended Winchester School and Rugby, where he won the Rugby Poetry Prize and the Balliol Scholarship. The following year he entered Balliol College, Oxford, where in 1843 he won the Newdigate Poetry Prize, earning a B.A. in Literae Humaniores in 1844. In 1845 he was elected a Fellow at Oriel College, Oxford, where he taught classics. From 1847 to 1851 he served as private secretary to a liberal politician, Lord Lansdowne, who was chief educational officer. During this time he published *The Strayed Reveller, and Other Poems* anonymously, but soon withdrew the volume. In 1851 he married Frances Lucy Wightman and took a post as inspector of schools, a position he held for the next 35 years. In 1852 he published *Empedocles on Etna, and Other Poems,* but again withdrew the volume. He realized his limitations as a poet, writing his sister that his poems were fragments just as he was, whereas she was whole. In 1853 he published, under his own name, *Poems,* which included his epic episode *Sorhab and Rustum* and a preface that is considered one of the most important critical texts of the nineteenth century. In 1855 he published *Poems, Second Series.*

In 1857 he became the first layman to hold the elected position of Oxford Professor of Poetry, a position he held for two five-year terms, but he declined a third. He published at least 13 books of essays, poetry, and literary criticism during the last 20 years of his life. Of his many publications, the most important was *Essays in Criticism* (1865), which established him as the chief English critic of his day. He held that "poetry is at the bottom a criticism of life."

In 1883–1884 he received a government pension of 250 pounds a year and began a lecture tour in the United States, after which he published *Discourses in America* (1885). He died in 1888 at Liverpool, having established himself as Victorian England's greatest man of letters. (Anderson and Buckler 1966)

 # ARREBO, ANDERS

Danish bishop and poet, author of the religious epic *Hexaëmeron* (ca. 1622, publ. 1661), describing the six days of creation. Arrebo was born in 1587 in Denmark, and was educated in theology, Latin, French, and the classics. He became bishop of Trondheim (Norway), and his epic contains descriptions of

North Norway. Based on the sixteenth-century French poet Guillaume du Bartas's *La Semaine,* the epic was completed about 1622 but not published until 1661, long after his death in 1637. In addition to his theological writings and his epic, Arrebo translated the Psalms into Danish. (Brogan 1996)

See also *Hexaëmeron (2).*

ARTHUR

A legendary king of Britain revered for at least 1,400 years. He is the hero of the medieval cycle of legends bearing his name. The core of the Arthurian legend derives from Celtic mythology, apparently originating in the British Isles, particularly in Ireland and Wales, before spreading to the European continent in the sixth and seventh centuries. Arthur and his court are mentioned in the writings of the chronicler Gildas (ca. 540); the poem "Gododdin" (ca. 600); *Historia Britonum* by Nennius (ca. 800); the tenth-century poem "The Spoils of Annwn;" the Latin history of Wales, *Annales Cambriae* (ca. 955); "Kulhwch and Olwen," a twelfth-century prose romance found in the *Mabinogion;* William of Malmsbury's *Chronicles of the Kings of England* (12th c.); Geoffrey of Monmouth's *History of the Kings of Britain* (12th c.); *Roman de Brut,* a verse chronicle by the Norman poet Wace, based on Geoffrey's work; the English priest Layamon's *The Brut,* the first English-language version of Wace's work; the twelfth-century French poet Chrétien de Troyes's *Lancelot* (Lancelot, the knight of the cart), *Eric et Enide, Cliges,* and *Yvain* (Chevalier of the lion); the thirteenth-century German poets Wolfram von Eschenbach's *Parzival* and Gottfried von Strassburg's *Tristan;* the prose *Vulgate Cycle* of the same period; the fourteenth-century anonymous works *The Alliterative Morte d'Arthur* (ca. 1360) and *Sir Gawain and the Green Knight,* a poem that ranks as one of the greatest Middle English works; Sir Thomas Malory's fifteenth-century prose version of *Le Morte d'Arthur;* sixteenth-century Edmund Spenser's *The Faerie Queene;* and nineteenth-century Alfred Lord Tennyson's *Idylls of the King.* (Barber 1961; Hubert 1980; Rutherford 1987)

ASPREMONT
(Also *Aspromonte* in the later Italian version)

French chanson de geste (early 13th c.) by an unknown author. The poem, containing 12,000 lines, is one of the Charlemagne cycle, later retold in Italian as *Aspromonte.* The historical events recounted are those upon which Boiardo's *Orlando Innamorato* and Ariosto's *Orlando Furioso* are based. The poem *Aspremont* is set in Calabria. When African king Agolante, accompanied by his son Almonte, invades Italy from Sicily, Charlemagne and his paladins march south to intercept him. Charlemagne's nephew Orlando wants to go along, but the

Aspremont, a 12,000-line early-thirteenth-century chanson de geste, a French style of poetry that glorified chivalry in battle, recounts events in the life of eighth-century Frankish ruler Charlemagne (742–814), who united much of Europe through successful campaigns. He is also the subject of a medieval German poem, *Karlmeinet*. This hollow gold and jeweled bust from about 1350 was to contain fragments of Charlemagne's skull.

king refuses because the boy is too young. However, Orlando disobeys his uncle and saves the Christians from defeat. He slays King Agolante's son Almonte, a friend of Hector of the *Iliad*. Hector, in fact, has given Almonte his sword. In the victory, Orlando is awarded not only Almonte's helmet, but also Hector's sword Durendal (Durindana). With the pope's blessing, Charlemagne founds the Frankish kingdom of Sicily and Apulia, so that Norman achievements in South Italy are now attributed to the Franks. (Ariosto [Vol. 1, Reynolds Intro, 1975] 1973)

AṬIKAḶ, IḶAṄKŌ

See Iḷaṅkō Aṭikaḷ.

 ATTA TROLL, EIN SOMMERNACHTSTRAUM
(Atta Troll, a summer night's dream)

German mock-epic (1841, publ. 1843) by Heinrich Heine (1797–1856), who wrote the poem during a summer visit to Cauterets in the Pyrenees. It appeared its final form in 1847. Containing 27 Kaput (chapters), the poem is written in fluent unrhymed trochaic four-line stanzas.

The poem opens with an account of the escape of a dancing bear, Atta Troll, from its master. The crude and unkempt Atta Troll personifies the Tendency poets, whom Heine regarded with derision. The poem describes the bear hunt with great digressions into a dream vision in which three female temptresses appear to the hunter. Eventually Atta Troll is shot and subsequently "honored" in an epitaph parodying the style, loaded with participles, of Lugwig I, König von Bayern.

In "The Bear Dance at Cauterets," the noble Atta Troll, "stiff and earnest, grave and solemn," dances with his mate Mumma. Her own dancing has "a suspicion/of the cancan . . ." making it "something scarcely moral," so that the trainer-keeper, who is forcing them to dance in the open marketplace, has to keep reprimanding her by whipping her for such brazen behavior.

"The Escape of Atta Troll" describes the bear's bursting his fetters, sending people scattering. The angry keeper is left with only the "black and wretched Mumma," whom he beats in his rage.

"In Roncesvalles" describes the "noble valley" where "Frank and Saracen meet headlong." There, "by the yawning gap of Roland," hidden in the brush, is the hole of Atta Troll.

In "Atta Troll Amuses," the bear lies in his hole among his dear ones, sucking his paws and pining for Mumma. He describes to his children evil man and tells them to flee from him: "Never trust the thing, my daughters,/That approaches you in breeches!"

In "Atta Troll's Republic," the bear describes to his children the way things will be when they overthrow the despots. Even Jews will share in civil rights, but it will be illegal for them to dance in the market because, ". . . the race is sadly lacking/In a sense of style. . . ."

In "Atta Troll Swears His Son, One-Ear, on the Altar," in the dark of night, Atta Troll takes his youngest son, Sir One-Ear, to a stone where Druids once offered up human sacrifices. He bequeaths his hatred of man to his son, making One-Ear swear eternal hatred.

In "Lascaro the Bear-Hunter," the scene shifts to the poet accompanying Lascaro in a search for the bear, which takes them across the bridge from France into Spain. They reach a small *posada* (inn) where a supper of chickpeas is served. They are as heavy as bullets, "taxing even the digestion/Of a German reared on dumplings." The two retire to a bed that is "with insects peppered."

"The Witch Uraka" relates how the poet and Lascaro paddle across the lake to the hovel of Lascaro's mother, Uraka. She crouches by the fire, melting lead, "casting fatal bullets destined/For the death of Atta Troll."

In "The Eve of St. John: Herodias" (Saint John the Baptist's Eve), while sleeping on a straw mattress in Uraka's hut the poet dreams of a spectral hunt in which many spirits fly by: King Arthur, Sir Ogier the Dane, slender naked nymphs with leafy wands, medieval damsels riding sidesaddle and holding chained falcons, a cavalcade of women with "rouged and wanton cheeks." But three beauties excel all others: the Greek goddess Diana, the Celtic goddess Abunde, and most fetching of all, Herod's wife Herodias, who carries the charger holding the head of John the Baptist. The poet laments not being able to follow her.

"Death of Atta Troll" relates how Atta Troll, awaking beside his children, tells them he has dreamed that he is lying under a tree that drips honey. In the tree are seven bears with wings. When they sing, Atta Troll's soul leaves his body. When he finishes telling his dream, he jumps to his feet. He hears the voice of his beloved Mumma and rushes from the hole, only to be shot by Lascaro. Uraka has imitated the voice of Mumma, luring him into range. But all is well: King Louis will erect a monument to good, religious Atta Troll.

In "Epilogue," dedicated to August Varnhagen von Ense, the poet describes his poem as "perhaps the last unfettered/Woodland song of the Romantic!" (Heine 1966)

See also Heine, Heinrich.

 # ATTAR, FARID AL-DIN

Persian poet, attributed author of a number of epics, of which perhaps at least nine are his. Attar's most famous epic is *Manteq al-tair* (The conference of the birds, or bird parliament, ca. 1177). Details of his life are much disputed. Traditionally, he was born about 1120 in Neishapour. He is said to have been educated at Mashad at the theological school by the shrine of Imam Reza. Later he traveled to Raghes, Egypt, Damascus, Mecca, Turkestan, and India. He returned to Neishapour, where he ran a pharmacy and wrote poetry, among them *The Conference of the Birds, The Book of Affection,* and *The Book of Secrets.* Late in life he was apparently convicted of heresy, because he was banished and his property seized. However, he returned and appears to have died in Neishapour about 1220 at an advanced age, possibly at the hands of Mongol invaders. He wrote only one work in prose, the *Tadhkerat-al auliya* (Memorial of the saints), a collection of the deeds, sayings, and parables of 38 Ṣūfī saints. (Attar 1984)

See also *The Conference of the Birds.*

AUBERON
(Oberon, Alberich)

Auberon, or Oberon, was the king of the elves (faerie) in medieval French folklore. In German legend he was known at times as Alberich, a dwarf-king of elves living in the woodlands and having magic powers. In the legendary history of the Merovingian dynasty, Oberon was a magician. In German lore Alberich was the dwarf who guarded the underground treasure of the Niblungs (*q.v.*). He has also been sometimes identified with Andvari, a dwarf who lived in a waterfall.

In an early medieval romance Oberon (Auberon) was three spans high, the son of a great warrior, Julius Caesar, and Morgan le Fay (or according to another version, the Fairy Lady of the Hidden Isle, Chapalone). Centuries earlier she had been married to a king of Egypt and mothered Alexander the Great.

One of his fairy godmothers decreed that he stop growing at the age of three, but also that he should be the most handsome of all creatures. Another gave him the power to read people's hearts and minds. The third gave him the power to assume any form he wished. The fourth gave him the power that made all creatures obey any of his commands. He also was never to grow old, and he had the power to produce anything at a moment's notice and to travel great distances as fast as thought. None of his gifts would turn to harm.

Oberon is best known as the King of the Fairies in Shakespeare's *Midsummer Night's Dream,* with Titania as his consort and Queen of the Fairies. He had the traditional gift of swift travel anywhere (he had just come from India and could compass the globe faster than the wandering moon), he was amorous of a mortal, he could control the weather, he had power over the unborn, and he had subjects (knights in his train who trace the forest). (Briggs 1978; Hulpach 1970)

AUCASSIN ET NICOLETTE

French romance epic (12th or 13th c.) by an unknown author. This is the only story extant using the "chant-fable" style of alternating prose and verse in seven-syllable assonant lines. It tells of the love of the noble son of Count Gavin of

Beaucaire, Aucassin ("Aucassin the frank, the fair,/Aucassin of the yellow hair"), for the Saracen prisoner Nicolette ("with straight brows and yellow hair"), bought from freebooters but in reality the daughter of the king of Carthage. (She asks him, "Aucassin, my love, my knight,/Am I not thy heart's delight?") The count wants a nobler marriage for his son, so he imprisons Nicolette, but she escapes and takes flight. Aucassin follows, and after enduring many hardships, including capture by Saracen pirates, he is shipwrecked near his home. He learns that his father has died and that he is now the count. Meanwhile, Nicolette is taken to Carthage, where it is learned that she is the daughter of the king, and she is betrothed to a Saracen. But ("Then she cut her curls of gold,/Cast them in the dungeon hold . . .") she escapes once again and, disguised as a wandering *jongleur* (minstrel), makes her way to Beaucaire, where she and Aucassin are reunited. ("When Aucassin heareth now/That his lady bright of brow/Dwelleth in his own countrie,/Never man was glad as he.") (Burgess and Cobby 1989; Hibbard 1942)

 # AZTLAN

Aztlan, the White Place, was the mythical home of the original Aztecs, located, according to different versions, anywhere from the state of Jalisco in Mexico to the upper Missouri River Valley. In the legend, the Aztecs went out of Aztlan in the old days, guided by Huizilopochtli, their war god, son of Coatlicue. Coatlicue was a mortal woman made immortal for her son's sake; she was appointed goddess of all herbs, flowers, and trees, and lived in a cavern on the peak of the mountain. Her dress was of serpents.

Aztlan was an island in a lake close by a place called Culhiacan. On this island was a mountain called Chicomoztoc, a religious center. In the mountain were seven caverns, from each of which came a specific Aztec tribe. The mountain was surrounded by waters filled with fish, flocks of ducks, and birds with green and yellow plumage. On the waters there were barges on which grew maize, beans, and fruits. The caverns of the mountain, where the people dwelt, were filled with precious stones. The years were tied together in bundles of five. When the people went outside the caverns they went in canoes among the floating gardens. When they departed Aztlan they took with them the bundle of years and many of the plants. They encountered stones and jaguars and plains filled with thorns and deserts on their way to Lake Tezcuco, where they subdued the tribes and built a city. (Brundage 1972; Colum 1930; Southey 1909)

 # BAGRITSKY, EDUARD
(Real surname: Dziubin)

Russian poet, author of *The Lay of Opanas* (1926), an epic about the Russian civil war. He was born in 1895 in Odessa into a Jewish family. He fought in the Russian civil war and in 1925 settled in Moscow, where he joined a literary group called Pereval, which was dedicated to Communist principles. He wrote several autobiographical collections over his life—*The Southwest, The Victors, The Last Night*—all of which were published in 1932, after he had become severely ill. His epic, *The Lay of Opanas*, published soon after he finished it, is written like a Ukrainian folk epic, a *byliny*. He died in 1934 of tuberculosis. (Bristol 1991)
> **See also** *The Lay of Opanas*.

 # *BAHAT-KATHĀ*
(Or *Brihatkathā*, Great tale)

Indian epic by Gunādhya (A.D. 50?–300?) written in Paiṣācā dialect. The poem served as a source for many plays and romances. (Van Buitenen 1959)

 # BALAGTÁS, FRANCESCO
(Also Francisco Baltazar)

Philippine Tagalog poet, author of the *awit* (narrative poem) *Florante at Laura* (full title *Ang pinagdaanang buhay ni Florante at Laura sa kahariang Albanya)* [Of what befell Florante and Laura in the kingdom of Albania, 1838]. Balagtás was born in 1788 in the barrio Pañginay in the municipality of Bigaa, Bulacan Province, 30 miles north of Manila in the Philippine Islands. His parents were Juan Balagtás and Juana de la Cruz. His was a poor family—his father was a blacksmith—so he moved to Manila in 1799 to enter the domestic service of a Trinidad family, who provided him with an education. In 1812 he finished the course in canon law at the Colegio de San José of the Jesuits in Intramuros, where one of his teachers, Father Mariano Pilapil, was a celebrated Latin scholar and Tagalog literary figure. After graduation he worked in several municipal offices.

About this time young Balagtás began an acquaintanceship with a popular native poet nicknamed Joseng-Sisiw because he often wrote love poems for lovesick swains. Under this influence, young Balagtás began writing verses himself. He was to become the first Philippine native to achieve prominence as a poet.

In 1835 or 1836, he moved to Pandacan in the suburbs of Manila, a place frequented by artists and musicians. At the age of 50 he fell in love with a beauty named María Asunción Rivera ("Celia") to whom he dedicated his epic poem. A rival in the courtship, a local *cacique*, had him imprisoned for some months on a trumped-up charge.

After his release, he moved closer to Manila, where he published *Florante at Laura*, written during or just after his imprisonment. Unfortunately, his love married another man. His epic poem, published in 1838, was inspired by a Spanish tale. By setting the action in Albania, the poet was able to describe the unpleasant conditions existing in the Philippines under Spanish colonialism and to make social commentary about colonialist tyranny—particularly that which he had so recently suffered in prison—without fear of censorship. The dedicatory poem "Kay Selya" (To Celia) is considered one of the finest lyric poems in the Tagalog language.

In 1840 he moved to Bataan, where he became an assistant to a justice of the peace, and then assistant to the court clerk. On 22 July 1842, he married Juana Tiambeng of Orion, by whom he had 11 children. In 1856–1857, as agricultural judge and *teniente primero,* he was appointed official translator of the court. In his official documents he always used the surname Baltazar rather than Balagtás, the Tagalog name by which he had been baptized, probably when in 1849 the governor-general ordered all natives to use Spanish names.

Shortly thereafter, he was imprisoned a second time after being charged with cropping the hair of a female servant, probably as punishment for doing something that displeased him. He served six months in the jail of Balanga and then was housed at Bilibid prison in Manila. Released after four years, he was jobless and impoverished from the expenses of defending his case. For two years he turned out many literary works to support himself and his family. He died in 1862, having written more than 100 *comedias* and scores of poems and *corridas,* earning a reputation as the "prince of Tagalog poets." (Quirino 1964)

See also *Florante at Laura.*

 # BALBOA, SILVESTRE DE

Spanish poet, author of *Espejo de paciencia* (*Mirror of Patience*, 1608). He was born in Spain about 1570, and came to the New World, settling in Cuba, where he wrote his epic poem about Cuba. Specifically, the poem relates, in two cantos of 145 epic octaves, the ordeal of Friar Juan de la Cabezas Altamirano, who was kidnapped by the French pirate Gilbert Giron in 1604. Balboa labels the freebooters who raided Cuba "Lutheran pirates." The first canto describes the patience with which the bishop suffers. In the second canto, vengeance is wreaked: A "little Creole Negro" deceives Giron into bringing the ship ashore, where the French are attacked by Indians. In the final furious battle, an Indian is the only casualty of the pirates. Then a "Creole savior, honorable Negro" drives a lance into Giron's chest, killing him. When the freed bishop returns to Cuba, the mythological gods receive him with flowers and fruits from the Cuban countryside: "O happy island of Cuba!" In his prologue, Balboa confesses that he has imitated Horace. He died about 1640. (Anderson-Embert 1969; Jones 1966)

See also *Mirror of Patience.*

 # BALBUENA, BERNARDO DE

Spanish bishop and poet, author of *La grandeza mexicana* (The grandeur of Mexico, 1604) and *El Bernardo o la victoria de Roncesvalles* (1624). Balbuena was born in Valdepeñas, Spain, in 1568. When he was very young he was taken to Mexico, where his uncle Don Diego was canon of the cathedral. There Bernardo received his education, during which he developed a lively interest in Italian literature. At the age of 17 he won a literary contest. Although he was influenced by Ariosto, he developed his own brand of Baroque poetry. In 1604 the first edition of his epic *The Grandeur of Mexico* was published by Melchor Ocharte in Mexico. Bernardo returned to Spain in 1607 and received a Doctor of Theology degree from the University of Sigüenza. In 1608 he was named abbot for the island of Jamaica. That same year another of his works was published in Mexico: *El siglo de oro en las selvas de Erifile* (The golden age in the forests of Erifile), a collection of ecologues. In 1620 he was named the first bishop of Puerto Rico, and he brought to Puerto Rican culture the influence of the golden age. In 1624 he presided over a meeting of the provincial synod held in his diocese. That same year, his epic *Bernardo, or The Victory of Roncesvalles* was published, the first literary epic of Puerto Rico. The work earned him the reputation as Puerto Rico's premier literary figure. His library was so esteemed that Lope de Vega mentioned it, along with Balbuena's literary accomplishments, in his *Laurel de Apolo* (1630). However, in 1625, Balbuena was forced to flee when Dutch pirates sacked San Juan, burning his residence and destroying his library, which contained most of his books and writings. He died in 1627 in Puerto Rico. (Peña 1968; Rioseco and Rael 1960)

See also *La Grandeza Mexicana.*

 # BARBOUR, JOHN

Scottish cleric and poet, author of the Scottish national epic *The Bruce* (*The Actes and Life of the Most Victorious Conqueror, Robert Bruce, King of Scotland, wherein*

also are Contained the Martiall Deeds of the Valiant Princes, Edward Bruce, Syr James Douglas, Erle Thomas Randel, Walter Stuart, and sundrie others, about 1375). Barbour was born about 1320 in Scotland. The earliest extant record of him is a 1357 passport in his name, to King Edward III of England from David II of Scotland, for Barbour and three companions to travel to Oxford for study. Barbour is described as archdeacon of Aberdeen in the document. In 1364 he and four knights received another passport to once again pursue studies at Oxford. In 1365 he and six others were granted passports to pass through England on a visit to Paris, probably to take advantage of that city's reputation as a center of learning. In 1368 he again obtained a passport for passage through England to France for study.

In 1372, when he was 52, he was appointed auditor to the Scottish king's household and, on occasion, auditor of Scotland's national exchequer. In 1376 he was awarded 10 pounds from Robert II, possibly in recognition of having finished the first half of *The Bruce*, which he apparently took great pains in researching. The work covers the period in Scottish history from 1286 to 1332.

In 1378 the king awarded Barbour amd his heirs an annual pension of 20 shillings, although Barbour was unmarried and had no children. Possibly he had finished the epic by then. Two years later he assigned the grant to the Cathedral Church in Aberdeen for the performance of mass for his and his relatives' souls, and "all the faithful dead." In 1399, King Robert granted him an annual pension of 10 pounds for the duration of his life. He died in Aberdeen in 1395.

In a work written by Andrew Wyntoun about 30 years later, mention is made of another work by Barbour, *The Brut*, probably a fabulous account of British kings from their supposed ancestor Brutus, great-grandson of Aeneas of Troy. This work has not survived. Barbour is also supposed to have written *The Stewartis Orygynalle*, a fictitious history of the Scottish royal house. This work, not extant, may have been the original source of the characters of Banquo and Fleance, later used in Shakespeare's *Macbeth.*

Barbour is sometimes referred to as the father of Scottish poetry. As a man and as a poet he was noted for his religious commitment and strong faith, unmoved by the kind of ecclesiastical ambitions so common in his time, as well as for his learning and scholarship, his relish for scenes of violence and adventure, and his fervid patriotism and pride in being a Scot. (Douglas 1964)

See also The Bruce.

 # BARLAAM UND JOSAPHAT

Middle High German epic (ca. 1225) by Rudolf von Ems (d. 1252/1253). The poem, consisting of some 16,000 lines, was inspired by a Latin poem that Rudolph received about 1220/1223 from Bishop Wido of Chappel (near Zurich). The Latin poem in turn was inspired by a Buddhist legend that reached Europe during the Crusades.

It relates the story of Josaphat, a noble heathen prince, who is converted to Christianity by Barlaam, a Christian teacher. Josaphat renounces wealth and lusts of the flesh, and achieves serenity through communion with God.

Another version of the poem, *Laubacher Barlaam,* was written by Bishop Otto of Freising, Bavaria (d. 1220). (Garland and Garland 1986)

See also Rudolf von Ems.

 # BARLOW, JOEL

American poet and public official, author of *The Columbiad* (1807) and a mock-heroic poem, *The Hasty Pudding* (1796). He was born in 1754 in a Redding, Connecticut, farmhouse, the son of Samuel Barlow. In 1774 he enrolled at Yale University, well known for its conservatism. There he met Joseph Buckminster, a tutor, who encouraged his attempts at writing poetry but also warned him against liberal attitudes. Barlow graduated as class poet in 1778, taught school at New Haven for a year, and then returned to Yale to work on a Master's degree and write poetry. He considered an epic about an ancient or biblical character, then one about America, which became *The Vision of Columbus.* To provide time to write, he obtained a license to preach and was accepted as chaplain for the Third Massachusetts Brigade. He won the attention of George Washington and other officers after preaching a sermon on patriotism following Benedict Arnold's betrayal. That winter he returned home to be married—secretly, because of the opposition of her father—to Ruth Baldwin (1781).

By the end of 1782, Barlow was out of the army, and moved to Hartford, Connecticut. He became known as one of the "Connecticut Wits," along with Noah Webster and the poet John Trumbull. In 1786 he passed the bar examination and published a popular satire on the confusion surrounding Shays's Rebellion. From the profits he published his long-delayed *Vision of Columbus.* His law practice took him to Paris, where he met Thomas Jefferson, who would become his lifelong friend, and he renewed his friendship with Lafayette. Barlow became involved in European politics, especially of France. In England, he associated with Thomas Paine, Mary Wollstonecraft, Joseph Priestley, and other radicals, becoming alienated from his old Yale friends. He returned to France to aid the revolution, and stood as an unsuccessful candidate for delegate from Savoy. During the Reign of Terror, he probably escaped the guillotine because he was an American citizen. In Paris he met James Monroe, who would become another lifelong friend. Through Monroe's influence, he was appointed consul to Algiers, where he negotiated the release of Americans seized by the Turkish pirates and secured the opening of shipping lanes. When relations between the United States and France threatened war, Barlow wrote attacks on the Federalists, which led to his being regarded as a traitor by the Americans.

At this time he and his wife had taken into their home the young painter Robert Fulton, who was involved in plans for systems of canals, a submarine,

American Joel Barlow, 1754–1812, based on a painting by Robert Fulton

and a steamboat. The canal system won the support of Barlow, who saw in it an instrument of democracy. With the election of Jefferson, Barlow and his wife returned to the United States in 1804 and moved to Washington, D.C. He advocated building a university in Washington that would combine research and teaching. He now expanded his *Vision of Columbus* to an epic, with illustrations by Fulton; it was published in 1807 as *The Columbiad.* The poem expressed his vision of a utopia, which included freedom of the seas, an inland canal system, and a university of scholars.

In 18ll, President Monroe appointed Barlow minister to France to cement relations with Napoléon during the War of 1812. After traveling to Lithuania to conclude a treaty, just as Napoléon had met defeat there, Barlow fled ahead of the French army. He became ill in Poland and died of pneumonia on 21 December 1812. He was buried there in an obscure grave. (Ford 1971; Woodress 1958)

See also The Columbiad.

 # BASÍLIO DA GAMA, JOSÉ

Brazilian poet, author of *Uruguai* (The Uruguay, 1769). He was born in 1740 near a small town in Minas Gerais, Brazil, a mining region in the southwest once rich in gold and diamonds, later rich in the so-called "School of Minas" poets: Basílio da Gama, José de Santa Ritta Durão (*q.v.*), Thomas António Gonzaga, Claudio Manoel da Costa, Ignácio José de Alvarenga Peixoto, and Manoel Ignácio da Silva Alvarenga. Basílio da Gama came to Rio de Janerio at the age of 15 to study with the Jesuits. He had completed his novitiate at 19 when the Marquês de Pombal, Portuguese foreign minister, expelled the Jesuit missionaries (1759), and secularized their missions.

Basílio da Gama fled to Portugal and from there to Rome, gaining admittance to the Roman Arcadia (Academy). After several years he returned to Brazil, then to Lisbon, where the Jesuits were also banned. He was accused of Jesuitism, imprisoned, and sentenced to exile in Angola. However, he composed an epithalamium for the wedding of Pombal's daughter, thereby obtaining permission to remain in Lisbon.

Thenceforth he was an avowed anti-Jesuit. His epic poem *Uruguai*, composed a decade later, took a (defensive) anti-Jesuit stance, celebrating the swift campaign against the revolting Indians of the Jesuit missionary villages by Spain and Portugal. Using blank verse, the poet made a deliberate attempt to break with the style of Camões, poet of the Portuguese national epic *Os Lusíadas*, to create a new Romantic, patriotic, all-Brazilian style.

However, if Basílio da Gama paved the way for a Brazilian literature distinct from its Portuguese roots, the poet himself did not return to his native land. He continued to live in Portugal and died there in 1795. (Basílio da Gama 1977; Putnam 1948/1971)

See also Uruguai.

THE BATTLE OF FROGS AND MICE

(*Batrachomyomachia,* The conflict of the well-greaved
Batrachia and the swift-footed rodents)

Greek beast epic poem (ca. 5th c. B.C.) by an unknown author, although Pigres of Halicarnassus, brother of Queen Artemisia, is traditionally credited. The poem, a parody on the Homeric poetry style, is written in hexameter verse, with lofty words and traditional epithets.

In grandiloquent language it relates the story of a violent one-day war, so vicious that the gods, watching with growing concern, must intervene. The mice in the poem (whose hero-herald is named "Saucepan-invader," son of the "proud Cheese scooper") may represent the Peloponnesians, and the frogs the Athenians. Another mouse is "Lord Lickplatter," while his slayer is "the gallant Couch-in-the-Mudhole." When all seems lost for the hero-mice, Athena is unwilling to come to their assistance because they once gnawed holes in her Panathenaic robe, nibbled the wreaths, and drank the oil in her temple. The gods beg Zeus to intervene, so he hurls down a terrible lightning bolt. But the dauntless mice and frogs fight on. The battle is brought to a swift conclusion, however, by the appearance of the "skew folk," who are "nipper bejawed" and "slantwise walking" and look like armored tanks—in other words, crabs.

Although the poem is a parody of the inflated style of Homeric epics, it also parodies war itself and the poets who glorify war. (Highet 1962)

BEAST EPIC

(Bestiary)

An allegorical narrative, often satirical, written in mock-epic style, in which the characters are animals endowed with human qualities. Beast epics first came into favor in medieval times, with the appearance, about 930, of the Latin rhyming verse *Ecbasis captivi* (The prisoner's escape), which contains a fable within a fable. In Germany and France these fables developed into separate cycles satirizing certain social groups. The Latin *Ysengrimus,* written in Ghent in 1148, became the model for the longest and most famous beast epic, composed by various authors between about 1175 and 1205, with some as early as 1130. The French version, *Le Roman de Renart,* is 30,000 lines long. Further branches continued to appear as late as 1250, but these are generally inferior. The German *Reinhart Fuchs,* consisting of 2,000 lines, appeared in 1180. Later, Goethe wrote a free translation, *Reineke Fuchs* (1793–1794). (Hornstein 1973)

BEATRICE

In the *Divine Comedy* by Dante Alighieri, Beatrice is the poet's beloved, now dead, who has become an angel, one of the handmaidens of the Virgin Mary.

Symbolizing divine revelation, Beatrice guides him through Paradise. In real life, Beatrice was Bice Portinari, a great beauty whom Dante first saw when they were both nine. She married Simone de Bardi, and Dante saw her but a few times before the age of 25, but he idolized her as the epitome of divine grace and the vehicle of his salvation. (Dante 1949/1979, 1982/1984, 1986; Musa 1973)

BELINDA

The central character in Alexander Pope's *The Rape of the Lock*. She is a beautiful but rather useless young woman who loses a lock of her hair to the baron and creates a social storm in her rage over its loss. She has a smooth ivory neck and a soft white bosom, and she makes much use of cosmetics when she gets up in the morning. Her hair is shining and bright, and she especially "nourishes" two ringlets against her neck. It is one of these that the baron clips as a souvenir.

BELLO TROIAN, DE
(Or *Bellum Troianum*)

Long hexameter Latin epic (ca. 11th or 12th c.) by Joseph of Exeter that is a chivalrous romance about the Trojan War. The poem provided Chaucer with some of the material from which he wrote *Troilus and Criseyde*. (Highet 1976)

BELLUM CIVILE

See Pharsalia.

BENÉT, STEPHEN VINCENT

American poet, author of the epic *John Brown's Body* (1928) and the unfinished epic *Western Star* (1943). He was born in Bethlehem, Pennsylvania, in 1898, the son of army officer James Walker Benét and Frances Neill Rose Benét, and the younger brother of poet William Rose Benét. Throughout his childhood he lived at several army posts, and received his education from a military academy in San Rafael, California, and a coeducational academy in Augusta, Georgia. In 1915, at the age of 17, he sold his first poem to *New Republic*, published his first book of poems, and entered Yale University. The following year he was elected to the editorial board of *Yale Literary Magazine*, becoming its editor in 1918. With the outbreak of World War I he enlisted in the army, but was honorably

American poet Stephen Vincent Benét, aboard the *Ile de France* in 1928, the year his epic *John Brown's Body* was published

discharged because of bad eyesight. He worked for the State Department until the war ended, then reentered Yale, earning his B.A. degree. He worked for a while as a copywriter in New York City before returning as a member of Henry Seidel Canby's writing course to Yale, where he earned his M.A. degree. In 1921 he married Rosemary Carr, who later collaborated with him on some of his writing projects. In 1926–1927, with a Guggenheim Fellowship, he went to Paris and began work on his epic poem *John Brown's Body*, which was published in 1928 and won the Pulitzer Prize for Poetry. The following year he was elected to the National Institute of Arts and Letters. For two years he was a script writer in Hollywood, and in 1935 began reviewing books for major publications. He was a prolific writer of prize-winning novels, short stories, poetry, poetic radio scripts, and an operetta, *The Devil and Daniel Webster*, based on one of his stories. In his last years, he suffered from ill health, but engaged in the writing of a second epic, *Western Star*, about the odyssey of American wandering and seeking in the opening of the American West. He died of a heart ailment in the arms of his wife on 13 March 1943, with this second epic unfinished. Posthumously, he was awarded another Pulitzer Prize in Poetry for it in 1944. (Stroud 1962)

See also John Brown's Body; Western Star.

 # BERNARDO
(Full title: *El Bernardo, o la victoria de Roncesvalles*)

Spanish (Puerto Rican) heroic epic poem (1624) by Father Bernardo de Balbuena (1568–1627). Written in some 5,000 stanzas, the poem is an imitation of Ariosto's *Orlando Furioso*, or a Baroque version of the *Chanson de Roland*; it is a novelistic epic about the exploits of a medieval knight. The poem established its author as Puerto Rico's first literary figure. (Peña 1968)

See also Balbuena, Bernardo de.

 # BERTA AUS GRANDES PIES
(Berta of the big feet)

French chanson de geste (ca. 1270) by Adenet le Roi (fl. 13th c.). The poem consists of 3,482 verses. Its heroine is Berta of Hungary (d. 782), wife of King Pépin and mother of Charlemagne. The poem is neither a true epic nor a romance. The poet reveals that the plot is a story within a story, which he reads from a book belonging to a monk in the Church of Saint Denis.

It begins with Charles Martel, king of France, who has two sons. The first takes holy vows and enters an abbey. The second, Pépin, is short in stature but daring. Early in life he exhibits the qualities that will make him a strong ruler by slaying an escaped lion. Pépin ascends to the throne and marries a noble lady, who dies without giving him an heir. He assembles his nobles to help him find another wife. They suggest the princess of Hungary, Berta.

Pépin sets off with a party of knights for Hungary, where he wins permission from King Floire and Queen Blancheflor to take Berta back to France as his bride. Berta's mother gives her three servants to take with her. One is Aliste, who looks exactly like Berta. Before the party departs, Berta gives Queen Blancheflor a ring to remember her by.

When the party arrives in France, a magnificent wedding ceremony is held. But that night, as Berta waits for her bridegroom to come, her old maidservant Margiste convinces her that Pépin means to kill her. Margiste proposes substituting her own daughter, Aliste, in the marriage bed. When Berta agrees, Margiste rushes to Aliste's room to reveal her plan of making Aliste queen of France and, with the help of the third servant Tibert (a ruffian cousin), disposing of Berta for good.

That night Aliste conceives Pépin's child and Berta is framed and accused of attempting to murder "the queen." She is taken far away into the woods by Tibert and three guardsmen, who plan to behead her until they behold her beauty. The guardsmen overpower Tibert, release Berta, and kill a pig so that they may take its heart back to Margiste and Aliste as proof of Berta's death.

Berta stumbles through the forest in Germany, terrified. She prays to God, promising, if he will save her, never to reveal her true identity but to remain humble forever. After a cold night on a bed of leaves, she happens onto a hermit's cottage. Although he refuses to let her in, the hermit sets her on the path toward the house of Simon and Constance, who welcome her into the family. She is adored by their daughters Ysabel and Aiglente, with whom she is inseparable for nine and one-half years. Everyone agrees she is the most virtuous maid in all the forest.

Meanwhile, Pépin and Aliste have two "treacherous" sons, Rainfrois and Heudris. The French people loathe Aliste, who, with her mother Margiste, collects huge taxes from rich and poor alike.

At the same time, King Floire and Queen Blancheflor, now without an heir, send word to Pépin requesting that he send his younger son to Hungary to be groomed for kingship. But Aliste refuses to allow the boy to go. Queen Blancheflor has a nightmare that she interprets as a sign that her daughter is in danger. She decides to journey to Paris to see for herself.

As soon as she enters the country she begins to hear reports of how despised her greedy daughter is. When Margiste hears that Blancheflor is on the way, she puts Aliste to bed, and when the Hungarian queen arrives, Margiste tells her that her daughter is too ill to see her. After several days, Blancheflor insists on being taken to the queen's chamber, where she soon realizes that the "sick queen" is not her Berta. She snatches off the bedcovers to reveal Aliste's small feet: Berta has broad feet.

The enraged Pépin has Margiste tortured and burned and Tibert hanged. But because Aliste is the mother of his sons, he allows her to retreat to a monastery with all her gold.

He sends out a search party to look for some trace of Berta. Hearing of the search, Simon questions Berta as to her identity. Remembering her vow to God, Berta denies that she is the lost queen.

Pépin vows never to marry again. One day he sets out alone on a hunting trip to Germany, stopping at the chapel where Berta prays regularly that she will have the strength not to reveal her identity. Pépin sees her and becomes enamored, but Berta resists his overtures. He does not want to take her by force, so he knows he must win her by love. As he advances on her, she orders him to step back: "I forbid you to touch me. . . . I am no ordinary damsel. I am the wife of Pépin, king of France. . . ."

Pépin is overjoyed but, having been tricked by one woman, he is cautious. He follows her home, and Simon and Constance, unaware of his identity, have him hide behind a curtain while they question Berta. She denies that she is the queen, saying she told the story only to save her virginity. Disheartened, Pépin leaves.

Later Simon visits the king and, when he realizes that Pépin is the true king, suggests that perhaps Berta has taken a vow not to reveal her identity. The two agree that the best way to find out is to send for Berta's parents.

King Floire and Queen Blancheflor hurry to Mans, where they are led to Simon's house. When Berta sees her parents, she rushes to them, overjoyed. The secret is out: Berta is the queen of France.

There is great rejoicing in the city. Pépin makes Simon a knight and awards each family member large yearly stipends. Berta asks Constance and the girls to return to the palace with her. The party returns to France, where the Parisians rejoice for days: "There remained in the town not a bald nor a curly,/No monk nor abbot, no ordained nor renegee;/But joined the procession and the ceremony." (v. 3329)

Berta's parents return to Hungary, where Blancheflor soon gives birth to a baby girl, named Constance in honor of the woman who rescued Berta. This Constance grows up to become queen of Hungary.

Berta and Pépin have a daughter who marries Sir Milon d'Aiglent and bears a son, "the great hero Rollany, he who never knew cowardice. . . ." The second child of Berta and Pépin is a boy whom they name Charles. "He was the great Charlemagne." (Goodrich 1961)

See also Adenet le Roi.

 # BHĀRĀTAYUDDA

Javanese epic (12th c.) by Mpu Sēḍḍah and Mpu Panuluh, retelling in Old Javanese *kakawin* parts of the Indian Sanskrit epic *Mahābhārata*. The *kakawin* combines epic, lyric, didactic, and erotic forms in Hindu style. But whereas the *Mahābhārata* contains 100,000 stanzas, the *Bhārātayudda* consists of only 722 stanzas. The Javanese version omits the lengthy books detailing the deeds of ancestors and former exploits of the heroes, the Pāndawa and Kaurawa (Pāṇḍavas and Kauravas), the two sets of cousins, descendants of Bhārata, who both claim the kingdom. It begins instead with the final attempts at reconciliation between the two sides, and depicts in vivid detail the war that follows. It also omits the slain warriors' final redemption.

In the eighteenth century the Muslim poet Yosodipuro, writing in the court in Surakarta, recast the poem using modern Javanese idiom and form. (Dudley and Lang 1969)

 # BHĀRAVI

Indian poet (6th or 7th. c.), author of an epic in classical Sanskrit, *Kirātārjunīya* (Arjuna and the mountain man). Bhāravi probably lived in South India during the reign of the Pallava dynasty. His epic helped set the standard for Sanskrit literature in the south. It recounts the Pāṇḍava prince Arjuna's encounter with a wild mountain man, whom he engages in fierce combat. The mountaineer turns out to be the god Śiva. Bhāravi's work, although revered by Indian Classicists, is generally considered stylistically more difficult than Kālidāsa's. (Dudley and Lang 1969; Thapar 1966)

See also Kirātārjunīya.

 # BHAṬṬIKĀVYA

Classical Indian Sanskrit poem (ca. 7th c.) by Bhaṭṭi. The *kavya* style involved creating a story, usually taken from earlier epics, that was pleasing to both the imagination and the ear. As a style, the *kavya* employs a wide array of complex meters and verse forms and displays a broad knowledge of the arts and sciences. Bhaṭṭi's work in particular is considered a model *mahākāvya*, consisting of relatively short cantos, each composed in a meter consistent with its subject matter, and often employing plays on words and double meanings. It celebrates the exploits of King Rāma and his consort Sītā, as told in the ancient Hindu *Rāmāyaṇa*, but at the same time it illustrates all the principal rules of Sanskrit grammar and poetics in precisely the appropriate sequence. For a discussion of *Rāmāyaṇa*, see the *Encyclopedia of Traditional Epics*. (Brogan 1996)

 # BLAKE, WILLIAM

English poet and illustrator, author of the epics *Vala* (1797), *Milton* (1804?) and *Jerusalem* (1804–1820). He was born in 1757, the third of six sons and one daughter of a London hosier. He was baptized in the Church of St. James, Piccadilly. In 1761, at the age of four, he had his first vision of God. At the age of eight, he had several visions of angels. His family may have been followers of the Swedish visionary Emanuel Swedenborg (1688–1772), who spent much time in London prior to his death when Blake was 15.

Blake began writing poetry at the age of 12. He was disinterested in formal education; in fact, he held it to be wrong. His parents were apparently tolerant of his attitude, for when he was 14, they sent him to Pars's Drawing School, the best in art instruction London had to offer. His father advised him to become an engraver rather than a painter, and Blake was apprenticed to master engraver James Basire.

During his seven-year apprenticeship, Blake became acquainted with a number of books on comparative mythologies of the ancient world. At Battersea he met his future wife, Catherine Sophia Boucher, daughter of a Battersea market gardener. After his apprenticeship ended in 1779, he studied briefly at the Royal Academy, developing friendships with artist academicians Henry Fuseli and John Flaxman. In 1782 he and Catherine were married. The following year Flaxman and Reverend A. S. Matthews's wife, Harriet, financed the publishing of Blake's first and only poetry collection, *Poetical Sketches*. Blake was included in Mrs. Matthews's circle of Bluestockings, of which Flaxman was also a part.

Blake was also influenced by the German Theosophist Joseph Boehme. In 1784, Blake's father died and left him a small inheritance with which he set up a printshop with his brother Robert and James Parker, a former Basire colleague. With the help of his wife, Catherine, Blake printed his illuminated poetry and eked out a meager living as an engraver for the rest of his life. In 1784 he wrote a satire on the events of his early life: *An Island in the Moon*, which contained some material later used in *Songs of Innocence.*

In 1787 he nursed his brother Robert, ill with consumption, around the clock for two weeks. When Robert died, Blake saw a vision of his brother's soul rising through the ceiling "clapping its hands for joy." Later he attributed to Robert his discovery of illuminated printing. The following year he began to experiment with this new process of relief-etching with color washes and pen added.

Also in 1787, Blake and Flaxman and their wives attended the inaugural meeting of the New Jerusalem Church and signed its foundation manifesto.

His most popular poetry collection, *Songs of Innocence,* was published in 1789. It was the first major product of illuminated printing.

Among the freethinkers who formed a literary circle meeting at Unitarian Joseph Johnson's bookshop in St. Paul's Churchyard in 1790 were the feminist Mary Wollstonecraft and the revolutionary Thomas Paine. A number of Blake's poems criticized the political and social tyranny of the day.

In 1792, Blake's mother died. Both parents were buried at Bunhill Fields, the Dissenters' cemetery.

In 1800, at Flaxman's instigation, Blake, his wife, and his sister moved to Felpham on the Sussex coast under the patronage of a literary squire, William Hayley. The country life was conducive to the development of ideas for his prophetic *Milton,* which he engraved during 1804–1808.

In 1803 he was involved in an altercation with a member of the Royal Dragoons in his own garden. He and his wife returned to London, where he was charged by the dragoon with "assault and seditious words." In 1804 he was tried for sedition and acquitted.

In 1809 he held a several-month exhibition at his parents' old home; by this time, his brother James owned the hosiery business. The show was attended by Henry Crabb Robinson and Charles Lamb, but basically the rest of the world ignored both show and artist. Blake occasionally got a small commission, but he was so strapped for money that in 1821 he was forced to sell his 50-year-old collection of Old Masters prints. He died in 1827 and was buried near his parents in Bunhill Fields. His wife survived him by four years. (Blake 1991; Frye 1947)

See also Milton: A Poem in Two Books.

 # BLANK VERSE

The English heroic line of blank verse is unrhymed iambic pentameter, while the classical heroic line is the hexameter. Verses composed in either of these meters are called heroic verse. Blank verse was introduced into English literature in the translation by Henry Howard, Earl of Surrey (1517?–1547), of part of Vergil's *Aeneid*. The form is used in English for stately dignified verse. Blank verse has no stanza divisions; however, Milton and others grouped segments into "verse-paragraphs" using wraparound or run-on lines.

A distich in (English) heroic blank verse is called a heroic couplet, while a quatrain stanza is called a heroic stanza. Set forms of the heroic stanza are Italian and Sicilian Quatrain. Heroic octave forms are the Italian and Sicilian Octaves and the Ottava Rima. (Deutsch 1974; Padgett 1987; Turco 1986)

 # BLIGGER VON STEINACH

German poet (ca. 12th c.), author of at least one epic poem, now lost. The poem is praised for its formal qualities by Middle High German poet Gottfried von Strassburg (d. ca. 1210), who does not mention its title or subject. Bligger the epic poet may or may not be the same person as Bligger the lyric poet who served in Apulia and Sicily from 1191 to 1194 under Emperor Heinrich VI (1165–1197). The name Bligger was carried by all members of this Neckarsteinach family (near Heidelberg). (Garland and Garland 1986)

 # BLOK, ALEKSANDR

Russian poet and dramatist, author of the epic poem *The Twelve* (1918). Blok was called by some poets Russia's greatest poet of the twentieth century. He was born in 1880 in Moscow, the son of a law professor at Warsaw University. His parents separated and he was reared by his mother in St. Petersburg, where his maternal grandfather, Andrey Beketov, was rector at St. Petersburg University. His mother was a friend of the family of Vladimir Solovev, the philosopher of the doctrine of Saint Sophia. The poet would later say that his poetry was shaped by a mystical love for the Divine Wisdom, or Saint Sophia.

Blok married Liubov Mendeleeva, daughter of the famous chemist, but the marriage was not wholly successful for either. He began a friendship with Andrey Bely that became a love triangle. In 1906 his wife left him, and returned later, pregnant. His love affairs with Natalia Volokhova, an actress (1907), and Liubov Delmas, an opera singer (1914), made an impact on much of his poetry. For example, Natalia inspired him to write, in 15 days, a 30-poem cycle called *Snow Mask* (1907). He wrote a voluminous amount of poetry and several lyric dramas as well. Among the latter are *The Puppet Show* (1906), *The Stranger* (1906), *The King on the Square* (1906), *The Song of Fate* (1908), and *The Rose and the Cross* (1912). He died in 1921 after a famine winter. (Bristol 1991)

See also The Twelve.

Russian poet and dramatist, Aleksandr Blok, 1880–1921

BOCCACCIO, GIOVANNI

Italian poet, author of *Teseida delle Nozze d'Emilia* (1342). The son of Boccaccio di Chelino and an unmarried French mother, he was born in 1313 in Florence, Italy. Boccaccio was legally adopted and raised in his father's household near Florence. He was given an excellent education, preparing him for a successful business career in a city that had rapidly become a mecca for prosperous merchants but was also still under the spiritual influence of the exiled Dante. Under the influence of his tutor, and perhaps his stepmother, Boccaccio early decided to devote his life to poetry. But when his father was transferred to Naples, Boccaccio was taken there and apprenticed to a "great business man." Naples was also a mecca for scholars, and he soon had access to a culturally sophisticated court and a rich library.

Dissatisfied with Giovanni's progress as an apprentice, his father sent him to the Stadium to study canon law. Dante's friend, poet Cino da Pistoia, was one of the instructors there. Giovanni began to experiment with various genres, often, under Dante's influence, in the vernacular. Toward the end of his residence in Naples he began work on *Teseida delle Nozze d'Emilia* (The book of Theseus), apparently inventing the story of rivalry in love. In the winter of 1340–1341 he returned to Florence because of his father's financial downfall. He finished the poem the next year, despite serious money problems and continuing animosity between him and his father.

The next ten years were catastrophic for Florence, with dictatorship, revolution, financial hardship, political assassination, and the Black Death in 1348. During this somber period, Boccaccio suffered personal losses—the deaths of his father and his mistress Maria d'Aquino—and family difficulties. Nevertheless, he managed, between 1348 and 1353, to compose his *Decameron*, which brought him literary fame and civic posts. He also developed a fast friendship with Petrarch, whom he first met in Florence in 1350.

By the early 1360s he had traded an active public life for the austere existence of a scholar in Certaldo, his birthplace. A papal dispensation removed the canonical impediment (because of his illegitimacy) to priestly ordination. In August 1373 he gave a series of lectures on Dante, interrupted by his ill health. He returned to Certaldo in January 1374, where he learned of the death of his friend Petrarch. On 23 December 1375, he died and was buried in the little church of Saints Michael and James in Certaldo. He asked that his epitaph read: "His study was gracious poetry." (Branca 1976; McCoy 1974; Serafini-Sauli 1982)

See also Teseida.

 # BODMER, JOHANN JAKOB

Swiss history professor and writer, author of several unsuccessful epics, who nevertheless made a contribution to the development of a German literature in

Switzerland. Bodmer was born in Greifensee, Switzerland, in 1698. As a young man he traveled in Italy, and in 1720, at the age of 22, he became a Staatsschreiber (official) in Zurich.

In 1721 he and a colleague, J. J. Breitinger, founded a weekly literary journal, *Die Diskurse der Mahlern,* patterned after Addison's *The Spectator,* as a reaction against the Rationalist movement in literature. Their premise, using John Milton's *Paradise Lost* as their example, was that the imagination should not be dominated by reason. They continued the journal until 1723.

In 1725 he became professor of Helvetian politics and history at the Zurich grammar school, a post he was to hold for 50 years. In 1737 he became a member of Grosser Rat, or a city councillor.

Bodmer's most successful original writings were treatises of literary criticism. In 1732 his German prose translation of Milton's *Paradise Lost* was published. Later (1742) his verse translation was published, and it was revised in 1754. He also translated Homer, in hexameters.

He was so inspired by Friedrich Gottlob Klopstock's religious *Der Messias* (*q.v.*) that in 1750 he wrote a religious epic, *Noah.* This was followed the next year by *Jakob und Joseph* and *Die Synd-Flut,* and in 1752 by *Jakob und Rachel,* all unsuccessful attempts at epic writing.

He became interested in Middle High German poems such as *Parzival* and *Nibelungenlied,* the latter of which he published (Manuscript C) in 1757 without acknowledging Jakob Hermann Obereit, the discoverer of the manuscript. He then turned to tragedies based on the classics, and in 1760 wrote *Electra* and *Ulysses,* followed by *Julius Caesar* in 1763, all of which were less than successful. Finally, in 1771 he wrote an unsuccessful historical epic, *Conradin und Schwaben.*

Bodmer's demeanor, termed "mercurial and vocal," and his critical writings made him an influential national educator. His most important contributions to German literature were to engender a renewed interest in German antiquity and to help establish a German literature in Switzerland. For these attempts, he was respected by the literati of the times: Goethe visited him twice, in 1775 and 1779; Klopstock visited him in 1748; C. M. Wieland visited in 1752.

He died at Schönenberg near Zurich in 1783. (Garland and Garland 1986)

BOGDANOVICH, IPPOLIT FYODOROVICH

Russian poet, author of the epic verse tale *Dushenka* (1775–1783). Bogdanovich was born in the Ukraine in 1743 into an impoverished family of the gentry. At the age of ten he was taken to Moscow to work in service. At 15, he introduced himself to the poet Mikhail Kherashov (1733–1807), who helped him obtain an education at Moscow University. When he was 20, he translated Voltaire's "Poème sur le désastre de Lisbonne," which brought him some literary notoriety. He joined the political circle of Nikita Panin and worked for the Foreign Office as a translator.

In 1766, Bogdanovich went to Dresden for three years as secretary of the Russian legation. In 1773 he published his lyric poems in *The Lyre,* and a decade later he published the work that established his fame, *Dushenka,* relating the marriage of Psyche and Cupid, based on La Fontaine's *Les Amours de Psyché et de Cupidon* (1669). At Empress Catherine II's request, he wrote a *Collection of Russian Proverbs* (1785).

He worked in the government archives until 1795 and died in 1803. (Bristol 1991)

See also Dushenka.

BOIARDO, MATTEO MARIA, COUNT SCANDIANO

Italian poet, author of *Orlando Innamorato* (1483). Descended from a noble family, he was born in 1440 at Boiardo Castle, Scandiano, Italy. Beginning in 1476, he served the Estensi (the princely house of Este) at Ferrera for the better part of his life. He began his epic *Orlando Innamorato* in about 1476, planning to construct the work in three parts. In 1480 he was appointed captain of the forces of Borso duke d'Este at Modena, serving for two years. In 1483 the first two parts of his epic were published. In 1487 he was appointed governor of Reggio, where he remained until his death. He ordered the bells of the citadel rung to celebrate the invention of Rodamonte as the name of the pagan warrior in his poem. He died in 1494 without finishing the third part of his poem, which breaks off at the ninth canto. (Boiardo/Ross trans. 1989)

See also Angelica; *Orlando Innamorato.*

BOILEAU, NICOLAS
(Nicolas Boileau-Despréaus)

French poet and literary critic, and author of, among other works, *Le Lutrin* (The Lectern, 1674–1683), a mock-heroic epic. He was born in Paris in 1636, the son of a clerk to the *parlementu.* He was educated at the University of Paris. He studied law and became an advocate until 1657, when his father died, leaving him a sizable inheritance. Thereafter, encouraged by his brother Gilles Boileau, an established man of letters, he devoted himself to literature. His first works were his *Satires,* which were circulated among friends until a friend collected seven of them and had them published in 1666. Two others were published in 1668. A friend of tragedian Jean Racine, comedic dramatist Molière (Jean-Baptiste Poquelin), and poet Jean de La Fontaine, Boileau became a favorite (ca. 1670) of Louis XIV, who granted him an annual pension. In 1674 he published *L'Art poétique* (The art of poetry), a didactic poem illustrating the principles he espoused for fine poetry, modeled after Horace's *Ars poetica.* This poem is considered his master work. In effect he codified the principles of French

French poet, literary critic, and author Nicolas Boileau, 1636–1711

classical literature, and was thereafter called the Legislator of Parnassus. His highly entertaining mock-epic about a real-life squabble over where to put a lectern, *Le Lutrin* (1664–1683) (*q.v.*), became the model for Alexander Pope's *Rape of the Lock*. In 1677 the king made Boileau his historiographer. He was elected to the Académie Française in 1684. He is famous for his attack on pedantry, in which he said, "Let nature be our study." He died in 1711 in Paris. (Harvey and Heseltine 1959; Hornstein 1973)

See also Le Lutrin.

BRAXATORIS, ONDRÉJ
(Pseudonym: Andrej Sladković)

Slavic poet and dramatist, author of a national epic, *Marína* (1846), and a historical epic, *Dêtvan* (1853). He was born in 1820 near the town of Dětva, located in Central Slovakia in present-day Czechoslovakia. He was among a group of new poets of the Romantic generation writing in the Central Slovak dialects rather than in Czech or in Western Slovak, which had been the literary languages up until then. In 1846 he wrote a national epic, *Marína,* hailed for its freshness and individuality. A few years later Braxatoris wrote a historical epic, *Dêtvan,* which describes in idyllic but truthful terms the peasant life of Central Slovakia. He treated philosophical problems in his play *Sôvety v rodine Dušanovej),* in which the characters are personified concepts of Hegelian philosophy. He died in 1872. (Čiževskij 1971; Preminger 1974)

See also Dêtvan.

THE BRIDGE

American epic poem (1930) by Hart Crane (1899–1932). The poet depicts modern American life using the Brooklyn Bridge as a symbol of his country's aspirations and achievements. The poet once explained, "I feel myself quite fit to become a suitable Pindar for the dawn of the machine age." He first conceived of the poem while living in Columbia Heights, Brooklyn. Only much later did he learn that the house where he lived while he finished the poem had been owned by Washington Roebling, the paralyzed engineer of Brooklyn Bridge. Furthermore, Roebling had used Crane's room to watch the bridge's construction. When the book was published in 1930, it met with a "less than enthusiastic reception." However, in 1951, Stanley K. Coffman wrote the first of a number of criticisms championing its method, structure, and unity.

The poem is written in eight sections, preceded by a proem dedication, and is structured somewhat like a symphony. The poet makes use of real people from America's past, such as Columbus, Whitman, Poe, and Emily Dickinson, as well as people from his own past.

"To Brooklyn Bridge," a proem ode, begins with dichotomous images of a seagull over the industrial harbor. The predawn is an archetypal time bridge between night and day.

Section I contains one poem, "Ave Maria," in which Columbus returns to Spain from the New World with a great sense of destiny and an "incognizable Word" of hope and promise that "dissuades the abyss," manifesting as an "inmost sob, half-heard."

At the beginning of Section II, "Powhatan's Daughter" begins with a description of "Pocahuntus" taken from the seventeenth-century prose epigraph. The section contains five poems.

"The Harbor Dawn" vividly depicts the sights and sounds of the harbor at sunrise. It is also the awakening of the poet or protagonist, who makes love to his "woman of the dawn."

"Van Winkle," a morning sequence, reminds the poet of walking off to school, the characters of history and literature in his copybook. (Now Rip Van Winkle forgets both office hours and pay and "sweeps a tenement/way down on Avenue A.") The poet recalls stoning young garter snakes and launching paper airplanes; he remembers the smile his mother "almost brought" him from church, which "flickered" through the snow and "forsook her at the doorway," not returning when they kiss in the hallway.

"The River" depicts the *Twentieth Century Limited,* which spans the continent. It roars by and leaves three hungry hoboes plodding along the tracks. The poet describes ancient "rail-squatters" he used to see behind his father's cannery works. The river, flowing toward the gulf, "spends your dreams." Spanning the continent in another direction, the river is a "liquid theme that floating niggers swell." Eventually it "lifts itself from its long bed" and meets the gulf. Like the Mississippi, the river of time washes all away.

"The Dance" depicts in vivid language the medicine man Maquokeeta in union with Pocahontas while "twangs" of lightning delta down his "saber hair."

"Indiana," where "bison thunder," no more rends the dreams, presents the hardships of the westward movement, which bridges the continent overland. A pioneer woman returns to Indiana from the gold rush as a widow, only to have her one surviving son, Larry, "all that's left to me of Jim," go off to sea.

In Section III, "Cutty Sark," the era of the clipper ships is evoked by a nostalgic, boozy old sailor, the prodigal son of the "Indiana" poem, reminiscing to the poet in a waterfront bar on South Street. As dawn puts out the torch of the Statue of Liberty, the sailor heads for the Bowery and the poet walks home across the bridge.

Section IV, "Cape Hatteras," describes the "dorsal change/ Of energy—convulsive shift of sand . . ." as the calm of the native forest is interrupted by the "nasal whine of power" that "whips a new universe." Over the industrial-capitalist scene is "strident rule/Of wings imperious": the airplane, which shortly becomes the warplane, a recent reincarnation of the clipper ship. The sky warriors are perhaps "New integers of Roman, Viking, Celt—" and the pilot holds a bridge with the past: "Thou hast in thy wrist a Sanskrit charge/To conjugate infinity's dim marge/Anew! . . ."

American Hart Crane published *The Bridge,* an eight-section poem, in 1930. He used the Great East River Suspension Bridge, also known as the Brooklyn Bridge, here in an 1889 photograph with the Fulton Ferry building in the foreground, as a symbol of modern American aspirations and achievements.

Section V, entitled "Three Songs," presents three versions of the American feminine psyche, none of which is more than a stereotype. In "Southern Cross" it is the harlot who, despite abuse and exploitation, still believes in Love. The Cross is described as a "phantom, buckled" that "dropped below the dawn." "National Winter Garden" describes the exotic dancer as Magdalene, wearing "turquoise fakes on tinselled hands," against whose hips "pearls whip" in her frenzied dancing. She is "the burlesque of our lust—and faith." "Virginia" describes "blue-eyed Mary" and "Cathedral Mary," who leans "from the high wheat tower."

Section VI, entitled "Quaker Hill," describes the land developers who sell the Promised Land to the highest bidder, for example, turning the old Quaker Meeting House into the New Avalon Hotel. America, still believing in Love, would seem to be the harlot from "Southern Cross": bought and sold by suburban land developers.

Part VII, "The Tunnel," details a different sort of bridge, the subway under the river, and the nightmarish trip toward home, where "eyes take fright" and gongs rattle.

Part VIII, "Atlantis," was the reworking of an earlier poem entitled "Finale" (1923). The poet speaks of migrations and inventions that "cobblestone the heart." The bridge from the past leads inevitably into the future, which is "to be endured." History leads, the poet believes, from "the haven hanging in the night" toward some prophetic time in which the "Bridge to Thee, O Love" may finally be reached. (Crane 1933, 1966; Savage 1942; Walker [Jeffrey] 1989)

See also Crane, Hart.

 # THE BRONZE HORSEMAN
(*Medny vsadnik*)

Short epic poem (1833, publ. 1841), by Aleksandr Pushkin; one of the greatest narrative poems in Russian literature. The event described in the poem, the flooding of St. Petersburg by the Nevá River in 1824, in which many of its citizens perished, is based on fact. Pushkin, incidentally, was the first to call the city Petrograd.

The poem begins with a long introduction in which Tsar Peter surveys the Baltic shore by the Nevá River, on which he plans to build his new capital. The river, the city, and the bronze statue of Peter the Great at its center are anthropomorphized to the extent that the river "pounces" on the city, which rises "with waters lapping round his waist." The waves are described as "malicious" and "like thieves" that take revenge against Peter the Great for building the magnificent city. By the end of the poem, even the statue comes to life in the protagonist Evgeny's mind.

Evgeny (or Yevgeny) is the common man introduced in Part One, a poor helpless clerk living in this city of opulence, representing the power of the state. While the rain falls and the Nevá crashes against its banks, Evgeny lies in his bed, thinking of all that must be surmounted if he is ever to be free, famous, or wealthy. When morning comes, the Nevá explodes, "raging, yelling," as it lays siege to the unsuspecting city. At the time Tsar Alexander still rules "in glory." He appears on his balcony and admits, "A Tsar is no commander/against God's elements." Evgeny sits in the rain, watching in the direction of a cottage near the shore where his sweetheart Parasha lives with her mother. All the while, a bronze horseman rises above the waters.

In Part Two, as the waters recede, Evgeny hurries to the cottage but finds no trace of it. In shock, he goes on to work, where people are going about "in cold indifference," and the "daring bosses/of commerce" are unperturbed, planning "to take their heavy losses/out on their neighbor." The great bard Count Khvostov composed ballads about the Nevá's devastation. His wits unhinged, Evgeny does not go back to his room; instead, he sleeps every night by the water's edge, surviving on food scraps thrown from windows. Malicious children throw stones at him, and an occasional coachman lashes him with a whip. One night when it is raining much as it did on that fateful night, Evgeny wanders to the spot where the statue stands. In fury, he begins to address the horseman, "Take care . . ./you marvel-working builder. . . ." He takes flight without finishing, imagining that the tsar in "blazing anger" turns his face toward him. He races down the street, hearing the clattering of bronze horse hooves pursuing him.

After this, he is cured of rebelliousness. When he crosses the square, he takes off his worn cap in deference.

Later the flimsy cottage washes ashore. Near it, Evgeny's body is found. His "cold corpse" is committed to "that self-same ground." (Johnston 1983)

See also Pushkin, Alexsandr Sergeyevich.

 # *THE BRUCE*

Scottish national epic poem (1375–1378) by John Barbour (b. ca. 1320). Composed in the old Scottish dialect, the poem contains 20 books with 102 sections, each having 200 lines of rhyming iambic couplets. It tells the story of Robert the Bruce (1274–1379), the Scottish king who freed Scotland from British rule. Unlike most early romances, it is historically accurate about men and events mostly in Barbour's own lifetime, a Scotland under English domination.

In Book I (Sections 1 to 4), King Alexander of Scotland dies. When the barons ask Edward, king of England, to choose his successor, he takes advantage of the situation to annex Scotland. He offers the crown to Robert the Bruce if he will become his vassal. The Bruce refuses. Edward sets up his own Englishman, John de Balliol, to rule Scotland. James of Douglas learns of his father's imprisonment and death and goes to Scotland. The Bruce signs a contract with the barons, but John "the Red" Comyn betrays him to King Edward.

In Book II (Sections 5 to 8), the Bruce escapes from London and goes to Dumfries and kills Comyn. The English king orders that the Bruce be found and hanged, but, with the bishop Douglas (who has declared for the Bruce) and some friends, the Bruce proceeds to Scone, where he is crowned king (1306). The English move against King Robert at Methuen, and the Scots are routed. The English governor, Aymer, offers life and land to those who will swear fealty to the English king. Now an outlaw, the Bruce hides with a small company among the hills. The Scottish commons desert him. His queen, Isabel, joins him in Aberdeen.

In Book III (Sections 9 to 12), John of Lorne, cousin of Comyn, seeks revenge and attacks King Robert, who retreats. Three men waylay the king at a narrow place and are slain. King Robert rallies his men, reminding them of Scipio and Julius Caesar. He sends the earl of Atholl to take the queen and the ladies to the castle at Kildrummy. The king will go ahead on foot and with no horsemen. He crosses Loch Lomond with Douglas and reaches Rathlin, which submits to him.

In Book IV (Sections 13 to 18), Queen Isabel and her daughter leave Kildrummy and take sanctuary at Tain, but they are seized and taken to England. King Edward sends the prince of Wales to besiege the castle at Kildrummy and follows with an army. But the king becomes ill and dies. His son Edward II, now king, captures the castle, seat of Robert's sister; the dowager countess of Mar. Robert's brother Nigel is executed out of hand. A landing in Galloway results in the deaths of Robert's brothers Thomas and Alexander. Meanwhile, Douglas ambushes men at Arran carrying supplies from the English boats to Brodick Castle, and takes the castle. King Robert, who is nearby, is told that some strangers have recently raided the castle. He blows his horn; Douglas recognizes it and joins him. Robert sends a spy to Carrick, instructed to build a fire on Turnberry Point if it is safe to land there, but the spy does not build the fire. The king believes he sees a fire, and his men launch their galleys. While the king paces the sand, a fortune-teller tells him that he will drive the Englishmen from his land. The poet discusses astrology and necromancy, citing the Bible.

In Book V (Sections 19 to 21), the king lands at Turnberry, then learns the truth: The signal bonfire was lit in error, or by the enemy. The king's brother, Edward, attacks the town anyway, and slays all he can find. Friends at Carrick tell Robert about his wife's imprisonment. Douglas goes to Douglasdale and raids the castle as the occupants sit at their meal. Wine and blood mingle in such a flood that men thereafter call it the Douglas Larder. Aymer bribes a Carrick man with two sons to waylay King Robert as he takes his daily walk. The king sees them and kills them.

In Book VI (Sections 22 to 26), Aymer plots to take King Robert as he travels to and fro in Carrick, but watchmen inform the king, who sets a trap in a narrow place and picks off his attackers one by one as they pass through. His men find him sitting on the hillside, dead men all around. Like Tydeus at Thebes, the king has single-handedly held off his enemy. Back at Douglasdale, Douglas entices the defenders of the castle into an ambush, and Thirwall is slain. Meanwhile, John of Lorne plans to track down the king with a bloodhound. The king finds a burn and wades down into it to throw the dog off his scent. A nearby archer shoots the hound.

In Book VII (Sections 27 to 31), Robert and his man meet three men who pretend friendliness but really intend to kill him. They reach an empty farmhouse, where they eat. After the meal, Robert asks his man to watch while he sleeps, but the man falls asleep too. When the traitors attack, Robert sees them and slays them, but not before his man is killed. Douglas arrives, and they surprise a company of Englishmen and villagers, killing most of them. Aymer retreats to Carlisle. King Robert goes out to hunt with two hounds and meets three men with bows out to avenge their kinsman John Comyn. They aim their bows. The king shames them for attacking an unarmed man, so they cast their bows aside and wrestle the king, who kills them with the aid of one of the hounds. Aymer sends a woman dressed in rags to spy on Robert. She is seized, and she confesses the plot. When Aymer and his men charge, Robert and his men beat back their foe. Ashamed at being beaten by a force so much smaller, the English blame one another. Aymer tries but fails to reconcile them, and returns to Carlisle.

In Book VIII (Sections 32 to 35), Aymer sends Mowbray with a thousand men against Douglas, who attacks them. They flee, except for Mowbray, who escapes. Aymer challenges the king to meet him under Loudon Hill. The two armies meet. The English are defeated, and Aymer resigns his command. Now that his power is waxing, the king crosses the Month mountains and marches northward, leaving Douglas to win Douglasdale. The castle falls to Douglas.

In Book IX (Sections 36 to 41) King Robert falls ill. The earl of Buchan marches against him. The king suddenly declares himself well and defeats his enemies. He then takes Perth. The entire northern part of Scotland is now under the king's sovereignty except for the lands of John of Lorne and Argyle. Sir Edward Bruce, brother to the king, goes to Galloway to wrest it from the English. He wins it, putting the English to flight. Aymer rides off to England to obtain a greater force, and returns in secrecy. The two armies clash. The English scatter, and Aymer again goes back to England. Now that entire region is subject to Sir Edward's brother, King Robert. Douglas, coming to a house on the Water of Lyne, chances to hear Alexander Stewart, Sir Thomas Randolph, and Adam of Gordon discuss their intention of occupying the forest and chasing Douglas out of that country. Douglas takes them prisoner, but Gordon escapes. Douglas, for kinship's sake—the prisoners are related to the king—welcomes the two. Randolph remarks that if they are going to war against the king of England, they should do it in an open fight. For his insolence, the king puts him under close arrest.

In Book X (Sections 42 to 47), the king besieges Dunstaffnage Castle, home of John of Lorne. After its surrender he holds the castle for his own forces. Sir Alexander of Argyle now joins him, but his son, John of Lorne, escapes across the sea. A peel tower at Linlithgow Castle is used to provide arms and provisions for those passing between Edinburgh and Stirling. A farmer who resents the English takes a wain of hay with eight men hidden in it into the castle and seizes the castle for the Scots. The king makes a bargain with his cousin Randolph. If Randolph will serve the king as vassal, the king will forgive his insolence, make him an earl, and bestow on him the lands of Moray. Randolph is won over and proves to be loyal and a man of honor. Randolph now begins a siege of Edinburgh castle, which the king of England has given into the keeping of Sir Piers Luband of Gascony. When the occupants find themselves besieged, they think Sir Piers has betrayed them, so they put him in prison and choose a constable to lead them against Randolph. Meanwhile Douglas takes the castle at Roxburgh and destroys it. In Edinburgh, Randolph, with the help of William Francis, scales the castle wall in the night and takes it. The capture of the castle had been foretold years before by Margaret, queen of Malcolm III, who warned, "Gardez vous de Francais!"—which had been interpreted to mean the French, but is now explained as referring to William "Francis." The captors find Sir Piers in the prison and bring him to the earl, and he agrees to be King Robert's man. Meanwhile, Sir Edward subdues Nithsdale and all of Galloway, a peel in Rutherglen, and Dundee, and lays seige to Stirling, where Mowbray sues for peace until midsummer, when it is understood that if they have not yet been freed by the English, they will surrender.

In Book XI (Sections 48 to 51), Mowbray goes to King Edward and suggests that to save Stirling Castle, they have an open fight with the pick of knighthood, not only from England but from its allies as well. King Robert's men

Robert the Bruce, Robert I of Scotland, with his second wife, daughter of the Duke of Ulster, from *Seton's Armorial Crests*. John Barbour composed *The Bruce,* a 20-book poem relating the tangled history of Robert's successful battles to drive English forces from Scotland.

fight on foot, not horseback; horsemen would have difficulty among the trees.

In Book XII (Sections 52 to 56), the fighting is fierce. King Robert sets a leather hat with the crown high on his head so it is evident he is the king. Sir Henry de Bohun charges him. The king cleaves Bohun's skull in two, inspiring his men with courage. Hearing of the Scottish success so far, the English are shaken. In the battle at Bannockburn, the advance of the English vanguard is repulsed, with great loss of life.

In Book XIII (Sections 57 to 61), the English archers wreak much damage, but are dispersed and fall back. While the fight is at its height, the yeomen and youngsters behind in the park (the camp-followers) choose a captain from their midst, fasten sheets to poles to look like banners, and march to the battlefield. The English think reinforcements have arrived and begin to scatter. The English king flees, but Sir Giles de Argentine declares he will stay to fight. He rides straight at Edward the Bruce's host and is killed. The Bannockburn is choked with drowning men and horses. Some of the English escape to Stirling Castle, with Douglas in pursuit. The English king escapes in a boat, and the others take refuge at Berwick. Sir Philip Mowbray yields Stirling Castle and remains loyal to the Scottish king until the day he dies. The queen and her daughter Margery are restored, and Margery, heir apparent, is married to Walter Stewart (Walter the Steward). Their son (also Robert) will some day be king of Scotland.

In Book XIV (Sections 62 to 67), Edward Bruce sets out for Ireland, where he bargains with some Irishmen, who will make him king if he overthrows the English. With King Robert's consent and the help of the earl of Moray, Sir Philip the Mowbray, Sir John de Soulis, Sir John the Stewart, and others, he makes his way to Carrickfergus and overwhelms the flower of Ulster's men. A truce is made, and Ulster acknowledges Sir Edward as lord. Sir Edward now fares farther through the land, and 10 or 12 of the kings offer loyalty. However, they do not keep their word for very long. Two of them attack Sir Edward in a narrow pass, but are defeated. Knights in Dundalk prepare for battle, but Sir Edward and his men charge so sturdily that the Irish flee in confusion. The Scots then ride southward. A large English army seeks out Sir Edward, attacks, and is defeated. Sir Edward now rides to an Irish king who has sworn allegiance to him, but who really plans to betray him. He has driven away every animal, so there is no food; and he floods the place, so that the Scots nearly drown. But Thomas of Down takes Sir Edward and his men in his four ships across to the other shore, where they can hide. They raid a supply train and get food.

In Book XV (Sections 68 to 71), the Scots take the town of Connor. Sir Edward besieges the castle at Carrickfergus, which is relieved secretly by Dublin ships, captained by Sir Thomas Mandeville. During the night the English surprise the Scots, but Neil Fleming sounds a warning, and the Scots attack. Edward slays Mandeville, but Fleming is mortally wounded. The Irish are defeated. Sir Edward sails through Tarbert to the Isles. The dwellers in the Isles remember a prophecy that none shall be able to withstand a man sailing from Tarbert, and they yield, except for John of Lorne, who is found and captured.

Back in Scotland, Neville challenges Douglas in Berwick, but is slain. Douglas so despoils the town that he is known hereafter as Black Douglas.

In Book XVI (Sections 72 to 79), King Robert goes to Ireland to help his brother. Their successes depress the English, who retreat to Dublin. The Scots advance to southernmost Ireland, and no one in Ireland can withstand the two together. When they come to Limerick, the king hears a woman cry. She is in childbirth, so they build a tent for her, where she delivers. Everyone is impressed that the king would delay his journey for the sake of a humble washerwoman. Edward goes north. All but one or two of the kings of Ireland give him obeisance, and had he not been willful, all of Ireland might have fallen to his hand. Meanwhile, Douglas in Scotland keeps the marches well. Hearing that the king is in Ireland, an English earl advances to Jedwood Forest, but is surprised by Douglas and slain. Some English land at Inverkeithing but are repulsed. King Robert returns to Scotland.

In Book XVII (Sections 79 to 86), Douglas and Murray move again against Berwick. King Robert joins them and takes the castle, giving it to Sir Walter Stewart. The English king, Edward II, determines to retake Berwick. The English arrive in ships and begin a siege. King Robert tries to divert them by raids into England. At Berwick the English make an engine called "the sow." Sir Walter brings in equipment for defense or assault: great cranes, catapults, and shot, but he lacks a cannon; at that time, they were not in use in Scotland. King Robert decides to ride outside the town and lay havoc there so they will abandon the English and leave the siege. He nearly destroys Ripon and halts at Mitton. The men of Mitton bring together archers, burghers, yeomen, monks, friars, priests, clerks, and peasants, but when Douglas appears, the recruits become frightened and flee. The battle is known hereafter as "The Chapter of Mitton." The English push the "sow" toward the wall. The engineer catapults a stone, which smashes it. The men all rush out. The defenders laugh, "The sow is farrowing!" The English king retreats from Berwick.

In Book XVIII (Sections 87 to 90), in Ireland, Sir Edward rashly attacks a superior force under Clare, after telling Gib Harper to wear his armor that day. Sir Harper is overpowered and killed. The English look for the king's body to behead it, and finding Harper wearing his armor, behead him and take the head back to the English king, thinking it is Sir Edward's. The remnants of Sir Edward's army flee to Carrickfergus, where they board ships. English king Edward II invades Scotland again and reaches Edinburgh. Surprised by Douglas, he retreats and is defeated at Byland. Stewart pursues his army to York. King Robert pardons the Frenchmen. The Scots have defeated King Edward in his own country.

In Book XIX (Sections 91 to 97), William De Soulis conspires against King Robert and is sentenced to death, but dies in prison. King Robert proposes peace with the English now that he has conquered all of Scotland. They agree on a truce. Sir Walter Stewart dies. After 13 years of harassment to Scottish ships, King Robert declares the truce broken. The new English king, Edward III, marches to Scotland, but is met and defeated.

In Book XX (Sections 98 to 102), peace is again made. The two kings agree that David, heir to King Robert and scarcely five years old, will be married to young Dame Joan, sister to the English king, age seven. The marriage is to take place at Berwick. Meanwhile King Robert is struck with an illness, so he cannot attend the wedding. After the ceremony, Joan and David are brought to the king. While he is still alive King Robert calls a parliament to crown David king and order that, should David not produce an heir, Robert Stewart, his daughter's son, is to be king. The king dies (1329), requesting that his heart be taken to the Holy Land. Douglas accepts the mission. On the way he joins the Spaniards against the the Saracens. He throws the king's heart before him, fights his way to it, and is slain (1330). Douglas's bones and the heart are recovered and taken back to Scotland. The epic ends: "Thus died these great lords." (TAP) (Douglas 1964)

See also Barbour, John.

 # THE BRUT

Middle English verse epic (ca. 1205) by the English priest Layamon. It is an English rendition of Wace's Norman French *Roman de Brut*. A mixture of alliterative and rhymed verse, it is the first "literary" long poem in Middle English, although it lacks the courtly polish of Wace's work. The poem marks the first appearance of King Arthur in English, and relates the legendary history of Britain beginning with its founding in 689 by Brute (Brutus), a descendant of Aeneas. Among the other early legendary kings depicted are King Leir (Lear) and Cymbeline. (Siepmann 1987)

 # BURLESQUE
(Satire)

Comedic art in which an everyday topic is presented in exaggerated parody. As pertains to poetry, the mock-epic ridicules the manner and style of heroic epics by exaggerated imitation. Examples of the burlesque are Alexander Pope's *The Rape of the Lock* and Paul Scarron's *Virgile travesti*. Burlesque or satire mocks, lampoons, or parodies a subject. (Hornstein 1973; Turco 1986)

 # BŪSTĀN
(The orchard, or The fruit garden)

Persian mystical didactic epic (13th c.) by Sa'dī (Musharrif-uddīn Sa'dī, ca. 1184/1215–1291/1292). The poem consists of a number of wise tales, each having a moral, that are "dissertations on justice, good government, beneficence, earthly and mystic love, humility, submissiveness, contentment, and other excellences." The poem is written in a simple style, using a simple meter. The poet makes a disclaimer about his abilities: "I boast not the stock of my own excellence;/But hold forth my hand, like a beggar, for pence." He asks the reader to show mercy for the good and spare the sinner, like God, and "If thou, too, herein seest faults, be it thine/Like thy Maker to act; like Him be benign." (Dudley and Lang 1969; Sa'dī 1979)

See also Sa'dī.

BUTLER, SAMUEL

English poet and satirist, author of the most important mock-heroic epic poem in English, *Hudibras.* The son of a farmer, Butler was baptized early in 1612 in Strensham, Worcestershire, and educated at the king's school, Worcester. He was employed in the household of the countess of Kent in Wrest, Bedfordshire, where he was allowed access to her splendid library. Later, during the period of the Commonwealth and Protectorate, he entered the service of Sir Samuel Luke, a staunch Presbyterian and a colonel in the Parliamentary Army. During this period Butler probably encountered the various curmudgeons whom he lampooned in his satirical poems.

When the monarchy was restored in 1660, the earl of Carberry, Lord President of Wales Richard Vaughan, named him steward of Ludlow Castle, a position he held through 1661. During this time he married a woman of some means; however, her fortune was soon dissipated by bad investments.

Toward the end of 1662 the first part of *Hudibras* appeared for sale, although the first edition is dated 1663. It was highly successful, and the second part was published the following year. In 1674 the two parts, plus "The Heroical Epistle of Hudibras to Sidrophel," were published together. Meanwhile, Butler wrote a satire on the newly established royal society entitled "The Elephant in the Moon" (1676).

Supposedly, King Charles and Lord Chancellor Clarendon promised remuneration for *Hudibras,* but it never materialized.

Butler died in London in 1680, having nothing, according to one commentary, but "poverty and praise." (Encyclopedia Britannica 1983)

See also Hudibras.

BYRON, LORD GEORGE
(George Gordon, Sixth Baron Byron)

English poet, author of the mock-epic *Don Juan* and a great body of other poems. He was born in London in 1788. His father, "Mad Jack" Byron, deserted

Romantic English poet George Gordon, Lord Byron (1788–1824), who cultivated a romantic and adventurous lifestyle.

his family, so George was brought up in his mother's native Scotland. His exposure to Presbyterianism's predestination led to the alteration of his religious views. In 1798 he inherited the title and estates of his granduncle William. In 1801 he entered Harrow School in London, after which he attended Cambridge University, where he received an M.A. degree in 1808. The previous year, a volume of his poems, *Hours of Idleness,* was published to less than critical acclaim. An uncomplimentary review in the *Edinburgh Review* occasioned a retort in heroic couplets entitled *English Bards and Scotch Reviewers.*

In 1809 he took his seat in the House of Lords. In the summer of 1809 he began a two-year tour of Europe, which resulted in a poem narrating his travels, *Childe Harold's Pilgrimage: A Romaunt,* two cantos of which were published in 1812. That year he met Lady Caroline Lamb, who became his mistress. A dashing and handsome lord, he was pursued by many women of the aristocracy, some of whom bore him children.

In 1813 he spent several months with his half-sister Augusta Leigh, whose daughter may have been Byron's. That same year his narrative poems *Giaour* and *The Bride of Abydas* were published, followed by *The Corsair: A Tale* and *Lara: A Tale* in 1814 and *Hebrew Melodies* in 1815. By that time Byron had become an immensely popular poet. In 1815 he married Anna Isabella (Annabella) Milbanke, who gave birth to Augusta Ada (Lady Lovelace) that year and left Byron the next year. This legal separation left Byron ostracized by the very society that had previously idolized him.

He left his homeland, never to return, and went to Geneva, Switzerland, with his friends Percy Bysshe Shelley and Mary Shelley. He fathered another daughter, Allegra (b. 1817), by Clare Clairmont.

While in Geneva, Byron wrote the third canto of *Childe Harold* and the narrative poem *The Prisoner of Chillon.* After he moved to Venice, he produced, among other things, the first two cantos in ottava rima of the mock-epic *Don Juan* (1818–1821) and the fourth and final canto of *Childe Harold* (1818).

After 1819, Countess Teresa Guicciola abandoned her marriage to become Byron's mistress. The two traveled in Italy for two years before settling in Pisa, where Byron wrote the narrative poems *Mazeppa* and *The Island,* as well as two verse dramas. In 1823 he completed all 16 cantos of *Don Juan,* which is often considered his master work.

In 1823, Byron joined Greek insurgents against the Turks at Missolonghi. He died there in 1824. (Magill 1989)

See also Don Juan.

 ## CAMÕES

Portuguese epic poem (1825) by João Baptista da Silva Leitão de Almeida Garrett (1799–1854). The poem celebrates the life of Luís Vaz de Camões (ca. 1524–1580), author of the national epic of Portugal, *Os Lusíadas* (publ. 1572), and decries the neglect his countrymen showed him. The poet's great work received little attention in his lifetime. He loved his country so much that, after the Portuguese under Sebastian suffered ignominious defeat at the hands of the Moors in Africa, Camões wrote from his deathbed, "All will see that so dear to me was my country that I was content to die not only in it but with it." (Atkinson 1952; Preminger 1974)

See also Almeida Garrett, João Batista da Silva Leitão de.

 ## CAMÕES, LUÍS VAZ DE
(Camoëns)

Portuguese poet, author of the Portuguese national epic *Os Lusíadas* (publ. 1572), which celebrates the life of his distant kinsman Vasco da Gama. A member of the lesser nobility, Camões was born possibly in Lisbon about 1524, the year of the death of Vasco da Gama, to whom his family was related by marriage. It was an era of Portuguese merchant-adventurer expansion, in which his father had participated. During a voyage to India, the senior Camões was shipwrecked and drowned off the coast of Goa.

Luís studied the classics and Italian Renaissance poets at the University of Coimbra. In 1544 he returned to Lisbon, where he was accepted in courtly circles, performing his poetry, until an unwise love affair in 1846 ended in exile. He entered the army as a foot soldier, and in 1847 was sent to Ceuta in Africa. He was wounded and lost his right eye.

Two years later he returned to Lisbon to resume his courtly life, but in three years' time he was in trouble with the authorities again: He was involved in a street brawl and sentenced to prison. After serving nine months, he was pardoned on the condition that he serve in the army in India.

In May 1553 he sailed for India aboard one of a fleet of four ships. His ship was the only one to arrive safely, and even that vessel was shipwrecked on the return trip. Three years later he was sent to Macau in China, where he stayed until 1561. Hostilities in China forced him to Goa again, where he remained for six years. The man whose love of country was unbounded had already spent most of two decades separated from his homeland.

For a number of years during his exile, he had been at work on his epic *Os Lusíadas*, which traced the nation's history through that of da Gama. When it was completed, he set out for Lisbon in 1567 to have it published. The journey took three years, and the poem was not published until 1572. He received a small pension from King Sebastion, but the poem received little attention otherwise. Camões fell ill in 1579, dejected over Portugal's defeat in Africa. On his deathbed he wrote to a friend, "All will see that so dear to me was my country that I was content to die not only in it but with it." He died in 1580 at about age 56. (Atkinson 1952; Hornstein 1973)

See also Lusíadas, Os.

 # CANDBARDĀI
(Or Chand Bardāi)

Indian poet, author of *Pṛthvīrāja-rāso* (or Pṛthvīrāj Rāsau). He lived in the twelfth century in Lahore, a city now in Pakistan and the capital of Punjab. A member of the bardic tradition at the Rājput court, he wrote his epic in Hindi based on bardic material about the feats of Pṛthvīrāj, the last Hindu king of Delhi before the invasion of the Turks. Pṛthvīrāj died in 1192, so Candbardāi must have composed the epic shortly after the events it depicts. (Blackburn 1989; Thapar 1966)

See also Pṛthvīrāja-rāso.

 # *CANTERBURY TALES*

Middle English collection of tales, mostly in verse (begun ca. 1385; unfinished at poet's death), the most celebrated work of Geoffrey Chaucer (ca. 1340–1400). Two of the tales have some epic characteristics: *The Knight's Tale*, a chivalric romance, and *The Nun's Priest's Tale*, a mock-heroic beast epic. (Chaucer 1969)

See also Chaucer, Geoffrey; *The Knight's Tale*; *The Nun's Priest's Tale*.

 # *CANTO GENERAL*

Spanish Chilean epic (1950) by Nobel Prize–winner Pablo Neruda, a surrealist, lyrical poet. Neruda spent 14 years writing on the subject of freedom and its suppression, in his words, "singing the earth and the episodes of our country's history." He gathered his collection as one long poem, which American poet

Robert Bly labeled "the greatest long poem written on the American continent since *Leaves of Grass*." It portrays, in 15 books, American botany, zoology, archaeology, history, conquerors, liberators, and politics. As Neruda noted in a speech against González Videla, it began as *Canto General de Chile*: "If I wanted to insult the President of the Republic, I would do it within my literary work. But . . . in the vast poem that I am now writing . . . I will also do it honestly, and with the purity that I have always displayed in my political activities." But as the poet's vision broadened beyond Chile's borders, it became a poem about Latin America and a myth of origins.

In some passages, "Alturas de Macchu Picchu" (The heights of Macchu Picchu) and "Canto General de Chile" (General song of Chile), Neruda's power and intensity as a poet can be seen despite his sacrifice of lyricism to politics.

The poem has a chronological plot. The first book, "A Lamp on Earth," speaks of the land itself, "My land without name"; of the vegetation of "Arboreal America,/wild bramble between the seas"; and of the arrival of birds and beasts. Neruda speaks of a land "tattooed by rivers" and of the arrival of man.

The second book, "The Heights of Macchu Picchu," containing 12 sections, is a group of poems of conversion. Neruda climbed to Macchu Picchu in 1943 on a journey home to Chile from Mexico. The following year he published this section as a free-standing poem. Part III begins, "Like corn man was husked in the bottomless/granary of forgotten deeds. . . ." He speaks of scaling "the ladder of the earth," feeling great kinship with the land and the people who live there.

Book III, "The Conquistadors," takes up the history in 1493. The first section, called "They Come through the Islands," begins: "The butchers razed the islands." It follows the conquistadors in Part II, "Now It's Cuba": "Cuba, my love, they put you on a rack," and, in Part III, "They Reach the Gulf of Mexico" (1519), in which "The murderous wind takes wing to Veracruz." In Part IV, he calls Cortés "a chilling thunderbolt." He speaks, in Part VI, of Alvarado, who "fell upon the huts/with claws and knives." Part IX describes Balboa's death, his head impaled on a spear. Part XII relates the coming of Ximénez de Quesada and his men (1536), who tie up the *Zipa* and demand the jewels of the ancient god, "jewels that flourished/and glistened with Colombia's/morning dew." Beginning with Part XVIII, several sections are devoted to the invasion of Chile, where "My Araucanian ancestors . . . you had just raised/your ear to the gallop . . ./when Araucania's/lightning struck." Part XXI is devoted to Valdivia (1544), who "drove his dripping spear/into Arauco's stony bowels." In the remaining segments of Book III he describes Magellan's traversing the strait into the Pacific. He ends on an uncharacteristically optimistic note, enumerating some good the conquistadors brought: machinery, technology, paper, wheat. "The light came despite the daggers."

Book IV, "The Liberators," relates, in 43 sections, the history of Latin America from the time of Cuauhtémoc (1520), "youth shaken in Mexico's/metallic darkness," to the Brazil of 1945: "Today the hunt spreads/over Brazil again."

Book V, "The Sand Betrayed," mirrors many of the political events in which Neruda was involved beginning with the mid-1940s. He was elected senator in 1944 and became a member of the Chilean Communist party the following year. He campaigned for presidential candidate Gabriel González Videla, whom his party supported. But after Videla was elected, he reneged on his campaign promises and outlawed the Communists. In 1947, Neruda, still a senator, published an open letter in Caracas accusing Videla of betrayal. The president issued an order for Neruda's arrest for treason. The poet went into hiding for a year, during which he was writing *Canto General*, particularly Book V, which takes to task politicians and exploitative American corporations, namely Standard Oil, Anaconda Copper Mining, and United Fruit. Part V is called "González Videla, Chile's Traitor (Epilogue) 1949," in which the poet says, "In my country villany presides." He refers to Videla several times as a rat.

Book VI, "America, I Do Not Invoke Your Name In Vain," is a short book of 19 sections, all brief hopeful poems anticipating a new day in Latin America.

Book VII, "Canto General of Chile," is apolitical: a collection of love lyrics to the poet's homeland, to its physical features, its plants, its seas. Neruda was very drawn to the sea.

Book VIII, "The Earth's Name Is Juan," covers in 17 sections a number of common people, whom the poet attempts to show that communism serves: a shoemaker, a fisherman, a colonel, and a banana worker, among others. At the time, Stalin's atrocities had not been revealed to the world, and Neruda quotes him as saying, "Our best treasure/is mankind."

Book IX, "Let the Woodcutter Awaken," contains six long poems in the same vein as the previous book, praising Stalin and the Soviet Union.

Book X, "The Fugitive," relates the poet's horseback flight over the Andes to Argentina when he was charged with treason.

Book XI, "The Flowers of Punitaqui," contains 15 brief, disjointed sections describing various conditions with which peasants have to contend, such as drought and factory strikes.

Book XII, "The Rivers of Song," takes the form of letters to five men who, like himself, lived—and some died—in opposition to powers in charge: Miguel Otero Silca, Rafael Alberti of "Generation of '27" in Madrid, González Carbaldo, Silvestre Revueltas, and Miguel Hernández, the great shepherd poet.

Book XIII, in 17 sections, entitled "New Year's Chorale for the Country in Darkness," is Neruda's lament for his native Chile under Videla's rule. With intense homesickness he writes, "My heart gallops toward you/like a dark horse, my little land."

Book XIV, in 24 poems, returns to a subject never far from his thoughts: "The Great Ocean," which for Neruda is "the central volume of force,/.../the motionless solitude brimming with life." The captivating sea is the mother of all things, the well-spring of the unconscious, the source of unceasing wisdom.

Book XV, "I Am," the final 28 poems, is a brief autobiography of the poet's life from 1904 to 1949. He describes himself as "a slender child whose pale form/was impregnated with pristine forests and storerooms." (I) He depicts his arrival, at age 17, to a Santiago "vaguely impregnated/with mist and rain," a city where "The clothing of 1921 pullulated/in an atrocious smell of gas, coffee and bricks." (IV) He chronicles his life as student, as traveler to exotic ports as a Cuban consul, as an observer in 1936—later political activist—of the beginning of the civil war in Spain, as an explorer of temples while consul general in Mexico (1940), a country he loves with great passion: "I want my words/to cling to your walls like kisses." (XIII) He bids Mexico farewell with regret: "Because in my life, Mexico, you live like a little/lost eagle that circles in my veins." (XIII) Part XIV tells of his return to his house by the sea in Isla Negra. When he is forced into exile he writes a will of sorts, leaving his books "to the new poets of America." (XXIV) He asks to be buried in Isla Negra, "facing the sea that I know, every wrinkled area/of stones and waves that my lost eyes/won't see again." (XXV) The final poem says that the book "was born/of fury like a live coal. . . ." (Neruda 1991)

See also Neruda, Pablo.

 # THE CANTOS

Modern American classic, a collection of 117 poems plus one fragment, which its author, Ezra Loomis Pound (1885–1972), referred to as an epic. He first announced his intention to produce "a cryselephantine poem of immeasurable length" in 1915—one that would combine the development of a poetic vision with contemporary political and historical events. Pound described an epic as being a poem including history. Certainly this definition applies to *The Cantos*. His epic, a work of monumental erudition if not of widespread accessibility, was the labor of 50 years. It is an attempt to write an epic in a lyric mode.

The poems are colloquial; throughout the work, Pound, a symbolist, presents phonetic transcripts of American and English dialects. Canto XVI, for example, concerns a long passage in French. Canto VII quotes Ovid in Latin and also includes passages in French and Greek. Others include German (LXXXVI, for example), Chinese (LXXXVI), and music (LXXV). Canto LXXVII is followed by a "dictionary" of ideograms used in the text.

A draft of the first 30 cantos was published in 1930, when the poet was age 45. Prior to that time, an early version of the first three cantos had been published in 1917; a revised version appeared in 1920. Cantos VIII–XI were published in 1923, entitled "Maletesta Cantos." Cantos I–XVI were published in 1925. Eleven new cantos were completed in 1934, when the first collection was published. Three years later Cantos XLII–LI appeared; Cantos LII–LXXI in 1940; Cantos LXXII–LXXIII in 1944; Cantos LXXIV–LXXXIV, called the Pisan Cantos, written during his first three years of hospitalization, appeared in 1948; Cantos LXXXV–XCV, entitled *Rock-Drill de los Cantares,* appeared in 1955; Cantos XCVI–CIX, *Thrones de los Cantares,* appeared in 1959, and a fragment about "Olga," meant to be included in the work, was written in 1966. It was incomplete at the time of Pound's death in 1972.

Pound's combination of so many elements led him to describe the structure of the work as "rag bag." In fact, the collection—particularly the section "The Thrones"—has been criticized as being deliberately abstruse and so convoluted with arcane references as to be undecipherable. His intent, he claimed, was to produce a "didactic treatise for philistine Americans."

For Canto I he borrows the image of Odysseus as a man on an inner journey back into the time of myth in search of culture. Its beginning: "And then went down to the ship," suggesting the continuation of an action begun sometime before the poem begins.

Canto II alludes to characters from Ovid's *Metamorphoses* as his model for transformation. During a sea voyage, a young boy is brought aboard, hitching a ride to Naxos, "loggy with vine-must": "He has a god in him,/though I do not know which god."

A brief Canto III takes the poet through Tuscan and the Spain of El Cid, indicating incidents to come. In Canto IV he visits spots from classical times. Canto V touches primarily on Renaissance Italy, while Canto VI juxtaposes Renaissance France with ancient Greece. Canto VII skips to Britain, supposedly tying the poet to the epic's historical and cultural context.

An early concern of Pound's, and one that he tackles in a number of the first 70 or so cantos, is the evils of usury, along with other capitalist shortcomings in general. He also denounces warmongers and journalists. He spends 20 cantos linking the disciplined government of Confucian China with the disciplined government of Adams's America.

Following Pound's confinement on treason charges during World War II, he assumes his own identity as the epic's protagonist, assuming as well a degree of humility at his own mistakes: In Canto LXXXI he says, "Pull down thy vanity/How mean thy hates/Fostered in falsity."

Cantos XCVI through CIX, called "Thrones" and written in prison, are "an attempt to move out from egoism to establish some definition of an order possible or at any rate conceivable on earth." He made this explanation to his friend, New Directions publisher James Laughlin. However, this is the section criticized as being deliberately abstruse and undecipherable.

The last segment, entitled "Drafts and Fragments," is the poet's attempt to be comprehensible, but he is aware of his own failure. In his original canto he admits to having fallen short in his attempt "to write Paradise" and asks that those who love him "try to forgive what I have made." He admits that "I lost my center/fighting the world." (Pound 1970/1991)

See also Pound, Ezra Loomis.

 # CARAMÚRU

(Full name: *Caramúru: poema épico do descubrimento da Bahia;*
Caramúru [Sea dragon, or moray]:
Epic poem of the discovery of Bahia)

Brazilian epic poem (1781) by José de Santa Ritta Durão (1722/1737–1784), of the Minas Gerais school of poets. The poet left Brazil and went to Portugal to become rector of the University of Coimbra, but he never lost his longing for his homeland and wrote the poem "from love of country." He wrote in his *Reflexões Prévias e Argumentos* that "Brazil is no less deserving of a poem than the Indies." He set about writing a national epic that would chronicle the history of the Portuguese colony from the sixteenth-century discovery of Bahia to the expulsion of all foreign invaders.

Consisting of ten cantos written in ottava rima, the poem celebrates the fictitious discovery of Bahia by Diogo Álvares, a shipwrecked sailor who comes ashore amid cannibalistic Indians. Somehow his firearms are intact, and the Indians are awed by their power. He becomes a chieftain to the Indians, who call him "Sea Dragon" (Caramúru), so-named because he appeared out of the sea. The term "dragon," or "moray," has particular significance because of the messianic aspect of the symbol: The Anaconda (or water snake) is the mythic ancestor, life-giver, and source of power and transformation among many South American Indians.

Álvares marries an Indian princess. She becomes a Christian, and bestows her lands upon the king of Portugal. At one point, two of the Indian chiefs engage in a life-and-death struggle; in this passage, the poet attains truly Homeric or Vergilian heights.

With its vivid descriptions of Bahian scenery and its reverence for Indian customs, the poem is now considered a major work of Brazilian literature, one of the very first. However, it did not garner immediate critical acclaim, which deeply disappointed the poet. (Brotherston 1975; Putnam 1948/1971)

See also Durão, José de Santa Ritta.

CASTELLANOS, JUAN DE

Spanish poet, author of *Elegías de varones ilustres de Indias* (Elegies of illustrious men of the Indies, 1589), the longest poem in the Spanish language, and one of the longest poems ever written in the world. Castellanos was born in Spain in 1522 and arrived in the New World as a youth. He lived in Puerto Rico for a period, then Cubaigua, Maracaibo, and Colombia. He served as an acolyte and later as a parish priest, but his life experiences did not stop with the church. He was a pearl fisherman, a soldier, an adventurer, and, by his own admission, an enjoyer of Indian women. Eventually he became a humanist and a writer. His poem of 150,000 lines, *Elegies of Illustrious Men of the Indies,* completed in 1589 when he was 67, is not in the least elegiac. Beginning with Columbus, to whom he dedicated his poem, he wrote in ottava rima about great men, peasants, and scoundrels (pirates). He had read classicists Ovid, Vergil, Horace, and Seneca, as well as Spanish writers Juan de Mena, Garcilaso de la Vega, Ercilla, and more. He dedicated the sixth of his *Elegies* to Juan Ponce de León and Borinquén (Puerto Rico).

He loved his adopted homeland, and lived to age 85 in the New World. But he died in 1607 without ever seeing his poem in print; in fact, it was not published until the nineteenth century. (Anderson-Imbert 1969; Jones 1966)

See also *Elegías de varones ilustres de Indias.*

CATALOGUE OF WOMEN

Greek epic poem (ca. 6th c.), now extant only in fragments, erroneously attributed to Hesiod. The poem, consisting of five books in hexameter, is a continuation of Hesiod's *Theogony*. It relates the stories of women loved by the gods who have become mothers of heroes. Some parts survive on papyrus fragments, and other parts are known from quotations that have survived. (Howatson and Chilvers 1993)

See also Theogony.

CATHERINE
(Saint Catherine of Alexandria)

Heroine (ca. 4th c.) of the Czech epic poem *The Legend of St. Catherine*, written in the middle of the fourteenth century by an unknown author. Legend holds that she was born early in the fourth century in Alexandria of noble pagan parents. She received a fine education and, after her conversion to Christianity, engaged in learned arguments defending her faith. Roman emperor Maxentius, who was persecuting Christians, called in pagan scholars to dispute her and defend his actions. She was finally sentenced to be killed on the wheel, henceforth known as the Catherine wheel. (Dvornik 1962)

See also The Legend of St. Catherine.

CĀTTANĀR, CĪTTALAIC
(Merchant-Prince Shattan)

Indian merchant, poetry critic, and Tamil poet (fl. ca. 171 A.D., author of *Maṇimēkalaï*, a continuation of the *Cilappatikāram* of Iḷaṅkō Aṭikaḷ, his friend. Cāttanār was a noble merchant and one of the last members of the *Sangam*, a revered academy of Tamil poets. He was a protégé of Chēral king Ceṅkuṭṭuvaṇ who ruled for more than 50 years, according to the *Cilappatikāram*, making many conquests during that time. Cāttanār had his friend Aṭikaḷ's blessing to write his epic, which is mentioned in Aṭikaḷ's Epilogue. (However, the prologue and epilogue were frequently written by someone other than the poet himself, so it is entirely possible that Cāttanār wrote it.) The poet himself (called "Cāttan") appears in Ayikaḷ's poem: it is he, referred to as "the famed Tamil poet, / Caṭṭaṇ," who tells the story of Kōvalaṇ and Kaṇṇaki to Ceṅkuṭṭuvaṇ. (Shattan 1989)

See also Maṇimēkalaï.

ČECH, SVATOPLUK

Czech epic poet, novelist, and satirist, author of two epic poems, *Europa* (publ. 1878) and *Slávie* (publ. 1884). Born in 1846, Čech was influenced by the poetry of Jan Kollár (1769–1820), who worked to foster a Slavic mythology. Čech became the leader of the Nationalists literary tradition ("Stir"), centered around a literary magazine called *Ruch*. He preferred nationalistic and patriotic themes for his poetry, colored by his own liberal humanism. Often his lyric poetry dealt with the economic and political misfortunes of the common people. His two epic poems idealize Slavic characteristics and democratic principles. His prose satires revolve around a character named Mr. Brouček, who lampoons the country's middle-class philistinism and complacency. But he also employed satire in some of his poetry. One of his best-known works is a poetic satire, *Hanuman*, published in 1884 as a political lampoon. Another of his most popular works, *In the Shade of the Lime Tree* (*Ve stínu lipy*), portrays in idyllic scenes Czech country life. He died in 1908. (Preminger 1974; Siepmann 1987)

See also Europa; Slávie.

CHANSONS DE GESTE

Medieval Old French metrical heroic epic-romances, many of which recount the deeds of Charlemagne and his paladins. Others describe the exploits of other legendary and historical knights of the Carolingian era (principally the twelfth and thirteenth centuries). Some 70 works in the *Charlemagne Cycle* have been preserved. The early chansons were usually comprised of ten-syllable assonant or single-rhyme lines. The earliest chansons, in which women played little or no part, glorified chivalry in battle. By the thirteenth and fourteenth centuries, romantic love became a factor in many of the chansons, which are characterized by 12-syllable rhyming lines (the alexandrine). (Hornstein 1973; Preminger 1974)

CHATEAUBRIAND, VICOMTE FRANÇOIS-AUGUSTE-RENÉ DE

French literary genius and author, among other works, of a long prose epic, *Les Natchez* (publ. 1826), and the Christian prose epic *Les Martyrs* (1809). Chateaubriand was born in 1768 in Saint-Malo, the tenth child of an old Breton family. He spent his childhood at the family château of Combourg near Saint-Malo, studying intermittently at Dol, Rennes, and Dinan. At the age of 20 he took an army commission, went to Paris, and was presented at court. With the approach of the French Revolution, he left France in 1791 and set out for

America, planning to discover the Northwest Passage. When the monarchy fell in 1792, he returned to France to fight with the *Armée des émigrés,* whose core was the royalist army. He was wounded during the siege of Thionville and in 1793 escaped to England.

During his seven-year exile, he wrote *Les Natchez,* a prose epic in 12 books, which he intended to make part of his book of Christian apologetics called *Le Génie du Christianisme;* however, he later changed his mind. He also wrote a political work on the Revolution and did a number of translations to support himself.

In 1800 he returned to France; a year later, he published a tale about Louisiana, *Atala,* which was immediately successful. He also wrote a Romantic tale, *René,* which, like *Atala,* was originally intended to form a part of his epic *Les Natchez.* At the moment when Roman Catholicism was again to become the official religion of France, he published his book of Christian apologetics, earning him Napoléon's patronage and an appointment to the embassy in Rome. However, after Napoléon summarily had the duc d'Enghien court-martialed, shot, and buried at midnight (1804), Chateaubriand resigned in outrage. He traveled in Spain, Greece, and the Near East during 1806 and 1807. When he returned, he devoted himself to literature and journalism. Among his works of that period was a prose epic about early Christianity, *Les Martyrs* (1809). He also produced several works describing his travels, a biography of the famous Trappist Rancé (L'Abbé Armand-Jean De Le Bouthillier, 1626–1700), and a number of political and critical writings.

After Napoléon's downfall, Chateaubriand served as one of Louis XVIII's ministers at Ghent as well as ambassador to London. He died in 1848 in Paris, but at his request was buried in an island tomb off Saint-Malo. (Harvey and Heseltine 1959)

See also *Martyrs, Les; Natchez, Les.*

CHAUCER, GEOFFREY

The first great English poet, author of *Troilus and Criseyde* (ca. 1385), a long narrative poem based on an incident from the Trojan War, and *Canterbury Tales,* an unfinished collection of tales mostly in verse. He was born about 1342 into the household of a prosperous vintner. His father had connections at the court of King Edward III, enabling the young Chaucer (by 1357) to serve as page to the countess of Ulster, wife of Prince Lionel, the king's second son. Geoffrey Chaucer later rose to the rank of Esquire in the royal household. He became fluent in French, Italian, and Latin, and versed in law, accounting, astronomy, medicine, physics, alchemy, and philosophy. He served in the military in France in 1359, and was taken prisoner and ransomed in 1360, part of his ramsom paid by King Edward III.

In all likelihood, his interest in poetry was aroused during his stay in France. He began a translation of Guillaume de Lorre (fl. ca. 1st half 13th c.) and Jean de Meung's (d. ca. 1305) long allegorical poem on courtly love, *Roman de la Rose.*

In about 1366 he married Philippa Swynford, attendant to the queen and sister to Katherine Swynford, who became the mistress, and later the wife, of John of Gaunt. In 1367, he was awarded a lifetime stipend by the royal exchequer. He and Philippa had two sons: "little Lewis," so-called in Chaucer's *A Treatise on the Astrolabe* (1391), and Thomas, who became a prominent public servant. The couple may have had a daughter as well.

In 1369 he wrote his most important poem, *The Book of the Duchess*, an elegy on the death of Blanche, wife of his patron John of Gaunt.

Over the decade of 1367–1377, the king sent Chaucer on several secret diplomatic missions to France. In 1372, Chaucer undertook a diplomatic mission to Genoa, Italy, to negotiate a commercial treaty. This journey and another, five years later, introduced him to the works of Petrarch and Boccaccio, as well as those of Dante, all of which profoundly influenced his writing for the rest of his life. In *The House of Fame* (1374–1380) he used, almost for the last time, the octosyllabic couplets that had characterized his earlier works. *The Parliament of Fowls* (ca. 1377–1386) and *The Legend of Good Women* (1380–1386) also show Italian influence. His use of the decasyllabic couplet, which evolved into the heroic couplet, was the first known English usage of the form, and he used it for most of the *Canterbury Tales*. The most significant accomplishment of his so-called Italian period is *Troilus and Criseyde* (1385).

In 1374 he was awarded a house and designated controller of customs of the Port of London, with duties to oversee customs on skins, hides, and wools. In 1382 he was also made controller of petty customs overseeing, among other things, wines. In about 1385 he acquired a home in Kent, where he was first elected justice of the peace. He served briefly as a knight for the shire of Kent in Parliament (1385–1386). He resigned his first life pension in 1388, and the following year Richard II appointed him clerk of the king's works, overseeing maintenance of all public bridges and buildings. He resigned this post in 1391 and received appointment as deputy forester of a royal forest in Somerset. Three years later, Richard II bestowed a second life pension upon him. By 1895–1896 he was apparently in the service of Henry Bolingbroke, son of his former patron and brother-in-law, John of Gaunt—hence, Chaucer's wife's nephew. When Bolingbroke had Richard deposed and he acceded as Henry IV, he increased Chaucer's stipend.

Chaucer continued to work on the *Canterbury Tales*, probably until his death in 1400. His funeral at Westminster Abbey established a new tradition, for he was the first to be interred in what is now known as "The Poets' Corner." (Chaucer 1971; Hornstein 1973; Siepmann 1987)

See also *The Knight's Tale; The Nun's Priest's Tale; Troilus and Criseyde*.

 # CHOERILUS

Greek epic poet, author of the *Persica*. He lived on the island of Samos in the fifth century B.C. His *Persica*, now lost, probably chronicled the Persian wars as narrated by Herodotus. It is known that the work celebrated the Greek rout of the Cyprian army at the Battle of Salamis because the Athenians decreed that the poem should be recited along with Homer at the Panathenaea, a religious festival honoring Athena, at which a contest of poets was traditionally held.

Later, Choerilus was employed by the Spartan general Lysander to celebrate his exploits.

Very little remains of his work. In one fragment he laments the disappearance of epic poetry, of which he considered himself the last practitioner. He wrote one poem, "On the Crossing of the Darius Bridge," about a bridge across the Bosphorus not far south of the Black Sea entrance, which was constructed of boats by Choerilus's fellow Samian, Mandrocles. (Olmstead 1948)

 # CHRÉTIEN DE TROYES

French poet, the foremost narrative poet of the twelfth century. He is the author of three finished romances, *Erec et Enide* (ca. 1170), *Cligès* (ca. 1175), and *Le Chevalier au lion* (The knight with the lion, ca. late 1170s or early 1180s), as well as two unfinished romances, *Le Chevalier de la charrete* (The knight of the cart) and *Le Conte du Graal* (The story of the Grail, or *Perceval*), two extant lyric poems, and a number of lost works, mostly Ovid adaptations or translations. He may also have been the author of *Guillaume d'Angleterre* (William of England). He was born about 1140, perhaps in the city of Troyes. At the beginning of his romance *Erec et Enide*, he refers to himself as Chrétien de Troyes, indicating that he was perhaps born there or lived in the city, center of the province of Champagne and site of the court. He has been called the father of Arthurian romance and the creator of medieval romance.

The only information known about him comes from his own brief comments in his works. The opening of *Le Chevalier de la charrete* contains a long passage praising Marie de Champagne, eldest daughter of Eleanor of Aquitaine and Louis VII of France, and wife of Henry the Liberal, count of Champagne. Marie's marriage to Henry occurred in 1159, so Chrétien's poem had to be written after that time. The passage of praise establishes the fact of his close ties to the court, which probably continued until Henry's death in 1181.

His final and longest work, *Le Conte du Graal*—almost 9,000 lines are extant—is dedicated to Marie's cousin and confidant Philip, count of Flanders, who may have been the poet's patron after Henry's death. Philip became count of Flanders in 1168, left in 1190 on the Third Crusade, and died in the Holy Land the following year, so Chrétien must have begun this poem before 1191. That it was unfinished could indicate that he abandoned it when Philip died, but more likely he would not have abandoned such a long work honoring a hero unless he was physically unable to complete it. This suggests that he died somewhere around 1191 or soon thereafter.

Because of their order in a list of his works included in *Cligès*, the dates of his five romances can be surmised. All five are Arthurian romances, reflecting a familiarity with Geoffrey of Monmouth's *Historia regum Britanniae,* Wace's *Roman de Brut,* and Celtic oral tradition. That he was also versed in the classics is evident from the titles of his lost works: The names of most of them suggest that they are either translations or adaptations of Ovid's work. Since Chrétien began his literary career with a series of translations or adaptations from Latin into the vernacular, he was probably a scholar with a university education, perhaps from a cathedral school.

One other poem, *Guillaume d'Angleterre,* based on the life of St. Eustace, contains in the opening line and again 17 lines later a reference to the author as being Chrétien: "Christian [Chrétien] wishes to begin the telling of a tale," and "Christian, experienced in storytelling, tells of a king who lived in England." (Chrétien de Troyes 1990)

See also *Erec et Enide; Parzival.*

 # CID, POEMA DEL
(Also *Cantar de Mío Cid*)

Spanish epic poem (ca. 1140) by an unknown Castilian bard extolling the exploits of military leader Rodrigo (or Ruy) Díaz de Bivar (or Vivar) (ca. 1040/1043–1099), who at one time or another fought on both sides of the war between the Christian Castilians and the Islamic Moors.

The poem, consisting of 3,735 lines, is divided into three sections, or *cantares.* The opening pages of the poem are lost, but the beginning may be assumed from another document, *Chronicle of Twenty Kings,* that had originally been translated from the poem into Latin prose.

The historical Díaz de Bivar was born into a family of the landed aristocracy in Bivar and became an *alferez* (marshal) in Castilian king Sancho II's army in 1065. Later he served under Sancho's successor, Alfonso VI, who in 1081 exiled him for raiding Toledo, under Castilian protection at the time. The Cid then swore allegiance to the Moorish rulers of Saragossa, while preparing to invade Valencia. In 1094 he became ruler of Valencia, which remained a Christian stronghold until his death, when it again fell to a Muslim army. The name Cid is a corruption of the Arabic *Sidi,* meaning "lord," so his title was the "Lord Fighter." He was also known as *El Campeador* ("the Champion").

In the first cantar, King Alfonso sends the Cid to collect tribute from the Moorish king of Seville, who is being attacked by Count Ordóñez of Castile. The Cid defeats Ordóñez at Cabra, imprisons him, and returns to Castile with the tribute. But his envious enemies speak against him to the king, who believes their stories and informs the Cid by letter that he has nine days in which to leave the kingdom. Saddened, the Cid calls his family and vassals together to decide who will accompany him and who will remain behind. The party leaves Castile and arrives in Burgos, where no one will give them lodging because the king has warned the people not to help the Cid. Only one little girl dares to speak to him, telling him that he must leave. The Cid camps outside of

Rodrigo Díaz de Bivar, known as El Cid, was an eleventh-century Spanish hero memorialized in an epic written by an anonymous Castilian in the mid-twelfth century. Here El Cid, kneeling, is pardoned by the Spanish king, Alfonso.

town, sleeping on the shingle of the riverbed. One man from the town, Martín Antolínez, brings him food, supplied by a group of Jews. Impoverished, the Cid negotiates with the Jews for food, then tricks them by filling their coffers with sand.

He journeys on to Cardeña to say good-bye to his wife, Doña Jimena, and his two daughters, whom he is leaving destitute. A hundred Castilians arrive from Burgos to join him in exile. The company sets off and eventually arrives in the Moorish kingdom of Toledo, a tributary of King Alfonso. Taking the Moors by surprise, the Cid attacks and defeats them, but he takes no booty for himself, not wishing to anger King Alfonso further. He travels on to the lands of Zaragoza, dependencies of the Moorish king of Valencia. He defeats a number of provinces along the way, taking booty, which he offers to the king, but Alfonso still refuses to forgive him.

The second cantar describes the Cid's drive against Valencia, which he soon conquers. The king of Seville attempts to recapture Valencia but fails. The Cid sends new gifts to Alfonso, who finally relents and pardons the Cid's family. His wife and daughters are permitted to join him in Valencia, where they are met with a great celebration and installed in a fine castle. The Moors under Yúsuf launch a new attack against Valencia, but they are defeated and Yúsuf's enormous wealth is divided as spoils of war. Again the Cid sends a gift to Alfonso, and this time the king shows benevolence toward him. The Heirs of Carrión, the *infantes*, ask Alfonso if they can marry the Cid's daughters, and the king agrees. Alfonso and the Cid meet on the banks of the Tagus River, where the king formally pardons the Cid before asking him for the hands of his daughters in marriage to the Heirs of Carrión. The Cid gives his daughters to the king, who performs the marriage ceremony and commends the Heirs to the Cid.

The third cantar recounts the cowardly conduct of the Heirs, Fernando and Diego Gonzalo, who are afraid of a lion and even fear battle. In addition, they beat their wives and ultimately abandon them. Outraged, the Cid avenges his daughters' honor with a trial by combat for his worthless sons-in-law, pitting Fernando against Pedro Bermúdez and Diego against Martín Antolínez. The Heirs of Carrión, soundly defeated, leave in shame and deep disgrace. The poet says, "May whoever injures a good woman . . . and abandons her afterwards/suffer as great harm as this . . . and worse, besides." He then marries his daughters, Doña Elvira and Doña Sol, to the princes of Navarre and Aragon. (Merwin 1962)

 # CILAPPATIKĀRAM
(The tale of an anklet)

South Indian epic (ca. 600) written by Iḷaṅkō Aṭikaḷ in Tamil. The poem, consisting of 5,730 lines, is considered India's finest epic in a language other than Sanskrit. It is composed primarily in the *akaval* meter, also called the "master's meter"—*āciriyam*, the most common meter of epic poetry: lines of four feet, except the penultimate line, which contains three. This line indicates a canto's approaching close. Two other meters are used in the poem, which also contains some prose passages.

Following a prologue of 103 lines, the poem is divided into three books (*kāṇṭams*), which in turn are separated into cantos (*kātais*). Each book, set in the capital of one of the three Tamil kingdoms, represents a phase of the narrative: the erotic, the mythic, and the heroic. The plot revolves around the Jaina doctrine of karma.

Book One, "The Book of Pukār," contains ten cantos. Canto 1, "The Song of Praise," describes the city of Pukār where Kōvalaṉ and fair Kaṇṇaki, both from wealthy families, are married. Canto 2, "The Setting Up of a Home," relates how Kōvalaṉ's mother sets up Kaṇṇaki in a home of her own, where the couple lives for many years in happiness. In Canto 3, "The First Performance," the courtesan Mātavi offers for sale a garland of gold pieces presented to her by the king for her superior dancing. Whoever buys the garland will also get Mātavi for a wife. Kōvalaṉ buys the garland, and comes under her spell and leaves his wife. Canto 4, "In Praise of the Evening," tells of Kaṇṇaki, heartbroken at being abandoned. Canto 5, "The Celebration of the City of the Festival of Indra," describes the spring festival in Pukār, which Mātavi and Kōvalaṉ attend. In Canto 6, "Bathing in the Sea," after the festival the couple joins the revelers at the seashore. In Canto 7, "The Love Songs of the Seaside Grove," Mātavi plays her lute, then hands it to Kōvalaṉ, who sings about a woman who hurts her lover. She believes he sings about her, and thinks he no longer loves her. She sings about a woman betrayed, and he, believing she now loves another, leaves. In Canto 8, "The Coming of Spring," back home, Mātavi writes him, inviting him to return, but Kōvalaṉ refuses even to accept the letter when her maid Vacantamālai delivers it. In Canto 9, "The Nature of the Dream," Kaṇṇaki dreams of a disaster striking Kāvalaṉ. He returns home and confesses his infidelity and the squandering of his fortune. She forgives him. They decide to go to Maturai to start life anew, using Kaṇṇaki's ankle bracelets as capital. In Canto 10, "Country Scenes," as they are walking the 300 miles to Maturai, they meet a Jaina priest, Kavunti, who teaches them many things along the way.

Book Two, "The Book of Maturai," has 13 cantos. In Canto 11, "The Scenes of the Forest," they meet a revered Brahman who points the way to Maturai. Kōvalaṉ leaves his wife in Kavunti's care and goes on alone. In Canto 12, "The Song and Dance of the Hunters," Kaṇṇaki and Kavunti rest in the corner of a temple of Aiyai and watch the people of the forest dance. In Canto 13, "Waiting on the Outskirts," Kōvalaṉ returns to the temple and watches the dances to Aiyai. In Canto 14, "The Sights of the City," Kōvalaṉ goes to the city and walks the streets of the four castes. In Canto 15, "The Refugee," when he returns to the grove where the two wait, the Brahman Mātalaṉ arrives and informs him of the birth of Maṇimēkalai, his daughter by Mātavi. Kavunti places Kaṇṇaki in the care of the herdswoman Mātari. In Canto 16, "The Scene of the Murder," Kaṇṇaki fixes a meal for Kōvalaṉ, then he goes to the marketplace to sell an anklet. The goldsmith examines the anklet and hurries off to tell the king that he has found the thief who stole the queen's anklet. The guards follow the goldsmith back to where Kōvalan waits, and one of them slays him with a sword. In Canto 17, "The Round Dance of the Herdswoman," Mātari predicts to her daughter, "Some evil is about to happen." They perform a dance to the gods. In Canto 18, "The Wreath of Sorrow," Kaṇṇaki learns that Kōvalan is dead, accused of being a thief. In Canto 19, "Kaṇṇaki Goes Round the City," she finds her husband's body and embraces it. He rises to his feet, wipes her tears, and ascends to heaven. In Canto 20, "The Demand for Justice," she goes to the palace and proves that her anklet contains jewels, while the queen's only contained pearls. The king is grieved because the goldsmith tricked him, causing him to kill an innocent man, and he dies. Seeing him dead, the queen dies as well. Canto 21, "The Crown of Wrath," tells how, in a rage, Kaṇṇaki wrenches off her left breast and hurls it at the city of Maturai, which goes up in flames. Canto 22, "The Great Fire," describes the devastation. The goddess of Maturai appears before Kaṇṇaki to console her. In Canto 23, "The Explanation," the goddess tells her that Kāvalan, as Bharata in a former life, gave up his vow of nonviolence and beheaded an innocent man, whom he mistook for a spy. In great sorrow, the victim's widow jumped off a cliff. The goddess tells Kaṇṇaki that she will join her husband in heaven in 14 days. Kaṇṇaki leaves the city alone and, as foretold, in 14 days she ascends to heaven.

Book Three, "The Book of Vañci," contains seven cantos. In Canto 24, "The Round Dance of the Hill Dwellers," the peasants witness Kaṇṇaki's ascension and perform a dance. In Canto 25, "The Choice of a Stone," they meet King Ceṅkuṭṭuvaṉ and tell him what they have seen. "The famed Tamil poet,/ Cāttaṉ," who is also present, tells the king the story of the unhappy couple. The king realizes that Kaṇṇaki is a goddess and decides to erect a memorial stone from the Himalaya for her. He prepares to ride to North India for the stone, along the way attacking Ārya rulers who have belittled Tamil kings. In Canto 26, "Removing the Stone," the king leaves Vañci and marches north, defeats the Ārya rulers and reaches the Himalaya to get a stone. In Canto 27, "The Lustration," the king engraves the image of Kaṇṇaki as the goddess Pattiṉi and dips it into the Ganges to be lustrated. Hearing the news of his son's fate, Kōvalan's father gives away his wealth and enters a monastery; his wife gives up her life. Kaṇṇaki's father likewise gives away his wealth and takes holy vows. Within a few days his noble wife gives up her life. Hearing the news, Mātavi says, "I must now lead a virtuous life. Maṇimēkalai should be spared the life of a courtesan . . ." so she enters a Bhuddist monastery. Both Mātari and Kavunti take their lives because they failed to protect Kaṇṇaki. In Canto 28, "The Dedication of the Memorial Stone," the king installs the image in a temple and orders daily worship. In Canto 29, "The Benediction," the king endows the temple. The goddess herself blesses the occasion. In Canto 30, "The Granting of a Favor," the queen tells the king of Maṇimēkalai's great renunciation. They learn the karma of the mothers of the two lovers and of Mātari. The released Ārya kings ask that the goddess grace their country with her presence.

A voice from heaven says, "Your wish is granted." Some two dozen instructions similar to the Ten Commandments are offered: "Fear to tell lies./Avoid spreading rumors. . . . Despise/Bad company./Do not give false evidence. . . .

The poem ends in an epilogue, which mentions the *Maṇimēkhalaï,* a continuation of the story by Cāttaṉar. (Parthasarathy 1993)

See also Iḷaṅkō Aṭikaḷ; *Maṇimēkhalaï.*

 # CINQUE CANTI
(Five cantos)

Italian epic (1519–1532, publ. 1545) by Ludovico Ariosto (1474–1533), who intended the work as a sequel to his *Orlando Furioso* (1516–1532). He drafted the work sometime around 1519, and returned to touch it up in the mid-1520s, but he never published it. After his death, the work was edited by his illegitimate son Virginia from a manuscript that was missing one or more pages. It appeared as a kind of appendix to a 1545 edition of the *Orlando Furioso*. Like the *Orlando Furioso,* which leaves the reader in suspense, the *Cinque Canti* does not have an ending.

Canto 1 begins on the banks of the Ganges River, where the Fairies convene every fifth year, called together by Demogorgon, who rules them. After all the others have assembled, Morgana arrives alone, "mournful, dirty, and neglected," with her hair tousled, wearing "the same dress she had/been wearing on the day when Orlando chased/and . . . captured her." Alcina rises to speak, suggesting they find a means to avenge Morgana. Orlando slaughtered the dragon and the bulls at the fountain, and he took away Gigliante the Blond, whom Morgana loves more than anything else. Actually, Alcina has her own unspoken agenda: She has been jilted by Ruggiero and hopes that, in punishing Orlando, they may reach Ruggiero as well. Other Fairies speak. Dragontina recounts how Astolfo and other paladins robbed her of her prisoners. So many come complaining—some of Oliviery, some of Uggiero, some of Brandimarte, some of King Charles himself. All except Morgana, who has sworn an oath never to harm Orlando, approve Alcina's plan. Demogorgon consents to a general revenge: "Let Orlando, let Charles, let the lineage of/France, let the entire Empire be wiped out. . . ."

Alcina decides that Envy should be the one to bring down the Empire: Envy, working through Ganelon, who at one time was in high favor with Charles. Now he hates all the great paladins surrounding Charles. He knows so well "how to feign/goodness, with a humble voice and a counterfeit/smile. . . ." Alcina goes to a deep, dark ravine hidden amid the Himalayas; from there, through a dreadful cave, a straight path leads down to Hell. There are seven gates leading to Hell, and this one, over which Envy rules, is one of the best traveled. Alcina approaches Envy and tells her, "God has ordained a certain limit for mortal/achievement . . . but/passing beyond which it would be almost divine." Charles, she explains, has reached that point, adding, "if you bring down his/greatness, you will surpass all your former glory." Envy agrees to help. She appears in Ganelon's dreams and shows him all the adulation that Orlando is receiving from a large crowd of people, who then turn upon Ganelon and call him a coward. Ganelon awakens determined to destroy Orlando.

Meanwhile, Charles has presented all his followers with generous gifts for helping him defeat the Saracens. Again Ganelon is jealous, but he hides his feelings and pretends that he has made a vow to go to the Holy Sepulcher. In reality, he goes to find the caliph of Egypt and the king of Syria to discuss how the Holy Land might be taken from Christian rule. Next he goes to Arabia to incite the people to conquer Africa while Charles's forces there are sparse. He devises a strategy that will set every king of Europe against all others.

As he travels, his ship is blown off course and lands on an unknown shore. He takes a few men and walks inland to a forest, where he finds a band of lovely ladies accompanied by riderless squires. He follows them to a beautiful palace, built in one night by demons at the behest of the enchantress Gloricia. Her palace welcomes rich and poor, binding the wayfarers' hearts to her love. Gloricia makes Ganelon and his men welcome; she knows that Alcina has arranged for his ship to arrive on her shore. At Alcina's bidding, she has him and his men seized during the night while they sleep. They are put aboard a ship, which raises itself above the earth and flies through the air until it reaches the island of Alcina.

Alcina has the men put into a dungeon and sends for Ganelon, to whom she explains her plan. She makes him promise not to stop until he has delivered Ruggiero and Orlando to her as prisoners. She gives him a ring, inside of which is a goblin named Vertumnus who can change into any shape and will obey the wearer's command. So that the wizard Malagigi cannot help the paladins as he has in the past, she completely silences all the spirits, except a few of her own.

Ganelon and his men board the ship, which carries them to Alexandria. Ganelon has already encouraged Desiderius to invade France from the east, together with the Germans and Hungarians; he will make the Spaniard Marsilio invade from the west. Alcina hopes to find another fiend such as Envy to bring down King Charles.

In Canto 2, Alcina chooses Suspicion, "the worst of all evils," to enter the souls of Charles and the paladins. She captures Suspicion while he is asleep and transports him to her realm, promising to return him to his own castle after he has done her bidding. He enters Desiderius, king of the Lombards, who is already afraid of Charles's powers. He suspects war in his own household and can find "no surer remedy/. . . than to incite all his neighbors/against France."

Meanwhile, Charles receives reports of the various plots against him; he abandons his festivals and begins to plan. He does not worry so long as he is armed with faith. He sends his captains through every land to make a levy of warriors. He breaks open the treasury to buy horses and to pay craftsmen to make weapons. The first standard he sends out is against Lombards. He sends Orlando with infantry to take the Alps, but they find their enemies have already seized the passes. Orlando and his men make pretenses of planning to pass everywhere except their true location. They launch a ferocious attack, never letting up by day or night. In the Lombard camp is a young lord, Ottone of Villafranca, wearing rich vestments sewn by his wife, Bianca. Baldovina catches Ottone at a narrow pass and takes him prisoner. Rumor spreads in the camp that Ottone is wounded and near death. Penticone, son of the Lombard king, goes to Bianca's tent to console her. His desire grows boundless; he cannot resist it. He goes to see her every day. She does not wish to offend him, so she resolves to flee and lose everything else rather than lose her honor. An aged servant agrees to conduct her safely to the city of the Gauls by secret trails. He urges her to wait for two days, until he returns from a place he must visit. In the meantime, she may make all sorts of promises to Penticone, which she has no intention of keeping. The old man sneaks over to the French camp and speaks to Baldovino, who agrees to free Ottone in return for the capture of Penticone. That night Baldovino goes off to occupy a high hill from which they can see into the enemy camp. The old man hurries back to his lady to explain what he has arranged. When daylight comes, Penticone appears at her door again. This time she is dressed in gay attire, and she welcomes him graciously. The old servant goes to get Baldovino and his men, who swoop down and capture Penticone. Baldovino has left word for Orlando to follow with the rest of the army, which he does. When Desiderius learns that his son has been captured, he retreats from the Alps, heartbroken. Orlando attacks and slaughters the Lombard forces.

In the meantime, Charles leaves with his army for Bavaria and halts at Augsburg, sending a message to Tassillone, king of the Bohemians, that he is ready to fight. Tassilone is so taken by surprise that he gives himself and his entire state into Charles's power. The French collect tribute and leave with hostages, marching to Prague, where once before they had driven back and routed King Cardorano with little trouble. This time Cardorano makes Charles proceed more cautiously. The French camp between the banks of the Moldau and Elbe rivers, "a bowshot distant from the city." To keep the city from receiving supplies, Charles builds a long wall between one river and the other. He goes into the forest and chops down the precious trees where the Pagans' gods live.

Meanwhile, the villainous Ganelon has gone to the Holy Land to disguise his part in the grand scheme. He travels to Budapest and promises he will do everything he can so that Prague can hold out another month. From there he goes to Bohemia. He comes to Charles's camp and kisses his hand. Charles esteems Ganelon highly, and is unable to tell his false friends from his true.

In Canto 3, suspecting nothing, Charles tells Ganelon all his strategy. The traitor quickly discloses it to Cardorano by messenger, with advice on how to escape the peril. The Bohemian king sends a herald to the camp telling Charles there will be no honor in attacking because there are so few troops within the walls. He suggests instead a small combat between a few men on each side. Ganelon advises Charles to use ten men and to call for his very best: Rinaldo, Orlando, Ruggiero, Oliviero, and his sons Aquilante and Grifone. Charles agrees, and a date is set in May for the conflict. Meanwhile, the Bohemians will have time to call in large armies to assist them.

Ganelon summons Vertumnus from his magic ring and orders him to change his appearance. The goblin first transforms himself into Terigi, Orlando's squire. He delivers letters supposedly written by Orlando and Charles to Rinaldo, who is fighting near Morlaas. Rinaldo reads the letter supposedly from Charles to Orlando, which tells him that he has doubts about Rinaldo's loyalty and has decided to remove him from command. But first he want to pretend that he needs him in Prague. Vertumnus tells Rinaldo that Orlando plans to kill Charles. Rinaldo decides to arm troops and join the attack.

Vertumnus takes on a new disguise as Charles's courier, and bearing new letters goes to Marseilles to see Ruggiero, his wife, Bradamante, and his sister Marfisa. Marfisa is ordered to take her cavalry and join Rinaldo in Lisbon, where Charles plans to attack. Bradamante's letter assures her that Marseilles is safe. Ruggiero is to head for Spain, Marfisa for Morlaas, while Bradamante stays to guard Marseilles.

Meanwhile, Namo arrives in Rinaldo's camp and learns that he plans to attack Charles. Rinaldo welcomes him "with evil looks." When Namo calls Rinaldo a traitor, Rinaldo has Namo arrested and put in prison. He tears across the countryside, laying waste wherever he finds resistance.

Ganelon, hearing of Rinaldo's exploits, informs Charles. He also reports that Ruggiero has sailed with his fleet from Marseilles, headed for Gibralter, and that Marfisa is headed with her cavalry in the same direction and has joined her power to Rinaldo's. Ganelon urges Charles to arrest Bradamante before she causes trouble as well. He also advises Charles to send a message to Ricardo, commander of his fleet, to pursue Ruggiero. He should also send a courier to Orlando, bidding him to come quickly to France with all his troops.

Charles is considering whom to put forward in the duel of ten against ten instead of Orlando, Ruggiero, and Rinaldo. He chooses Ottone, Avolio, and his brother Berlingiero. Ganelon advises him to send to Judea for Sansonetto, who would be better than all three of Namo's sons combined. Ganelon wants Jerusalem unprotected against the attack the king of Egypt is preparing to make.

Ganelon offers to take Marseilles himself, and Charles agrees to send him. Ganelon sails for Marseilles with Vertumnus disguised as Ruggiero, so that when they land, Bradamante runs out to embrace her husband. Unarmed, she is easily taken by her enemies. The populace hears of her capture and assembles with arms, but Ganelon calms them, showing them Charles's orders. Ganelon hopes that, with Bradamante as bait, he can draw Rinaldo and Ruggiero into his net. He sets off for Mainz.

Two of Bradamante's squires mount their horses, one riding to take the news to Rinaldo and Marfisa, the other deciding first to look for Orlando. Orlando has received orders to leave his Lombard seige and rush to the aid of the French against Rinaldo, so he has already arrived on the banks of the Rhone. The squire finds him there and tells him that the wicked Ganelon has captured Bradamante.

Orlando mounts a different horse and leaves behind his familiar shield, clothing himself in pure white. He departs at night, and no one but his squire knows that he has left. He travels the back way and waits at a mountain pass for Ganelon to appear. He strikes Ganelon down but does not kill him, then turns on the other men, who quickly take flight. Without revealing his identity to Bradamante, he gives her Ganelon's helmet, shield, sword, and horse. Then he rides away, leaving Bradamante to bind Ganelon like a thief and lead him away.

That same evening she comes across the squire Sinibaldo, who had gone for help. She gives him the rope and allows him to lead the prisoner. She gives Sinibaldo all of Ganelon's jewelry, including the magic ring, about which neither of them knows anything. They travel by night and sleep by day. Finally Ganelon gets an opportunity to induce an innkeeper to send a message to Lupo, a kinsman, asking for help.

As soon as Lupo hears the news, he leaves Bayonne with a hundred knights and camps out in some old houses along the route. The innkeeper goes to find Bradamante and Ganelon, lest they take another route and escape the snares set by Lupo. The innkeeper encounters a knight accompanied by a valet and two damsels. He sees Bradamante approach and embrace the knight. The knight is Marfisa, who has come to help her sister-in-law. The innkeeper joins them and invites them to spend the night in his inn. He tries to signal Ganelon that help is nearby, but the squire sees him. Marfisa seizes him by the neck and makes him reveal the plot. Alerted to the nearby ambush, the two go out toward Lupo's hiding place with Ganelon between them. Marfisa leaps forward, and with a few blows of her lance kills seven men before she even takes out her sword.

In Canto 4, Marfisa cuts two men in half in one direction and another in half longwise. She stabs ten and strikes three clear through. She continues to hack, while Ganelon considers himself "a certain meal for . . . vultures." When the rout is over, the women drag him off to Montauban and drop him into the dungeon.

Meanwhile, sailing toward the west, Ruggiero sees a small island rise out of the sea. It is an enormous monster, which follows them for three days and nights. When they are almost to Lisbon, Ricardo's fleet arrives and attacks. In the battle that follows, Ricardo sets fire to the ships and Ruggiero jumps overboard. He is swallowed by the monster. In its belly he meets an old man who tells him he is Alcina's captive, one of four in the belly of this monster, all of whom have jilted her at some time, and that he has been here since he was a young man. Ruggiero meets the other two men, and recognizes one of them as Alsolfo. He tells of having fallen in love with a married woman in Scotland. He had arranged to have her kidnapped, but with the help of Alcina, her husband rescued her and threw him into the sea, where the monster was waiting.

Meanwhile, Charles is intent on the battle the Bohemian king is to have with him, but Cardorano has no intention of fighting. He is only stalling until help arrives from Hungary, Saxony, and elsewhere. Little by little he has supplies brought in, while the French grow careless, not realizing that an enormous force is massing against them.

In Canto 5, when Charles realizes peril from two directions, he boldly decides to defeat both. He divides his army into three parts. The right flank is given to Oliviero; Uggiero the Dane is given the left wing, while Charles commands the middle. On the other side, the Barbarian horde divides into three battalions. Charles would be left undone but for God, who provides unexpected and unhoped-for aid.

From letters that Ganelon carried, Marfisa and Bradamante have already found out that Charles is the instigator of the destruction. Burning with indignation, Marfisa resolves to rush to Bohemia and kill Charles. She tells Bradamante and Guidon, Bradamante and Ruggiero's half brother, what she plans to do. Bradamante decides to go along, taking Ganelon, who can hang with Charles on the same gallows. Guidon can't go with them and leave Montauban unguarded, but he sends a message to the sorcerer Malagigi to hurry to them. The squire Sinibaldo finally finds Malagigi at the top of a cliff. Malagigi is angry because he has twice asked the spirits whether Orlando has really become Rinaldo's enemy, and the spirits are quiet. He does not know that Alcina has quieted them all. After Sinibaldo arrives with the news about Ganelon's capture, Malagigi tries to contact the spirits again. This time Vertumnus, hidden in the ring the squire wears, and whose speech is not forbidden, tells of Ganelon's plots. Malagigi is astonished. He leaves immediately with the squire toward Rinaldo, who is laying waste to the countryside.

Meanwhile, Orlando and his men reach Rinaldo, whose men confront them. As the two sides clash, Rinaldo calls out, "Traitor." Over the battle's din, Orlando cannot hear why Rinaldo has called him a traitor. They agree to withdraw and put off the battle until the next day so as to certify with deeds and words which of them is a traitor. The next morning Rinaldo finds himself alone on the battlefield.

At this point there is a gap in the narrative. The canto resumes with Bradamante, Marfisa, and Guidon journeying toward Prague in search of Charles. They stop on a hilltop overlooking the whole field and watch the battle raging below. The French are retreating in dissarray. Charles is thrown off a bridge into the river. His good horse finally brings him to shore. Here the narrative ends. (Ariosto 1996)

See also Ariosto, Ludovico; *Orlando Furioso.*

 # *CĪVAKACINTĀMAṆI*
(The amulet of Cīvakaṉ, or The wish-fulfilling jewel)

Indian Tamil epic (ca. 10th c. A.D.) by Tiruttakkatēvar, an adherent of Jainism. The poem narrates an ancient story, depicting Jaina kings with their philosophy of nonviolence and salvation through self-sacrifice. The poem is meant to instill the four ends of humans as espoused by Jainism. The narrative contains elements of the supernatural as well as poetic descriptions of countryside and city. The poet speaks of the loftiness of his theme and his inadequacy to deal with such great purposes. He asks the reader to overlook the flaws in his rendition. (Parthasarathy 1993)

 # CLASSICISM

In the West, a term in literature originally referring to the style of classical antiquity, or the Greek fifth and fourth centuries B.C. and the Roman first century B.C. and first century A.D., when those cultures reached their artistic zenith. The term has evolved to include any similar formal style that stresses form over content and technical perfection, restraint, and rationality over emotional expression and inventiveness. Classicism is the opposite of Romanticism. (Siepmann 1987)

 # *THE COLUMBIAD*

American epic poem (1807) in ten books by Joel Barlow (1754–1812). The poem, written in iambic pentameter in rhymed couplets, was a revision and expansion of an earlier poem, *The Vision of Columbus*, published in 1787. Both are expressions of Barlow's political, social, and scientific utopian ideals.

In the first four books Barlow does not depart much from *The Vision of Columbus*, describing America and telling its history from the Inca Empire to the present day. The next three books, on the American Revolution, expand upon events from *The Vision of Columbus*. Book Eight is an address to the patriots who survived the war. Book Nine is a revelation by Hesper of a future progress by man through a time of error toward a millennium of reason. Book Ten scans the future to reveal a union of all men and an assembly of united nations.

Book I opens with a tribute to Columbus, who taught mankind where future empires lay, but whose dream was corrupted by those who exploited the new territory. An invocation to Freedom follows. Barlow then shows the imprisoned Columbus, deserted by the monarch he has served and recalling in a monologue the first voyage over a chartless main and riding roaring storms: the desperate, mutinous crew; then, in the distance, the golden banks. Columbus remembers the triumphant foes and dissembling friends back at home, the death of his friend Isabella, the crowds of tyrants fixing their domain in the New World, and Freedom flying from her infant realm. But as Columbus grieves, Hesper, guardian of the Western Hemisphere, appears and takes him to the mount of vision on the western coast of Spain. Across the Atlantic, America appears, resplendent in its wealth of natural resources.

In Book II, Hesper shows Columbus the natives of this world, some living concealed in thickets; some, vagrants and untamed; others in settled hamlets living in corn-clad vales; and still others living amid rising domes in a happier state. Hesper also shows him war-painted chiefs thirsty for gore, butchering their captives for food. Columbus asks Hesper if these could be nature's sons, unlike those people on his first discovered isle. Why this dissimilarity? Did they come from a common source? Hesper answers that the human body is made of varied elements, producing a diversity in men. The first to arrive in America were vagrant tribes until the realms were peopled and their arts begun.

Hesper next looks where the imperial Mexico rose, with Montezuma on his rich throne, then Cortés staining the fields in blood. Columbus cries out for the Indians to drive back the invaders, but Hesper promises that in the coming age, the tyrants will pass. Hesper shows Cusco in rich Peru, founded by Capac and Oella, children of the sun, and their remarkable institutions and system of laws—now ransacked by Pizarro.

In Book III, Hesper continues his history of the Incas: their tall temple of the sun in the Andes, their response to the threatening mountain savages by spreading their religious belief in one prime power over all humankind, and the offer of peace. He shows how the Incas overcame the worshippers of the volcano and rescued the king's son from their altar.

In Book IV, when Hesper foretells the destruction of Peru by the Spaniards, Columbus grieves, but Hesper comforts him again with a vision of the future: a Europe of new nations curbing the lords, and the flourishing of the arts and new sciences; Erasmus and Luther bringing benighted nations into day; Raleigh leading the way to Columbia (America), not to plunder but to wake a slumbering soil to fruitful life and plant the germ of a race predestined "to methodize and mold new codes of empire to reform the old" with the infant empire of liberty. It is a land where Man will find "a nobler sense of duty and of right" and where Freedom will fix the central goal of moral systems: equal rights and equal laws. Hesper also shows Delaware arriving with settlers for Virginia, where Earth "will draw her first clear codes of liberty and law" and where those persecuted for their religion will be safer.

In Book V, Hesper gives a history of the North American colonists, at first finding a smiling land, but soon encountering savage foes, settling down to build towns and cities and electing sires to assume the cares of state and rule with all the rights that Britons know. In Canada, Gaul's migrant sons explore and plant their posts on the Wabash and the Mississippi, settle in Louisiana, carrying with them their feudal genius. But soon the mother states transport their feuds to America, and the British and French are at war. The British are saved by the young Washington, destined to "a loftier stride." The British colonies span the whole north and crowd the West.

But a darkness comes—hostile Britons from across the main—and there is fraternal rage. Delegates from assembled states convene in Penn's city: Washington, Franklin, Adams, Hancock, and Jefferson. They talk of independence. Freemen raise an American army, with Washington, Wooster, Putnam, Gates, and many others. Montgomery is first to move, to Quebec, where he dies a hero's death. The Britons take possession of New York. Disease invades the American camps. Each day the ranks are decimated.

In Book VI, Britons torture and put to death their American prisoners. Washington retreats, then surprises the British in a recrossing of the Delaware despite the ice, storm, and mountainous waves. Hesper, guardian of Columbia's [America's] right, comes to his rescue and calms the waters, and Washington takes some British prisoners. This is the beginning of an American victory. Burgoyne and the British sail up the St. Lawrence, but the colonists are energized. Brave Arnold, though later treason absorbs his soul, rides foremost. Indians join Burgoyne's ranks.

Among the British, the youthful Heartly, confident of an easy victory by the British, has left his betrothed Lucinda housed in the camp, brought there that morning to wed. But one British general after another is killed, and Arnold rolls the enemy ranks and rules the day. The British are routed. From the rampart, Lucinda watches, spies her Heartly, and traces his movements until he vanishes in the warrior-crowd. She rushes to where she saw him last, but he has sought the rear of flight. When he is told that Lucinda has been seen in the western grove, he frantically seeks her, but Mohawks, out to plunder the battlefield, find Lucinda and scalp her. Heartly sinks delirious on her lifeless body. Are these your trophies? Hester exclaims to the absent General Carleton (British governor of Canada and superintendent of Indian Affairs).

In Book VII, Hesper shifts attention to Europe, where an expanding dawn waits a reasoning race. A school of sages theorize, hailing an era that relieves mankind—foremost among them, the French. Columbia's wrongs fire their imaginations, and they move to put into practice their theme: That in people dwells the sovereign sway; that equal rights are the only source of law. They bend the royal ear, and he, to humble the British power, with Spain and Holland, lifts his arm to save. Russia draws around her the Baltic states to declare neutrality.

As Columbus watches, at the Battle of Monmouth, Washington charges the Hessians from the field. But the Hudson still flows through British waters, so Wayne takes Stonypoint. Lincoln marches to besieged Charleston, but Cornwallis forces its surrender and rolls across Carolina. Patriot after patriot is defeated: Gates quits the field; the traitor Arnold joins the British. Then the French navy sails up Chesapeake Bay, begins a siege of Cornwallis at York and Gloster, and engages the British ships. On shore, Lincoln moves over the plain, with a band under Fayette. A citadel is blown up, and Cornwallis and his army surrender to Washington.

In Book VIII, Barlow sings a hymn to peace: Too long there have been groans of death and battle's discordant bray. He bids farewell to his brother, whose untimely fall he laments, praising him and the other parting spirits who were the saviors of their native land. But think not the patriot's task is done, or Freedom safe, he adds. There are foes yet who would divide, corrupt with power, infect the land, or by inattention, lose that hard-won Liberty.

Then Hesper hears the voice of his brother Atlas, the guardian genius of Africa. Hesper's children have prevailed, Atlas says, but they have also enslaved Atlas's people. They preach faith and justice, and invite all men to share their liberty, but enslave Atlas's tribes! How can freemen create a world while

Engraved for BARNARD's New Complete & Authentic HISTORY of ENGLAND; a WORK Universally Acknowledged to be the Best Performance of the Kind, — on account of It's Impartiality, Accuracy, New Improvements, Superior Elegance, &c.

Hamilton delin.

Thornton sculp.

The SURRENDER of EARL CORNWALLIS (Lieutenant-General of the British Army in North America) to GENERAL WASHINGTON & COUNT De ROCHAMBEAU, on the 19th of Oct. 1781 — whereby the Posts

American author Joel Barlow included the 1781 surrender of British forces under Cornwallis to General George Washington and French Count de Rochambeau at Yorktown in *The Columbiad*, published in 1807. This engraving for a 1783 history book shows Earl Cornwallis giving up his sword to the victors.

slave and master ruin the state? Atlas forecasts a heavy vengeance that will shake the world. See how Rome—treading down the tyrant, flushed with victory—chained the world, then herself wore the chains. Modern Europe with her serfs and vassals, when transplanted to Hesper's shore, has only brought feudal feelings and sable [black] serfs. Now that Freedom rears her head, Columbia should preserve her principles: Equality, Free Election, Federal Band.

Hesper now reverses the flight of time and takes Columbus back to when this American continent was in its savage state. With a wave of the hand, inland trade begins. After a while a venturous train dares the sea. Where broad savannas were, rice and tobago (tobacco) are planted and grown. Hulls are built and launched on the waves. Young schools of science rise and expand: Harvard, Yale, and Princeton. Homebred freemen establish a social plan, learn the broad plain truths, rights, and duties, and feel a moral fitness. The preacher molds religion to the moral mind to harmonize mankind.

The torch of science flames, unfolding world after world, in the hands of others: Franklin, Rittenhouse, Godfrey. Copley's pencil traces the charms of face. Taylor portrays rural seats and craggy shores. Stuart and Brown raise moving portraits. Wright's chisel brings the sculptured marble to life. Trumbull's satire stings pride, knavery, and dullness. On wings of faith Dwight revives old Canaan's promised land, and all the dark futurities of heaven are given in bright vision.

In Book IX, Hesper suspends the vision. It is night but they are still on the mount. Columbus inquires, Why this progressive laboring search of man? Why must he wind through devious paths? Why did bounteous nature not give all science to these sons of earth at their birth? To this Hester answers that Nature moves in a progressive march. We greet her works while they are still imperfect, in their parts. At the beginning, Chaos forced from his breast a bursting, dark, formless, impermeable mass. Millions of periods have since learned to measure, then sought and sorted out the principles of things, till light at last began and every system found a sun.

Mark thy native orb, Hester says. Her shell-rock ribs attest to her age. Millions of generations toiled and died to crust it with coral and salt her seas. Millions more passed before her soil began. Then rose her proud phenomenon, Man, frail at first. Time informed his footsteps and untoned his tongue, unfledged his lofty mind. But he was still wild, to every beast a prey. For countless ages he was forced from place to place, and scarce preserved his race.

At last he found a fixed soil: on the flowery banks of the Euphrates, the Ganges, the Nile. Brahma tamed the throngs, and Homer built more durable than the pharaoh's hills of stone.

But there was also the waste of ages before man could reach a height over the beasts—blank periods, when errors twined with science, and some monster umanned his soul and marred his works. He endowed with passions every force he could not control, and from hence rose his gods, with bloodstained altars, priestly power, and false morals. He next extended such faith to heaven-anointed men, and with creeds and feuds sowed the seeds of war with all its woes. Mystery, leagued with Science, planned a course of holy crimes.

Down the cramped corridor, man groped his way. He mounted and mounted and seemed to gain the skies, then fell backward. At last Elysium spread before his eyes, lured his sense with sweet decoys, fancies of eternal joys, and illusions. The Lama dispensed fate and ruled half of mankind. In India old Ganges choked with sainted sands, and the wife mounted the pyre to burn with her lord's body. The Delphian oracles rived an empire. Pilgrims to Mecca's dead prophet extended their faith by fire and sword. Phoenician altars reeked with human gore. Heroes and kings became gods. Man, Hesper says, is still an infant, and he must mature his manhood, and at last behold his reason ripen. But the wanderings are past. Columbus, however, has his doubts. Nations have risen only to fall: Babel, Nineveh, Tyre, Carthage, Syracuse, Greece, Macedonia, Rome, and finally, the nations of Europe, which may suffer the same sad fate. But perhaps in the future some new Columbus (more wise and virtuous) will steer toward that day and unfold a strange new world. There is a difference, Hesper says. The arts and sciences of the ancients were faulty. They flourished in only one small nation at a time and sank beneath the storms of war. Man has now assumed a steadier gait. Charlemagne planted schools. Alfred opened mines. England has produced liberty and laws. Universities have risen. War, affected by science, now follows a smoother way, transplanting arts from Hagar's race: free cities, international commerce, the printing press, the magnetic needle. A curtain has been drawn aside to reveal an infant world. Behold a broader way, Hesper says, aiming at the rules of right, the line for civil power. Its rising seat and model is in these American confederate states. Each land shall imitate this brotherhood and band together within a federal zone.

In Book X, Hesper resumes the vision and brings into view future ages, all the world plodding through various stages of change: tribes still roving savage wastes; cultured realms where arts and virtues reign: restless Tartars, Chinese despots, desert robbers, Africa with her tribes purloined away, Europe's cultured shores and wealth, and America's federated states. The different paths are a "long circling course" that in the future will close and "give the world repose": a federal union blending their powers, their passions, and their interest.

The first of these future stages, Hesper says, will be unfettered trade and freedom of the seas, then inland commerce with canals. The Bard will attend to moral charms, seek the total God, and unfold social and systemed worlds. The Sage will remold Nature's frames, conquer disease with its causes, tame subterranean heat, probe the earth, walk under the oceans, ride the air, repair the labored land, spread fruitful soil over sandy desert. No more will the patriotic mind be confined to narrow views, directing the public rage against neighboring lands, but work to see the strength and happiness of combined humankind. Columbus still has misgivings: The world is a babel of tongues; but Hesper reassures him that in the future, one pure language will extend through all the world. Teachers in the past kept man curbed and led him blinded, but now the race has shaken off their manacles.

In this, Columbus sees the biblical Apocalypse, but Hesper advises that that is another time. He then unrolls another train of years, where legates of all the empires meet beneath a spacious dome, exchange counsels, and shape their course. Nearby a figure of Genius stands. Graved on its pedestal are Man's noblest arts. Beneath it lie all destructive things, priesthood and the mace of kings. Each envoy here unloads some old idol from his native land: a crescent, swords, scepters, miters, crowns, false codes, stimulants to war.

Here, says Hesper, are the fruits of your long years of toil. Let these broad views compose your mind to "spurn the malice" of your foes. May all the joys of future ages "repay your labors and remove thy pain." (TAP) (Ford 1971; Woodress 1958)

See also Barlow, Joel.

 # THE CONFERENCE OF THE BIRDS
(Or The Bird Parliament, *Manteq at-Tair*)

Persian mystical allegorical epic of Ṣūfism by Farid al-Din Attar (ca. 1120–ca. 1220). The framework of the allegory is this: The birds of the world convene to seek a king. The hoopoe, on whom "King Solomon relied / To carry secret messages between / His court and distant Sheba's lovely queen," is picked as guide. The hoopoe tells them they have a king—the Simorgh—who lives far away, and the journey to reach him is long and hazardous. At first enthusiastic, the birds quickly begin to make excuses when they realize how difficult the journey will be. For example, the parrot, so beautiful that she has been caged, wants only freedom to find the stream of immortality without a king. The nightingale cannot leave his beloved. The haughty peacock, who once lived in paradise, wants nothing less. The hawk is satisfied with his current position at the court with earthly kings. Proud of being so clean, the duck cannot leave water. The timid finch is afraid. The hoopoe meets each excuse with an anecdote or two to counteract the fears.

The flock flies a little way, adopting the hoopoe as their leader. The birds decide to question him further about the quest before going on. Each section, except the opening and the epilogue, begins with a bird questioning or arguing with the hoopoe, and continues with the hoopoe's answer, which usually consists of two or three illustrative stories.

The last question concerns the length of the journey. The hoopoe describes the seven valleys of the Way: Search, Love, Mystic Apprehension, Detachment/Independence, Unity, Bewilderment, and Fulfillment in Annihilation. The birds set off, and only 30 arrive at the court of the Smorgh, where at first they are turned away. When they are admitted, they discover that the Simorgh is themselves: *Si* (30) *morgh* (birds).

The epilogue consists largly of self-praise, as is customary in Persian poetry of the time. (Attar 1984)

See also Attar, Farid al-Din.

A sixteenth-century miniature by Habib Allah echoes the theme of *The Conference of the Birds,* an allegorical epic of Ṣūfism by Persian Farid al-Din Attar.

AMERICAN RIVER COLLEGE

CONQUISTADOR

American epic (1932) by Archibald MacLeish (1892–1982). It is based on the account by Bernal Díaz del Castillo of Cortés's conquest of Mexico and on MacLeish's own firsthand acquaintance with that country and its people. The poet wrote part of the poem during a 1928–1929 trip by foot and muleback on the Cortés route. It was published in 1932, winning the Pulitzer Prize in Poetry. It is written as if it were a recital by an old soldier on the Cortés march, with lyric descriptions of the land, delineation of character through dialogue, attention to death images, and relationships between people. It is a portrayal of self-sacrifice, courage, and endurance on both sides, as well as of treachery and self-seeking. Both Cortés and Montezuma, and the Indian woman Marina, are heroic figures. It is written for the most part in occasionally rhyming triplets, in 15 books. MacLeish resorts to accent marks to indicate the rhythm of Indian and Spanish names.

In the first section, "Bernal Díaz's Preface to His Book," MacLeish begins his epic with a monologue by the old soldier, "an ignorant man," and his reaction to an account by a priest and "learned man" with "the school-taught skrip," who describes only "big names" with "imperial decorations." Instead, the soldier remembers graves, battles lost, unknown hardships, wounds, hunger, "lives forgotten."

The epic proper begins in the second part, "The True History of Bernal Díaz." The first book introduces Cortés in Cuba and his differences with the governor, and Cortés's success in raising an expeditionary force to Mexico, with its recently discovered Aztecs. They acquire supplies at Trinidad and Havana, despite Governor Velásquez's orders to arrest Cortés.

In the second book, Cortés and his men sail for Cozumel. On shore, all they find at first are a poor people. The gold is piled "far on to the west," so Cortés sends word to the chiefs that he means no harm, and he orders his men not to annoy them. The Indians row out to them and finger the Spaniards' beards. Cortés sends men ashore with trinkets to barter. They sail on. One day an old man rows out to their ship and identifies himself as Jerónimo de Águilar, a priest from Darien who has lived there for many years. They sail on to Tabasco, where they are received with arrows. Cortés claims the land in the name of the king.

In the third book, sick of fighting, the Indians come seeking peace. With them is a young girl, Malinál, whom the Spaniards name Marina. She knows the tongues of the Aztec Tenochtitlán and of Cintla, and becomes the mistress of Cortés. They sail on until they see the mountains. They know the place from Grijalva's soldiers, who have sailed there before. The natives are friendly and bring many, many gifts. One who is first and lord speaks to them, and Marina interprets. He tells them that Montezuma sends them treasure. Cortés thanks him and adds that he would like to meet the emperor. The messenger boasts that the emperor's land lies beyond the mountain, at Tenochtitlán, where "the gods are old" and where "none have conquered that land."

In the fourth book, the Cuban governor's men with Cortés are eager to stop now and return to Cuba. Cortés has no authority in this land, they argue, only a commission to trade. But Cortés's men say that they have come this far, and the governor Velásquez be damned, "Take you this land!" Cortés is persuaded. He builds a gallows as a warning and imprisons the governor's men. His followers write a petition to the king of Spain asking that Cortés be named governor, and that he, not Velásquez, be permitted to keep the profits. When Velásquez hears this, he sends troops, but Cortés's men slip by them. The messengers reach Spain, but the king is gone, so that time and help from the French work in Cortés's favor.

In the fifth book, Cortés tries to establish order among the rebellious by hanging the worst, then leaves the ships. Word comes of their loss to rust, rot, and worms. This breaks the back of the governor's men, but they attack him: "Did he think he is God? . . . Has he brought them out to be fed to idols?" They call him scurrilous names. Cortés turns to them and admits that "this is an undiscovered and dark land." He tells them to take the one remaining ship. "Take what you will of the store. Return to Spain! . . . Why waste your souls in the west?" He turns to the others and says, "Before us lies in the west that new world." None speak again of returning.

In the sixth book, they march from the sea, eating grass to survive. The land and the way are unknown. The plain rises ahead, while far to the south there is much snow, and to the west, mountains like a great wall. They climb. It rains. They eat roots. They follow the waters, cross the rocks, and there is snow. Hawks fly far down under them. Their beards sting with the sleet. The mountain has no descent, but to the west is level country.

They come to towns with yelping dogs, where old men stare at them, sniggering that there is "room within on the altars" for them. Answering Cortés's query as to where they are from, the answer comes, "Montezuma, the king's land." They, however, are Totómacs, once free-born men.

In the seventh book, they pass through valleys, canyons, and mountain after mountain, everywhere hearing that the Tlaxcaláns lie ahead: "a violent and harsh race." They reach Tlaxcalá; there is a vast meadow, rooted with rushes, woodless, where a city, Téhua, stands. There they meet an attack by Indians painted black, with death eyes, breastplates quilted with cotton. The Spaniards stand and take it until the Indians finally disappear. The Spaniards relax, then are attacked from the rear, ten Indians to each Spaniard. The Indians fall by the scores. Finally they flee, and their old man comes out to make peace. The Spaniards march on until they sight Cholúla.

In the eighth book, Cortés meets hostile Cholúla, city sacred to Quetzalcóatl, where the Spaniards are deceived by false friendliness, and in turn are almost destroyed.

In the ninth book, the Spaniards arrive at the pass and start downward. They march by hoed fields to the city lying on a lake, a stone dike dividing the waters. The king awaits them, sitting on his golden chair. Attendants bear reproductions of the sun to his forehead, on willow poles. Even the straps of his shoes are golden. The king turns, stands in the gates, and says to them, "Malinchi! These are your houses: Yours and your brethren's: You may rest a while."

In the tenth book, the old soldier remembers the royal city: the girls with the scented hair; the king's house the Indians gave them to dwell in, well-made with lime and stone; the lake grass; the painted cloth; the smell of sweet wood; the walls of pine painted with scarlet beams, the outer walls burnished to shine like coins; some houses built to the water with the light from the ripples; the cool canals poled with slow skiffs. All the isle is channeled and rings with the clang of oars as they bring the corn "through the water-streets" and "pole in heaped fish." Many men stand in the cool of the arcades of the market, where sellers deal with cooked dough, stone masks of the dead, blue clay for baking, red dyes. The land is a good land, the king "rich with young wives and gold" and gardens. He keeps marks on a stone for the sun's turning and the way with the stars. But the ground is silent for the Spaniards. In their foreign hands the dust is only a red stain. Their tongues are "unskilled to the fruits," while the Indians pass with their cries at dawn and their deep drums. And they see Indians pass by the stone courts and the cages, the temple reaching the sky— and a boy slain—the belly arched to a stone knife. The Indians sing like children, and they eat the limbs for a feast.

In the eleventh book, the Spaniards feel death everywhere and are afraid. They wish to live here secure. The king can be their safeguard, so they seek him out. They find him under the garden trees. He tells them he had fore-knowledge of them; therefore, their fears are unfounded. They can be one of his people, but he warns them against violence and force. How would it profit them to make war or "bind his limbs with steel?" Though "their metal might hold him," how "should they hold death?" Cortés had thought "their ills were done," and "the wheel of their luck had turned," but it is not so. The die is cast. Their lives will be lost, thousands slain.

In the twelfth book, the Cuban governor's ships arrive in Mexico determined to curb Cortés's growing power. Cortés's men march to Campoála to meet Velásquez's men, leaving Alvarado in charge. They defeat them, then learn that Alvarado has forged a writ from the king summoning many of the Aztec chiefs to a dance after leaving their arms in a priest's house. He has then locked the gates and slaughtered them. Cortés is enraged and promises to hang Alvarado, but he returns to an ominous silence.

In the thirteenth book, the Aztecs receive Cortés's men with deep drums. They descend upon the soldiers in droves. They die, but keep coming, tearing their hands on the Spaniards' swords. The Spaniards' only hope is the king. They go to Montezuma, who receives them smiling, but is slain. A fierce fight rages. The waterways are barred to them. The water-breaks are open and armored. The Aztecs hold all the roads.

In the fourteenth book, de Ávila orders the soldiers to raid the stone-room for its gold, bird pelts, jade, and painted cotton, and then to build a bridge of planks across the broken causeways. But the bridge bogs down. Many soldiers are lost, including some of their captains. Their powder is spent. The Aztecs beat their drums; they whistle and jeer. They drive the Spaniards up in the dust with their spears and herd around them, their plumes waving in the sun "like maize." The soldiers fight blindly out of the melee. They retire to the mountains for that year.

In the fifteenth book, in the spring, the Spaniards march against them, this time "by the books and the science." They burn the back towns, they cut the mulberries, and they take down the dikes, so that the pipes of the Aztec fountains are dry. The Spaniards lay "a Christian siege with the sun and the vultures," for 93 days. The Aztecs care nothing for the siege on their side. The place stinks with dung. The whole city grubs for roots, and the Indians' guts swell with tree bark. They crawl out by the rubbish, and the soldiers let them go. The town is gone, "no stone to a stone of it." The whole thing is "a beautiful victory."

The Spaniards square the streets "like a city in old Spain." They build barracks and shops and a conspicuous church. Those in Spain who had jeered at their youth now begin to come "like nettles and beetles." They run on the land "like lice staining it." They parcel the bloody meadows, bringing carts with oak beds and Spanish pots heavy with the stink of stewed grease. They come with their wives and children and build barns "like the old cotes under Córdova." Spanish cities rise on Mexican soil.

The narrator is "old . . . an old man sickened and near death: and the west is gone now: the west is the ocean sky. . . ." He concludes: "O day that brings the earth back bring again/That well-swept town, those towers and that island. . . ." (TAP) (Falk 1965)

See also Cortés, Hernán; MacLeish, Archibald.

CONRADIN VON SCHWABEN

German-Swiss historical epic (1771) by Johann Jakob Bodmer (1698–1783) of minor significance and no success. (Garland and Garland 1986)

CORONA TRÁGICA
(Tragic crown)

Spanish epic poem (ca. 1627) by the literary genius Lope de Vega (full name Lope Félix de Vega Carpio, 1562–1635), more well known as a prodigious dramatist. The poem celebrates the life of Mary Stuart (b. 1548), formerly queen of France, as wife of Francis II. She inherited the throne of Scotland and came to claim it after Francis's death (1660), but she was not a popular choice for queen because of her Roman Catholicism. In 1565, she married the unpopular Lord Darnley, which did nothing to increase her own popularity. He was murdered two years later and she was imprisoned. However, she escaped to England, where she was next in line for the throne held by her cousin Elizabeth I. Fearing Mary's followers would attempt to seize power, Queen Elizabeth kept Mary confined for 18 years before finally executing her (1587). (Hornstein 1973; Siepmann 1987)

See also Lope de Vega.

 # CORTÉS, HERNÁN

Spanish conqueror of Mexico, hero of a number of sixteenth-century Spanish-American epics as well as a modern epic, *Conquistador,* by Archibald MacLeish. Cortés was born in 1485 in Medellín, near Mérida, Spain, into a family of ancient lineage but little wealth. At the age of 14 he was sent to study at Salamanca. Excited by the stories of Columbus's voyages, he went to Valencia to serve in the Italian wars but wandered idly for almost a year. In 1504 he finally sailed to Hispaniola (Santo Domingo), where he became a farmer and the notary to a town council.

In 1511 he sailed with Diego Velásquez to conquer Cuba and was appointed treasurer, receiving a gift of land, Indian slaves, and the first house in Santiago. Soon, dissident elements found in him a leader, and he was twice elected mayor of Santiago. When Velásquez heard of the efforts of Juan de Grijalba to establish a colony on the mainland, in 1518 he sent Cortés, with the title of captain general, with help. Soon suspicious, Velásquez changed his mind, but not before Cortés had put to sea to recruit more ships and men to undertake his own mission.

Cortés sailed for Yucatán early in 1519 with 11 ships, over 600 soldiers and sailors, and 16 horses. Landing at Tabasco, he won over the Indians and found Malinál (called Marina or Malinche, "the tongue"), who became his interpreter, mistress, and mother of his son. He sailed on, founded Vera Cruz as a headquarters, and shook off the authority of Velásquez. Welding his soldiers into a cohesive force, and burning his ships to prevent disaffection, he set out across the mountains to the interior. There he found a political crisis: subject peoples resenting the Aztecs. He quickly acquired more than 200,000 Indian allies. Despite threats from the Aztec ruler, Montezuma, he entered Tenochtitlán, the Aztec capital. Montezuma received him with great honor, believing him the incarnation of the god Quetzalcóatl, but Cortés seized him to control the country and so influenced Montezuma that he became Cortés's willing and faithful ally.

Spanish envy and politics soon plagued Cortés. A Spanish force arrived from Cuba, led by Pánfilo Narváez, to take over command. Cortés and a captain, Pedro de Alvarado, defeated the newcomers, but on their return to Tenochtitlán, Alvarado massacred many Aztec chiefs during a festival. An Aztec uprising followed, and Cortés was compelled to retreat from the city with a heavy loss of men. Eventually Cortés was able to besiege the city and capture it (13 August 1521). With this victory came the fall of the Aztec Empire and the establishment of Cortés as absolute ruler. He was accepted by the Indians and popular as a benign ruler. Only his loyalty to the Spanish king kept Mexico from becoming an independent kingdom under Cortés.

In later years, Cortés tried unsuccessfully to conquer Honduras, at which time his property was seized by those he left in charge. Reports of their cruelty reached the ears of the Spanish king. Bureaucrats sent a commission under Luis Ponce de León to investigate, and he soon died. Accused of poisoning de León, Cortés sped back to Spain to answer the charge. While there he was named Marqués del Valle de Oaxaca. On his return, he found the country in a state of anarchy. After restoring some order, he retired to his estate at Cuernavaca, Mexico. In 1540 he returned to Spain, in debt. He decided to return to Mexico, but died on the way to Seville in 1547. (Cortés 1929)

 # COX, GEORGE C.

American minister and poet, author of *Lindbergh: An American Epic* (1927, publ. 1975). Cox was born about 1904 in Illinois. He left college at midterm in 1926 to devote himself to writing poetry. In 1927 his first book of poems, *Out of the Shadows*, was published to some critical acclaim. His second book, *The Voice of God*, was published in 1929, with a foreword by Gerard Manley Hopkins, who foresaw a bright future for him in poetry. However, that year he discontinued writing to enter the Christian ministry. In 1933 he married Lucile Elizabeth Cox. He retired in 1966 to devote himself to writing and music. Following the death of Charles A. Lindbergh in 1974, Cox discovered the epic poem *Lindbergh*, which he had written in 1927. He added a final section to the original poem entitled "In Memoriam." The epic was published the following year. (Cox 1975)

See also Lindbergh.

 # CRANE, HART

American poet, author of the epic *The Bridge* (1930). He was born in 1899 in Garrettsville, Ohio, the son of Clarence Arthur Crane and Grace Hart Crane. Clarence Crane became a wealthy candy manufacturer in Cleveland, where Hart Crane lived from the age of ten. By the age of 13, he was composing poetry.

In 1916, at the age of 17, he accompanied his mother, who had separated from her husband, to visit his grandfather Hart's fruit plantation on the Isle of Pines, south of Cuba. The following year he moved to New York with the intention of entering college and enjoying a carefree lifestyle.

When World War I broke out, he left New York and returned to Cleveland to work in a munitions plant and shipyard. After the war, he held various jobs and wrote poetry. His father did not approve of his lifestyle or his poetic bent, and Hart broke with him in 1920.

In 1926 his first collection, *White Buildings*, was published. Crane acknowledged his debt to the French Symbolist Arthur Rimbaud, who had also left home at a young age to write poetry in Paris.

Crane wrote the long poem "For the Marriage of Faustus and Helen," later incorporated in *The Bridge,* in rebuttal to T. S. Eliot's pessimistic view of the industrial age as expressed in *The Waste Land.* By now Hart's father had become reconciled to his chosen profession. Clarence Crane and philanthropist Otto H. Khan financed the writing of *The Bridge,* which was meant to meld America's past, present, and future into an optimistic portrayal of the American spirit.

He received a Guggenheim fellowship to go to Mexico City to write another epic about the Spanish conquest. While in Mexico he wrote one poem, "The Broken Tower," but he failed to produce the epic. In 1932, returning to the United States by boat, he committed suicide by jumping overboard. (Crane 1933)

See also The Bridge.

 # CRAZY HORSE
(Jas-hunca-Uitco)

American Indian chief of the Oglala Sioux, hero of Neihardt's *Cycle of the West.* Born about 1842, he was the brother-in-law of Red Cloud, one of the principal chiefs of the Sioux. Crazy Horse was one of the principal leaders of the hostile Indians, who for several years defied the authority of the United States. Although only about 30, he was the most respected man of the whole tribe. The name "crazy" is actually a poor translation of the Sioux word *witko,* which means "magic" or "enchanted," referring to his supposed special, sacred vision.

After the death of his brother in 1865, he left Fort Laramie to make war on the federal troops, quickly establishing a reputation as a brave and cunning warrior and ruling over a strong band of Sioux with despotic vigor. In 1876 he defeated Gen. George Crook at the Rosebud River. With Sitting Bull he surprised and destroyed General Custer's army at Little Big Horn (1876), then was pursued by General Terry into the Black Hills. Later, General Crook led an army against him, forcing his surrender at the Red Cloud agency, where he was murdered in 1877 by a frightened soldier after being brought there for a friendly meeting with the agency chief.

Crazy Horse was the poet Neihardt's favorite Indian hero, an ideal tragic epic hero. (TAP) (Beazley 1985)

See also Cycle of the West; Neihardt, John Greenleaf.

 # CRISEYDE

The sweetheart of Troilus in Geoffrey Chaucer's *Troilus and Criseyde.* Her character was adapted from Giovanni Boccaccio's Criseida, heroine of the romance *Il Filostrato,* although Chaucer's Criseyde is much more complex. She evinces both a practicality and a genuine loving fidelity not present in her character as she appears in Shakespeare's *Troilus and Cressida*. (Chaucer 1971)

 # CRISTIADA

Spanish Peruvian epic poem by Diego de Hojeda (1571–1615). The poet, who composed it in a monastery in Lima, summarized the theme of this vast work: "I sing to the Son of God, Human and Dead." Writing in ottava rima, he uses passages from the Gospels, amplifying them with elaborate Baroque ornaments. He borrows episodes from Homer and Vergil, applying them allegorically to the life of Christ. Christ's vestments, for example, include the shields of Achilles and Aeneas. The poet's sources also include the writings of St. Augustine and St. Thomas Aquinas, as well as those of Dante, Tasso, Ariosto, Boiardo, and many others. The descriptions are rich with sensory tenderness reminiscent of secular Renaissance works. In the Last Supper scene, where Jesus washes the feet of his disciples, the beauty of his hands is taken up by the light, the water, the flowers, "in a joyous tremor." Hojeda's sensitive portrayal of the immolation of Christ, with its description of his handsome unclothed body as he is taunted and flogged, is considered one of the most poetic episodes in all of the literature on the life of Christ. (Anderson-Imbert 1969)

See also Diego de Hojeda.

 # CŪLĀMANI

Indian Tamil epic written during the age of the Pallavas (ca. 300–900) by Tōlāmoḷittāvar, an adherent to Jainism. It depicts Jaina kings with their devotion to nonviolence and self-sacrifice. The epic contains a mixture of the supernatural and reality, and gives excellent descriptions of landscape and cityscape. (*Encyclopedia Britannica* 1983)

 # THE CURSE OF KEHAMA

English epic (publ. 1810) by Robert Southey (1774–1843) (*q.v.*). Southey began work on his epic (originally entitled *The Curse of Keradon*), an Indian fable, while in Portugal in 1801 to write his history of that country. He worked intermittently on it until 1809, and finally completed it at the instigation of his friend Walter Savage Landor; it was published in 1810. It consists of 24 books, with irregular but rhyming stanzas. It is generally considered one of the best, if not the best, of Southey's long poems, and one of the best of the English Oriental poems of its period, including those by Byron, Shelley, and Moore.

Book I, "The Funeral," begins with an elaborate picture of a midnight procession and the burning of the dead Arvalan, son of Kehama, and his living wives. The son has been slain by the peasant father of Kailyal after he violated the girl. With dreadful wrath Kehama follows the procession of his heir apparent.

Book II, "The Curse," begins with a colloquy between the dead Arvalan and his father, in which the young man laments his death and asks for vengeance. The father orders the peasant, Ladurlad, and his daughter to be brought forth, but the daughter, clinging to the image of a goddess, is knocked into the water. Kehama pronounces a curse.

In Book III, "The Recovery," as Ladurlad wanders along the river, he sees a woman floating, clinging to the image of a goddess. It is his daughter. Protected by the curse, he walks dry into the water and bears her to shore. She is puzzled and doubts his explanation of being protected until she sees he is not wet.

In Book IV, "The Departure," Ladurlad decides to test the curse further and steps back into the river. It recedes around his dry hand. Kailyal credits the wooden goddess for their good fortune and erects the image on the bank. They go farther away from their oppressor.

In Book V, "The Separation," the two lie down under a tree for the night. Ladurlad apparently goes to sleep, so Kailyal goes to sleep too. At this moment, the father seizes the opportunity to spare her his fate and leaves. She awakens and runs after him, but the ghost of Arvalan appears and chases her. She reaches the sanctuary of a good god, Pollear, a statue of an elephant. When the ghost of Arvalan seizes her, the statue tosses him into the wood. Kailyal stumbles against the root of a broad manchineel tree and falls senseless beneath its shade.

In Book VI, "Casyapa," a superhuman Glendoveer, floating near the earth in the moonlight, discovers the senseless maiden and bears her up to Mount Himakoot, where old Casyapa, the Sire of Gods, dwells underneath the Tree of Life at the source of the Sacred River (the Ganges). The spirit tells Casyapa of the rage and power of Kehama. Kailyal revives. Casyapa decides to defy Kehama, but lacks the power. He calls for a ship of heaven to convey the maiden to Swerga, the lowest heaven.

In Book VII, "The Swerga," the ship sails noiselessly through the air. At the Swerga, there are blue lakes and the palace of Indra (q.v.). Indra, however, is no more able to control Kehama than Casyapa. Since no mortal can inhabit the Swerga, Kailya must be conveyed back to earth. She is taken to the foot of Mount Meru, beside the source of the Ganges. She prays to be returned to her father.

In Book VIII, "The Sacrifice," Kehama offers a sacrifice that will give him dominion over the Swerga: the immolation of a wild horse. But he is interrupted by a man who saves the horse, thus spoiling the ceremony: Ladurlad. Kehama seizes him and, although Ladurlad begs for death, instead orders him back to his wanderings. Kehama then orders the massacre of his own guards for not stopping Ladurlad.

In Book IX, "The Home-Scene," Ladurlad reaches his home, now neglected. The ghost of Arvalan grins at him from the sky, and Ladurlad tries unsuccessfully to strike him. The ghost blows up hot sand on Ladurlad, but the Glendoveer appears, hews Arvalan to pieces, returns the father to his daughter, and sails with them to Mount Meru.

In Book X, "Mount Meru," at this sanctuary, Kailyal meets the spirit of her dead mother. The Glendoveer and Kailyal are attracted to each other, and an Indian Cupid shoots at them vainly with a bow of sugarcane strung with bees.

In Book XI, "The Enchantress," fleeing from the Glendoveer, Arvalan seeks an enchantress for help. She provides him with armor and a chariot drawn by dragons to take him to Mount Meru to find Ladurlad and Kailyal. As he draws near, however, his chariot and steeds are drawn aside by "all-commanding Nature" and dashed upon adamantine rocks. Arvalan falls into an ice-rift 10,000 miles below and is left to howl, unpitied and unheard.

In Book XII, "The Sacrifice Completed," Kehama gets another wild and untouched horse for sacrifice, and the frightened Indra and his attendant spirits evacuate the Swerga for a higher heaven. On their way they stop at Mount Meru to explain their migration and to inform Ladurlad and Kailyal that they must return to Kehama.

In Book XIII, "The Retreat," Ladurlad and Kailyal return to the lower earth to a sylvan retreat, where they await their trials. In the retreat is a beautiful banyan tree, and the elephant and tiger lose their fierceness before the beauty of Kailyal. Fed upon "heavenly fare," she becomes more than a peasant girl, with lofty thoughts and imaginings, although she retains a womanish and loverlike fear of being forgotten by the Glendoveer. A band of wandering priests traveling to find a bride for Jaga-Naut, the idol with seven heads, appears and carries her off.

In Book XIV, "Jaga-Naut," the party arrives in the city of Jaga-Naut, and a celebration of his nuptials begins, with shouting, dancing, and singing in a procession led by the giant idol in a chariot. Kailyal is shut up in the bridal chamber. Arvalan suddenly appears, and she shrinks from him. The Glendoveer comes down and dashes Arvalan to pieces, but Arvalan's enchantress appears with a host of demons, seizes and pinions the Glendoveer, patches up Arvalan, and encourages him to take his pleasure with Kailyal. The enchantress secures the Glendoveer in Tombs under the ocean. Kailyal seizes a torch and sets fire to the bridal bed. Her would-be lover screams in pain. Kailyal's father, protected by the Curse, appears and bears her away.

In Book XV, "The City of Baly," Kailyal hears that the enchantress has borne the Glendoveer to the Tombs of the Ancient Kings, a city built on the seashore by Baly, a mighty monarch of olden times. The sea had inundated it, and all that is left are a few mouldering towers and spires still showing above the waters. As a gift of the Curse, Ladurlad has received the power to walk under water, and he goes down to save the Glendoveer. Kailyal waits day after day.

In Book XVI, "The Ancient Sepulchres," Ladurlad wanders through the submerged city and arrives at the arched tombs of the kings and finds their embalmed bodies, each seated on a throne and holding a scepter. At the farther end he discovers the Glendoveer chained to a rock and guarded by a huge sea monster with two tails. It attacks Ladurlad. He is protected from injury by the

Curse, but is held fast in the coils of the monster. The struggle lasts for seven days, after which the monster is finally overcome by sleep. Ladurlad is immune from growing sleepy, also by reason of the Curse. Faint, the monster tries to crawl away, but Ladurlad hacks at it with an old sword he has found and kills the creature. He hacks at the fetters of the Glendoveer and sets him free. The two make their way back up to the surface of the waters.

In Book XVII, "Baly," one night a year Baly has a respite from his judicial duties in Hell. He walks over India, revisits his old city, and appears just as the father and daughter emerge from the waters. As he arrives, Arvalan also appears in fleshly form, with the enchantress. Arvalan attempts to return the Glendoveer to the Ancient Sepulchres. Baly intervenes, seizes the sorceress and Arvalan, and, stamping upon the earth, opens it to bear the guilty pair down to punishment in the World below.

In Book XVIII, "Kehama's Descent," Kehama hears his son's shrieks as Arvalan is seized, and rushes like a thunderbolt to his aid, smoking with rage. Standing over the abyss, he demands that Baly surrender Arvalan, but Baly answers from down below that Kehama's dominion ceases down there. Kehama then turns to Kailyal and tells her that she alone among mortals is doomed by fate to drink with him the Amreeta cup of immortality and must therefore become his bride. She refuses in disgust. Kehama curses, springs into the sky, and vanishes.

In Book XIX, "Mount Calasay," part of Kehama's curse is to cause Kailyal to develop leprosy. She is devastated when she thinks how this blight on her beauty will appear to the Glendoveer, but she hopes she can trust his affection and the effect of her inward merits. The Glendoveer makes his way to the throne of Seeva (Śiva), the Preserver, to tell him of Kehama's cruelty. The throne is at such a considerable distance that even Brama (Brahma) and Vishnu had to travel a thousand years to reach it. But Faith enables the Glendoveer to reach it quickly, and he lands at the foot of Mount Calasay. At the summit, reached by seven ladders, he finds no life or sound or visible presence. He prays to Seeva with eyes uplifted to where there should be something and strikes a silver bell. At once everything, including the mountain, disappears in a flood of light. The Glendoveer plunges headlong downward, while a Voice directs him to the throne of Yamen, where one finds the remedy for every woe.

In Book XX, "The Embarkation," the Glendoveer lands at the place he had originally left. Kailyal meets him but, aware of her now-repulsive appearance, repels his embrace and tells him of Kehama's revelation that she must share the Amreeta cup and his throne with him. The two, with Ladurlad, leave for Yamen's abode aboard a strange vessel across a gloomy ocean.

In Book XXI, "The World's End," the three land, met by a hideous crew of criminals awaiting judgment and hoping that Kehama will come, subdue the inexorable God, seize His throne, and redeem them from Padalon, this Underworld. A milder company is also there, brooding on their doom: innocent souls so soon enduring death, now expecting to soar to Indra's happy spheres. There is a dark gulf here, from which demons rise and catch those souls doomed to land there. Kailyal pales with fear and clings to the Glendoveer, who consoles her by telling her that the demons do not wait for them. Then, taking her in his arms, he tells her to be of good heart, that it is he that bears her. He spreads his wings and shoots down into the abyss.

In Book XXII, "The Gate of Padalon," Padalon can be seen, a Realm of Woe with gates through which the souls of mortal men must pass—some, condemned by Baly, due here for penance. Others, from Baly's voice absolved, are dismissed to seek their heritage on high, aboard the Ship of Heaven. At each of the eight gates stand wardens, awaiting the hoped-for Kehama. The Glendoveer carries Kailyal to the southern gate, leaving her in charge of the keeper until he returns with Ladurlad. He explains to the keeper why they are there. The keeper orders a chariot, wraps the Glendoveer, Kailyal, and Ladurlad in mantles, and sends them inside Padalon.

In Book XXIII, "Padalon," they pass though the gate and arrive at a vast gulf of fire over which there is no bridge, only a single rib of steel, sharp as the edge of a scimitar. Their car, self-balanced on its single wheel, rolls over this edge of steel, with blazing billows below. On the other side, they go over a raised causeway, walled with little vaults and dungeons tenanted by tormented souls. All around are the sounds of chains, lashing, groans, curses, and scenes of executions. At the end of the causeway, however, is a beautiful city of diamonds, brighter than the midday sun. Leading to it are eight brazen bridges crossing a fiery river that surrounds it. In the center is the palace of Yamen, where he sits alongside Baly, and a vacant gold throne supported by three living human statues. The Glendoveer, Ladurlad, and Kailyal pay homage to the god, and the Glendoveer asks for redress from tyranny. Seeva bids them approach Yamen's throne, where all wrongs are redressed. Yamen tells them to wait in patience.

In Book XXIV, "The Amreeta," there is a sudden silence followed by approaching, deepening strange sounds. Kehama has arrived to seize the throne of Padalon. His plan is to divide himself into eight separate rajahs, each to march to one of the eight gates of the city, advance through the streets, and meet Yamen at the palace in battle. The battle ensues, in darkness. Kehama is victorious. A prostrated Yamen is stretched before him, his neck beneath Kehama's feet. Kehama questions the living statues, who acknowledge the justice of their punishment and say they await a fourth of equal guilt, to share the empty throne beside them. Kehama renews his proposal to Kailyal, who again disdainfully rejects him. Kehama then calls for the Amreeta cup of immortality. A huge marble tomb opens, revealing a giant skeleton that slowly presents the cup to Kehama, saying it has been doomed for him only and for Kailyal. An elated Kehama eagerly drinks it. The Glendoveer impulsively springs forward to seize the cup but is prevented by the skeleton. As Kehama drinks, a burning anguish flows through his body, which becomes red-hot. The three statues set up a fiendish cry welcoming him as the fourth doomed to stand beside them. The skeleton then presents the cup to Kailyal, who drinks it, trusting in the Heavenly Powers. A stream of fragrance flows through her body, and she becomes immortal without having tasted the bitterness of death. She rushes to the arms of Glendoveer, to become his bride and his equal in immortality. Yamen bestows on them his blessing. Kailyal is concerned about her father, and Yamen assures her that after his death she will find him in her mother's bower. A car carries both the Glendoveer and Kailyal away to the Swerga. The Lord of Death smiles on Ladurlad. He lies down and sinks into a sleep, from which he awakens to find himself a disembodied spirit with all those whom he loved, his wife and daughter, to part no more. (TAP) (Jeffrey 1811; Scott 1811; Simmons [Jack] 1948)

See also Southey, Robert.

 # CYCLE OF THE WEST

American epic (1913–1941) by John G. Neihardt (1881–1974). An epic of westward expansion and the displacement of the Native American, it covers a period in American history from 1822 to the Battle of Wounded Knee in 1890.

Several themes run through the epic: the great settlement of the West as more than a regional or national event, one of the great archetypal movements in the history of the world; the Greek sense of fate and a cosmic plan; Neihardt's concept of an "Otherness," where spiritual force is the true reality and brings understanding that unites men with nature in a cosmic whole; and the universal problem of trying to reach dreams.

Cycle of the West is a long narrative poem, in rhymed couplets and iambic pentameter, 650 pages and 16,000 lines in length. It is divided into five "songs," published separately at first, each song subdivided into sections. It tells the stories of real historic events and, for the most part, real persons—mountain men, fur trappers, Indian traders, keelboat crews, soldiers, settlers—opening the West. It tells of the Indian tribes as well, religiously resisting the invasion, and in their desperation welcoming a new religion promising a savior who would restore their old way of life. It finds values common to both peoples.

The first song, "The Song of Three Friends," is the tragic story of three fur trappers—Mike Fink, Bill Carpenter, and Frank Talbeau, members of General Ashley's first expedition to the West—setting out from St. Louis in 1822. It is subdivided into eight sections.

In the first section, "Ashley's Hundred," Neihardt gives an overview of the excitement that swept over the nation in 1822: young men bewitched by tales of wealth "before the great wind woke to snuff them." In the second section, "The Up-stream Men," three friends set out from St. Louis: the witty, self-assured Fink, "God's Adamic Dream"; lanky Carpenter, six-feet-two, a "cedar of a man," slow of wit and something of a child but unusually competent; and wiry Talbeau, scarce five-foot-six and slim but fast of movement and able to hold his own against more bulky opponents who "wondered what his comrades saw in him." In a favorite ritual, a test of mutual love and skill, Fink and Carpenter face each other at 60 paces with a whiskey cup as a target on the head of one and the other shooting it off.

In the third section, "To the Musselshell," the trappers meet a group of Bloods, who ask them to send a party to the Musselshell River where they live.

The three friends volunteer. In Section Four, "The Net Is Cast," at the Indian camp Fink falls in love with the beautiful foster daughter of a chief, but it is Carpenter on whom the maiden fixes her fancy. In Section Five, "The Quarrel," Fink is enraged, and sulks in his tent. Talbeau tries in vain to restore the friendship, but Fink engages Carpenter in a bloody fistfight, which he loses. In Section Six, "The Shooting of the Cup," Fink broods througout the winter, but with spring peace seems to be restored. Talbeau suggests the old shooting-of-the-cup ritual to cement a restored friendship. Fink fires, and Carpenter falls dead. Fink throws down his gun, protesting he did not mean to kill Carpenter.

In Section Seven, "The Third Rider," Fink and Talbeau volunteer to scout for the "River of the West" beyond the Range, a region "immensely rich in furs." After a long day's ride, the two men camp. Fink dreams of Carpenter's ghost. In Section Eight, "Vengeance," Fink blurts out a confession that he killed Carpenter intentionally. Obsessed with the idea of revenge, Talbeau orders Fink onto a grassland charred by a fire. In his flight he is bedeviled with a fear of both Carpenter and Talbeau. Talbeau pursues, but begins to pity Fink and repent of his desire for vengeance. Then he frightens a swarm of feasting crows and stumbles on "a thing without eyes," and "pilfered sockets with a pleading stare." He utters a long, hoarse wail of anguish and despair.

The second song, "The Song of Hugh Glass," is the story of an old seasoned trapper/hunter and his young friend, Jamie. In the first section, entitled "Graybeard and Goldhair," Glass is riding ahead, and is badly mauled by a grizzly bear. Jamie and their party come upon him, near death. Needing to move on, the party delegates Jamie and the unscrupulous Jules Le Bon to stay with what they think is a dying man and dig the grave for him when he dies. But the old trapper lingers, and Le Bon persuades Jamie they must abandon him since he is rapidly weakening and their staying is increasingly hazardous. The frightened, demoralized Jamie agrees, and they desert the old man, first taking his rifle, knife, and gear, which will be of no use to a dead man.

In the second section, "The Awakening," Hugh struggles back to consciousness and awakens to find himself abandoned and without his belongings. In the third section, "The Crawl," half delirious and highly enraged, Hugh begins to crawl, dragging his broken leg, the hundred miles back to Fort Kiowa across a barren country of mountains, desert, and hostile sky. He finds a broken knife and carves a crude set of crutches. After encounters with wild animals, Hugh comes across an Indian village, which he watches from a bluff, crouched in fear. But as he observes the Indians go about their daily tasks, they slowly become human beings to him. Glass is famished, and when he comes across an old, tottering squaw, he is tempted to kill her for what is in her pack. But a whimsy holds him back, and he sees her as a human being. He thinks of the perfidy of Jamie and is again resentful; but memories of their friendship now turn his anger into a longing for that friend and a belief in the miracle of being loved at all. He experiences a softening and forgiveness. Suddenly Nature no longer seems hostile.

In the fourth section, "The Return of the Ghost," Hugh arrives at the fort, where an amazed major tells him how Jamie and Le Bon had reported him dead. He points out Le Bon to Hugh, who sets his finger on the trigger of his rifle while Le Bon cowers, expecting the roar of the gun. But Hugh only kicks him. "Come, get up and wag your tail. I couldn't kill a pup!" Then he turns to the major: "I had a faithful friend. Where's Jamie?" But Jamie has set out to search for Hugh after hearing of his survival.

In Section Five, "Jamie," Jamie has been blinded by the rifle Le Bon took from Hugh. Now in a Piegan lodge, sick and broken, he asks the Piegans to bring him a priest. Hugh finds the blinded Jamie, who mistakes him for the priest and begins a confession of guilt, asking for absolution. Hugh answers that life is too short for hatred, reveals his true identity, and asks Jamie, "Will I do?"

The third song, "The Song of Jed Smith," is the story of another old trapper as revealed gradually, but not chronologically, in the reminiscences of three old friends: Bob Evans, Art Black (historic persons), and Squire (Neihardt's invention). Each represents a different level of sensibility and understanding. Squire, the youngest, is mainly interested in food, drink, and excitement. Evans is the educated man searching for meaning in life. Black is the oldest and most practical. In the first section the three meet some years after Smith's death, at the site of an 1825 rendezvous, and sit around a campfire with a jug of "Taos lightning," gassing. In the conversational flow, Smith comes alive: clean-shaven, hawk nose, "lean six-feet of man-stuff," fond of reading the Bible and often retiring to the woods for private prayer. Seven years before, a band of Comanches had scalped him. They drink to his going "angeling."

In the third section they remember crossing South Pass, the snow horse-deep, and the awe as they emerged at the top and saw the vast expanse of the Great Salt Lake. In the fourth section, Black recalls the labored crossing of the desert to the sea, when Jed had pulled out his Bible and read "like anything that's true." In a valley Jed had returned with a dozen "lousy-looking" Mohave Indians and "treated them the same as folks."

In Section Five, Evans talks of the trip along the coast among the High Sierras through ice and snow, and Jed at a sudden precipice's edge, about to fall and scared, then smiling. They had descended to the desert, a "stinging smother in the sand and the swelter of the sun," and hallucinated, imagining people and villages and seawater, and old Jed, seeing "something beyond you." In one forsaken moment he had seen Jed weak and had begun to love him.

In Section Six, Black remembers the journey from the San Gabriel Mission in southern California up the Pacific coast to Oregon and the massacre of all but Jed and himself by the Umpqua Indians. They remember how Jed talked about retiring, but had made one last trip to join his brothers beyond the Cimarron River in Mexico and died, a feathered huddle buried in Comanches. Squire's voice rises in sorrow, then ceases. Sensing the sorrow, the dog by the fire lifts his muzzle to the sky and mourns.

The fourth song, the "Song of the Indian Wars," tells of the gradual displacement of the Indians as white men move into the West at the end of the Civil War, a story told impersonally but with compassion. It avoids the old stereotypes, and shifts between the Indians and the white men, each participating in a struggle that neither side fully understands. In the opening section,

"The Sowing of the Dragon," it is four years after Appomattox, and men are now looking westward beyond the Missouri to a land "clad with grain and jeweled with orchard"; and, "being of the Cadmian breed," they "sow the dragon-seed." Other men see the end of sacred things and with pious dread behold the dwindling of the holy places. Down the rivers war sweeps. Every day some ox-rig creeping California way is plundered and the homesick driver killed, fighting for his little brood.

In the second section, "Red Cloud," members of different tribes of Indians gather, torn between those who trust the treaties by the Great White Father and those who remember broken promises by the whites. Spotted Tail, respected as a seer, urges conciliation, mindful of the women and children who would suffer from war. But Red Cloud issues a call for war, which carries the day. The white commissioner rides through the lane of Indians, and an ancient squaw lifts a feeble fist at him and screams. In the third section, "The Council on the Powder," a Cheyenne called Black Horse comes to the Sioux village urging peace, but the braves beat him. Some moons later, Red Cloud renews his call for war, and Spotted Tail again urges peace. Then Sitting Bull speaks for war.

In Section Four, "Fort Phil Kearney," a log train near Piney Isle is suddenly attacked. Troopers from Fort Kearney roar down the draw and scatter the Indians. On the twentieth day, a lookout signals a warning. Captain Fetterman, who had boasted he would ride the whole Sioux Nation down with 80 men, takes over and rides out. In Section Five, "Rubbed Out," Fetterman and his men are massacred. In Section Six, "The Wagon Boxes," winter and summer wear on, and August comes. Across the Piney Fork, a mile from the fort, as a wagon train makes its way to the loggers' camp, Indians attack. The soldiers crouch behind the boxes and bales of hay. The Indians set fire to the hay with ignited arrows. After bloody fighting, the Indians withdraw.

In Section Seven, "Beecher's Island," summer comes with peace. The Great White Father speaks: Between the Missouri River and the Big Horn, the country will be closed to the whites. But Red Cloud is loath to yield. With the next spring comes news from Kansas of women captured and men slaughtered, of trains burned along the Santa Fe, of drivers scalped. Panic spreads among the whites. All summer the cavalry pursues dissolving trails. At Beecher's Island, Indians attack, and Beecher is killed. The soldiers are surrounded for five days, until the cavalry arrives from Wallace.

In Section Eight, "The Yellow God," the reputation of Custer spreads throughout the West after the Battle of Washita. For four years there is peace; then Custer moves upstream, leading his men to the Black Hills, that "paradise of deer and singing streams." He inspires dreams among the whites, and a "man-flood" deepens. Among the Sioux, young men chant to the drums, and many go to Crazy Horse and Sitting Bull on the Tongue and Powder rivers. In Section Nine, "The Village of Crazy Horse," Washington orders all Indians to gather on the reservation or be declared hostile. Crazy Horse's people stay where they are, so one moonlit night the cavalry rides down and sets fire to the sleeping lodges. The Sioux panic and flee up the steeps. Later they return, and the village grows again, a "miracle of patches."

John G. Neihardt's *Cycle of the West* details the nineteenth-century westward exploration and settlement of North America. The epic relates stories of mountain men such as the two pictured here in George Caleb Bingham's 1845 painting *Fur Traders Descending the Missouri.*

In Section Ten, "The Sun Dance," the news of the massacre of Crazy Horse's village sets the blood of all the young Sioux astir. The whole white world seems to sweep the prairie. The Indians raid them. Enemies of the Sioux, many Rees and Crows join the white forces, so the Sioux turn to the Great Spirit for help. They raise a sacred pole in the center of their town and perform the sun dance. In Section Eleven, "The Seventh Marches," the white army gathers forces to clear the path for Custer. In Section Twelve, "High Noon on the Little Horn," Custer proceeds recklessly without waiting for Major Reno, whom he has sent for reinforcements. The Indians attack. When the dust settles, bodies "gleam white the whole way to the summit" in a brooding silence. Too late, Reno scatters the Sioux, who flee to the Big Horn Mountains.

In Section Thirteen, "The Twilight," the Indians have lost heart. The people are listless, and there is now no hope but in flight. But whither? They turn eastward. General Crook follows diverging pole trails that reveal the hunted scattering "like quails before the hunter." The multitude of Crazy Horse and war chief Gall have vanished. Crazy Horse's people now turn west and reach the valley of the Powder River. Surely here they will find peace, but bleak January brings news of approaching soldiers. The Sioux flee to the head of Little

Powder River. Spotted Tail, a lover of the whites, comes to them, urging compliance with the whites, and Crazy Horse brings in his people. In Section Fourteen, "The Death of Crazy Horse," as the last great Sioux comes in, he says, "Now let my people eat."

One day news comes of how Nez Percé chief Joseph has fought the whites and reappeared down the Yellowstone, undaunted. The whites fear what Crazy Horse is thinking. He has left the reservation and gone to the camp of Spotted Tail to be with his people. The white officer asks him to return to Fort Robinson for a parlay, sincerely promising him that no harm will come to him. Crazy Horse believes him, but at the fort he is hustled among bayonets to a barred room. He struggles. A frightened soldier stabs him. Dying, he protests, "I did not want to fight." His old mother and father bear his body away on a pony-drag to lie somewhere among the badlands.

The last segment, "The Song of the Messiah," presents the final stage of this epic journey of the white man, beset by tragedies for both the white and the red man. The frontier is gone. The red man has been cut off from his relationship to the land, but seeks salvation through a spiritual force. It is the end of one world, and the beginning of another. In the first section, "The Voice in the Wilderness," ten years after the death of Crazy Horse, there is a sadness. In vain the holy men call upon their magic. There is hunger everywhere. Complaints to Washington are disregarded. Gall, Red Cloud, and Spotted Tail have become old and only tell stories, and Crazy Horse lies somewhere upon a lonely hill. Then a timid rumor out of the West wanders in, that there had been a man who once had died and traveled the Spirit Land, and who knew there would be a new earth and heaven.

In Section Two, "The Coming of the Word," emissaries from the Sioux return, convinced that this is the Messiah, with the tale of a living Tree. They stop to pray among the Arapaho and learn a new dance, the Ghost Dance, to make the dead return. In the third section, "The Dance," the Sioux join in such a dance around a "Holy Tree," actually a sapling cottonwood with branches lopped and topped with withered leaves. Young Black Elk, who has been sleeping, tells of a dream of two crossing roads, good and evil, beside this Holy Tree, with a ring of peoples in brotherly bliss. Hearing of the dance, the agent suspects some kind of devilment is being hatched. Surrounded by the Indian police, he tells them to stop it. A warrior cries, "Go back and bring your soldiers. The dance is our religion." The returning dead, immune to bullets, will fight beside them, he says. "Nothing can hurt us now." The agent leaves.

In Section Four, "The Soldiers," in November there are rumors of marching men. With the promised armies of the dead, the Sioux youths are eager for battle. Rumor has it that Sitting Bull will come. In Section Five, "Sitting Bull," Sitting Bull has had a disturbing dream and does not come. In the night, intruders trick him outdoors and murder him.

In Section Six, "The Way," Sitanka and the Messiah's band of Sioux flee southward and find only an abandoned village. In a feverish dream, Sitanka sees the Savior, and awakens to tell his people that he has news of the Ever-Living Dead. He saw many soldiers, a bloody rain of flame and smoke, the

119

dead beginning to rise, and wounded children running toward the soldiers to play. But even if the soldiers come to kill, the Spirit says they must love them still, for they are brothers.

In Section Seven, "Wounded Knee," Sitanka's people arrive at the camp of soldiers, and Sitanka's vision seems about to become real. The soldiers are friendly. The Soldier Chief brings them food and medicine, and his holy man makes medicine for the burning in Sitanka's breast. All the valley is a holy place.

In the night Sitanka is awakened to hear Yellow Bird's voice: "Why are you giving up your guns to these Wasichus? Are you cowards? They are not brothers. The Nations of the Dead are crowding to help us." A gunshot rips the hush. Then once again the rage of men. A soldier's face with blazing eyes raises his gun butt. Sitanka cries, "My brother!" Then his brain goes out. Around his body a fury breaks out, followed by a roaring until it ceases, triumphant bugles blare retreat, and iron-footed squadrons march away.

Darkness falls. A mounting blizzard breaks. All night it sweeps the bloody field of victory that "keeps the secret of the Everlasting Word." (TAP) (Aly 1976; Whitney 1976)

See also Hugh Glass; Neihardt, John Greenleaf.

 ## DAHLSTIERNA, GUNNO EURELIUS

Swedish poet, author of two epics, *Kungaskald* (Hymn to the king, 1697) and *Göta kämpavisa* (Heroic ballad of the Goths, 1700). He was born Gunno Eurelius in Sweden in 1661. He worked as a civil servant to support his poetry writing. Dahlstierna admired the elaborate Baroque style of Italian Giambattista Maríno (1569–1625), and when King Charles XI died, he composed his *Kungaskald* in the king's memory. This poem, which remains the most elaborate Baroque-style verse in Swedish, established Dahlstierna's reputation. During the Great Northern War against Denmark, Saxony, and Russia, King Charles XII achieved an early decisive victory over Russia in the Battle of Narca (1700), and Dahlstierna honored the event with the *Göta kämpavisa*. Following the success of this poem, the king elevated him to the nobility (1702), and he assumed the name Dahlstierna. He is credited with introducing ottava rima, usually in alexandrines, into Swedish poetry. He died in 1709. (Magill 1993)

 ## *THE DALIMIL CHRONICLE*

Czech epic (early 14th c.) by Dalimil, an ardent Czech patriot. The first chronicle to be written in the Czech language, the poem portrays the history of the Czech people. In stunning and impassioned language the author expresses strong patriotic sentiments and equally strong dislike for the Germans. The rhymed chronicle is an important source for understanding Hussite nationalism, when animosity grew between the Czech majority and the German minority, which held a large portion of the wealth and influence. During the Hussite period the epic was widely read, copied, and passed among the citizens. The form of most fourteenth-century Czech verse was an eight-syllable trochaic line with couplet rhymes, although chronicles showed some variation. (Čiževskij 1971; Dvornik 1962)

DALIN, OLOF VON

Swedish historian, poet, and playwright, author of the epic poem *Swenska friheten* (Swedish liberty, 1742). Dalin was born in 1708 in Vinberg, Sweden. His writing first appeared anonymously in Sweden's first literary periodical, the popular *Then swäska Argus* (1732–1734). When his identity was revealed, he became the focus of literary acclaim, becoming the preeminent figure in Queen Louisa Ulrica's salon and tutor to the crown prince (Gustavus III). His most popular work was a satirical allegory, *Sagan om hästen* (The tale about a horse, 1740), in which the horse represents the Swedish people and its owners represent Swedish royalty. His epic poem *Swenska friheten* appeared two years later but was not a critical success. His patriotic ballads, however, captured Swedish imagination. His most ambitious work was a three-volume *History of the Swedish Kingdom* (1747–1762). He is credited with opening the way in Sweden for the ideas of the Age of Enlightenment. He died in Stockholm in 1763. (Magill 1993)

See also Swenska friheten.

 # DANDIN

Indian Sanskrit poet and prose writer (fl. late 6th, early 7th c.), author of *Kāvyādarśa* (Mirror of poetry) and *Daśakumāracarita* (Tales of ten princes), a romance about ten princes and their quests for love and renown. A resident of South India, Dandin is credited with setting the standard for Sanskrit literature in the south. His poem was written with such skill that it could be read both forward and backward, in one direction narrating the story of the *Rāmāyaṇa*, and in the other, the story of the *Māhabhārata*. (Thapar 1966/1987)

 # *DANDSERINDEN*
(The danseuse)

Danish lyrical epic (1833) by Frederik Paludan-Müller (1809–1876). Written in ottava rima and awash in aestheticism, the poem was inspired stylistically by Byron's *Don Juan*. The mood alternates between playful irony and dire pathos, unlike the poet's later moralistic works. (Brogan 1996)

See also Paludan-Müller, Frederik.

 # *DANIEL VOM BLÜHENDEN TAL*

Middle High German epic romance by Der Stricker (1st half 13th c.). An Arthurian romance, it relates several unlikely exploits. Der Pleier (fl. 13th c.) is

thought to have written *Garel vom blühenden Tal* (ca. 1260–1280) as a retort because of unchivalric aspects of Der Stricker's poem. (Garland and Garland 1986)
See also Stricker, Der.

 # DANTE ALIGHIERI
(Also Durante)

Italian poet, prose writer, and philosopher, author of the *Divine Comedy* (ca. 1308–1321), one of the greatest poems in Western literature. He was born in Florence in 1265 into a family of noble lineage but modest means. His father, Alighiero di Bellincione d'Alighiero, was a money-lender in Florence and Prato, as was his grandfather. His mother, Belle, probably a member of the Abati family, died when he was young, and his father married Lapa di Chiarissimo Cialuffi.

At the age of nine Dante first met Bice Portinari, also nine, whom he called Beatrice. Although he saw her only a few times, she profoundly affected him, becoming the inspiration of his major works and, he believed, the agent of his salvation. However, he became betrothed to Gemma Donati when he was 12. He was reared in the artistic milieu of Florence, wrote poetry under the influence of the elderly statesman and man of letters Brunetto (Bruno) Latini and poets Guido Cavalcanti and Guittone d'Arezzo. He dabbled in painting and studied classics, medieval literature, and theology, possibly at the university in Bologna.

His father died sometime prior to 1283. Dante had reached his majority when he again saw Beatrice. He was swept away by her beauty, which he equated with a revelation of the nature of the divine. He had a "dream vision" of her death and saw it as the apex of nature's unsurpassable perfection. His prose poems of her represented a new style of love poetry, in which she became more than the human embodiment of Heaven's radiance. Over time, in fact, Beatrice became the vehicle bringing him to a state of glory.

He married Gemma Donati and they had four or five children, while Beatrice, of the angelic beauty, married Simone dei Bardi. Prior to Beatrice's death in 1290, he had a second vision of the event, so that when she actually died, he was convinced that she had departed "to the kingdom where the angels have peace."

In the meantime, as a Guelf (papalist) cavalryman in the first rank, he fought in the Battle of Campoldino (June 1289) against the Ghibelline (imperialist) city of Arezzo and in the capture of Caprona, the fortress of Pisa (August 1289).

However, after Beatrice's death, he spent an intense period studying philosophy and theology in "the schools of the religious and the desputations of the philosophers," as he describes them in *Il Convivio* (The banquet). In about 1293–1294 he published *La Vita Nuova (New life),* love lyrics and sonnets composed between 1283 and 1291, laced into an autobiographical prose "plot" describing his love—both earthly and spiritual—for Beatrice.

He immersed himself in politics, joining the Guild of the Physicians and Apothecaries (1295/1296), Guelf law requiring a guild membership to qualify for high government posts. In 1300, after acting as Florentine ambassador to San Gemignano to elicit that town's participation in the election of a new captain for the Guelf League of Tuscany, he was elected to the governing Priorate. But the Guelfs soon split into warring factions called the White Guelf, of whom Dante was one, and the Black Guelf. While he was out of the city in 1302, the Blacks seized power, tried him in absentia, and condemned him to exile, never to return to Florence on pain of death. He wandered the countryside, taking refuge first in Verona, later most probably in Bologna and Paris, before he returned to settle in Ravenna about 1317. During that time he worked on *Il Convivio*, a philosophical commentary on 14 of his odes, never completed. He also wrote a political treatise, *Monarchia*. He had probably begun work on his greatest work, *La divina commedia* (Divine comedy), an epic allegory about the soul's search for God, about 1308. The *Commedia* is peopled with characters from his life, particularly from the days of his political career. His great-great-grandfather, Cacciaguida, who was knighted by Conrad III and died in the Second Crusade, appears in it, as do many poets from earlier times. The epic was written, not in Latin—although the first seven cantos of the *Inferno* may well have been written in Latin—but in Italian, a language in which Dante explained, "even women can exchange ideas," meaning that it was written for the "common reader." *Inferno* was first circulated in manuscript form about 1311.

He accepted the invitation of the count of Polenta, Guido Novello, to live in Ravenna, where he was given his own house, about 1317. His sons Jacopo and Pietro and daughter Beatrice joined him. There, apparently, he completed *Purgatorio* and wrote the whole of *Paradiso*.

In 1321, Guida Novello sent Dante as an ambassador to Venice to negotiate a settlement between Venice and Ravenna. The mission failed, and the diplomatic party was denied a ship for the return trip. On the land journey home, Dante contracted malaria and died soon after his return (1321). The city of Florence, from which he had been exiled for life, laid claim to his remains, but Ravenna refused to honor the claim. Requests were refused again in 1396, 1429, and 1476. Finally, in 1514, by authority of Pope Leo X, the Florentines received permission to remove the body. But when the tomb was opened, no body was there, and envoys informed the pope that "in death he must have been received, body and soul, into one of those realms [*Inferno, Purgatorio,* or *Paradiso*]." The tomb was again opened in 1782 and in 1865, when the Florentines petitioned for permission to remove the body. Again they were refused, but a chest containing Dante's remains was found that had been hidden in a wall in 1677. The chest now resides in the Bibliotheca Nazionale, while Dante's remains were returned to the original sarcophagus in Ravenna, where they are to this day. (Musa 1973; Dante Alighiere/Sayers trans. 1949/1979)

See also Divine Comedy.

DE BELLO TROIAN

See Bello Troian, De.

DE OÑA, PEDRO

See Pedro de Oña.

DE VEGA, LOPE

See Lope de Vega.

THE DEMON

(Subtitled *An Eastern Story*, 1829–1841)

Russian long narrative poem by Mikhail Lermontov (1814–1841). The poem, Lermontov's greatest, is considered by many Russians to be the greatest poem in the Russian language. Like many Russians, Lermontov had a long-standing fascination with Georgia and the Caucasus. At about the age of 15 he began writing a poem set in the Caucasus, *The Demon*, based on an ancient Georgian legend that reciprocal love between Lucifer and a mortal woman will restore Lucifer to his former place in the God's divine hierarchy of archangels and cause evil to cease on earth. He continued to rewrite the poem in eight different versions throughout his brief life, which was cut short at the age of 27 when he was shot in a duel. The poem, which contains vivid descriptions of the Georgian countryside, was never published during his lifetime, but was circulated privately in several versions. Like Pushkin's *Eugene Onegin*, it can be said to be a verse novel, but it is much shorter than Pushkin's work. It is divided into two parts. Part I has 16 sections, or stanzas, of varying lengths; Part II has 16 sections, some of which contain a number of long stanzas.

In Part I, the poem tells of Lucifer's great love for a beautiful Georgian princess, Tamara, daughter of King Gudál, who has betrothed her to a Turkish prince. Lucifer appears as a more sympathetic character, with hopes, feelings (he floats "sadly above the sinful world" and evil leaves him "deeply bored"), even eagerness to give up his power. (He says, "I am he, whose gaze destroys hope,/As soon as hope blooms;/I am he, whom nobody loves,/And everything that lives curses.") On the way to the wedding, the bridegroom is tempted by the crafty Demon, and he fails to halt at a wayside chapel and pray for protection "from Moslem's knife." His caravan is sacked and he is killed. In a dream, the bereft Tamara is comforted by a voice promising to "fly to you and keep/tryst with you till the daystar flashes. . . ." Just before daybreak a stranger "in beauty clad not of this world," leans above her pillow.

In Part II her parents take her to a convent, where she takes monastic vows. But the Demon comes to seduce her with unearthly delights, promising that her love will regenerate him, causing evil to vanish from the world. He tells her, "I love you with no earthly passion," and asks, "What, without you, is life eternal?" She admits, "I find/your words set secret pleasure thrilling. . . ." She makes him swear, "from evil machinations,/you'll cease for ever, swear it now." He so swears and kills her "trembling mouth" and sets her "blazing." After she dies, an angel carries off her soul, depriving the Demon of his prize, saying, "Begone dark spirit of denial!/. . . for long enough your wicked pride/has triumphed—God will now decide" to whom her soul belongs. Now "on that circle of tombstones/no one now weeps, and no one moans." (Johnston 1983; Riasanovsky 1993)

See also Lermontov, Mikhail Yuryevich.

DER GROSSE TRAUM

See Grosse Traum, Der.

DER GUTE GERHARD

See Gute Gerhard, Der.

DER PFAFFE AMIS

See Pfaffe Amis, Der.

DER TROJANERKRIEG

See Trojanerkrieg, Der.

DÊTVAN

Slovak epic poem (1853) by Andrej Sládkovič (pseudonym of Ondrej Braxatoris, 1820–1872, a poet of the Romantic generation). Whereas traditional epics usually relate exploits in the lives of royal persons, this historical epic describes the life of the peasants in the central Slovak region around the town of Dêtva. The depiction is idyllic but not idealistic. (Preminger 1974)

See also Braxatoris, Ondréj.

 # *DEUTSCHLAND: EIN WINTERMÄRCHEN*
(Germany: A winter's tale)

German epic poem (1844) by Heinrich Heine (1796–1856). It is an irreverent chronicle of the poet's return to Germany for a visit in 1843, in which he takes swipes at Germany's backward social structure and spoofs German hard-boiled conservatism.

The poem consists of 27 caputs, or sections, written in four-line stanzas of iambic meter. The second and fourth lines are rhymed, often incorporating comic puns.

In the first caput, the poet describes his arrival in his homeland for the first time in 12 years. A girl playing a harp sings a light-hearted ditty, inspiring the poet to contemplate replacing church music with rousing songs about the good life.

In Caput 2 the poet compares prying Prussian customs officers with officials such as those who ban writings (his own had recently been banned). In Caput 3 the poet has traveled to Aachen, where he pokes fun at this pocket of medieval thinking and the rigidity of the Prussian military establishment. In Caput 4 he goes to Cologne, where legend has it that the bones of the Magi are buried in the cathedral, presided over by narrow-minded clergy who are anything but "Wise Men."

In Caput 5 the poet carries on a humorous dialogue with Father Rhine, which has been pulled this way and that by the Germans and French for centuries. In Caput 6, in a dream, he meets an ax-wielding overseer of his thoughts who destroys the outdated bones of the Wise Men (Caput 7). Heine then pays tribute to Napoléon as another destroyer of false, binding beliefs. In Caput 8 he goes to Westphalia, where he indulges himself in the hearty foods he has missed.

He travels on, in Caput 9, through Teutoburg Forest. He recalls that this ground was once the scene of the ninth-century Battle of Teutoburg Forest, when Arminus led German tribes in a massacre of three Roman legions under Varus (Caput 10). He speculates on what great heights Germany might have achieved under Roman influence. When his carriage breaks down (Caput 11), the poet finds himself encircled by a pack of wolves. In Caput 12 he makes a long speech declaring to the wolves that he is one of their kind. He sees a crucifix by the roadside (Caput 13), which prompts a discussion on the precarious fate of reformers.

The poet does not travel east to Thuringia, but he devotes the next four sections to a fanciful encounter with twelfth-century Roman emperor Frederick

I Barbarossa, whom legend says waits in Kyffhäuser Mountain with his men until the day they wake and march forth to defeat Germany's enemies. The poet brings the emperor up to date on political and cultural happenings, but the poet's own new ideas outrage the emperor, whose ideas mirror Germany's at Heine's time. The poet has to concede that, in many ways, life in the Middle Ages was preferable to today. He sleeps, but is attacked and repressed in his dream by an austere Prussian eagle (Caput 18).

In Caput 19 he reaches the muddy lowlands of the Weser River valley and the town of Bücheburg. He slogs through, the weight of the past as heavy as the mud. In Caput 20 he arrives at Hamburg and the arms of his mother, who sits him down to a succulent dinner. In Caput 21 the poet looks around Hamburg, where his uncle Salomon had once set him up in business, but which had been devastated the year before his return (1842).

In Caput 22 he has a fanciful meeting with an imposing woman walking the streets. He learns that she is none other than Hammonia, goddess of Hamburg. She asserts that she is the offspring of the great emperor Charlemagne. In Caput 23, Hammonia acknowledges the poet's accomplishments, even though his work has been banned locally. In Caput 24 she urges him to return home, where he will now be welcomed by a country at last emerging from the political and cultural Middle Ages. In Caput 25 she speaks glowingly of Germany's future and offers to show it to him in her magical chamberpot. But when the poet leans over the pot to look, the stench overwhelms him (Caput 26). In the final caput the poet warns the Prussian king to respect poets, for they have the power to condemn him to eternal damnation. (Untermeyer 1937)

See also Heine, Heinrich.

DIE KRONE

See Krone, Die.

DIE MINNEBURG

See Minneburg, Die.

DIEGO DE HOJEDA

Spanish poet and Roman Catholic Dominican cleric, author of a voluminous epic on the life of Christ, *La Cristiada*, considered the best sacred epic in the Spanish language. He was born in 1571 in Spain and received a wide education in religious studies, the classics, and Renaissance literature. He spent his writing years in a monastery in Lima, Peru, where he was prior of the Convento del Rosario. According to tradition recorded by the Peruvian writer Ricardo Palma, the first copy of *Don Quixote* to arrive in Lima was a gift to the count of Monterrey, viceroy of Peru, from a friend in Mexico. When the book arrived, the viceroy was gravely ill and bestowed the book as a gift to Friar Diego de Hojeda, who was at his bedside. Later, Diego composed his epic *La Cristiada*. His work shows not only influences of the church fathers, Castilian sermons, St. Augustine, St. Thomas Aquinas, and Suárez, but also of Homer and Vergil, and of Dante, Tasso, Ariosto, Boiardo, Du Bartas, Hernández Blasco, Girolamo Vida, and of course his Lima friend Diego Mexía de Fernangil. Due to some ecclesiastical misunderstanding, the saintly Father Diego was divested of his priorship and exiled to Huánuco. The experience hastened his death, which occurred in 1615. (Anderson-Imbert 1969; Leonard 1967)

See also Cristiada.

 # DIONYSIACA
(Also *Dionysiăcă*)

Greek epic in the classic epic tradition (5th c.) by Nonnus, a Helenized Egyptian living in Alexandria. It consists of 48 books in Homeric language and dactylic hexameters. Although its main subject is the expedition of Dionysos to India, with episodes of Dionysos's amorous exploits, it also digresses into other Greek myths. It was greatly admired for its fertile inventiveness and descriptive fantasy, dwelling a great deal on the sensual side of Greek legends. Nonnus's style, which has a lively singing quality, is also marked by new words, bold phrases, and striking metaphors, sometimes grotesque. Its basic theme is Dionysos as savior of the world from Chaos.

The first part of the poem, Books I to XII, deals with events preliminary to Dionysos's expedition to India. After the conventional invocation to the Muses, Zeus struggles with Typhoeus, who with his numerous heads and hands flails the heavens, then descends to flog the seas, and uproots the mountains—finally to be struck down by a thunderbolt from Zeus. Cadmus sets out to seek his sister Europa, a captive of Zeus, and arrives at the palace of Electra, where he meets Harmonia, daughter of Ares. The two sail on to the oracle at Delphi to ask where Europa is. The god tells him to cease his search, but to found a new city at the place where a heifer stops and lies down. When he finds that place, a dragon guards it. With Athena's aid, Cadmus kills the creature and, instructed by Athena, plows the land and sows it with the dragon's teeth, which turn into warriors that kill one another until only five are left. These are recruited by Cadmus. After fighting off attackers, he founds the city of Thebes, named for the city in Egypt. He weds Harmonia with gifts from the gods, and brings to Thebes great arts. Among the guests is Aristaios, whose son Actaeon will be turned into a stag by Artemis and slain by hounds. His parents will search for him to give him a decent burial, and he will appear to them in a vision and tell them to have a bust of him made from his bones. Cadmus and Harmonia have four daughters, among them Semele.

Zeus has a child by Persephone, horned Zagreus, who as a baby climbs upon the throne of Zeus. Hera, angered, enlists the Titans to destroy the child. He is reincarnated as Dionysos (also referred to as Bacchos or Lyaios in the epic), who reappears in many forms, finally as a bull, which is butchered piecemeal by the Titans. Zeus seizes Earth, the mother of the Titans, shuts up the murderers of Dionysos inside Tartaros, and ravages Earth with fire and floods.

Eros visits Zeus and shoots him with 12 arrows. Zeus consequently desires 12 women, one of them Semele. Eros visits Semele in a dream in which a bird bears a fruit to Zeus, who buries it in his thigh. It emerges from Zeus's thigh as a full-grown man. Zeus visits Semele and her dream comes true. She is wedded to Zeus, but Hera is smitten with jealousy and puts a wish in Semele's mind to see Zeus on his throne, which no mortal can do and live. Semele sees Zeus in an awful blaze of light and dies, but is transported to a place in the sky. As Dionysos breaks out of his dying mother's womb, Zeus sews him inside his thigh. When the child, a reincarnation of the earlier Dionysos, is born, Hermes carries him first to his aunt, Ino, then to Rhea, who nurtures him to manhood. Ino sets out to find Dionysos, but when she returns, she finds her husband, Athamas, has gone mad and killed their son. She flees with the dead boy and jumps into the sea. The gods save her, and she joins the divine company of the sea, thereafter helping seamen who lose their way.

Meanwhile Dionysos grows into a youth. One day, while hunting in a wood, he meets Ampelos, who becomes his friend. On another day Ampelos is carried off by a man-slaying bull. The grieving Dionysos is consoled by a Muse, who brings back the dead youth as a flowering vine.

The second part (Books XIII to XXIV) deals with Dionysos's expedition to India. Zeus sends Iris to the halls of Rhea to inform Dionysos that he must drive the Indians out of Asia. Dionysos assembles a large host of heroes to help him. Rhea arms all the ranks of heaven for Dionysos: Naiads, Hadryads, Corybantes, Dactyloi, Telchines (gnomes), Centaurs, Cyclopians, Pans, Satyrs, Bacchi. Dionysos dons the gear of war, leaves Rhea, and proceeds to India. The wagon drivers carry shoots of the new vine of Bacchos. They cross the Phrygian plain and march along the Gulf of Nicomedia until they reach the Hydaspes River, welcomed along the way by the humble and the noble.

Dionysos sets out to free the Lydians and Phrygians from cruel tyranny. Hera is angered, and she prods the Titans and other Olympians to war. In the fighting, many of the deities become thirsty and drink from the river into which Dionysos's drivers have poured juice from the Bacchian vines. They become drunk so that they battle fantasies, then fall into a stupor. Dionysos takes them prisoner and binds them. One of them, a nymph named Nicaia, disdains the safety of the women's room and goes among the rocks or in the forest, where a young cowherd, Hymnos, sees her and falls in love with her. She rejects his advances, and kills him with one of her arrows. Dionysos sees her swimming, falls in love with her, pursues her, and soon wins her. In time she bears him a daughter.

Dionysos turns his attention once again to Phrygia. When he arrives in Assyria, the king meets him and entertains him. Dionysos takes a tour of Assyria, but when he returns to the palace, he finds his host dead. He takes part in the funeral rites. He then marches past Tyros and Byblos and arrives in Arabia. He encounters Lycurgos, a ruffian who harasses travelers, so frightening the natives that they sacrifice to him instead of Zeus. Hera sees an opportunity; she sends Lycurgos a poleax and incites him to attack Dionysos. Lycurgos overwhelms Dionysos, who dives into the sea. Zeus observes all this and from on high rebukes Lycurgos. Lycurgos attacks Dionysos's Maenads anyway and is beaten. Zeus makes Lycurgos mad and blind, and he begins his wanderings. Dionysos comes from under the waves to aid Aiacos, who is in a battle with an enemy. The carnage is infinite. Hera is troubled, so she stirs up the river Hydaspes, who drowns many in Dionysos's army. Zeus intervenes, and Dionysos wins the day.

The third part (Books XXV to XL) deals with Dionysos's war with the Indians. Dionysos comes with a full force. In the Indian camp, King Deriades is shaken with fear. Cybele sends a messenger to Dionysos urging him to continue the battle, and gives him an armor from Hephaestos and a shield on which are depicted scenes from old Greek legends. While all sleep, Athena appears in a dream to Deriades, deceitfully promising him invulnerability. In the morning Deriades summons warriors from far-scattered regions. The city teems with people. Deriades inspires his army with a rousing oration, and they rush onto the plain. In the forest, Dionysos arranges his troops in order of battle and inspires them with a call to arms. Athena and Apollo join him. Hera and other immortals join the Indians.

Implacable, bloody conflict breaks out. The terrible noise rises even to the palace of Zeus. Hera sees that the Indians are being destroyed and gives Deriades invincible courage so that the Indian troops rally. They fight until the evening star comes out. At Rhea's nod, a vision appears to Ares, inciting him with the false news that another sleeps in his bed with his bride. Ares speeds to heaven, abandoning the Indians. When the sons of Hephaistos are wounded, that god leaps down from heaven and rescues them. Deriades and Dionysos meet, and Dionysos starts to retreat. Zeus sends Athena down to bring Dionysos back to battle. Inspired, he attacks so vehemently that the enemy begins to retreat from the carnage, awakening new resentment in Hera when she sees the scattered Indians. She turns her eye aside not to glimpse Perseus ferrying across to Libya.

Perseus circles in the air and dives into a cave where he beheads Medusa, releasing Pegasus. Hera hates Perseus and Dionysos, and determines on revenge. She hastens to Hades, finds Persephone, and tells her a crafty tale: that Zeus has refused to help her shackled son Ares, but has rescued his son by Semele, Dionysos, yet would not defend him when he was cut up; that he has given the starry heaven to Semele and Tartaros to Persephone. Persephone is angered and gives Hera one of the Furies. Hera flies to India with the Fury, who becomes even more furious when she sees the crowd of dead Indians. The Fury flies away to heaven until Zeus falls asleep. Hera then calls on Iris for aid, and between the Fury and Iris they keep Zeus asleep for one whole day. Hera goes to Aphrodite, jealous of woman-mad Zeus, and gets her help. Then Hera approaches Zeus and seduces him. Meanwhile the Fury harasses Dionysos into madness, torturing him with visions of vicious beasts. Artemis tries to help but is driven off by Hera. Tormented, Dionysos wanders the pathless mountains. Meanwhile, Deriades attacks the Bacchant women in Dionysos's army, and their whole army is thrown into confusion. Many of Dionysos's best men are slain, and panic sets in. Only Aiachos stays behind.

One of the Graces sees the madness of Dionysos and the Satyrs fleeing from the battle. She goes back to heaven and reports all this to her mistress Aphrodite, who sends her to Eros. Eros hastens to India. Spying King Moorheus, Eros sends an arrow into his heart. Moorheus looks around, falls in love with the Bacchant Chalcomede, and all thoughts of fighting leave him. He is even willing to throw off his ancient name of Indian and be a Lydian, even surrender to Dionysos. He abandons his wife. Chalcomede is afraid of this madman, and would have thrown herself into the sea but for the appearance of the sea nymph Thetis, who suggests another recourse: pretend to love Moorheus and postpone marriage until after the war. Moorheus is torn different ways: He fears Deriades; he should kill Chalcomede, one of the enemy; and he pities his wife Cheirobië.

The next morning he renews his attack. Suddenly he is confronted by a woman who hurls a big stone at him, which tears the image of his wife on his shield. He pursues the woman, who rejoins her army. Deriades pursues the Maenads and drives them to the wall, which they enter. Once inside, they put off their armor and become women, refusing battle. In the meantime Chalcomede has halted alone in front of the wall, where Moorheus spies her and runs after her. She teases him by feigning desire for him. He takes off his armor and plunges into the river to wash away the darkness of his skin and become desirable to Chalcomede. However, she stands on the shore, laughing. Moorheus tries to seize her, unsuccessfully. Hermes appears and leads the Maenads out of the town. Deriades awakens to find them gone and sets out in pursuit a second time.

Meanwhile Zeus awakens and discovers Hera's trick. He sees the Maenads fleeing, with Deriades close behind. Angrily he berates Hera and threatens both her and Ares, ordering Hera to drive away Dionysos's madness. Zeus now arms his allies and moves into the battle, again god against god. Dionysos returns to the battle. Deriades, seeing the Maenads again on the battlefield, rallies his fleeing captains. Then Zeus tilts the balance of battle. Dionysos attacks the mighty Deriades, changing shapes as he fights, so that he appears as a firestorm, as running water, as a lion, a pine tree, and a panther. Deriades fights bravely against these insubstantial phantoms, searching for some magic. He frees himself from the entangling vines that are really Dionysos. Darkness stops the fight. Dionysos sends to Rhadamanes for ships. Deriades calls a council, where Moorheus argues that the Indians have more prowess in naval warfare. So Deriades declares war by sea. The Indians stop their warfare on land.

Dionysos's army prepares pyres for their dead and holds funeral games, including a highly competitive chariot race, boxing and wrestling matches, foot races, and javelin throwing.

The war lasts seven years. Hermes comes to Dionysos with a message from Zeus, assuring him of victory. Dionysos questions him about a tale he has heard about Phaëthon, the son of Helios, who grew up mimicking his father by driving his little wagon, wheeling with burning torches around flowers. He would stroke Helios's horses, longing to manage them, and beg his father for a run with the fiery chariot. His requests would be kindly denied, until finally Helios consented, with careful instructions. Phaëthon then sped through the constellations, forcing them out of their orbits. Sadly, Zeus struck him down with a thunderbolt and placed him as a new constellation in the sky. Hermes finishes this story and returns to Olympos.

The ships from Rhadamanes arrive, and Deriades renews the battle. Dionysos rallies his army. There is carnage on both sides. Zeus inclines the balance of the sea fight toward Dionysos. The Indian host abandons their ships and moves to the land. Deriades confronts Dionysos and is slain. The Indian war is over. On his victory march back to the Mediterranean, Dionysos comes to Tyre, the home of his ancestor Cadmus, and sings a hymn to Heracles. Heracles answers with an account of the founding of Tyre.

The fourth part (Books XLI to XLVIII) deals with the later adventures and loves of Dionysos. Dionysos leaves Tyre for the city of Beroë, a primordial place where a primitive people dwell. It was here that Aphrodite gave birth to a daughter named Beroë, for whom the city was named. Eros shoots an arrow at Dionysos as he wanders in the wood where Beroë also walks. He follows her, afraid at first to speak to her, but eventually he approaches her, pretending to be a farm laborer, and offers to water her land. Later he proposes to her, but she covers her ears. He pleads, but to no avail. He goes to Aphrodite. Since her daughter has two suitors, she orders that they meet in combat. Triton is to oversee the contest. It is a violent match. Zeus finally grants the bride to the rival, Earthshaker. Dionysos sulks. Eros comes to him and tells him that Beroë was not a proper bride for him, and that he has kept a daintier bride for Dionysos in Phrygia.

Dionysos leaves and comes near Hellas, where he establishes dances. The noise reaches the ear of the king of Thebes, Pentheus, who arms a hostile host. The inhabitants quiver in fear, and Pentheus's mother, Agauë, remembers a prophecy that Pentheus, who has seized the kingship from his father, will be torn apart by wild beasts. The army seeks Dionysos, but Zeus looses the Furies on Pentheus. Dionysos is caught, bound, and brought before Pentheus. The Maenads unbind him. In the madness that follows, Agauë tears her son to pieces. Dionysos sees and, taking pity, gives the women a drink of forgetfulness.

He proceeds to Athens. Rumor precedes him, and he is welcomed with wild dancing. He goes to the home of Icarios, where a liquor is provided that maddens the countrymen. Believing they have been poisoned, they cut Icarios to pieces. In despair, his daughter hangs herself. Zeus places her among the stars in heaven.

Dionysos goes on to Naxos. Theseus has just sailed away and deserted Ariadne. Dionysos beholds her sleeping and falls in love with her. As Dionysos stands over her, she awakens and begins a lament, begging the wind to bring Theseus back. Dionysos tries to comfort her. She casts aside all memories and accepts the suit of Dionysos. They are wedded with deities as wedding guests, among them Perseus's father, who derides Dionysos. Hera incites Perseus to confront Dionysos. He marshals the people against Dionysos, but when Dionysos reaches out and touches the sun and moon, Perseus leaves Dionysos and fights the Bacchants. He shakes the head of Medusa and turns Ariadne into stone. Hermes effects a league of friendship between Perseus and Dionysos.

Dionysos quits Argos. Hera marshals the Titans against Dionysos. Dionysos fights them with fire. There is infinite tumult. Dionysos slays many, but has one more task: to kill Pallene's father, who has an unlawful passion for his daughter, whom Dionysos now loves and whom he wins in a wrestling match with her.

Dionysos leaves for Rhea's house. There the virgin Aura, while swimming with Artemis one day, criticizes the goddess's breasts and impugns her chastity. Angered, the goddess goes to Nemesis and asks punishment for the nymph. Nemesis agrees, with Dionysos as the instrument. Dionysos sees Aura as he wanders in the wood, forgets Pallene, and falls in love with Aura. So as not to frighten her, he creates a magic spring of wine. She drinks from it and falls asleep. When she awakens he has vanished, leaving her in despair. She sets out to find him, wreaking havoc along the way. She bears him twins. Dionysos departs, proud of his two Phrygian marriages. Angered, Aura lays the two babes in the den of a panther, but one is rescued by Artemis, who takes him to Dionysos. The baby will become the third incarnation of Dionysos.

Athens honors Dionysos as a god, with three celebrations of the three incarnations. Dionysos has not forgotten Ariadne, and he places her in Olympos. He ascends into his father's heaven and sits on a throne beside Hermes. (TAP) (Hamilton 1940; Nonnos/Rose 1962; Trypanis 1981; Wright 1932)

See also Nonnus.

 # DIVINE COMEDY
(Original title *La Commedia;* called *Divina commedia* after the sixteenth century)

Christian allegorical epic by Dante Alighieri (1265–1321). He began the poem about 1308, completing it shortly before his death in 1321. The work is a monumental achievement that combines threads of four story levels: an autobiographical adventure fantasy, an allegory of the poet's spiritual unfoldment, a theogony, and a morality play. Besides being the world's greatest Christian epic, it offers a comprehensive study of the medieval Christian world. Because the poet chose to compose it in vernacular Italian rather than the standard Latin used heretofore, the poem marks the beginning of Italian literature and stands as a landmark of Western world literature. It contains 100 cantos of terza rima divided into three books, or canticles, of 33 cantos each, plus an introductory canto in Part I.

In this canticle, entitled *Inferno,* on Good Friday in 1300, Dante discovers that he has strayed from the right path and is lost in the Dark Wood of Error. He attempts to escape by climbing a mountain but is turned back by a leopard, a lion, and a wolf. Finally he is approached by the spirit of Vergil, who offers to lead him through Hell, Purgatory, and Paradise (I). By now it is evening, and Dante soon loses heart and wants to turn back. But Vergil chides him: "These doubts breed/From sheer black cowardice. . . ." Vergil tells how Dante's beloved Beatrice, now an angel in service to the Virgin Mary, has sent him to save Dante (II). They continue to the gates of Hell, enter the Vestibule, where the Futile, who did nothing in life, "whose lives knew neither praise nor infamy," run aimlessly in dizzying circles after a whirling banner. They hurry on to the river Acheron (the joyless), where the ferryman Charon transports the souls of the damned across to Hell. But Charon refuses to take the living Dante until Vergil intervenes. At that moment an earthquake strikes so violently that Dante faints. It is about 7:00 P.M. on Good Friday (III). When he awakens, he finds himself across the river and on the edge of the Pit of Hell. He follows Vergil into Circle I, the Limbo, where live the unbaptized and the Virtuous Pagans— all the great Greeks and Romans—who lived before Christendom, their only punishment being never to experience the bliss of God's presence (IV). They ascend to Circle II, the first of the Circles of Incontinence, for those who sinned less by deliberate choice than by failure to embrace good. Minos, the judge of Hell, attempts to block them at the entrance, but Vergil speaks his word of power and they enter. In this place the Lustful are tossed and whirled around forever on the Black Wind. Vergil points out Queen Semiramis, who in life was "so broken to lascivious vice/She licensed lust by law, in hopes to cover/Her scandal of unnumbered harlotries." He points out Cleopatra, Helen, Achilles, Paris, Tristram—all victims of lust. Dante speaks to Francesca de Rimini, who became the lover of her husband's brother Paolo. Her husband found them together and stabbed them both to death. Dante swoons as he listens (V). At Circle III, where Dante finds himself when he wakes, he is in rain: "One ceaseless, heavy, cold, accursed quench," accompanied by "huge hailstones, sleet, snow, and turbid drench." They are amid the Gluttonous, who must lie wallowing in the black mire, forever bedeviled by the three-headed dog Cerberus (VI). At Circle IV, they are met by Pluto, god of riches and the underworld, and Vergil again uses a "word of power" to gain their admittance. Here the hoarders and squanderers shove great weights against one another. Vergil explains they have been wrangling over "the boon/that is delivered into the hand of Luck" of whom he says, "Her permutations never know truce nor pause." They go on, descending a cliff to the Marsh of Styx, Circle V, where the Wrathful are "tearing each other piecemeal with their teeth." They take a "wide arc" around them and arrive at the foot of a tall tower (VII).

In Canto VIII, a beacon atop the tower signals for a boat to transport Dante and Vergil across the Styx to the City of Dis, which rims the Pit marking Upper Hill from Nether Hill. Phlegyas is sent to ferry them across. On the way, they meet Filippo Argenti, a Florentine knight now residing in the Circle of the Wrathful, who tries to attack Dante. As they reach the red-hot walls of the city, they find it guarded by Fallen Angels who slam the gate in their faces. By now it is Holy Saturday. They are at the gates of Nether Hell: the circles of deliberately willed sin.

In Canto IX, while they wait for Divine Intervention, three Furies appear and, beating their breasts, threaten to fetch Medusa and turn Vergil into stone, for all who look on her turn to stone. Medusa represents despair. But with a shattering thunderclap, a divine being arrives walking on water "with unwet feet" and opens the gates of Dis. Dante and Vergil enter and find themselves in Circle VI amid the flaming tombs of the Heretics.

In Canto X, as they follow a track between the city's ramparts and the tomb fires, a Florentinian called Farinata tells them that souls, while unaware of the present, remember the past and predict the future. He foresees Dante's exile. It is early morning of Holy Saturday.

The two rest briefly, in Canto XI, before descending the cliff into the chasm of Circle VII. Vergil describes the three narrowing circles of Hell they face: the Circle of Violence (VII) and the two Circles of Fraud (VIII and IX). He points out that usury is a crime. It is 4:00 A.M. on Holy Saturday.

In Canto XII, as they ready themselves to descend the rocks to Ring i of Circle VII, they are met by the Minotaur, but they manage to slip past him. Vergil explains that the rocks were loosened during the earthquake at the time Christ descended into Limbo. At the bottom of the precipice they find Phlegethon, the river of boiling blood, guarded by Centaurs. Here the Violent against Neighbors, sinners who shed other men's blood in passion, are plunged. On their way around the river to the ford, the centaur Nessus points out various famous scoundrels.

In Canto XIII, having forded the river of blood and left Nessus behind, the poets enter the pathless Wood of the Suicides, Ring ii of Circle VII, where the souls of Suicides—Violent against Self—are encased in the trees, and "foul Harpies" nest.

They come, in Canto XIV, to Ring iii of Circle VII, to a desert of Burning Sand where fire rains unceasingly: the home of the Violent against God, who lie on their backs facing Heaven. The poets travel between the forest and the burning sand until they come to the banks of the boiling red stream, the effluent of the Phlegethon. Vergil explains that all three rivers—Acheron, Styx, and Phlegethon—originate in the world and empty into Cocytus Lake at the Pit.

In Canto XV, while crossing the hot sand atop a dike, Dante sees his old teacher Brunetto Latini, who warns him of his ill treatment by the Florentines.

In Canto XVI, they reach the edge of the cliff and hear a waterfall. Vergil throws Dante's rope girdle into the abyss, a signal to a strange shape, which swims toward them. It is Geryon (Canto XVII), up from the Circles of Fraud.

The poets climb onto his shoulders to be carried over the Great Stone Barrier to Circle VIII.

In Canto XVIII, Dante finds himself in Malbowges, a "dreadful cone" divided into ten bowges (trenches). The first is for Panders and Seducers, who run in all directions, scourged by demons. The poets cross the bridge over Bowge ii where Flatterers are "plunged in dung."

In Canto XIX, crossing Bowge iii, they see the Simoniacs, whose heads are stuck into rocks and whose feet are tickled by fire. Simony is the sin of selling sacraments or ecclesiastical offices.

In the Fourth Bowge (Canto XX), Dante sees the Sorcerers, with heads twisted to the back, so that they must walk backward. The moon is setting on Holy Saturday morning.

They cross the Fifth Bowge in Canto XXI, where the Barrators, who profited illegally by their public offices, are immersed in boiling pitch and guarded by demons with sharp prods. As there is no longer a bridge across the Sixth Bowge, Vergil goes down to speak to the chief demon Belzecue, who says the bridges were broken by an earthquake at the moment of Christ's descent into Hell. However, the demon gives the poets an escort of ten demons to a place where they can cross. It is between 7:00 and 10:00 A.M. on Holy Saturday.

They proceed along the bank of the Bowge in Canto XXII, during which two of the demons quarrel and fall into the pit. In anger they begin to chase the poets (Canto XXIII), who escape by scrambling down into Bowge vi. Here they encounter the Hypocrites, who must walk about wearing gilded cloaks lined with lead.

In Canto XXIV they climb out of Bowge vi and reach the seventh bridge, where they find Bowge vii filled with reptiles, some of whom are Thieves. One Thief, bitten by a serpent, turns first to ashes and then to his former self. It is the Florentine Vanni Fucci of Pistoia, who stole the treasure of Sir Jacopo from the church of San Zeno in 1293.

In Canto XXV, Vanni makes an obscene gesture at God, then flees with the monster Cacus in pursuit. In Canto XXVI the poets continue onto the bridge over Bowge viii, where the Counselors of Fraud are wrapped in flames. Both Ulysses and Diomedes tell their stories.

In Canto XXVII, Guido da Montefeltro, the Ghibelline leader who was excommunicated for his actions against the church, tells his story.

The poets pass over the Ninth Bowge in Canto XXVIII and see the Sowers of Discord being torn asunder by a demon with a sword. They cross the next bridge in Canto XXIX and descend into the Tenth Bowge, where the Falsifiers suffer from horrible diseases. They remain there in Canto XXX, hearing discourse from Falsifiers.

They have now reached, in Canto XXXI, the Well at the bottom of the abyss, ringed with giants whose upper torsos are visible. The poets are lowered over the Well's edge by Antaeus, a giant representing a "brainless vanity." It is now afternoon on Holy Saturday.

In Canto XXXII, they reach Circle IX, the frozen lake of Cocytus, which contains the souls of the Traitors. At the edge, the region of Caïna, standing neck-deep in ice are Traitors to Their Kindred. In the next level, Anlenora, are Traitors to Their Country; in the level of Ptolomaea, Traitors to Their Guests (Canto XXXIII). In the region of Judecca, Traitors to Their Lords are completely submerged in ice (Canto XXXIV). The poets see Dis (Satan) devouring Judas, Brutus, and Cassius. They climb over him and go through the center of the earth into a deep cavern through which runs the river of Lethe, the river of Oblivion, whose springs are in the Earthly Paradise. They follow the stream until they emerge on the island of Mount Purgatory in the Southern Hemisphere of Earth, directly opposite Jerusalem in the Northern Hemisphere. It is the evening of Holy Saturday. This concludes the First Canticle. (Dante Alighieri 1949/1979)

Canticle II, *Purgatorio* (The mountain of purification), Canto I, begins in Ante-Purgatory with a proem and invocation. The first four tercets begin very much like a classical epic, with a delineation of the subject and the invocation to one or more of the Muses. The poets are met by Cato and Utica, the mountain's custodian, who tells Vergil to "wind a smooth rush around [Dante's] waist and bathe/his face to wash away all of Hell's stains."

In Canto II, it is dawn. A boat comes, full of arriving souls. Dante recognizes a friend, Casella, whom he tries—but fails—to embrace. Casella begins to sing of love, but is rebuked by Cato. Dante and Vergil hastily depart.

In Canto III, Dante is frightened when only his shadow appears, but Vergil explains that shades have no substance. They approach the base of the mountain and meet the souls of the Late-Repentants, who were also Excommunicates. Manfred, grandson of Empress Constance, appears, repentant.

In Canto IV, after a difficult climb they reach the First Spur. They are with the Late-Repentants through Negligence. It is noon Sunday.

In Canto V they reach the Second Spur, where they encounter the Late-Repentants Who Died by Violence. In Canto VI they continue their exploration of the Second Spur.

They arrive in the Valley of the Rulers in Canto VII. These rulers who through negligence are among the Late-Repentants include Henry II of England, Rudolph I of Hapsburg, Henry I of Navarre, Philip III of France, and many other thirteenth-century rulers.

In Canto VIII, as the sun sets on the Valley of the Rulers, two angels appear and inform the poets that they come from Mary's bosom "to serve as the custodian of the valley/against the serpent that will soon appear." When the monster arrives, the angels do indeed drive him away.

The poets spend the night in the valley (Canto IX), and Dante wakes to find a guardian angel, who escorts them to the gate to Purgatory.

In Canto X, Dante enters Purgatory and makes a slow, labored ascent to the First Terrace, bordered by a marble wall and sculpted with the likenesses of the Virgin Mary, David, and Trajan, all examples of humility. The First Terrace is the abode of the Prideful, who must forever be bent under the weights of heavy stones. Dante meets several of the Prideful in Cantos XI and XII. On the pavement tombs he sees stone effigies of 13 examples of punished pride, among them Satan, Saul, Sennacherib, and Cyrus the Great. The angel of humility leads him to a place where he can climb onto the Second Terrace. Dante comments that he feels lighter. The angel answers that one of the "P's" has been erased from his brow, leaving only six.

Canto XIII finds them on the Second Terrace, home of the Envious, who are punished by having their eyelids sewn together with iron wires.

In Canto XIV they meet and speak with some of the Envious and hear voices calling out examples of the Envious, such as Cain.

At midafternoon they are guided by another angel up to the Third Terrace, abode of the Wrathful (Canto XV), where Dante has a vision of examples of gentleness: the Virgin Mary looking for Jesus in the temple; St. Stephen, who is stoned to death as a Christian; Pisistratus, who says, "What shall we do to one who'd injure us/if one who loves us earns our condemnation?" When Dante wakes from his vision, he and Vergil are overcome with black smoke.

They learn (Canto XVI) that the smoke is punishment for the Wrathful. During the ascent to the Fourth Terrace (Canto XVII), Vergil expounds on the difference between natural love, "always without error," and mental love. He explains Purgatory's seven terraces punishing the Seven Deadly Sins: pride, envy, and wrath brought on by perverted love; sloth brought on by defective love; avarice, gluttony, and lust from excessive love of earthly goods.

In the Fourth Terrace (Canto XVIII) they meet the Slothful, whose punishment is to run without ceasing. The Slothful shout examples of zeal: Mary (who "made haste to reach the mountain" to share with her elderly cousin Elizabeth, barren until now, the miracle of pregnancy at her age) and Caesar (who during the war against Pompeii rushes off to conquer Spain). They hear shouted examples of sloth: the Jews wandering in the wilderness and the Trojans in Sicily. Dante is overcome by sleep.

In Canto XIX he dreams of the Siren who claims she turned aside Ulysses: "who grows used to me/seldom departs—I satisfy him so." Finally a saintly woman intervenes and summons Vergil, who is able to waken him. They ascend to the Fifth Terrace, abode of the Avaricious and the Prodigal. The Avaricious must lie face down on the ground, bound hand and foot.

In Canto XX, examples of poverty and generosity are given (such as the Virgin Mary and St. Nicholas), as well as many examples of avarice. The mountain begins to shake, and the voices of the souls shout "Gloria in excelsis Deo."

Statius appears (Canto XXI) and explains the earthquake: "It only trembles here/when some soul feels it's cleansed, so that it rises/or stirs to climb on high, and that shout follows." Statius speaks reverently of the *Aeneid:* "it was mother to me, it was nurse.—" Dante introduces Statius to its author, Vergil.

In Canto XXII the angel of justice, having erased a "P" from Dante's forehead, directs them to the Sixth Terrace, home of the Gluttonous. On the way Vergil and Statius discuss Statius's sin, which is prodigality. When they arrive at the Sixth Terrace, an upside-down tree blocks their path and a voice from within the leaves cries out, "This food shall be denied to you." Examples of temperance are cited, including the Virgin Mary, who asked Christ to make wine for the wedding guests, and John the Baptist, who subsisted on locusts and wild honey.

From Donati (Canto XXIII), they learn that the Gluttonous are condemned to starvation.

They encounter a second tree in Canto XXIV, and a voice warns them not to come near—a reminder of Eve's gluttony punishment. The tree sprang from a seed of the Tree of Knowledge of Good and Evil. This canto contains examples of gluttony: the Centaurs and the 9,700 Hebrew soldiers whom Gideon rejected because they were so anxious to drink that they got down on all fours and drank like dogs.

They pass to the Seventh Terrace (Canto XXV) and encounter the Lustful, who must be purified by walking through flames. Little time is left of the day; it is two-thirds over. They see some souls approaching from the opposite direction (Canto XXVI) and learn that they are the Lustful who sinned through unnatural acts. At sunset, they approach the threshold of Earthly Paradise (Canto XXVII), where an angel informs them, "Holy souls, you cannot move ahead/ unless the fire has stung you first. . . ." Dante is afraid, but Vergil tells him, "My son, though there may be/suffering here, there is no death. . . ." They pass through the flames. Dante falls asleep and dreams of Leah and Rachel, representing the active and the contemplative life, respectively. When he wakes, Vergil tells him, "You have reached/the place past which my powers cannot see? . . . From now on, let your pleasure be your guide./Your will is free, erect, whole. . . ."

Dante, Statius, and Vergil arrive at the Earthly Paradise, the top of the Mountain of Purgatory, on the Wednesday after Easter Sunday (Canto XXVIII). Dante finds himself in a dense forest: the Garden of Eden. He approaches a stream, which blocks his path, and sees a lovely woman, Matilda (symbol of active life), who is gathering flowers on the opposite bank. Drinking the waters of this river causes forgetfulness of sins committed on earth. A great procession passes by (Canto XXIX). The symbolism of various elements in the procession is explained (Canto XXX). Vergil disappears, and when Dante looks across the stream for Matilda, he sees Beatrice (in real life Bice Portinari, his early love, who died in 1290 when he was 25; she was the inspiration for his *La Vita Nuova*, and represents here the contemplative life). She speaks to him from a chariot, shaming him for ascending the mountain: "Did you not know that man is happy here?"

In Canto XXXI, Dante confesses to being bedeviled by outward appearances. Matilda immerses Dante in the Lethe and helps him and Statius ford the stream. In Canto XXXII the entire company, "the glorious army," proceeds eastward. They come to a barren tree, the tree of Adam. Beatrice descends from the chariot, which is tied to the tree. At that moment the tree leafs and blooms, and the sun breaks through. As angels sing, Dante swoons at the beauty of the song. When he wakes, Beatrice tells him his mission: "When you have returned beyond, transcribe/what you have seen."

In the final Canto (XXXIII), Beatrice calls man's life on earth "a race to death" and makes a long prophecy that Dante cannot comprehend. Beatrice asks Matilda to lead Dante and Statius to drink water from the Eunoe (another stream from the same source as the Lethe) and "revive the power that is faint in him."

At the close of Canticle II, Dante speaks to the reader, explaining that he is unable to describe in such short space "that sweet draught for which my thirst was limitless." He returns to Beatrice "remade" and "prepared to climb into the stars." (Dante Alighieri 1982/1984)

Canticle III, "Paradiso," begins with a proem and invocation to Apollo: "Make me the vessel of your excellence." In Canto I, Dante passes heavenward with Beatrice. They arrive in the First Heaven, the Sphere of the Moon (Cantos II, III, and IV), where Beatrice answers some of Dante's questions concerning the souls' places in the Empyrean order. In Canto V they ascend to the Second Heaven, the Sphere of Mercury. In Canto VI, they encounter Justinian, who discusses the destinies of the Roman Eagle and the souls in Mercury whose "righteous" acts on earth were motivated by desire for fame. In Canto VII, as heavenly beings sing and dance, Justinian and the other spirits disappear, leaving Beatrice to explain Justinian's assessment of Christ's death as just vengeance: From Christ's human standpoint, his crucifixion was a *just* punishment of humankind for its original sin (of Adam), but from his divine standpoint, "none was ever done so great a wrong." She tells him, "Only man's sin annuls man's liberty." They journey on to the Third Heaven, the Sphere of Venus (Canto VIII), while Beatrice grows more beautiful with each ascension.

They meet Charles Martel, who prophesies concerning the Anjou family fortune (Canto IX). They learn that Rahab, the prostitute mentioned in Joshua 2:1–21 and 6:17, who helped Joshua's messenger escape from Jericho, was the first soul of the pre-Christian era to be taken up into the Heaven of Venus, when souls were freed from Limbo during Christ's Harrowing of Hell. They ascend to the Fourth Heaven, the Sphere of the Sun (Canto X), where the spirits of the wise dwell. St. Thomas of Aquino and 11 other spirits form a holy wreath around Dante and Beatrice. St. Thomas discusses his Dominican Order and relates the life of St. Francis, who founded the Franciscans (Canto XI).

In Canto XII, St. Boniventure tells of the life of St. Dominic. St. Thomas discusses the wisdom of Solomon (Canto XIII). In Canto XIV they ascend to the Fifth Heaven, the Sphere of Mars, where Dante sees a vision of Christ on the Cross. In Canto XV he meets an ancestor, Cacciaguida, who died on the Second Crusade in the service of the emperor Conrad. Cacciaguida relates the Florentine history during his times (Canto XVI). In answer to Dante's question about his own future (Canto XVII), Cacciaguida prophesies Dante's exile, but urges him to remain loyal to his own poetic vision and to his mission to describe what he has seen.

They ascend to the Sixth Heaven, the Sphere of Jupiter (Canto XVIII), and see an imperial Eagle take shape. Dante denounces evil popes. In Canto XIX the Eagle denounces various current rulers, and in Canto XX discusses just rulers from the past, among them King David, Trajan, Hezekiah, and Constantine the Great. The Eagle explains that Hezekiah's death was not forestalled by his prayers. Rather, the sequence of events was predestined. Predestination is further discussed in Canto XXI, when they ascend to the Seventh Heaven. They enter the Sphere of the Fixed Stars in Canto XXII, from whence Dante sees the Earth, "the little threshing floor/that so incites our savagery. . . ."

In Canto XXIII the radiant light of Christ appears "with such intensity—/ my vision lacked the power to sustain it." Christ reascends to the Empyrean, and Dante looks at the second brightest light, that of Mary, "the living star," until she too rises up to the Empyrean, where St. Peter is "keeper of the keys of glory."

In Canto XXIV, Beatrice asks St. Peter to test Dante concerning "the faith by which you walked upon the sea." Peter asks him a series of questions, which Dante answers, concluding with his creed and his profession of Faith. St. Peter blesses Dante. In Canto XXV, St. James appears. Beatrice asks him to question Dante on Hope. St. James asks three things: what Hope is, "how it has blossomed/within your mind," and what is the source of his Hope. Knowing Dante's worst failing is pride (see *Purgatorio* XIII), Beatrice answers the second question for him, lest he be arrogant. Dante answers the first question, "Hope is the certain expectation/of future glory...." His answer to the last question is that many writers have inspired him, chiefly David, whose psalms first instilled Hope in his heart. St. John appears. Dante, gazing on John's sun-bright flame, is blinded.

In Canto XXVI, John questions Dante on Charity, or Love, and once his answers are found satisfactory, Beatrice dispels the chaff from his eyes, restoring his vision. Adam appears and answers four questions concerning his own fate before and after his expulsion from the Garden of Eden. Gazing at Beatrice's smile, Dante is transported to the Ninth Heaven, the Primum Mobile, in Canto XXVII. Beatrice explains that the motion of the entire universe is generated in the Primum Mobile, and therefore time originates there as well.

In Canto XXVIII she explains the complicated hierarchies of the angels. After a silence (Canto XXIX), Beatrice explains Creation, the rebellion of the fallen angels, and the nature and number of nonfallen angels. In Canto XXX they rise to the Tenth Heaven, the Empyrean, "the heaven of pure light," the Celestial Rose. Dante is unable to describe Beatrice's beauty in this place. In Canto XXXI, St. Bernard appears instead of Beatrice, who has now taken her rightful place in the Rose of Paradise, "on the throne her merits have assigned her." They turn their attention to Mary, the Queen of Heaven. In Canto XXXII, Bernard instructs Dante on the ranks of the various souls present. Bernard urges Dante to pray to Mary to grant him the strength to withstand gazing upon God himself. In Canto XXXIII, St. Bernard prays Dante's prayer for him, asking that when he returns to the world after his vision, he will maintain his faith. Dante at last sees the Eternal Light. (Dante Alighieri 1986)

See also Dante Alighieri.

 # DÔ CÂN

Vietnamese poet, author of *The Story of Phan Trân*, an extremely long narrative poem employing alternating hexasyllables and octosyllables. (Brogan 1996)

DOMETT, ALFRED

New Zealand poet, author of the Maori epic *Ranolf and Amohia* (1872). Domett was born and educated in England, and migrated to New Zealand as a young man. Trained in the Romantic and Victorian traditions of the day, he wrote his epic in imitation of them. (Curnow 1960; Preminger 1974)

DOMIK V KOLOMNE
(A small house in Kolomna)

Russian humorous epic (1833) by Alexandr Pushkin (1799–1837). The poem relates in a relaxed, humorous style the tale of a widow's household into which comes a new cook, hired by the widow's daughter. All goes well until the cook is caught shaving: He is a man dressed as a woman so as to be near his lover, the widow's daughter. (Bristol 1991)

DON JUAN

English mock-epic (1818–1821) by George Gordon, Lord Byron (1788–1824), considered the poet's masterpiece. Pronounced "Don Joó-an" to respect the meter, the poem was begun in 1818 but was still unfinished when Byron died. A thinly veiled autobiographical poem, it consists of 16,000 lines in 16 cantos written in ottava rima. Byron used the stanza form so brilliantly that it has become known as the "Don Juan stanza."

Throughout the poem the hero interrupts the narrative to express his views on English politics and society, literature, wealth, power, and chastity. The poet uses burlesque imitations of classic myths to deliver his social criticism. He often interrupts his narrative with unexpected, flippant asides: "Trust not for freedom from the Franks—/They have a king who buys and sells." (3:XIV) Byron intended the poem to be "the comic epic of the human race." His best friends believed it was a disgrace to his reputation, but Johann Wolfgang von Goethe pronounced the poem "a work of boundless genius."

The satire, dedicated to poet laureate Robert Southey, whom he addresses as "Bob Southey," purports to be about the Spanish libertine Don Juan, but the hero is really Byron himself. Although Byron's Don Juan originates in Seville, at the age of 16 he has a scandalous affair with Donna Julia, an older woman, and is sent abroad by his widow mother, Donna Inez. But the ship encounters bad weather and he is shipwrecked, swept onto a Greek island, where Haidée, the beautiful daughter of a Greek pirate, rescues him. As she nurses him back to health, the inevitable romance develops, but they are discovered by Haidée's father, Lambro, "the mildest mannered man/That ever scuttled ship or cut a throat." While Haidée goes mad and dies of grief, he takes Juan prisoner and sells him to the Turkish sultan Gulbeyas of Constantinople. There, Juan, a slave of the amorous sultana, falls in love with a beautiful harem girl, Dudu, so inciting the jealous sultana that he must flee for his life. He escapes to the Russian army, fighting the Turks. His courage earns him a place in St. Petersburg at the court of Empress Catherine II, who chooses him for a diplomatic mission to England. From the tenth canto onward, the action is set in England. The poet had hinted that he planned for Juan to become a Methodist, but the poem breaks off before that occurs. (Grebanier 1949; Harrison 1967; Siepmann 1987)

See also Byron, Lord George.

 # DON RODERICK

English epic poem (1814) by Robert Southey (1774–1843). The poem, set in Spain in the eighth century, relates the story of Don Rodrigo (d. 711), the last Visigoth king of Spain (r. 710–711). He first quells riotous Basques to the north, then turns his attention to the south, confronting the Muslim invaders from North Africa under the leadership of General Tariq ibn Ziyād, a Berber herdsman of Musa. Tariq establishes his base on the Rock of Gibraltar, which is named for him: Jebel Tariq, or Gebel al-Tariq, meaning "Tariq's mountain." The Islamic forces best the Spaniards in Wadi Bekka near the Guadalete, Rio Barbate, near Cádiz. Rodrigo flees from the Muslims but is killed. (Grebanier 1949)

See also Southey, Robert.

 # DONELAITIS, KRISTIJONAS
(Also Donalitius or Duonelaitis)

Lithuanian poet, author of the epic poem *Metai* (The seasons, 1765–1775, publ. 1818). He was born in 1714 near Gumbinnen, East Prussia (now Gusev). At the age of 22 he matriculated at the University of Königsberg, where he studied classical languages and theology, graduating in 1740. Three years later he became pastor at Tomingkehmen (now Ilinskoye), where he remained for almost 40 years.

During that time Donelaitis composed his epic, *Metai,* in hexameter verse, never used in Lithuanian poetry until that time. He also wrote six fables and a verse tale, *Pričkaus pasaka apie lietuvišką scodbą* (Pričus's tale about a Lithuanian wedding). His works were not published during his lifetime. Since *Metai* was first published in 1818 it has been translated into many languages, and Donelaitis has been lauded as one of the greatest Lithuanian poets. He died in Tomingkehmen in 1780. (Rubulis 1970)

See also Metai.

DRAGONTEA

Spanish historical verse epic (1598) by Félix Lope de Vega Carpio (Lope de Vega, 1562–1635), which recounts the last voyage and death of Sir Francis Drake, the privateer whom de Vega saw as a "devilish dragon." Earlier in his career Drake had fought against the Spanish Armada (1588), earning the poet's everlasting scorn, because de Vega himself fought with the armada, which was defeated and largely decimated. Although a hero in England, to the Spaniards Drake was "the master thief of the unknown world." The poem relates the story of Drake's expedition against Spanish possessions in the West Indies. Two years after Drake undertook that ill-fated voyage, upon which he and many of his crew died of a fever, Lope de Vega, who usually based both his plays and his poetry on historical fact, wrote his scathing poem. Drake was buried at sea off the coast of Panama, a fitting end, according to de Vega, for "the devilish dragon." (Hayes 1967; Highet 1976; Magill 1994; Rennert 1937)

See also Lope de Vega.

DRANJA

Albanian epic cycle (1981) by contemporary Albanian Martin Camaj, in exile in Munich, where he holds the Albanology chair at the University of Munich. The *Dranja,* a collection of "madrigals" in poetic prose, relates the adventures of an "imperfect being" who appears as a turtle. The poem combines traditional mores of the poet's Gheg highland roots with mythology, wedding them with contemporary poetics. (Brogan 1996)

DREAM-ALLEGORY

A popular type of medieval poem, the most famous of which is *The Romance of the Rose* (ca. 1235, 1280), written by two French poets separated by 50 years, Guillaume de Lorris and Jean de Meung. The usual form taken by a dream-allegory is that the poet falls asleep while reading and dreams he is in a beautiful garden. From there he has various experiences with allegorical characters. At the end of the poem he awakes. Other well-known dream-allegories are Chaucer's "The Book of the Duchess," "The House of Fame, "The Parliament of Fowls," and the frame-tale (prologue) of "The Legend of Good Women"; William Langland's *Piers Plowman;* and John Bunyan's prose dream-allegory, *Pilgrim's Progress.*

DRYDEN, JOHN

English poet, dramatist, and critic, author of *Absalom and Achitophel* (1681), *Mac Flecknoe* (1682), and *The Medall* (1682). Dryden was born in 1631 at Aldwinkle in Northamptonshire to a country family steeped in Puritanism but with a Parliamentarian and Church of England background. In about 1644 he was sent to Westminster School in London, and in 1650 he entered Trinity College, Cambridge. Despite some difficulties with college authorities, particularly the vice-master, that led to disciplinary action in 1652, he received his B.A. degree in 1654.

His first noteworthy poem was *Heroick Stanzas Consecrated to the Memory of His Highness Oliver Cromwell,* written in 1658. A year later he honored Charles II with *Astraea Redux.* Although his poetry, and later his dramas, quickly brought him acclaim in intellectual circles, he had to struggle for years to eke out a living with translations and plays. Over time he became the outstanding man of letters of the Restoration period, and Dr. Samuel Johnson named him "the father of English criticism."

The more noteworthy of his heroic plays, written in rhymed couplets, are *The Indian Emperor* (1665), *Tyrannic Love* (1669), *The Conquest of Granada* (part 1, 1670; part 2, 1672), and *Aurengzebe* (1675). His comedies include *The Rival Ladies* (1664), *Sir Martin Mar-All* (1667), *Marriage à la Mode* (1672), and *The Spanish Friar* (1681). His *All for Love* (1678) is written in blank verse.

In 1670 Dryden was appointed poet laureate and historiographer-royal. Later he was also named customs collector for the port of London. These offices relieved his financial distress for many years. During his "golden years," he wrote several satires and mock-epics: *Absalom and Achitophel* (1681), *The Medall* (1682), and *Mac Flecknoe* (1682). In 1686 he became a Roman Catholic, and in 1687 he published a beast fable, *The Hind and the Panther,* which was a defense of his faith and of Catholic king James II.

However, after the Revolution of 1688, Dryden refused to take the oath of allegiance to William and Mary, resulting in the loss of all his public offices, including the laureateship. He had inherited a small property from his father, but he depended for funds primarily upon his writing, largely translations and criticisms although he continued to write plays and poetry. Thus, even stripped of his laureateship, he remained the grand old man of letters. He died in 1700 and was buried in Poets' Corner in Westminster Abbey. (Kingsley 1958; Dryden 1994))

See also Absalom and Achitophel; Mac Flecknoe.

DU, NGUYEN

See Nguyen Du.

DU BARTAS, GUILLAUME DE SALLUSTE, SIEUR

French poet, author of the epics *Judit* (1574), *Uranie* (1574), *Le Triomphe de la Foi* (publ. in 1574), *La Semaine* (1578), and the partial *Seconde Semaine* (1584–1603).

Du Bartas was born in 1544 at Montfort, near Auch, France. A scholarly young man and a dedicated Huguenot, he became a counsellor to Henri de Navarre in 1566 and took up arms in the Wars of Religion. He was sent on embassies and in 1587 was received with distinction at the court of James VI, king of Scotland. He remained a simple Gascon country squire consumed by the desire to write poetry with a Protestant bent, in which he implemented the new techniques of a group of poets led by Pierre de Ronsard (1524–1585) who called themselves La Pléiade. His first biblical epic, *Judit*, was published in 1574, followed by *Uranie* and *Le Triomphe de la Foi*. In 1578 he wrote *La Semaine*, or *La Création du monde* (The creation of the world), an epic of seven books in alexandrine couplets. The theme is taken from Genesis i–ii, but the poet expands upon it by using Greco-Roman poetry, science, and philosophy. This poem was much better received in Protestant England, where it appeared in 1605 in a translation by Joshua Sylvester entitled *Divine Weekes and Workes*. Edmund Spenser and John Milton were among the poets influenced by the poem. Du Bartas's next project was to be an encyclopedic history of humankind hung on the framework of the seven days of Creation. However, he only finished four of the days. The first was published in 1584, and the last in 1603, after his death. He died in 1590 in Coudons, France. (Harvey and Heseltine 1959)

DUENADCAT
(The twelve)

Russian *poema* (verse epic, 1918) by Aleksandr Blok (1880–1921). The epic celebrates the October Revolution of Russia's civil war. It was written in two days' time in January 1918. Set in the streets of Petrograd, the poem centers around the accidental shooting of a prostitute, symbol of Beautiful Lady, by a Red soldier who is her former lover. Red banners festoon the streets, while the past is symbolized by a fat, gluttonous priest and a hungry dog. Despite the terror and bloody devastation, the poem foresees good to come. The 12 rebels are also depicted as the 12 apostles.

The soldiers shoot at someone walking ahead of the 12: "Soft his step above the snowstorn,/Pearly-hued his snowy dusting,/White the roses of his crown—/Jesus Christ walks out ahead." The poem's rhythms were derived from popular songs of the day, particularly the factory song (*chastushka*).

At the time, Blok considered the poem his masterpiece, but his enthusiasm for the revolution turned to disappointment, as did his enthusiasm for the poem honoring the 12 revolutionaries. (Bristol 1991)

See also Blok, Aleksandr.

THE DUNCIAD

English mock-epic (1728; rev. 1729, 1742, 1743) by Alexander Pope (1688–1744). First appearing in 1728 in three books, this satire, in heroic couplets, attacked literary charlatanism in general and poetasters, publishers, pedants, and, in particular, Pope's critics. This same version, with revisions, was reissued in 1729 as *The Dunciad Variorium*. It evokes the barbarous days when people who had forgotten how to carve statuary either dumped classical masterpieces in the river or ground down the statuary to use in road-building. The chief dunce in these versions is a playwright, critic, and rival editor of Shakespeare, Lewis Theobald (1688–1744), son of the Goddess of Dullness.

The New Dunciad appeared in 1742, and the final version appeared a year later as *The Dunciad in Four Books*. In the final versions, Theobald has been removed as hero; the Monarch of Dullness is poet laureate Colley Cibber (1671–1757), known for his arrogance and lack of tact, who reigns over the empires of Emptiness and Dullness. In Book II, a burlesque of the *Aeneid*'s depiction of the funeral games for Anchises, two publishers compete in urinating, producing streams comparable to the noble rivers of Maeander and Eridanus (2:157–184). These games are in celebration of Cibber's coronation, which ends with poetry-reading, putting the guests to sleep. In Book III, Cibber himself falls asleep and sees his past, present, and future. In all three, Dullness (Dulness) prevails. In Book IV the court and Parliament fall to the mediocrity of London culture; indeed, the world is conquered by universal Dullness: over scholarship, science, art. Classical scholar Richard Bentley (1662–1742) is introduced as an example of Pedantry. The Goddess of Dullness, with a yawn, directs her ministers to discourage thought at all cost, and "Gothic ignorance" sets in as finally the world returns to Miltonic night and chaos: the triumph of the anti-Logos. (Pope 1939/1967)

See also Pope, Alexander.

 # DURÃO, JOSÉ DE SANTA RITTA
(Or Rita)

Brazilian poet, author of *Caramúru* (1781). He was born between 1722–1737 in Cata Prêta, Brazil, in the Minas Gerais region. He studied at the Jesuit College in Rio de Janeiro, then went to Portugal, where he attended the University of Coimbra, receiving a doctor of theology degree in 1756. He entered the Gratian Order of St. Augustine in 1758. Because the Jesuit priests had encouraged resistance of the Guaraní Indians when the Spanish ordered their mission village vacated—the king of Spain having presented them to his father-in-law, the king of Portugal—the following year, the Jesuits were expelled not only from Brazil but from Spain and Portugal as well. Durão protested this action and was himself expelled. He fled to Spain, where he was held as a spy (1762–1763). Upon his release, he traveled to Rome, where he was appointed a papal librarian.

In 1778 he was able to return to Portugal, where briefly he was professor of theology at Coimbra before he returned to the Gratian convent as its prior. There he composed his epic poem, confessing that it was "from love of country" that he wrote. Durão was of the Mineira school of poets: Reared in the gold rush days in Minas Gerais, these poets were educated in Portugal, becoming members of the literati. They wrote poetry in a pre-Romantic combination academic–Arcadian style. Durão returned to the classical ottava rima of the sixteenth century for his epic.

In 1781, Durão published his epic poem *Caramúru* in Lisbon. The poem glorifies the natural beauty of his homeland and depicts Indian culture with sympathy. It is now considered a major work of Brazilian literature, but at the time it was largely ignored. Deeply disappointed at its reception, Durão burned most of his other poetry. He died three years later in Lisbon. (Putnam 1948/1971)

See also Caramúru.

 # DUSHENKA

Russian epic verse tale (1783) by Ippolit Fyodorovich Bogdanovich (1743–1803). The poem, written in *vers libre,* is an elegant retelling of La Fontaine's *Les Amours de psyche et de Cupidon* (1669), with a Russian cast: The heroine, Dushenka (Psyche), youngest daughter of a Greek king, is to wed a monster of unknown identity whom she is forbidden to look at. She is a spirited but loyal beauty who goes through the marriage ceremonies in the palatial gardens, described as if they were Tsarskoe Selo. Dushenka's wicked sisters convince her to visit her monster-husband, carrying a lamp and a sword so that she may see what he looks like and, possibly, kill him. But the light reveals a god: Amor. For her sin of looking upon a god, she is cast into the wilderness and required by Venus to do penitential tasks. For instance, she must fetch "living and dead waters," which are guarded by a serpent named Zmey Gorynych, and she must fetch golden apples from the Tsar Maiden's garden. When she finishes her penitence and is reunited with Amor, she too becomes a deity and ascends to Olympus. The couple has a daughter called Pleasure by some, Joy or Life by others. Regardless of the name, all the world knows "what kind of issue must be born/to Dushenka and to Amor." (Bristol 1991)

See also Bogdanovich, Ippolit Fyodorovich.

 # DUTT, MICHAEL
(Michael Madhusudan Datta)

Indian Bengali poet and playwright, author of *Meghanād-vedh* (*Meghnadbadh*). He was born in 1824 in Sāgardanri in present-day Bangladesh into a cultured middle-class Bengali family. He was educated at the Hindu College in Calcutta, but at the age of 19 he converted to Christianity.

He began as a writer in English, but returned to his native language of Bengali at the age of 34 or 35. In 1858 he wrote a prose drama in Bengali based on an episode from the *Mahābhārata*. The play, called *Sarmishtha*, was well received, as was his narrative poem based on the story of Sundra and Upasundra, *Tilottamasambhab* (1860). In 1861 his masterpiece appeared: an epic poem based on the *Rāmāyaṇa* entitled *Meghnadbadh*. Other of his poetry was inspired by Hindu myths as well.

He is credited with introducing the Bengali sonnet and the poetical form *amitraksar* (blank verse with run-on lines and varied caesuras) and many innovative verse techniques. He is considered the first great poet of Bengali literature. He died in Calcutta in 1873. (Parthasarathy 1993)

 ## ECBASIS CAPTIVI

(Full name *Ecbasis cuiusdam captivi*, The prisoner's escape)

Latin beast epic (ca. 930–940), the first medieval beast epic, by an unknown author. Written in rhyming leonine hexameters, it concerns the now-familiar tale of the fox and the sick lion. However, the epic contains a tale within a tale. The central character is a greedy, slow-witted, uncouth, and slothful wolf, who is a monk. In later versions the wolf is given the name Isengrim. The epic is meant to satirize the degenerate excesses of the church at that time. (Hornstein 1973)

EILHART VON OBERGE

German poet (fl. late 12th c.), author of an early—probably the first—epic of *Tristant und Isalde* (ca. 1170). Eilhart was a member of a Brunswick-Hildesheim *ministeriales* family and a vassal of Henry the Lion, duke of Saxony. He is known primarily for introducing to German literature the story of Tristram and Iseult (*Tristrant und Isalde*), which became the basis for many later versions of the story. He composed his epic for Mathilde, teenaged wife of the duke of Saxony and daughter of Eleanor of Aquitaine. She may have suggested to Eilhart this legend from her mother's court. Too, Eilhart had accompanied her and the duke on a visit to Normandy, where he could have picked up the plot. To please staid ears, he played down the intensity of the love affairs. Since Eilhart could not read, but could only compose orally and memorize, some scribe must have recorded it. (Holbrook 1970; Salmon 1967)

See also Tristrant und Isalde.

EKKEHARD I THE ELDER

Swiss poet, hymnist, and monk, thought by some to be the original author of *Waltharius* (ca. 930), a Latin heroic poem dealing with the Germanic legend of Walter of Aquitaine, the Huns, the Franks, and the Burgundians. He was born about 910, probably in Toggenburg, Switzerland, of noble parents. He was educated at the Benedictine monastery in Sankt Gallen, Switzerland. Later he taught there, eventually attaining the position of dean. He wrote many hymns and was credited by Ekkehard IV, who edited the poem in 1030, with being the original author. Ekkehard I died at Sankt Gallen in 973. (Dickens 1915)

 # EKKEHARD IV

Swiss monk and poet who revised the heroic poem *Waltharius* in 1030, attributing it to Ekkehard I. Ekkehard IV was born about 980 in Alsace and educated at Sankt Gallen under the tutorship of Ekkehard I's nephew, Notker Labeo. In addition to revising *Waltharius,* he contributed greatly to the writing of a history of Sankt Gallen. He died about 1069 at Sankt Gallen. (Dickens 1915)

 # *ELEGÍAS DE VARONES ILUSTRES DE INDIAS*
(Elegies of illustrious men of the Indies)

Longest narrative poem ever written in the Spanish language (1589, publ. 19th c.) by Juan de Castellanos. It consists of 150,000 lines, making it one of the longest poems in the world. The poet wrote it late in life, drawing on his varied experiences as an acolyte, parish priest, pearl fisherman, soldier, adventurer, and womanizer among Indian women. Contrary to the title, it is not an elegy.

The poem is dedicated to Columbus, the first ever dedicated to an explorer. The opening verses, written in a vernacular rather than elevated style, describe Columbus and his voyage.

The English and French privateers, such as Drake, are depicted as cruel agents of the devil, the scourge of God. Castellanos describes the poetry-writing Spanish captain Lorenzo Martín, who encouraged his starving sailors with his own rhymes: "The verses left such a bad sound in their ears/that they judged them to be prose/with superfluous rhymes." Of the great conquistador Jiménez de Quesada, who supposedly wrote voluminously although all his writing has been lost, Castellanos says, ". . . he contended with me many times/that the old Castilian meters were/those fitting and proper for having been brought forth/from the bosom of that language/and that the hendecasyllables were alien newcomers, adopted/from a different foreign mother."

The poet makes use of Indian words such as *bohíos* (Indian huts), *macanas* (clubs), and *jagüeyes* (cisterns) to add color to the descriptions. He employs subtle irony in his mock-heroic recounting of the Spanish peasants brought by Las Casas to colonize the coast of Cumoná. The men, accompanied by their shepherdesses, are armed like knights, with red crosses emblazoned on their breastplates, but they are totally unprepared for battle and are destroyed by the local Indians.

Throughout the epic Castellanos sprinkles allusions from the works of Vergil, Ovid, Seneca, and Horace, as well as contemporaries Garcilaso de la Vega and Ercilla y Zuñiga. His historical references are taken from the works of Fernández de Oviedo and López de Gómara, two sixteenth-century chroniclers of the Indies. Castellanos compares the Amazon Indians to nymphs and maids "such as those that appear in poems." He describes the Indian women as being beautiful enough to attract gods, so that "Jupiter would desire to be their husband." The women see the Spanish conquistadors as "lascivious and lusty fauns."

Castellanos's descriptions of the earthquakes of Cubaqua, off the island of Margarita in the Lake of Maracaibo, are considered among his best writing. (Anderson-Imbert 1969)

See also Castellanos, Juan de; Ercilla y Zuñiga, Alonso de.

 # ELISEY, OR BACCHUS ENRAGED

Russian mock-epic (1771) by Vasily Maikov (1728–1778). The poem was the first mock-epic in Russian literature and the first poem to descend to farce and ribald comedy. The poet's purpose was much larger than merely satirizing the new state liquor monopoly, the apparent target of the humor. The greedy wine merchants are only a symbol of all those who prey on society. The poem also represented a spirit of defiance against the repressing, "safe" literary climate that existed at the time. The poem's appearance had a liberating effect on subsequent authors, which continued to be felt into the next century.

The poem relates, in the elevated alexandrine, or iambic hexameter, the exploits of one called a "special hero": Elisey, hapless peasant turned pugnacious St. Petersburg coachman, who is a drunkard, rogue, brawler, lecher, and philandering married man. When he is drunk, he causes "catastrophes most dreadful/At Bacchus's behest." He has been in the habit of going from inn to inn, where he "fought and furnished drinks for waiters and for louts." In one episode Bacchus dresses him as a woman and has him incarcerated in a reformatory for prostitutes, where he lustfully accosts the female director. Elsewhere he rescues his wife, who is as wayward as he is. He also cuckolds the wine merchant.

Two villages are pitted against each other. Elisey's heroic feat is the terrible destruction of the wine cellar: "In infamous defeat the cellar fell entire,/Its phials all aboil, the bottles upside down./All vessel hoops were burst, the wine flowed out of vats,/And not a drop that anyone could find. . . ."

In the climactic battle the wine merchants confront the poor coachman. The Olympian gods sentence Elisey to serve in the army as penance for such waste. Zeus denounces "unjust judges, thieves, and perfidious friends" in a society where public fistfights and bear-baiting are allowed. (Bristol 1991)

See also Maikov, Vasily.

EMS, RUDOLF VON

See Rudolf von Ems.

ENEIT

Middle High German epic poem (1189) by Heinrich von Veldeke (ca. 1140/ 1150–d. before 1210). Heinrich's principal work, it is an adaptation of the anonymous poem *Roman d'Enéas*, retelling the story of Aeneas, this time casting the Trojan and Latin heroes as medieval knights. The poet began the poem about 1170, but lent the manuscript to a countess of Cleves. Lost for nine years, it was returned to him at the Thuringian court about 1179, and he finished it in 1189.

As befits work written under the heavy papal hand of the times, the poem dwells on the passion of Dido and its ultimate destruction of her. It relates Aeneas's trip to the Underworld and the life of Lavinia, ascribing to Lavinia particular virtue for her filial devotion. The epilogue, perhaps by another hand, gives some information about its author. Both poem and poet were praised by contemporaries Gottfried von Strassburg, Wolfram von Eschenbach, and Rudolf von Ems. (Garland and Garland 1986)

ENFANCES OGIER

French epic poem by Adenet le Roi (13th c.) about the exploits of Ogier the Dane. The character of Ogier is based on a historical person—a Frankish warrior named Autgarius, who first fought against Charlemagne and later was reconciled to him.

Ogier is a hostage for his father the king at Charlemagne's court. By his heroic deeds in Italy, he becomes a court favorite. But when Charlemagne's son kills Ogier's son in a quarrel, in retaliation Ogier kills the queen's nephew. The paladins intervene before Ogier can kill the king as well. He is imprisoned, but is released to fight the Saracens. (Harvey and Heseltine 1959)

See also Adenet le Roi.

ENGELHARD

Middle High German romance/epic (13th c.) by Konrad von Würzburg (ca. 1225–1287). The 6,000-line poem, known only by a 1573 printed version, is based on a medieval Latin poem by the same name.

Engelhard and his boon companion and double, Dietrich, visit the Danish court, where Engelhard falls in love with Princess Engeltrud. They are discovered in a secret rendezvous by Prince Ritschier, who falsely accuses Engelhard of philandering. In a battle to defend his honor and prove his innocence, his friend Dietrich impersonates him and is victorious. Engelhard and Engeltrud are married, and she bears many children.

In the meantime, Dietrich has contracted leprosy, which can only be cured by the blood of children. Over Dietrich's protests, Engelhard sacrifices his own children to save his friend's life. But God intervenes, and as a reward for Engelhard's fidelity, restores the children's lives. (Garland and Garland 1986)

See also Konrad von Würzburg.

EPIC

Traditionally, a long narrative poem in which the language, characters, plot, and style are of grand, dignified, elevated, and heroic dimensions. The hero embodies characteristics representing national or ethnic ideals. The narrative is usually a combination of experiences characterizing a whole epoch in man's history. The theme is based on universal human predicaments. Traditional epics have certain conventions in common: a declaration in the opening lines as to the subject, an appeal to the Muse for inspiration, a plunge into the middle of the story's action (*in medias res*), a list of the warriors, long descriptive passages, lengthy dramatic dialogue, and the "epic [elaborate] simile." (Hornstein 1973)

THE EPIC OF SHEIK BEDREDDIN
(Also called *The Lay of Simavneli Kadtoğlu Bedrettin*)

Turkish poem (publ. 1936) by Nazim Hikmet (also Nazim Hikmet Ran, 1902–1963). The poem is based on a peasant uprising against the Ottoman Empire in the early fifteenth century. Sheik Bedreddin, Turkish mystic and Islamic scholar, inspired the uprising by believers in the oneness of all people and all religion, and in the abolition of private property. Turkish, Greek, and Jewish peasants, under the leadership of Bedreddin disciples Torlak Kemal and Börklüje Mustafa, seized land from feudal lords, worked it, and defended it until Sultan Mehmet's army crushed them. The poem's appearance landed its author in a Turkish prison for one of several periods of political incarceration.

Hikmet, who introduced free verse into Turkish poetry, used both free verse and *aruz* (Arabic-Persian prosody) in this poem.

The first section, a lengthy prose introduction, begins in the 1920s, with a story within a story within a story. The poet is in prison as he writes. He is reading an old treatise about Sheik Bedreddin. He repeats the story of Bedreddin's life: his birth in Eiderne, his education in Cairo, his return to Eiderne as a high-level judge until Prince Musa is murdered by his brother Mehmet, his subsequent exile to Iznik, his inciting of the peasants to revolt against Mehmet, and his capture, trial, and execution. He describes the terrible deaths of Mustafa and Kemal.

The poet turns back to his reading. He sees someone standing outside his cell window—an apparition, obviously, because his cell is not on the ground floor. This apparition takes him on a journey, back to the time of Bedreddin.

The next four sections, in free verse, describe in vivid language scenes from the fifteenth century. Section One describes Mehmet strangling his brother Musa with a bowstring, purifying himself "with his brother's blood in a gold bowl," and ascending to the throne. After that, the marketplace is in disorder, and the guilds lose faith in their masters: "In short, there was a sovereign, a fief, a wind, a wail."

Section Two describes an old man named Bedreddin sitting on a sheepskin in the poverty-stricken mountain village of Iznik, writing in Persian a treatise called *Foundations*. At a distance sit "tall and rangy Börklüje Mustafa" and "hawk-nosed Torlak Kemal," watching reverently "as if looking at a mountain."

Section Three relates how Bedreddin hears a barefoot woman crying because her fisherman husband has been chained in the castle for taking a carp. Bedreddin says, "The fire in my heart/has burst into flame/and is mounting daily." He calls upon the peasants to revolt: "Men of the land, we will conquer the land." The next day, as the fisherman is beheaded, Kemal and Mustafa ride off, "each with a naked sword at his side" and in each saddlebag a handwritten book: Bedreddin's *Illuminations*.

In Section Four, still flying with his guide over the days and years, the poet hears that Mustafa has given a speech to the peasants telling them, "The landowners have been slaughtered wholesale/and the lords' fiefs made public lands." The poet and his companion travel the land and see that "the earth that wept . . ./started to laugh like a child. . . ." They see figs "like big emeralds." They see the fish jumping into the reed baskets.

Section Five tells, in prose, how the poet and his guide meet three followers of Mustafa. They describe destroying the army of the governor, Sisman, who had attempted to return the lands to the lords. Elated, the poet and his guide return to give Bedreddin the good news. Bedreddin says, "Now it's our turn. . . . We'll leave for Rumelia." So they leave at night, with horsemen in pursuit, hiding by daylight and traveling only at night, until they reach the sea. There they set sail.

Section Six, in verse, describes the voyage on the Black Sea of the party, now swelled to five, "headed for the Mad Forest,/The Sea of Trees. . . ."

Section Seven, in verse, tells of the party's landing in the forest, where they pitch their tents. They send falcons to every village with the message, "You know why we have come,/you know the trouble in our heart." Soon the people begin to converge: "an army flowing to the Sea of Trees," making a great din.

In Section Eight, in prose, the poet and his guide leave Bedreddin's camp and swim the strait of Gallipoli to deliver a message to Mustafa. They meet four travelers and learn that Bayezid Pasha, "who led the Sultan's twelve-year-old son Murad by the hand," is gathering Anatolian soldiers. Farther along, they hear reports that Bayezid is headed for a battle against Mustafa. They spur their horses onward until they reach Mustafa's camp.

Sections Nine and Ten, in verse, describe the fierce, bloody battle between Bayezid and Mustafa, which occurs during hot, heavy cloudburst weather. Mustafa is "nailed/by his hands/naked on a bleeding cross/on the hump of a camel." While Mustafa watches, 2,000 men are beheaded: "Bare necks split like pomegranates."

Section Eleven, in prose, describes the poet and his guide going to Manisa, where Bayezid has also gone to capture Kemal and hang him, returning ten fiefs to the lords. As the poet passes the ten provinces, vultures circle over "fresh, bloody corpses of women and children," preferring them to the bodies of men lining the road. The poet and his guide recross Gallipoli in a boat.

Section Twelve, combining prose and poetry, describes the poet's panic when he learns that Sultan Mehmet is headed for the Mad Forest. He and his guide ride in frantic haste to reach camp, only to learn that Bedreddin has been kidnapped by three of Bayezid's men. They realize that one of the four men whom they met earlier (Section Eight) was the prisoner Bedreddin.

Section Thirteen, in poetry, describes the confrontation between Bedreddin and the sultan, who demands of the old man, "Account for your heresy." But Bedreddin tells him, "Words avail not./Don't draw it out." He demands his sentence.

In Section Fourteen, each verse begins with "The rain hisses." It describes Bedreddin's hanging. "The rain hisses" is repeated at the end of the section.

The next prose section, "The Lathe-Turner Shefik's Shirt," begins, "The rain hissed outside." The poet is back in his cell, and it is morning. He tells Shefik the lathe-turner of his adventure with Mustafa's disciple who had appeared outside his cell window. Shefik laughs and explains he hung his shirt out the window, and it is that which the poet mistook for a "guide." Another prisoner, Ahmet, says he should write down his adventure as an epic. He even offers a story of his own for the ending.

The last section, "Ahmet's Story," is written in first-person prose from Ahmet's point of view. He describes a journey to Rumelia that he made at the age of nine with his grandfather. They are stopped in a village renowned for having the "most pigheaded peasants in the world." They learn that a story has been passed down for generations to the effect that Bedreddin's body was accidentally nicked as it was being cut down from the tree and that there was no blood in it. This means that Bedreddin will come back again. The grandfather laughs and says that the same claim is made by Christians and even some Muslims about Jesus. The peasant calls that belief a lie, but says, "Bedreddin will be reborn without his bones, beard, mustache—like the look of an eye, the words of a tongue, the breath of a chest." He says that followers of Bedreddin believe that Bedreddin's "words, look, and breath will appear from among us." (Hikmet 1977)

See also Hikmet, Nazim.

ERCILLA Y ZUÑIGA, ALONSO DE

Spanish soldier and poet, author of *La Araucana* (1569/1578/1589/1590), the first epic poem of the New World. He was born in 1533 or 1534 in Madrid and received an excellent education in Spain in theology and Renaissance literature. He was a courtier of Philip II, helping the prince's courtship in England when he learned of the murder of Pedro de Valdivia (1500–1553) by Chilean Indians. He volunteered for the punitive army and in 1554 or 1555 sailed to the New World, eager to avenge Valdivia's death. Of his journey, he wrote, "I have passed many climes, I have moved under many constellations." He distinguished himself as a soldier in Chile during the wars against the Araucanian Indians, fighting in the army of García Hurtado de Mendoza, and began the poem based on his experiences even as he fought. He called the work, which he wrote sitting beside the campfire at night, *Octavas reales* (Royal octaves). Gradually, however, he began to respect and admire the Indians, and simultaneously to disrespect his commander, so the tone of his octaves began to change. He took the chronicler's view of the Spaniards, but began to develop a poet's view of the Indians, whom he ultimately began to praise in his octaves.

Rivalry with his commander culminated in his court-marshal in Chile. Barely escaping execution, he was sent back to Spain in 1563. He continued to work on his poem, taking revenge on Hurtado de Mendoza by excluding him from the 21,072-line poem almost entirely. He published the three books in 1569, 1578, and 1589, producing the complete edition in 1590 as *La Araucana*.

His epic inspired many others, but only Pedro de Oña's (1579–1643) *La Arauco domado* (Arauco tamed, 1596) even remotely approaches his in literary value. He gained broad acclaim on both sides of the Atlantic, having produced the first epic in which the author appears as a participant, the first that immortalized the founding of a modern nation, the first work of real poetic quality that was based in America, and the first in which the author is torn between duty and truth. He died in Madrid in 1594. (Ercilla 1945)

See also Araucana, La.

 # *EREC*

Middle High German epic poem (ca. 1180—1185) by Hartmann von Aue (or Ouwe) (1160–d. after 1210). The poem, of some 10,000 lines, is a free translation of the Arthurian romance *Erec* by Chrétien de Troyes. The narrative is divided into two parts. The first 2,431 lines relate the story of the knight Erec who, while riding with the queen, avenges an insult. As a reward, he receives the hand in marriage of Enite, daughter of a penniless nobleman. He brings her back to Camelot for a wedding celebration.

The rest of the poem becomes moralistic. Because of his slavish devotion to his bride, Erec neglects his chivalric duties, causing him disgrace and banishment from court, which he blames on Enite. The two set out in search of adventure so that Erec can prove himself. Enite is an unwilling companion who refuses to obey his injunction not to warn him of approaching danger. Each time she disobeys him, he chastises her. At length Erec, half dead from wounds received from a series of "morally unjustified" encounters, is left unconscious while Count Oringles "rescues" Enite. But when the count accosts her, her screams revive Erec, who rushes to her rescue and slays the count. Reunited, the couple continues on to other adventures. They come to the Garden of Love, where the knight Mabonagrin, bound by an oath, must remain for as long as he is undefeated. Erec bests him, thus releasing him from the garden and his oath to his lady. Having performed a morally justified act, Erec is restored to knighthood and received back into Arthur's court. He rules over his own land with Enite at his side. (Hartmann von Ave/Resler trans. 1987)

See also Erec et Enide; Hartmann von Aue.

 # *EREC ET ENIDE*

French medieval Arthurian romance (*roman breton*) (ca. 1168) by Chrétien de Troyes (ca. 1140–d. before 1200?). The poem, of 6,878 lines, is not only the poet's first, but *the* first Arthurian romance. It inspired, among others, both Hartmann von Aue's German poem and Tennyson's *Geraint and Enid.* In the beginning, the poet boasts that his poem will "be remembered as long as Christianity endures."

Erec is a knight of King Arthur's court. Arthur goes on a hunt for a white stag, reviving the custom that whoever can kill it has the right to kiss the most beautiful maiden in the court. Riding with the queen, Erec meets a disgusting dwarf who insults the queen's maid and whiplashes him. Wanting to right the wrong, Erec goes to the inn where the dwarf's master has stopped. He meets Enide, the most beautiful daughter of an impoverished knight. He asks to "borrow" Enide to compete in a yearly competition for a sparrow hawk. If he wins, he will take Enide as a bride and send riches from his father, the king of Lac, to restore the knight's fortune. He wins Enide as a reward for his prowess. After their marriage, they return to his father's kingdom of Outer Wales. He is aghast when he overhears her lamenting his lack of chivalric exploits; she believes that his devoted love has caused him to neglect his knightly duties. They set out together on a quest for knightly adventures whereby he can show his chivalry and at the same time test Enide. Each time danger approaches, she disobeys his warning to keep absolutely silent, and she informs him of approaching peril. To his great disgust, she even keeps watch while he sleeps. They encounter robbers, thieves, amorous counts, and envious nobility. Eventually she begins to see the need for silence. Her fidelity brings about in him an understanding of the meaning of married love and leads to their reconciliation, but not before Erec suffers many wounds. They have one last adventure, the Joy of the Court, when they meet Maboagrain and his lady. She has bound him with an oath of love-service so that he cannot leave the confines of their love garden until bested in a joust. Erec defeats him, freeing the couple from their restrictive love. Erec and Enide return to Nantes, and on Christmas Day they are crowned. At the end, Erec becomes king of Outer Wales, heading his own round table. (Chrétien de Troyes 1990)

See also Chrétien de Troyes; *Erec*.

 # EROTÓKRITOS

Greek epic (ca. 1586, publ. 1713) by Vitséntsos Kornáros. The poem was written sometime prior to 1587 and later revised. Although it was not printed until 1713, in Venice, numerous manuscripts were in circulation. Editions appeared in Athens in the middle of the nineteenth century. Written in the 15-syllable iambic rhyming couplets of Greek folk songs, the poem contains 10,000 lines in five parts. It is written in the East Cretan dialect of modern Greek, the language of the poet's birthplace. The story comes from the popular French prose romance of Pierre de la Cypède's *Paris et Vienne* (1478), probably an Italian translation. Other probable inspirations were Italian Renaissance poetry, especially Ariosto's *Orlando Furioso*, Cretan folk songs, the contemporary Cretan playwright Chortatis, and Byzantine verse romances. The setting is that of the Latins in the Levant. Greek names replace Turkish, Slavonic, and Wallachian names. Its Athens has nothing to do with the classical Athens.

In Book I, in the time of the pagan Hellenes, a King Herakles reigns in Athens with his queen, Artemis, and a daughter, Aretousa. His favorite among his counselors is Pezostratos, who has an 18-year-old son named Erotókritos (or Rotókritos). One day the son sees the king's daughter, and falls instantly in love. When he confides in his friend Polydoros, however, he is warned to forget it. Erotókritos ignores the warning and begins to haunt the palace at night, singing love songs under the windows. The king and queen enjoy the music, but so does Aretousa, who falls in love with the unknown singer. The king tries to capture him, without success. Alarmed, Erotókritos stops his serenades and tries to forget by helping on his father's estate and by going hunting with friends. Meanwhile the princess longs to find the singer, although the nurse tries to dissuade her.

Erotókritos's friend suggests that he go away and forget. Erotókritos tells his mother to protect certain writings in his wardrobe, which no one is to see, and they set out. His father falls ill with a fever, and the king and his daughter visit. Erotókritos's mother, forgetting her promise, leads the princess into the garden. Left to herself, the princess enters a little closet with a writing desk. She finds a paper on which are written the songs she has memorized. Back at the palace she confides to her nurse her suspicion that Erotókritos is the mysterious singer.

Meanwhile, Erotókritos gets a message that his father is ill and hurries back to Athens. He discovers from his mother that the princess has seen his verses. Polydoros advises him to keep out of sight while he scouts the palace to see if the king knows, and if so, to go into exile. The king does not know, but the princess confides that she knows. Erotókritos assumes that her friendliness is only the natural response of a beautiful woman to admiration, but both begin to exchange friendly glances when they meet.

Book II reflects the historic struggle between Venetian Crete and Turkey. A tournament is held with 14 champions, among them Erotókritos. One is a savage warrior from Karamania (Turkey) who starts a fight with a Cretan and is slain. The tournament is postponed a day, then is arranged so that three chosen entrants—the Cretan, Erotókritos, and the Cyprian—should each meet with a group of the others. Erotókritos is assigned three and defeats them, one by one. The three champions, all victors in their contests, must now meet. By lot, the Cretan is eliminated, and Erotókritos and the Cyprian engage. Erotókritos's helmet is shattered, but he unhorses the Cyprian. Aretousa gives him the wreath; their hands touch, and love overwhelms them both.

In Book III, Aretousa cannot sleep for a desire to see Erotókritos. The doctors say it is just her nature to grow so thin, but she tells the nurse she will die if she cannot see Erotókritos. The nurse says his victory was mostly luck; if he had had to fight the Cretan he would have lost. Besides, he is not of sufficient rank for a lady. Aretousa insists she wants to marry Erotókritos and will die if she cannot. She persuades the nurse to let her talk with her lover by night at the window, but only to ask about his songs. The two begin a series of meetings. Finally she tells her lover to have his father, of whom the king is very fond, go to the king and ask for her in marriage.

Infuriated, the king exiles the young man and announces that he has given his daughter to the prince of Byzantium. Aretousa determines to betroth herself to Erotókritos anyway, that night. When he comes, she gives him her ring. He visits her for three more nights, then leaves on his exile, calling upon the Heavens to burn up everything except Aretousa and to strike the king with a thunderbolt. The nurse shrugs; after all, what can one expect of a 13-year-old girl? Meanwhile the king dismisses her friends and servants, nails the windows, and boards up the doors.

In Book IV an embassy arrives from Byzantium to arrange the marriage, but Aretousa refuses to cooperate. The king beats her and threatens her with death, then gives her a day to think it over. She has thought it over already, she answers, so the king writes the ambassadors that his daughter has a consumption. Then he cuts off her hair, beats her again, and imprisons her, along with the nurse. The mother also turns against Aretousa, treating her cruelly. The princess is dressed in old clothes and given an old palliasse stuffed with hay and thorns for a bed. She is placed in the darkest and muddiest dungeon and fed only bread and water. The nurse tells her to be brave and weather it. Once a month the king checks with Aretousa to see if she has changed her mind. Her imprisonment, but not its cause, is known abroad.

Meanwhile Erotókritos is in miserable exile in Egripos, his thoughts always on Aretousa. Finally he sends letters to his friend in Athens, and to his father. After a day, the messenger returns with an answer from Polydoros with the news from Athens. He is saddened to hear of the princess's sufferings, but glad to know of her constancy. While in Athens, Polydoros scatters reports about Erotókritos that reach the nurse, who relays them to the princess—but only where Erotókritos is and that he is well, not about his suffering and careless appearance.

After three years, King Herakles quarrels with King Vlantistratos of Vlahia (Wallachia), who gathers a huge army and marches on Athens, ravaging the countryside. When Erotókritos hears this, he determines to help Herakles. From a witch in Egripus he obtains a lotion that blackens his face so that not even his mother would recognize him. He also obtains another lotion that will restore his whiteness. He arrives outside the walls of Athens and finds a secret place where he can arm himself and sleep at night. When there is a battle, he ventures out and, unrecognized, attacks the Vlachs. At nightfall he hurries back to his hiding place, a mile away. Herakles is pleased, but neither he nor Polydoros suspect the stranger's identity.

After several such forays, the Vlachs notify their king that with two more such assaults they are done for, so the Vlachs make a surprise attack. Herakles rushes out to help his army, confused in the darkness. They rally. The battlefield is covered with the dead, and the fortunes of the combatants waver. The Vlachs choose 22 of their best warriors to find old Herakles, dead or alive. With the help of Polydoros, the king fights like a lion but, outnumbered, he is unhorsed and Polydoros is badly wounded. They hear a great shout as Erotókritos charges and kills three with his lance. Taking up his sword, he scatters the others. Herakles and Polydoros remount. The Vlach king rides off. The badly wounded Polydoros leaves the battlefield, with Erotókritos in charge of Herakles. The trumpets sound the end of the battle. Both the king and Erotókritos remove their helmets, but although the king looks him in the face, Erotókritos is still unrecognizable. Herakles thanks him and offers to divide his kingdom with him and adopt him as his heir, but Erotókritos says that all he wants is to fight for the right and not for any reward.

The Athenians have lost 8,100 men; the Vlachs, 10,000. Both kings are seriously concerned over these losses, so they exchange a desire for a truce. Into the Vlach camp rides a knight, still beardless: Ariosto, son of the Vlach king's sister, who comes from the Franks to help his uncle. The Vlach king suggests that Ariosto and a champion from the Athenians meet in single combat and decide the matter at issue. Ariosto is pleased at the idea. Herakles decides to think the proposal over, and calls a full council. He tells them that the Athenians do not have anyone who can match Ariosto except for Polydoros, and he is badly wounded. A counselor calls attention to the strange knight. Erotókritos enters the camp to ask the king if there will be a battle the next day. When he hears about the proposal, he forgets about his banishment, kneels before the king, and declares that the king has a suitable champion in Polydoros. When he learns of that knight's injury, he then offers to take the challenge himself.

On the fourth day, the two prepare for the encounter, Herakles presuming to instruct Erotókritos on how to fight, although that knight knows more about it than the king. The Vlach king likewise tutors Ariosto in combat warfare. An agreement is reached by the two rulers that the king whose champion is slain is to become tributary to the other. The two champions charge, and the lances of both are shattered. They draw their swords. Each is slightly wounded. Erotókritos's horse is inferior, and Ariosto kills it. The two men dismount and begin a sword fight. They wrestle and stab. Erotókritos slips and falls underneath Ariosto. He stabs Ariosto. Ariosto stabs Erotókritos. Herakles rushes up, thinking the Athenian is dead, but when they take off the armor, it is Ariosto, and he dies in his uncle's arms. There is a clap of thunder and a whirlwind. The army wails. The Vlach king mourns and lays the lad in a silver coffin and buries him with a great procession.

In Book V, meanwhile, Herakles weeps over Erotókritos, who he thinks is dead, but actually the Athenian has only fainted. The doctors sew up his wounds, but declare he has only one chance in 50 to survive. They carry him on a stretcher to the palace and lay him on Aretousa's bed. His wounds begin to heal. Aretousa hears about the victory but has little interest in the unknown warrior, wishing it had been her lover instead. Polydoros also recovers and begins to visit the stranger. One day, after Erotókritos has grown much stronger, the king comes to find out more about him. Erotókritos tells him his name is Kritides and that he left home on account of a girl who died and that he has been a knight-errant ever since. When the time comes he will tell the king why he came to fight for him and his native land. Since he has saved the king's life, the king offers him anything he has. I want neither realms nor riches, Erotókritos says. But he does want the king's daughter, who he hears is kept in a dungeon. It is for her sake that he has come to fight the enemies of Athens. The king answers that his daughter refuses to marry anybody, although he wishes she would marry him. He suggests that the young man go to the prison and look at her; she has become dirty. If she should accept him, and he still wants her, the king approves. Erotókritos continues: If she should still refuse, he has one other favor to ask—that she be forgiven and released from prison. The king bursts into tears; he longs to take his daughter into his arms after these five long years.

The king sends two elders to the prison, where they find the princess pale, thin, and dirty. They tell her how the stranger saved the king and the country, and why they are there. She takes it as an indication that her father is still trying to torture her and answers again that she would rather die than marry the stranger.

Give him the throne and leave her in prison, she cries. If they persist, she will kill herself. The king is persuaded that his daughter will die. Erotókritos is secretly delighted to hear of the princess's constancy. He asks to go to the prison himself and ask her just once.

Aretousa is furious. The king sends her a new dress and asks her to make herself presentable. She tears the dress to tatters and smears mud on her face to disgust this suitor. Outside the cell, Erotókritos calls the nurse to the window, secretly gives her his ring, and tells her that if her mistress still does not want to see him, to return it to a messenger he will send the next day. When

Aretousa sees the ring, she pales, imagining her lover is dead. To find out, the princess sends word that before she will talk of marriage she must know where he got that ring. He answers that he will tell her the next morning.

Erotókritos goes alone to her cell and tells her a story of finding the ring in Egripos beside a knight dying from an encounter with two beasts. She cries out that now she has nothing to live for. Erotókritos decides it is time to reveal his true identity. He wipes the black from his face. She faints, and after reviving, they weep and talk together as of old. She sends word to her father that she will marry the stranger. Her parents send her fine dresses and bring her to the palace. Erotókritos asks that his old father and mother be brought. He washes his face with the magic lotion, and all are astounded to see his true identity.

The king turns over his throne to Erotókritos, who becomes a wise and beloved ruler. So roses grow out of thorns, and faithful love has its rewards. (TAP) (Mavrogordato 1929; Trypanis 1981)

See also Kornáros, Vitséntsos.

 # ESCHENBACH, WOLFRAM VON

See Wolfram von Eschenbach.

 # ETZENBACH, ULRICH VON

See Ulrich von Etzenbach.

 # *EUGENE ONEGIN*

Russian "Byronic epic" or verse novel (1833) by Aleksandr Pushkin (1799–1837). Pushkin introduced a new kind of epic, a "free epic," or humoristic epic. Written in octosyllabic rhyming 14-line stanzas, it contains eight chapters of from 41 to 60 stanzas. Claiming to be a friend of the hero, the poet tells the story in first person. The poem is a mirror reflecting the life of nineteenth-century Russian society, and Pushkin's life as well. The frequent presence of the narrator intimates certain autobiographical aspects in the poem. Eugene's movement from city to country echoes Pushkin's own experience, as do Eugene's bouts of requited and unrequited love. The poem became the prototype of later Russian Romantic novels.

Chapter 1 introduces the central character, Eugene, who has an aristocratic upbringing, about which the poet comments, "It's easy, without too much fooling,/to pass for cultured in our ranks." (1:V) To keep pace with St. Petersburg society, Eugene's father "gave three balls a year, and rather/promptly had nothing left to give." (1:III) He sinks deeply into debt, debts that he leaves Eugene to pay. But about that time Eugene's dying uncle, who has made him his heir, sends for him to say farewell. Eugene rushes to his uncle's country manor, only to find that the old man has already died. Overnight, Eugene turns "countryman," but in only two days he is bored with life in the country, the beauty of which the poet describes in lyrical passages. He shuns local residents and becomes a recluse.

Chapter 2 introduces Vladimir Lensky, "good-looking, in the flower of age,/ a poet, and a Kantian sage," (2:VI) who becomes his only friend. Vladimir has loved Olga Larin since boyhood, and he has been betrothed to her for a long time. Olga has an older sister, Tatyana, who lacks Olga's beauty and who is "shy as a savage, silent, tearful,/wild as a forest deer, and fearful." (2:XXV) She spends her time reading romance novels. When the sisters' father, Dimitry (Yorik), dies, Vladimir composes a madrigal for an epitaph.

In Chapter 3, Vladimir convinces Eugene to accompany him to the Larin estate. Eugene's presence triggers "general furtive chatter" (3:VI) that Tatyana has found her man. For her part, Tatyana immediately falls in love with Eugene, who pays her scant attention and finds his visit boring. After he leaves, she writes him a passionate love letter in French, for her Russian is "as thin as vapour." (3:XXVI) She waits for an answer, and finally Eugene appears.

In Chapter 4, Eugene explains to her that he is unworthy to be her husband, for he is too worldly. He tells her, "I feel a brotherly affection/or something tenderer, still, for you." (4:XVI) He assures her, "You'll love again, but you must teach/your heart some self-restraint. . . ." Meanwhile, Vladimir continues to woo Olga. Tatyana goes back to her books and Eugene retires to his estate to lead a hermit's life. Two weeks before Vladimir's wedding, Vladimir visits Eugene and, after singing Olga's praises, tells Eugene that he is invited to attend Tatyana's name-day celebration.

Chapter 5 describes the sumptuous banquet, which is much larger than the family affair Vladimir has led him to expect. In revenge, Eugene begins to dance with Olga, flirting shamelessly. Vladimir leaves the party in a rage.

In Chapter 6, when Eugene learns that Vladimir has left, he becomes bored with Olga and wanders off; meanwhile, Tatyana pines for him in her room. Eugene soon receives a challenge to a duel from Vladimir, which he accepts. He shoots Vladimir through the chest, is immediately devastated and bereft, and leaves to wander the countryside.

In Chapter 7, Olga marries a Lancer and leaves home. Tatyana visits Eugene's home, where the old housekeeper, Anisia, shows her around, leaving her to look through his books and read his marginal notes. She now understands more about his self-centeredness and his shallowness. Disillusioned, she returns home, unwilling to entertain other suitors. At length her mother takes her to visit an old aunt in Moscow, where there will be eligible bachelors. Her Moscow cousins "fluff her curls out in the fashion" and in general teach her to behave in a more sophisticated manner. She becomes the toast of Moscow society. A famous, if fat, general has his eye on her, to the delight of her elders.

Russian composer Pyotr Ilich Tchaikovsky transformed Aleksandr Pushkin's epic *Eugene Onegin* into an opera, here staged at the Bolshoi State Theater.

In Chapter 8, Eugene returns after more than a two-year absence and, to break the monotony, attends a ball given by the general prince. There he sees a beautiful woman, the center of attention. He asks his host her identity and learns she is Tatyana, the host's wife. Eugene is smitten, "deep in love, just like a boy," (8:XXX) and returns to her home to be in her presence as often as possible. But Tatyana is no longer interested. Eugene "starts to languish: / . . . Onegin wastes. . . ." (8:XXXI) Finally he begins to write letters to her expressing his great love, but she never answers. Eventually he visits her and throws himself at her feet. She weeps and accuses him of wooing her now because, with her rank and riches, she would be "a tempting plume for you to take?" (8:XLIV) She admits her love for him, "but I've become another's wife—/and I'll be true to him for life." (8:XLVII) (Čiževskij 1971; Pushkin 1979)

See also Pushkin, Aleksandr Sergeyevich.

EUROPA

Czech epic poem (1878) by Svatopluk Čech (1846–1908), a follower of the pan-Slavic poet Ján Kollár and the central figure in the literary circle that attached itself to the literary magazine *Ruch* (Stir). This group favored nationalistic themes and Czech native traditions, of which *Europa* is a good example. In Greek myth, Europa, famed for her beauty, was abducted by Zeus disguised as a white bull. Čech likens the tale to the rape of his beautiful homeland, which had been abducted by Tsarist Russia and the Hapsburgs. His country bore the brunt of the War of Austrian Succession. The poet portrays the political and social misfortunes of his people in powerful but hyperbolic language, at the same time depicting Slavic traits, democratic ideals, and the beauty of the countryside in passionate detail. (Brogan 1996)

EVANGELINE

American narrative poem (1847) by Henry Wadsworth Longfellow (1807–1882). It is one of the very few poems in English composed in dactylic hexameter, the meter of the classical epics. It is the fictional account of the 1735 deportation of French colonists by the British government of Nova Scotia. The poem consists of 1,399 lines containing a prologue and two parts, each divided into five cantos or sections.

In Part I, Section I, the poet depicts the small Acadian village of Grand Pré, where the parish priest walks among the matrons, maidens, and children as the laborers return from the fields at sundown. Apart from the village lives the wealthiest farmer, Benedict Bellefontaine, whose daughter Evangeline, "the pride of the village," governs his household. Among her many suitors, only one is favored: her childhood companion Gabriel Lajeunesse, son of Basil the blacksmith.

In Part I, Section II, winter is settling in. Benedict and Evangeline are sitting by the fireplace when Basil and Gabriel arrive to discuss the menacing English ships that have arrived on their shores. The notary arrives, while the lovers hold hands by the window.

In Part I, Section III, the notary writes the dower agreement for the couple, and they celebrate with a tankard of ale.

In Part I, Section IV, the next morning the priest, the notary, Benedict, and Basil watch from the porch while Michael the fiddler plays and the neighbors dance. When the church bell summons, they all go to church, the men entering and the women waiting outside. The guard from the ships marches into the church, where the commander announces, "All your lands, and dwellings, and cattle . . ./[be] Forfeited to the crown; and that you yourselves from this province/Be transported to other lands. . . ." As a sudden hailstorm rages, Basil rises and cries, "Down with the tyrants of England!" But a soldier smites him and pandemonium breaks out. Father Felrician enters and reminds his flock that they are to forgive their oppressors. Meanwhile, Evangeline waits in vain for her father and Gabriel.

In Part I, Section V, on the fifth day the people are herded onto ships. Basil and Gabriel are put aboard one ship, leaving Evangeline and Benedict behind. While the people on the shore and in the boats moan and wail, Evangeline and the priest discover that Benedict has fallen from his seat, dead. They bury him on the seashore.

Part II, Section I, takes place a year after the burning of Grand Pré. The Acadian exiles have wandered homeless from city to city, looking for family members and neighbors. Among them are the priest and Evangeline, who is looking for Gabriel, refusing to take the advice of others to settle for Baptiste Leblanc, the notary's son.

In Part II, Section II, it is May and the Acadians float down the Mississippi to Louisiana, into Plaquemine Bayou to the lakes of the Atchafalaya. Evangeline sleeps. Meanwhile, a swift boat speeds between the islands. At the helm is Gabriel. But "Angel of God was there none to awaken the slumbering maiden," and her boat glides away without meeting Gabriel's boat. When she awakes, she tells the priest she is sure that Gabriel is nearby. The priest advises her to trust her heart.

In Part II, Section III, a herdsman sees a priest and maiden approaching. As they near, they recognize each other: it is Basil, who tells Evangeline that Gabriel has left, but that they will follow and overtake him.

Part II, Section IV, describes the months and years during which they wander, through the Ozarks, up to Michigan, never able to catch up with Gabriel. At length Evangeline grows grey-haired.

In Part II, Section V, Evangeline lands in "that delightful land which is washed by the Delaware waters." René LeBlanc has died there. Evangeline finds comfort among the Quakers, although she has never forgotten Gabriel. She becomes a Sister of Mercy. When a pestilence falls over the city, she ministers to the dying. As she makes her way among the victims, she finds an old dying man whom she recognizes as Gabriel. He dies in her arms. Now the lovers sleep side-by-side in nameless graves. (Longfellow 1893)

See also Longfellow, Henry Wadsworth.

 THE FAERIE QUEENE

English Romantic epic (1596) by Edmund Spenser (ca. 1552–1599). Spenser was educated at Cambridge and is noted for innovative verse forms and for combining in his work Puritan morality with Neoplatonic delight in the mysteries of sensuous beauty. *The Faerie Queene* as it exists is only a fragment of the complete work Spenser intended. Appended to it as a preface is a letter to Sir Walter Raleigh (1552?–1618) in which he explains his general purpose: to educate the reader by showing the qualities of a noble person (however, he describes only the first three books). The principal figure around whom he will picture these qualities, he says, is King Arthur, and his concern in this first part of his work (he completed only a part) is with Arthur as a prince, preparing himself to reign. Central to this preparation is an attempt to seek out and visit with the Faerie Queene, who represents both glory and Queen Elizabeth, the latter in her two capacities of ruler and "a most vertuous and beautifull Lady." Arthur himself is to represent in particular the virtue of magnificence, and this virtue is to be seen throughout the work. The "private morall vertues," as Spenser calls them, are to have other knights as patrons, and it is these knights whose adventures are in the foreground of the work.

Spenser intended to set forth 12 virtues in as many books, but he completed only six. The epic is preceded by several Commendatory Verses, followed by 17 Dedicatory Sonnets. Originally there were only ten sonnets, but when the first three books were bound (1590), Spenser added the names of other politically powerful people to the list of dedicatees. Each book begins with a proem followed by 12 cantos of varying numbers of nine-line stanzas. The stanza form, called Spenserian stanza, is eight lines of iambic pentameters followed by a ninth of iambic hexameter (an alexandrine). The rhyme scheme is *ababbcbcc*.

In the letter, Spenser describes the beginning of the first set of events. The Faerie Queene is having an annual feast lasting 12 days. On the first day, a tall, rustic-looking young man asks as a favor that the Queene let him serve her in any adventure that should require service. Soon after, a young lady enters, riding a white ass and followed by a dwarf who leads a "warlike steed" carrying the arms of a knight. This lady tells the Queene that a dragon has imprisoned her parents; she asks for aid in gaining their release. She tells the Queene that she has with her armor that will fit only a Christian knight. The rustic-looking young man is offered the task of representing the Queene in this matter, and it is found that the armor, marked with a large red cross over the breast, fits him very well: "He seemed the goodliest man in all that company."

This story precedes the beginning of the poetry of the first book, which is subtitled "Contayning the Legende of the Knight of the Red Cross, or of Holinesse." The first line of Canto I of Book I is a very famous one: "A Gentle Knight was pricking on the plaine." The word *gentle* as used in this line means "noble" rather than soft-acting, and the word *pricking* means "cantering."

The Redcross Knight and the Lady are crossing the plain, she with a lamb beside her and a dwarf following, when a storm forces them to seek cover. They find it in a section of forest so thickly wooded that the storm cannot break through. Within this forest they lose their way. In trying to discover some way out, they come across a cave, which the knight feels he must explore in an attempt to find something that can help them. Both the lady and the dwarf, who know this part of the country better than the knight, warn him against entering the cave, but he is "full of fire" and boldness, and he enters. Within he finds an ugly monster, half a serpent, but "th' other half did womans shape retaine,/most lothsom, filthie, foule, and full of vile disdaine."

This creature, who has a long tail "with mortall sting," has about her a thousand young ones "sucking upon her poisonous dugs." When they see the Christian knight they creep into her mouth and disappear. When she herself spies the Christian knight she flees, but when she gets into the light she tries to turn back, for she hates the light. He forces her to stay where she is. She threatens him with her tail, and he strikes her with his sword. She is stunned, but manages to wrap him so completely in that tail that he is unable to move. At this point Spenser makes his allegory explicit by saying, "God help the man so wrapt in Errours endlesse traine."

The lady, who is watching this struggle, urges the knight to add faith to his force and strangle the monster. With this encouragement, he gets one hand free and begins to choke her; soon she has to loosen her hold on him. Either as a result of the choking or as another attempt to win the battle, the monster vomits "a floud of poyson horrible and black, full of great lumps of flesh and gobbets raw," which causes the knight to back away. Mixed in with her vomit are the thousand creatures who had earlier entered her mouth. Realizing that his peril is increasing with the decrease of his ability to maintain his composure and still fight, the knight makes a great effort with his sword and kills the monster. "A streame of cole black bloud forth gushed from her corse." The thousand creatures then devour their dam.

The lady hails her champion, and now that they have disposed of Errour, the two of them discover a beaten path leading them out of the deeply wooded area. A second adventure begins immediately.

They meet an old, apparently holy man who offers them lodging for the night in his hermitage. While they sleep, this old man, Archimago—presumably architect of images, so archmagician—calls up evil spirits, one of which transforms itself into a lookalike to the lady, whose name we now learn is Una.

This false Una attempts to seduce the Redcross Knight, and he is tempted, but he is also disgusted that the lady he has pledged to defend has turned out to be a loose woman. His disgust saves him from error.

The evil spirits return to their master, who then fashions them as a pair of lovers coupling, one of them still looking like Una. Seeing the woman he has come to love in the arms of another man, the Redcross Knight rides away. Una, finding him gone but not knowing why—yet knowing that she loves him—rides after him, but she cannot catch him.

Archimago is not through. He fashions one of the spirits into a semblance of St. George, the patron saint of England, and the other into a lady to accompany him, a scarlet lady ornamented in the manner of the Whore of Babylon in the biblical book of Revelation. When the new knight meets Redcross, the two engage in a fierce battle, which Redcross eventually wins. The lady, who now claims to be an emperor's daughter, throws herself on the mercy of the Redcross Knight. The other knight, she tells Redcross, forced her to accompany him, but she managed to retain her virginity.

He begins to feel sorry for the lady—his holiness is not yet sufficient to enable him to sense her falseness—and he lets her accompany him until she can find some place of safety. She plays coy and tries to stimulate desire in him, and after a while he is tempted to respond. In this enchanted forest he is warned off by a tree that was once a man taken in by a satanic trick much like the one being applied to the Redcross Knight.

Meanwhile, Una continues her search for the man she loves and the holiness he represents. She seems a true Bride of Christ (and so a symbol of the true church) but a Protestant one who may still be the bride of a Christian man. The way of the church is hard, as the way of the man who would be holy is a continual challenge.

With the help of Prince Arthur, Una and the Redcross Knight are reunited, and the Redcross Knight overcomes a giant, who seems to represent blasphemy and rebellion against heaven. He also overcomes the terrible enemy Despair. Redcross, now identified with St. George, is bruised by all his battles, but Una directs him to the House of Holiness, where the process of his sanctification is begun.

In the letter to Raleigh, Spenser says that Book Two is "of Sir Guyon, in whome I sette forth Temperaunce." Sir Guyon, the knight who is to struggle to embody this virtue as the Redcross Knight St. George does to embody holiness, is accompanied on his adventures by an old man who serves as an adviser, reminding the knight of the value of restraint and providing him with the practical wisdom of experience that he lacks.

Guyon meets one of his temptations in the Cave of Mammon, where he is invited to serve riches rather than God. The cave has great halls in which deformed creatures work feverishly and some who resemble courtiers step on each other's feet as they scramble for advancement. One vast chamber contains a silver seat; one critic, Elizabeth Heale, suggests that this chamber reveals an attempt to mingle the divine and the worldly and so to demonstrate against the biblical injunction against trying to serve two masters (62).

Sir Guyon's best-known temptation comes at the Bower of Bliss, which is a center for sensuous pleasures that when godless promote incontinence. Guyon's task is to find this Bower of Bliss in order to destroy it so that it does not draw other men astray.

He does destroy it, and in the course of that destruction wastes much beauty. Heale points out that "moderation and restraint are qualities we have come to expect from a temperate Guyon, but a tempering response to incontinence and its seductions is inappropriate."

Spenser's letter to Raleigh announces that his third book concerns "Britomartis [Britomart] a Lady knight, in whome I picture Chastitie." His reference is not to sexual purity alone, although it certainly includes that, and he sees it as a virtue attainable by the virgin or by people linked in Christian wedlock. Sexual purity has its greatest importance, he tries to show, in the spiritual purity that should accompany it and to which it contributes.

Just as the Redcross Knight encounters Guyon at the beginning of Book Two, at the beginning of Book Three, Guyon encounters Britomart. Guyon is riding with Arthur when he sees an armored knight approaching. Guyon challenges in what must have been a customary way, lowering his lance and charging. The other knight meets him and gets the best of the exchange. The poet tells Guyon that he should not be upset, since the other lance is enchanted: It is borne by Britomart, and the magic is the force granted her for her chastity.

Britomart, in armor and pretending to be a man, is searching for the man who is destined to become her lover, a man whose name we learn is Artegall. Britomart has had a vision of him, a mere glimpse, in Venus's looking glass, and now her quest is to find the man himself.

She sees six knights attacking one, and she asks why—what has this man done? The six knights ignore her, so she rides in and stops the fighting with her enchanted sword, although she and the man she is championing must overpower some of the knights before all fighting ceases.

She discovers that the six knights are attempting to take Redcross to their Lady. He is refusing out of loyalty to Una. Britomart says that he is right to be faithful to his own lady. The knights, however, insist that their Lady is beyond compare, and they will take no refusals unenforced by battle. Again, Redcross and Britomart defeat the six knights in combat.

Britomart and Redcross voluntarily visit the Lady's quarters, Castle Joyeus. It is a place of extravagant luxury and elaborate but pornographic murals. The Lady, whom we will come to know as Malecasta, attempts unsuccessfully to seduce both Redcross and Britomart, supposing the latter to be a man. (Britomart refuses to take off her armor since it makes a good disguise.)

Britomart is not tempted by the Lady, but she is tempted slightly by the six knights, whose names suggest the parts they might play in a seduction. The only one who creates genuine interest on Britomart's part is the first of them, whose name, Gardante, seems to be a play on the Italian word *guardante*, which means "looking." The other knights are Parlante (talking), Jocante (joking), Basciante (kissing), Bacchante (drinking), and Noctante (pleasures of the night).

Malecasta's name suggests a lack of chastity: *malus*—bad, *castus*—chaste. Clearly the allegory in this book centers on the contrast between false and pure erotic love.

When Britomart fears that the Redcross Knight may be close to yielding to Malecasta's seduction, she attacks her hostess physically. When the six knights attempt to punish this behavior, the two Christian knights, Redcross and Britomart, once again defeat their would-be controllers.

Perhaps the best-known aspect of Book Three is the description of the Garden of Adonis, which contrasts to the Bower of Bliss in many of the ways that true love does to false love. The Garden seems to be a place where nature is in harmony with God, the Bower a place where art is in the service of that which is shallow and unwise in man. One symbol is the ivy, which is real in the Garden, imitation in the Bower.

Both the Bower and the Garden appeal to the senses. C. S. Lewis, discussing the explicitly erotic imagery of these two settings, remarks that Spenser has been much misunderstood relative to this matter. Spenser "is full of pictures of virtuous and vicious love," Lewis says, "and they are, in fact, exquisitely contrasted." But, he goes on to say, the contrast is not what one might expect: "Most readers seem to approach him with the vulgar expectation that his distinction between them is going to be a quantitative one; that the vicious loves are going to be warmly painted and the virtuous tepidly—the sacred draped and the profane nude. . . . [But insofar as it is quantitative at all] . . . the quantities are the other way round. . . . For him, intensity of passion purifies; cold pleasure is corruption." (330-1) Lewis considers that, for the most part, the contrast between the two places is best seen in the attitudes of the people inhabiting them.

Two verses, numbers 45 and 46, in Canto VI provide a sample of the general flavor: "And all about grew every sort of flowre,/To which sad lovers were transformed of yore;/Fresh *Hyacinthus*, *Phoebus* paramoure,/And dearest love,/Foolish *Narcisse*, that likes the watry shore,/Sad *Amaranthus*, made a flowre but late,/Sad *Amaranthus*, in whose purple gore/Me seemes I see *Amintas* wretched fate,/To whom sweet Poets verse hath given endlesse date.

"There wont faire *Venus* often to enjoy/And reape sweet pleasure of the wanton boy;/There yet, some say, in secret he does ly,/Lapped in flowres and pretious spycery,/By her hid from the world, and from the skill/Of *Stygian* Gods, which doe her love envy;/But she her selfe, when ever that she will,/Possesseth him, and of his sweetness takes her fill."

Between Book Three, which has to do with Chastity, and Book Five, which deals with Justice, is Book Four, concerning Friendship or Concord. In Spenser's terms, friendship is broader than the erotic love it includes, and it extends beyond individual persons to social and civic entities. The knights who are heroes of this book are friends caught up in discord that divides before experiencing fully the friendly love that unites.

Elizabeth Heale points out that the two couples around whom the narrative is formed create "a figure of completeness containing within itself an example of every kind of friendly alliance." This design is effected by showing two brother-sister combinations in which each of the men is the lover of the other man's sister.

Book Five features Artegall, Britomart's envisioned lover, who appears to be Spenser's idea of a knight of justice. He is trained as a harsh ruler of the kind Spenser himself is supposed to have felt necessary in Ireland, where he served for some years as an official of the English government. Much of Book Five is political allegory relating to English and Irish affairs of the Elizabethan period.

Courtesy is the subject of Book Six, subtitled "Contayning the Legend of S. Calidore or of Courtesie." As Spenser presents this virtue, it includes far more than just politeness. Its chief component is perhaps grace—grace as in graciousness, but also as in a mental and spiritual equivalent of grace in physical movement. It is a social virtue, but also a quality of conduct as it relates to the self and the nonhuman world. One of the principal images is the appearance and dance of the Graces, who function as inspiration for courtesy.

The story is of a knight named Calidore, who embodies the topic, virtue, and must quest after and destroy the Blatant Beast. The plot consists mainly of incidents along the way in which Calidore perfects and practices his courtesy. On one occasion he saves a lady, caught in compromising position with her lover, from her father's anger.

Beyond the six books Spenser finished, he wrote two cantos, apparently in preparation for a book on the subject of change. These pieces have come to be known as the Mutability Cantos. They are considered similar in some respects to the Garden of Adonis section of Book Three in their showing of delight in change as appreciation of the stuff of life itself. (Heale 1987; Lewis 1936; Spenser 1978)

See also Spenser, Edmund.

THE FALL OF HYPERION: A DREAM

Unfinished English epic poem (1819–1820) by John Keats (1795–1821). In 1818–1819, Keats began a Miltonic blank verse epic about the Greek myth of Creation called *Hyperion*. The titanic majesty of the divinities depicted in the poem was inspired by the Elgin Marbles. The poem was to relate the story of the Titan god Hyperion, god of the sun, and his defeat and replacement by Apollo, part of a younger generation of gods headed by Zeus. However, Keats abandoned the poem midway through Book III. The grandeur of his *Hyperion* foreshadows a work that, had it been completed, might have equaled *Antony and Cleopatra*. In the summer of 1819 he began a revision of the poem, although the renamed *Fall of Hyperion* became quite a different poem. The poet approached the revised version as a more personal vision, using the first-person voice of the poet to relate the story as a dream. The style is completely different as well, the later poem being free of the heavy Miltonic influence.

Canto I extends the condemnation of the dreaming poet as portrayed in an earlier poem, *Lamia.* In an enchanted dream vision, the poet defeats death by overcoming the obstacle of the "immortal steps" leading to the altar of the veiled priestess Moneta. He asks her ("the veiled Shadow"), "What am I that I should be so saved from death?" Furthermore, he does not understand why he alone has been granted this grace: "I sure should see/Other men here, but I am here alone." She explains that the others "are no dreamers weak," whereas the poet: "Thou art a dreaming thing,/A fever of thyself—" She parts her veil and he sees a "wan face," "bright-blanched/By an immortal sickness which kills not." He aches to know what "high tragedy" could "touch her voice/With such sorrow."

By the fall of 1819, Keats's tuberculosis had progressed so far that he no longer considered producing new work and did little but revise old work, preparing it for publication. *The Fall of Hyperion* was left uncompleted. (Anderson and Buckler 1966)

 # THE FALL OF TROY

(*Posthomerica, Ton Meth Omeron,* or *Ta met' Homeron*)

Greek epic poem (4th c.) written by Quintus Smyrnaeus (Quintus of Smyrna, fl. ca. 375). The poem shows a saturation with the spirit of Homer's poem, although with deviations. The first manuscript ever discovered was found in the fifteenth century. It was lost, but hasty and imperfect copies were made. The most ancient and the best was discovered at a later date. Probably Quintus knew the poems of the Cyclic Poets before him—whose works have not survived—but his epic is no remodeling of theirs; it is an independent and original poem. Quintus is in his element when describing a battle scene, but he omits many of the most important events in Homer. The story is told in 14 books in classical meters.

In Book I, Penthesileia, Queen of the Amazons, joins the Trojan forces out of friendship for Priam. She boasts of the havoc she will wreak on the Greeks, even on Achilles himself, and leads her Amazons into battle. She is so successful that the Trojan women are eager to join her, until one Trojan woman warns them of their inexperience at warfare. The Greek ships are set afire. Aias (Ajax) and Achilles enter the battle. The Greeks are heartened by their appearance and rally. They and Penthesileia rush at each other, and Penthesileia is killed. Her helmet falls off, exposing her lovely face and wringing pity from the victors. Angered and grieving, her father, Ares, darts down from Olympus but is stopped by Zeus. The Greeks gather their dead. Thersites attacks Achilles for killing the Amazon and is slain by him. The body of Penthesileia is borne to Troy and rendered funeral rites by a grieving city.

In Book II, Memnon, son of Tithonus and Dawn (Eos) and king of the Aethiopians, comes to the aid of Priam with a mighty host. In Olympus, Zeus warns the gods against becoming involved, advising them to leave the outcome to the fates. The Trojans, Aethiopians, and their allies arm for battle. The Argives speedily prepare themselves; amidst them is Achilles, like a giant

Titan. The two sides grapple; heroes on both sides are slain; among them is Antilochus, killed before his father's (Nestor) eyes. His brother drives at Memnon, but Eos protects him. Memnon slays throngs of Argives. Nestor goes to Achilles, urging revenge. As they engage in single combat, Thetis, mother of Achilles, intervenes, only to be stopped by Zeus. Finally Achilles kills Memnon. The Trojans flee, pursued by Achilles. Eos mourns her son as her gods bear his body away. His Aethiopian comrades are also winged away as the Trojans marvel. On the other side, the Argives grieve over Antilochus. Eos, with her deities, grieves as her gods bear Memnon's body away. The Aethipos bury their lord, and Eos resumes her daily journey accompanied by the Pleiades.

In Book III the Argives bury Antilochus, but Achilles is eager for vengeance and resumes the battle, making havoc among the Trojans. On Olympus, Phoebus is angered and comes down to warn Achilles to turn back. Achilles defies him and speeds after the fleeing Trojans. Phoebus vanishes into a cloud and shoots Achilles in the ankle. Achilles falls, shouting, "Who shot me? I fear it is Phoebus, as predicted by my mother." Hera upbraids Zeus for favoring Troy. He does not answer and sits aloof from the gods who favor the Greeks. The wounded Achilles still longs to fight, but none of the Trojans dare draw near to him. He leaps up and slays more Trojans before he dies. Even as he falls, the Trojans stare at him with dread and shrink away. Paris strives to rekindle their hearts, reminding them of Hector's death at the hands of Achilles.

The Trojans come forward to drag Achilles's corpse to Troy, but Aias (Ajax) bestrides the body and fights them off, joined by a host of Greeks who battle the Trojans furiously, with great loss of life on both sides. In the fight, Paris is wounded by Aias and borne safely back to Troy by his comrades.

Aias and the Greeks bewail the death of Achilles and vow to destroy Troy. All night the Greeks mourn the dead hero and then prepare the body for burial, laying it on a bier, around which woeful captive maidens are placed to wail. Briseis, Achilles's couchmate, tears at her flesh, weeping. Thetis clasps the body to her and kisses him. They light the pyre, and Achilles's body is consumed. From the ocean Poseidon rises and tells Thetis that her son dwells with the gods.

In Book IV, from afar the Trojans watch the great funeral fire with great joy. On Olympus, Hera complains to Zeus that he has been helping the Trojans, but Zeus is silent, aware of the fate that awaits Troy and pondering the ruin he will visit on the victors. Aias is battle-eager, but is reminded that funeral games are proper now. The Greek champions are summoned, but first the feats of Achilles are reviewed. Among the contestants are all the Greek heroes. They engage in wrestling, foot-racing, boxing, archery, javelin casting, and chariot-driving.

In Book V, when all other contests were over, Thetis lays down Achilles's arms in the midst of the contestants. On them are pictures of hunting, wars, the works of peace, the myriad tribes of men in cities and fields, banquets with their dancers, ships sailing the sea, and Poseidon amid sea-monsters. Zeus is depicted on the crest of the helmet. There are also an unpierceable corselet, a sword of hardened steel, and Achilles's spear, which had shed the blood of Hector. Thetis promises these as an athletic prize. Each champion claims them, but Aias seems the mightiest. He calls upon Idomeneus, Nestor, and

Amazons, right, represented on the Krater of Ruvo, fight Greeks during the Trojan War, an event included by Quintus Smyrnaeus in *The Fall of Troy*, written during the fourth century.

Agamemnon to act as arbiters. Odysseus, his chief rival, agrees. They decide to let the two chief rivals settle the matter in single combat, but Aias is angry, reviewing his history of heroic deeds. Odysseus answers that he is the better in wit and speech. Aias answers indignantly with instances of his might.

Suddenly dark bewilderment falls upon him, and in a fury he dons his mail, clutches his sword, and thinks to set the Greek ships afire and slaughter all the Argives, Odysseus first. (Pallas, caring for Odysseus, has smitten Aias mad.) Aias slaughters sheep right and left, thinking one of them is Odysseus, then stabs himself to death. The Greeks gather around him and mourn. Among them is his princess bride, who fears that now she and their child will be taken by the enemy and enslaved. Odysseus eulogizes Aias, and they carry the body to Mount Ida, where it is burned on a pyre. Again the Trojans watch from afar, rejoicing.

In Book VI, Menelaus summons all the Greeks, and surrenders all claim to Helen, whom he no longer loves. He recommends that they abandon the war; however, this is only to test the Argives. They rally, sending for Achilles's son; they will win a victory. In the meantime, Eurypylus, grandson of Hercules, joins the Trojans, bringing memories of the great feats of that hero. He gathers champions with him, and they charge the Greeks. From their ramparts, the Greeks, behind Agamemnon, at first push the Trojans back, but Eurypylus rushes forth, slaying many great Argives, and they flee to their ships.

In Book VII the Greeks take refuge behind the rampart of their ships, awaiting the arrival of Achilles's son Neoptolemus. However, his mother, Deïdameia, remembers how Odysseus and Diomede prompted Achilles to join the forces against Troy and thereby widowed her, so she opposes her son's helping the

Argives for fear he too will perish. But Neoptolemus kisses her and sails to Troy. Immediately after he arrives, he begins a charge against the enemy, with Odysseus, Diomede, and others at his side. Eurypylus, however, concentrates on the Greek ships, storming them with huge stones. The Greeks are terrorized but do not flinch, and they stand fast. Eurypylus taunts them, but the Trojans see in Neoptolemus Achilles's giant self again. They waver, then stop. Eurypylus urges them on. Pallas on Olympus hurries to Troy and inspires the Greeks, especially Neoptolemus. The Trojans pull back. The battle is at a standstill. Neoptolemus looks over the bloody battlefield, and a passionate longing for his father seizes him. Exulting, the Trojans extol Eurypylus.

In Book VIII, Neoptolemus clads himself in his father's arms and rouses the Greeks. Thetis is overjoyed. Neoptolemus boards his chariot and speeds toward the Trojans, followed by a thousand other chariots, like a mighty ocean wave. The earth groans beneath Trojan corpses, but Eurypylus is everywhere, a multitude falling beneath his spear. He and Achilles's son meet face-to-face. Neoptolemus leaps from his chariot and the two clash, battling for a long time. Finally Neoptolemus's spear passes through Eurypylus's throat, and he falls. Neoptolemus stands over the body and laughingly recalls Eurypylus's boast of destroying the Greek ships and men. He springs back into his chariot. Trojans fall like unnumbered leaves beneath the charge of his steeds. Trojans flee within their gates, but, unnoticed by the other gods, Ares appears, eager to help them. He cheers them on to face their foe. They flee no more but turn to face the Greeks. Deadly, bloody strife continues.

Ares wishes to meet Neoptolemus himself, face-to-face, but Pallas swoops down, ready to close with Ares. Zeus steps in and taunts them both. They both withdraw from the battlefield. The Argives pour to the very gates of Troy and take a breathing space. Within their gates, the Trojans withstand the assault. The Greeks might breach the Trojan walls, but Ganymede in Olympus, anguished for his fatherland, pleads with Zeus to help them. Zeus veils all Troy with a thick cloud. Frightened by Zeus's help to the Trojans, the Greeks retreat to their ships.

In Book IX the Trojan Antenor prays to Zeus that if it is their destiny to be destroyed, not to draw out the agony. Zeus hears him, and since he has already determined that Troy should be destroyed, he grants this boon. Priam sends to the Greeks asking a truce while they bury Eurypylus. Afterward, the Greeks attack again. The Trojan women watch the battle from the high walls. Helen sits in shame in her bower with her maids. Neoptolemus faces Deiphobus, son of Priam, who is saved by Phoebus with a cloud that hides him. Cloaked with clouds, Phoebus rushes to destroy Neoptolemus, but Poseidon intervenes and prevents him. Advised by the prophet Calchas, the Greeks draw back to their ships because it has been foreordained that Troy should not fall until war-wise Philoctetes comes to aid them.

They send Odysseus and Diomede to Philoctetes in Lemnos, where he was left by the Argonauts. He still suffers from wounds and, like a wild beast, he is unwashed and haggard. Odysseus and Diomede wash him, tend to his wounds, and bring him to Troy.

In Book X the Trojans prepare for a renewal of battle, led by Paris, who slays many a famed Greek. From the Greeks, Philoctetes smites many a Trojan. Finally, the two meet, and Paris is fatally wounded. Leeches are applied to his wound without any success. His only hope lays with Oenone, the nymph who was his wife before he left her for Helen. According to prophecy, only she can heal him, so Paris goes to Mount Ida, where she lives. But Oenone's heart is steeled with resentment, and she sends him away. As he stumbles back down Mount Ida, Hera sees him, rejoicing in his fate. Paris dies on the slopes of Ida. A herdsman carries the news to his mother, who wails in grief. Helen weeps. Far away, Oenone also weeps and flies to the pyre to leap upon it.

In Book XI, even though Paris is now dead, the young men of Troy fight on. Apollo comes to Aeneas and Eurymachus in the shape of a woman, encourages them, then vanishes to watch from on high. They are flooded with such new courage that Ares, watching, laughs, and Apollo rejoices. Neoptolemus presses against the Trojans but is hurled backward. Aeneas faces him, but Neoptolemus—influenced by Thetis, who in turn respects Aphrodite, patron of Aeneas—does not raise his spear against Aeneas; he turns his fury elsewhere. In the confusion, all would have perished, even by their fellows' swords, had not Zeus intervened and cleared the dust from the air. The Greeks raise their shields over their heads, ranged side-by-side like a solid roof, and advance to the Trojan wall. From above, the Trojans hurl huge stones, which, like the spears they hurl, roll harmlessly to the ground until Zeus interferes. With thunderbolts he rends mountain boulders down, dashing the Greek battle wall to fragments.

In Book XII the Greeks are frustrated, but Calchas argues that force will not win the war; only cunning strategy will prevail. He proposes building a great horse in which they can conceal themselves and ambush the Trojans, after burning their own tents and sailing away, pretending to abandon the seige. Neoptolemus argues that brave men choose battle. Odysseus sides with Calchas. The Greeks proceed with this stratagem. In the meantime the Olympian gods take up the conflict, partisans of Greeks and Trojans against one another: Ares against Athena, then the others. Angered, Zeus sends Themis with the threat to bury them all beneath the ruins of a shattered earth.

Achilles is the first into the Horse, followed by all the Greek heroes except Nestor and Agamemnon, who stay to keep order as the ships sail to Tenedos. Seeing the smoke from the burning Greek tents and the vanished ships, the Trojans run joyfully to the deserted beach and discover the Horse. Beside it is Sinon, left behind to trick the Trojans into bringing the Horse inside their walls. Sinon tells a false story of having been marked for slaughter by the Greeks to win from the sea powers a safe return home. He also says the Horse has been built to propitiate Athena's wrath for the Greeks' theft of her image from Troy. Suspicious, Laocoon warns the Trojans that this is a fraud. Angered, Athena torments him, so the Trojans proceed to roll the Horse inside the city. When Laocoon continues to warn them, Athena looses monsters from a cave, who bear down upon Laocoon, strangling him and his sons. Dreadful signs appear but are unheeded, except by Priam's daughter Cassandra, who also warns them about the Horse. Mocked, she rushes with a firebrand to the Horse, but Trojans pluck it from her hands. She turns and flees under a rain of darts.

In Book XIII night falls on Troy. Sinon draws near the Horse, unlooses the bars, and the Greeks leap out silently, pouring into the city. They set fire to the temple and palace, then proceed to the gates and slay the slumbering guards. When their friends arrive from the ships, aided by Thetis, and join them at the gates, they march to the fortress, slaying all they meet. Blood runs in torrents. Women shriek and wail. Many an Argive also falls. Neoptolemus slays all Priam's sons, and finally finds Priam by Zeus's altar, and lops off his head. The Greeks find Hector's baby and fling him off a cliff, then drag Hector's widow to slavery. Only Aeneas survives, forsaking the town with his father, Anchises, and his son—guided by Aphrodite and spared by Calchas's pleas to the Greeks. Helen flees and hides, but Menelaus finds her, cowering. At first he hungers to slay her, but Agamemnon stops him, blaming Paris and not her. On Olympus the gods mourn for Troy, except for Hera. Among the ruins, Theseus's mother, a Greek in Troy, identifies herself to the Greeks and is reunited with her grandsons. Laodice, Priam's daughter, is saved by the gods. Electra is shrouded in a mist and taken into the skies.

In Book XIV the conquerors return with spoils from Troy, Menelaus with Helen, Agamemnon with Cassandra, Odysseus with Hecuba. The Greeks offer sacrifices to celebrate their victory. Helen pleads with Menelaus to forgive her, and he does. The shade of Achilles joins in the festivity and, at his request, Priam's daughter Polyxeina is led to his tomb and offered as a sacrifice. The Greeks sail away. But Athena, angry at Aias the Lesser, approaches Zeus and asks for the use of his thunderbolt. With the help of Aeolus, God of the Winds, there is a mighty storm at sea that founders some of the Greek ships. Athena hurls a thunderbolt at the ship of Aias the Lesser, shivering it. Aias clings to a ship's plank and would have survived had Poseidon not buried him with a falling mountain. Athena is appeased, but Poseidon continues wreaking havoc, and thousands of Greeks perish. Athena fears for Odysseus. Poseidon swells the sea and rolls it toward Troy while Zeus pours rain from heaven. Apollo leads all the streams from Ida's heights into one channel and floods the Trojan walls until they vanish. The storm-dispersed Greeks sail on to their homes. (TAP) (Quintus Smyrnaeus 1913)

See also Quintus Smyrnaeus.

 # FÉNELON

(Full name: François de Salignac de la Mothe-Fénelon)

French theologian, archbishop, man of letters, author of *Télémaque* (1694–1696, publ. 1699). He was born in 1651 in the province of Périgord in France to a poor but aristocratic family of distinguished lineage. Little is known of his childhood except that he was trained in classical languages. In 1663 he began study with the Jesuits at the Université de Cahors. His father died that same year, and his uncle, the marquis de Fénelon, assumed the major influence on the young man. In 1665, Fénelon changed to the Collège du Plessis in Paris, concentrating on theology and philosophy. In 1672 or 1673 he entered the Séminaire de Saint-Sulpice and was ordained into the priesthood in 1674 or 1675.

Apparently, however, the young man had other ambitions. For one, he dreamed of missionary service in an exotic place, a dream never realized. Instead he was assigned to Les Nouvelles Catholiques in Huguenot territory for the rehabilitation of Protestants. There he wrote his first works, treatises on methods of education.

In 1689 he was chosen preceptor to Louis XIV's grandson, at which time he began to write original compositions that would teach in a pleasing and attractive manner. One of the first was his *Fables*. Another was Fénelon's version of *The Odyssey*. Finally, sometime between 1694 and 1696, he composed the *Télémaque* (*Les Aventures de Télémaque*), the best known of his works.

By this time he had established a reputation as teacher and orator, and in March 1693 he was elected to the Académie Française. In 1694 he was given a benefice and in 1695 named archbishop of Cambrai. However, in the meantime he had aroused the enmity of Madame de Maintenon by becoming interested in the ideas of Madame Guyon, a Quietist. As a result, Fénelon, who had written a book, *Maximes*, under this influence, was declared a heretic and deprived of his title and pension as preceptor and subjected to papal condemnation (1699). In the same year, circulation of his *Télémaque* led to its publication. It was judged to be a satire on Louis XIV, although Fénelon maintained that it was a pirated and unauthorized edition. The work was confiscated, and Fénelon was prohibited from further communication with any member of the royal family. The rest of his life was spent in exile at a small parish in Cambrai, where he had leisure time for writings of a philosophical nature. He died there on 7 January 1715. (TAP) (Davis 1979)

See also Télémaque.

FIRDAUSI, ABU'L QĀSIM
(Also Ferdausi, Ferdowsi, Firdawsi, Firdowsi, Firdausi)

Persian poet, author of the Persian national epic *Shāh-Nāmah* (1010). Firdausi is the author's pen name, a poetical appellation meaning "the Paradisal" or "the heavenly one." His honorific title was Abu'l Qasim (or Abo'l-Qāsem, or Abūol-Qāsem Manṣūr or Ḥasan or Aḥmad). His personal name is unknown, and the dates of his birth and death are uncertain. A poet named Neẓāmī-ye 'Arū't visited his tomb and birthplace and compiled the legends extant about his life. He was born about 935–940 in a village on the outskirts of the city of Tūs in the province of Khorāsān in northeast Iran to a family of moderate means belonging to the 'Dehqā (land-owning class, or people who cultivated their own land).

The 'Dehqāns educated their sons and passed on Persian history by oral and written tradition. Firdausi lived comfortably on income from his estates, was married, and had at least one daughter.

During early manhood, Firdausi wrote a prose version of Persian history called *Shāh-Nāmah* that was derived and translated from an earlier Pahlavi work called *Khvatāy-Nāmak*, with additions that carried the history a century farther. At the request of Sultan Maḥmūd ibn Sabuktagin, he began his own poem on the history of Persia, a project that would require 35 years to complete. In its text he incorporated 1,000 verses written by another Tūs native, ad-Daqīqī, who was the first poet to undertake an epic history. Ad-Daqīqī, a Sāmānid court panegyrist, was murdered by a Turkish slave before he could complete his epic, but his work is given acknowledgment in Firdausi's poem. When Firdausi completed the poem (1010), he presented it to the Turkish sultan Maḥmād of Ghazna, the Ghaznavids having conquered the Sāmānids by that time. There is great irony in the fact that Firdausi had to dictate his poem to the Turkic destroyers of the empire of which he wrote.

When the sultan paid Firdausi 20,000 dirhams, less than half what had been promised, the embittered poet divided the money between a bathhouse attendant and a beer vendor and left the country, at length taking refuge in Mazanderan at the court of the Sepahbād Shahreyār, descendant of the Sāsānians. There he composed a 100-verse satire of Maḥmūd, which he added as a preface to his epic. However, Shahreyār bought the satire for 100,000 dirhams and had it deleted from the poem. After a nine-year exile, Firdausi returned to Tūs, where he lived to be more than 80. According to 'Arūẓī, Sultan Maḥmūd was later persuaded to make amends to Firdausi, and sent 60,000 dinars' worth of indigo by royal camel caravan to Tūs. But the reward arrived during the funeral procession. His daughter refused the sultan's gift, which was eventually spent for repairs to a way station on Tūs's border.

Denied burial in a Muslim cemetery because of his heretical Shī'ite tenets as expressed in the poem, the poet was buried in a garden on his own estate, outside Tūs. (Levy 1967)

See also Shāh-Nāmah.

FLAŠKA, SMIL

Czech poet (fl. 14th c.), author of *Nová rada* (New council). He was born in or near Pardubice, a town in the eastern Bohemia region of Czechoslovakia. His work shows that he was familiar with the literature of Western Europe. Flaška was the leader of a school of didactic poetry; his intent in his epic was to defend the rights of Bohemian nobility against the encroaching power of the king. His chief work was *Nová rada,* an allegorical epic of 2,116 verses, the composition of which bears French and English influence. Other of his works are *A Father's Admonition to His Son* and a collection of old Czech proverbs. (Dvornik 1962; Kuntsman 1955)

FLORANTE AT LAURA

Filipino Tagalog epic (1838) by Francesco Balagtás (Francisco Baltazar), universally recognized as the greatest Tagalog poet. Widely popular from the beginning, it appeared in a dozen editions in the last century, mostly pirated or published without permission and usually hispanicized. Consequently many errors appeared. In 1906 a corrected version by a reputable Tagalog scholar, assisted by the poet's son, was published, using accepted Tagalog spellings. During World War II, however, all these were destroyed. Cheap, thin paper copies do exist, but they are rarities. In 1901, at the request of a captain in the U.S. army, Apolinario Mabini, a Filipino political philosopher and statesman in exile in Guam, made a hand copy of the poem with minor differences from early versions. It is the basis for the English translation.

In the original Tagalog, the poem reads naturally following an organic cadence and no accentual prescription, and is best translated into English with iambic tetrameter. The lines are dodecasyllabic with caesuras midway each line. It exploits the natural liquid flow of the Tagalog language. The original rhyme scheme is quatrains in monorima (*a-a-a-a*), sometimes approximating what in English are called half-rhymes. There are 399 quatrains.

The poem opens with an address to "Celia," actually María Asunción Rivera, with whom Balagtás was in love at the time. In stanzas 1 to 12, the story begins with a description of Florante, an Adonislike youth in love with Laura, daughter of a king. In stanzas 13 to 32, Florante is shackled to a tree in a forest, lamenting the loss of his love, Laura, and the "treason [that] has flung his tyrant-bond" over his native Albania. Ambitious Count Adolph has usurped the throne and seized the dukedom of Florante's father. He has also replaced Florante in the affections of Laura. In stanzas 38 to 68, Florante resumes his lament, recalling the vow Laura made to him, the service he rendered as warrior for the rightful king (her father), the design Laura sewed with golden threads on his armor (with prayers to protect him), and the precious jewels she fixed on his turban, topped by a flashing diamond "set to the 'L' that [headed] her name." He also recalls her taking him to her garden and hanging a garland of flowers around his neck. He longs for her embrace again and resents her "falsehood to [his] trust."

In stanzas 69 to 76, into the forest strolls a Moor, "a warrior of patrician mold," turbaned and garbed like a Persian, who divests himself of his shield and lance and sits down beneath a tree. Suddenly he springs to his feet, calling out, "O Flerida! All joy is dead!" In stanzas 77 to 82, he begins his lament. If Flerida had "been stolen by man of whom I were not son," he would have dealt that man a thousand deaths. Had that man not been his father, he would have "[seen] how all-unsparing spear could be!"

In stanzas 83 to 84, the Moor hears a moaning. It is Florante, who has resumed his lament. Florante broods over the brutality of Count Adolph, torturing his father, and his father's lonely death. Betrayed by his former friends and followers, as Florante's father was dying he "called to heaven . . . that his son be spared." In stanzas 97 to 104, after hearing Florante's tale, the Moor pours forth his own lament, contrasting the love of Florante's father for his son with his own father's ill will, stealing his love and wishing his death.

In stanzas 108 to 127, two panting lions have tracked the helpless Florante. Florante spies them and, thinking he will die, wails, "Adieu, Albania, wretched state of sin, of treachery, of hate." He hopes his country may never know "the smite of fatal spear [or] foeman's spite." Although he finds scorn for "the vows [he has] sworn to lay for its blood," he wishes it well. Florante also bids a loving farewell to Laura, although she is "false" and Adolph is "fiercely bent."

In stanzas 128 to 173, hearing Florante, the Moor hews and hacks his way through the tangled brambles to save him. The lions, "goaded by hunger and wont to kill," leap upon Florante, their "hair on end" and "whip[ping] their tails." The Moor slashes and thrusts at the lions until they drop lifeless into the dust. He cuts the shackles from Florante, who appears dead. The Moor folds Florante's hands on his breast, soothes his face, and prays for his recovery. As he gazes upon the prostrate youth, he ponders the noble face and wonders who this young man is. Florante awakes, and immediately calls out, "Where is Laura?" "Come, set me free," he cries, "when I am dead, yet think of me." Then, more alert, Florante sees the Moor and exclaims, "Am I in hands profane?" The Moor reassures him that although of a creed "noxious" to Florante, he would be "mean" not to help him. He, a Persian, recognizes Florante as an Albanian, but "common fate weaves friendly ties." Although he is a Moor, he is still "subject to heaven's creed" and "commiserates with those in need." The pair is "hushed," and each feels sympathies. The Moor returns to the place where he has been abiding and picks a fruit for their repast. At first reluctant, Florante eats, then lies down to sleep. When morning comes, he embraces his rescuer. The two exchange good wishes, and share their life stories.

In stanzas 174 to 346, Florante tells his story. He was born to a duchy in Albania, heir to Duke Briseus, his father, and Floresca, his mother, a native of Crotona. Florante's father was a confidant and counselor to the king, Linceus. His parents were loving and generous. Once, when he was an infant, a vulture seized him. Aroused by his mother's screams, a cousin killed the predator with an arrow. Another time, a falcon carried away a diamond the baby wore on its breast. When he was nine years old, he would roam the hills with his bow and arrows and bag game. He would stop by a spring and listen to the Naeads' song. Reminding the mother that a pampered child becomes spoiled, the father sent him to Athens when he was 11. He was assigned a good tutor named Pittacus, who helped him overcome his homesickness. Among the students was another from the same town—Adolph, son of Count Silenus, two years older than he, "genteel, his manners never loud." He always walked with bowed head, was soft-spoken, "liked by all the crowd," level-headed even when provoked. But his evasive heart was kept well hidden, and Florante felt a loathing he could not explain.

Days ran their course, and Florante excelled in his studies, outdistancing Adolph, so that after six years his reputation for learning was well known everywhere. Although pretending admiration, Adolph could not keep his jealousy secret very long. In a play in which he played Polynices to Florante's

Eteocles, to their roles as enemies Adolph added a line to the script, "Thief of my honor, be thou dead!" and sprang upon Florante with such force that if Florante had not dodged he would have been stabbed. The teacher intervened, and Adolph was sent back to Albania. Florante spent one more year in Athens, then received a letter that his mother had died. He fainted, and mourned her for two months. His father then sent a boat to bring him back to Albania. As he left, his tutor warned him to beware of Adolph. His best friend, Menander, accompanied him.

As his father welcomed him with a warm embrace, news arrived from the king of Crotona, his mother's homeland, asking aid against foes who were marching on that country—foes who, Florante adds, turning to the Moor, were being led by the Moor's countryman, Aladdin. At this point, the Moor smiles and says that rumors are often untrue, or if true, are magnified. Though brave and famous, he adds, Aladdin is but human, mortal, and the toy of fate. Florante answers that such a famous brave man should be spared.

He continues with his story: Upon hearing the news from Crotona, his father went to the Albanian king, Linceus, accompanied by Florante, "for battle braced." Introduced to the king, Florante was embraced and appointed commander of the troops to fight the Muslims in Crotona. As they sat down to converse, a goddess appeared and announced that Laura had not been faithless, adding, "I know not why she has forgot." Florante's troops "were sent Crotona's way," but he had a moment with Laura. "In tender loving phrases [he] confessed [his] love." His words moved her, but "her 'yes' was left unspoken." They parted in pain.

When Florante arrived in Crotona, the citadel was well-nigh gone, but his men hurled upon the besiegers. Their general, Osmalik, "finding how fierce [was his] onslaught," hacked his way to Florante. They met in single combat, and the Muslim was slain. With the help of Menander, the Albanians were victorious. The city now flung open its gate. The king and his subjects came out to greet and thank them, especially when they learned that Florante was the grandson of their beloved king. After five months in Crotona, Florante returned to Albania, hoping to see Laura again, but when the men sighted the city ramparts, the Christian banner was not in sight—the crescent waved! The city had fallen to Aladdin.

As the troops rested, a Muslim band approached leading a maiden bound with cords, to be beheaded. Florante feared it was Laura, so he raided the band to discover that it was indeed she; Laura had spurned the emir's lust. Florante loosed her bonds, and for the first time heard, "Florante, dear." Her father was in jail, as was his own father. Florante hurled his army against the Muslims, and "Albania was again [its] own." He freed the king and his father, as well as Adolph and the rest of the nobility. Only Adolph was angry, irked by the praise heaped upon Florante. Eager to win the crown and Laura, Adolph brooded, his jealousy from the days in Athens still festering.

Not long after, invaders from the Turkish side appeared. Laura grieved that Florante might die, but "Heaven granted that [he] should win over the great Miramolin." Later, Florante rode to Aetolia, where he won another victory, but received word from the king to hurry back. Leaving his troops with Menander, Florante returned, arriving in the deep of night, and encountered treason. He did not have time to draw his sword. They tied him and put him in prison. The king had been slain and his father taken, and Laura had been sworn to wed Count Adolph.

He spent 18 days in captivity. Then they took him out to the forest and bound him to a tree. Now he awakens to find himself in the Moor's lap, recounting his life's story.

In stanzas 347 to 369, the Moor begins his story. He is actually Aladdin himself, of Persia, son of Al'Adab, the great sultan. Again he calls out the name of Flerida. Florante breaks into tears, "outweeping Aladdin."

For five months they wander the forest. One day while exploring, Aladdin resumes his story: He had won the love of Flerida, a Diana among nymphs, but his father's love intruded. When Aladdin returned from the Albanian victory, his father imprisoned him, saying that Aladdin had abandoned his troops without leave. When news arrived that the Albanians had regained their capital, the sultan pronounced sentence on Aladdin's head, followed by the word that exile instead of death was his lot. He wandered for six long years in this forest, until he learned that his love was incarcerated and waiting to be beheaded. Aladdin rushed back to the king and prostrated himself to beg his father's pardon. The king's answer was that "Till [Aladdin] was wont to [accept] his love, reprieve was none." To keep Flerida alive, he had yielded, but he was still to be banished. He therefore went to Persia and had been roaming for many a year.

In stanzas 370 to 392, Florante and Aladdin cease their discourse, hearing voices drift their way. Laura and Flerida appear. Laura relates her life back in Albania since he left. Vague rumblings have risen and swept over the state to the throne itself. Mobs, then troops, have besieged the palace, shouting, "Death to Linceus the king!" Adolph was behind this, producing a forged document, supposedly from the king, ordering the closure of the granary. The king has been seized and executed, and his staff beheaded. The tyrant count has risen to the throne and threatened Laura with death if she disowned his love. She sought to call Florante from Aetolia, disguising her disgust and hate and seeking five months' time before yielding to his love—planning suicide if Florante should fail to come. She sent a letter to Florante, but he returned only to fall into the clutches of Adolph and ended up bound to the tree in the forest. Menander, receiving the letter, hurried back, but a traitor loyal to Adolph bore her off to him. He would have forced her except for an arrow that from somewhere pierced his heart.

At this point, Flerida breaks in to tell how she heard a maiden's voice in fear and, seeking it out, found Laura struggling and shot her assailant with an arrow. Scarcely has she finished when Menander arrives with troops seeking Adolph. When they see Florante, their first cry of glee is "Long live the king of Albany! And Princess Laura!" They all go back to Albania, where Aladdin and Flerida are christened and, along with Florante and Laura, married. Sultan Ali

Adab dies, and Aladdin hurries homeward. Florante is king of Albania, with his bride, Laura, at his side.

"Under this new monarch's reign,/Peace o'er the kingdom spread again. . . ./ Their people were with kindness blest./They went through life harmonious, aye,/Until Elysium bade them nigh. . . ./Cease, Muse, and unto Celia fly;/ Seek her out, bringing her my cry!" (TAP) (Quirino 1964; Subido 1964)

See also Balagtás, Francesco.

 # FLORIDANTE

Italian epic episode (1587), originally by Bernardo Tasso (1493–1569), meant to be a part of his epic *Amadigi* (1560), but left incomplete at his death. After his death, his son Torquato Tasso (1544–1595) reworked the episode and published it as *Floridante* in 1587. (Durant 1953/1981; Siepmann 1987)

See also Amadigi; Tasso, Bernardo; Tasso, Torquato.

FRANCIADE, LA

Uncompleted French epic poem of four cantos (1572) by Pierre de Ronsard (1524–1585), the central figure in French Renaissance poetry. Although the poet perfected the 12-syllable or alexandrine line, he did not use it in writing his epic, which was intended to be the national epic. It was written in decasyllabic verse, reportedly at the request of King Charles IX. Modeled after Vergil's *Aeneid*, the poem relates the legend of the son of Hector of Troy: Francus, the fabled progenitor of French kings. The first four cantos were published in 1572, but the poem was abandoned after Charles's death in 1574 because Charles's successor, Henry III, was not enchanted with the poet's work. (Harvey and Heseltine 1959)

FREE VERSE

A type of poetry in which the line does not follow a set, repeating metrical pattern, but it can be—and often is—rhymed. A single line may contain several types of feet; its rhythms follow the natural cadence of the spoken word. Although free verse is associated with modern poetry, such as that of Ezra Pound and T. S. Eliot, it was used by Goethe, Milton, Walt Whitman, and Matthew Arnold, as well as by the composers of the Psalms and the Hebrew Song of Songs. (Hornstein 1973)

FRESE, JACOB

Swedish poet, author of the religious epic *Passionstakar* (*Thoughts on the passion*, 1728). He was born about 1690–1691 in Finland, or of Finnish parents. He is hailed as Sweden's first significant subjective-emotional poet. His lyrics and hymns, as well as his epic, are steeped in a gentle emotional pietism that reflected the prevailing trend of eighteenth-century thought. He died in 1729. (Magill 1994)

FRITIOF'TAGER ARV
(*Frithiofs saga* or *Fridthjófs saga*)

Swedish lyrical epic cycle (1825) by Esaias Tegnér (1782–1846). Based on an old Icelandic saga, it is considered one of the masterpieces of Scandinavian Romanticism and remains a popular Romantic love poem with the Swedish people. The hero Frithiof, "the heir of peace," although perhaps largely the composite product of Tegnér's creative mind, combines the highest qualities of nobility and gentility with those of valor, virility, and patiotism, making him a popular ideal in nineteenth-century Scandinavia and beyond. The Frithiof cycle consists of 24 poems composed in a variety of meters, notably hexameter (six-foot catalectic dactylic lines), and a variety of stanza forms tailored to fit the circumstances depicted in each poem. By the beginning of the twentieth century the epic had been translated by some 50 different people into 11 foreign languages. (Preminger 1974; Siepmann 1987)

   See also Tegnér, Esaias.

FROST THE RED NOSE

Russian populist epic poem (1863) by Nikolay Nekrasov (1821–1878). This popular narrative poem, classified as a "civic poem," depicts the death by exposure of a peasant widow while she is gathering wood in the forest to build her husband's coffin. The "civic poem," which has no counterpart in the West, depicts the ugly aspects of reality in literary imitation of folk epic. The widow's death is described with reverence and detachment rather than with sentimentality. Nature is depicted as a monumental force. (Bristol 1991)

GARRETT, JOÃO BATISTA DA SILVA LEITÃO DE ALMEIDA

See Almeida Garrett, João Batista da Silva Leitão de.

THE GAUCHO MARTÍN FIERRO

Argentine epic poem in two parts (1872/1873 and 1879) by José Hernández (1834–1886). Part I, consisting of 2,316 lines, bears the publication date 1872 but was not actually published until 1873. By 1878 the poem had gone through 11 printings, with more than 50,000 copies in circulation. No other Argentine publication, particularly poetry, has become so popular. In fact, it was so well received that in 1879 a sequel was published, entitled *La vuelta de Martín Fierro* (The return of Martín Fierro).

Part One, entitled *El gaucho Martín Fierro,* or *La ido* (The flight), contains 14 cantos. Canto I is an introduction sung by the gaucho Martín Fierro—he accompanies himself on the guitar—asking the reader to listen to a story told by "a gaucho on the run." He describes himself as a hard-working and willing father and husband, yet still people take him for an outlaw.

In Canto II, Martín continues the introduction, describing the life of the Argentine cowboy whose work was once more like play. Now things are different, and the gaucho has to hide to keep from being beaten or being sent to the frontier with the army.

In Canto III, Martín continues his story: He once had children, cattle, a wife. Then he is sent to the frontier by the government, to fight the Indians. He is chosen because the judge has a grudge against him for failing to vote when the judge was running for office. The judge promises the men will serve only six months. Martín leaves his wife and children, stripping their home bare, loading up everything he has except his cattle, which he leaves in the care of his wife.

On the frontier, the men discover there are no barracks, and they are given no guns, no supplies. The colonel sends them out to work in his own fields.

191

Martín sows wheat, builds a corral, cuts adobe for a wall, and performs other back-breaking labor for more than a year. Since the colonel keeps the guns locked away, the Indians come and go as they please, stealing anything they want, taking prisoners and skinning them alive.

In Canto IV he tells how the gauchos growl about their poverty. Martín does not even have a shirt. The commandant even takes his horse. Another year goes by. Martín doesn't get paid because he isn't on the lists.

In Canto V he is tied to the stakes: "They stretched me out/just like a piece of fresh hide!"

In Canto VI, after almost three years, one night he grabs a horse and escapes. Back home, he finds nothing left of his place. A neighbor tells him the government took his land from his wife and sold his cattle. They hired his sons out as peons. His wife is gone, "flew off/with some ladies' man" so as to have bread to eat. Martín has no recourse.

In Canto VII, with no place to live, "without even enough to buy a smoke," he wanders in search of his sons. One night he enters a dance hall where he finds many friends. He gets drunk and insults a black couple, calling the woman a cow and singing a nasty song: "God made the whites;/St. Peter, the mulattoes;/but the devil made the blacks. . . ." The black man attacks him, and after a vicious fight, Martín kills him.

In Canto VIII, in another barroom brawl, he kills a smart-mouthed gaucho who has connections with the commandant. Thereafter he is on the run.

In Canto IX, Martin tells how he lives as as an outlaw. One night the police track him down. He makes a valiant but futile effort to fend them off until one of the men, Cruz, joins him against them, saying, "I won't let you bastards/kill a brave man like this!" The two of them kill many of the attackers and drive the rest away.

In Canto X, Sergeant Cruz takes up the story, also in song. He once had a woman until his friend, the commandant, took her from him after sending Cruz on missions far from home. When he returns and catches them together, he leaves home for good.

In Canto XI, Cruz continues his story: He wanders around "like an orphan" until one night at a dance a gaucho provokes him with some unflattering song. In the brawl that follows, Cruz kills him.

In Canto XII, Cruz is hunted by the police until a judge friend hands him a *placamation* and makes him a sergeant in the police force. But Cruz's sympathies are all for the gauchos who are often "hounded/without mercy by the law. . . ."

In Canto XIII, Martín Fierro is again speaking. He suggests that they sneak off to Indian territory, where they can survive handily as members of a tribe. He says, "Anyone who can handle the *bolas*,/or throw a lasso,/or sit a half-wild horse,/. . . can't be too bad off."

The narrator resumes the story, describing how Martín slings down his guitar, splintering it: He is through singing. Martín and Cruz round up a string of horses from a nearby ranch and cross over the frontier. As they look back at the last of civilization, two tears roll down Martín's face.

In Part Two, *La vuelta,* Martín tells of traveling with Cruz across the pampas and the desert into Indian territory. They plan to make friends and become useful members of a tribe, but they are given no chance. They are ambushed while they sleep, taken prisoner, and their horses and gear stolen. They are held separately and tortured for two years by the Indians. Then a tolerant chief allows them to pitch a tent and bunk together with Indian guards standing outside. The Indians force them to ride in raiding parties against the settlers.

The Indians contract smallpox from the settlers. The chief who befriended them is one of the victims. Nursing him, Cruz contracts the disease himself and dies.

Alone again, Martín escapes, rescuing a woman who has been whipped with the intestines of her own dead baby. They travel for miles to the pampas, where they come upon a ranch. Martín leaves the woman there and heads for home.

He discovers that the judge who sent him to the army has died and that he is no longer a wanted man. Elated, he goes to the races and there meets his long-lost sons, who tell him the sad news that their mother is dead. They, too, have been cheated and tortured by the government.

His older son sings his story of being unjustly arrested and imprisoned for a killing. He has spent many grinding years in prison.

His younger son sings about inheriting some property from an aunt. The unscrupulous judge appoints a tutor, Vezcacha, who robs the boy, and beats and starves him. The boy ends up wandering the countryside until he is picked up by the army and sent to the frontier, where he receives the same treatment the others have endured.

A young man, Picardia, appears and sings his song about the tortures he has endured at the hands of the army officers. He reveals that he is Cruz's son. They celebrate the reunion with wine and revelry. A black man joins them and engages Martín in a singing contest.

The black man sings that he has come to avenge the death of his brother, whom Martín killed years before. But before another fight erupts, other gauchos intervene and send Martín and his party away.

The four soon part, each to lead his own life. Martín advises his sons and Picardia to be loyal to their friends, respectful of the property of others, obedient to the law, honest in all things, and, should they find a woman, to be faithful and respectful. As the four part, each takes on a new name. Martín sings his final song and lays down his guitar forever. (Hernández 1936, 1974)

See also Hernández, José; Martín Fierro.

 # GAUTIER D'ARRAS

French poet (fl. 12th c.), author of epic romances, some inspired by the political aspirations of Eleanor of Aquitaine and Henry II of England. Gautier was a contemporary of two other French poets of note: Marie de France and Chrétien de Troyes. He belonged to the family of the castle bailiffs of Arras. He was an official, at least as early as 1160, of the court of Philippe d'Alsace, count of Flanders, under whose auspices he began his romance *Eracle,* which has a Byzantine background and is a mythical account of the life of Byzantine emperor Heraclius. It was begun about 1176–1178 as a romance for Marie de Champagne and Thibaur V of Blois; however, by the time it was completed (ca. 1179–1181), it was probably intended for Baldwin V of Hainaut. Another, *Ille et Galeron,* in a pseudo-Breton setting, was written for Beatrix of Vienne, wife of Frederick I Barbarossa. Although Gautier lacked the skill and depth of Chrétien, his work attempted to mediate between the austere tradition of old heroic epics and the contemporary predilection for secular legends and Persian fairy tales. Gautier died in 1185. (Harvey and Heseltine 1959; Heer 1961)

 # GAUTIER DE METZ
(Also Gauthier de Més en Loherains)

French poet and priest of Metz (fl. 13th c.), usually credited as being the author of *L'Image du monde* (The mirror of the world, ca. 1246 or 1247), an "encyclopaedic poem" describing the universe. The lengthy poem, also known as *Mappemonde,* is based on the medieval Latin work *Imago mundi* by Honorius Inclusus. Written in 11,000 octosyllabic verses, it tells the story of creation, mixing in geography, astronomy, cosmology, monsters, and treasures. The poet concludes that it is impossible to understand a universe that its Creator will always control. Gassouin, a Flemish theologian, is credited by some as being author of the work. (Harvey and Heseltine 1959)

 # *GAWAIN AND THE GREEN KNIGHT*
(Also *Sir Gawain and the Green Knight*)

Middle English alliterative metrical romance (ca. 1370) by an unknown poet who was a contemporary of Chaucer. It is considered the masterpiece of medieval alliterative poetry and the greatest of the Arthurian legends. Some scholars theorize that its author was the poet of "The Pearl and Its Jeweler," because the story is found in another Middle English manuscript that begins with "The Pearl." Several poets have been suggested as its author: John Donne, Hugh Prat, Hughown, Ralph Strode, and Hugo de Masci (Hugh Mascy). The author was well read, for he united themes from Latin, French, and Celtic literature. Two well-known central incidents, the Beheading Game Challenge and the Temptation with Exchange of Gifts, are combined to form the plot.

Told in stanzas of varying lengths, the poem is divided into four sections, called Fits. Each long alliterative line is divided in half, each half containing two strong accents and an unlimited number of unaccented syllables in the manner of Anglo-Saxon verse. In French fashion, each stanza ends with five short rhyming lines (*ababa*).

In Fit I, the New Year's revelry at King Arthur's court is interrupted by the appearance of the Green Knight, "an awesome fellow," who is "the handsomest of horsemen" with "hips and haunches" that are "elegant and small." He is dressed in green, trimmed in fur. He sits astride a "mettlesome" green horse and holds an ax of green hammered gold and steel. He announces to the assembly, "I crave in this court a Christmas game." He dares any knight present to strike him a blow with the ax, on the condition that he can return the blow one year later. The king's nephew Gawain, sitting beside the beautiful Queen Guinevere, accepts the challenge and lops off the knight's head. The knight picks up the head, which instructs Gawain to meet him at the Green Chapel in one year, and departs.

In Fit II, ten months later, after All Saints' Day, Gawain sets off in search of the Green Chapel to fulfill his bargain. On Christmas Eve he arrives at a marvelous castle whose master, Lord Bertilak (or Bercilak), invites him to spend the holidays with him and his wife ("most beautiful of body and bright of complexion . . . excelling Guinevere"). Also present is an older woman whose body is "stumpy and squat,/Her buttocks bulging wide. . . ." The castellan tells him that the Green Chapel is only two miles away, an easy ride on the appointed day of his confrontation. The lord of the manor proposes that Gawain rest at the castle each day, entertained by the beautiful wife, while he goes hunting. At the end of each day, the men should exchange what each has won during the day.

In Fit III, while the host goes on three hunts for deer, boar, and fox, the wife visits Gawain's bedroom three times, tempting the noble knight's virtue. But although she tries hard to "win him to wickedness," the two only "laugh and play," and Gawain receives only her kisses, which he gives the host in exchange for the animals from the daily hunt. On the third day, the lady presses Gawain "so hotly" that he is sorely tempted. Not only is he concerned for his courtesy, "lest he be called caitiff/But more especially for his evil plight if he should plunge into sin/And dishonor the owner of the house treacherously." When the wife fails to seduce Gawain, she persuades him to accept her girdle of green silk, claiming that "As long as he laps it closely about him,/No hero under heaven can hack him to pieces,/For he cannot be killed by any cunning on earth." Gawain accepts the gift but fails to mention it to his host during the evening's exchange.

In Fit IV, on New Year's Day, Gawain goes to the Green Chapel, where he again meets the Green Knight. The knight strikes him three blows to the neck. The first two do not touch him, but the third nicks his neck. The knight reveals himself to Gawain: it is his host, Bertilak, who was sent to Arthur's court by the sorceress Morgan le Fay, the old woman, in order "to grieve Guinevere and goad her to death." The first two blows have missed because Gawain resisted temptation twice. The third nicked his neck as a reproof for his failure to reveal the gift of the girdle. Now that the challenge is over, Bertilak begs Gawain to return to his castle, but Gawain refuses. He returns to Arthur's court, vowing to wear the girdle as a reminder of his moral lapse, a "mark of shame." He tells the story to his peers at the Round Table. They gather around to comfort him, judging that he acted honorably and vowing also to wear green girdles for his sake. The manuscript closes with the motto of the Order of the Garter: "Honi soit qui mal y pense" (Evil to him who evil thinks). (Stone 1959/1974)

 # GEORGE THE PISÍDIAN
(Also George Pisides, George Pisid, or George of Pisidia)

Byzantine deacon, archivist, and poet (fl. early 7th c.), author of the religious epic *Hexaëmeron* (Of six days) and works chronicling the reign and celebrating the exploits of Byzantine emperor Heraclius (610–641). Under the patriarch Sergius (610–639), George was deacon, skeuophylox, and chartophylox (archivist, in other words) of Hagia Sophia, the great domed basilica of Constantinople. In addition, he was a remarkable poet whom later Byzantines compared to Euripides. He made use of new meters, particularly 12-syllable iambic verse, in imitation of classical Greek poetry. It became the chief meter of medieval Greek poets.

He was an eyewitness to much of the history of the time, because he accompanied Heraclius on his first campaigns against the Avars, a raiding tribe of the Caucasus. In 622 he chronicled the emperor's victorious expedition against the Persians in a eulogy entitled "The Expedition of Heraclius against the Persians." In 626 the Avars attacked Constantinople but were repulsed, an occasion George celebrated with a poem in iambic trimeter. In 627 he wrote a three-canto panegyric called *The Heracliad* (or *Heraclias*) commemorating the emperor's victory over the Parthians and the recapture of the Holy Cross, which the Parthians had taken during an earlier raid on Jerusalem.

His masterpiece was the *Hexaëmeron,* retelling the biblical creation story. (Gibbon, Vol. II n.d.; Ostrogorsky 1969)

 # *GEORGICS*

Latin didactic poem (ca. 37–30 B.C.) by Vergil. Ostensibly on the subject of agriculture, the poem is composed in four books and is based on Hesiod's *Works and Days.* In one sense it is a reply to Lucretius's *De rerum natura,* describing the devastation wrought by a plague in Athens. Vergil is not presenting an instruction book for farmers; rather, he is depicting the country's farm life as the ideal life. The *Georgics* has been called the finest sustained tribute ever paid to a country by one of its citizens. One of the main themes of the book is that the ideals of Rome should spread to and enhance all of Italy.

Book I begins with the assurance that the enterprise has been favored by the gods. It gives general tips on agriculture: the raising of crops and the reading of weather signs; however, the poet cannot put aside his patriotism nor resist commenting on the current political situation, praying that Augustus (Octavius Caesar) will save the Romans, strife-torn since the time of the assassination of Julius Caesar, from civil war.

Book II speaks of the care of grapevines and fruit and olive trees, but goes far beyond that. It is an eloquent paean to Italy, to its heroes and to the produce of the soil.

Book III begins with the poet's resolution of rededication to his task. He discuses the care of livestock and their reproduction. The book ends with a description of a cattle plague in the Alps that wiped out all livestock life for a while.

Book IV discusses the raising of honeybees, describing the sacred significance of the miracle of regeneration and depicting the bees as examples of the ideal Roman community: "little Romans." Within this framework the poet expounds his philosophy concerning death and resurrection by using a myth within another myth: the episode of Aristaeus, together with the story of Orpheus and Eurydicē. The legend is that the bees belonging to the beekeeping god Aristaeus all die. His mother, the sea goddess Cyrene, sends him to Proteus for advice. Proteus informs him that the dryads have killed his bees, avenging the death of Eurydicē from a snakebite she received while fleeing from the amorous Aristaeus. Proteus tells the story of Orpheus and his wife, Eurydicē; how Orpheus goes to Hades, where Pluto and Persephone agree to let Eurydicē return to earth with him if he will not look back. But Orpheus forgets his promise and looks back to see if she is following him, thus losing her forever. (Vergil's is the oldest account of the story of Eurydicē.) Cyrene suggests that Aristaeus make a sacrifice to the two as atonement, so Aristaeus sacrifices four bulls and four heifers to the ghosts of Orpheus and Eurydicē. Nine days later, a swarm of bees fly up from the rotting carcasses. (Highet 1976; Howatson and Chilvers 1993; Siepmann 1987; Virgil/Dryden, Vol. V 1979)

See also Vergil.

 # *GERUSALEMME LIBERATA*
(Jerusalem delivered)

Italian epic poem (1581) by Torquato Tasso (1544–1595). The epic was finished in draft form in 1575, revised, and published in 1581. Although Tasso continued to revise the poem and finally published a drastically altered version as *Gerusalemme conquistata* (Jerusalem conquered), the 1581 edition is considered the definitive version. It consists of 20 cantos, in ottava rima. It is an account of the First Crusade, its main episodes and characters historical except for Rinaldo. It was written for the express purpose of exhorting the Christian peoples of Europe to unite against the heathen. Tasso intended to rival Ariosto's *Orlando Furioso* and to produce an epic in the true classic model. Despite its religious orientation, its poetic focus is on the love stories, healthy and physical.

In Canto One, after an invocation to the Heavenly Muse, in the seventh year of the Crusade, Godfrey of Bouillon is chosen by the archangel Gabriel to lead the Crusaders. His army marches on Jerusalem, where they lay siege to Aladine, prince of Judaea.

In Canto Two, Aladine seizes an image of the Virgin Mary and places it in one of the royal mosques as a magical safeguard, but someone steals it away. Unable to discover the culprits, Aladine sets out on a general massacre of his Christian subjects, including Sophronia, who accuses herself to save her fellow Christians. With her lover Olindo, she is tied to a stake for burning, but Clorinda, an Amazonlike warrior from Persia with the Pagans, intercedes on their behalf. Aletes and Argantes, ambassadors from the king of Egypt, come to the Christian army to inquire as to their purpose, and are not satisfied. Aletes returns to Egypt, but Argantes goes to Jerusalem to assist the Saracens.

In Canto Three, the Crusaders arrive before Jerusalem. Clorinda sallies out against a party of their foragers. Godfrey sends Tancred against her. Meanwhile, from the top of a tower, Erminia, daughter of the king of Antioch, identifies the principal Christians for Aladine. Dudon, captain of the Adventurers, drives the Pagans back, but is killed by Argantes. The Christians begin to build siege machines.

In Canto Four, Pluto (Satan), indignant at the Christian successes, calls a council, then sends his devils to harass the Christians. One of them, Armida, also an enchantress, goes to the Christian camp and attempts to seduce their chiefs. Introduced to Godfrey, she gives him a fictitious account of herself and asks for assistance to win back the Syrian kingdom of which she has been dispossessed. Godfrey refuses, then partially relents, and permits ten of the Adventurers to aid her.

In Canto V, Eustace, brother of Godfrey and in love with Armida, persuades Rinaldo, of whom he is jealous, to solicit the position of Captain of the Adventurers after the death of Dudon. Influenced by one of the devils, a rival, Gernando, disparages Rinaldo, who kills him. Godfrey promises punishment to Rinaldo, so upon the advice of Tancred, Rinaldo quits the camp. Armida accompanies him, with the companions given her and scores of others, including Eustace. News arrives of an Egyptian expedition and of the interception of the Christian supply convoy by the Arabs. Famine threatens the Christians.

In Canto Six, Argantes challenges the Christians to send one of their knights into single combat. Tancred is named. On the way, Tancred is entranced by the sight of Clorinda, who is stationed with a corps of a thousand men to watch the combat. Otho takes Tancred's place, is unhorsed by Argantes, and taken prisoner. By nightfall both Tancred and Argantes are wounded, and action is suspended for six days. Erminia, who has fallen in love with Tancred, the enemy, is torn between love and honor. Wearing Clorinda's armor, she goes to the Christian camp to cure Tancred's wounds. She is discovered and flees, pursued by Tancred, who thinks she is Clorinda.

In Canto VII, Erminia takes refuge in a shepherd's camp by the river Jordan. Tancred loses her trail, and is led by a treacherous guide to Armida's castle on an island in the Dead Sea, where he is imprisoned. The combat between

Argantes and Tancred is resumed, with Raymond, count of Toulouse, substituting for Tancred. God sends an angel to protect him. The Devil assumes the shape of Clorinda and wounds Raymond. Godfrey comes to his aid and almost defeats the Pagans, when the Devil raises a storm that confuses the Christians and permits Clorinda to return to the charge. The Christians retreat with great losses.

In Canto VIII a survivor brings news of the Arab massacre of troops under Sven, prince of Denmark, and of Sven's death and miraculous burial by some supernatural agent. He has brought Sven's sword to Rinaldo to avenge that death, but a patrol arrives with news of Rinaldo's apparent death, supposedly by the machinations of Godfrey. The Italian, Argillan, incites his troops to mutiny. Godfrey quiets the tumult and imprisons Argillan.

In Canto IX, Alecto, an aide to the Devil, leads the Turkish sultan Solyman to a night attack on the Christian camp. Godfrey hastens to meet the assault. God sends the archangel Michael to drive the demons back to Hell. Clorinda distinguishes herself in battle. Meanwhile, Argillan has escaped from prison and hastens to the battle scene. He is killed by Solyman, but his followers win the battle. Aladine calls off his troops, who are pursued amid great slaughter.

In Canto X, Solyman decides to join the Egyptian army, which is now advancing on the Christians. On the way, he meets the sorcerer Ismen, who conveys him in a magic chariot to Jerusalem, which he enters, invisible in a cloud. He goes to the council chamber of the king, where they are debating. Submission to Godfrey is suggested when Solyman, becoming visible, tells them he will join them. They will fight the Christians together. The king resigns his throne to Solyman. William of England tells Godfrey about Armida's enchantments and how Rinaldo delivered them from captivity. Peter the Hermit confirms that Rinaldo is alive and well, and foretells his future glories.

In Canto XI, Peter the Hermit urges a Christian assault and leads the army to a mass on the Mount of Olives. Godfrey assumes the dress of a private footsoldier to share their dangers, and the other princes follow suit. The assault begins, and the Christians make a breach in the walls. Clorinda, Solyman, and Argantes lead the Pagan defense. Godfrey is wounded and has to leave the field, but Tancred turns the Pagans back. An Angel from Heaven miraculously heals Godfrey, who returns to the combat. At nightfall he withdraws his army.

In Canto XII, Clorinda determines to burn the Christians' large wooden siege tower. The eunuch Arsetes tries to dissuade her by telling her of her birth as a Christian but upbringing as a pagan. Unpersuaded, she continues her assault, with Argantes, and sets fire to the tower. She flees back to the city, only to find that in the confusion she has been shut out. Tancred has trailed her, and they engage in single combat. He kills her, but before she dies he baptizes her. When he discovers what he has done, he despairs and tries to kill himself. He is rebuked by Peter the Hermit, but consoled by Clorinda in a dream. Argantes vows revenge.

In Canto XIII, Ismeno, the sorcerer, peoples the only available forest with demons, who frighten the Christian artificers repairing the damage done to the siege machines. Alcasto, a Swiss, tries to break the charm but retires in confusion. Tancred then undertakes the task, entering the forest and preparing to cut down a tree, when a demon in the guise of Clorinda asks him to stop. Peter the Hermit predicts the trials will soon cease, but heat and drought continue to plague the Christians, and the troops begin to desert. Godfrey prays to God and, moved by his entreaties, God orders that the sufferings end. It rains.

In Canto XIV, Godfrey is transported in a dream vision to Heaven, where he interviews Hugo, deceased commander of the French forces, who assures him of future success and tells him to recall Rinaldo. Charles, the Dane, and Ubaldo, one of the Adventurers, are sent to look for Rinaldo. Following Peter the Hermit's instructions, they go to the Ascalon River. They find an old man walking on the surface of the water. He takes them to his habitation under the bed of the river, then tells them what happened to Rinaldo since he left the camp: how he was ensnared by Armida, who fell in love with him and carried him away to an enchanted palace on the Peak of Tenerife. The old man instructs them how to reach Rinaldo and free him.

In Canto XV, Charles and Ubaldo embark on a ship steered by a mysterious female and sail through the Mediterranean, enter the Atlantic Ocean, and land on Tenerife. They climb a mountain guarded by wild beasts and covered with snow. At the top they find a perpetual spring and the Fountain of Laughter with two nymphs bathing in it. They resist the nymphs' allurements and enter the palace of Armida.

In Canto XVI, Charles and Ubaldo trace a maze, enter the magic garden, and find Rinaldo and Armida together. Armida retires, and, seized with shame, Rinaldo follows the knights out of the palace. Armida pursues them and pleads with Rinaldo, who rejects her and leaves. She tries her incantations, to no avail, then follows him to the seashore and begs him to take her with him, again unsuccessfully. In anger she vows revenge, destroys her palace, and, mounting her car (chariot), flies through the air to her castle on the Dead Sea to join the Egyptian army at Gaza.

In Canto XVII, the caliph of Egypt reviews his troops. Armida arrives unexpectedly with her auxiliaries, and Emiren, a renegade Christian, is appointed commander of the army. Armida offers her hand to anyone who will kill Rinaldo. Adrastus, an Indian king, and Tissaphernes, a distinguished Egyptian soldier, pledge to carry out her wishes, but they are jealous of each other and begin to quarrel. The caliph intervenes. Meanwhile, Rinaldo and the two knights land in Palestine, where they meet the old man who had entertained them in Ascalon; he is a magician. He gives Rinaldo a suit of armor and a shield with the exploits of Rinaldo's ancestors, the House of Este. Charles gives him Sven's sword. They proceed to the camp with Peter the Hermit, who foretells to Rinaldo the glories of his descendants.

In Canto XVIII, Godfrey welcomes Rinaldo, and Peter the Hermit tells him how to overcome the enchantments of the monsters of the Enchanted Forest. He climbs the Mount of Olives, offers up his devotions, and proceeds to the forest, where he begins working on the siege machines. He is hampered by enchantments and a demon in the shape of Armida, but when he cuts down a tree the enchantments cease. New engines are constructed by the Pagans, and Ismene makes artificial fire. A carrier pigeon pursued by a hawk takes refuge in Godfrey's bosom. Under its wing is a letter from the Egyptian general to the Pagan king, promising help if they will hold out a few more days. Godfrey orders an immediate assault and sends Tancred's squire Vafrine, disguised as a Syrian, to spy on the Egyptian army. The assault begins. Tancred mounts the wall, followed by Eustace. Ismene resorts to incantations and is killed on the wall, two sorceresses at his side. The archangel Michael appears to Godfrey and shows him invisible armies on his side. Godfrey gains a foothold on the wall and is confronted by Sultan Solyman, who unexpectedly retreats. Godfrey plants the cross on the wall of Jerusalem. Tancred does the same elsewhere, but Raymond is less successful on the southern side. When the Pagan king hears the Christian shouts of victory, he retires to a strong tower. The Christians pour in on all sides and begin a dreadful slaughter.

In Canto XIX, Tancred and Argantes meet on the wall, retire to a distance from the city, and engage in single combat. Argantes is slain, and Tancred faints from loss of blood. Jerusalem is sacked by the Christians. The Pagan army and much of the populace take refuge in Solomon's Temple, into which Rinaldo forces his way, slaughtering many of the refugees. Solyman and Aladine retreat to the Tower of David, and Raymond, attempting to force an entrance, is stunned by the sultan but rescued by his own soldiers. At nightfall Godfrey calls off his troops. The next day he sends Vafrine to spy on the Egyptians, now camped near Gaza. He discovers Erminia with Armida, and she escapes with him. She tells him of an Egyptian plot against Godfrey and confides her passion for Tancred. They discover Argantes's body and the wounded Tancred. With her attentions and care, Tancred recovers. Soldiers arrive and carry Tancred and the body of Argantes into the city. Vafrine reports his findings to Godfrey, who proceeds to blockade the citadel where Aladine has taken refuge.

In Canto XX, after a day of rest the Crusaders begin the battle. Each commander, Godfrey among the Christians and Emiren with the Egyptians, exhorts his troops. The fortunes of the contestants waver back and forth. An attempt on the life of Godfrey is foiled and the attacker slain. An endeavor by the Egyptians to surround the Christians is checked by Rinaldo. He passes by Armida, who, despairing and fearful of being made a prisoner, retires from the battle, escorted by Altamore, one of her suitors. Solyman, accompanied by Aladine, wreaks havoc. He fells Raymond. Tancred rises from his sickbed to protect Raymond, who revives and kills Aladine. Rinaldo kills Solyman. Armida flees to a secluded place, followed by Rinaldo, and is on the point of killing herself when Rinaldo persuades her otherwise. Her fondness for Rinaldo returns. He offers himself as her champion, and she offers herself as his handmaid. The Egyptians are totally routed. Emiren, their commander, is slain by Godfrey, and King Altamore is taken prisoner. Godfrey goes to the temple with the entire army. "Thus conquered Godfrey." He hangs up his arms, and drops to his knees before the Holy Sepulchre to pray and perform his vows. (TAP) (Bowra 1961; Nash 1987; Tasso/Nelson n.d.)

See also Tasso, Torquato.

THE GESTES OF STILFRID AND BRUNCVIK

Medieval Czech epic poem (ca. 14th c.) by an unknown author. The poem is an adaptation of the German traditional epic *Nibelungenlied,* the tale of Sigfried and Brunhild. A synopsis of *Nibelungenlied* can be found in the *Encyclopedia of Traditional Epics.* (Dvornik 1962)

THE GHOST DANCE

The Sioux Ghost Dance religion, which plays a part in *Cycle of the West* by John Neihardt, was a special phenomenon out of the Sioux war with the white man, and an offshoot of the Messiah cult founded by a Paiute in Nevada sometime between 1869 and 1872. The founder claimed to be the son of a white man, a *capita* (Spanish captain?), who did some preaching and introduced a new religious dance, and whose teachings laid the foundation for a Messiah religion. Indians from Oregon and Idaho helped spread his influence. When he died in about 1870, his son, Wovotka, 14 years old, was taken into the home of a white man, Dave Wilson, who gave him the name of Jack Wilson, a name by which he was known to the whites. In later years he assumed the name of his paternal grandfather, Kwohitsauq, but has generally been known by his original name, and to the Indians as the Messiah.

When he was about 18, Wovotka claimed that God took him in a trance to heaven, where he saw all the people who had died. He was to go back and tell his people to be good and love one another, and to live in peace with the whites. He then given the dance, which he was to take back to his people. If the people faithfully obeyed these instructions, they would at last be reunited with those in the other world. The dance spread to the Sioux in 1880.

The dance opened with a prayer to the Messiah. Participants were decorated with red paint by the medicine man, and they wore eagle feathers, which would waft them over the earth. In the center of the dance circle was a tree, where the dead would come. Peculiar to the Sioux was the wearing of the ghost shirt. The basic principle of the dance was to bring on the time when all Indians, living and dead, would be reunited upon a regenerated earth free from disease, misery, and death. A spiritual power ruled over men of all races, seeking universal peace.

Under the influence of Sitting Bull, however, the movement became hostile to the whites. With the return of the "ghosts" the whites would be annihilated, because the Indians would be reinforced by the dead. The white man's gunpowder—through a sympathy with Nature—would no longer have the power to penetrate the Indians' skin. Another faction, to which Big Foot (Sitanka) belonged, believed in discarding all warlike activities and seeking happiness by practicing honesty, peace, and goodwill among themselves and with the whites: In the new world, both races would dwell in peace together. A struggle between the two factions frightened the soldiers, resulting in the massacre at Wounded Knee. (TAP) (Mooney 1965)

See also Cycle of the West.

 GITAGOVINDA
(Song of the cowherd, or Song of Lord Govinda)

Indian Sanskrit epic or dramatic poem (ca. 1200) written by Jayadeva. The poem, into which are interspersed 24 religious/erotic lyrics, is based on the *Bhāgavata-Purāṇa*. The form of the poem is that of the mahākāvya, which typically consists of a number of relatively short cantos, each using a meter appropriate to the subject of the episode described in the canto. The cantos are characterized by alliteration and lyricism.

The poem describes the love of Krishna, the divine cowherd, and Rādhā, his consort and favorite of the *gopis* (wives and daughters of the cowherds). During the poem, erotic human love becomes transmuted into divine love.

It begins with Krishna's attraction for the beautiful Rādhā, follows their estrangement and Krishna's abandonment, and Rādhā's deep yearning that ensues: "While her body lies sick/From smoldering fever of love,/Her heart suffers strange slow suffocation. . . ./When exhaustion forces her to meditate on you,/On the cool body of her solitary lover,/She feels secretly revived. . . ." Finally, with the aid of a sakhā (Rādhā's confidant), they are reconciled.

Hindus see the poem as profoundly religious, speaking of the divine dimension of human love that Rādhā symbolizes for all who seek union with the divine (Krishna). The songs of the *Gitagovinda* continue to be sung in the temples and during festivals—particularly at the festival in Krishna's honor in Bengal. (Miller 1977)

See also Jayadeva.

 GODFREY

Godfrey (Godefroi) of Bouillon, who appears in *Gerusalemme liberata* by Torquato Tasso, was a descendant of Charlemagne and son of Count Eustace II and Ida, daughter of Duke Godfrey II of Lower Lorraine. Although named Godfrey IV, duke of Lower Lorraine, by his uncle (ca. 1060–1 July 1100), the Holy Roman Emperor gave Godfrey only the lordship of Bouillon until 1089, when Godfrey helped the emperor in his war with the Saxons. With his brothers Eustace and Baldwin, he joined the First Crusade in 1096, and was chosen one of its leaders. After the capture of Jerusalem in July 1099, he was named first Latin ruler of Palestine after a refusal by Raymond of Toulouse. However, he refused the title of king and accepted instead the designation *Advocatus Sancti Sepulchri* (Defender of the Holy Sepulchre). Eventually he alienated most of the other leaders, who returned to their homelands or to other parts of Palestine, leaving Jerusalem defenseless. He beat off an Egyptian attack. He also acknowledged himself a vassal of Daimbert, patriarch of Jerusalem, thereby involving himself in fratricidal struggles among allies for control of Palestine. Despite his weakness as a ruler, he was idolized in legend as the perfect Christian knight, the hero of the Crusade. (TAP)

See also *Gerusalemme liberata.*

 # GOETHE, JOHANN WOLFGANG VON

German poet, dramatist, critic, scientist, and novelist; author, among his many great works, of two epic poems, *Reineke Fuchs* (1794) and *Hermann und Dorothea* (1797) and an unfinished epic, *Achilleis* (1799). A polymath, considered a genius in many fields, Goethe distinguished himself in optics, mineralogy, anatomy, and botany, as well as in the literary arts. He was also a musician and painter.

Goethe was born in 1749 in Frankfort, Germany, the son of prosperous and educated middle-class parents. His father, Johann Kaspar Goethe, was a retired lawyer, formerly an imperial councillor. His mother, Katharine Elisabeth Textor, was the daughter of a Bürgermeister, a fashionable tailor of Frankfort. As a lad, Goethe was taught Latin, Greek, French, and Italian, and later he learned English and Hebrew. The French occupation of Frankfort afforded Goethe an early introduction to French theater, still in the midst of its neoclassicism phase, which style Goethe copied with his first dramatic efforts. At the age of 16 he entered the University of Leipzig to begin a three-year study of law, among many other things. During his stay in Leipzig he produced a songbook, *Das Leipziger Liederbuch,* some poems, and plays in the popular rococo mode.

Illness forced him to drop out in 1768 before his studies were completed, but during his recuperation at home in the next year and a half, he took up the study of chemistry and alchemy and dabbled in astology and occult philosophy. In 1770 he resumed his legal education at the University of Strassburg. He came under the influence of Johann Gottfried Herder, who preached against the literary rules and confinement of French neoclassicism in favor of the natural spontaneity of Romanticism. Literature was suddenly awash in emotions. Goethe became recognized as a leader in the literary movement later known as *Sturm und Drang* (Storm and Stress).

When he completed his studies in 1771, he returned to Frankfort, where he practiced law for the next five years. But he had already distinguished himself by writing some fine love poetry. At the time he was already at work on *Faust,* and he was helping to edit the *Frankfort Scholarly Review.* In 1773 he published the most powerful work of the *Sturm und Drang* period: a play called *Götz von Berlichingen,* about the medieval knight of the same name. The following year he published a short autobiographical novel, *Die Leiden des jungen Werther* (The sorrows of young Werther), about a hopeless love affair with one Charlotte

Buff, who was betrothed to another. During his five-year stay in Frankfort he also wrote numerous hymns, plays, operettas, and poems. He also became engaged to a rich banker's daughter, Lili Schönemann.

The structured social climate soon weighed heavily on his free spirit, and he went to Weimar in 1775 at the invitation of Duke Karl Augustus, who was interested in his work. The visit became permanent when Goethe was assigned as an important cabinet poet. He directed the Weimar theater and performed a heavy load of administrative tasks, all of which restricted his literary production. He fell in love with Charlotte von Stein, wife of a cabinet official, and she became the greatest influence of his life.

After many years years in Weimar, Goethe made a trip to Italy (1786–1788) that marked a turning point in his art away from Herder's influence and back toward a form of classicism.

When he returned to Weimar, he was relieved of most of his administrative duties, but he remained the court's cultural maestro for the rest of his life. In 1788 he took Christiane Vulpius, the daughter of a minor official, into his home. She bore him several children and years later became his wife.

He wrote a number of plays, and in 1990 published the first version of *Faust*. (Part I of *Faust* was published in 1808 and Part II in 1832, a few months before his death.) In 1794 he began a close friendship with Friedrich von Schiller, poet, dramatist, and historian. Until Schiller died (1805), the two were responsible for the movement called Weimar Classicism. During this period Goethe produced his two epic poems, *Reineke Fuchs* (1794) and *Hermann und Dorothea* (1797/1798), as well as the novel *Wilhelm Lehrjahre*. In 1799 he attempted another epic in the classical vein, *Achilleis*, which he never completed.

He continued to write prodigiously, concentrating during his last two decades on an autobiography entitled *Aus meinem Leben, Dichtung und Wahrheit* (Poetry and truth from my life, 1811–1833). He was the first to use the term "world literature." The term "leader in world literature" was aptly applied to him. He died in 1832 in Weimar at the age of 83. (Lewes 1965)

See also *Achilleis; Hermann und Dorothea; Reineke Fuchs.*

 # GORSKI VIJENAC
(The mountain wreath)

Serbian epic in dramatic form by Prince Petar Petrović Njegoš (1813–1851), Montenegrin count and bishop. The poem, the poet's greatest work, is a synthesis of Montenegrin life. (Čiževskij 1971; Preminger 1974)

 # GÖTA KÄMPAVISA
(Heroic ballad of the Goths)

Swedish epic poem (early 18th c.) by Gunno Dahlstierno (Gunno Eurelius, 1661–1709). Written in ballad form, the poem is an account of the victory during the

Great Northern War of Swedish king Charles II at the Battle of Narva (November 1700), which drove attacking Russian troops from the Swedish trans-Baltic provinces. (Magill 1993)

 # GOTTFRIED VON STRASSBURG

Middle High German poet (fl. 13th c.), author of the unfinished epic poem *Tristan*, or *Tristan und Isold* (13th c.). Little is known of his life. He was referred to as *meister* rather than *herr*, so he was probably not of knightly birth. The name Dietrich is spelled out in an acrostic at the beginning of the poem, indicating that Gottfried's poem was probably written for him. Gottfried's work shows evidence of his acquaintance with the French language, the classics, and epic poets Heinrich von Veldeke, Hartmann von Aue, and Bligger von Steinach and lyric poets Reinmar and Walthier von der Vogelweide. Although he was not a cleric, he may have been educated in a monastery school. He died about 1210. (Garland and Garland 1986)

 # *GRAF NULIN*
(Count Nulin)

Russian mock epic (1825, publ. 1827) by Aleksandr Pushkin (1799–1837). The poem is a whimsical parody on the life of the rural gentry. It is based on Shakespeare's dark poem *The Rape of Lucrece* (1594), itself taken from the Roman legend about Lucretia who, having been raped by the son of the king, declares her disgrace before her father, husband, and friends Valerius and Junius Brutus, then stabs herself. Brutus calls for an insurrection by the populace to resist tyranny. It occurred to Pushkin that world history would have been different had Lucrece slapped Tarquin as he tried to rape her. He probably would have desisted, Lucrece would not have committed suicide, Brutus would not have called for an insurrection, and Rome might not have become a republic. In the Pushkin version, the wife is spunky and is championed by a neighbor, Lidin. However, Pushkin wrote the poem only a few days before the Decembrist Revolt, an attempted coup d'état against the new tsar, Nicholas I.

The scene is a Russian country house. The heroine, Natasha Pavlova, is a young woman who sits beside her window holding an unread novel, pining because her husband is absent on a hunting expedition. A visitor arrives: Graf Nulin, on his way to Petropol. He is invited to stay the night by the bored and lonely young Natasha. After an entertaining dinner, they retire, but the count cannot stop thinking about Natasha's warm hospitality. He is sure that he will be welcomed if he goes to her bedroom. He slips down the hallway, makes a bold entrance into her room, and approaches her bedside, but as he kisses her hand, she slaps his face. He withdraws in "ignominious flight."

When the husband returns, he urges the count to stay on, but Nulin quickly takes his leave. Afterward, Natasha confesses to her husband what Nulin has done. The husband vows to hunt him down with his pack. Meanwhile, in a hilarious deadpan ending, the young neighbor, Lidin, laughs; it is he who "champions" Natasha for ending the tyranny. (Johnston 1983)

See also Pushkin, Aleksandr Sergeyevich.

GRAIL, HOLY

See Holy Grail.

LA GRANDEZA MEXICANA
(The grandeur of Mexico)

Epic poem (1604) by Bernardo de Balbuena (1568–1627). The poem describes the capital of New Spain during the closing days of the sixteenth century. The poet summarizes the contents of the eight divisions of the poem: "The site of the famous City of Mexico,/The origin and grandeur of buildings,/Horses, streets, social intercourse, manners,/Literature, virtues, variety of occupation,/Pleasures, occasions of joy,/Immortal spring and its tokens,/Illustrious government, Church and State—/All are included. . . ."

The poet describes walking through the new capital city, which is "soothed by a gentle and fresh breeze." He describes the streets, teeming with affable, courteous people whose speech is sweet. The ladies are beautiful, chaste, and modest. In the third canto, the poet describes at length the fine, spirited, well-bred horses with restless feet and fiery natures.

He speaks of the highly developed art and skill of the craftsmen, artists, poets, doctors, actors, architects.

The poem was published in Mexico in 1604, then all but forgotten until the nineteenth century, when five editions were published: three in Madrid, one in New York, and one in Mexico. (Peña 1968)

See also Balbuena, Bernardo de.

THE GREAT LEGEND
(Mahāpurāṇa)

South Indian Sanskrit epic of high quality composed in the ninth century by Jinasena and Guṇabhadra, followers of Jainism. The poem, in the style of the Hindu Purāṇas, was written under the reign and patronage of King Amoghavarṣa, also a poet and follower of Jainism. Jinasena was a teacher of

MEXICO.

Bernardo de Balbuena wrote *Le Grandeza Mexicana* (1604) about Mexico City, called Tenochtitlán by the Aztecs and capital of New Spain following the conquest of Cortés over Moctezuma in 1532. This map of Mexico City, with its central plaza and causeways, was published in 1576, just 44 years after the conquest.

the Digambara, one of the two principal sects of Jainism (the other being the Śvetāmbara). One notable difference between the two is that Digambaras own no property and wear no clothes, while the Śvetāmbaras wear white robes or loincloths.

The Great Legend consists of cosmology and legends of the patriarchs, called Tirthaṅkaras, and other great men. It also contains a number of philosophical passages expounding the tenets of Jainism. For example, in defense of the

Jainas's position that there is no Creator, Jinasena writes, "If out of love for living things and need of them he made the world,/Why did he not make Creation wholly blissful, free from misfortune?"

The poem relates the hierarchy under four groups of gods: Bhavanavāsīs, Vyantaras, Jyotiṣkas, and Vaimānīkas (house gods, intermediaries, luminaries, and astral gods), who are subservient to the Tirthinkaras (founders of the faith). Jainas believe that 24 Tirthinkaras, who had achieved spiritual liberation, lived during the cosmic age. The last was Vardhamāna Mahāvīra, founder of Jainism. The lives of the patriarchs are related in the poem, particularly the last two, Mahāvīra and Pārśvanātha. The latter lived 250 years before Mahāvīra. These are the only historically verifiable figures mentioned in the hierarchical section. (Jinasena 1951)

See also Jinasena.

GROSSE TRAUM, DER
(The great dream)

German epic poem (1946) by Nobelist Gerhart Hauptmann (1862–1946), poet, novelist, and leading German dramatist of his day. The author, who wrote in the new Naturalist idiom, considered this epic his most profound visionary revelation. Modeled after Dante's *Divine Comedy* and composed in terza rima with much symbolism, the ambitious, somewhat autobiographical work is the author's philosophical attempt to relate his own life to the contemporary milieu, with its worship of science and industrialization as saviors of humanity and its scorn for dire poverty and deplorable living conditions brought about by that very industrialization. He perceived the dichotomy in his own languid existence made possible by wealth and the lives of the poor whom he depicted. He saw in the lives of some laborers glimmers of his own heritage: His grandfather was a Silesian weaver, and he himself had worked as a farmer while in his teens. The experience gave his work authenticity. (Hornstein 1973; Siepmann 1987)

See also Hauptmann, Gerhart.

GUERRAS DE CHILE
(Wars of Chile)

Chilean Spanish epic poem written in 1610 and attributed to Juan de Mendoza Monteagudo (d. 1619). The poem recounts some of the same history of the wars between the Araucanian Indians and the Spanish conquistadors that is the subject of Alonso de Ercilla y Zuñiga's famous epic *La Araucana*. However, *La Araucana* celebrates primarily the battles waged by the Araucanian chief Caupolicán, whereas *Guerras de Chile* covers the more than 50-year struggle between the two peoples that began with the death of Governor Pedro de Valdivia and the defeat of his followers by the Araucanians under Lautaro (1553). After Caupolicán's capture and execution (1558), the Indian wars continued. In late 1599, following two guerrilla raids on the Indian fort of Paparlén, the Indians, 5,000 strong, attacked Valdivia and several other Spanish cities. They surrounded La Imperial for one year, cutting off supplies, so that everyone died except 20 men who surrendered. Of the 13 existing cities, six were destroyed by the Indians. Finally they set fire to Villarrica, took all the women as prisoners, and killed all the priests. (Anderson-Imbert 1969; Garcilaso de la Vega 1966)

 # GULISTĀN
(The rose garden)

Persian Ṣūfī didactic epic collection (1258) written in prose and verse by Sa'dī (Sheikh Mosliku'd-din Sadi of Shiraz, 1184–1291). Written in a style of elegant simplicity, it is considered Sa'dī's most important work. It is not an epic in the traditional sense, in that it does not narrate one story; rather, it contains many prose (a few verse) stories, accompanied by poetry, illustrating Çūfī tenets. The narratives are, in Sa'dī's words, "of rare adventures, and traditions, and tales, and verses, and manners of ancient kings, and I have expended some portion of precious life upon it."

The book consists of a preface, which is an interspersion of prose and poetry, and eight "chapters" followed by a conclusion.

The preface, set up like the chapters with sections of prose followed by poetry, explains the poet's motive for writing the *Gulistān:* "Perhaps, hereafter, for this pious task,/Some man of prayer for me to grace shall ask."

Chapter I, "On the Manners of Kings," consists of 41 stories, each followed by poetic stanzas of varying lengths, all illustrating attributes of national leaders. The poems are done in the manner of a moral or an explication of what the reader should glean from the story.

Chapter II, "On the Qualities of Dareweshes," contains 49 stories plus "couplets" (so labeled) stating the moral and "stanzas" (so labeled) explaining them.

Chapter III, "On the Excellence of Contentment," contains 29 stories plus "couplets," "distichs," "stanzas," and "apophthegms."

Chapter IV, "On the Advantages of Taciturnity," contains 14 stories with accompanying poems illustrating the virtue of taciturnity in the lives of ordinary people such as a merchant, poet, astrologer, preacher, Jew, servant, sage.

Chapter V, "On Love and Youth," contains 11 stories and as many or more verses. The last story, told in verse, is about a "gallant youth" pledged to a maid "beyond compare." The two go sailing and fall into a whirlpool. When the boatman tries to rescue the youth, he instead pleads that the boatman save his love. As a result, both the lovers perish. The poet asks, "Hast thou a mistress? her then prize,/And on all others close thine eyes."

Chapter VI, "On Decrepitude and Old Age," contains eight stories with poems that do not paint a flattering picture of old age.

Chapter VII, "On the Effect of Education," contains 19 stories and poetry. The final "story," the longest in the book, is entitled "The Dispute of Sa'dī with a Presumptuous Pretender as to the Qualities of the Rich and the Fool."

Chapter VIII, "On the Duties of Society," contains no stories. Instead, it consists of 106 maxims, plus explanatory poetry. The final, very brief maxim is: "Two persons died remorseful: He who possessed and enjoyed not, and he who knew but did not practice." It is followed by an explanatory stanza.

In the conclusion, the poet asks for the reader's prayers. (Sa'dī 1979)

See also Sa'dī.

GUṆABHADRA

Indian Sanskrit poet (fl. 9th c.) of South India; author, with Jinasena, of the great Jaina epic *Mahāpurāṇa* (The great legend). (Jinasena 1951)

GUNĀDHYA

Indian poet (fl. A.D. 50?–300?), author of *Bṛhat-kathā (Great tale)*, written originally in the Paisācī (Paisachi or Prākrit) dialect, a popular form of Sanskrit in preclassical times. This very early epic was a compendium, or cycle, of stories, romances, and fables—including beast fables—which is now lost except for retellings in later versions. It served as a great source for later plays and romances. (Van Buitenen 1959)

GUNDULIĆ, IVAN FRANOV

Yugoslavian (Croatian) poet and dramatist, author of the epic poem *Osman* (1626). He was born in 1588 or 1589 in Dubrovnik, Dalmatia. As a young man, he was both poet and patriot, active in local government affairs. He occupied several government posts in Dubrovnik during the golden period of Ragusan (Dubrovnik) poetry. This era was the Renaissance of art and literature, during which time Dubrovnik produced a circle of great poets and earned the title "South Slav Athens." Gundulić was certainly the leading poet on the basis of his masterpiece *Osman,* but this prolific writer earned recognition from other works as well. He wrote a number of fine lyric poems; his poem "The Tears of the Prodigal Son" is regarded as the best religious lyrical poem of the age. His best dramatic work is his pastoral drama *Dubravka,* in which the poet glorifies his native city and sings a proud ode to liberty.

In 1626, Gundulić was inspired by Torquato Tasso's *Gerusalemme liberata* to compose his epic *Osman,* but it was not published until 1826. The poem describes the Polish victory over the Turks at Chocim in 1621 and the assassination of Sultan Osman. Gundulić died in 1638 in Dubrovnik, which still honors him as the greatest poet of its golden age and the most outstanding poet of the Republic. (Dvornik 1962; Gazi 1973; Preminger 1974)

See also Osman.

 # GUTE GERHARD, DER
(Good Gerhard)

Middle High German epic (ca. 1220) by Rudolf von Ems (d. 1252/1253). The poem, of almost 7,000 lines, relates how Emperor Otto I is warned by an angel against hubris and conceit, citing the example of Gerhard. The king then hears the story from Gerhard himself. A rich merchant, he has earned the title of "Good Gerhard" because he has been charitable with his wealth at home, and has also journeyed to the East to pay ransom to the Muslims for captives (victims of the Crusades). Among those he redeems is a beautiful Norwegian princess, the betrothed of the missing English king William. Two years pass and King William has not returned, so Gerhard allows his son to become betrothed to the princess. However, on the eve of the wedding, William appears. In deference to the king, Gerhard withdraws his son's betrothal. (Garland and Garland 1986)

See also Rudolf von Ems.

 HAFT PAYKAR

Medieval Persian romance epic (1197) by Nizāmī Ganjavi (ca. 1190–1203), considered the poet's masterpiece. Written in 53 cantos containing 10,090 lines in *mas̱navī* form (rhyming couplets, as *aa bb cc*, etc.), the poem was dedicated to the ruler of Maragha who commissioned the work, 'Alā al-Din Körp Arslān. According to the poet, it is a gift of advice to the prince: a complex allegory of moral and spiritual development.

The historical character on which the story is based is Sassanian emperor Bahrām V Gūr (Gōr) (r. 421–439), son of Yazdigird I (r. 388–420). Bahrām was brought up at the court of the Lakhmid kings of Hira, who supported his claim to the Sassanian throne against Prince Khusraw. Bahrām appointed the minister Mihr Narseh (Narsi in the epic) and defeated the Hephtalites, or White Huns (the "Chinese" invaders found in Cantos 27 and 40).

The first eight cantos are introductory. Canto 1 is an invocation, praising God; Canto 2 is "In Praise of the Chief among Prophets," Muḥammad; Canto 3 describes the prophet's *mī rāj* (ascent to Heaven). Canto 4 is an account of the poem's composition. Cantos 5 and 6 are "In Praise of the August Ruler" and "An Address to Homage." Canto 7 is "In Praise of Discourse." Canto 8 is a long poem of advice for the poet's own son, as: ". . . know yourself, that you may taste the Spring of Life. . . ."

The story begins with Canto 9, where a son, Bahrām, is born to the aging Iranian king Yazdigird. Learning from a horoscope that his son is to become king of the world, Yazdigird sends him to the Lakhmid ruler Nu'mān (d. 418) and his son Munzir (r. 418–452?) to be educated for his future role.

In Canto 10, Nu'mān has the beautiful palace Khavarnaq built for him. When it is finished, the architect suggests that he could have built an even better one. Fearing the architect will indeed go elsewhere and build a better one, Nu'mān has him cast over the wall to his death.

In Canto 11 the king's vizier, a Christian, tells him that, "to know one's God aright/is better than all-owning might." Once he has found such wisdom, the vizier says, he will tear himself away from worldly goods. The king repents of his greed and disappears into the desert, leaving his son Munzir to rule.

In Canto 12, as he grows older, Bahrām becomes very skilled at hunting and branding wild asses (onagers).

In Canto 13, Bahrām, who has earned the title Bahrām Gūr (onager: gūr), slays a lion and an onager with one arrow.

In Canto 14, Bahrām chases a female onager to a cave guarded by a dragon. He slays the dragon, slits its belly, and finds the onager's foal. The onager leads him into the cave, where he discovers a great treasure.

In Canto 15, back home, Bahrām finds a secret room in the palace, where he sees portraits of the Seven Beauties: princesses from India, Chīn (China, Turkestan), Khwārazm, Siqlab (Slavonia), the Maghreb (North Africa), Rūm (Byzantium), and Persia. His portrait is in the center. He visits the room often in secret.

In Canto 16 he learns that his father, Yazdigird, has died. He has been such a bad ruler that the Iranians have placed an outsider on the throne as his successor.

In Canto 17, aided by Munzir, Bahrām raises a mighty army and marches to the Persian capital to claim his rightful throne.

In Canto 18 the usurper sends Bahrām a letter explaining that he never wanted the job as ruler, but was pressed into service. He has been working hard, while Bahrām, who has been raised on hunting and wine, is not fitted for the job. The late king was so tyrannical that he was called "the Sinner" by his subjects, so that "no one now will praise his seed."

In Canto 19, Bahrām gives a gracious answer, explaining that he is not guilty of his father's crimes, and that he will be a good ruler. The priests agree that his is the rightful claim, but they need proof of his worthiness. He proposes a test, placing the crown in an arena between two starved lions. "Whoever seizes it shall be worthy of crowning. . . ."

In Canto 20 the old usurper lays down his crown, not wishing to be killed by lions. His priests decide that Bahrām alone must face the test. If he fails, the ursurper will reign. In Canto 21, Bahrām seizes the crown from between the two vicious lions. In Canto 22 he ascends to the throne, promising to be a good king.

Canto 23 describes how he administers justice in his realm, even though he spends only one day a week on state affairs, the rest on love and pleasure. His subjects begin to forget about thanking God for their bounty.

In Canto 24, during a year of famine, he shows great compassion for his subjects. Thereafter the kingdom prospers.

In Canto 25, Bahrām goes hunting with his slave-girl harpist Fitna, asking her, "What think you of the feat you've seen?" When she fails to heap praise on him, he decides to get rid of her. But "lion-brave warriors do not slay/weak women," so he orders an officer to do it for him, to take her to his own abode and "snuff her like a candle's flame." But Fitna convinces the officer to hide her in his palace instead, pretending that she is a servant. Every day thereafter she carries a newborn ox up to his tower, continuing for six years until the ox is huge and she is very strong.

In Canto 26, Bahrām goes hunting and comes to a feast in the officer's tower. Fitna, wearing a veil, appears carrying the ox, to Bahrām's amazement. She reveals her identity and the two are married.

214

In Canto 27 the ruler of Chīn believes that Bahrām's devotion to pleasure is a sign of weakness and invades, but he is defeated. In Canto 28, Bahrām rebukes his generals for believing he is weak, then rewards them.

In Canto 29 he sends his messengers to seek the beautiful princesses from the Seven Climes, whose portraits he has seen. In Canto 30, at a winter feast, the architect Shīda suggests building seven domed pavilions to house his seven new brides. Canto 31 describes the seven domes and how Bahrām takes his pleasure there, feasting, drinking, loving, and hearing a tale from each of his brides as entertainment.

In Canto 32 the king spends Saturday in the Black Dome, hearing the tale of the King of Black, in mourning for a lost love, the beautiful Turktāz. In Canto 33 he spends Sunday in the Yellow Dome, hearing the tale of a king who overcomes a prediction of danger in marriage and weds his favorite concubine. In Canto 34 he spends Monday in the Green Dome, hearing the tale of a man on a pilgrimage to purify himself from a lustful temptation who kills a godless, evil man. Returning the man's belongings to his widow, he finds she is the object of his earlier temptation and marries her. In Canto 35 the king spends Tuesday in the Red Dome, hearing the tale of a prince who defeats many secret talismans guarding a Russian princess, earning her hand in marriage. In Canto 36 he spends Wednesday in the Turquoise Dome, hearing the tale of a handsome Egyptian prince, Māhān, led astray in the desert by a demon. After suffering many misadventures, the prince appeals to God and is led home. He dons blue robes and renounces the world. In Canto 37 the king spends Thursday in the Sandal Dome, hearing the tale of a man named Good who is robbed and left for dead by his traveling companion, Bad. A Kurdish princess rescues him. He marries her, and later becomes king. When he encounters Bad, he forgives him, but a Kurd kills Bad. In Canto 38 the king spends Friday in the White Dome hearing the tale of a man thwarted by many incidents in pursuit of his love for Bakht, until he realizes the cause of his frustration is the illicit nature of his desire. So he marries Bakht.

In Canto 40, after many rounds through the domes, Bahrām emerges at last and holds court in the spring, described in Canto 39, to celebrate the New Year. In Canto 40, in his absence, the evil vizier has left the kingdom in disarray. Again the Chinese ruler invades. But Bahrām's treasury is empty, and his army revolts.

In Canto 41, returning from an ill-timed hunting trip, Bahrām stops for a drink at the hut of an old shepherd, who tells of hanging his trusted guard dog after discovering the dog has been rewarding a she-wolf with his sheep in exchange for sexual favors. The king perceives a lesson for himself: He has trusted his vizier to protect his "flock," his subjects.

In Canto 42, Bahrām brings the vizier to trial, hearing testimony from victims unjustly imprisoned by the vizier. Cantos 43–49 contain the testimony of seven victims of the vizier's skewed justice. In Canto 50 the king executes the vizier. In Canto 51 the Chinese ruler withdraws his troops and sends his apologies.

In Canto 52, Bahrām renounces his seven brides, turns their domes into temples, weds himself to Justice, and goes hunting—this time to seek and slay his own faults. Again a female onager lures him to a cave, where he disappears forever. His mother leads a search for him, then turns the kingdom over to his successor.

Canto 53, an epilogue, contains a lament for the poet's first wife, the Kipchak slave Āfāq, and a prayer for the good fortune of the ruler for whom he has written his poem, ending, "as your fortune waxes, may / your end be true felicity." (Nizāmī 1995)

See also Nizâmî.

HANNE NÜTE UN DE LÜTTE PUDEL
(Hanne Nüte and the poodle)

Lower German dialect (Mecklenburger Platt) verse epic (1860) by Fritz Reuter (1810–1874). The poem relates the story of Hanne Nüte, who is in love with Fike, both of whom are in close contact with the world of birds. When Hanne is accused of committing a murder, the birds come to his rescue by revealing the true perpetrator of the crime. (Garland and Garland 1986)

HARPIES

Mythical winds having wings and the shape and characteristics of carrion birds, but with the faces of women. They frequently swoop down and snatch away food, possessions, even persons. They appear in the works of Homer, Hesiod, Apollonius of Rhodes, and Vergil. (Hornstein 1973; Siepmann 1987)

HARTMANN VON AUE
(Or Hartmann von Ouwe)

Middle High German poet, author of two Arthurian epics, *Erec* (late 12th c.) and *Iwein* (ca. 1200), and the narrative poem *Der arme Heinrich,* considered his finest work. He was born between 1160 and 1170 in Swabia, possibly at Eglesau on the Rhine in Canton Zürich. He was well educated in the classics and in French, probably in a monastery such as Reichenau. Hartmann was in the service, as a *ministeriale,* of a great lord who died, possibly on a crusade, leaving him emotionally distraught. He then participated in a crusade himself, either in 1180–1190 or 1197, after which he seems to have recovered his emotional equilibrium. His last work, the Arthurian epic *Iwein,* was composed about 1200. In addition to his epics, Hartmann wrote a verse essay on love called "Das Büchlein"; a religious legend in verse, "Gregorius"; three *Kreuzlieder* (Crusaders' songs); and a large number of *Minnelieder* (love songs.) Gottfried von

Strassburg's *Tristan* referred to Hartmann in 1210, so it is presumed that he died after that time. His death was mourned by Heinrich von dem Türlin in his *Diu Crône*. (Garland and Garland 1986)
  See also Erec.

HASANI BIN ISMAIL

Swahili poet, author of *Swifa ya Nguvumali* (The medicine man) (P. Lienhardt's edition, 1968), in which the poet attempts to interpret Swahili society and culture. The poem focuses on the conflicts between Islam and African traditional religion on the Tanzanian coast. (Allen 1981)
  See also The Medicine Man.

HAUPTMANN, GERHART

German dramatist, poet, and novelist, recipient of the Nobel Prize for literature, and author of epics *Till Eulenspiegel* (1928), *Der grosse Traum* (Part 1, 1942), and an early Romantic epic, *Promethidenlos* (1885). He was born in 1862 in Obersalzbrunn, Silesia (now Szczawno [or Salzbrunn] Zdrój, Poland), where his father owned the principal resort hotel. The elder Hauptmann had traveled widely in his youth; in 1848 he had witnessed the storming of the barricades in Paris, an event that made a lasting impression on his social conscience. In fact, his neighbors called him "the red Hauptmann." Gerhart's mother greatly influenced her son as well, with her Moravian piety.

The young Hauptmann was a weak student; he quit school at the age of 15, having failed in agricultural studies. He took up farming, and studied sculpture at the Breslau Art Institute before traveling to join his older brother, Carl, at Jena to study science, history, and philosophy. He became interested in the theater and, after a season in Rome as a sculptor (1883–1884), he went to Berlin to study acting.

In 1885, at the age of 23, he married the wealthy Marie Thienemann, and the couple settled in the outskirts of Berlin. He wrote one Romantic epic, *Promethidenlos* (The lot of the Promethides), in 1885 before turning to the more realistic style then in vogue.

He wrote his first successful play, *Vor Sonnenaufgang* (Before dawn), in 1889 on a Naturalistic theme, showing environmental and hereditary factors that control man's fate. He followed that play with several others, including *The Weavers* (1892), based on the lives and struggles of Silesian weavers, as related to him by his weaver grandfather. It is his best-remembered work. During these years he and Marie had three children.

In 1904, Hauptmann and his wife divorced and he married the actress and violinist Margarete Marschalk. He was 42; she was 30 and the mother of his

Gerhart Hauptmann, German Nobelist in literature, 1928

four-year-old son. They had been cohabiting for three years in a newly built mansion in Silesia. He strayed again only one year later, when he had a romantic interlude (1905–1906) with a 17-year-old actress, Ida Orloff, after whom he patterned many characters in his novels and plays.

He continued to write prolifically and to travel frequently. By 1912 his reputation as the most prominent German dramatist of his time was secured when he was awarded the Nobel Prize for Literature, one of many international honors he received over his lifetime. Although he continued to write and direct plays and to write novels, in 1928 he composed an epic, *Till Eulenspiegel,* based on the legendary German folk trickster-hero.

With the rise of Nazism, Hauptmann was criticized for not leaving by émigrés who fled Germany during Hitler's reign. However, he remained politically neutral, although privately he opposed Nazi ideology. His presence was only tolerated by the Third Reich.

In 1946, Part 1 of *Der grosse Traum (The great dream)* was published. Hauptmann considered this ambitious work his most profound and visionary revelation. It is a philosophical, symbolic work, written in terza rima, modeled after Dante's *Divine Comedy.* In it the author relates his life to the milieu of his time, which obviously encompassed the war years in Nazi Germany.

He died in 1946 in Agnetendorf, Germany, and was buried on the isle of Hiddensee. (Block and Shedd, 1962; Hornstein 1973; Siepmann 1987)

See also *Grosse Traum, Der; Till Eulenspiegel.*

 # *HAZZ AL-QUḤŪF*

(Full title: *Hazz al-quḥūf fi sharḥ qaṣīd Abī Shādāf,* or *The shaking of skullcaps*)

Egyptian mock-epic poem (17th c.) by Yūsuf al-Shirbīnī. The poem is a colloquial-language parody employing the hyperbolic formulas and rhythms of the oral poet to satirize the *Sīrat Banī Hilāl* and the peasants celebrated by that epic (see the *Encyclopedia of Traditional Epics*). The poem is accompanied by a mock-scholarly commentary in literary language.

The poet, who escaped his own *Saʿīdī* peasant upbringing by the only route available to village boys of his class—the route to Cairo and al-Azhar to enter the religious heirarchy of the *ʿulamā* to become a religious shaykh—turns his back on his own kind and directs his work toward an urbane audience.

In lofty language Hazz al-Quḥīf attacks the Nile Valley dirt farmer in dung-encrusted clothes. The poem describes Egyptian farmers as being so crassly materialistic that they neglect family and religious responsibilities in favor of caring for livestock and dredging canals. According to the poem, the peasants are so distrustful and exploitative that they form few friendships, and they do not honor *amān* (the pledge of security for refugees). They oppress their neighbors and are respectful of those who oppress them.

After the 1952 revolution in Egypt, this poem became popular with leftists and populists as an example of the "true" character of the peasant, who had been seen up till then as passive, sheeplike, even stupid. (Connelly 1986)

 # HEINE, HEINRICH
(Chaim Harry Heine)

German poet and critic known for his lyric poetry, but also the author of two mock-epics, *Deutschland: Ein Wintermärchen* (Germany: A winter's tale, 1844) and *Atta Troll, Ein Sommernachtstraum* (Atta Troll, a summer night's dream, 1847). Heine was born in 1795 in Düsseldorf, Germany, of Jewish parents of moderate means, Samson and Peira von Geldern Heine. However, the boy also enjoyed the off-and-on favor of a wealthy banker uncle, Salomon Heine. Heine took his early education at the Düsseldorf Lyceum and made an attempt at both banking and retailing. Eventually his uncle was persuaded to send him to the university. He attended university at Bonn, where he began his first book of poems. He next went to the university of Göttingen but left after only six months because of a duel, fought against the rules.

The young Heine was under the influence of more exciting preoccupations than those offered by the business world of his uncle Salomon. He was also influenced by his uncle Simon von Geldern, an inveterate traveler who had even been an Arab chief in Africa. In Berlin, he fell into the company of a wealthy Jewish matriarch, Rahel Varnhagen von Ense, who entertained a brilliant intellectual circle devoted to the works of Goethe.

Eventually he returned to Göttingen and earned a doctorate in law at the age of 30; however, much of his studies had been in the areas of history and the literary arts. In order to procure a government job—not available to Jews at the time—he renounced Judaism and became a Lutheran. Still he failed to get a civil service appointment.

He wrote a number of Romantic poems, which in 1927 were collected in the *Buch der Lieder* (The book of songs). This collection established his literary reputation. The poems have since frequently been set to music.

For a while he went to England, Holland, and later Italy. From 1826 to 1831 he wrote six volumes of *Reisebilder* (Travel pictures). Because of his outspoken views on the subject of freedom, he was far from popular in official Germany, and he was unsuccessful in finding work there, which forced his imposed exile from his fatherland. In 1831 he settled in Paris, where he earned a meager living as an author, editor, and journalist. In his career as a journalist he wrote articles about France's new capitalist regime under Louis-Philippe. He had an abiding passion for liberty and democracy, and his writings critical of his homeland resulted in a ban of his works in Germany.

In 1834 he fell in love with Cresence Eugénie Mirat, whom he called Mathilde, a *grisette* (shopgirl) who spoke no German. He finally married her in 1841. In 1843–1845, he wrote a longer mock-epic, *Atta Troll, Ein Sommer-*

nachtstraum, about the death of a trained bear, which was a brutal but witty spoof of pompous radicals and a depiction of the ironic complexity of his own rebellious spirit against the Germany he still loved.

In 1848 he took to his bed with a nervous system disorder that eventually left him partially blind and paralyzed. He continued to write, dictating to a woman whom he called *La Mouche* (the Fly), who also read his proofs and read books and newspapers to him. His unschooled wife was unable to read a word of his poetry.

After eight years of physical torment confined to what he called his "mattress grave," he died in 1856 and was buried in Montmarte cemetery. (Heine 1966; Untermeyer 1937)

See also Atta Troll: Ein Sommernachtstraum.

HEINRICH VON GLÎCHEZAERE

Middle High German poet, author of a beast epic, *Reinhart Fuchs* (late 12th c.). Only the name Heinrich is a certainty. The appellation Glîchezaere may have been added in error by a late-thirteenth-century copyist. Heinrich's original title for the poem was *Isengrînes nôt.* Only fragments of the original remain, preserved at Kassel, and nothing more is known of its author. (Garland and Garland 1986)

HEINRICH VON VELDEKE

Middle High German poet, author of the *Eneit* (1189). He is believed to have been born between 1140 and 1150. He was a Rhenish knight from the region of Maastricht, in present-day southeastern Netherlands. About 1170 he began work on the *Eneit,* based on *Roman d'Enéas,* an anonymous French metrical travesty of the *Aeneid.* The incomplete poem was lent to a countess of Cleves, but it was lost in 1174.

In 1183, Heinrich was in attendance at the court of Landgrave Ludwig von Thüringen when the manuscript was returned to him. He completed the poem in 1189. When Ludwig died on a crusade to the Holy Land (1190), his younger brother Hermann, who had been acting in his stead during his brother's absence, succeeded him. Hermann was a great patron of literature, and of Heinrich von Veldeke's work. Heinrich wrote a poem on St. Sercatius and some lyric poetry, as well as a poem entitled *Salomo und die Minne,* now lost, but attributed to him in the anonymous poem *Marie von Craûn.*

He was well thought of by his contemporaries; Wolfram von Eschenbach and Gottfried von Strassburg both praised his work, while Rudolph von Ems credited him with writing "the first proper verse." Heinrich is believed to have died before 1210. (Garland and Garland 1986)

See also Eneit.

HEKTOROVIĆ, PETAR

Yugoslavian poet, author of the pastoral epic *Ribanje i ribarsko prigovaranje* (Fishing and fishermen's talk, 1555). He was born in 1487 in Starigrad, Hvar Island, Dalmatia, to an aristocratic land-owning family. He was educated in Italy, where he became interested in the Italian adaptation of the forms of classical literature for vernacular writings. He became an important figure in the Ragusan (Dubrovnik) Renaissance of Slavic literature. He collected Dalmatian folk lyrics and interspersed them in his chief work, *Ribanje i ribarsko prigovaranje*. He died in Starigrad in 1572. (Čiževskij 1971; Gazi 1973)

See also *Ribanje i ribarsko prigovaranje*.

HELIAND

Old Saxon epic poem (ca. 830) by an unknown author. The extant poem, which consists of some 5,984 lines of alliterative verse, was said to have been written at the behest of Frankish emperor Louis I the Pious (r. 813–840). The title means "Savior" in Old Saxon. The poem is a rewriting, in 71 "songs," of the life of Christ as if it had happened in the author's own place and time; thus, Christ is portrayed as a German king.

Song 1 tells of the four heroes whom God picks to "write down the evangelium in a book. . . ." No one else is to attempt it other than Matthew, Mark, Luke, and John. The old man Zachary is introduced: a man always obedient to God's will.

Song 2 describes Zachary's encounter with the angel Gabriel, who tells him that his elderly wife will bear a child who will become "a warrior-champion of the King of Heaven." But Zachary doubts that his wife of 70 years will at long last bear a child.

In Song 3, angered by Zachary's doubt, Gabriel punishes Zachary so that he will not be able to say a single word "until your old woman bears you an earl. . . ." Zachary immediately loses his speech. His wife becomes pregnant, and a message from God tells her to name the baby John. When the child is born and named, Zachary regains his speech.

In Song 4 the angel visits Mary in Galileeland, announcing, "You are to become the mother of our Chieftain here among human beings." In Song 5 the angels announce that the Chieftain of mankind is born "at David's hill-fort." In Song 6 the mother, Mary, "the loveliest of ladies," and father, Joseph, take the child to the shrine, where two people, Simeon and Anna, recognize him as the Chieftain of Clans, the Lord of People. In Song 7 three thanes, "earls from the East," follow a star. In Song 8 the thanes present their gifts to the holy Child.

In Song 9, Herod sends a command throughout his kingdom to decapitate the two-year-old boys around Bethlehem.

In Song 10, on a trip to Jerusalem, the Son of the Chieftain, now age 12, becomes separated from his parents, who find him later at the shrine questioning the elders.

In Song 11, meanwhile, John announces Christ's coming to Middlegard. In Song 12 the Chieftain is baptized by John.

In Song 13 "the horrible enemy," Satan, tempts Christ three times.

In Song 14 the mighty Chieftain chooses Andrew and Peter, James and John, and Matthew as his first warrior-companions. In Song 15, Christ the Rescuer calls 12 warrior-companions, naming also Thomas, two Judases, his cousin James, Simon, Bartholomew, and Philip.

In Song 16, from a mountain the Chieftain gives instructions to the "earls in front of Him," giving them eight "Good Fortunes." Songs 17 through 23 continue the instructions on the mountain.

Song 24 depicts the marriage feast at Fort Cana, in which Christ's words and actions in turning water into wine are intentionally hidden from all so that they cannot be remembered or repeated from generation to generation.

Song 25 describes Christ's healing of a commander's "household lad" at hill-fort Capharnaum. At Fort Naim he raises the dead son of a widow (Song 26). In Song 27 he commands the wind and the sea. A cripple is lowered through the roof of the house where he is staying, and he heals the man in Song 28.

Songs 29, 30, and 31 tell the parable of the sower. Song 32 describes the attempt by "grim-hearted Jews of Galileeland" to throw Christ off a cliff. In Song 33, John the soothsayer is beheaded at the request of the king's niece and her mother.

Song 34 relates the Chieftain's feeding a great throng of earls with five loaves and two fishes. Song 35 tells of the Chieftain and Peter walking on the water. In Song 36 the Chieftain heals the daughter of a woman of the Canaanite clan.

In Song 37 the Lord gives Simon Peter, whom he calls "best of thanes," heaven-kingdom's keys so that he will have "all authority over the Christian people."

Song 38 depicts the mountaintop transfiguration of Christ.

Song 39 describes Christ's instructing Peter to cast a hook into the sea, catch a fish, and remove the golden coins from its mouth with which to pay the king's head-tax. In Song 40 the rich young man asks what he should do to get to the heaven-kingdom and is told to sell his treasure hoard and distribute it to the poor.

Song 41 tells a parable of the rich man and the beggar Lazarus. In afterlife the rich man burns in Hell, calling to Abraham to send Lazarus, who sits "blissfully" on Abraham's lap, with water, but Abraham refuses.

Song 42 relates the story of the workers who come late to the vineyard being paid as much as those who labored a full day, as a parable of those who come to Christianity late in life being rewarded as much as those who have been faithful for all their lives.

In Song 43, Christ foretells to his thanes his torture and death. On their way toward hill-fort Jericho he heals two blind men.

Song 44 is an author's sermon on the significance of healing the blind man.

In Song 45 "the Chieftain of human beings" enters Fort Jerusalem and fore-tells its downfall. In Song 46, Christ observes the poor widow "of uncompli-cated mind, of good will," who puts two bronze coins into the shrine's treasury, and he praises her. He advises the thanes to pay the taxes of the emperor from Fort Rome. In Song 47, Christ the Chieftain refuses to condemn the adulteress. In Song 48 he leaves the shrine because of quarrels over his teachings among the "arrogant Jews." Mary and Martha send for him because their brother Lazarus is ill. Christ tells his warrior-companions that Lazarus "has given up this light." Thomas accepts the warrior's fate to go along and die with Christ. In Song 49, Christ raises Lazarus from the grave.

Song 50 describes the clan-gathering of Jewish warriors who decide to kill Christ.

In Song 51 "the Chieftain of human clans" goes to Bethany to teach. In Songs 52 and 53, Christ describes the coming of doomsday.

Song 54 is called "Passio," meaning "Passion." Judas betrays his chieftain to the southern people, "slithery-hearted thanes." Christ arranges for a ban-quet, at which he washes the feet of his earls and thanes. Song 55 describes the last mead-hall feast of the warrior-companions. As soon as Judas, "that mean criminal," takes the food Christ offers him, "cruel things started going into his body, horrible little creatures, Satan wrapped himself tightly around his heart. . . ." The author warns, "This is the woeful situation of people who, under heaven, change lords."

In Song 56, Christ's words give three great powers to the bread and wine. First, they signify the means of salvation; second, they are a magic thing, a holy image of Christ; third, they are a means of overcoming the limitations of time and fate.

In Song 57, Christ goes up to the high Olivet mountain to pray, choosing three thanes to go with him: "James and John and good Peter—daring war-riors." He returns to find them sleeping.

In Song 58 "the grim Jewish army" captures Christ the Chieftain, while Peter, "the noble swordsman," flies into a rage and chops off Malchus's ear and opens his head. Christ "skillfully put the parts of his body back together." The wounds quickly heal.

In Song 59, Peter denies he is Christ's warrior-companion. Christ is brought before the assembly in iron bands in Song 60. He stands in chains before Pilate of Pontusland, while a remorseful Judas hangs himself (Song 61). In Song 62, Pilate questions Christ, while the Jews tell him, "He is . . . enormously impu-dent!" In Song 63, Christ is brought in iron shackles before King Herod, who sends him back to the other clan people. In Song 64 the Jewish warriors threaten Pilate with the will of the noble emperor Caesar of Fort Rome. In Song 65, Satan sets off for the home of the military governor, where he shows "mysteri-ous signs very clearly to the governor's wife" so that she will help Christ to remain alive. Satan knows that if Christ dies, He will take away Satan's power and he will no longer hold sway over the "broad middle-world." The governor's wife sends word asking her husband to spare Christ. He washes his hands of the matter and turns Christ over to the Jews. They whip and torture him and lead him to his death.

In Song 66 the Chieftain Jesus from Fort Nazareth is hanged on the criminal tree. In Song 67 the Chieftain of mankind dies and his spirit escapes. In Song 68 the body is removed from the gallows tree and buried in the earth. At night Christ's spirit returns to the corpse, and he rises. At sunrise the two Marys go to visit the grave and are met by an angel.

In Song 69, God's angel pushes aside the stone from the grave and tells the women that the Chieftain is on his way to Galileeland. In Song 70 the Jews bribe the grave guards with jewels to prevent them from revealing that Christ has risen. Peter, John, and Mary Magdalene come to the grave. Christ stands beside the weeping Mary, but she does not recognize him until he speaks her name. She is overjoyed.

In Song 71, Christ meets the warrior-company of earls on the road to Emmaus Castle. Then he rises to heaven, from where "the ruling Christ observes everything that happens in the whole world." (Murphy 1992)

 # HENRIADE, LA

French epic poem (1723, rev. 1728) by Voltaire (François-Marie Arouet, 1694–1778). It was an early work written when the poet was in his twenties. In 1717 Voltaire was arrested and put in the Bastille for writing inflammatory lines about the regent, and while in prison, he wrote the first version of *La Henriade*. He was released the following year. In 1720 he read parts of the epic at a gathering and, when the poem was criticized, he threw it into the fire. The poem was rescued from the flames by François Hánault. Voltaire was able to put the criticism behind him when he was allowed a reading to the regent himself. He continued to read excerpts at various social gatherings, including one at the country villa of exiled Lord and Lady Bolingbroke, who said his epic surpassed all poetical works that had appeared in France. In 1724 the poem began to circulate among the intelligentsia. It proved to be so popular that the regent awarded him a pension. It also earned him the favor of the young queen, Marie.

Composed in ten cantos and told in a lofty manner after Vergil's *Aeneid* and Homer's *Iliad*, the poem celebrates the struggle of Henry of Navarre to attain the throne. It depicts the assassination of Henry II and the religious wars with the Holy League, formed to defend Roman Catholics against the French Protestants and to put Henry of Guise on the throne. Once Henry of Navarre was king of France, he was revered by his subjects for having ended the religious wars by defeating the league at Arques and Ivry and, eventually, becoming a Catholic himself, an act of which the poem approves.

However, the poem criticizes the papacy, terming it "inflexible to the conquered, complaisant to conquerors, ready, as interest dictates, either to absolve or to condemn."

François-Marie Arouet Voltaire composed *La Henriade* during his imprisonment in Paris, which began in 1723. The poem is about the 1572 massacre of Protestants in Paris on St. Bartholomew's Day by Catholic followers of Henry of Navarre.

The poem uses the Massacre of St. Bartholomew as a text, flashing back to religious crimes from the time of Molocj, when mothers sacrificed their babies to fire, and to Agamemnon who, in exchange for a wind to propel his ship, was willing to sacrifice his daughter to the gods. It recalls the Romans persecuting Christians, who in turn persecuted heretics. It moves back to France, where Catholic followers of Guise were willing slaughterers of kings.

The poem praises Elizabeth for aiding Henry of Navarre. It describes Henry's clemency, his liaison with Gabrielle d'Estrées, and his siege of Paris. In imitation of the classics, the hero visits Hell, and after the fashion of Homer, the gods intervene in the war.

The poet was very much taken by the poem's reception: One French critic proclaimed it better than the *Aeneid,* and Frederick the Great said that "a man without prejudice would prefer *La Henriade* to the poem of Homer." In fact, Voltaire himself wrote to a friend, "Epic poetry is my forte, or I am deceived."

Voltaire was exiled to England, via Calais, in 1726 for having engaged in a fight with Chevalier de Roban, who made fun of his pen name. During his two-year stay in England, he decided to publish the poem. Jonathan Swift solicited subscriptions to pay for the printing, and among those subscribing were King George I and Princess Caroline. By the time the poem was published (1728), Caroline was queen. Voltaire dedicated it to her with an acknowledgment as well to George II. As a result, George II sent a gift of 400 pounds and invited him to attend royal suppers.

In three weeks, three printings of the poem, at three guineas per copy, had sold out. From his share of this English edition, Voltaire made 150,000 francs.

This formed the nucleus of the large fortune he later amassed. (Durant and Durant 1965)

See also Voltaire.

 # HERCULES

Swedish epic (1648, publ. 1658), the principal work of Georg Stiernhielm (1598–1672). The poem, a didactic allegory written in hexameter verse, was the poet's highly successful attempt at a marriage of classical myth and the new emerging Gothic nationalism, honoring Sweden's cultural heritage and stressing the qualities of honor and virtue. The epic retells, within the spirit of humanism, the classical Herculean narrative, personifying classical gods as national figures, reviving old Swedish words in the text, and alluding indirectly to current social and political problems of seventeenth-century Sweden.

Although it was completed in 1648, it was not published until 1658. Its publication established a trend in Swedish poetry, influencing the style of Esaias Tegnér (1782–1846) and Nobel Prize–winner Carl Gustaf Verner von Heidenstam (1858–1940). (Brogan 1996; Preminger 1974)

See also Stiernhielm, Georg Olofson.

HERE UNDER THE NORTH STAR
(*Täällä Pohjantähden alla*)

Finnish epic trilogy (1959–1962) by Väinö Linna (b. 1920). It relates the history of modern Finland, which gained independence from Russia after the Russian Revolution in 1917 but was plunged into civil war, beginning with the Battle of Tammerfors (1918) and lasting for a year. Finland became a monarchy with German prince Frederick Charles of Hessen as king for a short time, until Germany was defeated. Finally, Kaarlo Juho Stahlberg became president of Finland (1919–1925). As a result of the Winter War, Finland had been reunited, but the differences were not healed until the postwar era of the poet's time (1926), when a minority government granted a general amnesty. (Brogan 1996; Magill 1993)

HEREKALI
(Also *Utendi wa Tambuka,* The poem of the Battle of Tabuk)

Oldest extant Swahili epic (dated 1141, meaning A.D. 1728) written by Bwana Mongo. Rooted in Arabic literature, it is an account of Muḥammad's legendary campaign against Byzantine Heraclius in 630. It consists of 1,145 octosyllabic four-line stanzas. The poem is characterized by "raw energy and superficial religiosity." (Gírard 1976; Westley 1991)

 # *HERMANN UND DOROTHEA*
(Hermann and Dorothea)

German epic poem (1797) by Johann Wolfgang von Goethe (1749–1832). Written in hexameters in nine cantos, it is set during the French invasion of Germany after the French Revolution.

The First Canto, entitled "Calliope," begins with the landlord and his wife, proprietors of the Golden Lion, who sit at their door and watch the refugees struggle past. The apothecary and the parson stop by and tell them of the human misery they have seen. The landlord feels protected from the French by the Rhine as well as "by valiant Germans" and by God. He is more concerned, he tells the parson, about his son Hermann, whom he wants to see "making up his mind and bringing a bride to your altar."

In the Second Canto, entitled "Terpsichore," Hermann arrives and describes going to deliver emergency supplies to the refugees. He tells of meeting a young woman driving a cart holding another woman who had just given birth, and of giving all his supplies to her. The landlord expresses the desire that Hermann bring home a rich wife—one of the neighbors' daughters. But Hermann says the daughters humiliated him and laughed at him, and he never wants to see them again. He leaves in a determined huff while his father calls after him all that he expects in a daughter-in-law.

In the Third Canto, entitled "Thalia," the landlord bemoans the fact that the younger generation doesn't care to better themselves or improve the town the way the older generation does. He comments, "He who does not press forward, falls back!" His wife goes in search of their son, chiding the landlord for being so hard on the boy. The apothecary describes all the improvements he would make if he had the money.

In the Fourth Canto, entitled "Euterpe," while the men talk, the mother goes to look for her son. She finds him sitting under a tree weeping, saying he plans to join the army and fight the French. Eventually she persuades him to confess that he loves the poor refugee, whom he knows his father will never accept. The mother urges him to return to the house with her to speak to his father.

In the Fifth Canto, entitled "Polyphymnia," after the mother takes up her son's case, the parson steps in and reaffirms the boy's right to choose his own wife, saying the boy has always been prudent and thoughtful. The apothecary agrees, and after the son makes an impassioned declaration of his love for the girl, he suggests to his father that the parson and the apothecary go to the village and investigate her. The father reluctantly agrees, and the son drives the two men to the village outskirts in his buggy, where he waits while they go ahead on foot. The men meet an old refugee, a judge, who tells them of the people's hardships. The parson stays to listen to the old judge while the apothecary goes on to search for the girl.

In the Sixth Canto, "Clīo," the judge tells the parson of the bloodthirsty behavior of both sides, but he recalls one act of bravery: It is a young woman who saves herself and several girls in her care from ravishment by grabbing a Frenchman's sword and slaying all the attackers. The apothecary returns to say he has found the girl matching the son's description caring for refugee babies. The judge affirms that she is the same young woman he has just described. The two friends rush back to the waiting Hermann to tell him the young woman is worthy of being his wife. By this time, Hermann has doubts as to whether such a treasure of a woman would accept his proposal. He sends the two men home in the buggy, telling them he will walk home.

In the Seventh Canto, "Erato," as Hermann stands there, the girl, whose name is Dorothea, comes to the well to draw water. Lacking the courage to propose to her, he asks her to come home with him to work for his mother. She agrees to do so, saying, "Lucky's the girl who gets used to it, so that no errand's too irksome,/. . . And she lives only for others, forgetting herself altogether!" She takes the water to the village, says her farewells, and leaves to walk back with Hermann to his house.

In the Eighth Canto, "Melpomene," on the way home Dorothea asks Hermann to describe her future employers. He tells her that his father is "very keen . . . on outward appearance" with "rather a liking for airs." As they approach the house, she stumbles and twists her foot, saying, "I could really have done with a luckier omen!"

In the Ninth Canto, "Urania," the couple arrives home where the parents and the two friends wait. The father greets Dorothea as a future daughter-in-law. Believing he is making fun of her, she bursts into tears and determines to return to the village. Hermann confesses to the pastor that he has not proposed to her, but has brought her home under the subterfuge that he is hiring her as a servant. He begs the pastor to intervene and tell her the truth. But the pastor has a better plan. He tells Dorothea that it is a servant girl's duty to endure a master's teasing, explaining, "It's a common enough thing,/Surely, to tease a young lady for liking the looks of a young man." Dorothea confesses that she does like Hermann's looks—indeed, she has fallen in love with Hermann and knows a person of her station could never be his wife. Hearing her confession, Hermann steps forward and declares his love. The pastor betroths them then and there, after which Herman vows to leave immediately to fight the French: "If I know you are here to look after our home and our parents,/Why, then with confidence I shall go out and confront our attackers." (Goethe 1995)

See also Goethe, Johann Wolfgang von.

 # HERNÁNDEZ, JOSÉ
(Full name José Hernández Pueyrredón)

Argentine poet, author of the epics *El Gaucho Martín Fierro* (*La ido*, The flight, 1872) and *La Revuelta de Martín Fierro* (*La revuelta*, The return, 1879), later published as a single epic. He was born in 1834 in Chacra de Pueyrredón, Buenos

Aires. At the age of 14 poor health drove him from Buenos Aires to the pampas, where he learned the ways of the *gaucho* (cowboy). From the age of 19 he became active in the provincial governments' struggle for power with the central government in Buenos Aires. He served in the military, became a government official of Corrientes Province, and published a periodical, *El Río de la Plata* (1869).

In 1870 he participated in the unsuccessful coup against President Domingo Sarmiento. Afterward, he took self-imposed exile in Brazil (1871), where he wrote *El Gaucho Martín Fierro*, focusing on the oppression and injustice suffered by the gauchos. The poem documents the historical significance of the gaucho, whose land and livestock were expropriated by the privileged classes, and who was forced into military service to fight for principles he did not espouse.

In 1872 Hernández returned to Argentina and published his poem, which received immediate acclaim, although not necessarily for its considerable artistic merit; his political adversaries panned it, but were overruled. (One early commentator compared it to Harriet Beecher Stowe's *Uncle Tom's Cabin*.)

Seven years later he wrote a "sequel" entitled *La Vuelta*, in which the gaucho returns to become a part of society. This poem is published as Part II in some editions of the first poem. However, by the time the poems appeared, the gaucho had all but vanished from the Argentine pampas for good.

Hernández died in 1886 in Belgrano, near Buenos Aires. (Hernández 1974)
See also **The Gaucho Martín Fierro.**

 # HEROIC COUPLET

An English verse form of two consecutive lines of iambic pentameter whose end-words rhyme. Two kinds of heroic couplet are: the "closed couplet," which presents a complete thought or sentence not dependent on what precedes or follows it; and the "open couplet," also called the "run-on couplet," which is related to and/or dependent upon that which precedes or follows.

 # *HERZOG ERNST*

German medieval epic poem (late 12th c.) by a cleric possibly in Bamberg. The original poem exists only in two fragments; however, there is much evidence as to the contents of the rest. Ulrich von Etzenbach wrote a version based on the original poem. Odo, a priest of Magdeburg, wrote a Latin version of it in the thirteenth century, and another version in Latin prose exists. The latter was translated into German prose and became a popular Volksbuch (1493). During the nineteenth century, Ludwig Uhland (1787–1862) wrote a verse tragedy, *Ernst, Herzog von Schwaben* (1817). More recently, playwright Peter Hacks (1928–) wrote a play, *Das Volksbuch vom Herzog Ernst oder Der Held und sein Gefolge* (1953) based on the 1493 Volksbuch.

The first part of the poem evolves from two historical incidents involving revolts of sons against kings: Duke Liudolf's quarrel with his father, Otto I, in 953/954, and Swabia duke Ernst I's revolt against his stepfather, King Konrad II, in 1026 and 1028, which resulted in Ernst's death in 1030. Parts of these two events have been combined to make the first part of the story.

In part one, Duke Ernst's mother marries Emperor Otto, but a minister of the court, Pfalzgraf Heinrich, convinces Otto that his stepson is untrustworthy. Ernst, with his loyal companion Wetzel, takes revenge against Heinrich, killing him. Otto outlaws Ernst, who eventually sets out on a crusade.

The second part of the poem relates Ernst's journey to the Orient and his various escapades along the way. He rescues an Indian princess, held captive by people with bills like cranes. He and his companions barely escape death when their ships are sucked into a stony magnetic bluff. He comes into possession of a precious stone, the *lapis orphanus,* which has magical properties and which will later adorn the king's crown. For a while he enters the service of the king of Arimaspi, engaging in encounters with an assortment of peculiar adversaries. At length he returns and is reunited with the king. (Garland and Garland 1986)

 # HESIOD

Greek poet (ca. late 8th c. B.C.), called the father of Greek didactic poetry; author of *Works and Days* and *Theogony.* He was the son of a poor farmer who had gone to sea and finally migrated from Asia Minor to Boeotia (Greece). When the father died, Hesiod and his younger brother Perses divided the family farm. But they quarreled over the property and could not resolve their differences. Perses took their case to the ruling court, which he bribed to award him the larger portion of the land. However, he was lazy and as a result fared poorly. Hesiod, on the other hand, worked hard and lived frugally. The difference in the two men's styles and the economic results are depicted in his poem *Works and Days,* written to his brother. A didactic poem written in Homeric verse form, it gives maxims for living and precepts on farming as well as, briefly, on navigation. The poem inspired Vergil's poem on agriculture, *Georgics.*

Hesiod's *Theogony,* also called *Genealogy of the Gods,* is an important source of information on early Greek religion.

Legend says that Hesiod competed with Homer in oral poetry and defeated him. Legend also says that he traveled abroad and met a violent death. (Hornstein 1973; Siepmann 1987; Wender 1973)

See also Theogony.

 # HESPER

According to Joel Barlow in a note to his epic *The Columbiad,* Hesper and Atlas were brothers and Titans, sons of Uranus or Japetus, the sun. Atlas became a mountain in northern Africa to support the heavens. Hesper often visited the mountain in the study of astronomy, then disappeared and, having become a beautiful young man, was placed in the western sky as the Evening Star. Accordingly, his name was given to the western regions of the earth: Italy was called Hesperia by the Greeks, and Spain was called Hesperia by the Romans. (TAP) (Barlow 1970)

 # *HEXAËMERON* (1)
(Greek: Of six days)

Byzantine epic by George the Pisidian (fl. 7th c.). The work, thought to be the poet's masterpiece, is a retelling of the biblical creation story. In imitation of classical Greek poetry, the poet used 12-syllable iambic verse, which became the chief meter of medieval "classical" Greek poets. (Ostrogorsky 1969)

 # *HEXAËMERON* (2)

Danish religious epic (ca. 1622, publ. 1661) by Anders Arrebo (1597–1637). Based on sixteenth-century poet Guillaume Du Bartas's *La Semaine*, the poem describes the six days of creation, placed in a Scandinavian context, including elements of folk life and nature. It is written partly in twice-rhymed hexameter and partly in alexandrines. (Brogan 1996)

 # HIAWATHA

Hero of an American poem, *Song of Hiawatha* (1855), by Henry Wadsworth Longfellow. In Onondaga legend, Hiawatha is the hero/chief and founder of the Iroquois League of Five Nations. He is thought to have been a historical shaman/statesman who lived around 1450. Some legends say that he was originally a member of the Mohawk tribe, which rejected his teachings, forcing him to leave and live with the Onondaga. A powerful chief, Wathatotarho, opposed his attempts to unify the five nations of the Iroquois. After Hiawatha defeated him, the chief killed Hiawatha's daughter in revenge. (Erdoes and Ortiz 1984)
See also Longfellow, Henry Wadsworth; *The Song of Hiawatha*.

HIKAJAT PRANG KOMPENI

Sumatran epic poem (1873) about the Atjehnese Holy War of 1873, written by one of the participants. The poem exists only in manuscript form in the University Library at Leiden, Codex Ordinensis 8727B. It begins with a dream of the sultan's, which only the *oelama* (religious scholar) Teungkoe Koetakarang can interpret; he foresees in the dream the destruction of Atjeh by the Dutch. The king soon hands over his authority to the foremost territorial rulers, of *oelèëbelang*. The rest of the poem follows the deeds of various leaders, most of whom eventually die. The poem contains scenes following the Dutch invasion, the homeless villagers of Atjeh searching for shelter, and pictures of the leaders. The author wrote the poem along the way, adding new events as they occurred; he was killed before the war ended. (Siegel 1979)

HIKMET, NAZIM

(Also Nazim Hikmet Ran)

Turkish poet, author of *Human Landscapes* (1941–1945) and *The Epic of Sheik Bedreddin* (1936). He was born in 1902 in Salonika, the son of an official of the Ottoman government. He was raised in Istanbul, Anatolia. For a short while during World War I, he attended the naval academy. Following the war, during the Allied occupation of Turkey, he left Turkey and eventually ended up in Moscow, where he studied political science and economics at the University of Moscow, mingling with artists and writers from all over the world. He was already writing poetry at this time and had had at least one great love by 1924.

After Turkish independence, Hikmet returned home (1924), where he began working on a leftist magazine, for which he was arrested. However, he escaped and returned to Russia, where he continued writing poems and plays. He was greatly influenced by the poetry of Vladimir Mayakovsky (1894–1930), who created a verse system based on stress, wherein a word, rather than a line, is the unit (syllabic meter).

Following a general amnesty in 1928, Hikmet returned to Turkey, working as a journalist and proofreader on a number of journals, and as a translater, playwright, and poet, sometimes from prison. Turkish secret police constantly harassed him, and during the next ten years he served a number of short terms totaling almost four years. In letters to his wife written in prison he referred to her as "red-haired lady of my heart" (1933).

During the same ten years, he published nine books of poetry—five collections and four long poems, including *The Epic of Sheik Bedreddin,* the publishing of which, in 1936, landed him back in prison. His introduction of free verse greatly influenced Turkish poetry.

In 1938, when Turkish cadets were discovered reading his poems, Hikmet was arrested, charged with inciting the Turkish army to revolt, and sentenced to 28 years in prison. By this time he had married his second wife, Pirayé, and had at least one son. During the incarceration in Chankiri prison, when he heard about Hitler's invasion of Russia he became convinced of the need for an epic: the history of the twentieth century. Between 1941 and 1945 he completed a 20,000-line epic, *Human Landscapes from My Country* (or *Portraits of People from My Land*), which was smuggled out piecemeal. Parts of the epic were lost or destroyed during the process of being smuggled out, so that only about 17,000 lines are extant.

In 1949 a worldwide committee of writers and artists was founded that included Pablo Picasso, Pablo Neruda, and Jean-Paul Sartre, and the committee began a campaign for his release. In 1950, although Hikmet had suffered a heart attack, he nevertheless went on a hunger strike. That same year he was awarded the World Peace Prize. In a general amnesty that year, he was freed.

But in 1951 he was threatened with draft into the Turkish army at the age of 48. He fled the country, leaving behind his family, including his infant son, Memet, and went to Moscow. By that time he was married to Münevver Andac, who was prevented by the Turkish government from joining him in exile. (Born in Sofia, Bulgaria, and educated in France, she later moved to Paris and translated many of his works into French.) The rest of his life was spent in exile, during which he traveled and wrote novels, plays, and even children's stories.

During the last years of his life he lived with a young woman named Vera Tulyakova in Moscow, although he continued to travel widely. Hikmet was still writing poetry two months before his death in Moscow in June 1963. (Hikmet 1977, 1982)

See also The Epic of Sheik Bedreddin; Human Landscapes.

 # HIPPOLYTA AND HIPPOLYTUS

In Greek legend, Hippolyta is queen of the Amazons, a race of women-warriors who live in Scythia (the Caucasus) and kill all their male offspring. In one version they are offspring of Ares. Theseus invades her land. After an early show of resistance, Hippolyta submits and returns with Theseus to Athens, where she bears him a son, Hippolytus. On another occasion, one of the labors of Heracles is to bring back the girdle of Hippolyta. When he arrives in Scythia, she receives him kindly, but Hera stirs up trouble. Thinking Heracles is going to carry off their queen, the Amazons attack him. In reaction, Heracles kills Hippolyta, although she has tried to draw the Amazons away from him. He sails away with her girdle around his brows.

Hippolytus appears in Vergil's *Aeneid* (vii), Ovid's *Metamorphoses* (xv), Chaucer's *The Legend of Good Women*, and Edmund Smith's *Phaedra and Hippolytus*. After the death of Hippolytus's mother, his father, Theseus, marries Phaedra, who falls in love with Hippolytus. When Hippolytus spurns her, she makes false accusations about him to Theseus, who orders Poseidon to punish him. As Hippolytus flees, Poseidon's sea-calves frighten his horses, overturning his chariot and killing him. (Colum 1930; Hamilton 1940; Zimmerman 1961)

 # *HIROONA*

Caribbean epic poem (19th c., publ. 1930) by Horatio Nelson Huggins (1830–1895), a native of St. Vincent. The poem, of 12 cantos running 348 pages, is based on the 1795 rebellion of St. Vincent Caribs against British rule in the wake of the Haitian revolution. That rebellion led to the British deportation of 5,080 Caribs in 1797.

The title is adapted from the Carib name for St. Vincent, "Hiroon." The poem begins with an introduction that contrasts the beauty of the island and the "clear transparent sea" with the plight of the natives and the slaves the white man has brought: "the black man's chains, the red man's ban."

The hero, Warramou, is a nobly born warrior's son, leader of the revolt. The heroine, Ranèe, is a gentle Carib maiden who has been raised partly "by white men." She is in love with Norman, a white man. Her tender Christian heart leads her to thwart her tribe's human sacrifice.

In Canto XII, Warramou makes a final prophecy that the Christian God will avenge the wrongs done to his people by causing an apocalyptic explosion of St. Vincent's volcano in 1812. (The poet was writing after the fact.) He warns: "There comes, and quickly comes the day/When England's heel shall spurn these isles/. . . Her millions spent shall reckon lost . . ./Her battlements in slow decay/Uncared shall crumble day by day. . . ."

He predicts: "See! See! Yon mountain burst in smoke/. . . And all the mountain's sides ablaze. . . ." (Burnett 1986)

See also Huggins, Horatio Nelson.

 # *HISTORIA DE LA NUEVA MEXICO*
(History of New Mexico)

Spanish epic poem (1610) written by Don Gaspar Pérez de Villagrá, who was inspired by the conquest of New Spain.

The poem, consisting of 34 cantos in blank verse into which writs, royal decrees, and other documents are inserted, describes the conquest of New Mexico for Spain by Don Juan de Oñate. The poet-historian, a captain, accompanied the expedition and participated in the action. The poet relates that there were two factions among the Acoma Indians, one advocating friendship with the Spanish and the other favoring their extermination. In January 1599, Vicente de Zaldívar planned a frontal attack on the Acoma pueblo atop a cliff. He himself led a band of 11 up the deserted side of the cliff, while on another side of the mesa, protected by an 18-foot gorge, Spaniards placed a beam across the chasm so as to cross. When only 13 men had crossed, the beam was pulled away. The poet leapt the gorge and replaced the beam so that the others could cross.

The Spanish were assisted by the apparition of St. James wielding a sword and riding a white horse. The pueblo was destroyed, and 600 Indians were taken captive. Oñate and other leaders took part in the celebration performed by the Penitentes, an order that practiced flagellation during the dramatization of the Passion commemoration. The poet relates that Oñate and the other leaders joined in the customary self-torture.

The epic was originally published in Spain. Because of its historical significance, the epic was reprinted by the National Museum of Mexico in 1900. (Beck 1962; Peña 1968; Hammond 1927)

HOLY GRAIL

In medieval legend and literature the Sangreal, or Holy Grail, is the long-lost cup or dish, used by Jesus at the Last Supper, that various knights go on quests to recover. The earliest extant medieval Grail story is the French *Perceval* (ca. 1180) by Chrétien de Troyes. Wolfram von Eschenbach's German version, *Parzival* (ca. 1205), became the model for Wagner's opera *Parsifal*. Sir Thomas Malory's *Le Morte d'Arthur* (ca. 1470) was based on another French version, *La Queste del saint graal* (ca. 1210), author unknown. Alfred Lord Tennyson based his *Idylls of the King* on Malory's version. (Matarasso 1969)

 # HOMER

Ionian poet (ca. 700 B.C.?), the presumed author of the *Iliad* and the *Odyssey*, although there is dispute as to whether the two greatest epics of ancient Greece are the work of the same person, and whether such a person transmitted the poems by writing. The poet's use of formulaic language and themes places him within the tradition of oral poetry, but whether poems of 15,000 and 12,000 lines could have been composed without writing is disputed. Numerous early biographies were fabricated about Homer; eight of these are extant. These argue his birthplace as Chios, Smyrna, Cyme, Rhodes, Argos, Athens, Salamis, or Colophon. The *Hymn to Apollo* presents its poet as a blind Chiote, giving rise to the tradition that Homer was blind. As to his authorship, not only is there reason to believe that both poems are not the work of the same poet, a few scholars insist that each epic was the work of a number of poets. Greek epic poetry of the Homeric age was the end-product of a long period of accretion by generations of bards. Some scholars believe that, in the case of the *Iliad* and the *Odyssey*, this process continued until the sixth century B.C., when Pisistratus caused them to be codified for recitation at the Panathenaic festivals in Attica. Those who hold a different view credit the composition of the *Iliad* and at least the inspiration for the *Odyssey* to Homer. The most widely held position today is that each poem, although comprised of traditional material, is the work of a single author. The poems' blend of Ionic and Aeolic dialect and references in the *Iliad* to Ephesus's river Cayster and to a Carian woman, as well as a knowledge of the Troad, suggest that an important stage in the poems' composition took place in the eastern Aegean. For synopses of the poems, see the *Encyclopedia of Traditional Epics*. (Bowder 1984)

 # *HUDIBRAS*

English mock-epic or "burlesque" poem (1663, 1664, 1678; unfinished) by Samuel Butler (ca. 1612–1680). The popular and much imitated satire was published in three parts: Part 1 in 1663, Part 2 in 1664, and Part 3 in 1678. Written in heroic couplets (rhymed pairs of ten-syllable lines), it pokes fun at the Puritan army in particular and mankind in general for its pedantry and folly. Hudibras, the hero, is a Presbyterian knight bearing some similarity to Don Quixote. His squire, Rolpho, is an Independent, with whom he constantly bickers over petty and absurd religious differences. The two embark upon a series of comic misadventures in which their own ignorance, cowardice, and inept bumbling land them into worse trouble. The first part of the work, published anonymously, was so successful that it was immediately imitated.

When Part 2 appeared the following year, it was accompanied by an epistle entitled "The Heroic Epistle of Hudibras to Sidrophel." The poet characterizes Fame as "a tall long-sided dame,/That like a thin chamelion boards/Herself on air, and eats her words." (Part 2, Canto 1: 45, 47–48) He shows his disdain for pedantry: "Nor will you raise in my combustion/By dint of high heroic fustian." (Part 2, Canto 1: 585–590) The last part appeared in 1678. King Charles II was so pleased with the poem that he promised the poet a large monetary endowment; however, it was never awarded. (Highet 1962)

 # HUGGINS, HORATIO NELSON

Caribbean poet, author of the epic poem *Hiroona.* He was born in 1830 on the island of St. Vincent, the son of Lieutenant Horatio N. Huggins (1787–1861) of the Southern Regiment in St. Vincent, later a captain in the Trinidad Militia Regiment. The father owned land in Trinidad in the 1830s, when the family probably moved there. As a child in St. Vincent, the younger Huggins heard stories about the deportation of Carib Indians by the British and about the eruption of the volcano, which he would later use in his epic.

In 1864 the younger Huggins became rector of St. Phillip and St. Peter in Savonetta, Trinidad, serving until 1867. Then he became rector of St. Paul's, San Fernando, and chaplain of San Fernando Hospital. Late in life he composed his poem, which was published by his descendants in 1930. He became a canon sometime after 1891 and died in 1895. (Burnett 1986)

See also Hiroona.

 # HUGH GLASS

A character who appears in John Neihardt's *Cycle of the West,* Glass was originally a sailor who was taken prisoner by Jean Lafitte and forced to join the pirate's band. Escaping on the Texas coast, he was captured by Indians. While visiting St. Louis with a delegation of the tribe he regained his freedom.

In the spring of 1823 he joined General Ashley's second Missouri River expedition and was in the two battles with the Arikaras. In August he joined Major Henry's party on its return to the mouth of the Yellowstone River. Temporarily separated from the party, Glass was attacked by a grizzly bear and so injured that his death was expected momentarily. Pressed for time, Major Henry left Glass in the care of two of the trappers and proceeded on his march.

According to tradition, these two trappers were young James Bridger, age 19, and a certain Fitzgerald. These men took Glass's rifle and equipment and rejoined the party, announcing that Glass was dead and that they had buried him.

However, Glass slowly recovered his strength and after some days began crawling to Fort Kiowa, over a hundred miles away. He eventually got there and recuperated. Vowing revenge, he joined an expedition to Major Henry's new post on the Bighorn. There he found Bridger, whom he soon forgave. He found Fitzgerald some months later at Fort Atkinson, but by now his anger had cooled, and when he recovered his rifle from Fitzgerald, he declared the account closed. Later he engaged in a number of trapping ventures in much of the West. He became the subject of a great deal of folklore about encounters with Indians, and was admired for his integrity, truthfulness, and courage. He is thought to have been killed by the Blackfeet Indians on the upper Yellowstone River in 1833. (TAP) (Botkin 1975)

HUGO, VICTOR-MARIE

French novelist, dramatist, and poet, author of the historical epic *La Légende des siècles (The legend of the ages)*. He was born at Besançon in 1802, the son of Joseph-Léopold-Sigisbert Hugo, a general in Napoléon's army, who was stationed in Besançon at the time. He spent his first three years at Elba, then was moved to Paris for another three years. In 1807 he joined his father at Avellino. In 1809 he was sent with his mother to Paris, but they joined his father in Madrid in 1811. When his parents separated in 1812, he returned to Paris with his mother and brothers Abel and Eugène. At the age of 13 he was sent to boarding school, but he spent more time writing verse than on his studies.

In 1819 he began publishing a literary journal with his brother Abel, and in the same year became engaged to Adèle Foucher. They were married in 1822, the same year in which he published his first volume of *Odes et poésies diverses*, which earned him a small pension from Louis XVIII. The next year his novel *Han d'Islande* earned him another pension. Thereafter he was fully launched on a literary career, interrupted only briefly by the revolution of 1830. From 1826 (the date of the publication of his third collection of poems) onward, he produced an amazing variety of novels, essays, and travel literature, and five collections of poems. In 1841 he was elected to the Académie Française.

In 1845 he began to take an active part in politics. Originally a fervent Royalist, by now he had democratic leanings, although he supported the constitutional monarchy of Louis Phillipe as a step toward a republic. In 1845 the king made him a peer, but when the Revolution of 1848 broke out, he gave it his full support. However, when the new prince-president, Louis Napoléon, failed to offer him a high office in his government, he was deeply disappointed. When the 1851 coup d'état established the Second Empire, Hugo disguised himself as a workman and left France in disgust, taking with him his family and his mistress, the actress Juliette Drouet. Eventually he settled in Guernsey (1853), where he composed his sharp satires against the second Napoléon, his famous

French author Victor-Marie Hugo, 1802–1885, relates a tale to his grandchildren in an illustration by Reginald Bathurst Birch.

Les Misérables, most of the epic *La Légende des siècles* (1859), and the two religious poems that complemented the epic: *Dieu* and *La Fin de Satan.* With the fall of Napoléon in 1870 he returned to France, where he was elected to the Assemblée Nationale by 214,000 votes. He continued to write, including a second (1877) and third (1883) series of the *Légende.* Although his political influence soon waned, he was established as the greatest poet of nineteenth-century France, perhaps of all French literature. When he died in Paris in 1885, his was a national funeral, the celebration of an immortal. Paris was draped in black and a flood of flowers and portraits of Hugo lined the streets. His body lay in state under the Arc de Triomphe, and he was buried in the Pantheon. (Hugo 1907; Josephson 1942; Richardson 1976)

See also *Légende des siècles, La.*

 # HUMAN LANDSCAPES

(*Human Landscapes from My Country,* also *Portraits of People from My Land*)

Turkish epic poem (1941–1945) by Nazim Hikmet (1902–1963). Originally consisting of some 20,000 lines in five books, the poem was composed while the poet was in prison on trumped-up political charges. It was smuggled piecemeal out of the prison, and in the process some portions were lost. The extant poem consists of some 17,000 lines.

When Hikmet learned of Hitler's invasion of Russia, he became convinced of the need for an epic relating the history of the twentieth century, meaning primarily a history of Turkey since the Constitution of 1908. He envisioned beginning with Hitler's attack, then backtracking to the Boer War and working forward, continuing the epic until his own death. Consequently, there is no single hero, but a composite "fighter," which includes, for example, an epic poet, Jelal; a farmer, Kazim; a worker in handcuffs, Fuat. The "War" of the poem is a composite of World War I, the defeat of the Ottoman Empire and the occupation of Turkey by the Allies, the Turkish War of Independence establishing the Republic, World War II, and the political "war" that Hikmet and his fellow prisoners waged.

The episodic plot is told using cinematic techniques (the poet was also a screenwriter and playwright). Book I begins at Haydar Pasha Station in Istanbul in the spring of 1941. Attention focuses on one man who stands on the station steps: the master worker Galip. The "camera" pans to the other people he sees, and each is described in terse but rich detail. The passengers—including a group of prisoners as well as the unemployed, the dispossessed, factory workers, students, and soldiers—board the lower-class train. Galip sees Fuat's handcuffs and offers him a blessing: "May God . . ./see that all ends well."

During the train ride the whole spectrum of lower class social life is depicted, as well as the passing countryside between Istanbul and Ankara. Suddenly the train stops in the middle of nowhere. Aladdin, the engineer; the conductor; and Ismail, the fireman, get off to retrieve the body of a man who has jumped off the train. They put the body in the baggage car and continue their journey.

In Book II, meanwhile, at Haydar Pasha Station, a famous author, Hassan Shevket, sits drinking his *raki,* talking to a "thumb-sized man" (his conscience), who suggests to him that he is jealous of others who have made so much more money than he, such as Nuri Jemil, whom he spies on the platform waiting for the first-class express train. Nuri Jemil, in return, is jealous of Tahsin, a doctor and member of Parliament, who boards the sleeping car of the Ankara Express. Nuri Jemil enters the red velvet first-class car. To make it to this car, "he had fought for fifteen years" with people like himself, people "like packs of jackals." As the express train follows the same route as the other train, the poem follows the conversations, some in French, of the people of the upper and middle classes: senators, industrialists, doctors, professors' wives, merchants. Along the way the train passes by sites of major battles in the Independence War, triggering recollections by the passengers of historical events.

Among the passengers is Dr. Faik Bey, formerly a doctor for the police, who is going to his new assignment: chief of staff at a hospital on the steppe. He regales another passenger with the unsavory histories of some of the other passengers.

Meanwhile, the first train arrives at Ankara Station. The prisoners and their guards get off the train and part company, the prisoners being assigned to various prisons: Melahat, a female, to Ankara; Suleiman, to the east; Fuat, to the north; Halil, to a prison on the steppe. The others console Melahat that Ankara prison is fairly comfortable and that she will be able to send for her daughter to join her.

Book III begins with a panoramic view of the steppe, where the flowers have all withered and the locusts sing "the most hopeless of songs." All morning Nigar, carrying her six-month-old baby, has been running away from her husband's village with her lover, Mustafa. By late afternoon Mustafa has convinced her that the death of a six-month-old baby isn't a death, so, tired of carrying the infant, "her husband's seed," she drops it into a well. But soon she and Mustafa are both taken prisoner.

The poem continues in this vein with stories of other inmates in the prison on the steppe. Outside the walls, peasant women wait to see their husbands, begging guardsmen to take them the food they have brought. When the guardsmen ignore them, they become violent: "A mad woman is like a Kurdish dog— /the bravest horseman is no match for that." The guardsmen knock the women down with rifle butts.

On the second floor of the prison, Halil writes a letter to his wife, Aysha, describing what he can see from his window. Later he is sent to the hospital because of his eyes. He and Dr. Faik Bey sit in chairs on the landing, looking at the stone steps. The doctor remarks that the hospital is better than the government, because peasants have to squat against a wall at the government's door, whereas "at least here they can sit on the stone steps."

The poet describes an operation the doctor performs on a peasant's wife. Halil tells him that the woman and her husband and most of the people on earth are "condemned to a half-animal, half-vegetable" existence because they have to work so long and hard that they are "deprived of the happiness of thinking a lot." The peasant husband, Dumel, comes for his wife, but the doctor refuses to release her, even though she is lawfully Dumel's property and he wants her to come home to care for her two babies. Besides, Dumel explains, he has to harvest his crop. But when he sees her lying in bed, he says, "Nothing left in her now. . . . She's gone bad." He leaves and never comes back. Three days later she dies. The doctor, who is seen as the enemy by the suspicious steppe peasants, later commits suicide by taking poison.

Halil hears a scream and looks into a room to watch a baby being born. He feels embarrassed and wonders, "So Ausha gave birth this way, too?" His heart fills with joy as he hears the most beautiful sound in the world: "the first victory cry of the newborn."

In Book IV, back in prison, Halil has a visitor: the 13-year-old worker Kerim, who comes regularly for arithmetic lessons. From the barred windows they watch the migrating birds. The poem follows the birds' flight across continents, then shifts down to radio antennas, to the Voice of America broadcast. Thus the greater world's crises—in this case, the beginnings of World War II—intersect the lives in a Turkish town.

Book V begins with Aysha waking, watching her daughter Leyla sleeping. The day before, she received money from Halil, sent from prison. She writes him, ". . . it hurts to know / you're working to support me." She tells him about life on the outside: people smuggling money to Switzerland, Turkey shipping wheat to Germany. Meanwhile, Halil is depressed because a peasant, imprisoned for not paying his road tax, has hung himself. He reads Aysha's letter, then rereads her old ones. Each letter not only describes elements of Turkish daily life, but follows various incidents in the lives of people. Halil has flashbacks of things that have happened in prison.

In the final section of the epic, Fuat is released from prison. He is ecstatic at first, but on the fifth day of his freedom, as his train approaches Istanbul, he feels sick with sorrow, remembering all those still in prison, especially Halil.

A siren screams, and the poem follows the paramedic Hassan Killitch through the town to a neighborhood of unpainted houses, into a stinking place that houses six families in five rooms, where he finds a family suicide. A tanner has poisoned his whole family. All are dead but one girl. As they rush her to the hospital, Hassan is planning how he can get in on a black market drug deal. (Hikmet 1982)

See also Hikmet, Nazim.

 # HUON OF BORDEAUX
(Also Huon d'Auvergne)

A legendary figure at the court of Charlemagne who appears in the epic *Oberon* by Christophe Martin Wieland. Huon was reputed to be one of two sons of

Séguin, duke of Bordeaux, and as such had been educated by his mother at the court of the emperor Charlemagne. From his birth, Auberon (Oberon) had a special interest in him. When Huon came of age he was made duke of Guyenne, vassal of Charlemagne. An enemy of the family, Amaury, baron of Hautefille, conspired against him and turned the emperor against him. He was the subject of medieval romances in which he survives many troubles with the help of Auberon and marries Esclairmond, daughter of the Babylonian king. (Bullfinch 1970; Hulpach 1970)

HUSENI

Swahili epic poem in 1,209 stanzas, recounting the life and death of Ḥusayn ibn ʿAlī, Shīʿite Muslim hero, grandson of Muḥammad through the Prophet's daughter Fāṭimah and her husband, ʿAli, the fourth caliph. In A.D. 680, Ḥusayn was assassinated at Karbalā by the rival Umayyads under Yazīd, an event that shook the Muslim world with rebellious outbreaks of retribution for years. The Swahili poem is taken from the *ta'ziya,* a passion play festival commemorating the life and death of Ḥusayn, which is performed in Iran, Iraq, India, and Turkey. (Gírard 1976)

HYBRIS
(Hubris)

Excessive pride, to which ancient Greeks attributed the fall of many heroes. An act of *hybris* was met with swift retribution by the gods. In the *Iliad,* Agamemnon's *hybris* in refusing to return his war prize, Chryseis, causes Apollo to visit a plague upon the army. Achilles's *hybris* in refusing to participate in the battle after Agamemnon takes his war prize, Briseis, indirectly brings about the death of his dearest friend, Patroklos. Patroklos himself suffers from *hybris* and ignores Achilles's command to return to him as soon as he has turned back the Trojans. "Pride goeth before destruction" is found in the biblical book of Proverbs. In Christian belief, pride is considered the most venal of the seven deadly sins. (Jackson 1994)

HYPERION

English epic poem (1818–1819; unfinished) by John Keats, in which the poet employed the entire theogony of the classical Greeks. The poem, consisting of two and one-half books in Miltonic blank verse, is based on a Greek legend: the overthrow of the Titan sun god Hyperion by the sun god Apollo. The first two books were written during his brother Tom's lingering illness and death, and the third book was abandoned during a particularly bleak period following his brother's death and the complications of the poet's love life. Later in 1819 Keats returned to the subject with the intention of reworking the poem under a new name, ridding it of its heavy Miltonic flavor. The titanic majesties of the divinities in the poem were inspired by the Elgin Marbles, which he was taken to see in 1817 by the painter Haydon. The grandeur and repose of the Parthenon sculpture inspired in the poet a larger scope for his poem. (Anderson and Buckler 1966; Highet 1976)

See also The Fall of Hyperion: A Dream.

 # IBN ḤAZM, 'ALI IBN AHMAD

Andalusian poet and theologian, author of the combination poetry and prose epic on "pure love" *Ṭawq al-ḥamāmah* (The ring of the dove, 11th c.). Based on his own personal experiences, Ibn Ḥazm composed the epic in Spain during the 'Abbasīd reign. He was born in 994, the grandson of a Spaniard who converted to Islam. He began as a poet, his best-known work being his epic on chivalrous love. Ibn Ḥazm belonged to the strict fundamentalist Zāhirī sect, which interpreted the Koran literally. He became the chief minister at Córdoba, but his attacks on theological opponents led to his resignation, the public burning of his books, and his withdrawal from public life. He commemorated the book-burning in Seville by writing an epigram. He wrote an important book on comparative religion, *The Book of Religious and Philosophical Sects* (11th c.), pointing out inconsistencies in the Old and New Testaments. In his epic he expressed the theme of Udhrah love (*ḥubb 'udhrī*), or mystical love, said to be based on his own intimate experiences, in which the lover wishes to die on the path to the beloved. Ibn Ḥazm died in 1064. (Dudley and Lang 1969)

 # IḶAṄKŌ, AṬIKAḶ
(The venerable ascetic prince)

Traditional South Indian author (ca. 5th c.) of the Tamil epic *Cilappatikāram*. However, his name appears only in the *patikam*, or prologue, which scholars believe is a later addition to the poem. The author of the poem was probably a Jaina, since the poem itself is laced with the Jaina doctrine of karma. Nothing else is known about the author, although the convention of early Indian literature is to ascribe authorship to a prince of the royal house of Cērals. However, Iḷaṅkō possibly put a story from oral tradition into writing. (Blackburn and Ramanujan 1986; Parthasarathy 1993)

ILIAD

Greek epic (ca. 9th c. B.C.?) traditionally attributed to Homer. It tells, in 24 books of dactylic hexameter verse, of the events just prior to the end of the Trojan War. For a synopsis, see the *Encyclopedia of Traditional Epics.*

 # IMAGISM

A poetry movement that came into vogue about 1909 or 1910 among a number of American and English poets, following the lead of Ezra Pound and T. E. Hulme. The movement was primarily a reaction against sentimental Georgian poetry with set formulas about nature and the bucolic life. Imagism eschewed mere description in favor of the exacting image, and it abandoned set forms and rhythms and rigid discipline in favor of a "controlled" free verse and, in the words of Pound, "the sequence of the musical phrase, not . . . the sequences of a metronome." Imagist poems were often no more than four or five lines long, presenting a single, precise, but highly original metaphor.

Among other Imagists were Hilda Doolittle, Richard Aldington, John Gould Fletcher, William Carlos Williams, Amy Lowell, and F. S. Flint. In 1914, Pound edited the first of several Imagist anthologies. By 1918 the movement had run its course, but it nevertheless exercised a great, liberating influence on modern poetry, particularly the work of such poets as T. S. Eliot, Wallace Stevens, and Hart Crane. (Perelman 1994)

 # INBER, VERA

Russian socialist poet, author of the "epic" *The Pulkov Meridian* (1943). She was born in 1890 in Odessa, the daughter of a publisher. She spent the years 1910 to 1917 in Paris, during which she was influenced by the French and Russian Symbolists. Her first book of poems, *The Wine of Melancholia,* was published in Paris in 1914. During the years of the Russian civil war, she was in Odessa. In 1922 she moved to Moscow, becoming an avid constructivist. Her next collection, *The Aim and the Way* (1925), shows her realist leanings.

In the late 1920s, Inber began working as a journalist in Paris, Brussels, and Berlin. Her writing, which included prose and short fiction as well as poetry, became autobiographical. Her collection *To the Son I Do Not Have* (1927) sees communal life from the sentimental standpoint. She published a collection of lyrics, *The Soul of Leningrad,* in 1942. Her long narrative poem, *The Pulkov Meridian* (1943), depicts in a simple style the blockade of Leningrad during World War II, including graphic descriptions of the first artillery fire. The poem gained such popularity that in 1946 she published a prose account called *Almost Three Years.*

Inber devoted the 1950s to writing prose and poetry for children. In 1960 she published a collection about Lenin called *April.* She died in 1972. (Bristol 1991)

INGEMANN, BERNHARD SEVERIN

Danish novelist and poet, author of the epic cycle *Holger Danske* (Holger the Dane, 1837) and several historical novels, two of which are in verse. He was born in 1789 in Torkilstrup, Falster, Denmark, and educated at the University of Copenhagen to be a schoolteacher. He taught at Sorø Academy (1822) in the medieval town of Sorø, where he developed an abiding interest in Danish history and chivalric customs. He wrote six historical novels that were popular for several generations. The first, *Valdemar den store* (or *Seir*) (Waldemar the Great, or The victorious, 1824), is in verse. The next four are in prose. The last, *Dronning Margrethe* (Queen Margrethe, 1836), is also in verse. In 1837 he published a patriotic verse cycle that epitomized the Danish medieval character of chivalry and nationalism. In the next few years he published two collections of simple lyrics, *Morgensange for Børn* (Morning songs, 1837) and *Morgen og Aften* (Evening songs, 1839), which have continued to be much admired by the Danish people.

In 1846 he was named director of Sorø Academy, in which position he remained for a number of years. Although his works were beloved by the Danish people, he is best known in the English-speaking world for a hymn, known in translation as "Through the Night of Doubt and Sorrow." He died in Sorø in 1862. (Siepmann 1987)

INTREPID CORTÉS
(*Cortés valeroso*)

Spanish epic poem (1588) about Hernán Cortés's conquest of the Aztec empire written by Gabriel Lobo Lasso de la Vega (1558–1615). (Anderson-Imbert 1969)

ITALIA LIBERATA DA GOTTI, LA
(The liberation of Italy from the Goths)

Italian epic poem by Giovan Giorgio Trissino (1478–1550). The first modern epic in classical style, the poem consists of 27 books written in blank verse. It describes Eastern Roman Emperor Justinian's defeat of the Goths, who occupied Italy in the sixth century. Written in the style of a medieval romance, it is tinged with both Classical and Christian influences. Although the epic was once a very famous poem, Gilbert Highet terms the author "a bad poet" with a feeble imagination, whose verses are "flat," whose plot is "boringly arranged." (Highet 1976)

ITALICUS, SILIUS

See Silius Italicus.

IWEIN

Middle High German epic (ca. 1200) by Hartmann von Aue (ca. 1660/1670–d. after 1210). An Arthurian epic of some 8,000 lines, it was the poet's last work. The poem was inspired by *Le Chevalier au lion* by Chrétien de Troyes.

It relates the story of Iwein, a noble knight, who learns of the hazardous exploit experienced by Sir Kalogreant at the site of a magic well. Always in search of a challenge, Iwein sets off to see the well and its defender for himself. He succeeds in defeating the knight who is defending the well, chasing him into his castle walls. The knight subsequently dies, leaving Iwein trapped inside. A maid-in-waiting, Lunete, gives him a ring that makes him invisible so that he can elude the knight's men. But when the invisible Iwein sees Laudine, the knight's beautiful widow, he is smitten. With Lunete's help, he woos and wins her as his bride.

Eventually King Arthur and his retinue, including Gawain, visit the love-struck Iwein to remind him not to neglect his knightly duties. Iwein leaves Laudine, promising to return in one year. But when he forgets that anniversary, Laudine sends Lunete to upbraid him and to fetch her ring. Iwein is so devastated by this turn of events that he becomes mad, wandering about in the woods like a wild man. A noble lady upon whom he chances cures him with a magic ointment. He rescues her from her captors, then saves a lion that is about to be eaten by a dragon. Thereafter the lion becomes his loyal companion. He engages in other exploits, including rescuing the maid Lunete from execution.

At length, driven by desire for Laudine, he returns to the magic well, and he and Laudine are reunited. (Garland and Garland 1986)

See also Hartmann von Aue.

 ## JAKOB UND JOSEPH AND JAKOB UND RACHEL

German/Swiss unsuccessful religious epics of minor importance by Johann Jakob Bodmer (1698–1783). (Garland and Garland 1986)
 See also Bodmer, Johann Jakob.

 ## JALAL UD-DĪN RŪMĪ

See Rūmi, Jalal un-Dīn

 ## JĀMĪ, NŪR AL-DĪN 'ABD AL-RAHMĀN

Persian poet, mystic, and scholar, considered the last great classical Persian writer during Persia's golden age, author of *Haft Awrang* (Seven thrones), a set of seven epic poems modeled after Nizāmī's *Khamseh* (Quintet). He was born in 1414 in a village near Samarkand. After studying theology in Samarkand and Herāt, he became a Ṣūfī mystic, a member of the Naqshbandi order. His best-known prose work is *Nafahāt al-Uns* (Breaths of friendship), biographies of some 600 Ṣūfī saints. His most famous work is *Haft Awrang,* of which at least two poems have been translated: *Salāmān and Absāl* and *Yusuf and Zuleika,* love allegories about the mystic's quest for God. Jāmī won the patronage of Sultan Husayn Bayqara, Timurid ruler of Herāt (1469–1506), who founded a college especially for him and appointed him professor. He also enjoyed the friendship of Husayn's adviser, epic poet Nawā'ī. He died in 1492 in Herāt. (Dudley and Lang 1969; Kritzeck 1964)
 See also *Yusuf and Zuleika.*

JAYADEVA

Indian poet (fl. late 12th c.), author of the Sanskrit lyric epic *Gitagovinda* (Song of the cowherd). He was born about the mid-twelfth century in the Bengal village of Kenduli. His father, Bhojadeva, was a Brahman, a member of the Hindu priestly caste. Jayadeva was married to Padmāvatī and lived at Nadia, attached to the royal court of King Lakśmaṇasena (ca. 1178–ca. 1205). It was probably at the king's instigation that he composed his famous erotico-religious epic about the love affair between Rādhā and Kṛṣṇa. Because his poem is characterized by *bhakti* worship (impassioned worship of a personal God), it is conjectured that it may have originated in a more secular milieu, later being given a Sanskrit revision. Jayadeva is still honored in Kenduli, where an annual festival is held in his honor, at which songs from his epic are sung. (Miller 1977; Thapar 1966)

See also Gitagovinda.

 # JĀYASĪ
(Malik Muhammed Jāyasī, or Jaisi)

Indian Muslim Hindi poet, author of *Padmāvatī*. According to the poet, he was born during an earthquake in 1494, possibly in the city of Jayas, where he later lived. His house is still preserved. He began his first poem after the age of 30 following an association with Hindu scholars, who inspired him. He began his masterpiece, *Padmāvatī*, in the year 1540, and, according to him, was an old man when he finished it, probably after 30 years. He also mentions the loss of an eye and the loss of hearing in one ear, probably from smallpox. In later life he became a religious ascetic in seclusion in the jungle of Ramnagar, about 20 miles away (probably the longest journey in his life). The previously childless raja in nearby Amethi had a son, which he attributed to the prayers of Jāyasī; consequently the poet was treated as a saint and miracle worker. His tomb is venerated to this day. According to popular belief, he assumed the form of a tiger during his evening prayers and was shot.

Jāyasī told the story of Padmāvatī in the form of an allegorical Ṣūfī *masnavī*. His religious reputation is due to the epic's preservation. Deeply affected by Hindu yoga philosophy and Muslim lore, he was also revered as a Muslim saint by Muslims. In this meeting of Muslim and Hindu cultures, Jāyasī became the poet of unity and tolerance, a pioneer in Hindu-Islamic cultural rapprochement and collaboration. *Padmāvatī* is an illustration of this meeting of traditions. The poet was himself a Muslim Hindu. The epic is based on the Muslim invasion of India and the heroic resistance of a Hindu Rāsput prince, and a Muslim sultan's fascination with a Hindu princess.

Jāyasī is the oldest vernacular poet of Hindustan, and also the author of *Akhiri Kalam* and *Akharawat*. (Sherriff 1944)

See also Masnavī; Padmāvatī.

JED SMITH
(Jedediah Strong Smith)

A character who appears in the American epic *Cycle of the West* by John Neihardt. He was born in 1798 in Bainbridge, New York, where he received a fair education. At age 13 he became a clerk on a Lake Erie freighter, where he met traders returning from the Far West. When General William Henry Ashley organized his Rocky Mountain trade in 1823, Smith joined the venture. In 1826, Ashley sold his business to Smith and two other men, who carried on the trade until 1830, when they sold out to other mountain men.

In this period, Smith made his reputation as an explorer. He first investigated the Southwest and Oregon country for a trade route from California to Oregon. After reaching the Great Salt Lake, his party of 17 men passed through the Mojave Desert to the San Gabriel Mission. Under suspicion of spying by the Spanish California governor, he escaped imprisonment through the intervention of a captain from Boston, but his plan to go north to Oregon was frustrated. Instead, he proceeded northeastward in an unsuccessful attempt to cross the mountains. Smith left his main party on the American River, and with only two men made a successful attempt farther north, but it meant crossing an unrelieved desert back to the Great Salt Lake. A month later he retraced his route with 18 men, but was attacked by Mojave Indians, who killed ten men. With the eight survivors, Smith joined the men he had left on the American River, now in sad plight. With the Spanish governor's permission, he stocked new supplies and proceeded northwest to the coast. Crossing the Umpqua River on his way to the Willamette, his party was attacked by Umpqua Indians, who massacred all but Smith and one other man. They joined a third survivor on the Willamette, finally making their way to their rendezvous at Pierre's Hole. Smith retired from Rocky Mountain trade the next year, but in 1831 entered the Santa Fe trade. That year, at a water hole near the Cimarron River, he was surroundeded by Comanches and killed.

Smith was the first explorer of the Great Basin, the first American to make his way from the east into California, and the first to make it out from California. (TAP) (Lewis [Oscar] 1958)

See also *Cycle of the West.*

JERUSALEM, THE EMANATION OF THE GREAT ALBION

English epic poem (1804–1820) written, engraved, and printed by William Blake (1757–1827). Begun in 1804 and finished in 1820, the poem is one of his two longest works, and his last book. It is easier to understand the work in the context of Blake's other so-called "prophetic books," which include: *America* (1793), *Europe* (1794), *The Book of Urizen* (1794), *The Book of Los* (1795), and *Milton: A Poem in Two Books* (1804–1809). In *Milton*, Blake continued to pursue the idea, explored in the earlier works, of the arts as the chief mode of communication with eternity. He depicts Milton's spirit entering Blake. He uses "Jerusalem" to represent ancient times.

Blake envisions an ideal social order, "The New Jerusalem," which goes beyond mere social and political reforms to encompass a new respect for humanity and a spiritual grace that supplants old conventional authority. He depicts the devastating effect the Industrial Revolution will have on the quality of life of poor laborers. The Giant Albion represents the English nation and, by extension, all men. Although he is concerned by the infringement on individual rights by the government, the church, and even family, he is most concerned about industrial exploitation of the worker.

The poem, four chapters of free verse, has neither plot nor true characters, and his symbolism is often murky. Chapter one consists of 26 sections, plus an opening section entitled "To the Public." As it begins, Albion, once a great giant living in blissful harmony encompassing the whole universe, has fallen because he rejected Jerusalem, his feminine aspect. Thus he remains less than whole. He calls her "deluding shadow of Albion!/Daughter of my phantasy! Unlawful pleasure! Albion's curse!" (1:23) Instead, he chose the daughter of Luvah, Vala, who represents nature as divorced from eternity. Jerusalem asks him, "Why hast thou hidden me/Remote from the Divine Vision, my Lord and Saviour?" The remorseful Albion admits, "I have erred! I am ashamed! and will never return more./. . . I will give myself for my children!/Which way soever I turn, I behold Humanity and Pity!" (1:23) Albion finds himself in a hostile world. He falls into a chaotic state of sleep while Los, with tongs, anvil, bellows, hammer, and fiery furnaces, attempts to bring order.

A section preceding Chapter two is addressed "To the Jews," in which the poet asks, "Was Britain the Primitive Seat of the Patriarchal Religion?" If it is true, then "it is also True, that Jerusalem was and is the Emanation of the Giant Albion." He tells the Jews that their ancestors from Abraham to Noah were Druids. "Albion was the Parent of the Druids, & in his Chaotic State of Sleep, Satan & Adam & the whole World was Created by the Elohim."

In Chapter two, Los opens his seven Furnaces of Death to show the dreaming Albion that "the accursed things" within are "his own affections/and his own beloveds." Los describes himself thus: "Thou wast the Image of God surrounded by the Four Zoas./Three thou hast slain. I am the Fourth: thou canst not destroy me." "Zoas" is derived from *zoe*: life. They are based on the "Four Living Creatures from the Book of Revelations and the four-faced man of the Book of Ezekiel." The Zoas once stood around the "Throne Divine." Their English names were Verulam, London, York, and Edinburgh. With divine intervention, Los attempts to re-create from "an endless labyrinth of woe" the structure of eternity.

A short sermon, "To the Deists" precedes Chapter three, in which the poet calls the Deists "the Enemies of Christianity" and also "The Enemies of the Human Race & Universal Nature."

In Chapter three, Los, weeping over Albion, continues to rebuild. Albion continues to see visions of the chaos he has caused, while the Great Voice of

Eternity asks questions such as, "What is a Wife & What is a Harlot? What is a Church & What/Is a Theatre? are they Two & not One? can they Exist Separate?/Are not Religion & Politics the Same Thing? . . ." There are visions of Mary, Joseph, and Jesus; of the "Giants & the Witches & the Ghosts of Albion [who] dance with/Thor & Friga. . . ." Los sees a vision of all the Daughters of Albion becoming one in Vala, who has "the Druid Knife of Revenge & the Poison Cup/of Jealousy." She puts her hand upon the Looms and cries, "The Human is but a Worm!" She takes the distaff and spindle and, "with the Flax of/Human Miseries," turns "fierce with the Lives of Men."

Blake illustrates the scene with a plate showing two angels weeping over a world "Continually Building, Continually Decaying because of Love & Jealousy." Beneath a serpent are the words "Women, the comforters of Men, become the Tormentors & Punishers."

Preceding Chapter four is a sermon, "To the Christians," which says in part, "To Labour in Knowledge is to Build up Jerusalem, and to Despise Knowledge is to Despise Jerusalem & her Builders." Blake calls Jesus "the giver of every Mental Gift."

In Chapter four Albion asks Jesus, "O Lord, what can I do? my Selfhood cruel Marches against thee. . . ." Jesus replies, ". . . unless I die thou canst not live. . . ." Albion throws himself into the "Furnaces of Affliction." The Furnaces become "Fountains of Living Waters flowing from the Humanity Divine." Albion wakens, is reunited with Jerusalem, and recovers his state of bliss, harmony, and universal knowledge. (Blake 1991)

See also Blake, William; *Milton: A Poem in Two Books.*

JERUSALEN CONQUISTADA
(Jerusalem conquered)

Spanish epic poem by Lope de Vega (Lope Félix de Vega Carpio, 1562–1635), who is known chiefly as Spain's most lyrical golden age dramatist. The style of the epic is reminiscent of Torquato Tasso's *Gerusalemme liberata* (Jerusalem liberated, 1575) and the less successful *Gerusalemme conquistata*. (Preminger 1974)

See also Lope de Vega.

JINASENA

Indian Digambara teacher and poet (fl. 9th c.), author of *Mahāpurāṇa* (The great legend), a text of Jainism. The epic, written in excellent Sanskrit, is modeled on the Hindu *Purāṇas*. The Digambaras, or "Spaceclad," are one of two sections of Jainism. As a sign of asceticism, its monks were completely nude. Today the Digambaras are located primarily in the Deccan, specifically in Mysore. (Embree 1988)

JOCELYN

French narrative poem (1835) by Alphonse de Lamartine. The poem is a fragment of an uncompleted epic that was to begin with *La Chute d'un ange* (publ. 1838). The protagonist, Jocelyn, is a young seminary student who escapes the revolution and hides out in the mountains. He gives refuge to a boy named Laurence, who turns out to be a girl in disguise. The two fall in love, but Jocelyn cannot turn his back upon duty. His former mentor, the bishop, is imprisoned and awaits execution. The bishop wants to ordain Jocelyn so that Jocelyn can administer the last sacrament to him. Jocelyn confesses his love for Laurence, but acedes to the bishop's wishes and is ordained a priest.

After the Terror, Jocelyn is appointed priest in a remote Valneige parish, while the abandoned Laurence turns to a life of dissipation in Paris. One day Jocelyn is called to an inn to the deathbed of a woman, whom he recognizes as his long-lost love. He gives her absolution and reveals his identity before she dies.

A few months later, Jocelyn succumbs to an epidemic and dies as well. His parishoners bury him beside Laurence. (Harvey and Heseltine 1959)

JOHANNES DE BACTGEZANDT
(John the Baptist)

Dutch epic poem (17th c.) based on the life of the biblical John the Baptist, written by Joost van den Vondel (1587–1679), called the greatest of Dutch poets. The poem is written in alexandrine couplets utilizing internal rhyme and repetition of diminutive endings. (Preminger 1974)

JOHANÛZ DEM VIRGIERE

Middle High German verse epic (ca. 2nd half 14th c.) by an unknown poet, possibly from Rhenish Hesse. The poem, some 3,000 lines long, tells of a beautiful boy-child who is discovered by the emperor Sigemunt in his royal gardens. The boy is reared as a knight and shows his valor and fealty in battle. He is discovered to be the son of the count of Artois. He is rewarded with the emperor's daughter in marriage, and he becomes the next emperor. The poem was inspired by an earlier Flemish poem. (Garland and Garland 1986)

JOHN BROWN'S BODY

American epic (1928) about the American Civil War by Stephen Vincent Benét (1898–1943). The poem, in eight books, is written in three basic meters: traditional blank verse for serious episodes; heroic couplets for most of the Wingate episodes; and a rhythm close to ordinary speech for a variety of topics. Benét also uses some passages of rhythmic prose to sum up background developments. Songs and ballads are inserted for variety. The epic's meaning is embodied in the central character, John Brown, a legendary and historical symbol, and in the frequent multifaceted Phaethon imagery, symbolizing the divine humbling of pride, and the regenerative power. The epic also portrays the terrible suffering and great courage on both sides, the insane and brutal irrationality of war, and its tragic waste.

The invocation, written in ballad form, addresses the "American Muse," as "various as [its] land." The prelude opens with a monologue by a slaver reading his Bible, interspersed with a Negro spiritual.

In Book One we are introduced to the Yankee Jack Ellyat and the Georgia-born Clay Wingate, central figures in the epic. We hear the prayer of John Brown before his raid on Harpers Ferry and his capture. We are also introduced to the Negro majordomo of Wingate Hall who is proud of white folks and wonders why Brown wants to kick up such dizziness. "Nigger-business ain't white folks' business." Brown is hanged with a final speech: "The crimes of this guilty land will never be washed away." Then we hear the singing of "John Brown's body lies a-mouldering in the grave. . . . It marches on."

In Book Two, dashing General Beauregard has just bombarded Fort Sumter, and the war has begun. Jefferson Davis, with his gentility, and tall, lanky Lincoln—"whose wit was a coonskin of dry, tall tales"—assemble their cabinets. The press screams noisily; preachers howl for blood. North and South assemble with youths too ready to die. Clay Wingate likes "the crisp new toys of fighting," the brag and the girls, like Sally Dupré. In the cabins, Zachary cannot sleep. He is mighty fond of his white folks, but he "wants to be free." In Pennsylvania, slow-thought-chewing Jake Diefer rises from his bed, hitches the wagon for his boys, says good-bye to his wife, kisses her clumsily, and rides off to the army. Up in the mountains, Luke Breckinridge, rifle on his shoulder, slips from the forest into town. He's not sure whom he is going to fight. It ain't the British, nor Indians. Up North, a crowd gathers, singing, "We'll hang Jeff Davis on a sour-apple tree!" Jack Ellyat, marching in the parade, is followed by his dog. They have to kick it away as he boards the train. Plump Curly Hatton in another column is not used to marching; there is so much of the road and it is so dry. But he is in love with Lucy, and this makes him into a man.

The Congressmen come out to see the Union rout the Rebels at Bull Run. In the Henry House, aged Judith sees the soldiers go by, but she is too old to worry. As the guns begin to roar, they carry her to a ravine where she will be safe. Luke Breckinridge sees a woods full of blue-coated dolls. Shippy is too scared to shoot, and runs. Jack Ellyat's heart knocks. His shot might kill rebels, but he doesn't like it. A man he hardly knows falls in front of him. It feels wrong just to leave him there. They move Judith Henry back into the house. Its walls are riddled with bullets, enough to give her five sudden wounds and leave her dying. Curly Hatton is shot, and there is no more Lucy for him. The Union troops retreat.

A contemporary illustration shows abolitionist John Brown, his smoking rifle raised, facing capture by marines at Harpers Ferry, Virginia, in 1859. Stephen Vincent Benét titled his 1928 epic about the Civil War *John Brown's Body* for the fiery abolitionist who was tried for treason and hanged.

For Clay Wingate it has been a harsh, tense dream, everywhere relics of Yankees: a burst canteen, a woman's locket, bloody brains, a dead cat. You don't fight a war with a tabby cat. He closes his eyes, but a bugle sounds and he rides toward the sound.

In Brooklyn, Walt Whitman reads of the defeat and in his mind's eye sees the beaten men, the tired women, the sleeping boy still clutching his musket. Horace Greeley writes a hysterical letter to Lincoln, who gathers up the scraps, puts them together, and patches up the lost courage.

In Book Three, nine months have passed since Bull Run. Jack Ellyat is homesick, the only Westerner in Tennessee with a strange regiment of Illinois farmers—sick of war and the mud. Handsome McClellan is relieved of the command. Old "Cap" Grant of Galena, Illinois, a stumpy, middle-aged clerk in a faded army overcoat, writes the War Department offering his services, and is not answered, so he volunteers. Under Halleck he forces the unconditional surrender of Forts Henry and Donelson. The Confederate *Merimac* nears Washington and sinks the *Cumberland,* but the Union ironclad *Monitor* forces its withdrawal. The war wavers between the two sides. Something eats at Ellyat. He sees the sleeping, rough, lousy, detested soldiers—"like infants in warm quietness." He looks with untouched eyes before they wake and he can hate them again. Gray strangers burst into the tents, and Jack is taken prisoner, but as the column of prisoners march, Jack and a companion drop to the rear and escape.

Seventeen-year-old Melora Vilas and her family have moved to Tennessee from Kansas, finding a refuge in the woods where Pop can hide his son from the recruiters. Today she is out calling the hogs. Ellyat, lost in the woods, spots her. She is half-frightened, but seeing he is hungry, brings him to her family's cabin, where he stays for six days until he is well and strong. He tries to figure out his hosts. The father is all wrong, yet not weak. When a war comes, you fight on your side. He likes the mother and the boy, but he should get back to his regiment. Yet when Melora comes in, he looks at her and stays. One day at the spring, they kiss. Ellyat is troubled. He cannot stay with Melora, nor can he take her back home. There ought to be a wedding dress, a preacher, and a gold ring. If the father shot him there might be a tablet: "Here lies Jack Ellyat, shot and killed by an angry father for the cause of the Union." He decides to go as far as the road. He reaches a bridge. A round stick jabs his back. A voice says, "He's a spy. Let's string him up a tree!" "Naw," says a companion. "He's got good boots." They take the boots and let Ellyat go.

In Book Four, back at Wingate Hall they prepare for the return of old Marse Billy. In the slave quarters, little children play at chasing Yanks to Kingdom Come. Three stout pillars hold up the tradition of Wingate Hall: the black majordomo, Cudjo; black Aunt Bess, who petted and punished the children and closed the eyes when a Wingate died; and the mistress, Mary Lou Wingate, slightly built but hard to break, never well since her last child died and bearing her body's pain. She loves her tiny hands. She works even in the dead of night, doctoring, guiding the cooking, sewing, watching over the births and deaths in the Negro quarters, always gracious, never raising her voice to a servant. She is gentle, but she can hate, hate the North. The house is busy, to welcome the gentlemen back from killing. When Wingate arrives, he sees it all with altered eyes. He has seen only one battle, but he hears a whisper that he does not wish to hear: "This is the last. Hurry. Drink the wine. Kiss your sweetheart." He rides to the hall. Mary Lou embraces him. That night they all dance, but "Wingate Hall must tumble down." After the dance Lucy Weatherby can only recall its happiness. She hardly remembers Curly, who died at Manassas.

That night a slave named Spade leaves his master. He meant to kill him, but the signs weren't right. He goes all night long. When morning comes, he feels safe. He draws his master's face and spits on it. Up North he will be free!

Sally Dupré waits from the high porch of her house. As Clay rides by, he turns his horse around. Lucy Weatherall rides up, and the mood is broken. Sally dreams of stabbing a cloth doll with Lucy's face.

The war goes on with Union victories, although Vicksburg is still untaken. Overseas, however, watchers intervene for the cotton from the South. The blockade is broken, although the Union controls the Mississippi. In the East the outcome is uncertain. Jack Ellyat lies in a Southern prison, a gaunt, bearded, dirty old man who stares at the flies on the wall and tries to remember his green homeland. There are frequent deaths among the prisoners and disheartening rumors of Union defeats. They dream of escape.

"John Brown lies dead in his grave. It is nearly three years since he died, and he does not stir. There is no sound in his bones but the sound of armies. Go down, John Brown, and set that people free!"

In Book Five it is hot in Washington. Bull Run again, and 18 months of war. Still no end to it! "They come and talk to me of God's will," Lincoln says. "What is God's will?" He has never been a churchgoer, but now he asks divine guidance. "God's will be done!"

The escaped slave, Spade, swims a river to safety, but on the other side he encounters only indifference, even hostility. He is forced to work on the road at meager pay and threatened with enlistment in the Union army.

Melora Vilas, pregnant, hangs onto the hope that Ellyat is still alive and will return to her. The Abolitionists are now uncertain about the war and un-enthusiastic about Lincoln. The mills up north are idle because there is no cotton. Recruiting lags. Elections go against the president. The Army of the Potomac is bewildered by the frequent changes in command. In the prisons, there are rumors and charges, some true, some false. Jack Ellyat at last is in a prisoner exchange. On the march, some die. As they cross the river, they pass a boat with the sick Confederate exchanges on their way back to the South. As they pass, two weak voices from the crowd shout at each other. Ellyat says, "They look pretty bad. . . . They ain't such bad Rebs at that."

In Book Six, Cudjo polishes the Wingate silver. The family is in hard times: They have stripped the house to make ammunition for the Confederates, even taken the old mule. Sally Dupré's hands are colored with dye. She is tired of slogans and saving. She wants to dance all night in a new dress and forget about the South and courage. She will wait like a fool for bitter love to come home. If they hurt him, she will tend him. She would kill the man who fired the bullet, then sit by his bedside all night.

Wingate, on leave, sits by a smoky fire, mending a stirrup with rusty wire. What else to do? He remembers the feel of his horse slumping under him. He touches his sleeve, which the bullet tore, and remembers the Yankee who died speaking Irish. "This is Virginia's *Iliad*."

Up north, Jack Ellyat looks out at the snow-covered ground and recalls the smells and sights of prison. He wonders what happened to Melora. He will have to go back there soon.

The sleet beats down as Melora gives birth. Her mother eyes the baby as if to say, "You aren't respectable. What are you doing here?"

With spring, the sluggish armies begin to stir, but they are tired. Next time we'll lick 'em, each side thinks. Finish it!

Grant gnaws at Vicksburg. He—quiet and deadly holder-on—and Sherman—nervous, explosive, passionate, and slashing—make a good pair of hunting dogs. Tall Lincoln reviews endless columns, on his horse with his farmer's seat. He looks sad. In Richmond, a mob of angry women riot for bread and peace. Davis gets on a wagon and calms them, but the next day they riot again and the troops fire on them weakly. A few are arrested. The curtain is going up on a battle that will decide this war. Behind it lies a great colored quilt of states, battle-worn, but the plows go ahead, factory chimneys smoke, a new age boils and pours into rails of steel. Covered wagons move westward in this last war year. Behind the flat screen is the song of breath.

Shippy, the peddler and spy, creaks by Pollet's Hotel, with papers in his boots, carrying fate through the Rebel lines. He is caught by Clay Wingate. He thinks they couldn't be going to hang him, but he is wrong. Stonewall Jackson lies dying for four long days.

In Book Seven, two months have passed since Stonewall died. There are rumors that the Rebels are moving north: They are only a mile from Philadelphia, they are burning York, they are marching on Baltimore. Meanwhile Lee rides through Cumberland and arrives at Gettysburg, where 160,000 breathing men wait on two hostile ridges. Jack Ellyat sees the war coming toward them. "By god!" he cries. "You're not going to get this hill." Something hits him. He is down on the grass, and black night runs over him.

Melora Vilas sits by the spring with her child. The drafters ride up to the house and find her brother Bent in the barn. He'll make a good soldier yet, they say.

On Cemetery Hill, Ellyat regains consciousness. He turns to the man beside him and asks for a drink from his canteen, but the man has only half a head. At night a lantern approaches. "He's dead, all right," someone says. Ellyat yells, "I'm alive, damn you!" They take him away on a stretcher.

Pickett leads a charge. He goes with 15,000, comes back with 5,000. Wingate waits for the enemy and thinks of Lucy. The bugle sounds. Something trickles into his eyes. He comes to himself in a battered place. He asks who won. He is told they got whipped. "I wish I could sleep ten years," he says. It is the third day and the battle is done. The Army of Northern Virginia tramps back with their wounded, "one long groan of human anguish six miles long." "Each dusty road leads to Appomattox now."

In Book Eight, Grant comes east to take his last command. The siege of Petersburg begins. Grass grows over Charleston wharves. In the North, factory chimneys smoke, hotels are full; but in the Shenandoah Valley, mill wheels rot, chimneys stand alone and blackened. Lee knows it is over. Deserters begin to leave the Confederate armies. Luke Breckinridge deserts and starts home. When he arrives, he finds only Sophy and a house with empty rooms. They left last night, she says. "We've had no business and the nigger said the Yanks were coming." They leave together. After two days, they are stopped by an officer who asks for Luke's papers, then, debating a while, rides off.

John Vilas, his daughter, and the child ride a rickety cart down the road, spawning tales that he is the wandering Jew, a skipper who brought the first slaves—an old man destined to roam forever; that she seeks her soldier, that she is a Barbara Allen.

Lucy Weatherby packs her clothes; her brother Henry packs razors, shirts, and his "silly books." She must write to Clay and others, that they leave for Henry's "health."

Sherman marches to the sea. There are bullet marks on an old oil portrait. Thieves carry dead children's clothes on their bayonets. A looter hangs from a pine tree. Blacks stray from lost plantations, grinning, singing, following the blue soldiers, stealing from lonely cabins. Some wander to strange deaths; some stay a while, starve, then come back; some stay by the old plantation, not working, waiting for a friendly heaven to rain down a mule and 40 acres. Cudjo buries the silverware at night while Mary Lou Wingate holds the lamp. She prays for justice to strike all Yankees dead and for mercy for the faithful servants.

Bailey, tramping with Sherman's men, comes to Wingate Hall, where he finds a slight, grey-headed woman dressed in black, who calls him 50 kinds of thief and Yankee devil. He yells, "Shut up, old lady. This is war!" "That's right," she says. Bailey digs for buried valuables and finds none. They leave after setting the hall afire. Sally Dupré watches from her bedroom window and rushes to help Cudjo and the women vainly fight the fire.

Wingate wearily rides with his men down a road and meets soldiers at the top of a hill. A volley fells him. He wakes with a throbbing leg, then sinks again into unconsciousness.

Richmond falls. Lincoln walks the streets. A long blue column marches singing "John Brown's Body." On the way to Appomattox, the ghost of an army staggers down a muddy road. At first Davis is with them, then he leaves, invisible. An aide-de-camp seeks a suitable house for a council. Two chiefs meet—Lee, erect in his dress uniform; chunky Grant in mud-splashed private's gear. They talk of their days together in Mexico. The terms are agreed upon, and they leave. The room explodes with laughing and shouting. The order comes and the gray army falls in for the last time, stacking its arms.

Jake Diefer plows his farm, the stump of his left arm aching in the wind. A Negro leans on the fence. Does Jake need a fieldhand? "I ain't paying much," Jake says. They call me Spade, the Negro says. Jack Ellyat reaches home, leaning on a stick. He imagines he sees Melora. He sees a slow cart creaking up the hill driven by a woman with large eyes. Edmund Ruffin, the man who fired the first gun against Sumter, hears of the surrender, walks in his garden, takes a flag, cloaks it around his shoulders, cocks his pistol, and shoots himself. Lincoln dreams he is standing on the deck of a black boat moving out to sea. That night he goes to the theater and sits in a flag-draped box. A shot rings out, and the black boat carries him away. Sally, waiting at Appleton, sees Wingate coming down a weed-grown path and smiles.

"John Brown's body lies a-mouldering in the grave./Spread over it the bloodstained flag. . . ."

"Out of his body grows revolving steel,/Out of his body grows the spinning wheel/. . . the new mechanic birth." (TAP) (Fleming 1974; Stroud 1962)

See also Benét, Stephen Vincent.

 # JOSEPH OF EXETER

Author (ca. 12th c.) of a long hexameter poem, *De bello Troiano*, written in Latin. (Preminger 1974)

JOURDAIN DE BLAIVIES

Medieval chanson de geste, the second part of which is a recasting of the Greek romance *Apollonius of Tyre,* itself the inspiration for Shakespeare's *Pericles.* (Harvey and Heseltine 1959)

 # *JUDITA*

Croatian epic (1501) by Marko Marulić (1450–1524), the earliest epic in Dalmatia. Written with dodecasyllabic lines, it shows the influence of Italian Renaissance poetics. The poem retells the biblical story of Judith, Hittite wife of Esau (Genesis 26:34) with allusions of a parallel between conditions in biblical times and those in his native land, where the Turkish threat loomed. (Čiževskij 1971; Dvornik 1962)

See also Marulić, Marko.

 # *DER JUNKER UND DER GETREUE HEINRICH*

Middle High German verse tale (14th c.) consisting of some 2,000 lines by an unknown poet. The protagonist, a generous, free-handed young knight, finds himself in continual financial straits from which his faithful servant Heinrich invariably rescues him. The knight possesses a magic stone with which he can turn himself into a bird. He enters a jousting tournament and wins the hand of the princess of Cypress in marriage. (Garland and Garland 1986)

 ## KAISERCHRONIK

Early Middle High German poem of 17,000 lines chronicling the Roman rulers, as well as German rulers from Karl I der Grosse (Charlemagne) to Konrad III (r. 1138–1152). The poem, written in Regensburg, was at one time attributed to the priest/poet Pfaffe Konrad, but it is now believed to have been the work of several priests, probably under the patronage of Duke Heinrich der Stolze of Saxony (between 1135 and 1150).

Although the poem abounds in fantasy and legend and includes some emperors from fable, it ranks as Germany's first historical chronicle and is in no sense a precourtly poem of romantic chivalry. The "good" rulers are not heroes in the classic sense, but rather benevolent (Catholic) kings. However, Heinrich IV (r. 1056–1105), whom Pope Gregory VII twice excommunicated, comes in for a particularly severe drubbing. (Garland and Garland 1986)

 ## KALEVALA

Finnish national epic. See the *Encyclopedia of Traditional Epics.*

 ## KĀLIDĀSA

Indian dramatist and poet (fl. ca. 4th or 5th c.), the greatest Sanskrit writer and possibly the greatest Indian writer of all time, author of the epics *Raghuvaṃśa* (Dynasty of Raghu), probably his masterpiece, and *Kumārasaṃbhava* (Birth of the war god); three plays, of which *Sakuntalā* is his masterpiece; and two shorter poems. Although practically nothing is known about his life, evidence derived chiefly from characteristics and qualities of his work—the society reflected is that of courtly Indian aristocracy—indicates that he may have lived at the court of the great patron of the arts, Chandra Gupta II (r. ca. 380–ca. 415) and that he may have been a Brahman priest. The poet's art consisted in adapting the ancient, staid Brahman religious tradition to worldly and colorful Hinduism. Obviously he was widely traveled. The dates of his lifetime are fixed by two writings: the hero of one of his dramas, Agnimitra, lived about 170 B.C. The Aihole inscription, dated A.D. 634, praises Kālidāsa, so it is certain that he lived between those two dates. (Kālidāsa 1955)

See also Kumārasaṃbhava; Raghuvaṃśa.

 # KARL

Middle High German epic by Der Stricker, who lived during the first half of the thirteenth century. The poem is an adaptation of *Rolandslied* (The lay of Roland), an early Middle High German poem by Pfaffen Konrad, which itself is a translation of the French *Chanson de Roland* (ca. 1100; see the *Encyclopedia of Traditional Epics*). Der Stricker's epic, an extremely popular work, is thought to be the older of his two epic poems, the other being *Daniel vom blühenden Tal.* "Karl" refers to Karl I der Grosse, Charlemagne. (Garland and Garland 1986)

 # KARLMEINET

Medieval German poem (ca. 14th c.) of some 35,000 lines recounting the life of Frankish king Karl I Der Grosse (Charlemagne). The author, an unknown poet in the lower Rhine region, compiled a number of different legends into one poem, which was untitled until 1858, when it was given the title of its first section.

"Karlmeinet," the first section, is based on a French poem that had been translated into Flemish. It tells the story of young Karl, who takes refuge in Spain to escape persecution by regents. He earns knighthood fighting under Galafer, then goes home to win his own kingdom. He returns to Spain for Galafer's daughter, with whom he elopes and marries.

"Morant und Galîe" is based on a Middle High German epic (ca. 13th c.), of which some 500 lines survive. The knight Morant is accused of illicit relations with Galîe, but the perpetrators of the slander are found out and punished.

The third section, based on a Netherlands translation of *Speculum historiale* by Vincent of Beauvois, describes Karl's Frankish wars against Lombards, Saxons, and the Moors in Spain.

"Karl und Elegast," based on a Low Country legend, depicts Karl's divine command to undertake robbery. In the process he encounters a treason plot and realizes the fealty of his former knight, Elegast, who had been outlawed.

The fifth section retells the story of Roland, derived largely from Der Stricker's thirteenth-century *Karl,* which is itself an adaptation of *Rolandslied.*

The final section recounts Karl's death in Aachen (814) and is derived from *Speculum historiale.* (Garland and Garland 1986)

See also Stricker, Der.

KARNARUTIĆ, BRNO

Croatian poet (17th c.), author of the epic *Vazetje Sigeta grada* (The fall of the city of Szigeth, or Szeged). In the golden age of Ragusan (Dubrovnik) poetry, the poet, a captain of the Venetian cavalry from Zadar, wrote his epic about the death of the Croatian hero *Ban* Nicholas Zrinski and the capture of Szeged by the Turks. (Dvornik 1962; Gazi 1973)

KATHĀSARITSĀGARA
(Oceans of the streams of story)

Indian Sanskrit epic story collection by Somadeva (11th c.), a Kashmiri Brahman. This vast work is one of the treasures of Indian poetry, and one of the three known Sanskrit versions of the lost vernacular work *Bṛhat-kathā* (Great tale) of Guṇāḍhya.

The poem is a "frame story," in which the principal narrative serves to introduce a multitude of subsidiary tales (the published version of the work requires ten volumes). The collection is built around the adventures of King Udayana of Vatsa. The work is so vast that one of the subsidiary stories, *Vetālapañḍaviṃsatika* (Vikram and the vampire), is itself a frame story for yet more tales with titles like "The Faithful Suitors," "The Transposed Heads," "The Three Sensitive Queens," and "The King and the Spiteful Seductress."

One of the tales in *Kathāsaritsāgara*, called "Devasmitá," concerns a rich merchant who assembles many Brahmans for advice on how to obtain a son. They advise him to perform a sacrifice, which he does, and a son, Guhasena, is born. When the boy grows up, father and son travel to a far land in search of a proper bride. They find a fair maid named Devasmitá, whose father disapproves of her moving so far from home. But Devasmitá likes Guhasena's looks and steals away in the night with him and his father. They are married, and soon the father dies. Guhasena is urged by his relatives to go off to the country of Katáha to trade. His wife, fearing he will become attracted to another woman, disapproves of the trip. Both go to the temple to perform a vow in hopes they will receive divine guidance as to what to do. Śiva appears to them in a dream, giving each a red lotus, and advises both that should either be unfaithful, the lotus in the hand of the other will fade; otherwise, it will not. The two awake to find they are holding red lotuses. Guhasena sets off for Katáha to buy and sell jewels. Four merchants, noticing the red lotus in Guhasena's hand, get him drunk so that he will reveal the story behind it.

The four rascals set out to Guhasena's town to seduce Devasmitá in her husband's absence. They seek the help of an old woman ascetic named Yogakaramdiká, who says she will procure for them the object of their desire, and she even gives them her house to live in. She gains the confidence of Devasmitá and feeds her dog a piece of peppered meat, which causes it to cry. She tells Devasmitá the dog is weeping because it recognized her as a companion in a former life. She claims that Devasmitá and the hound were both wives of a certain Brahman who frequently traveled to other countries on business for the king. While he was gone, the woman lived naturally and pleasurably, not cheating the elements, so she has been rewarded with a remembrance in this life of her former existence. However, the other wife, through ignorance, confined all her attention to preservation of character, and therefore in this life has been downgraded to a member of the canine race.

Devasmitá senses a trap, but nevertheless asks the old woman to procure for her an interview with a charming man. The old woman tells her of the four young merchants. Devasmitá instructs her maids to bring wine mixed with Datura and then to have a dog's foot made of iron as quickly as possible. While the maids execute their duties, one of the maids dresses up to resemble her mistress.

The old ascetic chooses one of the four men to go to the house of Devasmitá. The young man meets the maid in disguise, who offers him a drink of the doctored wine, which quickly robs him of his senses. The maids steal his clothes, leaving him stark naked; then they brand him on the forehead with the mark of a dog's foot, carry him off into the night, and dump him into a filthy ditch. When the young man wakes, he is ashamed to tell his friends the truth, so he wraps his head in a turban and tells his friends he was robbed on the way home.

Each of the other men takes his turn at the house of Devasmitá, all receiving the same treatment and all reacting the same way. They leave without revealing to the old woman their ill-treatment, hoping she will suffer the same.

The next day the old woman goes with her disciple to Devasmitá's house, delighted with her accomplishment. Devasmitá receives her courteously and offers her a cup of drugged wine. When she and her disciple are intoxicated, the chaste wife cuts off their ears and noses and flings them into a filthy pool.

She fears that the young merchants may go and slay her husband, so she confides to her mother-in-law what has occurred. The mother-in-law agrees that some misfortune may happen to her son, so Devasmitá dresses up like a merchant and sails for Katáha. When she arrives she sees her husband talking to a group of merchants. When he sees her, he thinks, "Who may this merchant be that looks so like my beloved wife?"

Full of curiosity about the new merchant, the king assembles all the citizens and asks Devasmitá, "What is your petition?" Devasmitá tells him that four of her slaves have escaped, and she has come to search for them. They can be recognized by the mark of the dog on their turban-covered foreheads. She seizes the four merchants and, to prove that they are her slaves, orders that their head-wrappers be removed. When the dog's foot marks are revealed, the king, who knows the merchants, asks what this all means. Devasmitá confesses the truth to the assemblage, and the king laughs and says, "They are your slaves by the best of titles." The other merchants take up a collection to redeem the four, and Devasmitá and her husband return home, never to be separated again. (Runes 1961; Van Buitenen 1959)

See also Somadeva.

KAZANTZAKÍS, NIKOS

Greek poet and novelist, author of the epic *Odéssia* (1938). He was born in Candia (now Iráklion), Crete, in 1885, during a time of great unheaval, when the island of Crete was in revolt against the Ottoman Turks. His family fled to the island of Názos. When he was 17, Kazantzakís began a four-year study of law at the University of Athens. At the age of 22 he traveled to Paris to study philosophy under Henri Bergson.

In 1909 he traveled widely in Europe, North Africa, Russia, and Japan. In 1926–1927 he traveled to Italy, Egypt, Sinai, Jerusalem, and Cyprus, meeting Mussolini and Constantin Cavafy. He finally settled down on the island of Aegina in the 1930s. His *Odéssia*, written there in 1938, consists of 33,333 lines and is a modern sequel to Homer's *Odyssey*, beginning where the classic epic ends.

In 1947–1948 he moved to Paris to serve with the United Nations Educational, Scientific, and Cultural Organization (UNESCO), then in its infancy. He then moved to Antibes, France, where he wrote several other novels, the most famous in the West being *Zorba the Greek*; philosophical essays; poetry; and translations of Dante's *Divine Comedy*, Goethe's *Faust*, and several ancient Greek classics. He also wrote travel books, which were published posthumously. He died on a trip to China in 1957, and was buried on Crete. His second wife, Helen Kazantzakís, wrote his biography in 1968. Most of his work has been translated into English, as: *Zorba the Greek; The Fratricides; Freedom or Death; The Greek Passion; Japan-China: A Journal of Two Voyages to the Far East; Journeying: Travels in Italy, Egypt, Sinai, Jerusalem, and Cypress; The Last Temptation of Christ; Report to Greco; Saint Francis;* and *The Poor Man of God*. (Kazantzakís [Helen] 1968)

See also Odéssia.

KEIN HÜSUNG

Short German epic poem (1857) by Fritz Reuter. The poem contains 13 cantos of short rhyming lines in the Low German dialect of Mecklenburg, where the poem is set. It is the story of a squire who, angry at his serf, will not help the serf's daughter Mariken and her intended, Jehann, get a domicile so that they can marry. In a confrontation with the squire, Jehann stabs him with a pitchfork and flees, leaving Mariken with the troublesome problem of a child to rear alone. Eventually she kills herself. Later Jehann returns to claim his son. (Garland and Garland 1986)

KETAKĀDĀS

Indian Bengali poet (fl. 17th c.), author of a 12,000-line *Manasā-maǎgal*, a poetic cycle eulogizing the Bengali snake goddess Manasā. (Brogan 1996)

KHAMSEH
(Quintet; also *Panj Ganj,* Five treasures)

Persian collection of five epic poems by Nizâmî (ca. 1140/1141–ca. 1203/1209). The collection, written in *masăavî* form (rhyming couplets, *aa bb cc,* etc.), consists of his long, narrative, ethico-philosophical poem *Makhzan al-Asrâr* (The treasury of secrets, ca. 1163–1176), and four epic romances, *Khusraw u Shîrîn* (ca. 1180); *Laylî u Majnûn* (ca. 1188–1192); his masterpiece, *Haft Paykar* (The seven beauties, 1197); and *Iskandarnâma* (Book of Alexander) in two parts (ca. 1200–1202). The poems of the *Khamseh* were widely imitated by later poets. (Nizâmî 1995)

See also *Haft Paykar; Khusraw u Shîrîn; Laylî and Majnûn.*

KHERASKOV, MIKHAIL

Russian poet, author of the epic *The Rossiad* (1779). He was born in 1733 in Pereslavl to a nobleman of Wallachian extraction. He was educated at the Cadet Corps school in St. Petersburg. Kheraskov obtained an administrative position at Moscow University, where he directed the library, theater, and press. Always interested in enlightenment and literature, he established two literary magazines. Three collections of poems appeared in 1762 and 1764. Because of his Freemasonry activities, he was transferred to St. Petersburg, where in 1772 he established another magazine. He wrote *The Rossiad* (1779) to fill a longstanding need for a national epic. In 1779 he returned to Moscow University as the rector. His verse plays—nine tragedies, two comedies, and five sentimental dramas—were popular, as were his three novels. He died in Moscow in 1807. (Bristol 1991)

See also *The Rossiad.*

KHUSRAW U SHÎRÎN
(Also Khosraw and Shirin)

Medieval Persian minor epic romance by Abû Muhammad Ilyâs ibn Yûsuf ibn Zakî Mu'ayyad, whose pen name was Nizâmî of Ganja (Nizâmî Ganjavi, ca. 1140–1141–ca. 1203–1209). The poet wrote five long poems, four of them romances, all written in *masnavi* form and collected under the title *Khamseh* (Quintet), or *Panj Ganj* (Five Treasures). *Khusraw u Shîrîn* was the first romance. Although its date is uncertain, the poet addresses the Seljuk sultan Toghrïl II and others and tells of being summoned to speak with Ganja ruler Jahân Pahlavân and his brother Qïzïl Arslân, the latter bestowing a village as reward for the poem's composition.

Persian poet Nizâmî composed five epics at the end of the twelfth century; one was based on ill-starred lovers, Laylî and her cousin Qays. Qays, distressed that he cannot marry his cousin, goes mad and becomes known as Majnûn. Fifteenth-century artist Bihzad detailed Laylî and Majnûn at school.

The poem is based on a story from Firdausi's (d. 1020) great epic *Shāh-Nāmah* (Book of kings), about the love of the Sassanian ruler Khusraw II Parvîz (r. 590–628) for the beautiful princess Shîrîn. The poem's depiction of Shîrîn is said to be one of the most beautiful portrayals of woman in Islamic literature. The poem celebrates love as a cosmic force that brings about justice and harmony. It also deals with the issue of kingship and the theme of human perfectibility at the level of both king and subject. (Nizami 1995)

KIM-VÂN-KIÊU
(Also *Nguyen Van Vin*, The tale of Kieu)

Vietnamese epic (1813) by Nguyen Du (1765–1820), considered the greatest Vietnamese poet writing in *Nom* (non-Chinese characters). The poem, consisting of 3,253 lines in couplets of six and eight syllables, and written in southern characters called *chu-nom*, is considered by the Vietnamese people as the Vietnamese national poem and their supreme literary masterpiece. Almost a verse novel, the poem is based on a Chinese historical novel of the Ming period about two lovers, Kim and Kiêu, which the poet translated into Vietnamese poetry. The title is formed from the names of the three central characters. However, the poet goes beyond merely translating the original love story into poetry; he expresses his own personal angst and abiding humanism as well. The poem shows the influence of Confucian ethics and explores the Buddhist doctrine of karmic retribution for past sins: ". . . in this life span on earth/Talent and destiny are apt to feud./You must go through a play of ebb and flow/And watch such things as make you sick at heart." (Brogan 1996; Dudley and Lang 1969)

See also Nguyen Du.

KINGDOM OF THE LEOPARD
(*Kingdom of the Leopard, An Epic of Old Benin*)

West African epic cycle in English (1994) about the ancient West African kingdom of Benin by contemporary Nigerian poet Chi Chi Layor. The epic, consisting of 21 poems, relates both legendary and historical incidents from the various rulers and consorts of Benin, a kingdom that existed from about the thirteenth century forward in an area now within the boundaries of Nigeria. The poems appear in random order unrelated to their linear chronology.

"Oba Overami" tells of the visit to the kingdom by three white men with a trade treaty from the "exquisite British queen." Overami, the *Oba* (king, fl. 1888), refuses their gifts and the treaty. He consults an oracle, who sees fire and blood engulfing his empire, so he tightens security. Years later, more white men appear during the *iguen* festival, when *Obas* do not receive guests. The *Oba* sends his chief warlord to deter their arrival until the festival is over. But the warlord slays the white men, claiming they advanced beyond a given point. The prime minister advises the *Oba* to prepare for war. Soon angry white troops arrive and the *Oba*'s valiant men are "mowed down like grass." The "home leopard" (*Oba*) goes into hiding, but is found and tried. He denies ordering the warlord to slay the white men, but is found guilty and banished to Calabar. He is allowed to take only three wives from his huge harem. He dies "a commoner's death" in Calabar.

"Emotan," in two parts, takes place during the reign of Oba Ohen (ca. late 14th c.). Part I concerns beautiful Elere, whose father wants her to marry the *oliha*, an officer of the court whose duty it is to crown the *Oba*. But Elere and the *Oba* are in love and want to marry. The *Oba* devises a plan: During a performance by the masked *Ekoko* dancers, he and Elere will don costumes and masks and dance into the palace. The plan suceeds, and Ohen and Elere are married before her father finds out.

After their sons are born, Elere's love for Ohen wanes, and she slips away to her village, never to see the *Oba* again.

Elere has a beautiful cousin, Uwaraye, who can spin thread "finer than cobwebs" and make melon butter. Although she is slow and hates housework, she has many suitors, whom she turns down. Her father finally chooses a husband for her, the *Azama*, a man of royal blood. The *Azama* makes Uwaraye his second wife. The first wife, Arabe, resents the lovely new wife. Uwaraye is unhappy and her union with the *Azama* produces no children. Arabe taunts her, calling her "good-for-nothing." Because Uwaraye serves his meals late, the *Azama* renames her Emotan, meaning "lazy and slow."

Part II takes place in the fifteenth century. During Oba Ohen's 20-year rule, he has become lame. Since *Obas* are supposed to be "faultless and free from human failing," he keeps his debility secret from all but his closest servants, who carry him about and see to it that he is always first to arrive and last to leave every appointment. The *Iyase* (prime minister) becomes suspicious and hides behind a door before an official ceremony. But the royal guards spot him and bring him before Oba Ohen, who rants and orders his immediate execution.

The other chiefs are terror-stricken, and plot to get rid of Ohen. They dig a pit beneath the throne, which they conceal with only a thin covering. When the *Oba* sits on his throne, he crashes into the pit, and the chiefs and people stone him to death.

Following Ohen's death, his four sons are to rule in turn. Three sons are weak. The strong one is Ogun, son of Elere, the "runaway wife." The chiefs want an *Oba* they can manipulate, so they get Ogun's weak second brother to send him away, and he becomes *Oba*. Ogun is still in exile when the weak brother dies, so the youngest brother becomes the new *Oba*. Meanwhile, the *Azama* dies.

The first wife, Arabe, and her children inherit the house, leaving the aging Emotan homeless. She begins selling melon butter in Oba market. Her fame spreads and she is called "queen of Oba market."

One evening after closing time, an unkempt man arrives at her shop and begs for food. After she feeds him, he reveals he is Prince Ogun, home to assume his rightful throne. She warns him of his brother's spies. He goes to see a chief, Ogiefa, who secretly summons the *Oba*'s men to apprehend the prince. But the chief's head slave helps Ogun escape, and he hides out in Emotan's hut.

The *Oba* sends spies to search for Ogun and to kill anyone suspected of aiding him. Emotan secretly rounds up Ogun's supporters. During a festival when the *Oba*'s procession passes by Oba market, Ogun disguises himself as one of the dancers. When he is close enough, he plunges a spear into his brother's chest. Soon the chiefs rally around him and he is crowned Ewuare the Great (1440). But Emotan does not live to see him crowned. For her kindness and courage, Oba Ewuare deifies her and plants a tree in her memory. Today a bronze statue has replaced the tree near Oba market in Benin City.

"Iden and Oba Owyakpe" takes place in the eighteenth century. When the queen mother dies, the *Oba* buries 800 people with her, inciting the people of Benin to riot and throw him out. His wife, Iden, impresses the rioters with her courage as she stands by him. Afterward, she suggests that he consult an oracle as to how he can recover his crown. The oracle decrees that he must sacrifice someone to the gods. As there are no slaves remaining in the palace, Iden offers to be the sacrifice. At first he is reluctant to accept her offer, but finally he agrees. She is buried alive, and instantly he regains his throne.

"A Battle and a Dance" recounts events during the reign of Oba Esigie (r. 1504–1550), who learns that the king of Idah plans to attack him. His mother, Idia, tells Esifie to stay at home and let her fight. When her slave tries to hold her back, she draws her dagger and slays him. With her troops she marches on Idah, quickly subduing the king, who begs for peace. But Idia fights on, until the Idahs stage a special, colorful dance, the *Ekassa,* to placate her. She is so delighted that she invites the dancers to Benin. She asks that the *Ekassa* dance be performed at her funeral. Each year the dance that ended a bloody war is given.

"Imaguero" also takes place during the reign of Esigie, who marries his daughter to his warlord, the *Oliha*. Soon the *Oliha* takes a fifth wife, Imaguero. Although the *Oba* warns the warlord that women are "sneaky-sly," and that Imaguero has already betrayed her marriage vow, the *Oliha* is sure that Imaguero is the most faithful wife in all of Benin. The argument escalates into a duel, which ends in a draw. By now the *Oliha* is suspicious and calls in all his wives, eliciting a confession from the princess-wife that she plotted with her father, Esigie, against Imaguero. As punishment the *Oliha* kills the princess. Imaguero confesses that she has indeed been unfaithful because Oba Esigie threatened to kill her parents if she didn't come to him. She asks her husband to kill her too. Although he pardons her and curses the *Oba,* she cannot live with guilt. She drinks poison and dies in his arms.

"Adesua" takes place in the eighteenth century during the reign of Oba Akengbuda (r. 1750–1804). Adesua, who is betrothed to the *Oba,* is the beautiful daughter of the *Ezomo* (second in command after the prime minister, and generalissimo of the state army). A minor ruler, the *Obi* of Oboro-uku, becomes enamored of Adesua, but she jeers and calls him a "bush ruler." The angry *Obi* eventually has her killed. To avenge her death, Oba Akengbuda sends his troops against the town of Oburo-uku. After fierce fighting, the head of the *Obi* is sent to the *Oba* as a gift.

"Why Women Don't Rule in Benin" takes place in the fifteenth century, after the death of Oba Ewuare (r./fl. 1440). When his sons cannot assume the throne, his eldest daughter, Edeleyo, is given the title of *Edaiken* and prepared for coronation in Uselu. On the journey to Uselu, she falls ill, but "quick as a bullet," her bodyguards form a "human fence" around her because *Obas*, being superhuman, are not allowed to be sick. Days later she dies, and it is decided that women must not rule in Benin.

Although other parts of the epic up to this point are based on historical rulers or those around them, "The Native Doctor Who Ruled Benin" tells the legendary tale of an *Oba* "not born like others," who leaps from his mother's thigh with a medicine gourd in his hand. He is crowned king and rules for centuries, refusing to step down. When he is finally ready to leave, he wants to "walk into heaven/in style." A large procession follows him toward heaven until some short men "carrying pots on their heads" turn the *Oba* back, saying humans cannot walk into heaven without angering the gods. The *Oba* turns back and dies with all his retinue.

"Ovia River" relates the legend of Ovia of Ohen, "a delectable dame," who, being too good for the local men, decides to marry the king of Oyo. Her father sends her off with a pot, a parrot, and a dog, telling her to use the pot in emergencies.

Although the king of Ohen has a "house overflowing with wives," Ovia soon becomes his favorite. The other wives fume, particularly the senior wife, who tricks Ovia into catching snails in her white cloth, ruining it. The senior wife shows the cloth to the king as evidence that Ovia has a strange disease and should be avoided. Ovia is devastated by the king's neglect. Then she remembers the pot her father gave her. She climbs into it and is transformed into water. She flows back home to her father.

Today she is a river. The dog is used as a sacrifice to her. Her worshippers wear the parrot's feathers in their headdresses, and there are snails in Ovia River.

"IkpOba River" tells of Okpese, favorite wife of Aba Ewuare (r. ca. 1440–1473), of whom the other wives are jealous. They pay a medicine man to prepare a spell for Okpese. The spell makes her "break wind in a spectacular way,/shaking everyone. Okpese leaves the palace in disgrace, despite the *Oba*'s protests. She weeps and rolls on the ground until she becomes "a fast-flowing river."

"Ekpenede" takes place during the reign of Oba Ehengbuda (r. 1578–1608), whose only daughter, Isiuwo, marries Ekpenede, the *Iyase* (prime minister). Although Ekpenede has many children, he has only one son, and the number of sons is the measure of a man's virility. When this son has an adulterous affair with one of the *Oba*'s wives, he is executed. "Consumed with crazy shame," Ekpenede kills all his wives, his entire household, and himself. Thereafter, a law is passed prohibiting the *Iyase* from living near the palace.

"Ise and Oba Ozolua" relates how Oba Ozolua (r. 1481–1504), having slain a warrior, takes his wife and makes the warrior's son, Ise, his sword-bearer.

Later Ozolua kills the wife as well, and Ise chases him up a kolanut tree. Ise cannot cut down the tree because kola is used to appease the gods, so he sits down to wait while the king perches in a "piteous far-from-regal position." His former sword-bearer begs Ise to let Ozolua come down and they can settle their differences with a wrestling match. Ise is eager for the match, but with help from the ex–sword-bearer, Ozolua throws Ise down and beheads him. Hearing that his accomplice might tell the people of his cowardice, Ozolua slays him too. "Now Ise is remembered for his manliness."

"Master Thief" takes place during the reign of Oba Esigie (r. 1504–1550). Ata, a clever thief who has plagued the land, goes to the *Oba* to announce that he is leaving Benin for a place "with bigger challenges." The *Iyase* scoffs at his boasts, so Ata tells him to name a date, and on that date he will rob the *Iyase*'s house. The wager is made, and if Ata is caught, he will be killed. The *Iyase* names a date seven years away.

On the appointed day, the *Iyase* and his household go to bed so they can stay up all night. He locks all the doors and stands guard by the main door with his favorite wife. But Ata puts a spell on them so that they fall asleep. He steals everything in the house, even the clothes they are wearing. When they awake, they go "whining to the *Oba*," who reminds the *Iyase* of his bet with Ata. The thief divides the booty, giving half back to the *Iyase* and the other half to the state. He promises to leave Benin, but as a present to the *Oba* he will bring him an entire town.

Ata settles in the city of Ighan, where he charms everyone. For three years he does not steal. One day he steals the Ighan state drum and marches off beating it. The people chase him all the way to Benin, and after they are inside the palace courtyard, the *Oba* closes the palace gates. Ata is now a national hero, and the Igban drum is used during festivals and is named after the master thief. The Igban people settle down in Benin.

"The Greedy Hunter" is a morality verse-fable telling how a hunter, not satisfied with an elephant, a bush pig, and a bag of small game, tries to catch crickets as well, falls into the river, and loses all through greed.

"Joromi the Wrestler" is another verse-fable about an adolescent boy, Joromi, who wrestles with spirits who slay him. His sister revives him with magic leaves, and they escape. The spirit king chases Joromi and scratches his back with long nails, leaving a depression that people still have today.

"Eneka" is a typical hero verse-fable in which the baby Eneka is an enchanted child who, when he is grown, steals the *Ezomo*'s (generalissimo) sword and paralyzes his attackers, wrestles a giant, Igbadaken, and becomes a hero. One day he accidentally sees one of the *Oba*'s wives bathing, an offense punishable by death. As he awaits his execution, a rat he once saved helps him by persuading a viper to bite the *Oba*'s daughter, killing her. The rat then gives Eneka the herbal formula that will revive her. He saves the princess, marries her, and becomes a chief.

"Omafoma and Adese" is the story of a farmer, Omafoma, who has plans to marry three beautiful sisters. All three die before he can marry them. "Wild with grief," Omafoma wanders off toward Benin City, where Prince Imadasun lies gravely ill from a bull elephant goring. The *Oba* consults a wise woman, who says that if Imadasun drinks water from the bell that hangs around the beast's neck, he will be cured. Meanwhile, even the prince's twin sister, Adese, begins to sicken out of sympathy for her brother.

As Omofoma enters the city, he sees an old woman carrying a heavy load of firewood on her head. He carries it home for her, and in gratitude she tells him how to win the hand of Princess Adese. He is to make a musical instrument from a string and a piece of wood and take it to the forest. He does so and, encountering the beast, he whirls the wood at the end of the string, producing an eery hum that subdues the animal. When the owner of the runaway animal offers him a reward, Omofoma asks for the bell around its neck. Omofoma takes the bell to the palace, where Imadasun drinks from it and recovers. The jubilant *Oba* gives Adese to Omahoma for a wife, and he takes her and the old woman back to his hometown.

"Much Ado about a Woman" concerns a war between two rival towns, Ehor and Iruele. When Ovbioghumu, the leader of Iruele, visits the home of Okosun, leader of Ehor, Okosun's "winsome wife," Ibo, disgraces her husband by not having a meal waiting. Ovbioghumu prevents Okosun from punishing her, and according to custom, a guest's wish is always granted. But later, after the guest is gone, Okosun cuts off Ibo's hair and orders her to sit in the blazing sun and speak to no one. Ovbioghumu hears of this breach of promise and sends a servant to rescue her and bring her to Iruele. Furious, Okosun sends a servant, Atuke, to spy on Ibo and Ovbioghumu. When Atuke is caught, he is immersed in a pot of poison, and his ears are cut off. Atuke makes it back to Ehor to deliver his report before he dies. A war ensues, with charges and countercharges. Okosun commits suicide in disgrace, and his friend Esegbe becomes the new leader of Ehor. After a long war the two sides call a truce, and henceforth the two kingdoms are known for their great friendship.

"The Fighter," another poem about commoners in Benin City, concerns three brothers: Okougbo the farmer, Okohue the hunter, and Okodan the fighter. While the two older brothers work hard, the third only fights and robs his victims. One day he robs and kills the *Oba*'s eldest son. Realizing his blunder, he hides the corpse and asks his brother Okohue to take him hunting. But he backs out at the last minute, so that Okohue must go alone. Okohue fires his gun at a large sleeping animal, then discovers it is the prince. Frightened, he goes home to hide, but his younger brother, eliciting a confession from him, promises to keep him out of trouble if he will provide him with meat for the rest of his life. The hunter eagerly promises.

The fighter then goes to his farmer brother and tricks him into bashing someone he thinks is stealing his yams. It turns out to be the prince. Again Okodan becomes his confidant and promises to keep Okougbo out of trouble for killing the prince if he will provide him with yams for life. The oldest brother readily agrees.

Next Okodan takes the body to the palace, where the *Oba*, believing he sees a burglar, hits him over the head with a bronze statuette, only to discover the intruder is his own son. Horrified and heartbroken at what he has done, he hides the body. Okodan becomes his confidant as well and promises to get him out of his dilemma. He places charms on the corpse, then kills some chickens and hangs them around a wooden image. The *Oba* calls his chiefs and tells them his son has been ill and, although he has sacrificed animals to the gods, the prince has died anyway. The chiefs express their condolences to the *Oba*, who rewards Okodan by making him a chief.

"The Unlucky One," another folk poem, concerns an unfortunate boy who is named Omoegbebe, "Unlucky One," because his mother died in childbirth. His older brother Oboika, only seven, must raise him when the father dies as well. When they grow up, Omoigbebe has one terrible misfortune after another until he is finally under a double death sentence from the *Oba*. But a stroke of good luck with a wager makes him a rich man, and he returns to his village to share his fortune with his brother.

"Otolo" follows the typical hero-tale pattern, with a precocious baby, Otolo, of superior strength. At age two he wrestles and bests all the area's strong men and becomes known as the strong man of Ikhin. Omoweme, a "swashbuckling stranger" from Erara town, steals his mother's dog. Otolo stalks him down and they fight until they die. In the spirit world they continue to fight. Baba, king of the spirit world, finally passes judgment: Omoweme must stay in the spirit world; Otolo may return to earth, stripped of his superhuman strength. (Layor 1995)

See also Layor, Chi Chi.

 # THE KING'S FLUTE
(*I flóghera tou Vasiliá*)

Greek historical epic poem (1910, transl. 1966) by Kostis Palamás (1859–1943), who was honored as Greece's national poet. Inspired by the cultural and historical legacy of ancient Greece, Byzantium, and the heroic era of 1821, the poet wrote the powerful lyric epic in the vernacular in a highly rhetorical and poetic language. The poem garnered a nomination for the Nobel Prize for literature; in fact, Palamás was frequently nominated, but failed to receive it or to gain the international reputation his work merited. (Siepmann 1987)

See also Palamás, Kostis.

 # KIRĀTĀRJUNĪYA
(Arjuna and the mountain man, or Śiva as a hunter and Arjuna)

Indian courtly epic poem (ca. 6th or 7th c.) by Bhāravi. The poem, written in Sanskrit, is not as readable as Kālidāsa's epics because of its difficult language and style, with long descriptive digressions, but it is revered by Indian people as a classic, setting the standard for Sanskrit literature in the south. The poem describes the encounter between Pāṇḍava prince Arjuna (of the *Mahābhārata*) and a wild mountaineer. The two engage in combat, but the mountain man turns out to be the Hindu god Śiva. For more on the *Mahābhārata*, see the *Encyclopedia of Traditional Epics*. (Meister 1984; Thapar 1966)

See also Bhāravi.

 # KLOPSTOCK, FRIEDRICK GOTTLIEB

German poet, author of *Der Messias* (The Messiah), an epic in 20 cantos about the life of Christ, published in stages between 1748 and 1773. Klopstock was born in 1724 in Quedlinburg. From the ages of 15 to 21 he was educated at the boarding school of Schulpforta near Naumburg, where he received a thorough classical education. After reading Milton's *Paradise Lost,* he announced in his graduation speech (1745) his intention to write a great religious epic. He studied at Jena (1745–1746) before moving on to Halle (1746–1748). During this period he composed the first three cantos of his epic, which were published in 1748 in a Bremer weekly periodical. Written in classical hexameters, the poem gained him a reputation as a promising poetic genius.

Following his stint in Halle, he went to Langensalza as a tutor to his cousins (1748–1750). During this period, he began to compose odes to another cousin, Marie Sophie Schmidt, whom he called Fanny, but his amorous feelings were not reciprocated. He continued to write odes for the rest of his life, and these constitute his most lasting achievement.

In 1751, King Frederick V invited him to Copenhagen and presented him with a life pension. In 1754 he married a writer, Meta Moller, who died in childbirth four years later. After her death, Klopstock published her writings as *Hinterlassene Schriften von Margareta Klopstock* (1759). During the ensuing years he wrote six plays and two volumes of hymns.

In 1770 he left Denmark and settled in Hamburg, where a collection of his odes (*Oden*) was published the following year. The final cantos of *Der Messias* were published in 1773. In 1791 he married his late wife's niece, widow Johanna Elisabeth von Winthem, née Dimpflels. He died in Ottensen near Hamburg in 1803 at the age of 79. (Garland and Garland 1986)

 # *KLOSTER DER MINNE, DAS*
(The cloister of love)

Middle High German poem (ca. 1350) by an unknown author, probably a Swabian knight. The poem, consisting of some 1,800 lines, depicts a group of knights and ladies who form an order, the Cloister of Love, after the style of a religious order, observing strict regulations on conducting courtly life. It is generally believed that the poet is the same one who wrote an allegorical lament,

Klage um line edle Herzogin (ca. 1331), on the occasion of the death of Beatrix, duchess of Corinthis. (Garland and Garland 1986)

 # THE KNIGHT IN THE PANTHER'S SKIN
(Also The lord of the panther-skin, or The man in the panther's skin, *Vephkhis Tqaosani, vepkhistqaosani,* or *Vep'khis-iqaosani*)

Georgian Romantic epic (12th c.) by Shota Rustaveli (Shot'ha Rust'haveli, 1172–1216). The very long, narrative allegorical poem is the national saga of the Georgian nation and the sole surviving work of the national bard of the Caucasus nation of Georgia. It is the most enduring monument to Georgian medieval literature and history—much of the latter obliterated during Muslim occupation and later by the country's absorption by Russia. No early manuscripts of the poem have survived. In the centuries before its first printing in 1712, many copyists made small changes, so that now there are many versions. However, the basic poem survived and over time became the best-known poem in the Georgian language. Rustaveli is credited with helping to standardize the spoken language: Peasants could recite long passages from memory, and brides were required to memorize selections for their husband's entertainment. Many of the poet's aphorisms have become Georgian proverbs. The poem is considered a landmark in world literature as well. Unlike other poets of his time, Rustaveli was attached to the court of Queen Thamar (1184–1213) and was thought to be in love with her. Some critics dispute the traditional dating of the poet and his work, assigning them to a later period. This is due to the fact that the poet was influenced by Neoplatonism and the poem includes Iranian touches such as an Arabian knight; some churchmen regarded the poem as pagan and profane, and burned every copy they could obtain. However, the poem provides a vivid picture of the manners and ideals of medieval Georgia, the period in which traditionally Rustaveli wrote his epic.

The poem, consisting of some 1,576 to 1,669 quatrains—depending on the version—with 16-syllable trochaic lines divided in half by caesuras, has as its theme courtly love, knightly comradeship, and heroic quest. It relates the story of Rostevan, the aged king of Arabia, who has no male heir to the throne, and therefore prepares his beautiful and intelligent daughter Tinatin (Thinat'hin) for the role. She is in love with the noble knight Avtandil (Avt'handil), who is both commander of the army and courtier (called the "King of Arabia" but obviously a Georgian knight). One day while hunting, Rostevan and Avtandil meet a mysterious knight wearing a panther skin. Too depressed to talk, the knight cannot tell them his story. Unable to get the knight to speak, the king himself falls into a deep depression. Tinatin charges Avtandil to locate the mournful knight and bring him to the palace. Avtandil sets off on his quest, and after long wanderings, finds the knight (called the "King of India" but also obviously a Georgian knight), whose name is Tariel. Tariel tells him his sad tale: He is the son of a royal family, heir to the throne, and *amirbar* (admiral and military commander) of Indian king Parsadan. Tariel is in love with the king's daughter, Nestan-Darejan, but the king has decided to marry her to a Khvarizmian prince and proclaim him heir to the throne, even though Tariel is the legal heir. Nestan-Darejan convinces Tariel to kill his rival and take the throne by force, but her father finds out and has her severely beaten and sent to India. Tariel has engaged in a vain search for her and now, having lost all hope of ever finding her, he is returning to his own land. Frustrated in his own quest to win Princess Tinatin, Avtandil swears eternal friendship for Tariel and joins with him in his quest to rescue the fair Nestan-Darejan. Avtandil journeys to the land of King Nuradin-Pridon, a friend of Tariel's, who hears his story with great sympathy and provides him with a retinue, describing a beautiful woman he has seen being whisked away on a boat. Avtandil travels to Gulansharo (city of roses) and meets Fatima, wife of rich merchant Husain.

The poet admonishes, "Keep clear of Woman, if you have the strength and self-mastery! She will play with you, she will charm you, she will build trust . . . and then suddenly she will betray you and do you what harm she can. . . . Never should a secret be told to a woman in confidence." Fatima develops a passion for Avtandil ("sapling-fair hero"), writing him a love letter. He goes to her apartment to find her with another man. She begs him to kill the man, for she has dishonored herself, so he tracks down the man and kills him. Fatima tells him what she knows of Nestan-Darejan, now abducted by *Kajebi* (*jinn*, or demons, like those in the *Arabian Nights*), except that these are "not true *Kajes*, but mortal men who live secure among steep rocks." Avtandil returns to Tariel, and they journey to the land of the *Kajebi*, who hold the princess in an impregnable fortress. After many adventures, with the help of their friend Pridon they storm the fort and rescue Nestan-Darejan. They return home, where Avtandil marries Tinatin and Tariel marries Nestan-Darejan. They both become wise rulers of their own lands. (Rustaveli 1968, 1977)

See also Rustaveli, Shota.

 # *THE KNIGHT'S TALE*

English chivalric romance, one of Geoffrey Chaucer's *Canterbury Tales,* adapted from Boccaccio's *Teseida.*

See also Teseida.

 # KOCHOWSKI, WESPAZJAN

Polish poet and historian, author of the Baroque epic *Psalmodia polska* (1695). He was born in 1633 in Gaj, Poland. At the age of 17 he entered military service, serving for nine years, during which he fought battles against both Cossacks and Swedes. After his military service, he was appointed court historian for John III Sobieski (r. 1674–1696). In 1683 he was present when the king led 30,000 Polish cavalry against the Turks to save Vienna.

Fiercely patriotic, Kochowski believed the Poles were God's chosen people. His *Annales* describes the reign of King John II Casimir (1648–1668) and Sobieski's expedition to Vienna. He also wrote a collection of short poems reflecting the life of Polish gentry, *Niepróżnujące Próżnowanie* (Unleisurely leisure). In 1695 he wrote the epic *Psalmodia polska,* consisting of 36 psalms, the first example of the theme of Poland's manifest destiny, a popular subject of the Romantic nationalistic movement in Poland. He died in 1700 in Cracow, Poland. (Miłosz 1969/1983)

See also *Psalmodia polska.*

 # KÖNIG ROTHER

Middle High German epic romance/adventure (ca. 1150–1160), the earliest example of popular secular literature, by an author who is believed to have been a Bavarian priest writing for the entertainment of the nobility.

The young king Rother of Apulia decides to marry in order to produce an heir to the throne. He sets his sights on a beautiful princess, the daughter of Emperor Konstantin of Constantinople, who is known to execute would-be suitors. Rother sends 12 envoys to the emperor to ask for his daughter's hand, but before they leave he takes a harp and plays three tunes, which they are to listen for if in danger.

When the envoys arrive in Constantinople, they are promptly sent to prison. Rother assembles a great army and sets out for Konstantin's castle, assuming the name "Dietrich." He is accompanied by his faithful vassal Berchter, whose seven sons are among the imprisoned envoys.

On his arrival in Constantinople, "Dietrich" tells the emperor that he has been banished from Apulia by Rother. He manages to meet the princess and, learning that she wants to marry King Rother, reveals to her his true identity. The princess persuades her father to furlough the starving envoy prisoners for a period of three days. When they are released, Rother plays his harp to signal his presence. He effects their rescue and makes away with the princess as well.

But Konstantin sends a cunning *Spielmann* (minstrel) as emissary after them. The *Spielmann* tricks the princess into boarding his ship; then he sails away with her, returning her to her father.

Rother must then return to Constantinople in disguise and attempt to rescue his betrothed. But he is apprehended and sentenced to die. However, the faithful Berchter rescues him, and he escapes for a second time with his bride. (Garland and Garland 1986)

KONRAD, PFAFFEN

German priest and poet, author of the *Rolandslied* (ca. 1170), an Early Middle High German poem based on the French *Chanson de Roland* (ca. 1100). Konrad was probably a priest of Regensburg during the second half of the twelfth century, and his patron was probably Heinrich der Löwe, duke of Saxony from 1142 to 1180. It is supposed that Konrad composed the work for the duke and his consort about 1170. He first translated the poem from French into Latin and then into German. (For a synopsis of *Chanson de Roland*, see the *Encyclopedia of Traditional Epics*.) (Garland and Garland 1986)

 # KONRAD VON FUSSESBRUNNEN

Austrian nobleman and poet, author of the biblical epic *Die Kindheit Jesu* (ca. 1200), The poem, of some 3,000 lines written in rhyming couplets, describes Jesus's parental lineage, then relates the Annunciation, the Virgin Birth, the Flight into Egypt, and the Return to Nazareth. The author, a lay writer, used as one source an apocryphal gospel of the childhood of Jesus and acknowledges as another a work on the life of Mary by a "Meister Heinrich." (Garland and Garland 1986)

KONRAD VON WÜRZBURG

Middle High German poet, author of courtly epics, or verse romances, *Partonopier und Meliur; Engelhard; Der Trojanerkrieg;* the allegory of 32 eight-line stanzas, *Die Klage der Kunst;* and three verse legends of saints. He was born about 1225 in Würzburg of humble parentage. His prodigious output of poetry, which also includes love lyrics, didactic poems, verse romances, and shorter narrative poems, earned him several patrons, first in Strasburg and then in Basel, where he eventually settled. His poetry mentions many of his patrons, which included members of the clergy and of the new, wealthy merchant class. He died in Basel in 1287, having become one of the most influential craftsmen of his time. A century later, he was named one of the "twelve old masters" of medieval poetry from which the fourteenth-century *Meistersingers* claimed descent. (Garland and Garland 1986)

KORNÁROS, VITSÉNTSOS

Cretan poet, author of the Greek epic poem *Erotókritos* (early 17th c.). He was born in 1552 near Sitia on the island of Crete, probably the son of Jacob Kornáros, a Venetian-Cretan aristocrat. Documents in his hand indicate that he wrote in Greek with the Latin alphabet; therefore, his education must have been in an Italian school. He married Marietta Zeno and moved to Candia, where he joined the Academia dei Stravaganti. When the plague of 1591–1593 broke out, Kornáros was one of the few nobles to remain in the city, where he served as *Provveditóre all Sanita,* responsible for the health of the city during the crisis. The masterpiece of Cretan literature is his lyrical epic *Erotókritos,* a story of chivalrous love that is still recited today. He died in 1617, survived by two daughters. (TAP) (Trypanis 1981)

See also Erotókritos.

 # KRISTIJADE

Yugoslav religious epic based on the life of Christ by Ragusan (Dubrovnik) poet and dramatist Junije Palmotić (1606–1657), the last of the circle of great poets of Dubrovnik's golden age of literature. (Dvornik 1962)

 # KRONE, DIE
(*Diu Crône,* The crown)

Middle High German romance epic (ca. 1230) by Heinrich von dem Türlîn (or Türlein). The 30,000-line poem relates, in the first third, the fantastic adventures of Artus (King Arthur). The last two-thirds of the poem relates the miraculous exploits of Gawein (Gawain). As is usual with Arthurian matter, the weather seems perpetually springlike; however, the poet sets one adventure in the winter, on the snow-covered mountains of Carinthia, Austria, where he lived and wrote the epic. (Garland and Garland 1986)

 # KṚṢṆA DEVA RĀYA

Indian ruler and poet, author of the Telegu epic *Amuktamālyadā.* He was the son of Narasa Nāyaka, the powerful regent of the Vijayanagar empire in the Deccan region of India from 1490 to 1502, leaving his own sons in line to rule. Narasa's eldest son, Vīra Narasimha (r. 1503–1504), ordered the regent prince murdered (1503) and established the third dynasty of Vijayanagar. His younger brother, Kṛṣṇa Deva Rāya, succeeded him in 1509 and became one of the greatest Vijayanagar kings. He ruled the Vijayanagar empire from 1509 to 1529, during the golden age of Telegu literature. He completed his epic during his reign. As king, he allied his kingdom with the Portuguese for trade purposes, but refused to enter into a political alliance against the Muslims. Between 1504 and 1517 the explorer Fernando Magellan's cousin, Duarte Barbosa, visited Kṛṣṇa Deva Rāya and reported back to Portugal that the Deccan kingdom was a prosperous one. In about 1524, Kṛṣṇa Deva Rāya abdicated in favor of his son; however, the son was poisoned soon after. Suspecting a former chief minister, Kṛṣṇa Deva Rāya had the man and his family imprisoned and resumed the throne himself, ruling until his death in 1529. (Thapar 1966)

See also *Amuktamālyadā*.

 # KUDRUN

Middle High German heroic epic (ca. 1230–1240) of the Baltic coast—the Scandinavian and Frisian area—unrelated to the old Norse legends. It was written by an unknown Austrian poet. Written in stanzas resembling those of the *Nibelungenlied*, the poem is second in stature only to that work. It has the structure of a saga, in that it tells, in 32 *Aventiuren*, the story of three generations.

Aventiuren 1–3 relate the birth in Ireland of Hagen to Siegebant and Uote. Hagen is carried off by a griffin, which he later slays. He rescues three ladies, which the griffin has also carried off, and returns home with them. He makes Hilde, one of the three, his queen.

Aventiuren 5–8 tells of the birth to King Hagen and Queen Hilde of a daughter, also Hilde, of whom Hagen is very protective, killing any suitor who appears. King Hetel, a prospective suitor, sends an embassy headed by the warrior Wate, accompanied by the minstrel Horant, to woo the princess on his behalf. Won by Horant's music, the princess flees with the party of men sent by Hetel. Hagen pursues, but eventually relents and agrees to the marriage.

Aventiuren 9–32 tell the story of Kudrun, daughter of King Hetel and Queen Hilde, who accepts the proposal of Herwig, refusing another suitor, Hartmut of Ormanîe (Normandy). Hartmut kidnaps her and takes her home with him, pursued by Hetel's forces, whom he defeats in a battle on the Wülpensand. Kudrun refuses to marry Hartmut, and is held prisoner and mistreated by Hartmut's mother, Gerlint, for 13 years, her only companion the maid Hildeburg. Gerlint sends Kudrun to the seashore to do the washing, even though it is only March and there is snow on the ground. Kudrun learns that Herwig is on the way to rescue her, and she flings the clothes into the sea. Herwig and his army slay Gerlint, take Hartmut prisoner, rescue Kudrun and Hildeburg, and return home for a great wedding celebration. Hartmut is pardoned, and marries Hildeburg. Herwig, who must kill the father who pursues her, marries Kudrun. (Garland and Garland 1986; Hatto 1969)

 # KUMĀRASAMBHAVA
(Birth of [the war-lord] Kumāra)

Short Sanskrit epic poem (ca. 5th c.) by the great Indian poet and dramatist Kālidāsa. The poem, containing eight cantos, recounts the sometimes risqué story of the yearning for each other of Śiva and Pārvatī (Deva), the Father and Mother of the Universe, and of her seduction of him. A later poet added a sequel of nine cantos to the original poem.

In the first canto, the poet describes the Himalaya, animated by divinity, the winds "rising/from the mouths of caves,/Himālaya strives to sustain/the droning set of notes/that celestial musicians need for their singing." The ascetic Śiva, dressed in elephant hide like a beggar and free of all passion, is meditating in the Himalayas, but he is responsible for the generation of Pārvatī, his dead consort Satī, reborn as the daughter of the king of the Himalayas. As Pārvatī emerges in all her beauty, the sage Nārada predicts that she will become Śiva's wife. Pārvatī goes to the snowy peak where Śiva meditates, and she daily gathers grass and flowers for the ritual offering and carries water to clean the altar. Her gifts are a distraction, but Śiva allows her to serve him. Because of his respect for Himalaya, Śiva receives his beautiful daughter "even though she was an obstacle to his meditation,/for those whose minds are not disturbed even when temptation is near—they are truly firm." (1:56)

When Pārvatī ties a wedding cord to Śiva's wrist, "Śiva, manifest in his eight forms,/kindled fire with fuel of his own form—/the soul creator of austerity's fruit,/he practiced it with strange desire." (1:57)

In the second canto Brahma says, "Two things are capable of bearing/the seed of Śiva and my seed:/Pārvatī may bear Śiva's seed, and/Śiva's form as water may bear my seed."

The third canto, entitled "The Destruction of Kāma, the God of Love, by Śiva," describes how the "flower archer" places the "unfailing arrow called 'Fascination'" in his bow. From Śiva's third eye comes "a blazing glittering flame." The flame destroys Kāma, while Śiva, "wishing to escape from the proximity of women," disappears. However, although Kāma dies in the conflagration, his arrow has already struck Śiva. Pārvatī returns to her dwelling place, desolate to think that her own charm is so vain.

Following Śiva's temptation and the burning of love by the fire of Śiva's third eye, Kāma's mourning widow, Rati, voluptuousness personified, begs Śiva to revive her husband. She takes Kāma's ashes and smears them upon her body, preserving them so they can be revived later. (4:27,34)

However, Śiva's act destroys Pārvatī's desire: "The tip of love's arrow diverted by Śiva's roar/. . . struck a cruel blow in her heart." (5:54) She vows "to perfect herself by fiery penance," (5:2) even though her mother, Mēna, warns her, "Fiery austerities are alien to your body./A delicate mimosa flower can bear a bee's step,/but it cannot carry the weight of a bird." (5:3) The single-minded maiden retreats to the forest to "perfect herself until her penances bore fruit." She waters trees and feeds deer, finally going so far as to absorb herself into the elements until she brings her egotistical desire under control.

After a year, Śiva appears to her in the form of a young Brahman ascetic wearing a black antelope skin. He questions her about her love for Śiva and describes what a disgusting bridegroom he would be: "His body is monstrous . . ./his nakedness flaunts his poverty. . . ." (5:72) Enraged, Pārvatī defends her love: "Though destitute himself, he is the source of wealth;/lord of the universe, he

A tenth-century bronze sculpture represents Pārvatī, the consort of the Hindu god Siva. Indian poet and dramatist Kālidāsa wrote eight cantos in the fifth century B.C. about the love between the Father and Mother of the Hindu universe.

roams the haunts of ghosts/. . . He may glow jewels or be coiled in snakes,/ wear elephant hide or wild silk. . . ." (5:77,78) Won over by her arguments, Śiva assumes his godly form and tells her, "I am your slave,/won by your austerities." (5:86)

Her austerities have purified her for their wedding. In the sixth canto, as Pārvatī is prepared in finery, Śiva awaits the nuptials with impatience: "Even the Lord of Creatures spent those days with difficulty,/longing to unite with Pārvatī." (6:95)

In canto seven, Śiva politely refuses the wedding finery that is brought to him. Instead, he uses his own accoutrements: The skulls become a tiara, the ashes a perfumed sandalwood, the third eye a *tilaka* (dot of vermilion pigment on his forehead), and the serpents become ornaments, retaining the jewels in their hoods. (7:30–35) The women of Himalaya's city marvel at his beauty: "Kāma's body was not burned by Śiva. . . . Out of shame, when he saw Śiva, Kāma himself burnt his body." (7:67) At the end of their wedding, Śiva revives Kāma and gives him permission to use his love arrows, even against Śiva himself. (7:92–93)

In the eighth canto, Pārvatī's love and fear on their wedding night arouse Śiva's desire. (8:1) He carries her into the bedroom "with powers made great by his meditation." (8:81) In what is considered one of the most beautiful passages in Sanskrit literature, the poet describes the sunset over the Himalayas. As Śiva pauses to perform his sunset worship, Pārvatī pouts and sulks. (8:49–51) The poem describes their lovemaking: His power is so great that "Even when his passion was spent,/Śiva continued to make love to Pārvatī." (8:8)

The last nine cantos, written later by an imitator, contain passages concerning how Pārvatī conceives. Agni, in the form of a parrot, and the other gods interrupt the love-making, which deprives Pārvatī of a child. She weeps, and Śiva consoles her by wiping her tears with his loincloth. (9:11) Agni, who has received the spilled seed, is punished by the burning seed itself. He must be omnivorous, eat ordure, or suffer from leprosy. (9:16) He goes in pain to Indra and tells him, "Śiva restrained his passionate embrace of Pārvatī . . . because he was embarrassed./Then he placed in my body the seed which had fallen/. . . And that seed is never in vain . . . capable of burning the universe. . . ." Indra advises Agni, "If you plunge into the Ganges your pain will disappear."

It is said that the sages' wives become pregnant with Rudra's seed by bathing in the Ganges. (10:54)

Eventually the war god is conceived. The result is the birth of Śiva's son Skanda (Kumāra). Canto 15, "Kumāra's Fight against the Demon Tāraka," describes a confrontation between a "fearful flock of evil birds/ready for the joy of eating the army of demons" and "monstrous serpents, as black as powdered soot." The sun evinces joy at the death of the enemy demon. A thunderbolt lights heaven from end to end. The sky rains "torrents of red-hot ashes,/. . . mixed [with] blood and human bones." It is such a momentous occasion that "great elephants stumbled," horses fell, and "all the footmen clung together in fear." (15:14) (Kālidāsa 1955)

See also Kālidāsa.

KUNGASKALD
(*King-scald*, or Hymn to the King)

Swedish epic (1697) by Gunno Eurelius Dahlstierna (Gunno Dalstierna, 1661–1709), who wrote the poem in praise of King Charles XI on the occasion of his funeral. The poem is the most elaborate Baroque-style verse ever to be written in the Swedish language. The poet modeled it after the style of Italian poet Giambattisto Maríno, using ottava rima, primarily in alexandrines. Dahlstierna was the first to use the meter in Sweden. (Magill 1993)

KŬRVAVA PESEN
(Song of blood)

Bulgarian historical epic (1913) by Pencho Slaveykov (Penčo Slavejkov, 1866/1877–1912/1914), a member of the group of poets connected with the review *Misŭl* (Thought, 1892–1908). The magazine, which reflected contemporary Western ideas as opposed to Russian influences, was "intent on freeing art from parochialism and socio-political militancy." Slaveykov's epic, his greatest work, relates Bulgaria's history and its destiny; however, it was originally intended as a work of broader scope: European history. It was not completed. (Brogan 1996; Preminger 1974)

LA LÉGENDE DES SIÈCLES

See *Légende des Siècles, La.*

LA PUCELLE

See *Pucelle, La.*

LA SATANIADA

See *Sataniada, La*

LALLA ROOKH

English language epic (1816, publ. 1817) by Irishman Thomas Moore (1779–1852). The poem consists of four tales in verse with prose interludes and within a prose framework, interspersed with 26 songs of varied rhythmical patterns and rhyme schemes. The frame story is the journey of an Indian princess to her wedding, entertained en route by a young poet with the four tales. Its Oriental aura of splendor met the current taste, fed by such contemporaries as Lord Byron and Southey. This epic gave Moore a literary reputation rivaling that of Byron and Scott, and it earned what was then the highest price paid for a poem. However, Moore actually had little knowledge of the East and little interest in it *per se,* although he did find a parallel between the struggle of the Ghebers, the ancient fire-worshippers of Persia, against their Muslim masters and the Irish resistance to the English, a cause to which he gave himself throughout much of his life.

In the opening prose episode that introduces the framework of the epic, a marriage has been arranged for Lalla Rookh, daughter of the emperor Aurungzebe in Delhi, with the prince and heir apparent of Bucharia. At first bored by the journey to her wedding, the princess develops an interest in a youth about her own age, Feramorz, a great story-teller proficient with the *kitar*. He entertains her with tales.

The first, "The Veiled Prophet of Khorassan," contains 2,138 lines and is written in iambic pentameter couplets. Mokanna is a religious imposter who wears a veil to conceal his supernatural brilliance. He builds a large religious sect that assures its believers of eternal life in Paradise. Zelica is a beautiful maiden in love with Azim, who is reported to be dead. She is driven almost to madness by the presumed death, and enters the harem of the imposter Mokanna, expecting to win entrance to Paradise and reunion with Azim. Eventually, however, she discovers that Mokanna is a fraud. The caliph's army appears, alarmed by the false prophet and his host of infidels who hurl defiance at Islam.

In the ensuing battle the forces of Mokanna are destroyed, and he leaps to his death in burning waters. Zelica dons his veil to court death from the caliph's soldiers. A spear from one of the soldiers pierces her. The soldier is really Azim, who thinks he has killed Mokanna. He strips the Golden Veil from the dying girl and discovers it is Zelica. Azim grows old, haunted by her death, but when he finally dies, she appears in a vision, and they sleep side by side.

The tale ended, the great chamberlain who accompanies the princess is highly critical of the young man and suggests a different style of tale.

Several days elapse before the young man ventures his second tale, "Paradise and the Peri," a kind of fairy tale (in Persian mythology a *peri* is a fairy descended from evil angels). In this tale of 521 lines in iambic tetrameter couplets, a *peri* learns that she will be admitted to Paradise if she comes to the Holy Gates with "the gift most dear to Paradise." She comes first with a drop of blood from a young warrior who has died to free India from the tyrant Mahmood. Next she brings the sigh of an Egyptian maid dying from grief at her lover's death from the plague. Neither is accepted. Then she presents the tear of a hardened sinner who has repented of "many a ruthless deed; a ruin'd maid, a shrine profaned, oaths broken, a threshold stain'd with blood of guests! there written, all, black as the damning drops that fall from the denouncing Angel's pen." But now the man of crime watches an infant's play, followed by the vesper call to prayer, and sees the boy kneeling down, lisping the eternal name of God. The wretched man hangs his head and weeps with soul-felt penitence. The *peri* picks up the tear that falls on the sinner's cheek and offers it to the angel, who passes the *peri* through the gates. Heaven is won!

And this is poetry! the great chamberlain exclaims. It is a flimsy product of the brain, the story of a fantastical *peri*, he says. Lalla Rookh tries to soften the critic, without success. The travelers reach the city of Lahore, where the bride is received most enthusiastically with pageants and gifts. For some days after their departure from Lahore, a gloom hangs over the party, until the young story-teller sings a song accompanied by his lute. They camp in a grove of small Hindu temples, where an old tower is all that remains of an ancient fire temple built by the Ghebers (Persians), who had fled from their Arab conquerors, preferring liberty and their religion to apostasy. The chamberlain exclaims in horror at the account, and the young man proceeds to tell the tale of "The Fire-Worshippers."

This tale contains 2,226 lines, also in iambic tetrameter couplets. It is the story of the struggle of the Ghebers against Muslim rulers. Hafed, a Gheber, loves Hinda, daughter of a heartless Muslim emir, Al-Hassan. Hassan has been entrusted with the mission of stamping out the worship of Mithra. Unknown to him, his daughter Hinda receives a wooer, Hafed, each night in her high bower. She does not know that he is one of the hated Persians.

The princess is sad at the tale thus far, and the youth stops in the middle of it. The party continues their travel, now through a dreary country covered with jungle, where more than once a white flag flies from a bamboo staff, reminders that in that spot some human has fallen victim to a tiger. At sunset they arrive at a safe and lovely glen, where the young poet continues his tale, now in alternating rhymes.

The Ghebers have revolted. They will not stoop to be Muslim's slaves. The emir has the task of crushing the revolt, and Hafed is the leader of the rebellion, his only talisman, his only spell-word—"Liberty!" Vanquished, he leads the remains of his army to a mountain retreat. Hinda is captured by the Ghebers and discovers Hafed's role. A traitor reveals the retreat to the emir. Hinda watches the defeat of Hafed. He throws himself on a blazing funeral pyre, saying, "Freedom's God! I come to thee."

As she is conveyed by boat back to her father, Hinda leaps into the water. "Farewell to thee, Araby's daughter," a *peri* beneath the sea sings. The ocean *peris* "weep for the chieftain who died on the mountain . . . for the maiden who sleeps in the wave."

To the surprise of the others, the chamberlain has listened placidly to this story. He is organizing a plan of persecution for the young poet, whose recital, it seems to him, uses language and principles that are unacceptable. He plans to report him to the king immediately upon their arrival. If the king should not act upon this information, the chamberlain will see to it that there is an end to all legitimate government in Bucharia. For the moment he forgoes any criticism of the poet, surprising Lalla Rookh, who is expecting acid remarks. The entourage is not far from the forbidden river beyond which no pure Hindoo (Hindu) can pass, and the river rests in the rich valley of Hussun Abdaul. Lalla Rookh would be content to remain here forever, dreading the time when she will no longer see the poet. The party, however, is in a lively mood.

Not far away are the beautiful Royal Gardens. One evening as they are talking of the sultana Nourmahal, the Light of the Harem, who wanders among these flowers, mention is made of the reconcilement of a lovers' quarrel between her and the emperor during a Feast of Roses at Cashmere. This reminds them of a difference between Haroun-al-Raschid and his mistress, Marida, who reconciled by the music of Moussali.

The poet has forgotten his lute in the valley, so he borrows the *vina* of Lalla Rookh's little Persian slave, and tells this tale of "The Feast of Roses in the Vale of Cashmere," in 741 lines of alternate rhyming iambic tetrameter, changing temporarily in mid-tale to couplets whenever he speaks of the lovers' meeting: The valley is holding its Feast of Roses, a joyous time, with the beat of tabors, dancing feet, the minaret-crier's chant of glee, and the answering chorus from the neighboring harem. Jehan-Guire, Selim, son of the Great Acbar, speeds to the lake seeking the beautiful young Nourmahal. Nourmahal has quarreled with Selim, but hearing an enchanted song by Selim in disguise, she softens. He revives her love and they are reconciled. Reposing her head on his arm, she whispers with laughing eyes, "Remember, love, the Feast of Roses!"

At the tale's conclusion, the chamberlain remarks that he hopes he has heard the last of the young Cashmerian's poetry, which he calls "frivolous," "inharmonious," and "nonsensical." The subjects are bad, the themes are pagan. Whatever merits the young man has, poetry is not his avocation. The party ascends the mountains separating Cashmere from the rest of India. Because of the heat, they stop for repose and refreshment, with little time for any more tales. Lalla Rookh is depressed. Her ladies lament that meeting the king of Bucharia with pale cheeks will dampen their meeting, since she has been described to him in glowing terms.

They are met with gay pomp and processions. The roads are magnificently decorated, according to the taste of the young king that Lalla Rookh is to marry. It is night as they enter the city, and for the last two miles the hedges are festooned with rare roses, illuminated with tortoise-shell lanterns. They are greeted with fireworks. From this reception, the party deduces that the young king and bridgroom will make an exemplary husband. Even Lalla Rookh feels kindly, although she thinks how painful it will be for him not to be loved by her.

The marriage is fixed for the next morning, when she is to be presented to the king for the first time in the imperial palace beyond the lake Shalimar. After an anxious night, she is dressed by her ladies, and then, kissing a little amulet her father gave her, is conveyed by barge across the lake. Although the lake is covered with boats filled with minstrels and the shores are lined with rejoicing crowds, Lalla Rookh is melancholy. She tries to get a glimpse of the poet in the crowd. In the barge behind her is the chamberlain, his head full of the speech he will deliver to the king. They enter the canal from the lake to the domes and salons of the Shalimar; they glide beneath arches through the gardens, arriving where the king awaits his bride. She is agitated, and with difficulty walks up the marble steps. At the end of the hall are two thrones. On one of them sits the youthful king of Bucharia. The other is for the most beautiful princess. As Lalla Rookh enters, the monarch descends from his throne and extends his hand to take hers. She screams and faints at his feet. It is the young poet! He is the sovereign of Bucharia, who in disguise has accompanied his young bride from Delhi and won her love as a humble minstrel, thus deserving that love as a king.

The chamberlain is chagrined by this discovery, and his consternation is most pitiable. But he is too much the courtier not to be able to change his opinions. He immediately recants his criticisms, and he is suddenly seized with admiration for the king's verses. By the following week, he is swearing by all the saints in Islam that there never existed so great a poet.

There can be little doubt of the happiness of the king and queen of Bucharia after such a beginning. It is recorded that in memory of that journey, Lalla Rookh, to the day of her death, never called the king by any name other than Feramorz, the name by which she knew the young poet. (TAP) (Jordan 1975)

See also Moore, Thomas.

LAMARTINE, ALPHONSE-MARIE-LOUIS PRAT DE

French poet and statesman, author of two narrative poem-fragments of an uncompleted epic, *Jocelyn* (1853), and *La Chute d'un ange* (1858). Lamartine was born in 1790 at Mâcon, of an old family of landowners. His father, a Royalist, was imprisoned during the revolution. Following his release in 1794, he settled his family on a family tract at Milly, where the poet grew up. Lamartine attended school at Lyons, but ran away after the second year. In 1803 he went to Jesuit college at Belley for four years.

In 1816, while on a visit to Aix-les-Bains for his health, he fell in love with Julie Charles, the invalid wife of a Paris doctor. She appears in many of his poems as "Elvire." Her death a year later inspired him to write. His first volume, *Les Méditations poétiques* (1820) is generally considered the beginning of French Romantic poetry. The poems were an immediate success. That same year he received his first diplomatic appointment at Naples and also married a wealthy young Englishwoman, Maria Anna Eliza Birch.

His next volume of verse, *Les Nouvelles méditations* (1823), was not well received.

In 1825 he went to Florence as embassy secretary, but after the July revolution of 1830 he abandoned his diplomatic career and decided to enter politics. He made an unsuccessful bid for the Chamber of Deputies and decided to travel to Greece, Syria, and Palestine. During his absence, he was elected to the chamber. In 1833 he took his seat as a deputy and devoted himself to speechwriting. He discovered his gift for oratory and expressed his ideas on a society where liberty and justice prevailed.

In 1835 and 1838 he published the two narrative poems *Jocelyn* and *La Chute d'un ange,* which were to be part of an epic, but it was never completed. The collection *Recueillements poétiques,* published in 1839, was his last poetical collection. Thenceforth he devoted himself to political writings.

During the 1848 revolution he gained great power and renown for his rousing speeches, acting briefly as effective head of the provisional government. But in the elections the following year, no department was willing to stand him for candidacy, and he retired from public life. That same year he published a novel about his love for Julie Charles, *Raphaël,* as part of his effort to pay off a debt of 5 million francs. He sold the family estate and wrote for a living.

His wife died in 1863, leaving him in dire financial straits, but a government pension was awarded him in 1867. He died two years later in Paris. (Harvey and Heseltine 1959)

See also Jocelyn.

 # THE LAND OF MURAVIA

Russian mock-epic poem (1934–1936) by Aleksandr Tvardovsky (1910–1971). The poet's father was killed as a kulak during the period of the collectivization of the land; the poet wrote with the resolve to strengthen the morale of the people suffering hardships. Written in the style of folk tales with many of the narrative devices of the *byliny*, the poem tells the story of a foolish farmer who rejects life on the kholkhoz. He sets out to seek Muravia, the lost land of private ownership of land. After many unfortunate incidents on his journey, he learns that Muravia is only a myth, so he returns with a happy heart to the kholkhoz. The poem was praised by prominent critics of the time. (Bristol 1991)

 # LANDGRAF LUDWIG VON THÜRINGEN

Middle High German epic poem (ca. 1300) written by an unnamed priest for Duke Bolko I of Schweidnitz-Jauer. Based on historical but garbled facts, the poem, of some 8,000 lines, relates the heroic deeds of Ludwig III of Thuringia (d. 1160) on a crusade to the Holy Land. (Garland and Garland 1986)

 # LANGLAND, WILLIAM

English poet, presumed to be the author of the great Middle English alliterative poem *Piers Plowman* (ca. 1370–1387?). One early manuscript has a fifteenth-century annotation that associates him with the region of the Malvern Hills of the West Midlands in Worcestershire. He is thought to be the son of one Stacy (or Eustace) de Rokayle, a member of the gentry holding lands at Shipton-under-Wychwood. If he is identified as "Dreamer" in his poem (in fact, he calls himself "Long Will" in Passus XV), he may have been educated at the Benedictine school in Great Malvern because Will describes himself, in one version of the poem (the "C" text), as having received clerical training but as not being a priest. A self-professed poet and wanderer, he lived part of the time in the London slums with his wife and daughter, and the rest in the homes of people for whom he said prayers in exchange for room and board. References in the poem also suggest that he knew Westminster and Shropshire and make it clear that he had a thorough knowledge of theology. (Langland 1990)

LASSO DE LA VEGA, GABRIEL LOBO

Spanish poet and Mexico historian, author of *Cortés valeroso* (Intrepid Cortés, ca. 1588) and *Mexicana* (1594). He was born in 1558 in Spain and died in 1615. (Anderson-Imbert 1969)

LAUBACHER BARLAAM

Middle High German didactic epic poem (13th c.) of some 16,000 lines by Bishop Otto of Freisling, Bavaria (d. 1220). It relates the story of Josaphat, son of an oriental prince, who renounces worldly goods to follow the teachings of the monk Barlaam. He converts his father, then joins Barlaam as an anchorite. Inspired by a Latin version, the poem follows a more famous version by the twelfth-century poet Rudolf von Ems. (Garland and Garland 1986)

See also Barlaam und Josaphat.

LAY (LAI)
(Celtic: *loid*, song)

A medieval short narrative poem of about 1,000 eight-syllable lines (four-stress) of rhyming couplets, originally meant to be chanted to the accompaniment of a harp or lyre. The lays contain a folklore theme, an aura of Celtic fairy fantasy, with the element of chivalric love. The name *lai* and form were established by Marie de France (fl. 1165).

The term "Breton lay" was used in fourteenth-century England to describe any poem written after the fashion of Marie's and set in Brittany (for example, Chaucer's *Franklin's Tale*).

By the nineteenth century, the term had come to mean any short historical ballad (for example, Scott's *Lay of the Last Minstrel* imitates the verse narrative; however, it is meant to be read or recited without music).

Some epics contain the word *lay* in the title, as in the old Russian *Lay of Igor's Campaign* or the contemporary Russian *The Lay of Opanas*. (Deutsch 1974; Hornstein 1973)

THE LAY OF OPANAS

Russian epic poem (1926) by Eduard Bagritsky (real surname: Duziubin, 1895–1934). The poem depicts the Russian civil war, in which the poet fought. Ostensibly an imitation of the genre of Ukrainian folk narrative, the poem tells the story of Opanas, a Ukrainian rebel who joins the forces of the separatist Makhano, thus incurring the enmity of the Red commissar Kogan, a Jew. Eventually Opanas must confront Kogan in a duel in a lovely Ukrainian meadow: "Poplars in a gray flock standing,/... Steppe land stretching far and yonder,/ Grasses dry and bending,/... the sun of battle rises/... On that road but two men enter—/Opanas and Kogan."

In an epilogue the poet says, "Gone now are the years of duels/From Ukrainian pastures./Early waters rise no longer/With their din and rustle .../I do not know where our hero's/Bones do lie. ..." He concludes with praise for both contenders.

The poet was invited to rewrite his epic as a libretto for an opera. (Bristol 1991) *See also* Bagritsky, Eduard.

 # THE LAY OF THE DESTRUCTION OF THE RUSSIAN LAND

Russian epic (ca. mid-13th c.) by an unknown author about the Mongol invasion and conquest of Russia. Only the beginning of the poem has survived. This fragment is found with *The Life of Aleksandr Nevsky.* Nevsky (d. 1263), a prince of Novgorod, is praised in the *Life* as a hero of both the war of Mongol invasion and the wars with the Teutonic knights. The *Lay*, which borrows traits from the *byliny* and is noted for its use of rhymes, begins: "Oh bright and beautifully beautiful Russian land!" It describes the many beauties of Russia: "You are astounding with many lakes, with rivers and springs in hallowed places, with steep mountains, high hills, pure groves, wonderful fields. ..." It describes the inhabitants: "a variety of animals, innumerable birds, ... dreadful princes, honorable boyars, many courtiers." It concludes: "You are full of everything, O Russian land, O Orthodox Christian faith!" (Bristol 1991; Riasanovsky 1993)

 # LAYAMON

Early Middle English poet, author of *The Brut* (ca. 1205), a romance-chronicle of about 16,000 alliterative lines, the first example of Middle English in a secular poem. The poet, who flourished 1128–1207, was a priest living at Arley Kings in Worcestershire. His poem is an English verse translation of Robert Wace's Anglo-Norman verse *Roman de Brut* (ca. 1155), which itself was adapted from the Welshman Geoffrey of Monmouth's *History of the Kings of Britain* (ca. 1147), written in Latin. (Grebanier 1949)

LAYLÎ AND MAJNÛN
(Also *Laylā* [or *Lailî*] *u Majnûn*)

Persian romance epic (ca. 1188–1192) by Nizâmî (ca. 1141–ca. 1209). The poem is dedicated to the Sharvânshâh Akhsatân I (r. ca. 1162–1199 or later). It is based on a popular Arab legend about ill-starred lovers. The hero, the poet Qays, falls in love with his cousin Laylî, whom he cannot marry. He goes mad: "The maniac roams; with double speed/He goads along his snorting steed . . ." and goes to live in the desert, composing poems about his lost love. He is called Majnûn, which is Arabic for "possessed" or "mad."

Meanwhile, Laylî, "shielded by the harem screen,/The sweet Narcissus sad is seen:/Listening she hears, disconsolate,/Her father's words, which seal her fate. . . ." She is "given to be loved" by someone else in marriage: "a youth of royal presence, Yemen's boast,/Fierce as a lion, powerful as a host." At the wedding festivity all is a deafening celebration. "But Laylî, mournful, sits apart,/The shaft of misery through her heart. . . ." When the lovers die, they are buried in a single grave.

At one point the poet stops the action to warn about the fickleness of women: "For a while she looks upon you as a hero, and then, all at once you are nobody. . . . Never trust a woman." (Kritzeck 1964; Nizami 1995)

LAYOR, CHI CHI

Nigerian feminist poet, author of *Kingdom of the Leopard, an Epic of Old Benin* and *Oracles Don't Lie.* She is the daughter of political historian Mokwugo Okoye and novelist Ifeoma Okoye, a lecturer in English at the Institute of Management and Technology in Enugu whose many awards include the 1978 Macmillan Literature Prize and the 1984 ANA Best Fiction Award. Layor, who began writing poetry at age ten, graduated from the University of Benin. She worked as a news reporter for the *Guardian* newspapers and was self-employed in Enugu in the fields of advertising and marketing. She now serves in the Office of Social and Economic Development at the Baha'i World Center in Haifa, Israel. Her collection of feminist poetry, *Break Every Rule,* was published in 1989 in Nigeria. Her epic *Kingdom of the Leopard* records lore of the old kingdom of Benin, located in present-day Nigeria. Her epic *Oracles Don't Lie* is a cycle from the Yoruba. She has recently completed a Hausa cycle. (Layor 1995)

LE LUTRIN

See *Lutrin, Le.*

LEAVES OF GRASS

American poem (1855 version) by Walt Whitman (1819–1892). The poem, which Whitman continued to revise throughout his life, is his longest sustained effort in the bardic mode. The 1855 version consists of 12 untitled, unnumbered sections to be read as a single poem. Later, Whitman added the titles that head the sections on the 1881 edition. "Song of Myself," 1,336 lines long and comprising the first half or more of the work, is often considered Whitman's contribution to the American epic.

In the 1867 edition, the poet divided "Song of Myself" into 52 numbered chants, or sections. Since that time, various scholars have organized the narrative structure into seven, eight, nine, or ten parts. Editor Malcolm Cowley chooses to divide the narrative into nine parts, which he terms sequences, noted here with Roman numerals.

(I) Chants 1–4 comprise the first 72 lines. The poet begins by attempting to establish authority to speak: "I celebrate myself,/And what I assume you shall assume,/For every atom belonging to me as good belongs to you." (1–3) The poet goes on to describe his love for his natural self as well as his deeper self, or soul.

(II) Chant 5, lines 73–89, voices ecstasy: the union of poet, lying on the grass, and soul, expressed in terms of sexual rapture. He sees the spirit of God in every person, every creature, every leaf.

(III) Chants 6–19, lines 90–387, take the grass as a metaphor. In Chant 6 a child comes with hands full of grass asking, "What is grass?" The common grass becomes the central image, representing the divinity present in the meanest of things. The poet observes people, places, many living things. He relates to people and events both present and past: "In me the caresser of life wherever moving . . . backward as well as forward slueing. . . ." (226) He feels a kinship with the natural world. Watching various creatures, such as a hen turkey with her brood, or the sow's litter nursing, he says, "I see in them and myself the same old law. . . ." (245)

(IV) Chants 20–25, consisting of lines 388–583, concerns the poet in the body. He likes all of his aspects: ". . . hankering, gross, mystical, nude, . . ." (388) just like everyone else, both immoral and august. The sequence ends with the poet arguing with himself about his inability to express the ineffable about himself, finding that "the best I am" is beyond articulating.

(V) Chants 26–29, lines 584–646, describe ecstasy through the senses of hearing and touch. The poet decides to be completely passive, and "do nothing for a long time but listen." (584) After the mystical experience of being totally absorbed by sounds and "[l]et up again to feel the puzzle of puzzles,/And that we call Being," (609–610) he does the same for the sense of touch, which becomes the ecstasy of physical union.

(VI) In Chants 30–38, lines 647–973, the poet has gained the power of identification. Whereas his first ecstasy (Chant 5) afforded him the vision to see the infinite in the smallest, most commonplace things, the ecstasies in Chants 26–29 give him a vision far into space and time. Thus he sees himself in everyone who has ever lived.

(VII) In Chants 39–41, lines 974–1,049, the poet feels omnipotent, at one with the powers of the universe. He is the Answerer (Chant 39), the Healer (Chant 40), and the Prophet (41), announcing the godhood of men.

(VIII) In Chants 42–50, lines 1,050–1,308, the poet issues "[a] call in the midst of the crowd," (1050) offering his philosophy: "I am the acme of things accomplished, and I am an encloser of things to be." (1,148) In Chant 46 he says, "I know I have the best of time and space—and that I was never measured, and never will be measured./I tramp a perpetual journey. . . ." (1,198–1,199) He assures his listeners, "It is not chaos or death. . . . it is form and union and plan. . . . it is eternal. . . . it is happiness." (1,308)

(IX) In Chants 51–52, lines 1,309–1,336, having finished his sermon the poet prepares for death: "I bequeath myself to the dirt to grow from the grass I love." (1,329) He tells his listeners to look for him and, "Missing me one place search another,/I stop some where waiting for you." (1,335–1,336)

The other sections—some, but not all, divided into chants by the poet—will be described using his 1867 titles:

"A Song for Occupations," consisting of six chants of 178 lines, celebrates the various occupations. The poet asks, "Will you see afar off? You surely come back at last,/In things best known to you finding the best or as good as the best,/In folks nearest to you finding also the sweetest and strongest and lovingest. . . ." (164–166)

In "To Think of Time," in nine chants of 135 lines, the poet says, "I swear I see now that every thing has an eternal soul! . . . I swear I think there is nothing but immortality!" (131, 133)

In "The Sleepers," in eight chants of 204 lines, he relates sleep to death: "I will stop only a time with the night. . .and rise betimes." (201)

In "I Sing the Body Electric," in eight chants of 119 lines, the poet speaks of every man and every woman being "the start of populous states and rich republics." (100) He asks, "Who might you find you have come from yourself if you could trace back through the centuries?" (103) The body is sacred, and "Who degrades or defiles the living human body is cursed." (118)

In "Faces," consisting of five chants in 85 lines, he looks at people's faces and says, "I see your rounded never-erased flow." (37) He feels "the melodious character of the earth!" (83)

"Song of the Answerer," consisting of 54 lines, is not divided into chants. It answers the question "How should the young man know the whether and when of his brother?" (2)

"Europe: *the 72d and 73d Years of These States*" contains 36 lines. The poet warns, "Is the house shut? Is the master away?/Nevertheless be ready . . . be not weary of watching,/He will soon return . . . his messengers come anon." (24–26)

In "Boston Ballad," consisting of 41 lines, the poet describes going to Boston for a parade of "Yankee phantoms." He thinks there is one thing that belongs here: He envisions having King George's bones dug up, sent to Boston, glued together, and crowned. He tells the king, "You have got your revenge old buster!" (39)

"There Was a Child Went Forth," consisting of 33 lines, describes a child going forth daily, and the first object he sees, he becomes. "And that object became part of him for the day or a certain part of the day . . . or for many years or stretching cycle of years." (3)

In "Who Learns My Lesson Complete," consisting of 29 lines, the poet declares that all things are equally wonderful.

In "Great Are the Myths," consisting of five chants of 67 lines, the poet enumerates the things that are great, such as: myths, liberty, today, "the plunges and throes and triumphs and falls of democracy," (9) yourself, myself, youth, old age, day, night, poverty, wealth, the earth, language, English speech, the law, justice, goodness, wickedness, life, death.

He ends, "Sure as the stars return again after they merge in the light, death is great as life." (67) (Whitman 1959)

See also Whitman, Walt.

THE LEGEND OF ST. CATHERINE
(*Legenda o svaté Kateřině*)

Czech epic (ca. mid-14th c.) by an anonymous author. Consisting of 3,519 verses, the poem describes in vivid and lively imagery the life of the legendary St. Catherine of Alexandria, an early-fourth-century Egyptian of noble birth who becomes a Christian and protests Roman emperor Maxentius's persecution of Christians. Maxentius sends pagan scholars to debate her, but her scholarly arguments prevail. She is sentenced to die on a spiked wheel, henceforth called the Catherine wheel, but the wheel breaks. She is beheaded. Angels transport her body to Mt. Sinai, where it is found 300 years later. A great monastery is erected, which still exists. (Dvornik 1962)

LÉGENDE DES SIÈCLES, LA
(The legend of the ages)

French historical epic (1857, 1859–1883) by Victor Hugo (1802–1885), a result of his ambition to write a vast epic in which the central figure would be Man—in all his aspects of history, fable, philosophy, religion, and science—struggling upward from the darkness of barbarism to a golden age. Every epoch in its dominant characteristic and every aspect of human thought was to be expressed, a goal never really achieved. The result was a series of independent poems, different in kind—allegory, narrative, vision, didactic, lyric—in a great variety of verse forms, united in contributing to the overall theme. There are historical gaps, which Hugo tried to fill, only partly successfully, in a second series (1877) and a third series (1883) shortly before his death in 1885. The recognized canon contains 61 poems from all three series.

Egyptian-born Catherine of Alexandria, with a sword and spiked wheel, was the subject of a mid-fourteenth-century Czech epic. A Christian convert in the fourth century, she defended her faith against challenges by Roman Emperor Maxentius, who had her tortured for her beliefs.

The opening poems, "La Terre" (I) and "Le Sacre de la Femme" (II), fix man's condition before the Fall in Eden, with glimpses of Eve the Woman, then Cain and the torment of conscience, followed by portraits of women: Ruth and Boaz, and, finally, the women at Jesus's tomb. "Suprématie" (III) introduces the Indian concept of deity. "Entre Géants et Dieux" (IV) is the mythical expression of the cosmos. Jupiter the usurper has just overthrown the Giants, and Titan warns him of his precarious and temporary position at the summit of power. "La Ville Disparue" (V) deals with a lost Atlantis, a once great and glamorous civilization. "Aprés les Rois" (VI and VII) deals first with the historical emergence in the classical world of kings and the great city civilizations of antiquity down to Attila, and second, from Ramses to the Medicis. In "Decadence de Rome" (VIII) the decent of the soul of Man is represented by Androcles's lion within the decadence of Rome. In this period the struggle of good against evil reaches a nadir of pessimism. "L'Islam" (IX) focuses on the rise of Islam. "Le Cycle Héroique Chrétien" (X) deals with the excesses of medieval chivalry, when barons on the heights attack and pillage the plain. "Le Cid Exilé" (XI) portrays the ideal hero, the Spanish Cid, defying tyranny.

In "Les Sept Merveilles du Monde" (XII) the famous Seven Wonders of the World speak haughtily of their lofty domination of time, only to have the lowly earthworm enter and announce earth's finitude and ever-present death. "L'Epopée du Ver" (XIII) is a mock-epic celebrating the mastery of the worm, which devours not only the classic books but eventually the whole world. "Le Poëte au Ver de Terre" (XIV), however, refutes the claims of death and holds up a future hope. In "Les Chevaliers Errants" (XV) the poet shows the beginning of the march of history with a few admirable knights-errant and a series of rapacious feudal barons. In this period there are also many attempts by heroic figures to overcome evil.

"Les Trônes d'Orient" (XVI) is a series of portraits of Oriental despots, among them Zim-Zimri, a wicked potentate exalted in human eyes but morally base, who finally disappears in a column of smoke as the sun sets. Another, the sultan Mourad, is evil incarnate with monstrous power, who has slaughtered great numbers of women and children. He is faced with judgment but is saved by an almost accidental act of kindness: stooping to help a dying pig being tortured by flies. In Heaven he is saved by the pig's testimony. "Avertissements et Châtiments" (XVII) (Warnings and punishments) shows justice at work on evil rulers. "L'Italie—Ratbert" (XVIII) depicts evil-doers and usurpers of lofty positions of power. Ratbert and his henchmen have plundered and murdered, while flatterers praise him. But the stone statue of Satan smiles at their flattery. "Welf, Castellan D'Osborn" (XIX) is a solitary hero amidst all this evil. "Les Quatre Jours d'Elciis" (XX) and "Le Cycle Pyrénéen" (XXI) continue the depiction of evil barons. In "Seizième Siècle. Renaissance. Paganisme" (XXII), mankind is still a prisoner of fate. A character, the Satyr, dreams of liberation, a force dethroning the Olympian gods. "Je me penchai. J'étais dans le lieu ténébreuse . . ." (XXIII) is a hymn of hope. "Clarté d'Ámes" (XXIV) deals with the light given to prophets.

"Les Chutes" (XXV) deals with failures. "La Rose de l'Infante" (XXVI) describes the defeat of the invincible Spanish Armada as a wrecked fleet of drifting petals. The Infanta, essentially a tyrant, is redeemed because she is a child. "L'Inquisition" (XXVII) is based on a travel book about the Inquisition in South America and the Indian sacrifices at the Momotombo volcano. "La Chanson des Aventuriers de la Mer" (XXVIII) describes the pirates and their raids. "Mansuétude des Anciens Juges" (XXIX) deals with the use of torture to obtain confessions. "L'Échafaud" (XXX) shows the use of the scaffold. "Dix-Septièmbre Siècle. Les Mercenaires" (XXXI) describes the Swiss mercenaries—who seem as lofty and as noble as their Swiss mountains—with their bloody crimes in Italy and Hungary. However, the judge has given them authority in the name of law and justice, and the priests have assured them of God's sanction. "Inferi" (XXXII) is Hugo's version of the Inferno. "Le Cercle des Tyrans" (XXXIII), on tyranny, contains a paean to Liberty and a criticism of extravagant monarchies that rob their citizens. It looks forward to the Revolution.

"Ténèbres" (XXXIV) is a lyric about the darknesses, the griefs of Man. "Lá-Haut" (XXXV) is a dialogue between a star and a comet: one the light, the other the flame; one the symbol of harmony, the other of liberty. "Le Groupe des Idylles" (XXXVI) celebrates the idyllic in such great men as Solomon, Aesclepiade, Theocritus, Vergil, Catullus, Bion, Longus, Dante, Petrarch, Ronsard, Shakespeare, Voltaire, Diderot, Beaumarchais, and Chénier, and ends with an old man finding the language of babies, and with an idyll in the voice of a one-year-old child.

"Les Paysans au Bord de la Mer" (XXXVII) is a lyric landscape, where the sea wind blows and the peasant feels the sea mist; but also where the monstrous waves batter, the harsh wind blows, and deep dark caverns rest within the ocean. "Les Esprits" (XXXVIII) is at first a dialogue between two travelers, one a patriarch, the other a prophet, but wise only about things of the abyss. The patriarch proceeds to a plain, where he encounters God, and a dialogue ensues about the prophet he had met, who spoke only of dark things. He speaks for me, God says, where you need warnings. "L'Amour" (XXXIX) celebrates love as a human emotion, recorded in accounts of Thisbe and Berenice, in the poems of Horace, in the legends of Greece.

In "Les Montagnes" (XL) mountains like Mount Blanc inspire men to achievement. "Océan" (XLI) portrays a blind, howling creation tamed by Man, who has sailed that ocean to distant places, and overcome it just as he overcame the Flood and Babel—examples of the progress of which Man is capable. "A l'Homme" (XLII) urges Man, the son of Eve, who has climbed the highest mountains, and mastered the telescope and microscope, to probe a world more vast than the stars and search the infinite. In "Le Temple" (XLIII), a white temple is to be built on a spotless mountain, surrounded by the forest and the restless ocean. Diverse paths will lead to its summit. Within will be an image of a reality greater than Jehovah, Jupiter, or Brahma, where all dogma and all bibles will vanish. Within this temple, pagans, Christians, Parsi, Roman priests, and Buddhists will join in one religion. Other temples, corruptible and based on error, madness, and fable, will be destroyed. The statue of Reality, impassive and veiled, will—like a dream, heedful of the air, the forest, the ocean, the seeds, the sky, the clouds, the stars—stand open to the sky and to the air. Evildoers will be ill at ease before it, and all those whose hearts are great—the sages—will feel the plain light within their souls. Behind the statue will be an eternal lamp, and they will understand that it is the rising of an eternal morning.

"Tout le Passé et Tout l'Avenir" (XLIV) is a prophetic hymn, a conversation with a mysterious Being, answering doubts and offering hope for the future. "Changement d'Horizon" (XLV) proposes new horizons, replacing Homer as the poet, war as the law. Death is not the end of man. "La Comète" (XLVI) predicts that some day the comet, the flame, will return. XLVII passes rapidly over the sixteenth, seventeenth, and eighteenth centuries.

"Le Retour de l'"Empereur" (XLVIII) reflects Hugo's feelings about Napoléon, describing the popular enthusiasm over his return and the subsequent disillusionment, and is a paean to France as the mother of revolutions. "Le Temps Present" (XLIX) comments on recent French history, much of it satire, but, in "Le Cimitière d'Lau," also admiration of such heroes as a Vendean peasant chief who live and die for something higher than personal credit or success. "L'Élégie des Fléaux" (L) is an elegy: The battle, with its fury and massive bloodshed, is over (the defeat of France in 1870). France is without compass, without a sailing mast, without anchor, without pilot, without direction, at the mercy of the wind. But the human spirit cannot be broken. Heavenly order and human reason will prevail. France, dream on. You are great, it is your fate! "Voix Basses dans les Ténèbres" (LI) hears voices out of the darkness of the soldiers, the priests, all together, who will overcome, will recover. "Les Pauvres Gens" (LII) is an idyll expressing a hope for the future lying in the common man, embodied in a woman character whom the poet names Jeannie. "Le Crapaud" (LIII) uses as a symbol an ugly toad looking upward at the sky. Dazzled, it dreams. From its low station, without fear, shame, or anger, it looks at the sun. A man passing by, a priest with a book, steps on it. A woman stabs its eye with the point of her umbrella. Four schoolboys amuse themselves with torturing the creature. The toad drags itself down the path. Night begins to fall, and children see the toad and cry out, "Kill the bad animal because it is ugly!" They all laugh, as blood runs all over the body of a creature whose only crime is being ugly. It runs away, one leg torn off, and plunges into a deep rut. The children have never been so amused, and they run on in their play. One stops and returns to see what has happened to the toad. A cart pulled by an ass appears and rolls onto the rut where the toad lies. Stop! the child calls out. The ass stops, sees the toad, lowers its head sadly. The driver spurs him on, but the ass turns aside. The child drops the rock in his hand and calls after the ass, "You are good!" A diamond inside carbon. An ass the servant of God!

"La Vision de Dante" (LIV) is a monologue by Dante, who, in his grave, hears a voice asking him what it is like down there. Dante asks how long he has been there, and learns it has been 500 years. A vision appears to him, an angel with the word JUSTICE on his head. He calls the dead to rise. A crowd emerges, crying, "Justice on the earth!" Dante sees armies amidst the turmoil of clashing weapons. The shades shout "Murderers!" There are men in the robes of judges next to gibbets and pillories, then princes, kings, and, finally, a pope. All have been condemned to Hell. "Les Grandes Lois" (LV) (The higher laws) is a series of meditations on values and vanities. At its conclusion the giant sun speaks to a dwarf star: Without me the firmament would be but a shroud. I amaze infinity. The atom listens and answers, "God."

"Rupture avec ce qui Amoindrit" (LVI) (Break with that which diminishes) calls attention to the vanities that obsess men and urges opening the soul. The French Revolution, though mixed with horror, greeted the light, with, alas, the head of Louis XVI. In "Les Petits" (LVII) (The little ones), someone cries, "Death!" and the people crowd in. Petit Paul, only three years old, watches as his grandfather dies. He wanders through the village crying, "Papa! Papa!" Men make up the army that are the victors, but the children are their stay and the future. "Vingtième Siècle" (LVIII) (Twentieth century) has two sections. The first, "Pleine Mer" (Wide ocean), builds upon a huge contemporary ship, the Leviathan, intended for a thousand passengers and to be used to lay the Atlantic cable. In this poem it becomes a warship, a symbol of human achievement at the service of darkness and violence. The second section, "Plein Ciel," is an expression of optimism, a vision of man's conquest of the air, with a dirigible, that will destroy the barriers between nations and bring universal love and brotherhood. It is also a utopian faith in the power of science, another stage in the ascent of Man. LIV continues visions of the future.

"Hors de Temps. La Trompette du Jugement" (LX) (Beyond time. The trump of Judgment Day), originally the final and climactic poem of the first series, is an expression of a messianic faith in the coming of the revolution. In that future time, a sinister hand will emerge out of the shadows, out of infinity. It belongs to some archangel or seraphim, its feet planted in a hell but its face toward the stars. "Abîme" (LXI) (The abyss), the concluding poem in the second series, is an exchange between Man; Earth; Saturn; the Sun; the stars Sirius, Aldebaran, and Arcturus; a Comet; the North Pole; the Zodiac; the Milky Way; nebulae; Infinity; and God. It is a cosmic vision of the immense whole of Creation. Infinity comments that it all exists united within a clouded shadow. God makes the final comment: I have only but to blow and it will all be darkness.

As the poet Swinburne observed, this epic is an account of a tragic pageant of the centuries, from the legendary dawn when the first woman felt within her a child, to an ultimate justice in the likeness of the trumpet of doom; from Eve, the mother of men; to the Revolution, mother of peoples.

Hugo left two other pieces, which he intended as sequels: "La Fin de Satan" (The end of Satan) and "Dieu" (God), in which Satan is redeemed, and an offspring of God (goodness) and Satan (evil) unites both in a profound oneness of form, two sides to the same coin. (TAP) (Grant 1968; Richardson 1976; Swinburne n.d.)

See also Hugo, Victor-Marie.

LERMONTOV, MIKHAIL YURYEVICH

Russian poet, novelist, and dramatist, author of *A Demon* and *The Novice*. He was born in Moscow in 1814, the son of a retired army captain, Yury Petrovich Lermontov, and Mariya Mikhaylovna. His mother died when he was three and he went to live with his grandmother, Yelizaveta Alekseyevna Arsenyeva, on her country estate. During his years with his grandmother he traveled frequently in the Caucasus. When he was 13 (1827) his grandmother took him to Moscow to attend a boarding school for children of the privileged class. He studied painting and wrote poetry in the manner of Byron, a style he was to continue for the rest of his life, so that he became known as the "Russian Byron." In 1830 his first verse, *Vesna*, was published. He entered Moscow University the same year. The following year (1831) he wrote a play, *Stranny Chelovek*, which voiced a protest against the tsar and serfdom. He left Moscow University in 1832 and enrolled in the military cadet school in St. Petersburg, graduating two years later. He was appointed to the Life-Guard Hussars and was stationed near St. Petersburg.

In 1835 he wrote a play, *Maskarad* (publ. 1842), critical of aristocratic life. In 1837, when Aleksandr Pushkin was killed in a duel, Lermontov wrote an elegy that laid much of the blame for the poet's death on the system. When the poem reached the attention of the court of Nicholas I, Lermontov was exiled to the Caucasus. When he was allowed to return a year later, he wrote a number of Romantic and satirical poems as well as dramas. In 1840, using Caucasus images and themes, he wrote a novel called *A Hero of Our Time*, which established him as one of the founders of the Russian novel. That same year he was exiled again after a duel. Throughout most of his life he worked on a magnificent long poem entitled *The Demon*, set in the grandeur of the Caucasus.

In 1841 he was returned to his regiment, but at the age of 27 he was killed at Pyatigorsk in a duel with a fellow officer, N. S. Martynov. Lermontov has often been considered Russia's second greatest poet, successor to Pushkin. (Bristol 1991; Johnston 1983; Myers and Brodsky 1988; Riasanovsky 1993)

See also *The Demon; The Novice.*

 # *LES MARTYRS*

See Martyrs, Les.

 # *LES NATCHEZ*

See Natchez, Les.

THE LIBERATION OF ITALY FROM THE GOTHS

See *Italia Liberata da Gotti, La.*

THE LIGHT OF ASIA
(Or *The Great Renunciation*)

English epic (publ. 1879) by Sir Edwin Arnold (1832–1904). The poem, "by the medium of an imaginary Buddhist votary," introduced the Western world to the life and character of Prince Gautama (Prince Siddhārtha), the Buddha, and the philosophy of Buddhism. It consists of eight books in blank verse, with intermittent passages of rhymed lyric verse. It was Arnold's most famous work, and immediately popular. Although essentially concerned with the heights of the Buddha's wisdom, it is also an admixture of love poetry and luxuriant Oriental scenery drawn from Arnold's own experience when he lived in India from 1856 to 1861.

Book First tells of the reincarnation of the Buddha after 10,000 years, to be born as a son to Queen Maya and King Suddhōdana. The king is unaware of this origin, but when his dream-readers augur a special prince, he orders a high festival and names the son Prince Savārthasiddh, or more briefly, Siddhārtha. At his birth, a stranger, Asita, comes and bows down in worship, announcing that this is the Buddha. Eight days later the mother dies, and the king gives the babe to a foster-nurse. When the prince is eight years old, his education begins, but he is so precocious that even his teachers prostrate themselves before the boy and accept him as their teacher, although he keeps his reverence for them. He also excels in physical pursuits. One day, after a cousin shoots a swan with an arrow, the prince takes up the bird and draws the arrow from it. The cousin quarrels with him, claiming the bird as his trophy, but a priest awards the bird to the prince. The king takes the prince, a young man now, to see the realms, but all he sees is violence. He sits under a jambu-tree with ankles crossed and begins to meditate on the deep disease of life. A pity fills him, and his spirit passes into ecstasy, purged from sense and self and attaining Dhyāna, the first step of "the path."

In Book Second, the young man is 18 years old, and his father builds three stately houses for him. However, the father is troubled by memory of the prediction and sees two possible paths for his son: one, the sad and lowly path of self-denial and pious pains; the other, the proud path of a king of kings, with the Earth to rule. However, the young man, though amid these palaces, already turns his eyes wistfully to the first path. The king calls his ministers for advice. One suggests love as a cure for those "distempers." So the king commands a festival to which the realm's maids shall come as competitors for the heart of the prince. As they pass slowly before him, he sits passionless until young Yasōdhara comes. Her gait, her face, her form, her eyes cast such a spell upon the prince that his heart takes fire. When the king is told this, he immediately arranges their marriage. However, it is a law that whenever a maid of noble house is asked in marriage, the suitor must prove himself in martial arts. The king is dismayed, for among the other suitors are those who have excelled in such contests. However, the prince proves the best in archery, swordsmanship, spear-throwing, and horse-breaking. The young girl approaches the prince wearing a black and gold veil. Long after, when asked about this, the Buddha answers that in another incarnation they both had been tigers, he wooing and conquering her. The two are wed, and they live together in a luxuriant pleasure palace, night and day served rich feasts and entertained by sensuous dancers. The king orders that within that mansion there be no mention of death or age, sorrow, pain, or sickness. The three gates are bolted and barred, and an order is given that no man shall pass the gates, not even the prince.

In Book Third, although surrounded by luxury and protected from knowledge of any pain or death, from time to time the prince starts up and cries, "My world! Oh, world! I hear! I know! I come!" His wife then asks what ails him, but all he does is look at her, terror-stricken, then smiles, trying to calm her fears. But he hears the Devas sing a song about the woes in many lands, urging him to leave love and to wander in search of rest. One evening a maid, Chitra, tells the prince and his wife an ancient tale of a distant world. He asks Chitra more about that land, then orders that his chariot be brought. He emerges, and the people greet him joyfully. Midway in the road, creeping forth from a hiding place is a ragged wretch, an old, fleshless, toothless man, shaking with palsy. One skinny hand clutches a worn staff that props his quavering legs. He begs for alms. Horrified, those around the prince try to thrust the old man back, but the prince stops them and asks who the man is. They tell him that the man was once young, but old age has sapped his strength. Is this the fate of men? the prince asks. Shall I and my wife be thus one day? When the answer is yes, the prince begins to ponder as he returns to the court, and he lies sleepless that night. That same night the king has troubling dreams of a strong wind rending a flag bearing the mark of Indra; then of ten huge elephants trampling the southern road, with his son sitting on the foremost; then, of the prince sitting in a shining car snorting white smoke and fiery foam; then, of a wheel of burning gold turning and turning, with strange things written on its tire; then, of the prince beating a mighty drum with an iron mace, midway between the city and the hills; then, of the prince scattering gems from atop a tower that rises high over the city, crowned with clouds, while the whole world comes, striving to seize the jewels; and, finally, of a noise of wailing as six weeping men gnash their teeth and walk disconsolately.

The next morning, the king is angry because none of his wise men can tell him the meaning of his dream, but an aged man dressed as a hermit comes and explains it. The seven fears are seven joys that will come to his house. The flag is the end of old faiths and the beginning of a new one. The elephants shaking the earth signify the ten great gifts of wisdom with which the prince will shake the world. The car with horses are the fearless virtues that will carry his son to light. The wheel is the perfect Law, which he shall turn. The drum is the thunder of the Word he will preach. The rising tower is the growing of the Gospel of the Buddha. The jewels are the untold treasures of the Law. The six weeping men are the six chief teachers whom the prince will convince of foolishness. Rejoice, the hermit adds, for the fortune of the prince is more than kingdoms. Now happy, the king sends a gift after the hermit, but when the messenger arrives at the temple, he finds only a gray owl.

Determined to find new delights to bind his son to more worldly conquests, the king steps up the pleasures in the mansion and sets a double guard at the doors. But the prince is determined to see the world beyond the gates. He begs his father to let him view the streets of the city. The king consents, but gives orders to keep him informed. The prince mingles with the people. He hears a mournful voice from the roadside. It is a sick man. Inquiring, he is told of disease, which also afflicts mankind. How can Brahma make a world and keep it miserable? he asks. He returns home. When the king hears of this encounter, he sets a triple guard on the gates.

In Book Fourth, the princess is pregnant, and awakens the prince with her fears from a dream in which a bull invaded the streets and trampled the warders. She also dreamed of four Presences sweeping into the city while the flag of Indra fluttered and fell, and in its place rose a banner with new words and sentences. From the east a soft wind blew, opening the scrolls so that all might read them. In a third dream there was an unpressed pillow and empty robe. It all ended with a voice crying, "The Time is nigh." The prince tries to console her. He loves her, the mother of his babe, but he knows that the time has come when he must depart on the mission to which time has led him. He bids his horse, Kantaka, be brought to him. He mounts and reaches the gate with tripled brass, which rolls back silently. He passes free from the palace.

In Book Fifth, the prince, the Lord Buddha, comes to a cave, where he sits through all kinds of weather, wearing a yellow robe, eating scanty meals, homeless and alone, subduing his body with fasting, meditating silently while animals and birds gather around him. Then he makes his ablutions and goes into the town, in the fashion of a Rishi with begging bowl in hand. The townsmen notice his godlike face, and mothers bid their children fall to kiss his feet. He wends his way to sit upon his hill with holy men, to hear and ask of wisdom and its roads. In groves beyond the city but below the caves dwell Yogis, Brahmacharis, and Bhikshus—a gaunt band withered by disease but mortifying their bodies. The Buddha asks one of them why they are adding to their ills. The man answers that in this way they can purge sin's dross and purify the soul. Will you so loathe the flesh, the Buddha asks, that it shall not serve to bear the spirit on? We dwell by painful pasts to find the light. Abroad winds the better road, Buddha says. Onward he passes, sorrowful that men dare not love their life but plague it with fierce penances as if to please gods who grudge pleasure to man.

Down the mountain, white goats and black sheep slowly wind their way. As they stray, the herdsman keeps them moving. Why, the Buddha asks the herdsman, are you driving these flocks since it is usually evening that men fold them? He is told they are being herded to a sacrifice by a king to his gods. The Buddha goes with him, meeting a young woman whose child had been bitten by a snake and who had earlier sought him upon the hill to save the child. He had told her to find a black mustard seed. This she had tried to do, unsuccessfully. Now her child is dead. The Buddha tells her that the whole world weeps with her. He would pour his own blood if it could ease her pain. The Buddah tells the woman to go and bury the dead child.

The Buddha and the herdsman enter the city, carrying a lamb. The king thinks it is the sacrifice he has ordered. He waits with white-robed Brahmans before the altar and prepares a goat for the knife, but the Buddha stops the king and looses the bonds of the animal. He speaks to them of life, which all can take but none can give. All life is linked and kin, he tells them. The priests scatter the altar flames and fling away the sacrificial knife. The king issues an edict that henceforth there shall be no more sacrifices.

It is written in the holy books that when Buddha wore a Brahman's form, dwelling upon the rock Munda, drought withered all the land. The Buddha then spotted a starving tigress with two hungry cubs. The Buddha offered himself as meat to the mother and her cubs. Thus had been the Buddha's heart long ago. Now he bids cessation of the cruel worship of gods. The king, learning of his royal birth and holy search, asks him to stay there, but Siddhārtha says he must go to build the Kingdom of the Law, journeying to Gaya, where the light will come to him. The ascetics from the hill stay with him.

In Book Sixth, the Buddha lives once more in the forest, musing the woes of men, the ways of fate, the doctrines in the books, the lessons from the wild creatures. Once, he falls into a swoon and a shepherd boy comes by, shades him with boughs from the trees, and pours milk upon his lips. But he is a Sudra, of low caste, and is afraid of defiling the Buddha, until the Holy One tells him that all flesh are kin. The peasant's heart is gladdened, and he gives the Buddha the milk. On another day, a band of nautch-dancers trip down the forest path on their way to a festival. One with a *sitar* sings a song of joy that turns to sadness while the music dies. Buddha lifts his brow and says, "The foolish sometimes teach the wise." By the river dwells a landholder with a lovely wife but no male child, until, after her prayers, a boy was born, now three months old. A servant runs to her with news that a god is among the trees. She hastens to the Buddha and tells him of her vow to make an offering if she should be given a boy child; now, thinking the Buddha is a god, she will keep it. He blesses the child but insists that he is no god but a wanderer seeking the light. She describes herself as a faithful wife, for which the Buddha praises her.

He proceeds to the Tree of Wisdom, where woodland creatures hail him as the savior who will assuage the world's woes and greet the Night that the ages await. The Master sits under the tree, but Mara, the Prince of Darkness, knows that this is the Buddha who would deliver the world. Mara summons all his evil powers, who war with wisdom and the Light: the ten chief Sins—Self, Doubt, dark creeds, Passion (in the guise of sweet Yasōdhara, his wife), Hate, Lust of Days, Lust of Fame, Pride, Self-righteousness, and Ignorance. But the Buddha sits serene, attaining Sammā-sambuddh, beholding the ten great Virtues. Next he attains *Abhidjna,* insight into worlds where a Power rules all things according to the laws of virtue. In the next watch the Buddha finds the secret of Sorrow, where he who is wise bears meekly all ills until he achieves *Karma,* the total of a soul, nevermore needing a body and a place, and finally reaching *Nirvana*—sinless, stirless rest, change that never changes.

With the dawn the birds sing, and peace among men and animals comes. The Spirit of the Lord lies upon man and bird and beast. The Buddha arises and sings a song of deliverance from delusion.

In Book Seventh, the prince's father sits sorrowful over the absence of his son, and Yasōdhara laments the absence of her husband. A group of traveling merchants arrive who say they have seen the prince and worshipped at his knees. He has become a Buddha who saves all men, and men say he is traveling this way. The wife is elated. The merchant tells how the Buddha has been many places to teach the Way. At Yashti, King Bimbasāra believed him and set a stone carved in memory of his visit. When the prince's father hears all this, he sends nobles as messengers to his son, asking him to come unto his own in the realm. The Buddha receives the message and returns. Sobbing, the princess falls at his feet. The king, hearing how his son comes in mendicant's clothing, becomes angry, but when the son falls to his knees before him, he softens. He reminds his son that he is the heir of a spacious power and asks him why he wears the clothes of a beggar. His son replies that he comes of another descent, the line of Buddhas, and he offers his father a treasure: the path to *Nirvana.* That night they enter into the Way of Peace.

In Book Eighth, the Buddha sits on a hill by the city of his father, Suddhōdana, to teach the Law. He sits at the right hand of his father, surrounded by the lords and chiefs. Between his knees, his son Rahula smiles, and at his feet Yasōdhara sits. Thousands, including the narrator, come to hear him. The Buddha speaks in rhymed quatrains: Any searcher will find no light; there must be veil after veil. Within himself a man must seek his deliverance. He suffers from himself; no one else compels. Before beginning and without end is a fixed Power that moves toward good; its law endures. The heart of it is Love; the end of it is Peace and Consummation. Man goes unto *Nirvana.* This is the doctrine of the Karma. For those who would take the *Nirvāna-way,* these are the Four Noble Truths: Sorrow, Sorrow's Cause (desire), Sorrow's Ceasing (conquest of self), The Way. The Path is eightfold: Right Doctrine, Right Purpose, Right Discourse, Right Behavior, Right Purity, Right Thought, Right Loneliness, Right Rapture. The Path follows four stages: In the first, the climber knows the Noble Truths; in the second, he is made free from doubts, delusions, and inner strife; in the third, he is purged and pure, and his stately spirit has risen to love all things in perfect peace; in the fourth, he reaches the ultimate goal—the ten sins lie in dust. *Nirvana* is not to cease, nor is it to live. It is lifeless, timeless bliss. To live is to follow the Five Rules: kill not, give freely, bear not false witness, shun drugs and drink that abuse mind and body, touch not your neighbor's wife.

To those of the yellow robe, the Buddha teaches the Ten Observances and what a mendicant must know, laying the foundations of the Order of the Yellow Robe, which stand to this day.

All night he speaks. When he is finished, the king rises and bows low before his son and asks to be taken into his Company. Yasōdhara cries for the Buddha to give their son Rahula the Word for his inheritance. Thus the three pass into the Path.

In conclusion, the narrator speaks of the Master who has given Asia the light, and who in the fullness of time died but left for men the Path that leads to where he went, to *Nirvana,* where the Silence lives. (TAP) (Arnold n.d.; Elton 1920; Walker 1931)

See also Arnold, Sir Edwin.

 # LINDBERGH

American epic poem (1927, 1974, publ. 1975) by George C. Cox, a clergyman. The body of the poem was written in 1927, following Charles A. Lindbergh's historic flight across the Atlantic in his plane *The Spirit of St. Louis.* When Lindbergh died in 1974, the poet added the final section, and the book was published the following year. The poem is written in free verse, employing a variety of meters and cadences, sometimes an uneven pentameter shifting into shorter rhythms.

It consists of three cantos, two interludes, and a memoriam, all of which are preceded by two poems. The first, entitled "Gateway," is written as though it might have been spoken by Lindbergh: ". . . I seek to break/the bounds and barriers of earth/And fly ever upward. . . ." The second poem, entitled "A Brief Prelude to Canto One," expresses the poet's vision of a "master plan" for mankind from the "master Mind" whom he calls: "A Music Maker Who goes singing, dancing/Down all geologic ages. . . ."

Canto I, entitled "The Progress of Man," calls Lindbergh "God's Own Viking." In six sections it tells of the evolution of the earth and the history of mankind. The latter portion of Section V deals with the discovery of America by Vikings and with the dawn of the scientific age: "The old earth turns relentlessly on its axis./In silent contentment it takes its well ordered/Course about the sun, while on its surface/Man is continually seeking reality."

"First Interlude" returns briefly to Lindbergh and the "pursuit of the dreams of vibrant youth."

Canto II, entitled "Boyhood Days of Lindbergh," presents in two sections of colorful imagery not only Lindbergh's boyhood, but his young manhood as well.

"Second Interlude" is the poet's profession of faith in a divine Creator involved in the affairs of man.

Canto III, entitled "The Pilgrimage of Peace," describes Lindbergh's historic flight across the Atlantic, which the poet equates with man's flight through the ages: his fears and courage, his victories, and his final triumph over the unknown. He calls Lindbergh: "The great Archangel of Peace. He was not an American,/. . . but a great soul of/the ages, a citizen of the world. . . ."

Pilot Charles Lindbergh, subject of George C. Cox's 1975 epic *Lindbergh,* stands ready for his 1927 solo transatlantic flight from New York to Paris in his plane called the *Spirit of St. Louis.*

"In Memoriam," the final section, written in 1974 after Lindbergh's death, celebrates him as other heroes and saints have been honored throughout the ages. (Cox 1975)

LONGFELLOW, HENRY WADSWORTH

American poet, author of the narrative poems *Evangeline* (1846), *Song of Hiawatha* (1855), and *The Courtship of Miles Standish* (1858). He was born in 1807 in Portland, Maine, the product of two old New England families. His mother was Zilpah Wadsworth, whose father, a general in the American Revolution, could trace his ancestry back to John Alden. Longfellow's father, a lawyer, traced his ancestors back to a blacksmith who settled in Massachusetts in 1680. Longfellow attended Portland Academy, then entered Bowdoin College in Maine as a sophomore, graduating in 1825 with Nathaniel Hawthorne. During his school years he wrote and published poetry in national magazines, as well as translating poetry. This latter talent led to an offer of a professorship in languages at Bowdoin on the stipulation that he first study languages in Europe. This he did, ignoring his father's wishes that he enter his law office. He studied French, Spanish, and Italian, returning four years later (1829) to become professor and librarian at Bowdoin. In 1831 he married Mary Potter.

In 1835 he was offered a chair of modern languages at Harvard provided he would study abroad, an offer he accepted. He traveled to England, Sweden, and the Netherlands. His wife died during the trip to Rotterdam, and thereafter he settled in Heidelberg, Germany.

In 1836, Longfellow returned to Harvard, and in 1839 he wrote *Hyperion*, a Romantic novel whose heroine was modeled after Frances Appleton, whom he met in Europe. That same year he published his first collection of poems, *Voices in the Night,* and in 1842 he published his second collection, *Ballads and Other Poems*, containing "The Wreck of the Hesperus," which became very popular. In 1843 he made another trip to Europe and married Frances Appleton. For a wedding gift, her father bought them the Cambridge mansion called Craigie House where Longfellow was already living. They lived there for the rest of their lives.

Longfellow became increasingly interested in writing narrative verse. Inspired by Goethe's *Hermann und Dorothea*, he wrote *Evangeline* in 1847. The poem, written in dactylic hexameters, was immensely popular.

In 1854 he left his Harvard post of 18 years to devote himself to writing. Using the trochaic meter of the Finnish *Kalevala*, he wrote *The Song of Hiawatha* in 1855. In 1858 he wrote *The Courtship of Miles Standish*, which sold 10,000 copies in a single day.

At the height of his popularity, his second wife died after her dress accidentally caught fire (1861). Grief-stricken, Longfellow did not write for several years. In 1863 he published *The Tales of a Wayside Inn* after the manner of Chaucer's *Canterbury Tales*. The first poem, "Paul Revere's Ride," became very popular. He translated Dante's *Divine Comedy* (1865–1867), an outstanding translation at the time.

He died in 1882 in Cambridge, Massachusetts, one of the most popular U.S. poets of the nineteenth century. (Siepmann 1987)

See also Evangeline; *The Song of Hiawatha.*

 # LOPE DE VEGA
(Lope Félix de Vega Carpio)

Spanish dramatist and poet, called the Shakespeare of Spain, author of the historical epics *La dragontea* (1598), *Jerusalén conquistada* (1609), and *Corona trágica* (1627), the Romantic epic *La hermosura de Angelica* (1602), the burlesque epic *La gatomaquia* (1634), and some 1,500 plays. He was born in 1562 in Madrid, the son of Félix de Vega, an embroiderer, and Francisca Fernández Flores.

By the age of five he was composing poetry, and he wrote his first play, a comedy, at the age of 13. He began to study Latin and Castilian at the age of ten with the poet Vicente Espinel. At the age of 12 (1574) he entered Jesuit Imperial College to study the humanities. He probably also attended the University of Salamanca. Before the age of 14 he had already been involved in fighting the Portuguese. He found favor with the bishop of Ávila, who in 1577 enrolled him in the Universidad Complutense, the Alcalá de Henares, to study for the priesthood. He began in earnest to write comedies and translate Latin poetry. However, an affair with a married woman brought an abrupt end to Lope de Vega's studies.

When Félix de Vega died in 1578, his embroidery shop passed to his son-in-law, husband of Lope's sister, Isabel de Carpio. The poet later added the noble Carpio to his own name.

In his early twenties he began a long-term romantic relationship with Elena Osorio, daughter of a well-known theater backer who did not approve of his daughter's liaison with a struggling dramatist. Lope de Vega wrote several scathing attacks on the young woman's family, and they brought charges of defamation against him. In 1588, at the age of 26, he was sentenced to exile from Castile for two years and to exile from the court at Madrid for an additional six years.

In the midst of the exile he married Isabel de Urbina by proxy and left to fight with the Spanish Armada, undertaking various military adventures to the Azores, meanwhile writing at least one epic, a Romantic epic in 20 cantos, *La hermosura de Angélica* (The beauty of Angelica, publ. 1602), a sequel to Ariosto's *Orlando Furioso.*

After Spain's defeat, he returned to Valencia, site of a popular drama school, where he wrote many comedies and romances that he sent to his Madrid agent, Gaspar de Porres. By the time his exile was completed, he had earned the sobriquet "phoenix of the witty."

In 1590 he returned to Toledo and took a position as secretary to the duke of Alba. During his five years there, he wrote a novel, *La Arcadia* (publ. 1598). At about the same time, he began his real work as a playwright. In 1594 his wife died in childbirth. In 1598 he married Juana de Guardo, with whom he had three children. He wrote *La dragontea* (1598), an epic—an attack against England—telling of the last voyage and death of that "devilish dragon," Sir Francis Drake.

He returned to Madrid and began a liaison with Micaela de Luján, with whom he had seven children, and who appears in his poetry until about 1608 as "Camila Lucinda." However, during this time he remained married to Juana.

In 1605 he became secretary to the duke of Sessa, for whom he worked for 26 years. Between the years 1610 and 1613, in addition to writing such plays as *Fuenteovejuna, El acero de Madrid,* and *El perro del hortelano,* he wrote a historical epic based on the Third Crusade, *Jerusalén conquistada* (1609). He also wrote an important treatise, *El arte nuevo de hacer comedias en este tiempo* (The new art of writing plays, 1609), which had a profound influence on theater. He established the three-act comedy and founded the Spanish national theater.

His wife Juana died in childbirth in 1614, sending him into a deep depression that resulted in his decision to take up monastic orders. However, shortly afterward, he became romantically involved with a married woman, Marta de Nevares Santoyo, who appears in his poetry as "Amarilis." They maintained a relationship for ten years until Marta, who became both blind and mad, died at the age of 40. Lope de Vega then wrote his most famous tragedy, *El castigo sin venganza,* as well as a new epic, *Corona trágica* (1627), about Mary Stuart, Queen of Scots. In 1632 he published a largely biographical work written in prose and poetry, *La Dorotea.*

Although his work had taken a more serious turn, in 1634 he published the burlesque epic *La Gatomaquia,* a parody of the Italian epic concerning the romantic escapades of three cats.

He had, however, come to repent of his tumultuous life filled with many love affairs, elopements, abductions, marriages, and liaisons. Toward the end of his life he also lost both a favorite son and daughter. His last work, *Égloga a Claudio* (publ. 1637), is a critical reflection on his life. He died at age 73 in 1635 in Madrid. The phrase "Es de Lope" had become a synonym for perfection. Cervantes called him the "prodigy of nature." The quality and quantity of his work make him one of the greatest dramatists of all time. (Hayes 1967)

See also *Corona trágica; Dragontea; Jerúsalen conquistada.*

THE LORD OF THE PANTHER-SKIN

Georgian epic. See *The Knight in the Panther's Skin.*

THE LOUSIAD

English mock-epic poem by John Wolcot (1738–1819), who used the pen name "Peter Pindar" for this coarse, sometimes vulgar political parody. This sample is from Canto I; the speaker is George III on discovering a louse on his place at dinner: "How, how? What, what? What's that, what's that," he cries,/With rapid accent, and with staring eyes:/"Look here, look there; what's got into my house?/A Louse, God bless us! Louse, louse, louse, louse, louse." (Highet 1962)

THE LOVE OF TANDARIS FOR THE INDIAN GIRL FLORIBELLA

Czech epic poem (ca. 14th c.) by an unknown author. The poem was inspired by Konrad Flech's Middle High German *Floire und Blanscheflur* and by the thirteenth-century French metrical romance *Floire et Blanchefleur,* also told in the English metrical romance *Flores and Blanchefleur* and in Italian prose by Boccaccio as *Filocolo.* (Dvornik 1962)

LUČA MIKROKOZMA
(The ray of the microcosm)

Serbian philosophical epic by Montenegrin Price-Bishop Petar Petrović Njegošs (1813–1851). In this case the poet eschewed the styles of Romantic literature popular at the time, returning to more classical construction for the poem, which in subject matter is tied to the older European philosophy and treats a subject similar to Milton's *Paradise Lost.* (Čiževskij 1971)

LUCAN
(Marcus Annaeus Lucanus)

Silver Latin poet (from the post-Augustan Silver Age [ca. A.D. 18 to A.D. 133] in Latin literature), author of the epic *Pharsalia.* He was born in A.D. 39 at Corduba (Córdoba), Spain, into a wealthy, distinguished, and cultured family. He was the grandson of Seneca the Elder, a historian and writer on rhetoric. His father, a knight, rhetorician, and imperial finance administrator, was the brother of two renowned men: Seneca the Younger, Nero's tutor and virtual ruler of Rome during Nero's first eight years, and Gallio (Lucucs Iunius Gallio Annaeanus Novatus), governor of Achaea, to whom the Jews brought Paul in A.D. 51–52, accused of impiety. (Gallio refused to consider the charge: Acts 18: 12–17.)

Lucan studied philosophy in Rome under Stoic Cornutus, sharing tuition with satirist Aulus Persius Flaccus. In the late 50s he continued his education in Athens, but Nero called him to Rome to become a part of his inner circle. He was married to Polla Argentaria, to whom he wrote a composition, now lost.

In A.D. 60, he won a laurel wreath in a poetry competition at the first celebration of the Neronian Games for a poem praising the emperor. In about 62 or 63, Nero conferred upon him the religious post of *augur* and the financial post of *quaestor,* a clear honor since it was not usually conferred until the age of 30, and Lucan was then in his early twenties. The post also carried with it the right of enrollment in the senate. Also in about 62 or 63, he published three books of his epic about the civil war between Caesar and Pompey called *Pharsalia.* It has since been called the greatest Latin epic after the *Aeneid.*

However, the books contained some passages at which Nero might take offense, although nothing like the savage attacks that would appear in the later books. He fell out of favor with Nero, who considered himself something of a poet in his own right. Lucan was forbidden both to write poetry and to plead with the courts, thus effectively ending his literary and political careers. Thereafter, Lucan began lampooning Nero. In 64 the great fire of Rome broke out and burned for five days and nights, destroying over two-thirds of the city. Among the poet's lost works is a poem, *On the Burning of the City,* in which the poet may have accused Nero of setting the fire.

Lucan even joined in the conspiracy of Caius or Gaius Calpurnius Piso in 65 to assassinate Nero and put Piso on the throne. Piso was executed, and Lucan, despite trying to influence the emperor by denouncing his own mother, was compelled to commit suicide (A.D. 65), as were his father and both of his uncles. He opened his veins and recited some of his own poetry as his life ebbed away. Suetonius wrote his biography, depicting him as a brilliant and prolific writer. Now all his works except the *Pharsalia,* itself unfinished, are lost. (Suetonius 1981)

See also Pharsalia.

THE LUCIADS

See Lusíadas, Os.

LUCIĆ, HANNIBAL

Croatian poet, author of epics about the tragic destiny of Croatia after the battle of Krbava (1493), which left it under Venetian domination. Lucić was born in 1485 in Hvar. He was a nobleman who also excelled in lyric love poetry. A learned and accomplished poet, he translated Ovid and wrote the earliest secular dramatic work in Croatian literature, *Robinja* (The slave woman). The work is more a narrative poem in dialogue than a drama. He died in 1553 in Hvar. (Čiževskij 1971; Gazi 1973; Preminger 1974)

Portuguese explorer Vasco da Gama presents a letter from the king of Portugal to the ruler of Calicut in India during his voyage of discovery in 1498. Luís Vaz de Camões composed *Os Lusíadas* about the voyage in 1572.

 # LUSÍADAS, OS
(The Luciads)

Portuguese national epic (1571, publ. 1572) by Luís Vaz de Camões (ca. 1524–1580). The poem, consisting of ten ottava rima cantos, has been called the greatest Vergilian epic of the Iberian Peninsula, the backbone of Portuguese literature.

The poet, himself an explorer, based his *Aeneid*-inspired narrative on the figure of a distant relative, Vasco da Gama, and his voyage to India. However, Vasco da Gama represents the Portuguese people as a whole and their glorious achievements.

After an invocation to the Muse and a dedication to King Sebastião, Canto 1 describes a meeting of the gods on Olympus while Vasco da Gama sails up the east coast of Africa. Bacchus, who opposes the Portuguese, instigates a Muslim attack against the Portuguese at Mozambique. However, da Gama, who is favored by Venus and Mars, escapes and sails his ships to Mombasa.

In Canto 2 the islanders at first send an emissary to welcome da Gama: "The king of this island is overjoyed at your arrival. . . . Your fame has come before you. . . ." Bacchus dons the garb of a Christian to convince the sailors of the safety of entering the channel, while on land the Muslims ready their ammunition. But Venus and the Nereids send vicious winds that prevent the ships from entering the river's mouth. Da Gama says, "This is beyond question a miracle that has saved us from walking blindly into a trap. . . ." On behalf of the Portuguese, Venus appeals to Jupiter, who promises her, "Your people will embark on greater enterprises still, and will discover new worlds to mankind." Jupiter sends Mercury to Malindi to prepare a friendly reception for da Gama. The king of Malindi visits the ships and engages the captain "in one topic after another."

Canto 3 begins with an invocation to the epic Muse. Da Gama then describes to the king of Malindi the mythical founder of Lusitania, named for either Lusus or Lysa, "the sons—some say, companions—of Bacchus, who were the earliest inhabitants." He describes the first king of Portugal, Alfonso Henriques, and subsequent kings, their battles against the Moroccans, and their conquests. He tells of Alfonso's having Inés de Castro put to death because his son Pedro can think only of her. Pedro takes vengeance against her killer and becomes a severe ruler. But his son Gernando is a gentle ruler, who becomes infatuated with Leonor Teles de Menesea, wife of another man. Like Paris with Helen, Fernando carries Leonor away to be his wife. Da Gama says, "A weak king can sap the courage of a strong people."

Canto 4 continues da Gama's tale to the king of Malindi, describing uprisings after Fernando dies, and Castile's threat. The valiant Nuno Alvares Pereira rallies the people and is victorious at the battle of Aljubarrota. King João I ventures overseas and captures Cueta, then Alfonso V makes many conquests in North Africa and against Castile. He describes enterprises of João II and how Manoel I, after a dream about the Ganges River, sends da Gama around the Cape in search of India.

In Canto 5 da Gama tells of his voyage as far as Malindi; in Canto 6 the king entertains the visitors and supplies a pilot to cross the Indian Ocean. Bacchus descends to Neptune's court to stir up trouble for the Portuguese. Aeolus turns winds against them, almost capsizing the vessels, but after a prayer by da Gama, Venus and her nymphs pacify the winds. At daybreak the sailors sight India.

Canto 7 begins with praise for the Lusitanians: "neither peril, nor self-seeking, nor lukewarmness in devotion to Mother Church deters you from the conquest of the lands of the infidel." Portugal is compared favorably to Germany, England, France, and Italy. Da Gama lands and goes to the Samorin, proposing a treaty of friendship.

Canto 8 describes the banners flying from the fleet, depicting the heroes of Portugal, beginning with Lusus and going to Henry the Navigator. The Samorin's soothsayer poisons his mind against the Portuguese, saying they are pirates, while Bacchus prods the Muslims to plot their destruction. When da Gama is detained from returning to his ship, he begins to suspect treachery but assures the king he is not a pirate and that the gifts he brings are from King Manoel of Portugal. He is allowed to return to the ship and does not risk going ashore again.

In Canto 9 two groups of Portuguese traders are detained on the shore so that a fleet from Mecca can arrive to destroy all of da Gama's vessels. Warned of the plan, da Gama seizes Muslim merchants as hostages and exchanges them for the two groups of traders. He sets sail at once for the Island of Love, which Venus has arranged as a reward. Tethys and her Nereids are waiting for the mariners. Smitten by love, Tethys declares herself to da Gama.

Canto 10 describes a feast for the mariners and the Nereids. Tethys takes da Gama to a mountaintop and explains the universe, with Earth at its center. She describes Africa, Asia, Oceania, and Brazil as arenas of Portuguese discovery. Da Gama sails his vessels for home.

The poet laments the decline of the heroic persona: "This country of mine is made over to lusting greed." He appeals to Sebastião not to withhold his favor from those vassals who serve him overseas: "Observe how cheerfully they go forth, . . . spirited as lions and brave as bulls, exposing themselves to . . . all the uncharted perils of the universe. (Camões/Atkinson 1952)

See also Camões, Luís Vaz de.

 # *LUTRIN, LE*
(The lectern)

French mock-heric epic (1674, 1683) in six cantos by Nicolas Boileau (called Despréaux, 1636–1711). The first four cantos of the poem were published in 1674, the last two in 1683. The poem was inspired by a dispute between two ecclesiastical figures, the treasurer and the precentor of the Sainte-Chapelle in Paris, about the position of a lectern in the chapel choir.

The poem begins with a close imitation of the opening lines of the first and seventh books of Vergil's *Aeneid*. The poet describes the wrath of the treasurer Auvry, who feels the precentor has been taking over some of his duties. The poet models the anger of "Discord" and her indignant speech upon Juno's in the *Aeneid* (1:36–49). Her transformation into an aged servant to religion and her visit to Auvry are parodies of the demon Allecto's visit to Turnus in the *Aeneid*. (7:406–466)

Auvry devises a plot to belittle the precentor by restoring a huge lectern to its position directly in front of the precentor's seat, rendering him invisible to the congregation. This task is undertaken in the dark of night, infuriating the precentor when it is discovered the next day. The precentor takes his complaint to the chapter and has the lectern removed, after which the treasurer appeals to the sibyl "Chicanery" for help.

In Canto 5 the adversaries, with their seconds and supporters, meet in a bookshop for a duel, hurling at one another books by authors both ancient and contemporary. The poet, also a literary critic, manages to throw satirical barbs as his "duelists" heave their books, and it becomes a battle of the books themselves. With a wily strategy devised by "Chicanery," the treasurer prevails, and the two are finally reconciled. (Harvey and Heseltine 1959; Highet 1962)

 MAC FLECKNOE

(Subtitle: *A Satire upon the True-Blue Protestant Poet T. S.*)

English mock "epic," very brief (publ. 1682), by John Dryden (1631–1700). The poem, an attack on Protestant poet Thomas Shadwell (who, ironically, later succeeded Dryden as poet laureate in 1689) is a parody of a heroic theme. The "hero" of the poem is the poetic "dunce Mac Flecknoe." The title comes from an Irish priest known for his poor poetry, Richard Flecknoe (ca. 1600–ca. 1678). Dryden depicts Shadwell as Flecknoe's successor in the monarchy of nonsense, ridiculing the poet so badly that his reputation never recovered.

The two men had once been friends, but in 1681 Dryden had ridiculed Shadwell, along with others, in his *Absalom and Achitophel*. The following spring he published *The Medall,* a pro-Tory poem, which was answered by Whig Shadwell's savage poem *The Medal of John Bayes*. Dryden's *Mac Flecknoe* was his reply. It is written in rhyming couplets with no enjambment: "And when false flowers of rhetoric thou wouldst cull,/Trust nature, do not labor to be dull. . . ."

The coronation and consecration, by his predecessor Flecknoe, of a mighty king and prophet (Shadwell) is compared in somber terms with several greats: Aeneas's son Ascanius becoming the heir of Aeneas and building the capital Alba Longa; Hannibal, the Carthaginian general, succeeding his father Hamilcar Barca; Romulus ascending to the new throne of Rome; Elisha inheriting the mantle of Elija. "Sh— along my perfect image bears," says Flecknoe, and thus Shadwell becomes "the last great prophet of tautology." (Kingsley 1958)

 MÁCHA, KAREL HYNEK

Czech poet, author of the lyrical epic *Máj* (1836). He was born to poor parents in 1810 in Prague. As a schoolboy Mácha began to write in German, but he was most influenced by the works of Byron and Sir Walter Scott, as well as those of the Polish Romantics.

National Czech pride was emerging at the time, as was the Czech literary language, capturing his imagination. By the time Mácha was 20, he had begun to write poems, prose, and novels in Czech. Most of his prose works were uncompleted, although they show a perfection in language technique. In the field of poetry, he showed more facility, introducing iambic verse to Czechoslovakia.

In 1834 he journeyed to northern Italy, and two years later he attained a legal position in Littoměřice, Bohemia. However, he died of pneumonia in 1836, the year his masterpiece, *Máj,* was published. Although the poem was not well received at the time, Mácha is now considered the greatest poet of Czech Romanticism. (Čiževskij 1971; Dryden 1994))

See also Máj.

 # MACLEISH, ARCHIBALD

American poet and playwright, author of *Conquistador* (1932). He was born in 1892 in Glencoe, Illinois, to Andrew and Martha Hillard MacLeish. He was educated at Hotchkiss School, a preparatory school, and Yale University, where he distinguished himself both as a Phi Beta Kappa student and as an athlete. His first poem appeared in 1911 in the *Yale Literary Magazine,* which he later served as editor.

In 1916 he married Ada Hitchcock, and in 1917 he entered the army artillery with a hospital unit, seeing active duty at the front and rising to the rank of captain. While in France, he published his first book of poetry.

After the war MacLeish earned a law degree at Harvard and stayed to teach one year, then joined a distinguished law firm in Boston. In 1923 he left for France with his wife and two children. He stayed in France for five years, and came under the influence of nineteenth-century French poets and Ezra Pound and T. S. Eliot. These years produced several collections: *The Happy Marriage* (1924), *The Pot of Earth* (1925), *Streets in the Moon* (1926), and *The Hamlet of A. MacLeish* (1928).

In 1928 he and his family returned to the United States, and in 1930 he published *New Found Land,* a collection that showed considerable craftsmanship, increased skill in a variety of verse forms, and a deep concern with his American heritage.

From 1930 to 1938, MacLeish served as an editor on *Fortune* magazine. During the 1930s he directed his poetry toward a wider audience, with pieces that were frankly "public" poems, although he also continued to write personal lyrics. Following a trip to Mexico and after reading Bernal Díaz's account of Cortés's conquest of Mexico, MacLeish wrote his epic poem *Conquistador* (1932), directed to a wide audience. It won him his first Pulitzer Prize in Poetry, but it also involved him in a controversy with left-wing critics, in which his replies established his views on poetry and its relation to its times. During that time he also wrote several verse plays for radio, including *The Fall of the City* (1937) and *Air Raid* (1938).

MacLeish served as Librarian of Congress from 1939 to 1944 and was involved in the reorganization of the Library of Congress. In the last of those

Author and diplomat Archibald MacLeish, left, with Assistant Secretary of State Dean Acheson, 24 February 1945, during a radio broadcast.

years, he was assistant director in the Office of War Information. He showed himself to be deeply concerned with world affairs, participating in the establishment of the United Nations Educational Scientific and Cultural Organization (UNESCO), writing its constitution and chairing the committee to coordinate worldwide cultural activities.

In 1949 he was appointed a professor at Harvard University. He retired in 1962, but continued to speak out on national issues. His *Collected Poems: 1917–1952*, published in 1952, won a second Pulitzer Prize and the Bollingen Prize for Poetry.

MacLeish continued to write plays in verse; his verse *JB*, which had its debut on Broadway in 1958, won the Pulitzer Prize for Drama. In 1962 he published *Poetry and Experience*, an original approach to poetry. Another verse drama, *Scratch,* appeared in 1971, and *The Great American Fourth of July Parade,* a verse play, was performed on radio in 1975. His *New and Collected Poems 1917–1976* appeared in 1976, and his essays were collected in *Riders on the Earth,* published in 1978. Among other honors, he served as a lecturer at Cambridge University in England, assistant secretary of state, and president of the American Academy of Arts and Sciences. He died in 1982 in Boston. (TAP) (Falk 1965)

See also Conquistador.

MACPHERSON, JAMES

Scottish poet and forger (1736–1796), publisher of the *Ossianic Poems.* He was born in 1736 in Scotland. In 1760 he published what he claimed were translations of poems by the third-century Gaelic bard Ossian (Oisin), entitled *Fragments of Ancient Poetry Collected in the Highlands of Scotland and Translated from the Gaelic or Erse Language.* The poems aroused such interest that the author was able to collect funds from a number of literary figures to finance further trips to the Highlands to collect more epics. In 1762 he published *Fingal, an Ancient Poem in Six Books,* and in 1763, *Temora, an Epic Poem in Eight Books.* In 1765 he published a collection entitled *The Works of Ossian.* While some critics hailed the poems as a great discovery, others, particularly Samuel Johnson, believed they were fake. After Macpherson died in 1796, it was discovered that he had collected some fragments of early Gaelic poems, which he used as a basis for his own work. The poems had an important influence on the development of Romanticism in France, where Napoléon admired them, and in Germany, where Goethe's *Werther* was inspired by them. (Hornstein 1973; Siepmann 1987)

 # *MADOC*

English epic (1799, 1807, 1815) by Robert Southey (1774–1843). The first version, finished in 1799, consisted of 15 books with about 6,000 lines. Reconstruction of the poem began in 1803. At this time, it was divided into two parts; the first, "Madoc in Wales," had 17 sections, and the second, "Madoc in Aztlan," had 27 sections.

After some consideration, Southey decided against blank verse in favor of rhymed couplets. A second edition appeared in 1807, and a fourth in 1815. There were minor revisions, all unimportant.

The epic was based on two legends, for which Southey believed there was historical evidence. In the first, a Welshman had sailed to the West after a murderous vendetta in Wales between the sons of Owen Gwyneth, rival heirs to the kingship, in search of a better resting place (America?), from which he returned for a boatload of adventurers and settled in what is assumed to be the southern region of the Missouri River. Their descendants are said to be an Indian tribe still present during Southey's time (the Mandans?), retaining the language, complexion, and some of the arts of their ancestors. The second of these legends concerns the Aztecas, who forsook their homeland, Aztlan, to the north, and under the guidance of their leader founded the Aztec Empire to the south, taking the name of "Mexicans" in honor of their tutelary god, Mexitli. Their emigration is connected with the adventures of Madoc, both having occurred about the same time.

In section I of Part 1, "The Return to Wales," Madoc sails back to Wales; as he sights land, he recalls the events that led to his original departure: the seizure of the kingship by David, eldest son by a second wife of the deceased Owen Gwyneth. On shore Madoc is greeted by Urien, the old man who had fostered him, who tells him of the murder of Yorwerth, the elder son, and the exile of the other brothers. He also announces the forthcoming wedding of the usurper to a Saxon princess, a Plantaganet with British blood to pollute the Welsh royal line. Urien takes Madoc to the festivities, where Madoc's sister Goervyl sits sadly, and urges her to restrain Madoc from provoking David.

In section II, "The Marriage Feast," David receives Madoc warmly, but Madoc accuses him of complicity with the hated Saxons and the murder of their brother Hoel. In their anger, David is restrained by his bride, and Madoc by his sister. The bard sings a lay of ancient Welsh victories, rousing in Madoc dreams of days that are no more.

In section III, "Cadwallon," Madoc recalls the events that led to his departure from Wales: news of the strife that shook the royal house after their brother Hoel ascended to the throne, challenged by David. Madoc describes how he sped to the ensuing battle and found a bloody plain with no living soul; how one of their brothers was tortured and killed by David; how Cadwallon befriended him, warned him he was in danger, and took him to the shore and pointed to the west, where a nobler conquest than the overthrow of David could be won. Madoc answered that they would go together.

Section IV, "The Voyage," describes the original voyage: how Madoc sails westward with Cadwallon through many a tempest, finding land after four weeks.

In section V, "Lincoya," as they coast along the shore, the captive of a chief, Lincoya, rows out to their ship asking help for his people, who live up a mighty river. They sail up the river, cross leagues of fertile mead with a thousand herds, and hike over mountains to reach Lincoya's village.

In section VI, "Erillyab," Madoc meets the queen, Erillyab, who has lost her realm in warfare but has retained the old customs, giving them a deeper and religious character. Her people are still faithful and obedient. At her side stands her son, now near manhood. Many weapons hang on a tree by the door— her husband's war-pole, his moldering quiver and his stone-ax green with moss, but the bow-string still singing as it cuts the wind. An Aztec man, hooded with sable, his half-naked limbs smeared black, approaches and seizes a small boy and girl being claimed for sacrifice, their hearts to be plucked out and eaten. Madoc catches them up to protect them. The priest raises a menacing hand, but the queen calmly rises, takes the battle-ax from her husband's war-pole, hands it to her son, and calls upon her husband's spirit. The awed priest returns without his victims, bearing the news that the Hoamen have cast off their vassalage and defied the power of Aztlan.

The king of Aztlan sends for Madoc, who comes unarmed, with Lincoya as interpreter, to a beautiful and populous plain, where Aztlan lies on the shores of a broad lake, and behind it, a mountain-sized temple. From his throne the royal Azteca Coänocotzin welcomes Madoc, then takes him up the temple steps. From the top he indicates four towers piled with human skulls, and in the distance many cities ready to answer any call to arms. Madoc says that even if the Aztecas have ten times those cities, their arrows will be met with fire unless the Hoamen are freed. He will fight in God's cause. The king answers that the Aztec gods are not feeble.

In section VII, "The Battle," Urien suggests taking captives instead of wholesale slaughter, a strategy that will inspire both fear and gratitude. Meanwhile, Lincoya has raised a large host of Hoamen, stationing them at the entrance to the mountain straits. The Aztecs, in feather-mail and coronals of colorful plumes, attack. An arrow strikes the plated breast of Cadwallon and rebounds. The Aztec darts recoil, and their lances shiver. They flee when Hoamen arrows and spears pierce their thin gold-and-feather mail. Captives expect to be sacrificed, but soon learn that they will receive mercy. The next day, messengers come from the king. He has been stricken with a malady by the gods and asks that Madoc visit his sickbed, bringing healing and peace.

In section VIII, "Peace," old Iola, learned in the use of herbs, restores the king to health. Soon the king speaks of peace and friendship. He tells how his people came to those valleys, then only bleak heath, desert moor, wild woodland, and savannahs—a rude country of rude dwellers who provoked them to war. Should the Aztecs now submit to their old enemy? But Madoc insists that the Hoamen be freed. He has not come from his native island to wage a war of conquest. The Aztec king agrees, provided there is no destruction of the worship of his fathers. The priests are silent, but finally consent. The king announces that henceforth there will be no more blood sacrifice upon the altars.

Finishing his account, Madoc tells his fellow Welshmen that he has returned to their beloved native land to tell this story, but he plans to return to what has now become his home.

In section IX, "Emma," Madoc asks forgiveness and peace from his brother. This the king sullenly grants, provided Madoc communicates no more with the fugitives from the past civil war. Madoc's sister berates him for meekly accepting the fate of their brothers, but Madoc answers that all he has asked is that the remaining brothers accompany him in exile.

In section X, "Mathraval," Madoc seeks recruits for his return voyage.

In section XI, "The Gorsedd," Madoc and the king meet on a remote hilltop, where a bard, Caradoc, sings of days when sons of Britain had quit their native land to dare the ocean and had disappeared, whereas Madoc had found the world he sought. Madoc does not need to announce his enterprise, and news spreads of this land where plenty dwells with liberty and peace.

In section XII, "Dinevawr," Madoc meets his brother Ririd, who wants to go with him.

In section XIII, "Llewelyn," Madoc goes to an island where his forefathers lie buried, tells the abbot he will be buried in a distant land, and endows a yearly rite as a bond between him and his men and their mother isle. At the meal, Llewelyn, son of his murdered brother, asks to be excused from accompanying Madoc. As the rightful king, he must remain and save his people.

In section XIV, "Llaian," Madoc meets Llaian, Hoel's widow and mother of their young son. She asks Madoc to take the boy.

In section XV, "The Excommunication," Madoc stops at a monastery, where they are excommunicating Madoc's father for not having joined the Crusade. The priest urges Madoc to lay aside his project and join. But Madoc refers to the Welsh "loyalty to Christ before the coming of the Roman church," and refuses the curse. When his father's body is taken to be reburied in an unhallowed grave, he intervenes and buries his father properly.

In section XVI, "David," the king refuses to let their brother Rodri accompany Madoc, and they part in anger.

In section XVII, "The Departure," a boy comes to Goervyl's chamber and begs her to take him as her page. She leads him to her brother, who takes him into the entourage. The boy is really Serena, beloved of Caradoc. At the last banquet, Madoc bids farewell to David, who almost follows his impulse to release the brothers. The next day the king comes, saying he has given orders to release Rodri, but he has escaped. God be with you, he tells Madoc. They part with warm, brotherly feelings.

In section XVIII, "Rodri," a boat speeds to one of the ships, and its occupant asks for Madoc. It is Rodri, with Llewelyn, come to bid Madoc farewell. Rodri assures Madoc that the civil strife will soon end, and Llewelyn predicts that some day he will ascend the throne.

In section I of Part II, "The Return to Aztlan," Madoc returns and sails up the river to Cadwallon, who has been watching for him. In his absence a palace has replaced the queen's old hut.

In section II, "The Tidings," Cadwallon tells Madoc that as soon as he left, the priests began spreading rumors of evil signs and now even the prince rarely approaches the Britons. Lincoya comes with a warning, recounting how he was chosen as the sacrificial youth and given four maids in spousal, among them Coatel, whom he had come to love. She returned his love and on the eve of the sacrifice she drugged the food at the temple. Lincoya fled back home. He warns them to be wary of outward friendliness. Young Malinal, an Aztlan dwelling with them and estranged from the Aztlans, confirms that the Aztecs are planning some kind of treachery. Meanwhile Lincoya has found Coatel, who relates that Coänocotzin has stood at the shrine of Mexitli and offered up human blood, and secret vows have been made.

In section III, "Neolin," the queen welcomes Madoc, but her son disguises his true feelings. The priest Ayayaca warns that the Aztlan god wants blood, but Neolin, an Aztlan priest, claims that they only want to be able to worship their god. The queen's son Amalahta supports Neolin.

In section IV, "Amalahta," Amalahta falls in love with Goervyl, Madoc's sister, and asks Madoc for her as his wife. Cadwallon answers that, with the Britons, Madoc does not have the power to give marriage; she must be won by love. In silence Amalahta contemplates snares and violence. Madoc orders that a watch be set upon Amalahta and Neolin.

In Section V, "War Denounced," ambassadors from Aztlan await Madoc. Two declare their allegiance to their traditional gods. Malinal declares himself true to Madoc's faith and cuts off all ties, while his brother Yudhidthiton, "chief of chiefs," vows to restore the Aztec gods. Madoc repeats their wish for peace, but the Aztlans build a huge bonfire and pray to their gods.

In section VI, "The Festival of the Dead," as Amalahta advises, the Hoamen celebrate the traditional Feast of the Souls to appease their old gods, supported by Amalahta; but the queen intervenes: She is the ruler and the Aztecs have slain their children. Neolin calls for Lincoya as a sacrifice, but he is not to be found. Ayayaca offers himself in Lincoya's place, but the queen pulls him back. Neolin, looking for another victim, seizes a small boy and prepares to dash out his brains on the stone idol's head. A serpent advances with open jaws, seizes the boy, and glides to the dark recesses of his den.

In section VII, "The Snake God," a messenger from the queen speeds to Cadwallon and Madoc, who have received Lincoya. They go to the ritual and seize Neolin. The serpent emerges from the cave and protects Neolin within its coils. Madoc smites Neolin. The reptile drops the dead Neolin and flees back to its den. They enter the cave and kill it.

In section VIII, "The Conversion of the Hoamen," Madoc comes to the Hoamen with the Christian cross, and explains to them the One Eternal God. The queen and the priest Ayayaca announce their conversion and are baptized.

In section IX, "Tlalala," Caradoc leads a captive Aztec from the ships. "Let him go," Madoc says. "Today is no day for vengeance. Tell him their gods have fallen." They are to clean their temples, "put away their abominations," and accept the Christian cross. The captive, Tlalala, is defiant. We do not engage in wrongful war, Madoc tells him, but when we do war, to aid the feeble and oppressed, "we put our terrors forth." Loosed, the captive bounds back to Aztlan, where he informs the priests, but they only inspect the altar for the morrow's sacrifice. The victims' eyes are wild with terror.

In section X, "The Arrival of the Gods," Tezozomoc is led to the king after being immured within the forest for ten months as penance for public sin. He tells of his trance in which Coatlantona, mother of Mexitli, appeared and told him that the gods' anger requires the blood of the strangers for their banquet. Tezozomoc instructs Tlalala to waylay one of the Britons and bring him to be sacrificed. Ocellopan volunteers to accompany Tlalala.

In section XI, "The Captive," Tlalala and Ocellopan take Madoc and young Hoel captive.

In section XII, "Hoel," Hoel is taken to the temple for a ritual, then conveyed in a bark across the lake to a cavern, where he is forced inside.

In section XIII, "Coatel," Coatel sees what is happening and enters the cavern, but does not dare take Hoel away. She promises the boy she will return, then climbs out.

In section XIV, "The Stone of Sacrifice," Madoc is led to the altar, but Tlalala and five others ask to meet Madoc in combat as an offering to their god. The king consents. Madoc's foot is fettered down, and he is given a buckler, a sword, and a stout staff. The Aztecs fight aggresssively, but Cadwallon arrives.

In section XV, "The Battle," Cadwallon and the Aztlan army clash. The Britons' arrows pierce the Aztecs' feathered armor, but the Indians, knowing they must win or Aztlan will fall, fight fiercely. Then Lincoya arrives, leading the mountaineer Hoamen. The Aztecs flee, but the priests rush out and fight with zeal.

In section XVI, "The Women," in Madoc's house, Goervyl and the women agonize. Malinal, who has learned that Amalahta is coming with a band of disloyal Hoamen, rushes in and takes down Madoc's weapons. Goervyl fastens on a breastplate and is joined by the other women. Malinal rebuffs the invaders but is wounded. Amalahta seizes Goervyl, but Mervyn, the page, runs after him and fells him. The queen seizes her son for judgment.

In section XVII, "Deliverance," Coatel frees Madoc from his bonds and leads him to Hoel in the cavern. At the lake, thinking of Lincoya, Coatel almost accompanies them, but aware that her father would weep for her, leaves them. They set out in a boat. On the other shore Llaian is looking for Hoel and tells them that the Hoamen, hearing Madoc was in danger, have abandoned home duty to rescue him. Madoc speeds back to the village. Anxious about the battle, he hastily dons his arms and orders young Mervyn to do the same. Goervyl intervenes: "He is too young." "I was once such a boy," Madoc answers, "and in that day slew many a Saxon." The pseudo-Mervyn, wishing she had revealed her true identity, nevertheless dons the mail and takes a spear and sword, but her breastplate falls, revealing that she is a woman. Goervyl now insists that Mervyn (Serena) not go.

In section XVIII, "The Victory," the king of Aztlan, in his long feathered robe and helmet topped by a sculptured snake and plumes, comes out to meet Madoc, who is in mail and shield with blazoned eaglets. Madoc smites the king, but the blow glides off the plumes. He cleaves Coänocotzin's helmet, and the king dies. In the meantime the captive Urien, being carried to his death, shakes off his captors and fights like a younger man. Madoc and his men mow a path to the temple and shatter the giant idol. The Aztecs flee while Tlalala remains, still raging with fury. Yuhidthiton confronts his enemy, but Madoc calls off the pursuit.

In section XIX, "The Funeral," the scattered few who have escaped come back bearing the noble dead upon their shields to Mexitli's temple. After the priests have slain the beloved women and the slaves of the dead, they are laid on pyres. The priest holds up the ark containing the remains of their king and lays it in the temple tower. Yuhidthiton is anointed king.

In section XX, "The Death of Coatel," the chief priests insist that Madoc was freed, not by a god but by one of them—Coatel—and they drag her to be killed. Her father stabs himself and falls across the body of his daughter.

In section XXI, "The Sports," funeral games are held. Tezozomoc boldly enters the temple and comes back with the unbroken image of Mexitli and the banner of Aztlan. The people pray to the god to destroy their enemy.

In section XXII, "The Death of Lincoya," the Aztecs renew the war. Lincoya comes down from the hills and urges his countrymen to repossess the land of their forefathers. Coatel's nurse tells him of her mistress's death. He decides to join her in "the Country of the Dead" and jumps off a precipice.

In section XXIII, "Caradoc and Serena," Caradoc recognizes Mervyn as Serena.

In section XXIV, "The Embassy," the Christian cross now rises above Aztlan, and the Hoamen have repossessed their land, but Yuhidthiton warns that the Aztecs are not subdued. "Leave us," he says. "Choose your dwelling place in any direction. Atzlan will supply your wants and assist your departure. If, however, you persist, Aztlan will come in anger." Madoc answers that they have already won the Aztec city.

In section XXV, "The Lake Fight," the Aztecs and the Britons meet in a lake battle, in which the Britons splinter the Aztec vessels.

In section XXVI, "The Close of the Century," the Aztecs mourn their dead and feed funeral pyres. Despite protests by the high priest and Tlalala, the king opts for their departure. The priest announces this is the fifth Sun, when the Aztec empire was doomed to end. As they perform the proper ritual, the volcano erupts, burying Tezozomoc.

In section XXVII, "The Migration of the Aztecas," the king sends a messenger to Madoc to tell him he has won and that they will leave the land, but with one request: that he be permitted to take the ashes of his fathers. He orders a pyre built on the mountaintop, then applies a torch to it. He has one more request, that if the lake ever returns to its old boundaries, the ashes of the former king, Cöanocotzin, be respected. He announces that from now on there are to be no priests, no blood sacrifices. He bids his people farewell. Tears flow. The line is drawn between those who will stay and those who will go. All the youths choose to leave with Yuhidthiton.

On the third day, the Aztec priests appear, bearing the statue of Mexitli, followed by the ashes of the kings, then the king, with Tlalala at his side. Malinal awaits them. With a dark countenance, the king meets his brother, but the two are reconciled. Tlalala, who will not leave his native land, cries farewell, then stabs himself with his javelin.

"So in the land Madoc was left sole Lord," and "Yuhidthiton led forth the Aztecas to spread to other lands Mexitli's name and rear a mightier empire, and sets up again their idolatry till Heaven . . . sent among them the heroic Spaniard's sword." (TAP) (Brundage 1972; Colum 1930; Southey 1909)

See also Southey, Robert.

 # *MAHĀPURĀNA*
(The great legend)

Indian Jaina epic (9th c.) written in Sanskrit by the teacher Jinasena and modeled after the Hindu *Purāṇas*. Jainism, a very ancient tradition, was revitalized in the latter half of the sixth century B.C. by Mahāvīra. The Jains believe there is no creator of the universe, that the universe is maintained by natural principles. The poet asks, "If God created the world, where was he before creation?" (4:18) He instructs, "Know that the world is uncreated, as time itself is, without beginning and end. . . ." (4:37) (Embree 1988)

See also Jinasena.

MAIKOV, VASILY

Russian poet, author of *Elisey, or Bacchus Enraged* (1771), the first mock-epic in Russian literature. He was born in 1728, the son of a provincial landowner who was also an army officer and patron of the actors' troupe at Yaroslavl, northeast of Moscow. As a young man, Maikov was attached to the Semenovsky Regiment of the Imperial Guards, stationed in St. Petersburg. When members of the actors' troupe moved to St. Petersburg, Maikov became acquainted, through them, with the Sumarokov school of poets who brought the first wave of the Enlightenment to Russia.

In 1762 he began to contribute to the various literary magazines sponsored by Mikhail Kheraskov (1733-1807), leader of the Sumarokov school and later author of *The Rossiad* (1779). Maikov's first success was a satirical verse tale, *The Ombre Player* (1763), poking fun at the aristocracy's pastime of gambling. There followed a number of lesser political satires. His mock-epic *Elisey, or Bacchus Enraged,* published in 1771, attacked the wine merchants who held the monopoly on selling alcoholic beverages. It was his last major satire. After the Pugachev Revolt, he turned to writing poems that were pious instructions in the spirit of Freemasonry.

He also wrote two verse tragedies, *Agriopa* (1767), set during the Trojan War; and *Themistus and Hieronyma* (1772), set in Constantinople of the fifteenth century. His last major work was a pastoral comic opera, *A Country Holiday, or Virtue Crowned* (1777). He died in 1778. (Bristol 1991)

See also Elisey, or Baccus Enraged.

MÁJ
(May)

Czech lyrical epic (1836, trans. 1932) by Karel Hynek Mácha (1810–1836), said to be the greatest Czech poet. Mácha introduced iambic verse to Czech poetry. The poem, containing four cantos and two intermezzos, is a contrast between youth and age, love and death. Mácha employed inventive language for such things as names of colors, sometimes using translations of descriptions from other works.

The opening lines of the poem are the best-known lines in Czech poetry: "It was late evening, the first of May—/Evening May—it was the time of love./ The voice of the turtle-dove summoned to love/Where the pine grove wafted its scent." However, the idyllic time does not last; "The fury of the times bore that season far away,/Far off his dream. . . ./The fair childhood age of the dead."

Vilém, "the man of dread," is an outlaw known as the "forest lord." He kills the man who seduced his fair Jarmila, not knowing that the man is his own father. Vilém is sent to prison; bereft and lonely, he contemplates the meaning of life and nature's "mystical elements." Eventually he is beheaded. (Čiževskij 1971; Preminger 1974)

See also Mácha, Karel Hynek.

THE MAN IN THE PANTHER'S SKIN

See *The Knight in the Panther's Skin.*

 # MANASĀ-MAṄGAL

Although it is the generic name of Indian poems honoring the Bengali snake goddess Manasā, *Manasā-maṅgal* is also an epic of 12,000 lines by Bengali poet Ketakādās (fl. mid-17th c.)

Manasā, daughter of Śiva, desiring to be worshipped by men, defeats worshippers of other deities, including Kṛṣṇa and even Śiva himself, using snakes and bribery. When the merchant Cāndo refuses to forsake the worship of Śiva, Manasā destroys his crops, his ships, his seven sons, and finally Cāndo himself. Cāndo's wife pleads for his life, which Manasā restores on the condidion that the wife convince him to worship Manasā. (Dudley and Lang 1969)

 # MANIMEKHALAÏ

Indian Tamil epic (c. A.D. 171) by Cāttanār (c. 2nd c. A.D.?), also known as Merchant-Prince Shattan. The author was a friend of Prince Iḷankō Aṭikaḷ, author of *Cilappatikāram* (The ankle bracelet), of which this work is a continuation. It is considered both a verse epic and a didactic novel, containing traditional and legendary elements as well as historical ones. The story is set in three South Indian kingdoms—Chera, Chola, and Pandya—whose dynasties fade into prehistory.

The poem consists of a prologue and 30 cantos. The prologue sets the scene in the city of Puhâr. In canto I the annual festival of the god Indra is proclaimed in Puhâr to honor the god who has accomplished 100 sacrifices in his former existences. The kings of all neighboring countries are summoned. It is said that "if the festival were not celebrated, Puhâr's guardian genie would be consumed with wrath and molest all inhabitants."

In canto II, Chihitrâpati, Mâdhavi's mother, learns that her beautiful granddaughter Manimekhalaï and her daughter refuse to take part in the dances in Indra's honor and have decided to abandon the profession of dancer and prostitute to join the monastic life. Vasantamālā, Mâdhavi's faithful companion, tries to convince her: "For a girl destined by birth for art and pleasure to become an ascetic and mortify herself is an impious act. . . . The entire population of the city condemns Mâdhavi without pity." Mâdhavi explains that her former lover Kovalan has died and his legitimate wife, Kannaki, has also immolated herself upon his pyre, so for Kovalan's daughter Manimekhalaï, "the monastic life seems to me more fitting than the vicious commerce of her charms and the base acts which are the courtesan's life."

In canto III, for the first time Manimekhalaï hears the terrible fate of her father and his virtuous wife, and retreats to one of the city's gardens to shed bitter tears.

In canto IV, when the Chola prince Udayakumāra passes by in his chariot and learns that Manimekhalaï has entered the garden, he follows her. She hears the chariot's approach and says to her monastic companion Sutâmati, "Prince Udayakumāra seems to be infatuated with me." Sutâmati leads Manimekhalaï, "beautiful as a doll," to the garden's crystal pavilion and locks her inside.

In canto V, the Chola prince sees the girl's "charming body" through the transparent walls of the pavilion and is consumed with desire. After he leaves, Manimekhalaï rejoins Sutâmati, and soon appearing before them is the goddess of the ocean with a very similar name, Manimekhalâ. She has come to Puhâr "to amuse herself with the joyful din of the festival. . . ."

In canto VI, the goddess, who has adopted "the simple form of a townswoman," sweeps up Manimekhalaï and transports her to the isle of Manipallavam in the midst of the sea.

In canto VII, the goddess appears before the Chola prince, advising him to "cast far from you this blameworthy desire which draws you to Manimekhalaï, since she is destined for the monastic life." Then she returns to the garden and awakens Sutâmati, who has fallen asleep. The goddess instructs her, "Run and tell Mâdhavi of my arrival and of the spotless path for which her daughter has been chosen." Then she rises to the sky and disappears.

Meanwhile, in canto VIII, Manimekhalaï awakens on the island, frightened at being alone, and begins to weep and call for Sutâmati. She sees a vision of the Buddha on a divine pedastal and no longer feels abandoned.

At the sight of the jewel-encrusted pedestal, in canto IX, Manimekhalaï suddenly recalls her past life and is aggrieved.

In canto X, while Manimekhalaï wanders, burdened with sadness at her memories, the goddess reappears and explains that Prince Udayakumâra is the reincarnation of her former husband Rahul in her past life, in which she was called Lakshmi. The goddess explains how to free herself from her fears, teaching her magic formulas (*mantras*).

In canto XI, when the goddess departs, Tivatilanaï, divine protectress of the island, appears and presents Manimekhalaï with a marvelous magic bowl with which she must feed the destitute. The goddess tells her, "This magic bowl will only be filled in the hands of those whose charity, the fruit of their past virtues, is sincere."

In canto XII, taking her bowl, Manimekhalaï returns to her mother and her companion. They all go to visit the sage Arvana Adigal, who says of her magic bowl, "You now possess the . . . Cow of Abundance, which contains the substance of life. You must now go about the world to put an end to the pains of hunger suffered by living beings. There exists no more meritorious act towards gods or men than to assuage the pangs of hunger."

In cantos XIII and XIV, Arvana Adigal tells them the story of Aputra, the first possessor of the bowl, and how he received it from Chintâ, the goddess of knowledge.

In canto XV, the three women return to the city. As Manimekhalaï carries the bowl through the streets, the young people of the town, who are "stupid and loud-mouthed," ask, "How is it possible that Manimekhalaï . . . now roams the streets of Puhâr with a beggar's bowl in her hand?"

In canto XVI, the matron Atiraï pours alms into the bowl to be distributed to the poor in gratitude for the return of her husband Shaduvan, long thought to be lost at sea.

In canto XVII, the food placed in the magic bowl multiplies without ever running out; thus its possessor can feed a mass of poor people. One woman, Kayashandikaï, approaches and describes her insatiable hunger. Manimekhalaï satisfies her hunger, then leaves for the travelers' hospice called Ulaka-aravi.

When the prince learns of Manimekhalaï's whereabouts (canto XVIII), he visits the hospice. She thinks, "In my former life, this man was my husband, my dear Rahul. . . . It is therefore proper for me to greet him humbly." She bows before him. But the prince prostrates himself before her, saying, "My fate is in your hands."

In canto XIX, to escape the amorous prince, Manimekhalaï takes the form of Kayashandikaï, whose genie-magician husband had cursed her with insatiable hunger. She arrives at the city's prison and causes it to be transformed into a monastery.

In canto XX, Kanchana, Kayashandikaï's genie-husband, approaches Manimekhalaï, still in her disguise. When she is indifferent to him, he is dismayed. He sees the prince approaching, lusting after what he believes to be his wife, and he kills the prince with his sword.

In canto XXI, Manimekhalaï wakes to find the prince's body, and wails and laments. A statue possessed by a genie begins to speak, explaining that the prince's death is due to an action in his past life. The statue warns her that the king will throw her in prison and the queen will order her release in order to torture her, but Mādhavi will seek Adigal's help in obtaining her release, after which she will go to the city of Vanji in the disguise of a monk.

In canto XXII, as the statue predicted, the bereft king imprisons Manimekhalaï for causing his son's death. At the queen's insistence, Manimekhalaï is released into her custody.

In canto XXIII, on Manimekhalaï's advice, the king transforms the prison into a hospice. As revenge for causing the prince's death, the queen plans to drive Manimekhalaï insane, until Manimekhalaï explains that his death was due to "the grave fault committed by your son in his former life."

As predicted, Mâdhavi comes with Arvana Adigal to rescue Manimekhalaï (canto XXIV). He teaches the queen and the other women of the court the nature of *dharma* (the law) and instructs Manimekhalaï to leave for Apurta's kingdom.

In canto XXV, Manimekhalaï accompanies Apurta to the beautiful isle of Manipallavam, where she learns details of her own former life.

In canto XXVI, she takes the form of an ascetic and flies to Vanji.

In canto XXVII, in Vanji she studies religious dogmas from teachers of various sects.

In canto XXVIII, still disguised as a monk, she visits Kanchi and finds her mother and other women with Arvana Ardigal.

In canto XXIX, she discards her disguise and prostrates herself before Arvana Ardigal, who instructs her in the Buddhist *dharma*. She adopts a monastic life.

In canto XXX, Manimekhalaï practices austere self-denial and is freed from the cycle of births and deaths. (Shattan 1989)

See also Cāttaṉār, Cīttalaic.

MANTEQ AT-TAIR

See The Conference of the Birds.

MANUCARITRA

Indian Telegu epic (16th c.) by Peddana, the chief poet at the court of Vijayanagar ruler Kṛṣṇadēvarāya (r. 1509–1530). The poem is based on an episode in the *Mārkaṇḍeya Purāṇa*. It is the story of Pravara, a pious Brahman youth, who rejects the love of the heavenly damsel Varudhini, and of a spurned heavenly suitor of Varudhini's who assumes Pravara's form to win Varudhini for his bride. (Dudley and Lang 1969)

MARINO, GIAMBATTISTA
(Or Marini)

Italian poet, author of *Adone* (1623), an epic of 45,000 lines. He was born in Naples in 1569. His parents encouraged him to study law, but he never practiced his profession. He was apparently a witty and brilliant man who was able to charm influential people into becoming his patrons. After the age of 21 he led the dissolute life of a vagabond, traveling between French and Italian courts, often in debt or in trouble with the law. In 1596 he wrote *La sampogna,* a series of pastoral and mythological idylls; however, he was not able to publish it until 1620. His poetry, such as *Canzone de Baci,* was circulated in manuscript form and was widely popular.

He was twice arrested (1598 and 1600) on morals charges while he was working as a secretary to a Neapolitan prince; however, both times influential friends obtained his release. He traveled to Rome, where he became friends with Cardinal Pietro Aldobrandini, nephew to the pope. The two traveled to several parts of Italy. In Parma, Marino attempted to have some of his poems published, but the advent of the Inquisition put a stop to his plans. Eventually, in 1602, his early poetry appeared under the title *Le rime.*

He went to Torino in 1608, enjoying the patronage of the duke of Savoy for seven years. However, in 1615, after he wrote some satirical poetry (*La murtoleide,* 1615, publ. 1619) about another poet, Gaspar Murtola, Murtola brought charges and had him imprisoned. Again admirers secured his release, but he left and went to Paris, where he secured the patronage of Marie de Médicis and Louis XIII for the next eight years. During that time he published his most important work, *Adone,* the love story of Venus and Adonis. His flamboyant Baroque style, laden with elaborate metaphors and word play, was so imitated that the style became known as *marinismo* (later *secentismo*), and it dominated seventeenth-century Italian poetry.

Marino returned to Naples in 1623, where he died two years later. (Preminger 1974)

See also Adone.

 # MARTÍN FIERRO

Hero of the Argentine epic *The Gaucho Martín Fierro* (1872, 1879) by José Hernández (1834–1886). Martín is a poor gaucho who tells the story of his life, accompanying himself on his guitar. Because he did not vote for a local judge, he is drafted to fight Indians, suffering great privations in the army. When at last he is allowed to return home, he finds his home destroyed and his family gone. He finally locates his sons, now grown, to whom he offers advice, and sends them on their way. Then he lays down his guitar forever. (Hernández 1974)

 # *MARTYRS, LES*

(Subtitled *ou le Triomphe de la religion chrétienne,* The martyrs, or the triumph of the Christian religion)

French prose epic (1809) of early Christianity by Vicomte François-René de Chateaubriand (1768–1848). Written in 24 books, the epic is set in the third century, during the time of Emperor Diocletian's persecution of the Christians.

The story follows two young Greeks: Eudorus, a Christian, and the pagan maiden Cymodocea. Both are destined by God to be sacrificed so that other Christians may be saved (Book 3). Eudorus's early life in Greece and his adventures in Germany, Gaul, Egypt, and Rome are recounted in Books 4–11. Book 4 contains a vivid description of a battle between Franks and Romans, which historian Augustin Thierry (1795–1856) claimed was responsible for his schoolboy decision to become a historian. In Book 12, Cymodocea, who loves Eudorus, is converted to Christianity. They are married, but are soon separated by circumstances. After many hardships they are reunited in Rome, where they are doomed to become martyrs, suffering persecution and finally death.

From the arena where they perish, Emperor Constantine declares that Christianity will henceforth be the official religion of the Roman Empire. (Harvey and Heseltine 1959)

 # MARULIĆ, MARKO

Croatian poet and philosopher, author of Croatia's first epic, *Judita* (1501). He was born in 1450 in Split (Spalato), Dalmatia, to a noble family. After becoming a clergyman, he studied classical languages, literature, theology, and philosophy at the University of Padua, Italy, where he was greatly influenced by humanism. He returned to Split, where he became the epitome of the religious renaissance in Dalmatia. His didactic moral works, such as *Evangelistarius* and particularly his Latin treatise on how to lead a good and happy life, *De bene beateque vivendi*, made him known throughout Europe. The treatise went through 20 editions in Croatian, 12 in Italian, 6 in German, and was also translated into French, Portuguese, and partly into Czech.

Marulić also wrote a long plea to Pope Hadrian VI to unite all Christianity to fight against the Turks. He expressed the same sentiments in his long Croatian historico-religious epic *Judita* (*Istorija svete udovice Judit u versih hrvacki složena,* The history of the holy widow Judith), an epic in six cantos using the Old Testament heroine as an example to encourage his countrymen in their struggle against the Turks. The poem was first printed in book form in Venice in 1525, the first printed Croatian literary work. His vernacular verse marked the beginning of literature in the Croatian language.

He also wrote *Molitva* (Prayer) describing the suffering of the Croats under Turkish rule. In 1510, at the age of 60, he retired to a Franciscan monastery on the island of Šolta; however, he returned to Split two years later, where he died in 1524. (Čiževskij 1971; Dvornik 1962; Gazi 1973)

 # *MAŠNAVĪ*
(Also *mathnavi* or *mesnevi*)

The word literally means "doubled one." In Arabic, Persian, and Turkish poetry, *mašnavīs* are rhyming couplets; however the term has been extended to mean a long epic poem using rhyming couplets.

 # *MASNAVÎ-YE MA'NAVÎ*
(Spiritual couplets)

Persian didactic epic (13th c.) by Jalāl ad-Dīn ar-Rūmī (1207–1273), the greatest Persian mystic poet. The poem, inspired by Rūmī's Ṣūfī master, Ḥusām ad-Dīn

Chelebi, and dictated to him, is written in six books of nearly 26,000 couplets. It reflects all aspects of thirteenth-century Ṣūfism through its fables, stories, moral teachings, and philosophical musings, and is the poet's greatest work.

An example of the latter, entitled "The Music," is from Book I: "For sixty years I have been forgetful,/every minute, but not for a second/has this flowing toward me stopped or slowed./I deserve nothing. . . ."

"The Destiny of Man" answers the question of how to achieve immortality: by spurning life's joys; divesting oneself of hopes and fears, faith and doubt; ceasing both to love and to hate; merging one's "individual being" with "the Eternal's love."

In "The Question," also in Book V, one dervish asks another, "What was your vision of God's presence?" This sparks a story about choosing between walking through fire or through water. Most people avoid the fire, "and so end up in it."

"The Variety of Intelligences in Human Beings," in Book V, describes as an example of intelligence the Mind of the Whole, which gets a glimpse of "a lovely hunt going on, where God/is Hunter and everything else the hunted. . . ." The Mind sees and tries to quit hunting and "completely/be prey." To do otherwise is like a chess game. The poem describes the game in which "The queen has your king in danger. When you move out of check,/she takes the rook. . . ."

The poet asks the age-old question, in Book V, "Why Organize the Universe This Way?" He describes three companions: "Number one,/what you own. He won't even leave the house, . . ." "Number two,/your good friend. He at least comes to the funeral./He stands and talks at the gravesite. No further." The third is "what you do, your work" which "goes down into death to be there with you,/to help. Take deep refuge/with that companion, beforehand." In "Learning the Signs of the Zodiac" (Book V), he gives advice on avoiding fear of dying: "A stone is not so frightened of rain as a clod is." Another called "Display" in Book V contains the advice: "Better be quarry than hunter. . . ./ Don't try to be the sun. Be a dust mote."

In Book VI we find: "When one is united to the core of another, to speak of that/is to breathe the name *Hu,* empty of self,/filled with love." Also from Book VI, in "Those You Are With," the poet asks, "What is a real connection between people?" He answers, "When the same inner sight exists/in you as in another, you are drawn to be companions." He advises, "Always search for your innermost nature in those you are with." From Book VI in "The Phrasing Must Change," the poet uses the example of Zuleika, who loves Joseph so much that "she concealed his name/in many different phrases, the inner meanings/ known only to her." He says, "When one is united to the core of another, to speak of that/is to breathe the name *Hu,* empty of self and filled/with love." He quotes an old saying, "The pot drips what is in it."

Rūmī's fables are interspersed as illustrations. "The Merchant and the Parrot" tells the story of a man, about to embark on a trading mission to Hindustan, who asks his caged parrot what gift he should bring to it. The parrot answers that he should deliver a message to all parrots flying free in Hindustan asking for their help and counsel for their brother confined in a cage. The merchant goes off to Hindustan and, seeing a number of parrots in the desert, stops his horse and calls out the parrot's message. Immediately one of the parrots falls dead, saddening the merchant. When he returns home and relates the incident to his caged parrot, it too falls dead. As the merchant throws the body from the cage, the bird flies to a high branch. From there the parrot explains the message of the other parrot's actions: "Escape . . . from speech and articulate voice,/ Since it was thy voice that brought thee into prison." As the parrot flies back toward its homeland, it calls to the merchant, "Thou shalt one day be free like me!"

"The Greek and the Chinese Artists, on the Difference between Theologians and Mystics" tells of a debate between the Greeks and Chinese, whom the sultan puts to a test to settle the argument as to which are better artists. The two groups are put in separate rooms facing each other, door to door. The Chinese demand a hundred colors, so every morning the sultan opens his treasury and gives them their colors. The Greeks say, "No hues . . . are suitable for our work. . . . All we require is to get rid of the rust." They shut the door and set to work polishing, becoming smooth and unsullied as the sky. When the Chinese finish, they invite the sultan in to view the beautiful paintings. Then the Greeks remove the curtain between the two rooms so that the reflection of the Chinese paintings strike the walls from which they have polished away the rust. All that the sultan saw in the Chinese room is even lovelier here. "The purity of the mirror without doubt is the heart, which receives images innumerable. . . . They who have burnished their hearts have escaped from scent and colour; every moment, instantly, they behold Beauty."

"The Ṣūfī, the Fakir, and the Sharif, and How Their Solidarity Was Destroyed" tells how a gardener decides to divide three men whom he believes have come to rob him. He sends the Ṣūfī into the house for a rug. While he is gone, he turns the other two against the Ṣūfī. When the Ṣūfī returns, he is driven out. The gardener does the same with the Sharif, sending him into the house for waffles. When the Sharif has been driven out, the gardener berates the Fakir: "What sort of Fakir do you call yourself? You put to shame every fool alive. . . ." The Fakir agrees and tells him, "Beat me. This is the due recompense for one who breaks with friends." The poet offers this moral: "Whoever the Devil cuts off from the men of nobility, finding him isolated, he proceeds to devour him. To quit the congregation of the saints for so much as a moment— that is the chance for Satan's cunning. . . ."

"The Policeman and the Drunkard, on Spiritual Intoxication" tells of a policeman badgering a drunk whom he finds lying beside a wall. The drunk tells him to "leave me alone. . . . If I had the power to walk I would have gone to my own home. . . . If I had been in my right reason . . . , I would still be sitting on the bench, holding forth like the shaikhs." (Arberry 1961; Kritzeck 1964; Moyne and Barks 1984; Runes 1961)

THE MAXIMUS POEMS

American epic (1950–1970, publ. 1960–1983) by Charles Olson (1910–1970). The poem is divided into three books of more than 300 poems. The first volume was published in 1960, the second in 1968, and the third was completed shortly before the poet's death in 1970 and published in 1975. The epic takes the form of a series of "letters" from Maximus of Gloucester ("the Greatest"). The bardic figure of Maximus, a modern man, is modeled after Maximus of Tyre and represents in this case the voice of humanism. The fishing town of Gloucester, Massachusetts, represents for the poet a microcosm of contemporary America.

In composing the poem the poet set for himself the role of cultural revolutionary who would free the American twentieth-century race-mind, still mired in seventeenth-century Cartesian conventions. As Olson was beginning his work on *The Maximus,* he voiced the thesis of a fundamental contest between the essential secular humanism of the Renaissance mind and the inhibiting predatory commercialism, consumerism, and capitalism of the Calvinist mind, particularly as evinced in Puritanism. In other words, 250 years after the time of English Puritan colonization of America, the "second flowering" of the Elizabethan appears in the works of Melville or Whitman. The spirit of the Renaissance crossed the Atlantic and lingered in the mind of the common American breaking free of Calvinism during the Revolution, briefly thriving during the Jeffersonian era, suffering a setback by Hamilton and the Federalists.

Book One begins with a letter from "I, Maximus of Gloucester, to You." Through these letters, the poet acquaints the reader with something of Gloucester's history, beginning with when Gloucester was pure: "Gloucester, your first house was as Elizabeth's/England . . ." and the area—and by inference the American sensibility—was exemplified by the spirit of such as the independent fishermen of Gloucester. But Puritans, "the first of/the shrinkers," introduced competitive acquisitiveness.

"History Is the Memory of Time," in Book One, tells of the "fish rush." Now, in the same place, each generation is living "33 years/of shoddy &/safety—not at all/living. . . ." We are now "a nation fizzing itself/on city managers. . . ."

"Stiffening, in the Master Founders' Wills" speaks of things the Puritans savored, "like throwing people/out."

The "Renaissance humanistic mind" shifts to the Cartesian insistence on a sharp delineation: "grace versus work," spirit versus matter.

There is a bronze sculpture of a fisherman in Gloucester. As visitors stop before it, Maximus wants them to know: "A fisherman is not a successful man/ he is not a famous man he is not a man/of power, these are damned by God."

In grave irony he describes "Part of the Flower of Gloucester" (Book Two), which includes rubbish fermenting on the bottom of the harbor so that "bubbles/. . . keep coming up and you watch them break/on the surface and imagine the odor."

Olson describes the westward movement of humanism in the wanderings of Maximus as "from Tyre to Malta to Marseilles to Iceland to Vinland to Gloucester."

In Book Three, Olson assigns to "Norse" the essential European ethos: "Norse are/Anglo-/Saxons . . ./early Greeks . . ./Kelts . . ./Gauls . . . Rus." They are all Teutonic, he says, except Constantinople. Olson's thesis is that the Teutonic or Nordic person is the essential European or Indo-European.

The epic abounds in rich images of the sea and the fishing village. "Thank God," he says, "I chose a Protestant/*Federalist*/town/I come from the last walking period of man." Of his views on religion, he says, "I believe in religion not magic or science I believe in society/as religious both man and society as religious."

Some of the poems are concrete, and some only have a concrete element, as in the title:

Father   From My own old
Sky   Mother Earth   View point

which suggests both a boyhood viewpoint from the freshwater cove, the harbor, now obscured, and "Gloucester" (holistic, perhaps) versus Cartesian (left-brained, perhaps) viewpoints.

Toward the end of the last book, Maximus (modern man) compares his life to stone, lying face-down, or the ground beneath it. His life is buried "with all sorts of passages." It is the stone from which eighteenth-century Connecticut stone walls are built, the stone being "from the bottom such Ice-age megaliths. One finds oneself walking among relics that defy time." He discovers that time and life love space. It is, or so the poet would like to hope, "the initiation/of another kind of nation." (Olson 1983)

 # THE MEDICINE MAN
(*Swifa ya Nguvumali*)

Tanzanian epic written in Swahili by Hasani bin Ismail that interprets Swahili society and culture. It focuses on conflicts between Islam and traditional African religion on the coast of Tanzania. (Lienhardt 1968)

 # MENDOZA MONTEAGUDO, JUAN DE

Spanish poet, attributed author of *Guerras de Chile* (Wars of Chile, 1610). He was born in Spain in the sixteenth century and traveled to the New World in South America, where he engaged in the wars against the Araucanian Indians. Inspired by Alfonse de Ercilla y Zuñiga's (1534–1594) great epic poem *La Araucana*, it is believed that he wrote his own version of the Chilean wars in 1610. He died in 1619. (Anderson-Imbert 1969)

MESSENIACA

Greek epic poem (ca. 250 B.C.) by Rhianus (b. ca. 275 B.C.). One of five epics, now lost, this poem is the only one whose contents are known, although tiny fragments of both *Achaia* and *Thessalica* remain. *Messeniaca* deals with a war between Messene and Sparta in the seventh century B.C. It was used by Pausanias as a source for his history of Sparta. (Bowder 1984)

METAI
(The seasons)

Lithuanian epic (1765–1775, publ. 1818) by Kristijonas Donelaitis (Donalitius, 1714–1780). The poem, consisting of 3,000 lines in hexameters, presents in forceful language the life of the common people, emphasizing the sacredness of life and the earth. It contains vivid descriptions of nature. (Brogan 1996)

See also Donelaitis, Kristijonas.

METAMORPHOSES

Latin historical epic (ca. A.D. 8) by Ovid (Publius Ovidius Naso). The epic is written in Latin hexameter heroic couplets and is divided into 15 books.

Book One deals with the formation of the universe "when nature's face was blank; . . ." the emergence of life and then mankind; the various ages—"the age of gold," the silver age, the bronze age, the iron age "as slaughter spread;" the Giants' revolt and Jupiter's suppression of it; the great deluge; the tales of Deucalion and Pyrrha (only survivors of the Flood, who replenish mankind by throwing stones behind them), Apollo and the nymph Daphne; Jupiter and Io (whom he turns into a heifer to avoid Juno's suspicion of his love); and the parentage of Phaethon, Clymene, and Phoebus (Apollo, the sun god).

Book Two tells of Phaëthon (who for one day drives the chariot of the sun; his poor driving threatens both heaven and earth with destruction, so Jove kills him with a thunderbolt); the story of Callisto (who bears Jove a son, Arcas, and is changed by Jove into a constellation, Great Bear); the story of King Cecrops's daughter Aglauros, who discovers the secret of Pallas (which is the deformed Erichthonius, who has the tails of serpents for legs and whom Pallas keeps closed in a wicker chest); the story of Phoebus (Apollo) and Coronis (whom he kills after she lies with "some Thessalian lad;" he pierces her breast with an arrow, and as she lies dying she tells him she is carrying his child; he "snatches from death the child unborn" and takes it to the centaur Chiron to rear); the birth of Aesculapius to Coronis and Apollo; the prophecy and transformation of Ocyrhoë (changed into a mare by the gods, who are angry that she can foretell the future); the story of the shepherd Battus (seeing Mercury drive Jove's cattle away and hide them in the wood, he is transformed by Mercury into a stone); the story of Mercury's love for Herse, one of King Cecrops's daughters, "the fairest of the fair;" the story of the transformation of Aglauros into a statue by Hermes (Mercury) (while her sisters Herse and Pandrosos leap to their deaths from the Acropolis); the story of Europa and Jupiter (who transforms himself into a "comely bull" who so charms Europa that she climbs upon his back and is carried away).

Book Three tells how Europa's father, Agenor, sends his son Cadmus to find her. Cadmus searches the world and can't find what Jove (Jupiter) has hidden. He bests a dragon at Thebes and sows the dragon's teeth on the plain, with Minerva's help. An army of men spring up, and when Cadmus throws a stone in their midst, they begin killing each other in the confusion. Those who survive become allies of Cadmus and help him build Thebes. Diana is bathing in the river when the hunter Actaeon sees her. Angered, she changes him into a stag, and his own hounds tear him to pieces. Cadmus marries Harmonia and they have a son and four daughters. The youngest, Semele, is impregnated by Jove. Juno, consumed by jealousy, demands that Semele be killed, so reluctantly Jove "smote her mortal frame/With force unsufferable and blasting flame." Jove takes the fetus and sews it into his own thigh until it is time for the baby, Bacchus, to be born.

Other stories in Book Three are:

The strange experience of the blind prophet Tiresias, who becomes a woman for seven years before he turns back into a man. He prophesies such things as Hercules's greatness and Pentheus's death.

The tale of Echo, deprived of speech by a jealous Juno because she gossips about Jove's loves, and Narcissus, whom Echo loves but who does not return her love, so sated is he by his love for his own reflection. She pines away and is changed into a stone that can speak.

The story of the hostility of Pentheus to Bacchus. He refuses to acknowledge the divinity of Bacchus.

The tale of the ship captain Acoetes, whose crew finds Bacchus asleep and kidnaps him. He changes all except Acoetes into sea monsters.

The story of the death of Pentheus, who is torn to pieces by the Bacchae, who mistake him for a wild boar during their raucous ceremonies.

Book Four contains the story of the three daughters of King Minyas—Alcithoë, Leuconoë, and Arsippe—who will not acknowledge Bacchus's divinity, so they stay indoors and tell each other stories about failed lovers.

The first is the tale of Pyramus and Thisbe, two lovers in ancient Babylonia during the rule of Queen Semiramis. Although they live next door to each other, their parents forbid them to see each other. They run away, planning to meet outside the city walls at the tomb of Ninus. Thisbe arrives first but is frightened away by a lioness. She drops her veil, which the lion sullies with blood. When Pyramus arrives, he believes Thisbe has been eaten, and he kills himself with his sword. Thisbe returns and kills herself with her dead lover's sword.

Next is the story of the trick played on Mars and Venus. When Apollo sees their adultery he tells Venus's husband, Vulcan, who spins a net in bronze that snares the couple in bed. Vulcan throws the door open and invites all the gods to watch.

Next is the story of the loves of the sun-god.

Last is the story of Salmacis and Hermaphroditus, whom Salmacis loves. He refuses her advances, but when she sees him undress to dive into the water, she becomes inflamed with passion and dives into the pool, attaching herself to him so thoroughly that he becomes half-woman, half-man.

When the daughters of Minyas finish their tales, they are transformed into batlike creatures.

Juno, irritated that Ixion has to atone for his crimes with unending pain while "Athamas in wealth and pride may reign—/He and his wife . . . hold me in disdain," decrees that King Athamas will be at the furies' call and shall be raving mad, so that Cadmus's house will fall.

Exiled to Illyria, Cadmus kills a snake and is transformed into one. Harmonia asks him to use his power to change her into a snake as well, which he does.

When Andromeda's mother boasts that her daughter is more beautiful than the Nereids, Poseidon sends a sea monster to ravage the land. To appease the monster, Andromeda is chained to a rock near the sea to be eaten by the monster. Her uncle Phineus, to whom she is betrothed, lacks the courage to free her. Perseus sees her and falls in love. He slays Medusa, one of the three Gorgons, who has the power to turn people into stone. He places her head on Minerva's shield, where it still has the same power. He turns the sea monster to stone with the Gorgon head and frees Andromeda.

Book Five tells how, after Perseus frees Andromeda, Phineus comes to claim her, but Perseus wins her love and turns Phineus to stone as well. Perseus returns to his native land and fights the usurping sea monster Proteus. He then turns on Polydectes, who was rejected by Perseus's mother, Danae, but is planning to ravish her anyway. Perseus saves his mother and turns Polydectes into stone.

Urania, one of the nine Muses (of astronomy), tells Pallas (Minerva or Athene) about the nine daughters of Euippe and Piero, a rich couple in Pella, who challenge the nine Muses to a musical contest. Calliope, Muse of epic poetry, continues the story, telling about Ceres, goddess of agriculture, who is grieved when Pluto (Dis) abducts her daughter Proserpine. Ceres, "the fear-struck mother," searches land and sea in vain. When she learns from Arethusa, a nymph of the stream, that Pluto has abducted her, she visits Jove to plead for his intercession. Jove promises to restore Proserpine to her mother if Proserpine eats nothing in Hades. But Proserpine eats seven pomegranate seeds, so she must spend six months each year as Pluto's wife and six months with her mother.

Her worries over, Ceres turns to hear the story of Arethusa, a former wood nymph who, pursued by Alpheüs, the river god, prays to be turned into a stream.

After all the stories are finished, the daughters of Euippe and Piero are defeated by the Muses, and the nine daughters are transformed into magpies.

Book Six describes Arachne, a woman of Lydia who is the daughter of Idmon, a dyer. She is so skillful at weaving that she challenges Pallas to a contest. She depicts in her tapestry the love trysts of the gods, so angering Pallas that she rips the cloth to pieces. In despair Arachne hangs herself, but Pallas transforms her.

The next story relates the rivalry of Niobe and Latona. Niobe, who has many children, taunts Latona, who has only two, Apollo and Diana (Artemis). Outraged, Latona appeals to the gods for satisfaction. All Niobe's children except Chloris are slain, and Niobe is turned into stone. As a child, Niobe's brother Pelops is killed by his father, Tantalus, and served to the gods at a banquet to see if they can tell the difference. No one except Ceres, distracted with grief for her daughter Proserpine at the time, eats any. She eats a shoulder. The other gods bring Pelops back to life, replacing the shoulder with one of ivory, and send Tantalus to Hades for punishment. Latona, fleeing with her two children (by Jupiter) from Jupiter's wife Juno, comes to the country of Lycia. When the Lycians refuse to give Latona a drink, she asks the gods to change the people into frogs so they will have to live in water forever.

Marsyas the satyr, a skillful flute player, challenges Apollo, a lute player, to a musical duel, to be judged by the Muses. The victor can decide the loser's punishment. Apollo wins, ties Marsyas to a tree, and flays him alive. A river springs from his blood and the tears of the mourners.

King Tereus of Thrace marries Procne, daughter of King Pandion of Athens, his ally in a war against Megara. Tereus violates Procne's sister Philomena and cuts out her tongue so she can't tell. Philomena weaves a tapestry depicting her ravishment and sends it to Procne. The two sisters kill Itylus, son of Tereus and Procne, and serve him as meat to Tereus. During the meal Philomena tosses Itylus's head onto the table. The gods punish them all: Tereus is changed into a hawk, Procne into a swallow, Philomena into a nightingale, and Itylus into a pheasant.

Book Seven begins with the story of Medea, an enchantress at Colchis, where Jason and the Argonauts come in quest of the Golden Fleece. She falls in love with Jason and helps him win the Golden Fleece by performing certain tasks, such as sowing dragon's teeth, from which armed men arise to attack. She renders helpless the serpent guarding the Fleece, enabling Jason to take the Fleece. She restores his aged father, Aeson, to youthful vigor by boiling him in a pot of magic herbs, then persuades the daughter of Pelias, Jason's uncle, to let her do the same for him. But she deliberately does not use magic herbs, causing his death. When she and Jason are driven from Oilus, they go to Corinth, where Jason decides to abandon her and marry Glauce, daughter of King Creon of Corinth. Medea causes the deaths of both Creon and Glauce with a poisoned rope and diadem. She kills her own two children by Jason and escapes to Athens.

Minos II, king of Crete, decides to wage war on Athens because his son Androgeos has been killed there. He plans to exact a yearly tribute of seven youths and girls to be shut up with the Minotaur. He sends Cephalus to the island of Aegina to ask the people's aid in a battle against Athens. When the people of the island are destroyed by a plague, Jupiter repopulates it with people made from ants, called Myrmidons.

When Cephalus is asked about his spear by Phocus, one of the Aegina princes, he tells the story of how his wife's sister, Aurora, seduces him and spirits him away. When he comes to his senses, he rejects her. In revenge she sends him back to his wife, Procris. To test her faithfulness, he goes home in another identity so that she does not recognize him. Procris allows herself to be seduced by him, and when he changes back into himself she is so filled with shame that she exiles herself as one of Diana's huntresses. Minos gives her a hound that always finds its quarry and a spear that always hits its target. Later, when the couple is reconciled, she gives Cephalus the hound and lance. Cephalus goes hunting alone. When he tires, he rests and makes a speech to Aura, the breeze. Someone overhears and, thinking he is wooing Aura, whispers the slander to Procris. She goes out to spy; he, thinking she is prey, wounds her fatally with the lance. As she dies, she says, "Let not Aura . . ./Wife it in rooms that once belonged to me." He quickly explains the truth, and she dies smiling.

In Book Eight, Scylla, daughter of King Nisus of Megara, falls in love with King Minos, who plans to invade the country. She promises to deliver him the kingdom if he will marry her. Her father has a lock of purple hair upon which his strength depends. While Nisus is sleeping, Scylla cuts off the lock, thus killing her father. She delivers the kingdom to Minos, who is so repulsed by her act that she drowns herself. Nisus is turned into an osprey (sea eagle) and Scylla is turned into a lark or sea bird called Cires.

When Minos prays to the gods to send him a sacrificial victim in order to settle who will rule Crete, Poseidon sends him a bull. Minos takes the kingdom, but cannot bring himself to sacrifice the beautiful animal. Poseidon causes Minos's wife, Pasiphaë, to mate with the bull, and from that union comes the Minotaur, a man with a bull's head. Daedalus arrives on Crete and builds a labyrinth in which Minos can hide the Minotaur. It is fed seven Athenian girls and seven Athenian youths every nine years.

When Theseus comes to be sacrificed, Minos's daughter Ariadne falls in love with him and gives him a thread with which to find his way out of the labyrinth. He kills the Minotaur, comes out of the labyrinth, and marries Ariadne. But soon, his ardor cooled, he deserts her on the island of Naxos. However, Bacchus arrives to comfort her, placing her crown in heaven as a constellation called the Northern Cross.

Meanwhile, Daedalus, still in Crete, is homesick. When Minos won't let him go and confines him in the labyrinth, he invents wings made from feathers held together with wax for himself and his son Icarus. The two escape Crete, but Icarus flies too close to the sun and his wax melts, causing him to plunge to his death in the Icarian Sea. As Daedalus buries his son, a partridge claps his wings in glee: It is Talos, once a nephew and rival of Daedalus. Talos invented the saw and compass, inciting Daedalus to such a jealous pique that he pushed Talos off a tower, killing him. Talos has been changed into a partridge.

When King Oeneus neglects to sacrifice to Artemis, she sends a wild boar to ravage the land of Calydon. The king rounds up a band of heroes for a boar hunt, promising the hide to the boar's killer. The great huntress Atalanta wounds the animal first. Meleager, the king's son, kills the boar with his bare hands, but gives the hide and head to Atalanta, whom he loves. His mother's brothers begin to quarrel over the spoils, so Meleager kills them. When his mother, Althaea, learns that her brothers have been slain, she takes the brand and burns it. (The Fates had appeared at Meleager's birth and decreed that he would live so long as the brand that was on the fire was not consumed. Until that time Althaea had taken the brand from the fire, preserving it all these years.) When she burns the brand, her son Meleager is killed.

Baucis and Philemon, an old couple of modest means, entertain Jupiter and Mercury, in disguise because they have been repulsed by the behavior of the rich. As a reward for their hospitality, they are saved from a flood, their humble cottage is changed into a marble temple with a golden roof, and Baucis and Philemon are made the first priestess and priest. They request to die at the same time; when they die, they are turned into an oak and a linden whose boughs intertwine.

When Erysichthon cuts down a grove of trees sacred to Ceres, she curses him with insatiable hunger. He sells his daughter for food, but she appeals to Neptune, who changes her into a man, enabling her to escape her new master. She then turns into a girl once more. When her father learns of her ability to change form, he sends her here and there disguised as various animals, which he sells to buy more food. At last there is no more food, and he eats his own flesh.

Book Nine tells of the defeat of the river god Acheloüs by Hercules in a wrestling match to win the hand of Meleager's sister Deianira. After Hercules wins her, they leave and come to a flooded river. The centaur Nessus carries Deianira across and tries to rape her. Hercules kills him with an arrow poisoned with blood from the Lernean Hydra. As he lies dying, Nessus gives Deianira his bloodstained tunic, saying that the blood has the power to win back Hercules's love, should he ever be unfaithful. Later, when Hercules falls in love with Iole, Deianira sends the garment to Hercules. When he wears it, it causes his death. Jove addresses the gods, telling them to receive the hero Hercules as a god. They all approve, and Hercules is made a star.

Alcmene tells the story of Hercules's birth. Juno (Hera), jealous because her husband has fathered the child, appears as Lucina, goddess of childbirth, and keeps Alcmene in agonizing labor for seven days and nights. Galanthis, Alcmene's maid, sees Juno's fine hand in it and tricks Lucina into believing that the child has already been born, thus breaking the spell. Lucina punishes Galanthis for lying by changing her into a weasel.

Dryope, a nymph ravished by Apollo, is nursing her eight-year-old baby by him. She plucks a lotus, which bleeds: It is Lotis, a beautiful nymph who fled the lustful Priapus and was changed into a lotus tree. Dryope is turned into a poplar tree. When her husband comes looking for her, she tells him her ravishment is not her fault. She begs him to take the child and let some nurse care for him.

After Hercules's death, the Fates make his old comrade-in-arms, Iolaüs, young again.

Byblis, an old woman, falls in love with her twin brother, Caunus. As punishment, she is turned into a fountain.

Because Iphis's father, Ligdus, has ordered his wife, Telethusa, to kill their child if it is a girl, she is reared as a boy. Ianthe, a beautiful girl, falls in love with Iphis, so the mother begs the goddess Isis to turn Iphis into a man so the two can marry.

Book Ten tells of Orpheus's journey to the underworld to petition Pluto and Persephone to restore his bride, Eurydice, to him. They agree to do so, providing he does not look back when he leaves. But he forgets and looks around to see if Eurydice is following, thus losing her forever; Eurydice dies a second time. Bereft, Orpheus tries to cross the Styx again, but the ferryman refuses to take him. Orpheus sits on the bank for days, plucking his lyre. The trees, charmed by Orpheus's music, crowd around him. He sings to the trees about Ganymede, a beautiful Trojan boy loved by Jove, who takes the form of an eagle to transport Ganymede to Olympus where he becomes a cup-bearer to the gods.

Hyacinthus, a beautiful youth, is loved by both Zephyrus (the West Wind) and Apollo. When Hyacinthus chooses Apollo, in a fit of jealousy Zephyrus blows a discus Apollo has thrown so that it veers and strikes Hyacinthus, killing him.

Pygmalion carves an ivory statue so perfect that he falls in love with it, so he asks Venus to give it life. The goddess grants his request, and the statue, Galatea, comes to life. The couple have a daughter, Paphos.

After Myrrha's mother brags that the girl is more beautiful than Aphrodite, the goddess curses Myrrha with a great lust for her father. Through trickery Myrrha spends many nights in his bed. When he discovers the truth, he vows to kill her. She flees, so he kills himself. Pregnant, Myrrha is changed into a myrrha tree from whose trunk the goddess of childbirth, Lucina, brings forth Adonis. Adonis is so beautiful that Venus falls in love with him and bears him a son and a daughter. She warns him to be wary of the animals she hunts. He ignores her warning and is killed by a wild boar. A beautiful flower, called anemone, springs from his blood.

Atalanta desires virginity and says she will not marry any suitor who can't best her in a race. Those whom she bests, she kills. But Hippomenes takes up the challenge, carrying with him three golden apples Venus has given him. He drops them along the path. Unable to resist, Atalanta stops to pick them up and loses the race.

Book Eleven tells of Orpheus who, while singing, is brutally killed by the Thracian wives who are "with Bacchic rage possessed." His ghost seeks and finds his dead wife, Eurydice, with whom he walks the meads hand in hand.

King Midas foolishly requests of the gods that everything he touches be turned into gold. But when his food, even his daughter, turns to gold, he begs that the touch be removed. He is told to wash in the River Poctolus, and thereafter the river sands are gold. Midas attends a music contest between Apollo and Pan judged by Tmolus, who declares Apollo the winner. However, Midas disagrees with the decision; he prefers Pan. Offended, Apollo changes Midas's ears to donkey's ears.

The story of the founding of Troy is related.

Old Proteus has told the ocean goddess Thetis, "Be fruitful, ocean goddess: you shall be/the mother of a warrior son. . . ." Jove, fearing that a greater warrior than he might come from a union between himself and Thetis, bids his grandson Peleus to marry her in his stead. Thus the Argonaut Peleus is the only mortal ever to marry a goddess. The wedding is attended by all the gods. Three goddesses—Aphrodite, Athena, and Hera—contend for the golden apple marked "For the Fairest," which Eris (Discordia) rolls in. When they ask the Trojan Paris to judge who should receive the apple, he chooses Aphrodite, earning him the enmity of the other two, who help the Greeks in the Trojan War to come.

When Ceÿx is drowned in a storm at sea, his wife, Alcyone, learns of it in a dream. His body is washed ashore, and Alcyone is so bereft that both she and Ceÿx are changed into kingfishers.

Book Twelve tells the cause and beginning of the Trojan War: Paris brings home a stolen wife (Helen, wife of Menelaus who, with his brother Agamemnon, raises an expedition against Troy). The Greeks, stalled at Coulis by prevailing bad winds, are told by an oracle that because Agamemnon has killed Artemis's stag, his daughter Iphigenia must be sacrificed before the winds will change. As Iphigenia stands before the altar with weeping priests, Artemis relents and puts a deer in her place.

Cygnus, a Trojan ally, is invulnerable. Achilles is unable to kill him with darts, lance, or spear, so he suffocates Cygnus by tightening strangling cords around his neck. But later, when Achilles returns for the body, Cygnus has been transformed into a swan.

Wise Nestor tells the story of Caeneus, who receives from Poseidon the ability to change her sex. She becomes an invulnerable warrior fighting with the Lapithae against the Centaurs. She offends Jove, who buries her under a pile of trees and tranforms her into a bird.

Nestor relates to Hercules's son Tlepolemus how his father killed all of Neleus's 12 sons except Nestor.

After ten years of the Trojan War, Achilles, who has killed Hector, dies at the hand of Paris. Afterward, conflicts grow over who will get Achilles's arms. Ajax and Ulysses vie for them, so Agamemnon tells the chiefs to "sit as a body, to decide the case."

In Book Thirteen, a lawsuit develops over Achilles's arms. Both Ajax and Ulysses make speeches, each describing his own mighty deeds and telling why he should be awarded the arms. When the Greek leaders vote in Ulysses's favor, Ajax goes mad and kills himself.

The fall of Troy is related.

The story is told of Polyxena, who accompanies her father, Priam, when he goes to ask Achilles for the body of his son Hector. She is devastated when

Achilles is killed, and sacrifices herself at his tomb, after which she is claimed by his ghost.

Priam and Hecuba's youngest son, Polydorus, sent to King Polymestor for safety during the war, is murdered by the king at the war's end in order to keep the boy's treasure for himself. The body is thrown into the sea. It washes ashore and is brought to Hecuba. She appeals to Priam to avenge their son's death, but he is too cowardly. She takes matters into her own hands, luring Polymestor and his sons to her tent, where she blinds him and kills his sons. When Thracians attack her, she grows a muzzle and is changed into a bitch. She growls and barks and howls out her grief.

The story is related of Aurora's lamentation for her son Memnon, by Tithonus. She carries away his body after he is killed by Achilles.

When the war ends, Aeneas begins his wandering.

Polyphemus, a one-eyed giant, loves Galatea, daughter of Nereus. But she loves a young shepherd, Acis. When Polyphemus discovers the lovers together, he hurls a rock at Acis. Galatea sees the rock coming and turns Acis into a river.

Glaucus, a sea deity, falls in love with Scylla, a sea-nymph. Scylla appeals to Circe, who falls in love with Glaucus herself.

Book Fourteen tells how Circe pours poisonous herbs in Scylla's bathing waters, causing the part of her body that gets wet to be transformed into a hideous monster.

On his way to Italy, Aeneas is blown by the wind back to Libya, where he eventually marries Queen Dido of Carthage. When he is ready to continue his journey, she orders a pyre built and falls on his sword-point. Aeneas leaves Carthage in a hurry, "blown once more to Eryx, [where] at his father's tomb he paid/Due honors. . . ." Aeneas lands at Cumae, where he is helped by the Cumaean Sibyl, to whom Apollo has granted the gift of prophecy for 1,000 years. From there Aeneas goes to Sicily, where he finds his old friend Achaemenides marooned at the cave of Polyphemus. Aeneas takes him along and visits the ashes of his old nurse, Caieta.

At the town of Caieta, named for the nurse, Achaemenides encounters his old shipmate from the Ulysses voyage, Macareus, who proceeds to tell his story. In describing a sunset, he says, "Declining Phoebus now had dappled o'er/ With dying gleams the far Tartessian shore."

Returning home after the Trojan War, Ulysses visits Circe on her isle of Aeaea. She feeds his men a potion and all but Eurylochus are transformed into swine. Circe loves Picus, the son of Saturn. When he spurns her and remains faithful to Canens, she turns him into a purple woodpecker.

The wars of the Trojans in Italy are described.

Vertumnus, god of change, falls in love with Pomona, goddess of fruit. To win her, he tries various disguises, such as a laborer, reaper, pruner, plowman, and an old crone.

Amulius usurps the crown of Alba Longo from his brother Numitor. Later, Numitor's grandson Romulus kills Amulius and restores the throne to his grandfather. (The story of Romulus and his twin Remus and their founding of

Rome in 653 B.C. appears in the *Aeneid*.) Posthumously, the Romans name Romulus Quirinus. He disappears in a cloud during a thunderstorm. Those who witness the miracle build temples to him. A star sets Hersilla's hair aflame, and she joins her husband, Romulus, who renames her Hora.

Book Fifteen tells of Numa, second king of Rome, and his learning. His first wife is Tatia. When Tatia dies, Egeria gives him legal advice for governing Rome. They marry. When Numa dies, she melts into tears and is changed into a fountain by Diana.

When Hercules returns from Spain with Spanish oxen, he stops at his benefactor Croton's and enjoys his hospitality. Upon leaving, he says, "Upon this site . . ./A city shall your children's children see." Myscelus is told in a dream by the gods' cup-bearer to "Haste, bid your nature land good-bye and go/Where distant Aesar's pebbly waters flow." He leaves Argos and founds Crotana.

Pythagoras settles in Rome (ca. 530 B.C.) and founds his school.

Hyppolytus is the son of Theseus and Hyppolyte, who dies. Theseus then marries Phaedra; while he is away, she falls in love with Hyppolytus. As a devotee of Artemis, Hyppolytus has promised to live a life of honor and chastity, so he rebuffs Phaedra. She writes a letter to Theseus, accusing Hyppolytus of seducing her, then she hangs herself. Theseus banishes his son and uses one of the three curses Poseidon has given him to curse his son. As Hyppolytus drives his chariot along the shore away from the palace, a sea monster scares the horses. Hyppolytus is thrown from the chariot and dragged to death.

A Roman general sees horns on his reflection in a stream. An oracle tells him the horns are a sign that he will rule Rome. He calls his followers together, concealing his horns, and tells them a dangerous dictator must not be allowed into the city. He warns them to watch out for a man with horns. Then he reveals his horns. His followers groan but abide by his warning. They give him instead land outside the city, "As much as, plowing with his team of kine,/He might ring round from dawn to day's decline." They set bronze horns beside the city gates, in his honor.

The people of Latium, during an "air-borne plague" (293 B.C.), seek the help of Apollo (Phoebus). Amidst their prayers, a voice is heard: "You seek too far afield: look nearer home:/Not Phoebus, but his son, must succor Rome." They consult the books of Sibyl and send to the temple at Epidaurus in Argos for Aesculapius's cult, which establishes a temple, with a sanitarium, on the Tiber River's "Island," where the Tiber splits.

The achievements of Julius Caesar are listed: "Not his wars, with triumphs fitly crowned,/Not acts domestic, and a rule renowned," but, referring to Julius's son Augustus, "no work by Caesar done/Matched this, to be the sire of such a son." The poet continues, "To win more laurels than he well could wear—/What was all this, to raising such an heir?"

Of Julius Caesar's assassination the poet says, "Heaven with all its warnings had no power/To crush the plot, and stay the destined hour."

As for Augustus: "When great Augustus leaves the earth he sways,/And joins the gods. Yet still with loving care/From distant heavens shows favor to our prayer."

After the gods of Rome are invoked, the poet makes a prediction about his own immortality in letters: ". . . high above the stars, from death secure/Shall Ovid's name indelibly endure." (Watts 1980)

See also Ovid.

MEVLŪD-I PEYGAMBERI

(Also *Mevlid-i Serif* or *Mevlūd-i Nebi*,
Hymn on the Prophet's nativity)

Turkish religious poem about Muḥammad's life by Süleyman Çelebi (d. 1422–1429), Anatolian poet.

The *Mevlūd*, which borrows from eighth-century Arabian biographer Ibn Isḥāq, as well as other legends and poems, is an adulation of the Prophet. It tells the story of Muḥammad's birth, his life, his miracles, his death, and his journey to heaven. Written in unpretentious Ottoman Turkish vernacular, the poem is still chanted during observances of the Prophet's birthday and is often recited at Muslim Turkish funerals. (Preminger 1974)

MEXICANA

Minor Spanish epic poem (1594) by Gabriel Lobo Lasso de la Vega (1558–1615) relating the story of the conquest of New Spain by Cortés. (Anderson-Imbert 1969)

MICKIEWICZ, ADAM

Polish patriot, playwright, and poet, author of what has been called "the last epos" in world literature, *Pan Tadeusz*. He was born in 1798 in Nowogródek (or possibly in a nearby village, Zaosie), in the Grand Duchy of Lithuania. His father was a small-town lawyer; his mother, a former servant girl in a nearby manor house. As a child, Mickiewicz learned the folklore of the Byelorussian peasants, which was laced with the local Roman Catholic and Greek Catholic traditions. He went to a Dominican school in Nowogródek, where he was a mediocre student, but he excelled in games and theater performances. When he was 14, the Napoleonic army entered Nowogródek, and Napoléon's brother, Kieronymous, king of Naples, took up residence in the family house.

In 1815, at the age of 17, he entered the University of Wilno on a scholarship, first studying science, then switching to literature, and graduating in 1819. According to the stipulations of his scholarship, he became a high school teacher in a nearby town, Kowno. His years there were lonely and confining, and his love for the wealthy Maryla Wereszczaka was unfulfilled when she decided to marry a count instead of a poor schoolteacher—a decision she later regretted.

His first poems, written to amuse his friends, imitated Voltaire; he had even adapted *La Pucelle d'Orléans*. His first serious poems appeared in his collection *Ballady i romanse* (Ballads and romances, 1822) and opened the era of Romanticism in Poland. The poems were very successful with the lower strata of the population. His second volume, *Poezye* (Poems), appeared the following year. It contained two longer poems: *Grażyna* and parts 2 and 4 of *Forefather's Eve*, about *Dziady*, a folk ritual, which would become his major theatrical achievement.

That year, the tzarist authorities clamped down on youth movements in Lithuania, sending some students ages 12 to 15 to Russia for life as common soldiers. At school Mickiewicz had been active in the Philomaths, a literary group called "nonpolitical," but with some contact to Freemasonry. Along with his friends, he was arrested and held for about six months in a prison converted from a monastery of the Basilian fathers. He was ordered to Russia to serve in a teaching position.

Late in 1824 he arrived in St. Petersburg, where he immediately found friends among intellectual groups with which the Philomaths had maintained contact. It is also possible that he entered Freemasonry in Russia. As a poet he had already established a reputation in literary circles. He received a position at a *lycée* in Odessa, where he lived, in his own words, "like a pasha," surrounded by women. One in particular, Karolina (née Rzewuski) Sobański, who was also the mistress of General Witt, military commander in southern Russia, appears in his poetry. He wrote a cycle of 22 love sonnets that begins with his ideal love for Maryla, passes to the sensuous trysts of Odessa, and ends with bitter denunciation of his transitory affairs. An excursion to the Crimea in the company of General Witt and Karolina led to the popular *Sonety krymskie* (Crimean sonnets), published in Moscow in 1826 and soon translated from the Polish into Russian.

In 1826 he was transferred to Russia, where he made many valuable friends among the intelligentsia, among them Pushkin. A young poetess friend, Caroline Jaenisch (later Pavlova), was the first to translate his (and Pushkin's) poems into German. In 1828 in St. Petersburg he published a long epic poem, *Konrad Wallenrod*, a tale in verse presumably taken from old Lithuanian chronicles. The poem exerted strong influence on the younger poets, although there was some objection because the poem was said to glorify treason.

With the help of friends, he obtained a passport for travel in the spring of 1829. At the same time he brought out an Arabic-style poem, *Faris*, in St. Petersburg. While traveling in Germany, he visited Goethe, who received him cordially. He went to Rome and found an international community not unlike the one he had left behind. News of the insurrection in Warsaw reached him in Rome, but instead of going to Poland he went to Paris, perhaps carrying a diplomatic message. However, he was deeply disappointed by French politicians and left for the Polish border. But he did not, or could not, enter. By then it was 1831 and the Poles had lost the war. He had a love affair with Konstancja Łubieński and returned to Dresden. In 1832, he wrote part 3 of *Forefather's Eve*, which was published in Paris the same year. The completed work was introduced into the repertoire of the Polish theater by the reformer Stanisław Wyspiański (1869–1907). It became a kind of "national sacred play," at times forbidden because of its emotional impact.

In 1832 the poet returned to Paris, where his writing expressed the idea that Poland was to redeem the nations through her suffering. It also warned the French and English of the despotism that would subjugate all of Europe if it continued to be tolerated.

During 1832–1834, in addition to editing a periodical, the *Polish Pilgrim,* he wrote a poetic work, *Pan Tadeusz,* in 12 books of Polish alexandrine (13-syllable couplets). It has been called an epic, a novel in verse, a fairy tale, even a mock-heroic epic. The poem was not highly praised by the simple people for whom he wrote it. Polish exiles thought its tone was not elevated enough, although a few thought it was a masterpiece. The poet himself said, "I hope I will never again use my pen for trifles." But gradually the poem won recognition as the highest achievement in all Polish literature.

Mickiewicz wrote no more poetry. He continued to live in exile, and his books were smuggled into Poland, where even the mention of his name was forbidden. He married Celina Szymanowski, whom he had known in Moscow when she was a teenager. The two had several children, although the marriage was not happy. He became active in politics beginning in 1848, and in 1849 began editing a Socialist paper in Paris, *La Tribune des Peuples.* For a while he was librarian at the library of the Arsenal.

In 1855 he left for the Near East to aid the Polish and Cossack troops against Russia in the Crimean War, traveling with his friend Armand Lévy. While visiting a military camp near Constantinople, he contracted cholera and died suddenly in the arms of his friend Lévy. His body was taken to France, but in 1890 it was moved to Wawel Castle's cathedral in Kraków. (Miłosz 1969/1983)

See also Pan Tadeusz.

 # MILTON, JOHN

English poet and prose writer, author of *Paradise Lost* (1665) and *Paradise Regained* (1671). He was born in 1608 in London, the middle child and elder son of a Protestant scrivener and banker, John Milton, Sr. He received his education at St. Paul's School and Christ's College Cambridge, matriculating in 1625, earning a BA in 1629 and an MA in 1632. Because of his handsome but delicate features, he was nicknamed "The Lady" by his college classmates. There he wrote his first poem, "On the Death of a Fair Infant Dying of a Cough," on the death of his sister's baby.

Following his years at Cambridge, Milton returned to his father's, first to Hammersmith and then to his country place at Horton, where he studied, read, and wrote for the next six years (1632-1638). In 1638, his mother having died the previous year, he left England to travel in Europe. Upon his return in 1639, he settled in London, where he tutored nephews Edward and John Phillips, and began to think about composing a great poem about Britain.

In 1643 he married Mary Powell, the young daughter of an Oxfordshire Royalist who was in debt to Milton Sr., but a month after the marriage Mary returned to her father's home, remaining for two years. During this time Milton wrote some tracts critical of the Church of England, particularly in regard to its position against divorce. His wife returned in 1645 and later bore him a son, who died in infancy, and three daughters: Anne (1646), Mary (1648), and Deborah (1652). His wife died a few days after Deborah's birth.

Under Cromwell's Commonwealth Milton served as Secretary in Foreign Tongues to the Council of State, a position roughly the equivalent of Secretary of State in the United States. A large part of his duties consisted of translating official state communiques.

At the age of 43 Milton's eyesight, which had been failing for years, left him (1651). Although his blindness restricted his secretarial capacities, he continued to translate state letters for the Commonwealth until 1669.

In 1656 he married Katherine Woodcock, who died only two years later of complications following childbirth. Her death and his own blindness are the subject of some of his sonnets of the period.

With the coming of the Restoration government, Milton's own position was precarious; however, his life was spared, possibly because his friends were able to portray him as a harmless blind poet.

In 1663 he married Elizabeth Minshull. Two years later, during the plague of 1665, they moved to a house at Chalfont St. Giles, Buckinghamshire.

By this time Milton had abandoned the notion of writing a British epic, choosing instead a Christian theme. He began *Paradise Lost* ca. 1655-1658 and finished it in 1665. The first edition was published in 1667, again in 1668 and 1669. A second edition was published in 1674. In 1671 he published a lesser sequel, *Paradise Regained,* as well as a drama, *Samson Agonistes,* all in one volume.

Due to financial straits brought on by his loss of a government post, to poor health—primarily attacks of gout, to somewhat antagonistic relationships with his daughters, and to the lack of independence caused by his blindness, Milton's final decade was less than comfortable. But when he died just before his 66th birthday in 1674, his burial at St. Giles was attended by "all his learned and great friends of London." (Milton/Ricks 1968)

 # MILTON: A POEM IN TWO BOOKS

English short epic poem (1804, 1808–1809) of a little more than 2,000 lines written and illuminated by William Blake (1757–1827). It is evident from the title page of one of the four original copies of this book that at one time Blake planned to compose 12 books. He apparently changed his mind, because the epic is complete in two books. This poem is one of Blake's "prophetic books." The poet wrote in protest to industrialization, which he saw as authoritarian, dehumanizing, and denigrating to workers. He even wrote in protest to all conventional authority: family life, status, seniority, sex, religion. The poem, Blake's best-known, was set to music and entitled "Jerusalem" by Sir Hubert Parry.

Subtitled "To Justify the Ways of God to Men," the poem begins with a preface consisting of a prose exhortation: "Rouze up, O Young Men of the New Age!" It promises a New Age in which the "Perverted Writings" of the classics by the "silly Greek and Latin slaves of the Sword" will be seen in their proper light.

Following the preface are four four-line stanzas of four iambic-rhymed feet in which the poet, despairing from the industrial drudgery of the era, asks, "And was Jerusalem builded here/Among these dark Satanic Mills?" His term "Satanic Mills" was a metaphor for industrialization in general.

The poet early establishes a Christian context of good versus evil, upon which his poem is based. He attributes to Christ and his Apostles the notion that "there is a Class of Men whose whole delight is in Destroying."

Book I, consisting of 1,355 lines of free verse divided into 30 sections, begins with a plea to the Muses who inspire Milton to "Come into my hand." He asks, "What mov'd Milton . . . to go into the deep? . . ."

As in traditional epic poetry, gods and men interact, as do the past and present. Thus, as the inspired man, Milton appears, as do Wesley, Newton, Pitt, and Nelson, along with Jesus, Isaiah, and Ezekiel from the Bible, plus an elaborate befuddling mythology he constructed: the characters of Los, blacksmith, potter, visionary, creator and destroyer of forms; Urizen, aged reasoner and formulator of laws; Orc, fiery youth, spirit of energy; Vala, cruel goddess of nature; Jerusalem, the soul, bride of the "god within;" and Giant Albion, signifying Britain.

Book I is a description of the World of Los, "the labour of six thousand years," (1:31–64) which is flawed by man's inhumanity and exploitation of both nature and fellow man. When the Ancient Man sleeping on the Rock of Albion awakes, he is astonished and ashamed to hear sounds of war and to see his own children mocking Faith and denying Providence. Los instructs him to bind the sheaves (as in the Judgment Day hymn "Bringing in the Sheaves") into three classes, which have been woven since "under pretense of benevolence the Elect Subdu'd All." The classes are: the Elect, "who cannot believe in Eternal Life/Except by Miracle & a New Birth;" the Reprobate, "who never cease to Believe;" and the Redeem'd, "who live in doubts & fears, perpetually tormented by the Elect." (1.27:31,33,35,36)

Book II, consisting of 609 lines in 17 sections, is a book of prophecy in the style of Revelations. It describes Beulah land, a "pleasant Shadow" created at the request of the Emanations as a temporary rest, hidden from the unbounded life of Man. Milton sits on the Couch of Death conversing with the Seven Angels of the Presence who claim they are not individuals but states, compelled to combine by Satan, "the Spectre of Albion/Who made himself a God & destroyed the Human Form Divine." (2.35:12,13) They tell Milton that he is about to be created a state as well, called Eternal Annihilation. Milton has decided to redeem the Female Shade from eternal death. She is Ololon, described as a "sweet river & liquid pearl river of milk" located in Eden. Following Milton's track one sees the four states of Humanity in repose. They are: Beulah, where there is music and pleasant sleep on soft couches, with winged female forms in attendance; Alla, located in the heart; Al-Ulro, located in the "Loins & Seminal Vessels;" and the fourth state, which is dreadful, "terrible, deadly, unutterable," located in the stomach and intestines.

Ololon bemoans the "piteous Female forms compell'd/To weave the Woof of Death!" Ololon descends through Beulah to Los and Enitharmon into the Garden of Milton's track. But they cannot step into the Vegetable World "without becoming/the enemies of Humanity" except in female form. The Virgin Ololon seeks Milton, who has descended, driven from Eternity. His shadow appears. He speaks to Satan, whose purpose and that of his priests and his churches is "to impress on men the fear of death, to teach/. . . fear . . . constriction, abject selfishness." (2.43:38,39)

Satan comes in a cloud of fire, claiming to be God, "Oppos'd to Mercy, and the Divine Delusion, Jesus. . . ." (2.44:2) Milton calls for Albion to awake, subdue Satan, and cast him into the burning lake of Los. Albion, who has been sleeping on his couch in Beulah, looks over the world; then his strength fails and he sinks back onto his couch. The Virgin Ololon speaks to Milton, telling him she has seen him striving against those who seek to annihilate religion (Voltaire, Rousseau, Hume, Gibbon, and Bolingbroke), substituting "Natural Religion." She asks, "Is Ololon the cause of this? O where shall I hide my face?" (2.46:14) Milton tells her that it is time to cast off "the idiot Questioner" who "publishes doubt & calls it knowledge, whose Science is Despair." (2.48:15) These and others he calls "murderers of Jesus." Jesus Christ appears and weeps as he enters Albion's bosom. The time of the Great Harvest has come. (Blake 1991)

See also Blake, William.

 # MINNEBURG, DIE

Middle High German allegorical poem (ca. 1340) of 5,000 lines whose author cites the style of Meister Egen von Bamberg as his inspiration. The style, called *geblümter Stil,* is elaborate with ornamental metaphors and flowery expressions. Probably composed in the episcopal state of Würzburg in Eastern Franconia, the poem describes a love of great purity, depicting a war between virtues and vices and condemning unfaithfulness. (Garland and Garland 1986)

 # MIRAMONTES Y ZUÁZOLA, JUAN DE

Spanish soldier and poet (fl. 1615), author of *Armas antárticas* (Antarctic wars), written between 1608 and 1615. Miramontes y Zuázola took part in the Spanish-American struggle against the pirate Thomas Cavendish, an Englishman who in 1586 sailed to the Patagonian coast and through the Straits of Magellan, attacking and plundering Spanish settlements from South America to Mexico. Cavendish was actually the third person to circumnavigate the Earth. The poet must have had fine training in the classics, for he describes the conflict and his South American surroundings with the "dash and imagination" of one trained in the "finest techniques of the epic of the golden century." (Anderson-Imbert 1969)

MIRROR OF PATIENCE
(*Espejo de paciencia*)

Cuban Spanish religious-heroic epic poem (1608) by Silvestre de Balboa (1570?–1640?). Consisting of two cantos having 145 epic octaves (in hendecasyllabic lines), the poem is Cuba's first. It is singular for its creole, Cuban, and national character.

The only two extant (and greatly different) versions of this poem are in the handwriting of the poet and novelist José Antonio Echeverría (1815–1885). At one time it was thought that both the poem and the poet might be a hoax; however, it is possible that Echeverría may have copied the poem, modifying and modernizing it in the process.

Although it was doubtless inspired by Alonso de Ercilla y Zuñiga's (1534–1594) epic *La Araucana*, it is not about the Spaniards' battle against the Indians. Rather, it depicts the Spaniards' struggle against those Balboa calls "Lutheran pirates."

Canto 1 describes the suffering of the bishop, Friar Juan de la Cabeza Altamirano, whom the French buccaneer pirate Gilbert Biron kidnapped in 1604. The bishop is compared with Christ.

Canto 2 is about vengeance. It describes a "little Creole Negro" who deceives the pirate Giron into putting shore, where a tribe of Indians awaits. In the ensuing battle, only one Indian is killed by the French. Another "Creole savior, honorable Negro" kills the heretic Giron by thrusting a lance into his chest. When the bishop is freed and returns to Cuba, the mythological gods are there to welcome him with flowers and exotic fruits. (Anderson-Imbert 1969)

MISRAMA, SURYAMAL

Indian poet, author of *Vamsa Bhaskara* and *Vira satsaī*. He was born in 1872 in Rājasthān state, India, and wrote about the place where he lived. His *Vamsa Bhaskara* consists of the deeds of the Rājput princes who ruled Rājasthān, then called Rājputāna, during the poet's lifetime. His *Vira satsaī* is a cycle of heroic couplets extolling the deeds of historical heroes. Misrama is considered to be the originator of Rājasthāni literature. He died in 1952. (Dudley and Lang 1969)

Silvestre de Balboa composed a two-canto epic *Mirror of Patience* in 1608 about Cuba's resistance to attacks by "Lutheran pirates." Here French privateers burn and plunder a Spanish settlement in Cuba.

 # MONGO, BWANA

Swahili poet (fl. 18th c.), credited as author of the earliest known original Swahili epic, *Utendi wa Tambuka* (Lay of Tabuk, or The poem of the battle of Tabuk, 1728). The *utendi* form consists of four short hemistichs of which the first three rhyme together and the fourth carries a rhyme repeated as the terminal rhyme of each stanza. Mongo's poem, rooted in Arabic written literature, is written with "raw energy and superficial religiosity." It is preserved in the library of the Seminar für Afrikanische Sprachen, Hamburg, Germany. (Dudley and Lang 1969; Westley [RAL] 1991)

 # MOORE, THOMAS

Irish poet, author of *Lalla Rookh* (1817). He was born in 1779 in Dublin to a middle-class Catholic family that had been dispossessed of their lands in Bloody

Mary's reign. His mother's family were Irish Protestants who had fled to Ireland to escape persecution in Mary's time, but his mother converted to her husband's Catholic faith. Tom showed precocious tendencies early, composing verses at the age of 11. The family was musical, and he soon developed an ear for music as well.

The Dublin of his boyhood was a city of violent emotions. In 1781, Ireland got its independent Parliament and fought the British over the Catholic question. Inspired by the French Revolution, a revolutionary society called the United Irishmen was organized, its goal to overthrow English domination.

Moore began studies at Trinity College in January 1795. He formed a close friendship with Edward Hudson and Robert Emmet, both of whom later became involved in political intrigue (Hudson was imprisoned and Emmett died on the gallows). Charges of Moore's disloyalty to the Irish cause at this time produced a scorn for him among the more nationalistic Irishmen.

After completing his studies at Trinity, Moore sought a literary career abroad, first in London, where he met Thomas Godwin, Scott, Shelley, and Lord Byron (with whom he formed a lifelong friendship). Later he went to Bermuda, then the United States, where his disparaging comments provoked American antagonism.

The first number of his *Irish Melodies* appeared in 1808, and the tenth and last in 1834. These, which included such favorites as "The Last Rose of Summer" and "Believe Me If All Those Endearing Young Charms," were to earn him a reputation and an income that lasted a quarter of a century. Their appearance aroused sympathy for the Irish cause among the English, and Moore became a hero with the Irish nationalists.

In 1812, at the suggestion of a friend and influenced by Byron's poetry with Oriental settings, Moore began writing *Lalla Rookh,* finishing it in 1817. It immediately gave Moore a reputation rivaling that of Byron and Scott, and was easily the most translated poem of that time. Later works had political overtones (some were satires), and he devoted much of his time and energy to the Irish cause. He inherited Byron's memoirs, but he burned them to protect Byron, although he did publish *Letters and Journals of Lord Byron* and wrote his biography. He died in 1852 in Wiltshire, England. (TAP) (Jordan 1975; Strong 1937)

See also Lalla Rookh.

 # MORRIS, WILLIAM

English poet, author of *The Story of Sigurd* (1877). He was born in 1834 in Essex into the family of a wealthy London businessman of Welsh descent. The family home was a country house on the edge of Epping Forest, in which William took special delight as a boy. From the ages of 14 to 18 he attended school at Marlborough among the Wiltshire Downs. At Exeter College, Oxford, he soon formed a close and lifelong relationship with the painter Edward Burne-Jones.

The two soon discovered the works of John Ruskin, who inspired in them an enthusiasm for the life and art of the Middle Ages, a period that seemed to provide a sense of stability in the midst of the rapid changes of the Victorian Era.

At Oxford, Morris was a member of a circle of friends who came under the influence of the Socialist views of Carlyle, Ruskin, and Charles Kingsley, who found some of their inspiration for reforms in the Middle Ages. However, Morris resisted any final idealization of that period. His earliest poems and prose tales, which appeared in 1855, reflected this interest in the Middle Ages and his association with the pre-Raphaelites.

Soon afterward, with some of his old Oxford friends, he founded the firm of Morris and Company, manufacturers and decorators, where among other accomplishments he invented the Morris chair. Between 1865 and 1870 he wrote extensively. In the autumn of 1868 he met Eríkr Magnusson, a pastor who had come to England to supervise the printing of an Icelandic New Testament and who had begun some translations of Icelandic legends. Under Magnusson, Morris began to learn the Icelandic language, and soon they were collaborating on translations, including a prose version of the Sigurd story (1870).

In 1871, Morris visited Iceland with Magnusson and was deeply impressed by its rugged and desolate landcape, much of which he would later incorporate into scenes of *The Story of Sigurd*. Upon his return in 1873, he published translations of ancient Icelandic sagas, which contained a mass of legends, histories, and romances. After a year's work on it, in 1877 he published *The Story of Sigurd the Volsung, and the Fall of the Niblungs*, an epic poem retelling the Icelandic epic, the *Völsunga Saga*. It is generally considered Morris's finest poetic achievement, although it was not his only translation of an epic. He had translated Vergil's *Aeneid* in 1875, and would make a verse translation of the *Odyssey* in 1886–1887.

Occasionally his interest in Socialist reform and the ideals of the Middle Ages would creep into Morris's Icelandic work, like the flashes of social conscience in Sigurd. Most of Morris's last work was in the cause of socialism: his utopian *Dream of John Ball* (1887–1888) and *News from Nowhere* (1890).

Among his interests was the art of printing, especially (under the influence of Burne-Jones) the art of design and illustrated editions of books. In 1890 he established Kelmscott Press, which produced a revolution in book publishing with its beautifully illustrated books.

Morris continued to write up to the last days of his final illness. He died in 1896 at Hammersmith. (TAP) (Faulkner 1980; Mackail 1968; Noyes 1971)

See also Sigurd the Volsung.

 # MPU KANWA

Javanese poet (11th c.), author of the epic *Arjunavivāha* (Arjuna's wedding). Mpu Kanwa must have lived at the emperor's court during the time of Javanese ruler Airlangga (991–1049). The poet used the Indian epic *Mahābhārata* as a basis to write the life of Emperor Airlangga. He may have been chiefly responsible for the development of a national Javanese literature, written in courtly Javanese mixed with Sanskrit words, using Sanskrit meters and poetic styles. (Encyclopedia Britannica 1983)

   See also Arjunavivāha.

MTSYRI

See The Novice.

MUHAMADI

Swahili religious-epic poem by an unknown author, written in about the eighteenth century. The poem, consisting of 6,280 stanzas, is the longest written epic in any native African language. It is a versified account of the life of the prophet Muḥammad. (Knappert 1983)

 # NĀGARAKERTĀGAMA

Javanese epic (1365) by Prapanca (Prapañcha, 14th c.), purported to be a contemporary chronicle of the Majapahit Empire of East Java. A manuscript of the poem, originally called *Desá warnana* (The description of the country), was discovered in Lombok in the nineteenth century. The poem is an obvious attempt to venerate the king, emphasizing the element of royal divinity. It is considered the most important work of vernacular literature of the era. The epic covers the reign of King Kertanagara (r. 1268–1292) down through that of his great-grandson King Hayam Wuruk (r. 1350–1389), whose life and reign it details.

Kertanagara's birth to King Vishnuvardhana of Janggala and a princess of Kaḍiri is a unifying factor for the two chief factions of the realm. Thus he is named Kertanagara, meaning "Order in the Realm." Because according to Javanese cosmology a great king is to unite the two factions, Kertanagara is named king while he is still a boy (1254), prior to his father's death. The people of Janggala and Kaḍiri converge upon the capital city of Tumapel, named Kutaraja, thenceforth called Singhasāri. Tumapel is also known by the name Singhasāri.

Kertanagara's father continues as de facto ruler until Kertanagara comes of age in 1268. He marries a princess of Champa (South Vietnam). The epic depicts him as deeply religious, a follower of Tantric Buddhism. When Kublai Khan sends a demand for tribute (1289), Kertanagara refuses to pay and cuts the ambassador's face and ears. However, before Kublai Khan can retaliate, during a Tantric ritual drinking bout Kertanagara is killed by Jayakatwang, rebel leader of Kaḍiri (1292). In turn, Jayakatawang is overthrown by Kertanagara's son-in-law, who becomes known as Kertarajasa. In time Kertarajasa forces the Mongols to withdraw. Kertarajasa and his son rule with hardship, putting down several uprisings from the new capital of Majapahit.

The poet particularly praises the warrior Gajah Mada who, during the reign of King Jayanagara (r. 1309–1328), serves as head of the royal bodyguard, escorting the king to safety in 1319 during a rebellion led by Kuti, who captures the capital. Gajah Mada spreads the rumor that the king is dead, and when he sees how his subjects grieve and how unpopular Kuti is, he organizes an insurrection, ousting Kuti and placing Jayanagara back in power. But in 1328, after the king appropriates Gajah Mada's wife, Gajah Mada instructs the court physician, Tancha, in how to "treat" the ailing king. After the king dies, Gajah Mada has Tancha executed and places the king's daughter, Tribhuvana, on the throne.

When Tribhuvana comes to power (ca. 1328/1329–1350), Gajah Mada becomes chief minister. The poet, court poet and historian at the time, calls him "eloquent, sharp of speech, upright, and sober-minded." Through Gajah Mada's efforts, Javanese influence spreads to Sumatra, Borneo, and Bali. In 1350, Tribhuvana resigns in favor of her son, Hayam Wuruk, who reigns as Rajasanagara. The epic, composed during the height of Hayam Wuruk's reign, praises the era as Java's most glorious period.

One section describes the New Year's celebration, when visitors from India as well as notables from Java and emissaries of the vassal states attend a purifying ceremony in which the king is purged with holy water. Afterward, many fine speeches are delivered in which the ruler's role as the receptacle of divinity is emphasized. Royal divinity cleanses the world of impurities, enabling its inhabitants to fulfill their obligations to the gods. (Dudley and Lang 1969; Preminger 1974)

See also Prapanca.

 # *NATCHEZ, LES*

French prose epic (1826) by Vicomte François-René de Chateaubriand (1768–1848). The poem, consisting of 12 books, was written between 1794 and 1799 while the poet was in England. He originally intended it to be part of a work of Christian apologetics, *Le Génie du Christianisme* (1802), but he abandoned the idea. The poem continues the story of René, told in two other works: *René* (publ. 1805) and *Atala* (publ. 1801). In the former, the boy René, reared in idyllic surroundings with his beloved sister Amélie, is grieved when he learns the reason she has taken vows in a convent: her passion for him, which has escalated beyond sisterly affection. He leaves for the wilds of America, where he meets an old Indian, Chactas, and a missionary, Père Souël, to whom he relates his story. In the latter, a prose romance, Chactas tells how, as a youth, he is captured by a hostile tribe but is saved by the maiden Atala, a Christian convert who had promised her mother that she would take the veil. They flee together, finally reaching the mission of Père Aubry. Atala wants to marry Chactas but, remembering her promise to her mother, knows that she cannot, so she takes poison. The two men bury her in the forest. Later, Chactas learns that Aubry has been murdered and lies buried beside Atala.

Les Natchez continues the story of René and Chactas. The Natchez are the Indians after whom a Louisiana town, founded by the French in 1716, is named. The Natchez revolted against the colonists and were all but wiped out. (Harvey and Heseltine 1959)

See also Chateaubriand, Vicomte François-René de.

NAWÂ'Î
(Real name Mîr 'Alî Shîr)

Turkish poet, greatest poet of classical Chaghatay Turkish literature, author of five Romantic epics (1484–1485) modeled after Nizâmî's *Khamseh*. He was born in 1441 in Herât into an aristocratic family. After studying at Mashhad, he spent some time in Samarkand, returning to Herât in 1469 when his former classmate, Sultan Husayn Bayqara, came into power. He became the sultan's adviser, except for a brief period (1487–1494) when he fell out of favor. In addition to the epics, he wrote many occasional poems, collected into one volume in Persian and four in Turkish. He wrote *Lisân al-tayr* (The language of the birds), inspired by 'Attar's *Conference of the Birds,* and *Mahbûb al-Qulûb* (The heart's beloved), a satire of contemporary society written in rhyming prose, modeled after his friend Jâmî's *Bahâristân.* Largely due to his prose treatise "Contention of Two Languages," comparing Persian and Turkish for use for belles-lettres, Turkish was accepted during his day as a literary language. He died in 1501 in Herât. (Dudley and Lang 1969)

NEIHARDT, JOHN GREENLEAF
(Later changed to John Gneisenau Neihardt)

American poet, author of the epics *The Divine Enchantment* (1900), now lost, and *Cycle of the West.* He was born in 1881 on a farm near Sharpsburg, Illinois. As a boy he moved with his mother to his grandfather's farm in Wayne, Nebraska, where he later attended Nebraska Normal College. According to Neihardt, at age 11 he had a dream much like the visions of Black Elk, leading to his interest in poetry. In college he became interested in the classical epics and Hindu mysticism. This led to an epic drawn from the Hindu, *The Divine Enchantment* (1900). Dissatisfied with the work, he bought up all the copies he could locate and burned them.

He worked as an editor for a newspaper in Bancroft, Nebraska, and as a clerk for an Indian trader and land agent, a position that led to a close relationship with the nearby Omaha Indians. Out of these experiences he wrote short stories about the fur-trappers and Indian life, and lyric poetry. From boyhood he had a fascination with American rivers, and in 1908 traveled in his own boat down the Missouri River from Fort Benton, Montana, to Sioux City, Iowa, an experience described in his *The River and I* (1908). The river appears again in *Cycle of the West.* The latter work, written over a period of 28 years, fulfilled his dream of writing an American epic. He was also the author of *Black Elk Speaks* (1932) and a novel, *When the Tree Flowered* (1951).

For a while in the 1920s, Neihardt was a literary editor for the St. Louis *Post Dispatch.* In 1921 he was named poet laureate of Nebraska. From 1943 to the end of the war he served as director of information for the Bureau of Indian

Affairs. In 1949 he went to the University of Missouri at Columbia as poet-in-residence. In his last years he worked on his autobiography; the first volume, *All Is But a Beginning*, appeared in 1973. He was at work on a second volume at the time of his death in 1974 at Columbia. At his death, Sioux Indians, at their own request, held a sacred ceremony at the close of the funeral. (TAP) (Aly 1976; Whitney 1976)

See also *Cycle of the West.*

 # NEOCLASSICISM

A term that refers to a revival or adaptation of classical style in literature. In Europe, particularly in England and France, the revival occurred primarily in the seventeenth and eighteenth centuries, although the time frame varies in other countries. Neoclassicism is characterized by the same traditional established formula, fixed standards, discipline, restraint, objective reason, and polish that characterized the period of classicism. For example, English neoclassical poetry almost exclusively uses the flawless heroic couplet. (Hornstein 1973)

 # NERUDA, PABLO

Pen name of Chilean poet Ricardo Eliecer Neftalí Reyes Basoalto, author of *Canto General* (1950) and winner of the Nobel Prize in literature in 1971. He was born in 1904 in Parral, Chile. His father, José del Carmen Reyes Morales, was a railroad worker, and his mother, Rosa Basoalto, was a schoolteacher who died of tuberculosis when Neruda was less than two months old. Neruda claimed to have Indian ancestors whose culture inspired him. Two months after his mother died, the family moved to Temuco, where his father married Trinidad Candia Marverde. Neruda attended Temuco Boys' school from 1910 to 1920. Against his father's wishes, he began writing and publishing poetry at a young age, eventually assuming a pen name.

In 1921 he moved to Santiago to study at the Instituto Pedagógico, intending to become a French teacher. In 1923 he published *Veinte poemas de amor y canción desperada*, ardent love poems written in the vernacular that captured the imagination of people of all strata in Latin America and Spain.

Because he wanted to go to Europe, he applied for a post in the diplomatic corps. In 1927 he was accepted, but posted to Rangoon instead. Following a tour in Rangoon, he was sent to Colombo and then Singapore. During this period—a melancholy one for him—he wrote a major book, *Residencia en la tierra*, which revolutionized Spanish poetry and established him as a powerful surrealist poet. Although written in the 1920s, the collection remained unpublished until 1933. In 1930, while in Java, Neruda married María Antonieta Haagenar Vogelzanz, of Dutch descent. The couple had one daughter.

Neruda returned to Chile in 1932 and was soon named consul in Buenos Aires. During the next year, he met Spanish poet Federico García Lorca (1899–1936), who was touring Argentina, and the two became close friends. In 1934 Neruda became consul in Barcelona, and the following year he was transferred to Madrid. He became associated with a group of Spanish poets known as "The Generation of '27": Lorca, Rafael Alberti, Pedro Salinas, and Vicente Aleixandre, to name a few. He championed the shepherd-poet Miguel Hernández and was at the hub of a great surge of Spanish arts, which came to an abrupt end with the Spanish civil war. The year of Franco's revolt (1936) brought an end to his marriage—he had already become romantically linked with Delia del Carril, an Argentine whom he married in Madrid—and a beginning of his active commitment to politics. His friend Lorca's assassination (1936) was only one of the unspeakable Fascist acts that thrust Neruda into the maelstrom of political activism. He was dismissed as consul. He went first to Barcelona and then to Paris, organizing opposition to fascism in the artistic community. He returned to Chile (1937) and began marshaling the same kind of support for the Spanish republic. He also published a book about the Spanish civil war, *España en el corazón* (1937).

In 1939 his government sent him to Paris to help fleeing Spanish refugees find new homes. He returned to Chile in 1940, but very shortly was sent to Mexico as consul general. By this time he was widely known and respected not only as a poet, but as a cultural and political leader. His writing was greatly influenced by World War II and new Fascist atrocities.

In 1943 he published *Canto General de Chile*, which later became Book VII of his *Canto General*. On his way back to Chile that year, he visited the ruins of Macchu Picchu, inspiring his poem *Alturas de Macchu Picchu* (1944), later incorporated into *Canto General* as Book II. He was elected senator in 1944 and became a member of the Chilean Communist party, campaigning for González Videla for president, the candidate his party supported. But once elected, Videla reneged on his campaign promises and moved to outlaw the Communist party. In 1947, from Caracas, Neruda published an open letter calling Videla a traitor, and this action resulted in charges of treason against Neruda. An order was issued for his arrest, and he went into hiding for a year. He escaped on horseback over the Andes into Argentina in 1949, borrowed a passport from Guatemalan novelist Miguel Ángel Asturias, and traveled to Paris.

By 1950 he was back in Mexico, where he published the *Canto General* to great critical acclaim. While in Mexico he met Chilean Matilde Urrutia, who became his companion and later his wife. In 1953 he published anonymously a collection of love poems dedicated to her, *Versos del capitán*. During the next dozen years he traveled and wrote, championing political causes. Two of his later volumes, however, *Cantos ceremoniales* (1961) and *Memorial de Isla Negra* (1964), were nostalgic returns to his seaside home of Isla Negra.

When his old friend Salvador Allende became president, Neruda accepted a post as ambassador to France. That same year (1971) he received the Nobel Prize in literature. However, he contracted cancer and was forced to return to Santiago in 1972, gravely ill. There he witnessed Allende's downfall, aided by machinations of the U.S. government. Neruda died in Santiago in 1973. (Neruda [Intro, Roberto González Echevarría] 1991)

See also Canto General.

 # NEW COUNCIL

Czech beast epic (14th c.) by Smil Flaška of Pardubice (1348–1403). The poem, containing 2,116 verses, is an allegory and satire in which a parliament made up of various animals gives counsel to the lion king. Showing French and English influences, the epic provides the profile of a good prince, or a manual of conduct for princes in general. It was written to defend the rights of Bohemian nobility against the encroaching power of the king. (Čiževskij 1971; Dvornik 1962)

See also Flaška, Smil.

 # THE NEW WORLD AND ITS CONQUEST
(*Nuevo mundo y conquista*)

Spanish epic (ca. 1580) by Mexican poet Francisco de Terrazas (1525?–1600?). Terrazas was the firstborn son of conquistador Francisco de Terrazas (d. 1569), who came to Mexico as Cortés's majordomo, later *alcalde ordinario* (justice of the peace) of Mexico City. The poem, left unfinished at his death, is extant only in fragments, but it and other of Terrazas's work won the poet extravagant praise from Cervantes, Dorantes de Carranza, and others. The poem is written in octaves and was inspired by Ercilla y Zuñiga's *La Araucana* and probably by the courtly "Italian style" of Spanish poet Gutierre de Cetina, a guest in Mexico at the time, with whom Terrazas is presumed to have had close contact.

In begins "Not of Cortés and his mighty deeds,/Nor of the extraordinary victories do I sing,/But of those brave and invincible hearts/Whose valor amazes the world. . . ." In one fragment the poet refers to the Guanajos Islands expedition of Francisco Hernández de Córdoba. Another fragment contains a comparison of Cortés to Xerxes, emphasizing the small size of Cortés's army. It includes a vivid description of shark fishing and the speech Cortés made to the Indians of Cozumel through the interpreter Melchorejo. The most complete episode of the poem is the idyllic love story of Huitzel and Quetzal. The poet says of New Spain's treatment of the natives: "You have been a rigorous step-mother to your own/And a sweet, merciful mother to strangers. . . ."

Works written in Mexico at the time were not well received; most poets returned to Spain to write their poetry. Terrazas is considered the first native-born Spanish-American poet, and *The New World and Its Conquest* is the first epic by a native Spanish-American poet. (Anderson-Imbert 1969; Jones 1966; Peña 1968)

See also Terrazas, Francisco de.

Spaniard Hernán Cortés led a small force of conquistadors against the New World Aztec empire in Mexico in 1532. Francisco de Terrazas, son of Cortes's majordomo, wrote of the conquest in *The New World and Its Conquest*, an epic from about 1580. Gabriel Lobo Lasso de la Vega recorded his fellow countryman's exploits in *Cortés valeroso* (Intrepid Cortés) in 1588 and American author Archibald MacLeish published *Conquistador* (1932). A scene from the Lienzo Tlaxcala includes Cortés, seated, meeting emissaries from Tlateloco. His companion, Marina, translates while Spanish soldiers and native allies look on.

 # NGUYEN DU
(Full name Nguyen-Du Thanh-Hien; also To Nhu)

Vietnamese poet and statesman, author of the national epic of Vietnam, *Kim-vân-Kiêu* (trans. 1943). He was born in 1765 in Tien Dien, Vietnam. For generations his family had been mandarins serving the Le dynasty. At the age of 19, Nguyen Du passed the mandarin examinations and took a military post. Three years later a rebel uprising forced the Le regime out of office, and after efforts to restore it failed, Nguyen Du retreated to the area of his native village, settling in the Hong Link mountains nearby. In 1802 the powerful Nguyen family gained control, and its new ruler, Nguyen Anh, called Gia Long, summoned Nguyen Du to court. Returning to public life with reluctance, the poet was appointed to several positions. By 1813 he had been promoted to the position of Column of the Empire and was sent to Peking as head of Vietnam's official delegation.

In China he translated a historical novel from the Ming period into Vietnamese poetry. Written in couplets of six and eight syllables, the poem, *Kim-vân-Kiêu*, is more than just the love story of Kim and Kieu; it actually embodies much of Confucian teaching and was to become the national epic of Vietnam. He wrote other poems as well, many in Chinese.

Over the next seven years he was assigned twice more to ambassadorial delegations to Peking. In 1820, as he readied himself to depart on the second trip, he died in Hue. (Dudley and Lang 1969)

See also *Kim-vân-Kiêu.*

NIBELUNGENLIED
(Also *Der Nibelunge Nôt*)

Middle High German heroic epic poem (ca. 1200–1210) by an unknown author. The most powerful of the German epics of the Middle Ages, it consists of 2,300 rhyming four-line stanzas (*aabb*). Each line is divided into two sections, each section in the first three lines having three stresses, the last line usually extended. For a synopsis of *Nibelungenlied*, see the *Encyclopedia of Traditional Epics*. (Garland and Garland 1986)

NIZÂMÎ
(Also Nezāmī; full name Elyās Yüsof Nezāmī Ganjavī)

Persian poet, author of the *Khamseh* (The quintet), also known as *Panj Ganj* (Five treasures), a collection of five minor epic poems. He was born about 1141 in Ganja (present-day Kirovabad), Azerbaijan. His writing shows a wide knowledge of history, astronomy and other sciences, literature, and music, although he left Ganja only once in his life, to be presented to the ruling prince. His work earned him the patronage of several princes, as well as the reputation as the first great dramatic poet and the greatest Romantic poet in Persian literature. He established the *masnavī* a form for long and continuous narrative, setting a pattern imitated even into the seventeenth century.

Although much of his work has been lost, the surviving masterpiece is the *Khamseh,* comprised of 30,000 *masnavī* (rhyming couplets) making up five poems. The first, dedicated to Fakhr al-Din Bahrāmshā, was written about 1163–1164, although many of the dates are conjectural, based on dedications and mention in the works of current rulers. Entitled *Makhzan olasrār* (The treasury of mysteries), it is a didactic poem, the only one of the five that is not an epic narrative. The second, *Khosrow o Shīrīn*, a Romantic epic, was presumably written about 1180 because it praises Toghril II, Ganja ruler Muḥammad ibn Eldigüz Jahān Pahlavān, Qïzïl Arslān, and Nusrat al-Din Abū Bakr. The third, *Leyli o-Mejnūn* (The story of Leyla and Majnun), the retelling of the desert romance of Majnūn and Lailā, was written about 1188–1192, and is dedicated to the Sharvānshāh Akhastān I (r. ca. 1162–1199 or later). The fourth, his masterpiece, *Haft Paykar* (The seven beauties), is dated 1197 and dedicated to 'Alā' al-Dīn Körp Arslān, ruler of Maragha. The fifth, *Sikandar*, or *Eskandar-nāmeh* (Book of Alexander the Great), appeared about 1200–1202. This final poem is divided into two books, *Sharaf-nāmeh* (Book of honor) and *Iqbāl-nāmeh* (Book of fortune).

Nizâmî died about 1203–1217, possibly 1209, in Ganja, having set a standard for Persian poetry that would never be equaled except perhaps by Jāmī. (Browne 1983; Kritzeck 1964; Nizami 1995)

See also Haft Paykar; Khamseh; Maṡnavī.

NOAH

German religious epic (1750) by Johann Jakob Bodmer (1698–1783). Based on the biblical account of the Great Flood, the poem was inspired by Friedrich Gottlieb Klopstock's success with his portentous epic *Der Messias* (first part publ. 1728). However, Bodmer's poem was no more successful than his other religious or historical epics. (Garland and Garland 1986)

See also Bodmer, Johann Jakob.

NONNUS

Helenized Egyptian poet, author of *Dionysiăcă*, a Greek hexameter epic poem in 48 books. He was born about A.D. 400 in Panopolis, or Akhmīm, in Egypt. He lived most of his life in Alexandria. He was well read, possibly because of the famous library at Alexandria, and had a vast acquaintance with Greek classics and legends, from Homer to the Orphic hymns and the Latin Ovid. *Dionysiăcă* is one of the chief sources for our present knowledge of the Dionysiac cycle of legends. The monumental poem describes, in books 13–48, an expedition to India by the god Dionysus. The work was often imitated, earning him the reputation as the leading Greek poet of the Roman era, the last Greek epic period. Late in life, after he had converted to Christianity, Nonnus wrote a hexameter paraphrase of the Gospel of John called *Metabole*. His style, with daring metaphors and his vast acquaintance with legends and other literature, made him famous in his day, and he became a leader in the last Greek epic school. (TAP) (Howatson and Chilvers 1993; Trypanis 1981; Wright [F. A.] 1932; Wright [W. C.] 1907)

See also Dionysiaca.

THE NOVICE
(*Mtsyri*)

Russian epic poem (1837) by Mikhail Lermontov (1814–1841). The poet explained the title: "Mtsyri in the Georgian language means 'a monk who does not serve,' something in the nature of a novice." The poet first began writing the poem, at that time entitled *The Confessions,* in 1829 when he was about 15 or 16, but he never completed it. Five years later he wrote a second version entitled *Boyar orsha,* but apparently was not satisfied with it. In 1837 he visited an old monastery in Georgia, where he found a solitary monk in residence. The monk related his life's story, and Lermontov used it basically unchanged in the new version of the poem, which has been labeled Lermontov's spiritual and psychological autobiography. It contains 26 cantos written in a loose Romantic style.

In Canto I the poet describes the Georgian monastery, attended now by "just one old watchman, feeble and grey," whom both men and death have forgotten.

In Canto II, one day a Russian general rides down from the mountains on the way to Tiflis. He has with him a prisoner—a child who is ill. No groan escapes the child's lips: "In pride/and in silence he all but died." The monk takes pity on the child, keeping him at the monastery even after he recovers. One night the boy vanishes. After a three-day search, he is found on the steppe, thin, feeble, and febrile. He will not speak, and each day he grows weaker. His friend the monk comes and prays for him. The boy raises his head with his last bit of strength and speaks.

In Canto III the boy thanks the monk for coming to hear his confession. He has done no ill to others, he says. He has had one passion, for which he does not pray for pardon.

In Canto IV the boy expresses regret that he has been deprived of home, friends, parents, even native land. He once took an oath that at some time, just for a moment, his "burning breast" would be "pressed/against someone's" from his own land. Now he realizes that his dream is dead, and, "as I've lived, I'll find my grave/in alien soil, an orphaned slave."

In Canto V he regrets that he must die so young, while his passions are still sharp.

In Canto VI he lists all the sights he saw during the days after his disappearance. While he was looking at the "grey bastion—Caucasus," a secret voice told him that he once lived there. He begins to remember the past.

In Canto VII he remembers his father's hall, his village. He remembers guns, his father's armor, his sisters singing over his crib. He remembers the family gathered around the hearth in the evenings, listening to tales of men of long ago.

In Canto VIII he explains why he ran away: He wanted to *live,* if only for three days.

In Canto IX he describes running for hours, all night, until exhausted. Then he "slid/snakelike, away from man, and hid."

In Canto X he describes hearing "a hundred angry voices" at daybreak, and finding himself on the "sheer/brink of a frightful cliff" high above "an angry torrent."

In Canto XI he listens to the voices, nature's voices, but nowhere is "one single human tongue" to praise the morning hour's majesty. But soon he begins to "pine and thirst."

In Canto XII he sets off downhill to the water but hides when he hears a Georgian maiden's sweet singing.

In Canto XIII the girl, in humble dress, brings her pitcher to fill in the stream. He watches her take her full jug back to her cabin. He is filled with yearning.

In Canto XIV night comes and he falls asleep. In his dreams he sees the Georgian girl, and again he is filled with sweet yearning. He determines to walk until he reaches his native land.

In Canto XV he tears his way through the brush, but always on the horizon's edge are the same woods. He throws himself down in despair, determined not to make even the feeblest cry aloud.

In Canto XVI, as he lies crying on the ground, a snow leopard springs out, rolls on its back, and begins gnawing on a bone.

In Canto XVII he waits until the leopard, smelling an enemy, notices him and charges. The boy breaks his cudgel over the leopard's head. The animal falls, bleeding, but gets up again.

In Canto XVIII the leopard charges again. They wrestle and fall to the ground together. As the boy howls like a wolf, the leopard dies.

In Canto XIX the boy shows the monk the scars on his chest, then resumes the story of his quest for his native land.

In Canto XX the boy describes leaving the woodland knowing that "in the flower/of years . . ./I must . . . carry with me to the tomb/the longing for my home."

In Canto XXI, unlike the mighty horse that, losing its rider on a strange steppe, can find the straightest, shortest way home, the boy cannot go home, although daybreak comes and he can see.

In Canto XXII the boy hides in the grass as motes circle in the sun and vapor steams from white rocks.

In Canto XXIII he sees the cloister in the distance. He tries to rise, tries to shout, but can do neither. He seems to be in a river and to hear a fish's "small voice's silvery strain" enticing him to stay. Finally the "raving fit" leaves his body.

In Canto XXIV he relates how he was found and brought here. His only regret is that he will never reach his homeland.

In Canto XXV he asks the monk to hold his hand, saying he would barter eternity for a few moments among "those steep and strange/rocks where my childhood used to range. . . ."

In Canto XXVI he asks to be buried in the monastery garden facing the Caucasus. He hopes "some brother, or some friend" from his homeland will bend over him and sing to him about "that country, once my own" so he can sleep in peace. (Johnston 1983)

See also Lermontov, Mikhail Yuryevich.

THE NUN'S PRIEST'S TALE

Mock-heroic poem from Chaucer's *Canterbury Tales,* drawn from the fables of Reynard the Fox. A widow's rooster, Chauntecleer (Chanticleer) rules seven hens. He allows his favorite, Pertelote, to dismiss his warning dream of being captured by a fox. Don Russell, the fox, flatters him, enticing him to sing. When Chauntecleer closes his eyes to crow, the fox grabs him. Chauntecleer tricks the fox into opening his mouth to taunt the pursuing widow and her helpers, then flies to a treetop, resisting the fox's further flatteries. (Chaucer 1969)

OBERGE, EILHART VON

See Eilhart von Oberge.

OBERON

German romance epic (1778–1780) by Christophe Martin Wieland (1733–1813). The poem, consisting of about 7,000 lines written in 12 cantos of ottava rima, tells the stories of Huon of Bordeaux and Rezia, derived from a medieval prose romance, and of Oberon and Titania, influenced in part by medieval fairy lore and in part by Shakespeare's *Midsummer Night's Dream,* which Wieland had earlier translated into German. In it, the emperor Charlemagne serves as a deus ex machina. The poem was enthusiastically received by Romantic writers and was the inspiration for an opera by Carl Maria von Weber. The earliest published translation into English, in Spenserian stanzas, was by William Sotheby in 1798. However, the best translation into English, in the original ottava rima, was by John Quincy Adams, at that time minister to Prussia and later the sixth president of the United States. However, it was not published until 1940.

In this epic, around a medieval legend Wieland wove motifs drawn from past fantasies, from the Greek Heliodorus to later fairy lore, with magic and exotic details. The poem may also be viewed as a resurrection of the old moral tale, an allegory of continence and faithfulness, possibly reflecting Wieland's upbringing by a pietistic Protestant minister father.

Canto One opens with Huon's departure to the Holy Sepulchre in Jerusalem. On the way he meets Cherasmin, who accompanied Huon's father on his pilgrimage 18 years before but now joins Huon. Huon tells him how he incurred the anger of Charlemagne, who banished him and confiscated his estates, but promised a pardon if he would go to the caliph of Babylon, cut off the head of the person seated next to the caliph, claim the caliph's daughter in marriage, and bring back four of the caliph's teeth and a handful of his beard.

In Canto Two, Huon finds a resplendent palace in a forest, from which a beautiful boy rides in a silver chariot drawn by leopards. A voice warns them to go back, but Cherasmin persuades Huon to go on. They meet a group of evil nuns and monks, when suddenly a dwarf, Oberon, appears, leaning on the stalk of a lily with an ivory horn over his shoulders, which he blows. At once, everyone but Huon begins dancing. Oberon tells Huon that he has been his friend from childhood, and that he has the power to punish polluted souls like those of hypocritical nuns and monks. He waves his lily wand: The dancing stops. Oberon offers Cherasmin a draught from an empty golden cup. Cherasmin hesitates, but as soon as he puts the cup to his lips, it is full.

Oberon tells Huon to proceed with Charlemagne's mission; he gives him the ivory horn and cup with instructions to blow the horn if ever menaced by swords, whereupon his enemies will all be set to dancing. If he blows a louder blast, Oberon will appear to help him. The cup will fill up when put to the lips of an honest man, but will remain empty if held by knavish hands. Oberon admonishes Huon never to disgrace himself.

In Canto Three, Huon and Cherasmin meet the prince of Lebanon, who informs him that the giant Angulaffer lives in a castle nearby, where he keeps the prince's lady prisoner. Huon proceeds to free the lady, who tells him that the giant is now asleep, and that he can take the magic ring from the giant's finger and kill him. Huon refuses to kill a sleeping enemy, so he awakens the giant and kills him in combat. As Huon continues on his journey, he twice dreams of a beautiful lady, with whom he falls in love.

In Canto Four, as the two travel along the Euphrates River, they save the life of a Saracen being attacked by a lion. Huon offers him a drink from his magic cup, but it remains empty and burns the Saracen's hand. The Saracen blasphemes. Huon draws his sword but the Saracen flees, taking Huon's horse. In the next village Cherasmin buys an old mule, and they continue on their journey. At Baghdad, an old woman invites them into her home. She tells them she is the mother of the nurse to the sultan's daughter, who is to be married the next day to her cousin Babekan. However, the princess does not love the prince because she has dreamed of a dwarf with a handsome young man, with whom she has fallen in love. Besides, Babekan failed to keep a promise to kill a monster that has been terrorizing the land. Cherasmin advises Huon to forget the task given him by Charlemagne, and to concentrate only on winning Princess Rezia. Huon insists he will keep his word, but he is awake all night.

In Canto Five, Princess Rezia also has been awake all night, anxious about the wedding, but toward morning she falls asleep and dreams of the unknown knight. She tells her nurse, Fatme, that she will kill herself rather than marry the prince. Fatme tells her of a strange knight who spent the night at her mother's hut. The mother is called in to describe the stranger. They agree he is the unknown knight of Rezia's dreams.

Back at the hut, Huon awakens to find a suit of clothes fit for an emir, provided by Oberon so that Huon will be admitted to the hall. He proceeds to the court and recognizes Babekan, seated at the left hand of the sultan, as the Saracen he saved from the lion and who stole his horse. With one stroke he beheads Babekan. Huon and Rezia recognize each other as the persons in their dreams. Huon puts the giant's ring on Rezia's finger and claims her as his bride. Furious, the sultan and his attendants fall on Huon, so Huon blows on the horn. Immediately the whole court except Rezia begins to dance. When the spell of the horn wears off, Huon approaches the caliph and drops on one knee to ask in the name of Imperial Charles for four of his teeth and a handful of his beard. The caliph angrily asks who Charles is: "Let him pluck the teeth out himself." Huon offers a compromise: If the caliph and his people turn Christian, no more will be required of him. In a rage they all attack Huon until Cherasmin blows the horn, this time loudly. There is a terrible earthquake. The caliph and his attendants are struck motionless. Oberon appears and asks Rezia whether she wishes to remain with her father or with Huon. She chooses Huon. Oberon brings a coach drawn by four swans and driven by a child, and it carries Huon and Rezia through the air.

In Canto Six, Huon and Rezia land on the coast of Askalon. Oberon appears, giving them a casket containing the caliph's teeth and beard to take to Charlemagne. He tells them to take a ship nearby before the caliph can catch them. They are to speed to receive the nuptial blessing from the pope, but until then they must live as brother and sister, not as husband and wife. If they taste of the forbidden love, they will be separated from Oberon forever. Oberon then disppears.

Though somewhat dejected by these instructions, the lovers embark. Finding it difficult to control his feelings for Rezia, Huon occupies his time instructing her in the Christian faith. She is baptized and takes the new name of Amanda. But their passion waxes so great that Cherasmin plots with Fatme ways to bolster the virtue of Huon.

As part of the strategy, he tells Huon the January and May story of Gangolf and Rosetta, an old reformed rake married to a beautiful young girl. He is blind and so jealous that she turns to an affair with Walter, the old man's squire. One day she tricks her husband into helping her meet her lover. Oberon and Titania see what is going on. Indignant at the trick on the old man, Oberon rails against the treachery of women and declares he will punish Rosetta by restoring the husband's sight. Titania sides with the woman and declares that she will provide Rosetta with an explanation of her actions. His sight restored, Gangolf goes into a rage; Titania conceals Walter in a cloud. Thinking quickly, Rosetta tells Gangolf she has only been struggling with an evil spirit in the shape of a man in order to restore Gangolf's sight. The husband believes her, and they are reconciled. The angry Oberon tells Titania he will separate from her until a couple in love defy death or reject the glory of a throne rather than be false to each other. Despite Titania's entreaties, Oberon disappears. Since then, Oberon has dwelt in some natural retreat and makes it his pleasure to torment lovers.

Huon tells Cherasmin that if Oberon wants to be reconciled to Titania, he and Amanda are such a faithful couple. Cherasmin fears that his moral tale has had no effect.

In Canto Seven there are two ships at Lepanto, one bound for Marseilles and one for Naples. Annoyed by Cherasmin's intervention, Huon orders him to take the vessel to Marseilles and carry the casket containing the sultan's teeth and beard to Charlemagne with news that Huon will soon follow with the caliph's daughter. Then Cherasmin is to meet him in Rome. The lovers embark for Naples. Huon feels guilty about his treatment of his friend and takes it out on Amanda, treating her with reserve, much to her distress. But one night, after both are kept awake by their passion, Amanda goes to his cabin, where after a struggle they surrender to their feelings. Immediately there is a violent storm, and the ship is in danger of sinking. The captain calls everyone together to determine the guilty person. Amanda and Huon plunge into the sea together. The sea is instantly calmed.

At the very instant the lovers break their vow of chastity, the ivory horn and golden cup given them by Oberon vanish. However, the giant's ring, still on Amanda's finger, keeps them from sinking. After landing on a desert island, they live in a cave. Amanda discovers she is pregnant. In desperation Huon explores the rugged island, a fearful mass of cliffs and ruins, and barely escapes falling off a rocky cliff.

In Canto Eight, Huon finds a pleasant spot, a paradise, and a hermit named Alfonso, who has lived there for 30 years. Huon brings Amanda there. Alfonso tells his history as a prince of Leon who was shipwrecked with his wife, who bore him three sons, but all died in the plague. He fled to this barren place with an aged servant. They found this elysium built by Titania as a retreat after her quarrel with Oberon. Years later the servant died, and in solitude Alfonso has found God in Nature here.

When Huon tells Alfonso his story, Alfonso advises Huon to continue chastity in order to win back Oberon's favor. When spring comes, Amanda's time approaches. Titania has seen the couple arrive, and hopes they will be the couple needed to reunite her with Oberon. She has a grotto there, with her throne. Amanda discovers it, and, assisted by Titania and her fairies, delivers a baby boy. Titania then disappears. Huon finds the grotto and sees Amanda with the baby at her breast.

In Canto Nine the ship, from which Huon and Amanda were thrown, is wrecked on the coast of Tunis. Fatme is taken captive and sold as a slave to the king's gardener. Cherasmin arrives safely in Marseilles, but instead of delivering the casket to Charlemagne, goes to Rome. Huon is not there, so he disguises himself as a pilgrim and sets out to find him. He wanders for two years to many ports, finally arriving at Tunis and finding Fatme, who tells him all that happened until the lovers cast themselves into the sea. Hoping Oberon has saved them, Cherasmin waits in Tunis, hiring out as a laborer in the royal garden.

After Huon and Amanda have been on the island for three years, Titania learns from the stars of some misfortune to Amanda, so she steals the child and turns it over to her three fairies to keep in her bower. She plucks three rosebuds from the garland around her head, informing the fairies that when the rosebuds turn to lilies, they will know that she and Oberon have been reconciled. Huon and Amanda find Alfonso dead. The garden has disappeared, and all that is left are rocks and precipices. Amanda discovers that the child is gone. In their search they become separated, and Amanda is seized by Tunisian sailors who have landed to take on fresh water. When Huon hears her shrieks, he rushes to her but is overpowered by the sailors, who leave with Amanda, planning to sell her to the king of Tunis.

In Canto Ten, Titania is unable to help Huon but finds the magic ring Amanda has lost, the nuptial ring she gave to Oberon. Onboard ship, the captain is touched by Amanda's moans and assures her that she will become queen of Tunis. Titania appears to her in a vision and tells her that her son and Huon are both still alive. In the meantime, Oberon sends one of his attendant spirits to take Huon to the seraglio in Tunis, where he is reunited with Cherasim. He learns that Fatme is a slave there. Huon proposes to use some of the jewels in the casket to search for Amanda and purchase her release. Fatme arrives with news that a ship has been wrecked on the coast, its only survivor a beautiful woman, now with the king and queen; surely it is Amanda. Huon decides to work at the castle disguised as the gardener's nephew.

In Canto Eleven, Huon frequents the seraglio gardens where the women spend their evenings. When Queen Almansaris sees Huon, she falls in love and plots to bring him into the part of the harem she controls. King Almanzor falls in love with Amanda, but she is cold to him. The queen uses the king's lust, proposing that Amanda be lodged in a distant section of the harem where he won't be disturbed, but also where he won't disturb the queen. Fatme suggests to Huon that he send Amanda a *Maneh,* braided with the initiaLS A and H. It comes into the hands of the queen, who thinks the H stands for Hassan, Huon's assumed name, and the A for Almansaris. She sends word to Huon to come at midnight. He thinks the message is from Amanda, but when he reaches the harem, he is astonished to find the queen instead. Unsuccessful in seducing him, the queen is angered.

In Canto Twelve the queen plots to draw Huon into the garden while she is bathing and renew her efforts at seduction. Again he resists her, but she throws her arms around him with such strength that Huon is obliged to call upon Oberon to protect him. Discovered by the king, the queen accuses Huon of forcing her. The king orders that Huon be burned the next day. The queen comes to Huon and offers to set him on the throne if he will return her love. When Huon refuses, she storms out in a fit of rage.

Fatme tells Amanda of Huon's fate. Amanda flies to the king and begs him to spare the life of his gardener. Learning that Huon is Amanda's husband, the king agrees to do so if she will become his queen. When she refuses, he threatens that they will both perish in the flames. The next morning, when both are tied to the stake, there is a clap of thunder, the earth shakes, the flame expires, and the ivory horn suddenly appears around Huon's neck. He blows the horn, and all Tunis begins to dance, even the king, reluctantly, with the queen. A coach drawn by swans bears the lovers to the palace of Oberon, who no longer appears as a dwarf but as a handsome youth. Titania is there. Huon and Amanda have fulfilled Oberon's condition for their reconciliation: The lovers defied death and rejected a throne rather than be false to each other. Three nymphs descend, their rosebuds turned to lilies. Titania gives the lovers a garland of myrtle, a symbol of constancy: as long as they keep it they will enjoy happiness. The fairies appear with little Huonnet, whom Titania hands to his mother.

The next day Huon and Amanda are taken to Paris, arriving at a tournament given by Charlemagne, where Huon wins back his lands and shows Charlemagne that he has fulfilled the emperor's demands. The emperor is reconciled and declares, "May our Empire never want a princely youth like thee to guard and grace the land!" (TAP) (Adams [Faust, intro] 1940; Van Abbé 1961)

See also Huon of Bordeaux; Wieland, Christoph Martin.

ODÉSSIA

(Or *I Odysseia,* The odyssey; a modern sequel)

Greek epic (1938, trans. 1958) by Nikos Kazantzakis (1885–1957). Consisting of 33,333 lines in 24 books, the epic contains passages of great beauty, combining the vernacular of Greek fishermen and shepherds with legends and ballads rich in detail. Begun in 1925 and intended to be a reflection of the poet's philosophy, the poem went through seven revisions as Kazantzakis's philosophical attitudes developed.

He said that his work depicts modern man attempting "to find deliverance by passing through all the stages of contemporary anxieties and by pursuing the most daring hopes." It is in that sense an autobiographical allegory.

The poem begins with a prologue that is an invocation to the sun. Mediterranean light and Greek fire continue as images throughout the book.

The hero, a modern Odysseus, undertakes a journey of spirit, wandering in a world of philosophical thought, beset by nihilistic doubts, agonizing over the meanings of life and death, struggling to find truth and freedom.

Beginning with Book XXII, the story melds with the Homeric version at the point following Odysseus's slaying of his wife Penelope's would-be suitors. He continues his journey down the coast of Africa all the way to the South Pole, where he dies. (For a synopsis of Homer's *Odyssey,* see the *Encyclopedia of Traditional Epics.*)

It ends with an epilogue that is again an invocation to the sun. (Kazantzakís [Nikos] 1958)

ODILJENJE SIGETSKO

Croatian epic (1684) written by Pavao Ritter Vitezovic (1652–1713) and published in Linz. (Gazi 1973)

ODYSSEY

Greek epic poem (ca. 850 B.C.) traditionally attributed to Homer. For a synopsis see the *Encyclopedia of Traditional Epics.*

OGIER THE DANE

Hero of several epics. As Ogier de Danemarcke, he is the hero of a French chanson de geste, *Le Chevalerie Ogier Danemarcke,* which is part of the *Doon de Mayence* cycle; and of the French *Enfances Ogier* by Adenet le Roi. He is the hero of a fifteenth-century anonymous Middle High German epic that relates his childhood, his feats against the Saracens, and other adventures, including warring against Charlemagne. As Holger Danske, he is a Danish hero and the subject of a Danish folk song.

In the central story, he is held at Charlemagne's court as a hostage for his father, Geoffrey of Dannemarach (originally probably referring to the marches region in the Ardennes, later coming instead to be understood to be Denmark). He gains favor by his brave deeds in Italy, but after Charles's son kills Ogier's son during a quarrel, Ogier kills the queen's nephew in revenge. He is pursued and imprisoned, but later he is released to fight the Saracens in Spain. He is awarded the fiefs of Hainaut and Brabant.

The character is identified with a Frankish warrior, Autgarius, who fought against Charlemagne and later became his ally. For more of *Doon de Mayence,* see the *Encyclopedia of Traditional Epics.* (Garland and Garland 1986; Harvey and Heseltine 1959; Siepmann 1987)

See also Adenet le Roi; *Enfances Ogier.*

 # OLSON, CHARLES JOHN

American avant-garde poet, author of *The Maximus Poems.* He was born in 1910 in Worcester, Massachusetts. His father, Karl, was a letter carrier. He attended Wesleyan University and spent a brief period as a fisherman on the *Doris M. Hawes* out of Gloucester. He was an English instructor at Clark University in Worcester, and during the summers he worked as a letter carrier in Gloucester. Through poet Wilbur Snow, his professor at Wesleyan, Olson won an Olin Fellowship at Yale for his work on the papers of Herman Melville. In 1935 his father died, leaving him with the care of his mother. In 1937 he entered a doctoral program with F. O. Mattiessen at Harvard, enrolling in a newly established graduate American Studies program that, in a broad approach to studying American civilization, brought together disciplines from the humanities and sciences. He was awarded his first Guggenheim for a study of Melville in 1939. In 1940 he was living in Gloucester with his mother, but soon moved to Washington, D.C., where he stayed until 1951. In 1947 he published *Call Me Ishmael.* He married Constance Wilcock, half-sister to Doris Huffman, fourth wife of his friend Edward Dahlberg.

Beginning in 1952 he was first an instructor and later the rector at Black Mountain College in North Carolina, an experimental school attended and staffed by a number of avant-garde writers and artists. During this time he began to exert an influence on other poets: "The Black Mountain School of

Poetry" refers to Olson's poetical theory. Primary to his theory was his sense of phrasing to achieve the most forceful presentation, the implied use of vernacular, and thus the rejection of traditional forms. His *Projective Verse* (1959) outlined his concepts.

In 1960 he published the first volume of the epic *Maximus Poems*. The second volume was published in 1968; the third was completed shortly before his death in 1970 and was published in 1975. His other volume is *Distances*. He died in 1970 in New York City. (Christensen 1979)

 # OLYMPISCHER FRÜHLING
(Olympian spring)

German-Swiss epic (1900–1906, 1910) by Carl Spitteler (1845–1924). The poem, a modern "Greek" epic, was published in four volumes from 1900 to 1906, then revised in 1910. The poet devised his own metrical scheme for the poem: six-beat rhyming couplets. It is an allegory, presenting the human condition in mythological terms.

The Olympian gods, asleep in the underworld, are summoned by Fate and climb Mount Olympus. They meet the dethroned chivalry of Kronos coming down. Once on top, they compete for the throne and for Hera's hand. Zeus wins both. Hebe, with food for immortality, yodels like an Alpine maid: "And see, on the horizon far above the pasture,/The shape in the blue sky of a slender maiden,/In the dress and demeanor of a simple shepherd,/Yet shimmering like an angel from heaven./Her hollow hand like a shell held over her mouth,/While outside shouts of joy ring through the mountain side." (1.3) As the gods acquire their full strength and nature, they wander the world, exercising their powers in manifold activities, symbolizing growth from childhood to careless youth, and the difficulties and conflicts of growing into adulthood. It also symbolizes a civilization, bursting on the scene, energetic in its youth, that suffers heroic strife and is fated to decline, but may survive if it sends out a savior rather than dominating.

The poet conveys both a sense of lofty grandeur and impending doom. In the section entitled "Theme," a bell speaks: "Through the whirling winds I see/Human sorrow graced by soul./And thou wonderst why I toll?"

Finally, when the idyllic life on Mount Olympus begins to deteriorate, Zeus creates Heracles, sending him to rescue mankind from its suffering. In the section "Heracles Passing to Earth," Heracles promises his human brothers and sisters that he will live for work "and no reward, except upon accomplished deed,/A silent, knowing glance. . . ." (Highet 1976; Runes 1961)

 # OMEROS

Contemporary West Indies epic poem (1990) by St. Lucian poet and playwright Derek Walcott (1930–). The poem, Walcott's tenth and most ambitious book of verse, led to the 1992 Nobel Prize in literature. It is a commentary on the historical passage of the common life in the Caribbean, using St. Lucia to represent the West Indies as a whole. St. Lucia has been called the Helen of the West Indies, Walcott has said, leading him to attempt a Greek-style epic about everyday Caribbean life.

Book One, Chapter I, begins in the present, with Philoctete explaining to tourists, "who try taking/his soul with their cameras," how they cut the dugout canoes. They "wound" the first cedar tree, and they pass the rum "to give us the spirit to turn into murderers." The island landscape is an idyllic scene. One of the builders is Achille. The trees are "bearded elders [who] endured the decimation/of their tribe without uttering a syllable." The canoes are to serve fishermen: one for Hector, one for Achille.

In Chapter II, white-haired Philoctete, limping from an unhealed sore on his shin, watches the fishermen put out to sea in their pirogues. Seven Seas rises early to make coffee, envying the pirogues already miles out to sea. He thinks of other boats centuries ago, thinks of Omeros. Antigone, visiting from Greece, tells the narrator that Omeros is what they call Homer in Greece. The narrator thinks *Omeros* is the conch shell's invocation: *Mer* is "both mother and sea in our Antillean patois" while *os* is "a grey bone, and the white surf as it crashes. . . ."

In Chapter III, Hector is enraged because Achille took some old bailing tin from his canoe. Although Achille replaces it, Hector still wants to fight. The villagers gather around, "ranged for the slaughter." Achille knows the duel is "over a shadow" and its name is Helen. In front of Ma Kilman's bar sits a blind man, old St. Omere, who claims to have sailed around the world—hence the nickname "Monsieur Seven Seas." Philoctete comes to the bar so Ma Kilman can put vaseline on his wound and give him some alcohol to kill the pain.

In Chapter IV, Philoctete hobbles up to his yam beds, and when the dry leaves pierce his wound he screams in pain. As he tests his knife blade, the leaves recoil "in a cold sweat." Hacking them off at the root, he says, "You all see what it's like without roots in this world?" He lies on his back and asks God's pardon; he will be patient. If a horse can endure afflictions, so can man. At a white terrace restaurant, the narrator sees a woman in a madras head-tie, coming like a "padding panther," her "head proud," although she is looking for work. It is Helen.

In Chapter V, Major Plunkett and his wife, Maud, now pig and orchid farmers, sit drinking at their usual Saturday watering hole. He is a veteran of Field Marshal Montgomery's African campaign. He had promised himself that when the war was over, he and Maud would move to the other side of the world, "somewhere, with its sunlit islands,/where what they called history could not happen." Now he thinks, "We helped ourselves/to these green islands like olives from a saucer,/munched on the pith, then spat their sucked stones. . . ." It has been a lovely life. Only a son is missing. He and Maud don't go to the fashionable Victory, where the drinkers affect upper-class accents. They see Helen walking down the beach in a yellow dress Maud altered for her. She is the prize for whom Hector and Achille vie.

In Chapter VI, Helen inquires about work as a waitress in the beach restaurant, having quit the hotel because of fresh tourists. But the white manager thinks she is too fresh. Helen reveals to a waitress, "I pregnant,/but I don't know for who." She sets up shop on the street, braiding "tourists' flaxen hair with bright beads/cane-row style. . . ."

In Chapter VII, Achille and Helen are at the market. He does not want to carry her basket: "I not your slave!" He follows her onto the beach, rams her against a van. She scratches him, he tears her yellow dress. The van belongs to Hector, who leads her inside it, "a trainer urging a panther back to its cage." As the van drives away, Achille cries. He remembers the day he lost faith in her, when he is diving for forbidden conchs and sees her and Hector together on the high wall. He drowns the conchs and they sink into the sand "without any cries." He has suspected Hector for a long time.

In Chapter VIII, Achille begins diving to the wreck of an old galleon, weighting his heel with a piece of concrete to make him sink. "She go get every red cent," he says, but he wonders, what if her love is already dead? He finds no gold coins and knows he must take conch shells from the forbidden reef if he is to make any money. Philoctetes tries to make peace between the two men, saying they have a common bond: the sea. But neither man listens.

In Chapter IX, in the hurricane season, Achille gets a job shoveling out the Plunketts' pigsty, walking six miles to work, saving every penny he can. The monsoons come; he has seen the mare's tails in the sky. He is coming from Ma Kilman's with a bottle of kerosene when the rains hit, and he runs to his shack, where the rain hammers on the galvanized roof. He lies awake thinking about Hector and Helen. But Hector isn't with Helen; he is trying to save his canoe because its anchor rope has loosened in the storm. He lets the surf carry him where it will, and finally is swept up onto the sand. The storm rages through the night: The gods are having a fête. When it is over, the people come out to see "the mess the gods made in one night alone." Achille bails out his canoe.

In Chapter X, Plunkett watches the rain destroy the farm except for a few orchids, which Maud rescues. His employees go home when the rain abates. Plunkett takes the Land Rover, driving up by a volcano the locals call Ma Kilman because they believe the mountain is a sibyl, to the site of an old sulphur mine abandoned by his countrymen in 1836. He sees a yellow butterfly, like Helen, and wonders why she follows him. Maud thinks the mountain is "like Adam and Eve all over . . ./Before the snake. Without all the sin."

In Chapter XI, Plunkett, now a pig farmer, muses on the proud people of St. Lucia, who are not, like the empire, swinish. He thinks of Helen, their former maid and his mistress, and the yellow dress that Maud claims she stole, but which Helen claimed Maud gave to her. He decides that the place needs its true place in history, which he will research for Helen's sake. He sequesters himself in his room while Maud sits alone on the divan and does her needlework.

In Chapter XII the narrator reminisces about the house where he and his brother grew up; about the father, the poet; his bastard grandfather, whose people were from Warwickshire, "the Bard's country." His father tells him his history. Father and son walk toward the wharf. The father gives advice: "Measure the days you have left. Do just that labour/which marries your heart to your right hand." He advises him to simplify his life to one emblem only: "a sail leaving harbour/and a sail coming in." But he warns that "all corruption will cry to be taken aboard." He recalls the ocean liners at anchor, passengers tossing coins to boys balanced on logs, who dove into the sea after them; recalls women with pole-straight spines carrying baskets of coal on their heads up the gangway of the hull. In Chapter XIII he tells his son to write his couplets with the same slow ancestral beat. His duty is "to give those feet a voice."

Book Two, Chapter XIV, returns to Plunkett's research of history, times when a young officer on the *Marlborough* is sent to spy on the tonnage and arms of Dutch merchant ships sent through St. Eustatius to American colonies. Then he is to embark to Plymouth, "to serve with Rodney." This merchandise is French aid to the colonies. The information will be used by the admiral to wreak revenge on the Dutch Antilles and on Martinique, owned by the French.

After the Dutch defeat, Achille's ancestor, a laborer for the Redcoats, is trying to raise a cannon in position in a redoubt, pointed at the French on Martinique.

In Chapter XV the British and French ships engage in a sea battle. A young midshipman thinks there is "no war/as courtly as a sea-battle." As the carnage mounts, he is thrown against his own sword, then washed into the sea.

In Chapter XVI, Plunkett pays for a fancy crest to be fashioned, making him a blueblood. But he tells the shield-maker that there are no offspring—there will be no more Plunketts. Now he watches as Maud, always homesick, makes a quilt of birds, and he thinks, "This is her shroud, not her silver jubilee gift."

In Chapter XVII, Plunkett continues researching the battle between the British and French. He climbs to the fort, sees a lizard, and recalls that the original Arauc name of the island, Iounalo, means "where the iguana is found." He wonders, "Was the greatest battle/in naval history . . . fought for a creature with a disposable tail? . . ." He realizes that history will be revised "by black pamphleteers," making the British the villains. He continues his historical research in Ordinance, finding an entry about Plunkett, a midshipman, drowned at the age of 19. He has found a namesake, a son, from colonial times, the time of George III. But he won't tell Maud.

In Chapter XVIII, working on his history, Plunkett notices the Homeric repetition of details. He recalls catching Helen trying on Maud's serpentine bracelet. He thinks he is helping her people, but these, he remembers, "are the vows of empire." Thereafter, "every hour of the day,/even poking around the pigs, he knew where she was."

In Chapter XIX he tries to make Maud see the similarities of the Trojan War, fought over Helen, and the battle of the British and French over an island once called Helen. His house stands on the very spot where buglers stood on barracks steps. He likens the cannon to a penis, an instrument of rape of the island.

In Chapter XX two identical factions vie for local office: A Marxist and a Capitalist. Maljo says they are "two men fighting for one bone." He forms a third party, for workers' rights, called the United Force. He rents Hector's van and a microphone. Philoctete limps among the crowd at each stop handing out pamphlets. Seven Seas sings for him. Achille promises "to canvas for him in the depot/during domino games." Maljo, called Static because of the microphone he forgets to turn on, tells the crowd, "Every vote is . . . your free ride/ on the Titanic: a cruise back to slavery" on ships that are like hotels in which, he reminds them, "you cannot sit inside/except as waiters, maids." He calls the election "fried chicanery." Once again, two factions—Marxist Labor Party and Capitalist WWPP, one Greek, one Trojan—vie for Helen. He plans a big all-night rally, but on that night it rains, and the block party is ruined. He loses the election, pays Philoctete to clean up the mess, and leaves as a migrant worker for Florida.

In Chapter XXI, Achille dreads Friday night, when Helen goes out "selling herself like the island" and the village seems not to care that it is dying, "the way it whored/away a simple life that would soon disappear." Meanwhile, Plunkett hears the "contending music" from the village bars on one side and "across black water,/the hotel's discotheque."

In Chapter XXII, Helen leaves Achille and moves in with Hector, leaving one hairpin in her soapdish—a sign, Achille thinks, that she will come back. Hector has sold his canoe and bought a van, the Comet, with which to transport tourists to the airport. It has leopard seat cushions and a fur monkey, and a dashboard altar with a porcelain Virgin.

In Chapter XXIII, Helen, arrogant and proud, comes to ask Maud for the loan of $5 because she is pregnant. Maud asks about Achille, or Hector. Helen answers, "I am vexed with both of them, oui."

In Chapter XXIV, Achille is now sure Helen will never come back. He is on his boat, named *In God We Trust.* He is at home on the water. A swift, like one Maud is making on her quilt, leads the boat. He has left the island behind and is in the Atlantic. He feels as if he is heading home to Africa.

In Book Three, Chapter XXV, God gives Achille permission to come home: "Is I send the sea-swift as pilot." Achille is in the Congo. A man walks toward him, and he knows it is his father, Afolabe. Achille does not remember the name he was given before he went away, does not know what Achille means.

In Chapter XXVI, Achille hears the tribal history from "a white-eyed story teller," learns how he will pay for some blasphemous offense "by forgetting his parents, his tribe, and his own spirit/for an albino god."

In Chapter XXVI, Achille witnesses a slave raid, when 15 men are lost. Afterward, he walks through the dusty streets, where doors are "like open graves." He climbs a ridge and sees the "chain of men/linked by their wrists with vine. . . ." He kills one man, thinking, "I can deliver/all of them by hiding" and attacking the captors one by one. But he becomes entangled in vine.

In Chapter XXVIII the slave history continues. The men, from many tribes, have no tribe in the new land. Later they talk to the gods "who had not been there/when they needed them."

In Chapter XXIX, Helen takes dried laundry from Hector's line, "not Helen now, but Penelope," waiting for Odysseus's return. She lies on the bed and thinks about Achille. Meanwhile, blind Seven Seas recognizes Philoctete by the smell of his putrefied sore and asks him about Achille. Philoctete says, "They say he drown." Seven Seas says Achille is looking for "his name and his soul." He adds, "He go come back soon."

In Chapter XXX, Achille tells the mate he has been to Africa. The mate tells him he has had a sunstroke. While he was unconscious they have caught a kingfish, blue albacore. They watch a frigate bird steal a mackerel from a herring gull. Achille calls the gulls "white slaves for a black king." The mate scoffs, "You wish." But Achille's spirits are lifted. They return to shore, blowing the conch shell. Achille sees Helen leave.

In Chapter XXXI, raking leaves for Seven Seas, Achille learns about the meaning of the Pomme-Arac tree's name. Pomme means "apple" and Arac means the Arauc Indians to whom the land once belonged. He rakes across an old gravestone and hurls it away.

In Chapter XXXII the narrator visits his frail mother, reminding her that she has three children: Derek, Roddy, and Pam. He walks the street, with amnesia like his mother's, trying to understand patois again.

In Book Four, Chapter XXXIII, back in Brookline, the narrator is "like a Jap soldier in his Pacific island/who prefers solitude to the hope of rescue." He looks for a letter until he grows tired, "like wounded Philoctete/the hermit who did not know the war was over/or refused to believe it."

In Chapter XXXIV, on a trip west, the narrator likens love contracts to "treaties with the Indians,/but with mutual treachery." He cannot believe his relationship is over any more than the Sioux did when the Union Pacific came through.

In Chapter XXXV, in Georgia, with its Greek revival columns, he sees where the Trail of Tears started and thinks how Greek it was, "the necessary evil/of slavery . . ." with towns like Athens, Sparta, Troy. He thinks of the "bundles of women moving in ragged bands," headed for Oklahoma. He reads the letters to the Indian agent by Catherine Weldon about the Indians, who believed "the papers the Sioux had folded to their hearts/would be kept like God's word . . ." and that "peace would break out as widely as the moon." He likens Catherine Weldon to Achille on the river.

In Chapter XXXVI the narrator goes into the museum, with its Greek columns, and sees Achille on canvas, surrounded by sharks like Melville's whale. Outside, he hails a cab, "but cabs, like the fall, were a matter of colour." In New England he sees the "pale, alarmed look" of a woman at a bus stop. He sees the image of his father, who says, "Once you have seen everything and gone everywhere,/cherish our island for its green simplicities."

In Book Five, Chapter XXXVII, he visits Lisbon, reliving its glory days.

In Chapter XXXVIII he goes to London, and describes a down-at-the-heel bargeman, a sort of Odysseus. The bargeman curls up on a bench. He sees "under everything an underlying grime." With biting irony the poet asks a series of questions: "Who decrees a great epoch? The meridian of Greenwich. . . . Where is the light of the world? In the National Gallery."

In Chapter XXXIX in Ireland, the fields inherited by natives "hide stones white-knuckled with hatred."

In Chapter XL, from a ship off the Aegean coast, his heart "thuds like the galley-slaves' drums." On to Istanbul, but the place is not his, since he prefers "not statues but the bird in the statue's hair."

In Chapter XLI, recalling the Roman empire, he says the Romans had Greek slaves. He recalls all the injustices to American Indians whose smoke-prayer was "pushed back by the Pilgrim's pitchfork."

In Chapter XLII he visits Toronto, "a city whose language was seized by its police."

In Chapter XLIII, Catherine Welborn describes "a chain of men/linked by wrists to our cavalry." She likens an old Indian with a dry rattle to "white-eyed Omeros," thinking he must be deaf as well as blind. She sees a broken arrow and thinks, "Those were our promises." She says of history: "I had no power to change it."

In Book Six, Chapter XLIV, back in the Antilles, the narrator remembers all the sights and smells, and knows: "I lived there with every sense."

In Chapter XLV, Hector, speeding down the road in his Comet, tries to screech to a stop to avoid one of Plunkett's piglets. His van lodges against a tree; Hector does not move. The narrator, arriving on the island, is told of Hector's death by the transport driver. He sees how everything has changed. The beach now looks like everywhere else: Greece or Hawaii. The driver points out where Hector died. Hector has paid the price for giving up the sea. "A man who cursed the sea had cursed his own mother."

In Chapter XLVI, Hector is buried at sea, not far from where he and Achille had fought for a tin and Helen. Achille tells his friend good-bye while Helen watches. Pride sets her face like stone after this. Philoctete still suffers from his unhealable skin wound.

In Chapter XLVII, Ma Kilman goes to mass, thinking of the various healing herbs. She goes in search of a certain one. Once long ago a swift flew from Benin with a seed in its mouth. The swift dropped the seed on St. Lucia and the vine grew.

In Chapter XLVIII, Ma Kilman has all but forgotten the wisdom of her great-grandmother, but she takes off her wig, and the ants crawl upon her head and tell her secret wisdom.

In Chapter XLIX, Ma bathes Philoctete in the brew of the root, stewed in a cauldron from the old sugar mill, healing his incurable wound.

In Chapter L the Plunketts, planning a cruise, consider "level-voiced" London, which unnerves him, and Maud realizes she prefers gardens to empires.

In Chapter LI, Plunkett has an altercation with a motorist who calls him "honkey," until he sees it is Hector. He asks after Helen's health. After mass they stop for fresh bread.

In Chapter LII, Maud dies of cancer, devastating Plunkett. The narrator admits there was Plunkett in his father, and much of his mother in Maud. He admits "a changing shadow of Telemachus" in himself, in his "absent war."

In Chapter LIII the narrator attends Maud's funeral. Helen is there in a veil. Achille stands next to Philoctete. After the funeral Helen tells Achille, "I coming home."

In Chapter LIV the poet sees Major Plunkett whistling the next day. Someone says, "Collecting insurance." The major speaks to the poet, who realizes the major has been "caught out in the class-war." He feels contempt. The major had once trained them all as cadets.

In Chapter LV, it is the day after Christmas (Boxing Day), and Achille and Philoctetes, now healed, dress like women warriors, Achille wearing Helen's yellow dress. After their dance, Achille arrogantly sends Philoctete out to bow and pick up the coins. Philoctete weeps.

In Book Seven, Chapter LVI, from his hotel balcony the narrator sees the marble head of Homer rise from the sea. Homer asks him who told him the name Omero, "my proper name in the ancient speech of the islands?" When the poet answers that a Greek girl told him, Homer is pleased. He asks if they are still fighting wars, and the poet answers, "Not over a girl's love." Homer says, "Love is good, but the love of your own people is greater."

In Chapter LVII, blind Seven Seas ferries the poet through the ships in the bay. The island is again compared to Menelaus's wife (Helen), who struts because she knows that no one can claim her beauty any more than that of the Lucian bay.

In Chapter LVIII the poet sees the changes speculators are making on the island, on the heights the Plunketts loved. Seven Seas tells him that in every odyssey there are two journeys: "one on worried water" and one on paper.

In Chapter LIX the poet says he and Philoctete shared the same wound, the same cure. For Achille, work is a prayer of anger, as he refuses "to strike a pose for crouching photographers."

In Chapter LX, Achille must go farther and farther every day for his catch. He tells Philoctete they must keep heading south, perhaps even to the Grenadines. There, a whale lifts their boat, almost swamping it.

In Chapter LXI, Plunkett visits Ma Kilman, who sees his Maud walking by a lake. His grief, his wound, heals slowly. He knows that Maud is proud of him.

In Chapter LXII, Seven Seas hears sounds of a village "surrendering a life besieged/by the lances of yachts in the white marina." The island has become a souvenir itself. School history texts show a "cloud-wigged Rodney," but the builders, ancestors of Hector, Achille, and Philoctete, are not these.

In Chapter LXIII, Seven Seas sees from Ma Kilman's rum ship a new girl, Maljo's niece. Maljo has gone to Florida as a migrant worker, taking up with a Choctaw woman until a Choctaw truck driver tries to choke him. The pregnant Helen comes into the shop, and after she leaves, Ma says Achille wants to give the child, Hector's child, an African name. Philoctete will be the godfather.

In Chapter LXIV, Helen is a waitress at the Halcyon, wearing native costume. A triumphant Achille cleans his mackerels. Achille has no passport, since the horizon needs none. He never begged, is no one's waiter. He hates shoes. No one insults him and he insults no one. The poet would be honored if Achille will be one of his casket-bearers. (Walcott 1990)

See also Walcott, Derek Alton.

OÑA, PEDRO DE

See Pedro de Oña.

ORGANT

French mock-epic poem, published anonymously in 1789 by Louis Antoine Léon de Saint-Just (1767–1794), a French revolutionary leader and fanatical lieutenant of Robespierre. Written during a time of prerevolutionary unrest, the poem is in part autobiographical. It contains long passages of satirical and lewd political references in the vein of Voltaire's 1755 mock-epic *La Pucelle d'Orléans*. At the age of ten the poet lost his father. At the age of 21, disappointed in love, he absconded with some of his mother's valuables and went to Paris. His mother had him arrested and put in a reformatory. The poem was poorly received, even by his friends, and in a short time authorities confiscated the book. (Harvey and Heseltine 1959; Siepmann 1987)

ORLANDO

Hero of *Orlando Innamorato* by Matteo Maria Boiardo (15th c.) and *Orlando Furioso* (16th c.). He is the count of Brava (or Adglante), senator of Rome, nephew of Charlemagne, the mightiest of paladins. His love for Angelica is central to both works.

Orlando is the Roland who is the hero of the Old French epic *La Chanson de Roland* (The song of Roland). The legends about him grew up around the historical Hruotland of Brittany, leader of Charlemagne's rear guard in the Battle of Roncesvalles. For *The Song of Roland,* see the *Encyclopedia of Traditional Epics.*

See also *Orlando Furioso; Orlando Innamorato.*

ORLANDO FURIOSO
(Mad Roland, or Orlando in a mad frenzy)

Italian Romantic epic (1516–1532) by Ludovico Ariosto (1474–1533). It was published in 1516 with 40 cantos. In 1532 a longer version of 46 cantos was published. The cantos, totaling 38,736 lines of brilliant, flowing ottava rima, are arranged in stanzas of hendecasyllabic lines. It is a continuation and enlargement of Matteo Maria Boiardo's *Orlando Innamorato* (1482–1483), wherein, during a gathering of Charlemagne's paladins, the pagan princess Angelica, daughter of the Great Khan, tries to distract the Christian knights and lead them astray, weakening the Christian forces allied against the Saracens under the leadership of African emperor Agramante and King Gradasso. However, Orlando's story takes a back seat to the story of the pagan Saracen Ruggiero (called Rugiero in Boiardo's work) and the French Christian Bradamante.

In *Orlando Furioso*, the forest, where much of the action takes place, almost becomes a character. In the forests, full of magic and monsters, the paladins are seduced by their passions into fantastic adventures.

The poem begins with Angelica's escape from captivity. Charlemagne had placed her in the care of Bavarian duke Namo so as to avoid a confrontation between Rinaldo (Ranaldo in Boiardo's work) and his cousin Count Orlando, "who both languished in the throes/Of love upon Angelica's account." She must elude both Rinaldo and the Saracen knight Ferraù, nephew of King Marsillo of Spain, as the two knights take separate routes through the forest. Rinaldo is easy to avoid because he is afoot, having lost his horse. Ferraù, having just withdrawn from battle, bends over a stream to drink. His helmet, which he has stolen from Orlando, falls into the water. Angelica comes upon Ferraù, who is smitten by her as well. Rinaldo appears and the two duel, but neither can best the other. They call a truce as Angelica rides away. She meets Sacripante, also in love with her. He intends to seduce her but is interrupted by a knight who unseats him. His opponent is Bradamante, the woman warrior who is Rinaldo's sister.

In Canto II, Rinaldo appears and duels with Sacripante, but is duped by a hermit's sprite. Again, Angelica rides away during the battle. Rinaldo rides to Paris, and Charlemagne sends him to Britain to solicit military aid. During the channel crossing he is tossed by a terrible storm.

Bradamante, ancestress of the House of Este, is loved by Ruggiero, whom she loves in return. Once a warrior on the side of the Saracens, he has become a Christian. Bradamante meets a sorrowful knight, Pinabello, nephew of Gano (Ganelon). Believing her to be a man, he tells her that a flying knight (Atlante, an African magician and Ruggiero's guardian) kidnapped his fair damsel and imprisoned her in a high tower. Pinabello is "of all true knights the foe./ . . . In acts of treachery he was the worst." (II.58) He tells her that two knights, Ruggiero and Gradasso, challenged Atlante, but were bedazzled by a magic shield and captured. Intent on rescuing Ruggiero, Bradamante offers to help Pinabello. When he discovers who she is, he plots to betray her, convincing her to lower herself into a cave while he holds the rope. But he lets go, and she is knocked unconscious in the fall.

Canto III begins with a tribute to the Estensi dynasty, whose ancestress is Bradamante. She does not die, but rises and enters a larger cave like a chapel. Melissa, a benign sorceress, welcomes her and takes her to Merlin's tomb. She conjures visions of Bradamante's descendants, the Estensi, and foretells their greatness. Then she tells Bradamante that King Agramante has given the sorcerer Brunello a magic ring stolen from Angelica. Brunello has agreed to try to free Ruggiero for Agramante. But Melissa tells her, "It is . . . you alone/Who'll rescue him from the enchanter's hand." (III.71) Bradamante is instructed to kill him and take the ring. She is also warned against Atlante. Melissa tells her how to overcome him. Bradamante leaves and meets Brunello at an inn.

In Canto IV, Bradamante ties Brunello to a fir and takes the ring, but she spares his life. She goes to Atlante's castle in the Pyrenees and challenges him. Despite all his magical tricks, the ring she wears makes her invulnerable. She pretends to fall from her horse, and when he dismounts, leaving his magic shield tied to the hippogriff he rides, she overpowers him. She spares his life but claims his shield and hippogriff and makes him destroy his castle, although he begs either to keep Ruggiero or be killed. Bradamante frees the captives, but when Ruggiero mounts the hippogriff, it carries him away, much to her alarm.

The scene shifts to Rinaldo, who survives the winds and tumbling sea and lands on the Scottish coast. He travels until he reaches an abbey, where the monks tell him of the plight of Ginevra, daughter of the king of Scotland. An evil lord has told the king that he has seen her bring her lover to her balcony by rope. By law she is condemned to burn to death for such an act, unless within one month a knight appears to challenge the report. The monks urge Rinaldo to champion her. Incensed by such a harsh law, he says, "Death rather to such damsels as refuse,/But not to her who loves and life renews." (IV.63) He sets out to rescue her. On the way he stops to rescue Ginevra's maid-in-waiting, Dalinda, who is about to be killed by some ruffians.

Canto V begins with a treatise on the evils of violence to women. Dalinda tells how she came to be the victim of ruffians. She has been in love with Polinesso, duke of Albany, who has pretended love for her to hide his ambition to marry Ginevra. The princess, however, loves Ariodante, an Italian cavalier at the court of St. Andrew's in Scotland, who loves her in return. Polinesso convinces Dalinda to disguise herself as Princess Ginevra so that Ariodante and his brother Lurcanio can observe her let down a rope from Ginevra's balcony for Polinesso. When Ariodante sees this, he is so bereft that he attempts to kill himself. He leaves the court, and a stranger reports to the princess that Ariodante has "flung himself head first into the sea." (V.57) Ginevra is so grief-stricken that she rends her garments and tears her golden tresses from her head. Lurcanio, hearing of his brother's death, denounces Ginevra. When Rinaldo hears Dalinda's story, he is all the more resolute to champion Ginevra. He rides to St. Andrew's city where Lurcanio, still angry at the princess, is being challenged by an unknown knight, who bests him. Rinaldo defeats Polinesso in a joust, and Ginevra is vindicated. As Rinaldo removes his helmet, the king asks the other knight to identify himself as well.

In Canto VI the unknown knight is revealed as Ariodante, who did not die in his plunge into the sea. He and Ginevra are wed and his king names him duke of Albany. Rinaldo begs for leniency for Dalinda. She is spared and becomes a nun in Denmark.

Meanwhile, Ruggiero has been carried by the hippogriff to the island realm of Alcina, a sorceress. He ties the hippogriff to a myrtle, but the tree speaks and asks him to unbind the creature, which is mutilating the myrtle. The tree is revealed as Astolfo, son of King Otto of England and cousin of Orlando and Rinaldo. Astolfo tells of his capture and enchantment by Alcina after she tires of him as a lover. Ruggiero goes to Alcina's castle. He learns of Alcina's sister Logistilla, Morgana, and Arthur (of the Round Table), who defrauded Alcina of her kingdom. He determines to go to her aid, despite the menace of Erifilla, a giantess guarding the bridge from Alcina's to Logistilla's realm.

In Canto VII, Ruggiero meets Erifilla, who is mounted on a wolf. They fight and he slays her.

Bradamante searches for Ruggiero and learns from Melissa that he has succumbed to Alcina's evil charms. Resolving to rescue him, Melissa has herself conveyed to the island. With the magic ring she conjures a demon horse and disguises herself as Atlante. She rebukes Ruggiero for succumbing to Alcina's beauty, reminding him of his destiny to father the House of Este. She gives him the magic ring by which he sees Alcina as old and hideous, and he breaks free of her spell. With sword and shield he mounts the hippogriff and heads off to fight Logistilla.

In Canto VIII, Ruggiero forces the outer gate and kills the guards. Melissa frees Alcina's captives, including Astolfo. She heads for Logistilla's ahead of Ruggiero, riding over wasteland.

In Scotland, where Rinaldo has come to plead for troops to fight against the infidel, the king offers him all the forces under his command. Rinaldo proceeds to London, where the prince of Wales also pledges forces to help.

The story shifts to Angelica, in flight from a hermit, whose horse is possessed by a demon and plunges into the sea. She is washed to the island of Ebuda, where the hermit assaults her, but the Ebudans capture both her and the hermit. She is chained to a rock, where, as is custom, she is to be sacrificed to Proteus.

Back in Paris, Orlando still searches for Angelica. During a fitful slumber, he dreams of her calling for help, and he leaves Paris immediately, telling no one where he is going. Charlemagne is furious, but his friend Brandimart goes in seach of him.

In Canto IX, searching for Angelica, Orlando meets a damsel who tells of the cruel Ebudans who hunt women to feed to "a voracious beast." Fearing Angelica may be a prisoner of the Ebudans, he volunteers to join the force going to the island. But their ship is blown to Antwerp, where he meets Olimpia, daughter of the count of Holland. He goes to Holland on her behalf to confront Friesland king Cimosco, who has killed her father and brothers, imprisoned her love, Bireno, and taken the country. Orlando skewers six men and the troops flee, as does Cimosco, firing a cannon that kills Orlando's horse. Orlando pursues him on foot and kills him. Bireno and Olimpia are reunited, while Orlando resumes his quest for Angelica.

Canto X takes up the fate of Olimpia and of Bireno, who, feigning love for Olimpia, lusts after other women. They set out for Zealand but a storm casts them off on an island. The next day he and the crew sail away, leaving Olimpia alone on the island.

The scene shifts to Ruggiero, headed for Logistilla's realm with Alcina's fleet in pursuit. He reaches Logistilla's palace walls while the queen's forces defeat Alcina's fleet. He meets Astolfo, who is also eager to depart toward the west. Logistilla teaches them how to control the hippogriff. Ruggiero travels overland to London, where he sees the forces allied to fight the Moors. He flies to the Hebrides and sees a naked girl chained to a rock: It is Angelica. She watches as the giant orc rises from the seas to attack him. The hippogriff is drenched as Ruggiero fights valiantly. He puts Bradamante's ring on her finger to keep her from harm as he unleashes the dazzling magic beam of his shield, which blinds the orc. The hippogriff carries Ruggiero and Angelica away to Brittany. Smitten by her charms, Ruggiero tries to seduce Angelica, but is prevented by his clumsy armor.

In Canto XI, anxious to escape Ruggiero's advances, Angelica recognizes the ring and puts it into her mouth, which renders her invisible. She escapes to a cave, and the hippogriff flies away, leaving Ruggiero. As he returns home on foot, he sees a vision of Bradamante fighting a giant. The vision is Atlante's ruse, luring him to an enchanted place where other knights and ladies are held captive. He loves Ruggiero like a son and wants him kept safe.

Orlando has cast Cimosco's cannon into the sea, but it will be discovered some day and, when it is used to make war, chivalry will be dead. Setting out to find Angelica, Orlando comes to the island of the Ebudans and sees a woman tied to a tree. The giant orc appears, intent on swallowing him, boat and all. Orlando flings the anchor into the orc's mouth, wedging it open, then he slashes the orc and drags it ashore, where it dies. The outraged islanders attack Orlando. He kills 30 of them, then frees the naked damsel as Irish king Oberto's army arrives to attack the Ebudans. Orlando discovers that the damsel is Olimpia, who tells of being abandoned by Bireno. King Oberto falls in love with her and promises to punish Bireno. He finds clothes for her, and they return to Ireland, where he slays Bireno. He and Olimpia are married. Orlando continues to look for Angelica; in a forest in St. Malo, he hears a shriek of terror.

In Canto XII, Orlando sees a knight carrying a struggling maiden whom he believes to be Angelica. The knight enters Atlante's palace of illusions with Orlando in pursuit.

Ruggiero, seeking Bradamante, reaches Atlante's palace. Angelica also nears the palace. She cannot decide between Orlando and Sacripante as protector; she finally chooses Sacripante. Ferraù also arrives. All the knights are looking for Angelica, but at their approach she uses the magic ring to disappear. Ferraù plans to win Orlando's helmet in a joust, but while the two fight, Angelica steals the helmet. Sacripante leaves, thinking she has ridden ahead. Both jousting knights are indomitable. When they stop, Ferraù thinks Sacripante has stolen the helmet and rides off in pursuit. He finds the helmet and dons it.

Meanwhile, Orlando meets the African forces and kills many of them before resuming his search for Angelica. He sees a light on a cliff, climbs up and finds a beautiful girl inside a cave, guarded by an old crone. The damsel sobs out her story.

In Canto XIII the damsel, Spanish princess Isabella, tells of her love for Scottish prince Zerbino, brother of Ginevra. The two fell in love while he took part in a joust in Galicia. When he returned to Scotland, he sent a knight, Odorico, to bring Isabella to join him. But they were shipwrecked off La Rochelle, where Odorico became consumed with lust for her. He sent the other survivors on errands so that he could have her to himself. But pirates arrived and carried her away to this cave.

At that moment the pirates return. Orlando slays the leader, hurls a heavy stone down on others, and hangs seven more, while the old crone escapes. Orlando and Isabella set out together.

At Marseilles, where Bradamante has been fighting the pagan horde, she grows pale when Melissa returns without Ruggiero. Melissa comforts her by telling her about her famous progeny.

Canto XIV describes the parade of Spanish and African troops. Tartar king Mandricardo joins African king Agramante outside Paris. Hearing reports of the deaths of some of his men, Mandricardo visits the battle site, then searches for the knight in black responsible for the slaughter. He meets Princess Doralice, escorted from Granada by knights. Mandricardo kills the knights and abducts Doralice. He woos her and, although she is betrothed to Algerian king Rodomonte, she weakens and spends the night with him in a shepherd's hut. Later they wander about, coming upon two cavaliers and a fair maid.

King Agramante begins a siege on the gates. Charlemagne prays for deliverance. Angels intercede, and Rinaldo arrives with help. The Saracens under Rodomonte are defeated and burned to death. Rinaldo slays King Dardinello of Zumara.

In Canto XV, while Rodomonte rages at his losses and Agramante's assault on one of the gates of Paris is repelled, Astolfo leaves Logistilla's realm and sails through the Persian Gulf to the Red Sea. A hermit warns him of the magic net of the monster Caligorante. Astolfo continues, pursued by Caligorante, who falls into his own net. Astolfo binds him, leads him behind his horse, and ties him to an oak tree. Later Caligorante is taken to Palestine and given to the king of Persia, who gives Astolfo gifts in exchange. Along the way they encounter the monster-robber Orrilo, fighting brothers Grifone and Aquilante. Astolfo recognizes them and cuts off Orrilo's head. They all travel to Palestine, where Grifone receives news of his lover Orrigille's infidelity. He leaves in secret to go after her.

In Canto XVI, Grifone meets Orrigille and her lover Martano, whom she says is her brother. They go to the festival in Damascus.

In Paris, the British reinforcements arrive, led by Rinaldo, and a bitter battle rages. Charlemagne goes to the citadel's defense.

In Canto XVII, Charlemagne enters the citadel. Eight Christians attack Rodomonte.

In Damascus, when Grifone and Martano are challenged to fight by eight cavaliers, Martano flees. Ashamed of Martano's cowardice, Grifone defeats seven. His joust with the eighth is halted and he is declared champion. While Grifone sleeps, Martano returns, steals his armor and horse, and goes to the palace to be honored in Grifone's stead. The king gives him and Orrigille sumptuous apartments in the palace. Grifone wakes, dons Martano's armor, and goes to court where a banquet is being held. Martano suggests that Grifone, whom he calls a coward, be hanged. Grifone is seized, while Martano and

Orrigille depart. The mob insults Grifone, but as soon as he is freed, he grabs up his sword.

In Canto XVIII, on a rampage of revenge, Grifone kills 30.

In Paris, the siege continues. As Rodomonte's troops dissolve, he plunges into the Seine. He wades ashore and sees a dwarf from whom he asks news of Doralice. The dwarf tells him, "No longer mine or yours." When the dwarf relates how a knight has stolen her away, Rodomonte flies into a rage.

Grifone, still fighting the mob in Damascus, earns the king's admiration. The king gives Grifone half his kingdom for the shame he has suffered unduly. A Greek traveler arrives who tells Aquilante of Orrigille's whereabouts. Grifone has already disappeared, and Aquilante suspects that his brother is in pursuit of Martano. Aquilante himself pursues Martano and Orrigille and, when he finds them, takes them prisoner, returning them to Damascus. The people revile them and they are cast into a dungeon. Martano is flogged. Aquilante finds Grifone recovering from his wounds. The king announces a new tourney in one month.

Word of it reaches Astolfo and Sansonetto, who vow to attend. On their way to Damascus, they meet the warrior-maiden Marfisa, Ruggiero's sister, who accompanies them. In Damascus, she recognizes her own arms offered to Grifone as a trophy; she had left them to pursue Brunello. She seizes them and charges into the hostile crowd. Grifone and Aquilante attack her, Astolfo, and Sansonetto, and are unhorsed. Marfisa and her allies retreat, pursued by the mob, but Aquilante recognizes Astolfo and all hostility ceases.

Marfisa and the paladins leave for Cypress, where they are caught in a violent storm.

In Paris, where the siege continues, Rinaldo kills King Dardinello. While Charlemagne's paladins celebrate victory, two Saracen youths, Cloridano and Medoro, appear, wanting to bury their dead king, Dardinello. When night falls, the two brothers slay many sleeping Christians to avenge Dardinello's death.

In Canto XIX the Scottish knights arrive and kill Cloridano and wound Medoro, leaving him for dead. Angelica, traveling with the protection of the magic ring, finds Medoro. She takes him to a herdsman's hut to tend his wounds, falling in love with him in the process. When he is well, they marry and leave. She gives her bracelet to their shepherd host. As they head to Barcelona, they encounter a madman covered with mud who leaps up to attack them.

Meanwhile, Aquilante, Marfisa, and Grifone are caught in a storm at sea. They are blown to Laiazzo, which is ruled by women who either kill all prisoners or make them slaves. The women plan a jousting tournament. Marfisa defeats nine opponents, then jousts with the tenth, but they are evenly matched. When his identity is revealed, the knight is found to be only a youth. Marfisa reveals that she is a woman.

In Canto XX, Marfisa discloses her name. The knight, Guidone, tells how women came to rule. She suggests that he join with her friends to break free. They make plans to escape, but when they set sail, Astolfo is nowhere to be seen and he is left behind. When the ship arrives at Luni, Marfisa leaves them to go her own way while the others go on to the palace at Marseilles. Marfisa meets Pinabello and his lady. She defends Gabrina, Isabella's guardian, against the mockery of Pinabello's lady, defeating Pinabello. She meets Zerbino, brother of Scottish princess Ginevra, whom she challenges and defeats as well for mocking Gabrina's ugliness. She leaves Gabrina with him as his charge.

After Marfisa rides away, Zerbino laments the loss of Isabella, but Gabrina hints that Isabella has been tarnished by at least 20 men. The two travel on and meet a cavalier.

In Canto XXI the cavalier, Ermonide of Holland, challenges Zerbino and is defeated. He tells of Gabrina's infatuation with his brother Filandro, who resisted her advances. When Filandro was wounded, he recuperated at the castle of Gabrina's husband, Argeo, where Gabrina tried to seduce him. After he left, Gabrina lied to Argeo, saying Filandro had made advances to her. Argeo pursued Filandro and took him prisoner. While he was in prison, Gabrina visited him, but still he resisted. He was tricked into killing Argeo, and when she showed him the body, he yielded to her to avoid infamy. Her love then turned to hate. She poisoned him and he died. After hearing the story, Zerbino apologizes to Ermonide but remains Gabrina's champion, even though he detests her. They ride away, hearing the sound of combat.

In Canto XXII, Zerbino comes across a knight lying dead.

The scene shifts to Astolfo, traveling across Europe, whose horse is stolen while he rests by a spring. He is lured to Atlante's palace, searching for his horse. He uses the magic book given to him by Logistilla to try to break the spell of the enchanted palace. Atalante resists, but Astolfo blows his horn and breaks the spell. He finds both his horse and the hippogriff, which he decides to ride, giving the horse to a friend.

Meanwhile, Ruggiero and Bradamante are reunited. Ruggiero plans to be baptized, and they set off to Vallombrosa for that purpose. On the way they meet a lady in tears who tells them that before the morrow a youth will be slain at Pinabello's castle. Eager to help the youth, Bradamante travels to Pinabello's. While Ruggiero fights four warriors, she spies on Pinabello, pursues him, and kills him. Then she searches for Ruggiero, whom she cannot find, although she does find his horse.

In Canto XXIII, while searching for Ruggiero, Bradamante finds Astolfo and takes charge of his horse for him. She sets off alone for Vallombrosa, but on the way meets her brother Alardo. She goes home to Montalbano with him, where her mother and brothers welcome her. She sends her friend Ippalca on to Vallombrosa with Ruggiero's horse, but on the way Ippalca encounters King Rodomonte, who takes possession of the horse.

The story returns to Zerbino. Finding a knight lying dead, he goes in pursuit of the slayer. He returns to Gabrina and the body, which is that of Pinabello. They travel to Altaripa, where Gabrina accuses Zerbino of the deed. He is arrested and sentenced to death, but as he is led to his execution, Orlando and Isabella arrive. Orlando kills 80, while 40 more flee. Zerbino is released, and he and Isabella are reunited.

Orlando departs in search of the Tartar king Mandricardo. When he finds him, the king does not recognize him. Mandricardo challenges Orlando for his sword (originally Hector's, of the *Iliad*). Orlando accepts the challenge, and hangs the sword on a bush during combat. But about that time, Mandricardo's horse goes berserk and charges off. Orlando again goes in search of the king, asking Zerbino to wait there for three days before he leaves. He enters a forest and sees carvings of Medoro and Angelica on the trees, making him violently jealous. He enters a grotto and reads Medoro's verses of love. He stops at the shepherd's house and learns that Medoro and Angelica enjoyed many nights upon the very bed where he is to sleep. When he sees the bracelet Angelica gave the shepherd, he is bereft. During the night he leaves, weeping. In a blind rage, he smashes the grotto and the trees and dams up the stream, then he tears off his armor and clothing and throws down his weapons. Barehanded, he begins uprooting trees.

Canto XXIV begins with a warning against love, described as "madness after all." Bereft of his wits, Orlando kills shepherds and tears up trees. A hostile crowd attacks him, but he kills 20, then roams the countryside, berserk.

Zerbino and Isabella, meanwhile, meet two cavaliers guarding a prisoner. It is Odorico. Isabella tells how, when the vessel sank, she and three men survived. Odorico had tried to "force her will," but she was carried away to the pirates' den. The two cavaliers bow, recognizing Zerbino as the royal knight of Scotland. Zerbino recognizes them as Corebo and Almonio, whom he sent to protect Isabella. Almonio tells how they lost Isabella, and how they captured Odorico. Odorico pleads for mercy, and while Zerbino tries to decide what to do with him, the evil crone Gabrina rides up shrieking. As punishment Zerbino puts Odorico in charge of Gabrina for one year. But only one day later Odorico hangs her; a year later, Almonio will do the same to him.

Zerbino finds Orlando's coat and other traces of him. Princess Fiordeligi joins them, telling of her search for her husband, Brandimart. She recognizes Orlando's horse and armor. Zerbino hangs Orlando's weapons on a tree with an inscription warning "Hands off. . . ." But the pagan Mandricardo rides up with Doralice and grabs the sword. He and Zerbino fight, and Zerbino is wounded twice. Doralice begs an end to the strife. As Zerbino dies, Isabella falls across him, screaming out in grief. A hermit comes along and decides to take Isabella to a nearby convent.

Rodomonte, who loves Doralice, arrives to challenge King Mondricardo. They joust until Rodomonte kills the king's horse. Doralice pleads with Rodomonte to stop. The two swear a truce.

Canto XXV begins with a declaration on the benevolent influence of Love. Ruggiero, who has thrown his magic buckler down a well, is summoned to help Agramante. He is in a quandary, because he has promised Bradamante to go to Pinabello's to rescue a condemned youth. He decides to go on to Pinabello's, arriving at the scene of the execution, where he mistakes the youth for Bradamante. After he rescues the youth, slaying dozens in the process, he asks who he is. The youth reveals that he is Ricciardetto, Bradamante's twin brother. He relates the time when Spanish princess Firodispina, mistaking

Bradamante for a man, fell in love with her. Ricciardetto substituted for his sister and won Fiordispina. Now Ruggiero and Ricciardetto ride to the castle belonging to Buovo d'Antona and guarded by his bastard son Aldigiero. Aldigiero greets them with the news that his half brothers Vivian and Malagigi have been captured by Ferraù, who has given them to his cruel mother, Lanfusa. She has agreed to sell the two to Bertolagi. Ruggiero vows to rescue them, but again he remembers the message urging him to help Agramante. He also remembers that he has promised to rendezvous with Bradamante at Vallombrosa's shrine. He sends her a letter explaining that his king has requested his aid. As soon as he is released from service, he will embrace the Christian faith and ask her father, Aymon, for consent to marry her. He asks her to wait 15 or 20 days. Then he, Aldigiero, and Ricciardetto set off to Bayona, where Vivian and Malagigi are to be handed over to Bertolagi.

Canto XXVI begins with a paean to the noble love of Ruggiero and Bradamante. Ruggiero, Aldigiero, and Ricciardetto meet a strange knight who offers to help them. It is Marfisa, but they do not know she is a woman. They meet a band of Moors with the two prisoners. After a lively battle, Vivian and Malagigi are set free, and Marfisa's identity is revealed. They dine beside a magic fountain of Merlin's in which they can see the futures of many European countries. A lady approaches: It is Ippalca, who says that an African took her horse, Frontino, belonging to Bradamante. Outraged, Ruggiero goes with her in search of the horse. He learns that it is Rodomonte who took the horse. The two rescued brothers, Marfisa, Aldigiero, and Ricciardetto remain at the fountain. Rodomonte, Mandricardo, and Doralice ride up. Mandricardo decides to claim Marfisa for Rodomonte. The two rescued brothers attack Mandricardo and are quickly unhorsed. Ricciardetto charges, but his horse stumbles. Marfisa calls for her shield, arms, and steed, and fights Mandricardo herself. Finally Rodomonte intervenes, asking for a deferment while they go to help Agramante. Marfisa readily agrees.

Ruggiero, searching for the stolen horse Frontino, sends Ippalca on her way bearing a letter to Bradamante and returns to the fountain, where he finds Rodomonte riding the stolen horse. He challenges, but Rodomonte refuses to yield the horse or to fight, because all hands are needed now to free Agramante from the clutches of Charlemagne. Mandricardo sees the shield of Hector that Ruggiero bears, which was formerly conferred upon Mandricardo at the Castle Perious, and challenges Ruggiero. The two fight until Rodomonte joins in. Marfisa intervenes, but her horse slips. Malagigi sends a demon into Doralice's horse, which bolts away. Rodomonte and Mandricardo chase after her. Ruggiero vows to catch up with them later, bids the others good-bye, and sets off for Paris. Marfisa also leaves for Paris, without farewells.

In Canto XXVII, Rinaldo leaves Paris to search for mad Orlando and Angelica. Satan plans a slaughter of the Christians and, perceiving Rinaldo's absence, sends one demon to speed Rodomonte and Mandricardo to Paris, and another to retard the progress of Marfisa and Ruggiero. The pagans attack the Christian camp, and after a gory battle the Christians retreat into the citadel.

In the pagan camp, the newly arrived Ruggiero, Marfisa, Mandricardo, and Rodomonte all want to duel and put their cases before King Agramante as to whose fight should take precedence. The affair is decided by lot. Mandricardo is to fight first with Rodomonte (over Doralice), then with Ruggiero, and finally with Marfisa. Gradasso, fastening armor on Mandricardo, sees the name "Durindana" on his sword and claims it as his. He and Ruggiero begin to fight Mandricardo until Agramante intervenes and asks Gradasso if Mandricardo can at least use the sword during the jousts. Then Sacripante, fastening on Rodomonte's armor, recognizes the horse Frontino, which had originally been his. The two fight over the horse until again Agramante intervenes. While they try to sort out whose horse it is, Marfisa comes in and recognizes Sacripante and learns that Brunello was the thief who stole not only the horse but her sword. She vows to get even. She defies Agramante, grabs up Brunello, and rides off with him, threatening to hang him. Agramante's adviser, Sobrino, tells him not to try to stop her. Instead, Agramante turns to the rivalry of Mandricardo and Rodomonte over Doralice. He persuades each to abide by Doralice's choice. She chooses Mandricardo and, grief-stricken, Rodomonte leaves. Ruggiero wants to follow him and get the horse, but remembers that he is to fight Mandricardo.

However, Sacripante is under no such obligation, and he follows Rodomonte. But he sees a woman fall into the Seine, and while he jumps in to save her, his horse wanders off. By the time he catches it, he has lost the trail to Rodomonte, who rides along ranting against women. He arrives at an inn where the landlord tells a tale of women's perfidy.

Canto XXVIII is the landlord's tale, which the ladies are advised not to read because it is about women's depravity. When he finishes, another guest defends women, reminding everyone of the sins of husbands. Unconvinced, Rodomonte leaves. He meets the hermit escorting Isabella to the nunnery. He is smitten by her.

In Canto XXIX, when the hermit attempts to protect Isabella, Rodomonte kills him. He woos Isabella, but she vows to remain true to her dear, dead Zerbino. She proposes to make a potion that will make him invincible if he will promise not to violate her. He pretends to agree. She brews the potion and offers to test it herself. After she has drunk it, she asks him to try to cut off her head. He wields his sword and lops off her head. It bounces three times, calling Zerbino's name. God praises her for choosing a brave course. Remorseful, Rodomonte builds a mausoleum for her, a tower for himself, and a narrow bridge across the Tiber at the perilous pass. He challenges all who cross it, stripping Saracens of their armor with which to adorn the monument, and holding prisoner all Christians to be sent to Algiers.

When mad Orlando arrives, naked and on foot, Rodomonte tries to push him off, not knowing who he is. But Fiordiligi, searching for Brandimart, appears, and she recognizes him. She watches them wrestle and fall into the water, then rides on. The poet relates the adventures that have befallen Orlando in his maddened state.

In Canto XXX, because Ruggiero and Gradasso both challenge Mandricardo, Agramante persuades them to draw lots so that only one man fights for them both. Ruggiero wins, and the joust takes place. Both combatants are gravely wounded. Mandricardo dies, and Ruggiero is awarded Mandricardo's arms. He gives the horse Brigliadoro to Agramante, who has Ruggiero placed in his tent.

Meanwhile, Ippalca has delivered Ruggiero's message to Bradamante, who fears for his life.

In Canto XXI, Rinaldo is reunited with his family, who form a band and ride to Paris. They meet a knight in black whom Rinaldo fights until he learns the knight is his brother Guidone. They join forces and advance at night on Agramante's pagans, attacking in a bloody encounter. Agramante retreats to Arles, taking the wounded Ruggiero. Anxious to win the horse Bayardo from Rinaldo, Gradasso challenges him. The two prepare for combat at dawn.

In Canto XXXII the poet apologizes for the distraction of so many threads of the story.

Marfisa, who has taken Brunello by force, refrains from hanging him. She delivers him instead to Agramante, who is so delighted to have her aid in fighting Charlemagne that he has Brunello executed for her.

Meanwhile, Bradamante hears a rumor that Ruggiero is to marry Marfisa. In a rage she vows to meet him in battle. Taking Astolfo's magic lance, she sets out for Paris astride Rabicano. She is met by three kings and Ullania, a messenger from the queen of Iceland. She hears the story of the Icelandic queen and the golden shield. She meets a shepherd who points the way to Tristan's castle, where one must joust with any claimants for lodging. Three kings challenge her for a room, but she unseats them. She enters and reveals that she is a woman. But as she and Ullania enter the hall, Ullania is asked to leave, since only the most beautiful woman may stay. Bradamante challenges the rule, telling the diners that she won her place as a cavalier; how can they be sure she is not a man? Ullania is allowed to stay.

In Canto XXXIII, as Bradamante leaves the castle the next morning, she is challenged by the same three kings, whom she unseats once more. She travels on to a castle near Paris.

Meanwhile, Rinaldo and Gradasso prepare to fight, the victor winning Orlando's sword and the horse Bayardo. They are interrupted by a flying monster that causes Bayardo to gallop away. Both men go after the horse. Gradasso captures him, rides swiftly to Arles, and sets sail on a galley.

In the meantime, Astolfo flies down to Ethiopia where he enters King Senapo's (Prester John's) castle. The king is wealthy and powerful but blind, punished by harpies for his youthful pride. Astolfo vows to try to lift the curse if the king promises to thank God alone for it. As they prepare to partake of a feast, the harpies appear. Astolfo stops the king's ears and blows a blast on his horn. The harpies flee, and he follows them to the gates of Hell.

In Canto XXIV, Astolfo enters Hell and meets a spirit named Lydia, damned for rejecting her lover Alcestes, which caused him to die of sorrow. Astolfo escapes from Hell, flies to Paradise where he meets St. John, hears the reason for Orlando's madness, and learns he can find a cure for it by flying with John to the moon. There Astolfo finds Orlando's wits and his own. He takes them both and returns to Paradise, where he sees the fates spinning skeins. An ancient man takes them away as fast as they are spun.

In Canto XXXV, St. John reveals that the skeins are lives. A golden skein is to be the life of Ippolito d'Este.

As Bradamante rides to Provence, she meets Fiordiligi. Mistaking her for a man, he asks her to save Brandimart. Bradamante agrees to help. She arrives at the bridge guarded by Rodomonte. Vowing to avenge Isabella, she fights Rodomonte, unseating him in one charge. She hangs his arms in Isabella's shrine, removes those of the paladins, and puts up a new sign indicating that the bridge is free. She offers to escort Fiordiligi to Arles, asking that he restore the horse Frontino to Ruggiero and deliver her challenge to him, concealing her identity. At Arles, she waits at the border, sounding her horn in challenge. Ferraù, Grandonio, and Serpentino answer, all of whom she unseats.

In Canto XXXVI, Ruggiero accepts her challenge, but Ferraù reveals her identity to him. However, Marfisa rushes out to challenge her. The two fight during several long encounters. At length Ruggiero intervenes and fights Marfisa until Atlante's voice from the tomb reveals that they are brother and sister. The two embrace; she learns of his love for Bradamante, whom she also embraces. Ruggiero tells her their ancestry, and she resolves to become a Christian but agrees that for the time being he should continue in Agramante's service. As Ruggiero rides away to Arles, they hear a cry of distress.

In Canto XXXVII the poet discusses men's envy of women and decries that men obscure women's fame. He mentions many famous women from ancient times down to his day. He tells women that they themselves must praise women.

Hearing a cry of distress, Ruggiero and the two women find three women whose skirts have been cut off at the waist. Bradamante recognizes one of them as Ullania, who says that the three kings have done this—and worse—to them. Ruggiero and the women enter King Marganorre's castle, capture him, and overthrow his kingdom. Marfisa makes all the inhabitants swear that henceforth wives will be masters in that kingdom. She forces Marganorre to leap from a tower to his death.

In Canto XXXVIII, Ruggiero reports to Arles while Bradamante rejoins Charlemagne's forces with Marfisa, who is baptized.

Astolfo returns to Earth from Paradise with Orlando's wits. St. John has shown him an herb that will restore Senapo's sight, so he mounts the hippogriff and flies to Nubia, restores the king's sight, and receives assurances of help against the pagans. He traps the wind in a wineskin, then deploys the Nubian troops. They sweep North Africa, burning, sacking, taking prisoners.

Agramante realizes that he has left his own realm unguarded. His adviser, Sobrino, suggests they end the bloodshed with a duel: Ruggiero against any Christian knight Charlemagne chooses. It is agreed, and since Orlando is not available, Rinaldo is chosen to fight Ruggiero. Ruggiero vows that if anyone intervenes on his behalf, he will no longer serve Agramante, while Rinaldo vows that if Charlemagne removes him from the fight before he or Ruggiero is defeated, he will swear allegiance to Africa. The joust begins.

In Canto XXXIX, Ruggiero is in a quandary: If he kills Rinaldo, his promised bride's brother, she will hate him forever.

Melissa uses her magic to disguise herself as Rodomonte and convinces Agramante that Ruggiero can't win against Rinaldo and that he should stop the duel. Believing that Rodomonte is now there to help his cause, Agramante stops the combat, while Melissa disappears. Immediately both sides begin fighting, but many of those on whom Agramante has counted have disappeared.

In Africa, Astolfo routs the African troops and takes Algaziers king Bucifar prisoner. Out of leaves he creates a fleet of ships, which the Dane, Dudone, will command. As his enormous army prepares to set out to sea, a shipload of Rodomonte's prisoners lands, among them Orlando's brother Oliver, Brandimart, and Sansonetto. Suddenly a madman appears, whirling a heavy cudgel. A damsel gallops up. It is Fiordiligi, who has traced her husband, Brandimart, to Africa with the help of his adoptive father, Bardino. She recognizes the naked wild man as Orlando. The men finally subdue him. Astolfo puts the vial of wits to his nose; he inhales them and comes to himself. While they dress him, Bardino tells Brandimart that his real father, King Monodant, is dead, and that he is needed to rule in the Levant. But Brandimart says that first he must help save Charlemagne's realm. Orlando and Astolfo plan strategy for the siege of Biserta.

In France, Agramante is deserted by his troops and flees, pursued by Bradamante and Marfisa. He jumps on a ship, and his fleet sails for Africa. On the sea his fleet is met by Dudone's fleet, which attacks with great fury. The pagans try to escape.

In Canto XL the battle continues. Agramante manages to escape, taking his adviser, Sobrino, with him.

In Africa, Orlando leads the siege of Agramante's kingdom of Biserta, which is sacked. When Agramante learns that his capital is burned, he considers suicide, but Sobrino tries to encourage him that all is not lost. They sail east and take refuge on an island where another boat, bearing Gradasso, has landed. The two friends embrace, and Gradasso offers to engage Orlando in single combat to conclude the war. He vows to drive the Nubians back across the Nile using Arabs, Chaldeans, Iranians, and Macrobians. Agramante agrees to everything, except that he himself will challenge Orlando. Gradasso and Sorbino want to fight as well. Orlando agrees, choosing his brother Oliver and Brandimart. As they plan their strategy, they see a pilotless vessel arriving.

In France, Ruggiero discovers it was Agramante who broke the pact and suspended his duel with Rinaldo. But seeing his king so defeated, he decides not to desert him now. He rides to Arles, hoping the fleet will take him back to Africa, but the ships are gone. He goes to Marseilles, where he sees Dudone's armada, with seven captive kings. Ruggiero attacks and kills 100 men. Dudone hears the noise and goes to fight. Ruggiero does not want to hurt the Dane, because his bride is Danish on her mother's side.

Canto XLI gives an account of the chivalrous beginnings of the Estensi before returning to the battle between Ruggiero and Dudone. A truce is called on Ruggiero's terms, and the seven kings are freed and sail back to Africa with Ruggiero. But a terrible storm sends the men into lifeboats. Ruggiero swims for shore. When the storm is over, the pilotless ship sails on to Africa. It is this ship that Orlando sees as they prepare for their battle with Agramante. They board the ship and find only weapons, armor, and the horse Frontino aboard. Orlando gives the horse to Brandimart for the battle and distributes the weapons and armor. Both sides go to Lampedusa, the battle site.

Swimming to shore, Ruggiero vows to become a Christian. When he reaches land he meets a holy hermit who foretells his future: From the day of his baptism he will live seven years, to be ambushed by Mazanzans to avenge Pinabello's death, which Bradamante, not he, caused. His descendants—and Bradamante's—are foretold: the mighty House of Este.

At Lampedusa, Sobrino is wounded and left for dead. Gradasso slays Brandimart. Oliver is pinned under his fallen horse.

In Canto XLII, raging over Brandimart's death, Orlando slays both Agramante and Gradasso. He hears Brandimart's last words: "Remember me, Orlando, when you pray." He adds, "To you I commend/My Fiordi—" but dies before he can speak his wife's name. Orlando rescues Oliver and has Sobrino carried to his tent.

Meanwhile, Bradamante is in anguish when she discovers that Ruggiero has broken his vow and remained loyal to Agramante.

Rinaldo, who loves Angelica, sets out to find her. He asks the help of the magician Malagigi, who tells him Angelica is married to the Saracen Medoro, destined to be king of India. He sets out to find her. In the forest of Ardennes, he is attacked by a monster but is rescued by a cavalier who refuses to reveal his identity. They reach a fountain from which Rinaldo drinks, curing him of his love for Angelica. The knight then reveals that his name is Scorn; instantly he disappears. Rinaldo hears of the final combat and sets out to reach Orlando. When he arrives in Italy, a cavalier invites him to his palace, which is adorned with statues of illustrious Italians. At dinner he is offered a magic potion that will tell him if his wife Clarice is virtuous.

In Canto XLIII, Rinaldo refuses the goblet. The host relates an early episode in Melissa's life. Instead of going to bed, Rinaldo takes a riverboat to the future site of Ferrara, hears the boatman's tale, then journeys on to Ravenna, rides to Ostia, and sails for Sicily, eventually reaching Lampedusa, where he sees a battlefield. He joins in the procession at Brandimart's funeral. Fiordiligi joins Brandimart in his tomb and dies. After the funeral Orlando must find a doctor for Oliver, whose foot was crushed by the fallen horse. They hear of a hermit near Sicily who can heal him. Orlando, Rinaldo, Oliver, and the wounded Sorbino arrive in Sicily and find Ruggiero there as well. Oliver is healed, and when Sorbino witnesses the miracle, he is converted, baptized, and healed of his own wounds. They recognize Ruggiero and pay him special honor. He has been baptized.

In Canto XLIV the hermit advises Rinaldo to accept Ruggiero as his brother-in-law. Rinaldo agrees and promises Bradamante to him, unaware that his father awaits his consent for her to marry Leone, prince of the Levant. The five take leave of the hermit. Orlando restores Ruggiero's weapons and the horse Frontino.

Meanwhile, Astolfo dismisses the troops and returns to France, sets the hippogriff free, and travels to Marseilles, arriving the same day as Orlando, Rinaldo, Oliver, Sorbino, and Ruggiero. A grand procession is held in the victors' honor. Duke Aymon and Duchess Beatrice are furious to learn that Rinaldo has promised his sister to Ruggiero. Bradamante is in a quandary, not wishing to disobey. Ruggiero, who has no wealth to offer, is tormented. Bradamante sends him a letter, pledging undying love. She asks Charlemagne not to allow anyone to marry her unless he is able to best her with lance or sword. Her parents whisk her away to Rochefort, while Ruggiero devises a plan to win her.

He goes to Bulgaria, arriving in Belgrade just as Constantine and Leone, to whom Bradamante has been promised, are about to attack the Bulgars. When he sees the Bulgars routed, he rallies them, killing many Greeks and Constantine's nephew. Leone retires to a hillside to watch, admiring the valiant Ruggiero. When the Greeks retreat, Ruggiero agrees to be the Bulgars' king, but first he sets after Leone, who has fled. After a long pursuit, he arrives at a city ruled by Unigardo, who recognizes him.

In Canto XLV, Unigardo, a loyal vassal of Constantine, has Ruggiero taken prisoner and handed over to Theodora. While Bradamante grieves about his absence from court, Leone rescues him. Ruggiero swears loyalty to Leone and, despite his anguish, agrees to take Leone's place in the combat against Bradamante.

He knows that he must die. He does not use his lance or sword, does not ride Frontino, which would give away his identity. He wears Leone's coat and enters into battle with his beloved Bradamante. But although he never aims a blow at her, he fends off hers and is declared the victor. Leone thanks Ruggiero for winning him his bride, while Bradamante sorrows. Ruggiero retreats to the forest in grief.

Marfisa goes to Charlemagne, refuting Leone's claim to Bradamante because she and Ruggiero are already wed. (XXII:34) When Charlemagne questions Bradamante, she neither denies nor admits it. Aymon refutes the betrothal because Ruggiero was not a Christian at the time. Marfisa proposes that Leone fight Ruggiero. Leone agrees, because he now has the unicorn, which guarantees his victory. He sends scouts to find Ruggiero.

In Canto XLVI, anxious to see Bradamante and Ruggiero marry, Melissa leads Leone to Ruggiero, who has been fasting and is near death. He reveals for the first time that he is Ruggiero, who would have killed Leone in Bulgaria if he had caught him. Ruggiero explains that while he lives, Bradamante is not free to marry, so he is doing the honorable thing and starving himself to death. His chivalry astonishes Leone, who relinquishes his claim to the maid. Melissa conjures food, which revives Ruggiero. Leone helps him onto Frontino, who has sought out and found his master.

The Bulgars send ambassadors to France to bring back Ruggiero as their king. Leone and Ruggiero arrive in Charlemagne's court where Leone tells the king, without revealing his identity, that the knight with him is the unknown champion who bested Bradamante in battle. Marfisa leaps up and says her brother Ruggiero is the only true mate of Bradamante. Anyone else, she says, will have to fight her. Ruggiero removes his helmet, revealing his identity, and there is great rejoicing in the court. Duke Aymon changes his mind and welcomes Ruggiero as his son-in-law. The Bulgars declare him their king.

A big wedding is prepared. On the wedding tent Cassandra embroiders a prophecy about the birth and life of Cardinal Ippolito d'Este, a descendant of Ruggiero and Bradamante. At the wedding banquet Rodomonte appears and challenges Ruggiero, saying he is a traitor to his lord. Bradamante fastens Mandricardo's armor on her husband, who refuses the aid of the paladins. After a ferocious battle, Rodomonte is slain. (Ariosto [Vol. 1] 1973; [Vol. 2] 1977)

 # *ORLANDO INNAMORATO*
(Roland in love)

Italian Romantic epic (1482–1483) by Matteo Maria Boiardo, Count Scandiano (1434–1494). The poem of 35,440 lines, written in Ferrarese dialect in octaves, was intended to consist of three books. Book I, containing 29 cantos, and Book II, with 31 cantos, were published in 1482. Thereafter the poet undertook Book III, but it was left unfinished at the ninth canto at the time of the poet's death. The poem represents the first attempt to blend the Carolingian stories of chivalry (legends of Charlemagne and his paladins) with the Arthurian stories of romance. In the sixteenth century, Francesco Berni (ca. 1497/1498–1535) translated the poem into Tuscan. Because the original Ferrarese dialect was less facile, Berni's version was the more popular for many years. The year after Boiardo's death, his widow issued Book III—eight cantos and a partial ninth. Eleven years later a Venetian poet, Nicolo degli Agostini, wrote a fourth book. Before he could finish a fifth and sixth book, another poet, Raphael da Verona, had written his own fifth book. The poem was the inspiration for Ludovico Ariosto's *Orlando Furioso*, the finest Italian epic. The poet keeps several plot threads going at once, skipping back and forth, adding to the suspense.

Book I is entitled "Containing the Various Adventures and the Cause of His Falling in Love, Translated from the True Chronicle of Turpin. . . ." Turpin was the legendary archbishop of Reims in France, whom Boiardo and others credited with writing a chronicle of Charlemagne's reign.

Canto I introduces a mighty king reigning in the Orient, Gradasso, who wants two things: the horse Bayardo belonging to Ranaldo, and Durindana, Orlando's sword. He chooses 150,000 knights to accompany him to France, although he seeks to duel alone with Charlemagne. Meanwhile, King Charles sits at his Round Table surrounded by knights, including the treacherous Gano and Ranaldo, the poorest one, and their various wives. The beautiful Angelica arrives with her brother Argalia, whom she introduces as "Uberto." She has been sent as a decoy by her father, King Galafrone of Cathay, to entice the knights to joust against her brother with his invincible lance, offering herself as the prize if Uberto is unhorsed. Her purpose is to distract the Christian knights, rendering them vulnerable when the Saracens attack. Orlando is smitten by the bewitching princess, as are all the others. But Malagise, Ranaldo's magician cousin, sees the true character of Angelica and predicts destruction for Charlemagne's court. He sees that Galafrone has given his son a ring that, held in the mouth, makes a man invisible; worn on his finger, it breaks spells. Later, at the pagan camp outside the town, Malagise sneaks up on Angelica, who is napping. He casts a spell over her giant guards, but she is wearing the ring, and it protects her. Argalia appears and ties up Malagise. They transport him magically to Cathay, where Galafrone locks him in an ocean rock. With Malagise's book of spells, Angelica wakes her giants.

The paladins draw lots to joust against Argalia. English duke Astolfo is defeated first. Feraguto, nephew of the king of Spain, is next, but he refuses to quit even after he is unhorsed. Angelica's giants step in, but Feraguto defeats all four.

In Canto II, Feraguto's refusal to yield disrupts the plan to defeat all the paladins, so Angelica and Argalia decide to return to Cathay, leaving behind the magic lance. Astolfo retrieves it, unaware of its magic power. Meanwhile, Ranaldo, who has drawn third, hurries to Arden Wood to catch Argalia to joust. Orlando frets for fear that Ranaldo will win Angelica before he has a chance to joust. He sneaks off to Arden Wood to find her first.

Charlemagne calls for a joust between Christians and pagans. During the joustings, Ogiere the Dane falls, so terrifying Gano that he slips away. Charles is furious because Ranaldo, Orlando, and Gano are all absent. Astolfo, returning from his defeat at the hands of Argalia, volunteers to uphold the Christian honor, but Charles sees Astolfo as an embarrassment and is distressed.

In Canto III, Astolfo defeats Grandonio of Morocco, using the lance that he doesn't realize is invincible. Thereafter he defeats several others. The joust suddenly turns into a brawl; Charles has to intervene to restore order. He jails Astolfo.

Ranaldo arrives at the wood and, finding no one, spies a fountain and takes a drink, not realizing that it is Merlin's magic fountain. Any cavalier in love who drinks from it will hate the one he once adored. After he has drunk, Ranaldo decides that he hates Angelica. He lies down and goes to sleep. Angelica arrives and falls in love with the sleeping prince. When he wakes and sees her, he leaps upon his horse Bayardo and rides away, ignoring her cries of love. She lies down in his spot and sleeps.

Feraguto arrives and does battle with Argalia, who is fatally stabbed. Argalia asks to be relieved of his armor and thrown into a stream. Feraguto obliges, having first received permission to wear Argalia's helmet for several days.

Orlando comes across the sleeping Angelica. As he admires her, Feraguto appears wearing Argalia's helmet. They do not recognize each other and begin fighting. Angelica awakens and takes flight.

In Canto IV, as the two fight, Spanish princess Fiordespina rides up and tells her cousin Feraguto that King Gradasso has arrived from the Orient and is sacking Spain. Feraguto asks Orlando to postpone the duel so that he can rush off to Spain to help defend it. Orlando also leaves, to look for Angelica.

Charlemagne sends Ranaldo with an army to Spain to help King Marsilio against Gradasso's attack. In a great battle Ranaldo routs 200,000 pagans, then battles a mob of seven square miles. The battle gets down to a duel between Ranaldo and Gradasso, who wants his horse Bayardo. But even in the biblical Samson's armor, Gradasso cannot defeat Ranaldo on his fantastic horse. Ranaldo sees his brother Ricciardetto being held prisoner by Orione.

In Canto V, Ranaldo slices Orione in half. Gradasso suggests a new battle the following day—on foot. If Ranaldo wins, all the prisoners will be released. If Gradasso wins, the horse Bayardo will be his. Ranaldo agrees.

Angelica has conjured a sprite to take her back to Cathay, but she cannot forget Ranaldo. She goes down to the sea and rescues Malagise from the rock, telling him she will free him and restore his book of spells if he will make Ranaldo come to her. Malagise agrees. A demon transports him to Barcelona, where his cousin Ranaldo is encamped. He begs Ranaldo to come make love to Angelica and thus buy his freedom, but Ranaldo refuses. With the help of demons, Malagise lures Ranaldo aboard a ship that transports him swiftly east to a garden by the sea.

Orlando, also traveling east in search of Angelica, meets a palmer who laments that a giant has just stolen his son. Orlando rescues the boy, and in return the palmer gives him a gold book containing the answer to everything. Orlando then fights a monster who asks two questions: What creature walks but has no feet? and What walks using four, then two, then three? After he has killed the monster he refers to his book and finds that the answer to the first question is a seal. The answer to the second is a human being who first crawls on all fours and as an old man uses a cane. He rides on until he meets a giant guarding the Bridge of Death. The two begin to fight.

In Canto VI, Orlando kills the giant, but not before the giant releases a net that traps Orlando, causing him to drop his sword Durindana. He calls to a passing friar to use the sword to cut him down, but the friar is too weak, and he runs away as a giant cyclops arrives. The giant throws the sword at him, cutting the net and freeing him, but Orlando, enchanted, can't be killed. The two face off, the giant using the magic sword Durindana and Orlando using a club. Orlando spies a spear, which he hurls at the giant's one eye, felling him. He retrieves his sword and the friar comes out of hiding to show him the cave where the giant keeps prisoners. After he has freed them, Orlando rides off. He soon meets a courier who tells him that Angelica is in hiding so as not to have to marry a Tartar as her father has arranged. Orlando hurries on but is met by a damsel on a bridge. She holds a crystal cup from which he must drink before he can cross. When he drinks, he forgets everything and becomes the damsel's slave.

Meanwhile, when Ranaldo disappears, Gradasso returns to camp, vowing to raze Paris if he doesn't get the horse Bayardo. Ricciardetto, believing his brother Ranaldo must have been killed, leads his troops back to the French frontier. In Paris, Charlemagne prepares for Gradasso's attack. Ogieri the Dane leads 12,000 men through the gate. An enormous battle ensues.

In Canto VII, Ogieri fights the pagans fiercely, but is wounded and must retreat. Charlemagne rides Bayardo. Gradasso unseats him, but Bayardo gallops off to Paris. Gradasso captures many knights and the Christian army retreats. Gradasso tells Charlemagne that he will release his prisoners if they will send him the horse Bayardo and, when Orlando returns, the sword Durindana. Charlemagne agrees and sends a messenger to town for the horse. But Astolfo, who has vowed to defeat Gradasso himself, has the messenger locked up. He sends a challenge to Gradasso, who accepts and agrees to release his prisoners and go home if he loses. Astolfo defeats him with one stroke of the magic lance. Gradasso releases the prisoners and takes his troops all the way to Africa, while Astolfo sets out to find Ranaldo and Orlando.

In Canto VIII, Ranaldo reaches the garden on the island of the Pleasure Palace, where he is met by a maiden who leads him into the palace. He is dined and entertained by maidens. One tells him the palace has been built for him by Angelica. Hearing this, Ranaldo leaves at once and reboards the ship. It sails swiftly away, bringing him to a distant shore, where a grizzled old man begs him to rescue his daughter, kidnapped by a highwayman. Ranaldo chases the thief, who drops the girl when he sees the paladin coming and sounds a loud horn. At that, a nearby castle drops its drawbridge and out stalks an evil giant, who attacks Ranaldo. The giant triggers a trap and Ranaldo falls in. The giant catches him and carries him toward the castle. On the drawbridge an old crone appears who tells the story of the castle: how a lustful knight, her husband, falls in love with the castle's chatelaine and conspires to kill the woman's husband. The chatelaine and the knight's wife serve the knight his own children for dinner. He kills the chatelaine and then rapes her. From that seed a devil monster is magically born who guards their dungeon tombs. Ranaldo, who is to be fed to the monster, asks permission to fight the beast. During the bloody battle he is wounded four times.

In Canto IX, Malagise returns to tell Angelica Ranaldo's answer to her offer and of his fate. She is furious and threatens to have Malagise killed, but he explains how only she can rescue Ranaldo. She flies to the grate above the dungeon and drops glue into the monster's mouth, thus enabling Ranaldo to strangle the brute with his bare hands. He escapes the dungeon and is walking along the shore when he hears a damsel crying in distress.

Astolfo, still traveling east on the horse Bayardo, comes to the Tartar kingdom of Agricane, who also loves Angelica and wants her for his wife. She hates him and has sent out a plea for someone to come to her aid. King Sacripante of Circassia, also in love with her, is the first to arrive with his troops. He wants Astolfo to join him, but Astolfo refuses unless he can lead. Sacripante decides to follow him and get his horse and sword. Astolfo rides until he meets a great Saracen knight, Brandimart, accompanying a lovely damsel. Astolfo challenges Brandimart to a joust. The Saracen's horse falls and dies on the first clash and, thinking he has lost the damsel, Brandimart prepares to stab himself. Astolfo assures him that he does not plan to take his woman, causing Brandimart to weep: "My shame is doubled, lord: You've twice/Conquered me—now with courtesy. . . ." Sacripante appears and, seeing the fair damsel, challenges Brandimart for her. Since Brandimart has no horse, Astolfo challenges Sacripante for his horse and easily bests him. He gives the horse to Brandimart and the three ride away. The damsel begs them to change course because the River of Forgetfulness lies ahead, but they relish adventure. They come upon Dragontina, an enchantress with a crystal cup, guarding the river bridge. Astolfo threatens her; the bridge bursts into flames. The damsel leads them farther to another bridge. They reach a garden gate, which Brandimart batters down, and they find the prisoners, including Orlando, all with no memories. A brawl ensues. Astolfo escapes Orlando's sword when Bayardo bounds over the wall. Orlando gives chase.

In Canto X, unable to overtake Astolfo, Orlando returns to the battle site. Dragontina gives Brandimart a drink drawn from the demonic stream and he forgets everything.

Thinking that Orlando is still chasing him, Astolfo gallops for two days. He comes upon an encamped army and learns that the assembled kings are set to help Agricane lay siege to the citadel of Albraca, where Angelica is hiding. He rides to Albraca; Angelica embraces him, but says she wishes he were Ranaldo. When the kings and their huge army attack, Astolfo goes to meet them single-handedly. But he is soon unhorsed and Agricane gets the horse Bayardo. King Sacripante arrives with his army.

In Canto XI, Agricane, who has been trying to stop his army's retreat, invites Sacripante to a duel. The two fight until the king of Turkey rouses the others to intervene. In the melee Sacripante's army retreats to Albraca, where Angelica admits them. But Agricane and 300 of his men also get in. Recuperating from a loss of blood, Sacripante goes to help drive out Agricane.

Coming from Castle Cruel, Ranaldo meets Fiordelisa, a maid needing help to fight nine knights trapped in the River of Forgetfulness. One is Orlando. Ranaldo agrees to go with her.

In Canto XII, Fiordelisa tells a love story of Iroldo and Tisbina. As she finishes they hear an ear-splitting howl.

In Canto XIII, Ranaldo confronts a giant guarding Argalia's horse and wounds him. The giant releases two griffins that have been chained on either side. One flies away with the giant while Ranaldo attacks the other, finally killing it. He descends to the cave entrance and finds the body of a damsel with a message challenging him to right her wrong. Entering the cave, he finds a magnificent horse tethered and a book telling the story of the treacherous king of Baghdad, Trufaldino. He releases the horse Rabicano, and returns to the damsel. They travel on, stopping to sleep in the forest. A centaur appears. Ranaldo wakes and attacks the creature, which grabs the damsel and gallops away.

In Canto XIV, Ranaldo gives chase to the centaur, which throws the damsel in a river and turns to fight. He easily bests it with his sword Fusbert, then resumes his quest for Orlando.

Trapped inside the city walls at Albraca, Agricane battles Sacripante. Torindo of Turkey joins the fray against Agricane. Seeing the enormous slaughter, Angelica decides to seek help. Promising Sacripante and the others that she will return in 20 days with help if they will continue to guard her citadel, she puts the magic ring into her mouth, becomes invisible, and slips out. She rides off and meets an old man whose son lies dying in a house close by. Angelica knows herbal remedies, so she follows him, unaware that he has tricked her: He must pay a tribute of 100 women every year to his king. He locks her in his tower with the other captives. Among them is Brandimart's love, Fiordelisa, who tells her where Orlando and the others are being held captive by Dragontina. Angelica again uses the ring to make herself invisible and slips out before the bridge door closes. She rides to Dragontina's hideaway and slips in. She finds Orlando sleeping and places the ring on his finger, canceling out his enchantment. She tells him how he came to be there and asks him to help her fight Agricane and save her city. After disenchanting the other prisoners, they all set off to confront Agricane.

Trufaldino, king of Baghdad, finds his friends Sacripante and Torindo asleep and throws them in the dungeon. He sends a message telling Agricane, who is insulted: he wants to win by force and courage, not by trickery.

Orlando, nearing Agricane's troops, blows his horn. Believing that Angelica's father, Galafrone, has come to reclaim his castle, Agricane covers Bayardo with mail and prepares for the battle.

In Canto XV, in the fierce fighting, Angelica is captured when she forgets to use her ring. Trufaldino agrees to open the citadel if Orlando promises to be his champion against any challenger. At Angelica's behest, Orlando agrees. They enter the citadel and prepare for another battle the next day.

Canto XVI depicts the battle between Agricane and Orlando, which lasts six hours. Agricane wears a helmet made by Solomon, which saves his life. Galafrone's arrival to reclaim Albraca interrupts the duel. With his army is Marfisa, a woman warrior who has sworn to wear arms until she bests Gradasso, Agricane, and Charlemagne. As Galafrone begins to fail, Angelica sends for help from Orlando.

Meanwhile, Ranaldo sits beside a spring grieving for a friend destined to die.

Canto XVII explains that the friend is Iroldo, enamored of Queen Falerina, who holds visitors captive in a garden guarded by a serpent. Iroldo was held captive for four months until ransomed by Prasildo, who took his place. Now Iroldo means to attack to save his friend from the dragon, and Ranaldo vows to help him. After Prasildo's rescue, both men worship Ranaldo as if he were a god. Ranaldo converts the men and Fiordelisa to Christianity, then expresses an intention to find Falerina's garden, although the damsel warns him that it is enchanted and guarded by a dragon, a bull, an ass, and a giant. She advises him to try to free Orlando instead. He agrees, and they all set out, but find the garden destroyed. They meet a man who tells them what happened, and they know that Orlando has survived. They ride on and meet the woman warrior Marfisa, who challenges all three knights together.

In Canto XVIII, Prasildo charges first but is thrown from his horse. Iroldo falls next. Ranaldo then charges, and they have a ferocious battle like Ranaldo has never had before.

Orlando goes to Galafrone's aid. He and his paladins turn the meadow red with blood. Then he resumes his duel with Agricane, while the Tartar's army is being destroyed. Their battle takes them far afield into the night. Finally they agree to stop until dawn. They talk about Christianity and of "worthy and chivalric manners." But neither can endure another man being in love with Angelica, so before dawn they resume their duel.

In Canto XIX, Orlando eventually strikes the mortal blow against Agricane, who begs to be baptized before he dies. Orlando carries him to the stream and baptizes him. After the king dies, the horse Bayardo approaches Orlando, who mounts him, leading his own horse by the reins. He enters the forest and meets three giants leading a camel carrying a girl prisoner. He determines to free her, battling two giants while the third guards the girl.

Agricane's troops disperse in disarray. Galafrone frees the captives, among them Astolfo. Angelica thanks them for their help. Astolfo, Ballano, and Antifor ask for horses and go off to avenge their imprisonment. Astolfo meets and kills a Tartar in his armor. He dons his own armor and goes on to do great deeds.

Ranaldo and Marfisa are still fighting with no intention of yielding. Galafrone, in pursuit of Agricane's fleeing troops, stops to watch. He sees Rubican, the steed his own son, Argalia, was riding when he was killed. Believing Ranaldo must have killed his son, he charges. Marfisa is enraged to have the duel disturbed and charges Galafrone. Brandimart and Antifor arrive and, presuming Marfisa to be one of Agricane's warriors, charge her. Seeing her outnumbered, Ranaldo offers aid. Fiordelisa arrives, and she and Brandimart slip into the woods to make love. Afterward they fall asleep.

In Canto XX a wizard, Palmer, sneaks in, drugs Fiordelisa with a magic root, and steals her. Brandimart wakes and rides off to rescue her. He comes across Orlando and the three giants with the maid on a camel. He attacks and, with Orlando's help, defeats them. But he finds that the woman he has rescued is not Fiordelisa.

Marfisa chases all the knights, even Astolfo, into the citadel. She calls on Ranaldo, who is inside the walls, eliciting his help in fighting Trufaldin, the traitor. Ranaldo sounds his horn and calls him out.

In Canto XXI the knights inside the citadel do not feel right defending a traitor, but they have given their word. They especially feel badly about killing their friend Ranaldo—for they outnumber him seven to one. But Ranaldo will not back down.

With magic herbs Leodilla, the damsel whom Brandimart and Orlando saved, heals the head wound Brandimart sustained in the battle. She tells of her two suitors—one old, one young—between whom she proposes a race: Whoever bests her will win her. But the old man, Foldorico, enchants her with golden apples, tempting her off her path, so that he wins. She vows to finish her story later.

In Canto XXII the three go in search of Fiordelisa, whom the wizard Palmer has carried off to a cave. But a lion in the cave tears Palmer to shreds. Fiordelisa runs away and meets a large man who ties her to a tree.

Leodilla resumes her story to Orlando and Brandimart: Foldorico, the old man who wins her as a wife, locks her in a fortress. Ordauro, the young suitor who also vied for her, buys a palace nearby and builds a tunnel to her fortress, and the two become lovers. Ordauro invites Foldorico to his palace to meet his new bride. Leodilla dresses like a bride and races through the tunnel to the palace, where Ordauro introduces her as Leodilla's twin sister. After Ordauro, claiming that he must escape the unhealthy sea air, leaves with his "wife" for the inland, Foldorico finds Leodilla and his treasure gone, and he hires a young man to follow them. The young man lures Ordauro away while he grabs Leodilla. He takes her to a gloomy valley where three giants surprise him.

Leodilla halts her story when the great stag of the Treasure Fairy appears. Enchanted by its beauty, Brandimart gives chase for hours. But at night he loses it and lies down to sleep.

In Canto XXIII, the next day, Brandimart finds Fiordelisa tied to a tree. He fights and slays the Wild Man. As the two ride off to find Orlando, they tell each other of their recent adventures.

Ranaldo, fighting Grifone, begins to lose when Aquilante and Chiaron join against him. Marfisa evens the odds by helping him.

In Canto XXIV, Leodilla, who has been telling her story to Orlando, is disappointed at his lack of interest in her. All night he ignores her. The next morning a maid appears who presents him with a book and a horn that will aid him in battle. Three times he must sound the horn. The first two will bring great tests and pain. The third will make him "a happy man for life." He blows the horn and two bulls emerge from a boulder. He reads in the book that he must yoke the bulls and plow the adjoining field, or he will die. He performs this feat and blows the horn again. A dragon appears, which Orlando's book says he must behead and sow its teeth in the field. From these teeth armed men spring up, and he must slay them. After they all die, they are absorbed in the earth.

In Canto XXV, when Orlando blows the horn the third time, a white hound appears. When nothing else happens, Orlando throws the horn away. The damsel tells him the hound is owned by the fairy Morgana, who has hidden gold in the mountain, and it can lead him to the stag, which, when caught, can bring the hunter great wealth. Orlando tells her he will not hunt the stag because those who "set their minds on wealth/. . . never can be satisfied." He rides off with Leodilla behind him. They meet her lover, Ordauro, who takes Leodilla. Orlando rides on to Angelica's citadel, where she gives him a bath and a feast, then begs him to defend her from Marfisa, who has developed a hatred for her. He vows to do so. Aquilante and Grifone appear and tell him that Ranaldo is coming. Orlando grows jealous to think that Ranaldo may also love Angelica. He weeps, knowing that one of them must die. Three hours before dawn he goes out to meet Ranaldo.

In Canto XXVI the various knights are arrayed against each other. Ranaldo kills Trufaldino. Orlando, astride Bayardo, cannot make the horse obey so long as Ranaldo is around. Brandimart arrives with Orlando's steed, Brigliador, which Orlando mounts. Brandimart leads Bayardo back to the citadel. Orlando and Marfisa fight until Ranaldo appears, dragging part of Trufaldino's body. Orlando challenges Ranaldo, who does not want to fight his kinsman, but is finally provoked to duel.

In Canto XXVII the two exchange insults, then engage in a ferocious battle lasting until nightfall. They decide to return the next morning. Orlando returns to the citadel, and when he tells Angelica that Ranaldo is outside, she trembles and begs to be allowed to watch the duel the next day. She wants Marfisa to guarantee her safety for the duration of the duel. Sacripante rides out into the night to arrange a peace pact with Marfisa. The next morning Angelica promises to let Orlando have his way with her if he will grant one wish on the battlefield.

In Canto XXVIII again the knights exchange insults, then battle for hours. Eventually, as Orlando is about to strike the fatal blow, Angelica intervenes, reminding him of their promises of the night before. She tells him to leave at once for the realm's edge, where he will find a magic garden guarded by a dragon, which he must slay. He gallops off, and when Ranaldo revives, he wants to ride after, vowing revenge. Distressed when Ranaldo refuses her invitation to go to the citadel to have his wounds tended, she asks a maid to return Bayardo to Ranaldo. But Astolfo intercepts the maid, taking the horse for himself.

Orlando meets a knight guarding a damsel dangling by her hair over a river.

In Canto XXIX the knight, named Uldarno, tells of how the damsel, named Origille, tricked him and two others into fighting her brother on behalf of her father, who wants him dead. All four men are sentenced to die because Origille's scheme is illegal. Still, Orlando vows to rescue the damsel, but after he does, she tricks him, steals his horse, and leaves him afoot on the plain.

Book II is entitled "The Second Book of Orlando Innamorato Continuing the History Already Begun, Tells of the African Attack on Charlemagne and Introduces Rugiero the Third Peer, Founder of the Renowned House of Este."

Canto I recounts the genealogy of King Agramante, who calls together 32 kings, telling them they will win no fame unless they go to France to fight Charlemagne. The old men try to dissuade him, while the young ones want to go. The aging king of Garamanta says they must find Rugiero, without whom they can't win the war.

In Canto II, while Agramante and his brigade search for Rugiero in Africa, Ranaldo, Astolfo, Prasildo, and Iroldo ride off to search for Orlando. They meet a maid crying for her sister who has been carried off by a knave and tied to a tree above the river. Three knights disappear into the river struggling with the knave while Astolfo looks on in horror. He and the maids leave the scene and travel on until they hear a trumpet blast.

Grifone and Aquilante, riding ahead of Orlando, come to a pretty garden and a palace where they spend the night. Origille rides in on Orlando's horse, telling the lie that she has found the horse beside Orlando's slain body. During the night all three are captured by unknown assailants. As they are led away, they see a cavalier coming on foot but do not recognize him.

Marfisa and her men still lay siege to Angelica's citadel. Marfisa cuts Oberto (Angelica's brother) in two. Sacripante and Marfisa face off.

In Canto III, Marfisa and Sacripante are fighting when word comes that King Mandricardo and his son have killed Sacripante's brother and threaten to take his kingdom. Sacripante asks leave to go save his kingdom, but Marfisa refuses, saying she will not stop until she has destroyed Angelica. So the fighting resumes.

In Africa, Agramante is having no luck finding Rugiero, so he consults the seer Garamanta, who tells him of Angelica's magic ring, which will allow them to find Rugiero and the secret garden. He warns against trying to invade France without Rugiero, but "Haughty Rodamonte" decides to go on to France alone. He takes his men to Algiers and prepares to cross the sea. Brunello, the dwarf king, vows that he will find the ring.

Orlando, on foot, sees some men leading prisoners: Grifone, Aquilante, and Origille, riding his stolen horse. He learns from their captors that the prisoners are to be fed to the dragon in Falerina's garden at Organa. When he is recognized, he has to draw his sword to keep from being taken prisoner as well. He fights so valiantly that the captors flee, leaving the prisoners. Origille and Grifone have fallen in love, but Orlando sends him and Aquilante on their way. A lady rides up on a white horse and warns him of the nearby enchanted garden. He asks how to get in.

In Canto IV the lady tells him he must remain chaste if he wants to enter the garden, and that he can only enter at sunrise. She gives him a book and leaves. That night while Orlando sleeps, Origille steals his magic sword and horse and goes to look for Grifone. Orlando wakes at sunrise and tries to enter the garden by clubbing the dragon to death. His book tells him to follow the nearby stream to exit. He meets Falerina, who refuses to tell him where the gates are. He ties her to a tree and consults his book. So that he can't hear the siren's deadly song, he stuffs his ears with roses. When the siren, part beast, emerges from the water and sings, he pretends to falls asleep. When she nears, he grabs her and cuts off her head. With her blood, he stains his skin and armor to protect himself from the bull guarding the gate. He kills the bull and an ass with gold scales, then faces two giants.

In Canto V he ties the giants to the bridge and, instead of leaving, wonders how he can destroy the evil garden. He reads about a tree that will cause the garden to disappear if he can snap off its topmost branch. He accomplishes this deed. Falerina, tied to a tree, explains why she built the garden: to punish the knight Ariante and his "lying wench," Origille. She tells Orlando that if she dies, the bridge and her prisoners will disappear.

While Marfisa and Sacripante continue to fight, Brunello, sent from Africa by Agramante, reaches Angelica's walls, intent on stealing her ring so they can find Rugiero. While Angelica watches the fighting, Brunello sneaks up and snatches the ring. When Marfisa and Sacripante take a break, Brunello steals Sacripante's horse and Marfisa's sword. Angelica takes out after him.

Caramano, leading 200,000 troops from Turkey, is bent on killing Angelica. Galafrone tells her to seek Gradasso's help, so Sacripante, in pilgrim's garb, slips away to find him.

In Canto VI, despite a storm at sea, Rodamonte sets off from Algiers with his troops. But the ships are scattered at sea.

In France, Charlemagne plans for Agramante's invasion. He sends Duke Namo, Ansuardo, and Ranaldo's sister Bradamante to guard Provence.

Rodamonte's ships are blown to Monaco, where the locals attack them. Arcimbaldo of Cremona sends for help, and Lombard's Desiderio and Bavaria's Namo lead their armies toward Monaco.

In Canto VII, Namo's forces attack. Bradamante's lance can't penetrate Rodamonte's armor. Desiderio and his troops attack.

Falerina and Orlando reach the river of the fata (fairy) Morgana and see Ranaldo's armor hanging on a tree, where Aridano (one of the nine kings escorting Angelica to Albraca) hung it after he defeated Ranaldo, Iroldo, Prasildo, and Dudone. Orlando vows to avenge his cousin Ranaldo, but Aridano grabs him and leaps into the lake with him.

In Canto VIII they sink to the bottom and reach a grotto and a new land, where Orlando manages to kill Aridano. He travels through the cave to an exit, which he takes despite a warning sign that he won't be able to leave unless he catches the fay with a bald spot on the back of her head. He finds Morgana, who fits the description, sleeping. He also finds Dudone, Brandimart, and Ranaldo imprisoned behind a crystal wall. He chases Morgana into a stormy, rocky wilderness.

In Canto IX, Orlando meets a woman named Penitence, who plans to thump and whip him as he chases after Morgana. He chases the fay despite the whipping, finally catching her by the forelock. Immediately the whipping ceases. Morgana gives him the key to release the captives, but begs that he not release her love: Ziliant, Brandimart's brother. Orlando releases the others while Ziliant weeps at being left behind. Ranaldo, trying to take gold out with him, is repulsed by a strong wind, so he relents and leaves the gold behind. He goes to Montalbano, while Orlando is determined to go to Angelica's aid, with Brandimart at his side. Ranaldo and his men reach Manodante's realm, which they cannot leave until they fight the giant magician Balisardo for a day.

In Canto X, Iroldo and Prasildo both fight the giant Balisardo and lose. Then Balisardo manages to trap Dudone in the hold of his ship. The giant takes on a disguise as Dudone and faces Ranaldo, who does not want to fight him. Eventually Ranaldo, too, is caught in the snare and hauled below deck. They sail to Manodante's realm, where Astolfo is already imprisoned.

On their way to see Angelica, Orlando and Brandimart encounter Marfisa chasing the thief Brunello.

In Canto XI, Brunello, the thief Agramante sent to steal Angelica's ring, rides by on the horse he stole from Sacripante and grabs Orlando's sword and horn. Orlando and Brandimart see Origille across the river, and Orlando again falls in love with her. Origille begs him to forgive her. He heads downstream to battle the giant Balisardo, who takes the shape of a demon and lures him onto the prison ship. But Brandimart follows, rescues Orlando, cuts off the giant's legs, and throws him into the sea. The prison ship captain surrenders, telling them that Manodante, the richest king in the world, has lost two sons: one kidnapped by the slave Bardino, the other by the fairy Morgana, who loves him. But she has promised to release him in exchange for Orlando. Orlando and Brandimart decide to sail to the king's island on the pretense of delivering Orlando to him. Origille, who loves Grifone, learns he is in Manodante's prison.

In Canto XII, to obtain Grifone's release, Origille tells Manodante of Orlando's plan to trick him. Manodante has Orlando and Brandimart drugged and thrown into the dungeon. There Orlando recites the Bible to Brandimart, converting him to Christianity. In return for saving his soul, Brandimart promises to save Orlando's life. He offers to exchange names so that Orlando will be set free. Brandimart remains in prison while Orlando sails for Morgana's land to retrieve the king's son, Ziliant.

Astolfo asks to see the king, but Brandimart, to avoid being exposed, tells the king that Astolfo is mad. Finally Brandimart confesses that he is not really Orlando and is chained in a tower.

On his way to Morgana's, Orlando sees a dead dragon and a woman mourning it. Another woman rides up and asks for his aid.

In Canto XIII, Morgana is the damsel holding the dead dragon; Brandimart's love, Fiordelisa, is the other. Morgana has used magic to turn Ziliant into a dragon, but the transformation killed him. Orlando tells Fiordelisa where Brandimart is. Morgana resurrects Ziliant as himself and kisses him tenderly. Orlando grabs Morgana by her forelock, making her vulnerable, and demands Ziliant. When Orlando and Ziliant get away, they find Fiordelisa still praying. The three sail to the island of Manodante. Manodante learns that he has held his own son, Brandimart, in prison. The two brothers, Brandimart and Ziliant, embrace, and Brandimart and Fiordelisa kiss. Count Orlando baptizes the whole family. Astolfo, Ranaldo, and all the other prisoners are released. A pretty damsel enters: Brandimart's sister Leodilla.

After many days Dudone calls the cavaliers to fight off Agramante. Ranaldo and Astolfo answer the call, but Orlando does not. Brandimart is determined not to desert Orlando. Ranaldo, Dudone, and Astolfo come across Morgana's sister Alcina fishing. She falls in love with Astolfo and invites him to climb aboard a whale. Then she says some magic words and the whale carries him away. Ranaldo and Dudone attempt to rescue him.

In Canto XIV, Dudone almost drowns, but Ranaldo rescues him and carries him ashore, knowing he can never find Astolfo now. He leads his troops to aid King Desiderio in defending against Rodamonte's invasion of France.

In Canto XV, Rodamonte and Ranaldo meet and duel until King Charles arrives. Rodamonte leaves to fight Charlemagne until nightfall, then he looks for Ranaldo in Arden Wood. Ranaldo follows him, but Rodamonte loses his way and the Spaniard Feraguto confronts him instead. Ranaldo comes to a field where a naked youth sings to three maids dancing around him. They throw their flowers at Ranaldo, then the maids and the youth beat him until he is helpless. One of the maids tells him she is Pasitea, a servant of Cupid, the youth. Ranaldo, who has been loved without loving in return, "must then love but not be believed." He is instructed in how to free himself from "Love's contempt." He finds Merlin's fountain, where he drank once before, shunning Angelica ever since. Now he drinks again and is filled with desire for her. He mounts Bayardo and heads east. Soon he meets a lady and a knight.

Meanwhile, Marfisa still pursues the thief Brunello.

In Canto XVI, Marfisa must follow on foot because her horse has died. She comes upon a maid in white riding with a knight.

Brunello escapes onto a ship and sails for Africa, where Agramante fumes because his army will not leave without Rugiero, who is guarded by a wizard and can't be rescued without the magic ring. Brunello arrives and gives Agramante the ring and Orlando's horn; in return, the king awards him with a kingdom. They all leave to find Rugiero, high on Atalante's mountain. They sound their horns, and Rugiero appears, leaping onto the saddle of a fine horse.

In Canto XVII, while the Africans converge on the Christian lands, Rugiero enters a tournament at Mount Carena wearing Brunello's armor. He is not recognized until he is wounded. He returns to Atalante's cliff for a cure of herbs.

Brandimart and Orlando see a maid sitting by a fountain guarded by a knight on a nearby bridge. A pilgrim dares to cross and is challenged. He throws off his pilgrim clothes: It is Sacripante. The knight is Isoliere, "a daring youth" of Spain. Sacripante is looking for Gradasso. At the maid's request, Orlando stops them from fighting.

In Canto XVIII, Orlando leaves Isoliere behind and heads for Angelica's with Brandimart. They see the armies of several kings amassed before the citadel. After dark, Orlando sneaks into the castle. But when Angelica learns that Ranaldo has returned to France, she begins to think of reasons that Orlando should take her to France. They sneak out, no more than a party of 20. The company divides, Brandimart with Fiordelisa, and Orlando with Angelica, going their separate ways. Orlando encounters flesh-eating giants, whom he defeats. Brandimart rescues Fiordelisa from a group of giants, then rides to help Orlando.

In Canto XIX, Marfisa is furious because she can't catch Brunello, so she turns on Brandimart. When he refuses to fight a woman, she grabs Fiordelisa and threatens to throw her off a cliff. He trades his armor for Fiordelisa's safety. Marfisa rides off and meets two knights who lead her to France. Brandimart and Fiordelisa meet a band of thieves. Brandimart sees Agricane's dead body and takes his armor, leaving his crown. He duels with the leader of the thieves, slays him, and takes his horse.

Orlando and Angelica travel through Persia and Mesopotamia. At Beirut they find a ship bound for Cypress. As "Rotolante," Orlando agrees to help Norindino win Lucina in a joust.

In Canto XX, Orlando and Angelica leave the island secretly. A storm at sea lands them in Arden Wood, where Angelica drinks from Merlin's fountain. At once she detests Ranaldo. Ranaldo, who has chased Feraguto into the wood, sees Angelica and apologizes for his past behavior. He and Orlando prepare to fight for her.

In Canto XXI, as the fight begins, Angelica rides off and meets Charlemagne's army. She tells King Charles about the duel. He hurries to separate the two, promising them that the one who fights better in battle against the invaders will win Angelica. Meanwhile, Duke Namo will guard her. The army sets out for Paris.

In Africa, Rugiero emerges from Atalante's invisible castle to defend Brunello against charges of murder. Atalante predicts that Rugiero will become a Christian whose descendants will found the house of Este.

In Canto XXII, Rodamonte's ships return to Biserta with a prisoner, Dudone. Agramante thinks that Rodamonte is dead.

In France, Rodamonte is fighting Feraguto. They learn from a passing courier that Spanish king Marsilio, Feraguto's uncle, is attacking Montalbano in France. Rodamonte allows Feraguto to halt the duel, and offers to go with him to join Marsilio. They meet the magician Malagise and his brother Vivian, Ranaldo's cousins. Malagise conjures an army to deter the pagans, but they capture him and Vivian and carry them to King Marsilio.

In Canto XXIII, it is the custom of pagan kings to allow ladies in the camp. Rodamonte, enamored of Princess Doralice of Granada, performs deeds daily to attract her attention. Meanwhile, Charlemagne attacks, sending the warrior maiden Bradamante to attack the Saracens from behind.

In Canto XXIV, Charlemagne is unhorsed. Ranaldo fears that Orlando may reach him first and win Angelica, so he rides Bayardo at full speed, reaching Charles first, and helps him remount. Orlando reaches Charles too late, and turns to the battlefield, sweeping through like a black storm.

In Canto XXV, Bradamante leads 10,000 fresh troops in a search for Rodamonte, who killed her horse in Provence. She finds him just as he knocks Orlando unconscious.

Brandimart and Fiordelisa encounter a damsel signaling from a palace guarded by a giant and a dragon. Brandimart kills both creatures six times before they die. Paintings on the courtyard walls foretell the future. The damsel says he must kiss a dragon or die.

In Canto XXVI the damsel brings Brandimart and Fiordelisa to a sepulcher. She tells Brandimart that he must open it and kiss the dragon inside, or they will all fall into an abyss. As soon as he kisses the dragon, it changes into a woman: a fay named Febosilla. As a reward for releasing her from enchantment, she enchants his armor and horse. Brandimart and Fiordelisa accompany the other damsel, Doristella, to Syria, where her father is king of Liza. On the way she tells her life story. Thieves attack. Brandimart catches one, Fugiforca, who begs not to be taken to Liza.

In Canto XXVII the thief says he once kidnapped the king's baby and sold her. She was Doristella's baby sister. When they arrive in Liza, the queen recognizes Fiordelisa as the baby girl. Fiordelisa convinces her family to become Christians. Brandimart rides toward Biserta.

In Canto XXVIII, Agramante is dancing with fair ladies on a portico when Brandimart arrives. The two joust and then join together in hunting wild animals. During a feast a drunken drummer accuses Agramante of delaying his expedition, so the king resolves to embark immediately.

In Canto XXIX, Agramante's gigantic armada sails to Spain. From there they march to France, where Rodamonte is already fighting Charlemagne. Ranaldo fights Feraguto, the paladin Oliver fights Moroccan king Grandonio, and Bradamante fights the Saracens. Orlando sees a huge force approaching, and he rides off to meet them. Agramante orders his officer, Pinadoro, to capture several barons and bring them back unharmed so he can learn about the war. Pinadoro gallops off and meets Orlando, who bests him and sends him back with the message that Marsilio and Charlemagne are battling. Orlando sends a challenge, but Pinadoro advises Agramante not to go. Agramante's other kings rush forward anyway, so he follows, with Rugiero at his side. Charlemagne is stunned to see such a huge army approaching. He sends for Ranaldo and instructs him to go to the pass at the cliffs and start picking off the men as they enter.

Canto XXX describes the battles of the two sides, during which Orlando hides and prays to God that Charles's troops will meet defeat. Feraguto enters the woods where Orlando hides. Neither knows the other is there.

In Canto XXXI, Feraguto drops his helmet in the water, and Orlando offers to help him retrieve it. Feraguto manages to insult him by lauding Ranaldo's valor. Orlando rides off in a rage to help King Charles, who is contemplating retreating from Agramante's onslaught until he sees Orlando coming. Single-handedly Orlando dispatches the warrior kings. As he and Rugiero begin to tilt, the magician Atalante, Rugiero's guardian, conjures hordes of men to keep the Christians busy. Oliver is dragged away by a giant. Ranaldo is mortally wounded and carried away by the horde. Abruptly Orlando stops his fight to chase the enchantment of Atalante. After he leaves, the other Saracens return to the field and begin attacking the Christians. Orlando stops by a spring for a drink. In the water he sees women dancing in a crystal palace. He jumps in the water and goes through a door of gold and sapphires. The epic ends at this point. (Boiardo 1989, 1995)

OS LUSÍADAS

See Lusíadas, Os.

OSMAN

Ragusan (Dubrovnik) Croatian epic poem (1626) by Ivan Franov Gundulić (1588–1638). The epic, written in 1626 but not published until 1826, is considered the finest poem to come out of the golden age of Ragusan poetry. The poem was originally 20 cantos, although cantos 14 and 15 are no longer extant. It is composed in stanzas of four octosyllabic alternately rhyming lines (*abab*) after the fashion of Ludovico Ariosto and Torquato Tasso, using the Baroque artifices characteristic of *marinismo,* named for the poetic style of Giambattista Marino (1569–1625). Using a complex, interwoven plot like that of *Orlando Furioso* and *The Siege of Paris,* the poet weaves several stories around the battle of Chocim.

The poem relates contemporary incidents, celebrating the Polish victory over the Turks at Chocim (Bessarabia, Ukraine) in 1621. It also describes the assassination of Sultan Osman II, who, on pretense of making a pilgrimage to Mecca, in fact planned to raise a new army in Syria and Egypt to do away with the Janissary corps, whom he blamed for his 1621 defeat. But the Janissaries learned of the scheme, deposed him on 19 May 1622, and strangled him the following day. The poem not only exalts the Slavic Christian heroes of the struggle against the Turks, but also prophetically foretells the liberation of all southern Slavs. The outstanding composition of the era, the poem earned Dubrovnik the title of "South Slav Athens." (Dvornik 1962; Gazi 1973; Preminger 1974)

 # *OSSIANIC POEMS*

A series of poems published in Scotland by schoolmaster James Macpherson (1736–1796) purported to be translations from an ancient Gaelic bard, Ossian (or Oisin), of the third century. In 1760, Dr. Hugh Blair, Professor of Rhetoric and Belles Lettres at Edinburgh University, published Macpherson's *Fragments of Ancient Poetry, Collected in the Highlands of Scotland, and Translated from the Gaelic or Erse Language.* The heavy cadences of the poems thrummed with a wild, heroic, primitive power, inspiring an enthusiastic reception throughout Britain.

Money was collected to finance the author on further tours of the Highlands to collect more. Blair was convinced that the fragments pointed to the existence of a lost epic. Macpherson did indeed produce two epics: *Fingal* (1762) and *Temora* (1764). In 1773, Macpherson issued the poems again as *The Poems of Ossian.* These were presented in a poetic prose, expressing lofty sentiments with a pervasive melancholy.

However, some skeptics, such as Samuel Johnson, thought that Macpherson was deceiving the public. Now scholars agree that Macpherson used a few authentic Gaelic fragments as a foundation and formed around them his idea of what the Gaelic epics must have been like. But his idea has an eighteenth-century flavor.

Despite the cloud over the Ossianic poems, no other author did more to hasten the Romantic movement in Western Europe than Macpherson. William Blake, Napoléon, François René de Chateaubriand, Alfonse-Marie-Louis de Lamartine, Johann Wolfgang von Goethe, and Matthew Arnold all admired the poems. In Goethe's early novel *The Sorrows of Young Werther,* there is the statement, "Ossian has superseded Homer in my heart. To what a world does the illustrious bard carry me!"

From *Fingal* (1762): Fingal is described as "tall as a glittering rock. His spear is a blasted pine. His shield the rising moon." When Fingal speaks, it is "like a wave on a rock." The poem ends with Duchomar professing his love for Morna, rhapsodizing over her physical attributes: "Thy arms, like two white pillars, in the halls of the great Fingal." Morna insists that she loves only Cathba, whom Duchomar has slain. She asks Duchomar for his sword, still red with Cathba's blood. When he gives it to her, she pierces "his manly breast" and he falls "like the bank of a mountain stream." He asks her to pull the sword from his breast, but when she draws the sword out, he pierces "her white side" and spreads "her fair locks on the ground." The poem ends with the line: "The cave re-echoed to her sighs." (Grebanier 1949)

 ## *ÖSTERREICHISCHE REIMCHRONIK*

Middle High German epic (late 13th–early 14th c.) by Ottokar von Steiermark (ca. 1260–ca. 1320). The poem, of about 100,000 lines of rhyming couplets, traces Austrian history from the death of Emperor Friedrich II in 1250 to 1309, breaking off abruptly at that point. The most famous part of the poem describes the fall of Acre in 1291. The poet sees the divine hand of God in history and relates the story from the standpoint of the knightly class to which he belonged, developing his style from courtly models. (Garland and Garland 1986)

See also Ottokar von Steiermark.

 ## OTTOKAR VON STEIERMARK

Austrian knight, author of the Middle High German historical epic *Österreichische Reimchronik* (late 13th–early 14th c.) He was born about 1260 in Austria. In his works he mentions as his teacher one Meister Kuonrât von Rôtenbere, an otherwise unknown minstrel. In addition to the huge verse-chronicle, Ottokar also wrote a chronicle of the emperors, now lost. He planned a history of the popes as well, but apparently died before he could write it. (Garland and Garland 1986)

 ## OVID
(Publius Ovidius Naso)

Roman poet, author of *Metamorphoses.* He was born in 43 B.C. to a wealthy equestrian family of Sulmo, some 90 miles east of Rome. His parents had destined him for a career in law, and sent him to Rome for the rhetorical education necessary for a servant of the state, then on to Athens to complete his studies. But after holding several minor political offices, Ovid decided to become a poet. In a short time he became known as the most brilliant poet of his generation.

His first collection, *Amores*, consisted of love elegies. These were followed by the *Heroides,* in the form of love letters between such well-known couples as Hero and Leander and Paris and Helen. The *Ars amatoria* (The art of love) established him as the undisputed arbiter of elegance and grace and a popular member of the Roman social set. At this time he had almost completed his greatest work, the historical epic *Metamorphoses,* relating the history of the world from chaos to the time of Julius Caesar.

However, Emperor Augustus was apparently angered by something in the poem *Ars amatoria.* Ovid was banished from Rome and took up residence at Tomis, a bleak fishing village on the Black Sea, at the very edge of the empire. His epic is still recognized as one of the greatest books of Western literature.

Ovid was never allowed to return to Rome, and died in Tomis in A.D. 17 or 18. (Suetonius 1981)

See also Metamorphoses.

 ## *PADMĀVATĪ*

Indian Hindi religious epic (16th c.) by Malik Muhammad Jāyasī (Jaisi), a Muslim Hindi poet from the former Oudh state. The poem was begun in 1540, but its completion date is unknown; however, it is known that its author was by then an old man. In its present form it consists of 57 cantos and an envoy. The language is the dialect, and much of the imagery, from Ramnagar in north India, where the poet spent his later years. The epic is primarily a tale of love infused with Ṣūfī mysticism—half fairy tale and half historical romance. The main plot—the siege and destruction of Chitar by Alauddin—was derived from Indian history, principally the account by Amir Khusrav, an eyewitness. However, Alauddin's infatuation for Padmāvatī and his attempts to have her, except for a possible hint in Amir Khusrav's account, are probably the invention of Jāyasī.

The poet prefaces his tale, in Canto 1, with a devout paean to the "primal Maker who gave life and made this world," followed by a lengthy, traditionally Muslim account of Creation. He celebrates the coming of the prophet Muḥammad and the writing of the Quran (Koran), sings the praises of the Sher Shah, current sultan of Delhi, and introduces himself as a "follower of poets."

Canto 2 describes Simhala (Ceylon), where God created Padmāvatī, the "Perfect Woman." There are singing birds, ambrosial orchards and gardens, convents and temples where devotees mutter prayers, and beautiful maidens. The city is as bright as the heaven of Çiva (Śiva, Shiva), with streets built by Fairies. Its councillors are wise and speak in Sanskrit. The king's palace has pillars of diamonds and rubies.

Canto 3 describes Padmāvatī's birth, childhood, and growth into adulthood, when she is stirred by erotic feelings. Hirāmini, a parrot and a "great Pandit," serves as a confidant and adviser, giving the princess knowledge of good and evil. The king, her father, gives orders to kill the parrot, but the princess hides it until it seeks refuge in the forest.

In Canto 4, Padmāvatī sports naked in Mānasarodaka Lake surrounded by maidens with the faces of beautiful flowers and the virtues of Padmāvatī. In Canto 5 she asks her maidens to seek the parrot in the forest, but a fowler snares it.

In Canto 6, Ratna-sēna is born in Citra-pura (Citaur), the son and heir to the king, Citra-sēna. The pandits foretell his finding a mate in Simhala. In Canto 7, a merchant from Citaur comes to Simhala with a Brāhmana to trade. The Brāhmana meets the fowler, buys the parrot, and returns to Citaur. In the meantime the king has died, and Ratna-sēna, grown to manhood, is king of Citaur. Hearing of the parrot, he purchases it. In Canto 8 the queen, Nāgmatī, chief of the harem, has heard of Padmāvatī and asks the parrot who is the fairer. Learning the truth, she is enraged and, fearing that the king will hear this from the parrot, orders that it be killed. However, encountering her husband's rage, she has the parrot brought back. In Cantos 9 and 10 the king quizzes the parrot about Padmāvatī and is provided with an erotic inventory of the princess's physical features and charms.

In Canto 11 the king falls in love, and in Canto 12, leaves his kingdom as a Yogi, setting out for Singhala-dvipā (Simhala) with an army of yogi followers, a journey to spiritual emancipation as well as to love. Guided by the parrot, the king comes to the ocean where, in Canto 13, the king of Kalinga meets him with provisions and, in Canto 14, with ships.

In Canto 15 (an allegory of Haṭha Yoga practice), the king crosses the salt sea to the Seven Seas. Counseled by Hirāmani, the parrot, he masters turbulences of the soul to finally seize the tiller of the lead ship and sail out of the blackness of night into sunlight in the seventh sea, the Sea of Mānasar, where they find rapture.

In Canto 16 they reach Singhala-dvipā, where Ratna-sēna approaches the temple of Mahadeo, tutelary deity of the Rājputs and of Yogis, where anyone can obtain fulfillment of any wish. In Canto 17, Ratna-sēna prays that his wish for Padmāvatī be fulfilled. By the force of this Yoga, Padmāvatī falls in love in Canto 18 and, awake all night, searches in all directions for a vision of the one she desires. Appetite and sleep desert her for days. In Canto 19 the parrot comes to her, tells her of his escape from the fowler and his meeting the king of Citaur, Ratna-sēna, a sun worthy of the moon, Padmāvatī. He has left his kingdom and become a Yogi for her sake, and is now in the temple gazing for the sight of her. Padmāvatī immediately falls in love with Ratna-sēna.

In Canto 20 the princess proclaims a spring festival and leads a procession to the temple, but the Yogis, intoxicated with the wine of love, fall into a stupor. Palmāvatī puts sandal-paste on the unconscious Ratna-sēna to awaken him, but unsuccessful, writes, "You have not learnt the yogi of asking alms, so you fell asleep. If you are in love with the moon, come to her." The princess returns to her palace, where she dreams of a siege of a fortress, followed by the joining of the sun and the moon—foretelling a battle for her sake, then married bliss.

Ratna-sēna awakens (Canto 21). Seeing the writing on his body and realizing the princess has been there, he weeps and determines to immolate himself. In Canto 22, the god Mahes (Mahadeo, Śiva), the tutelary deity of Yogis, appears with his wife, Pārvatī, and puts out the pyre. Finding Ratna-sēna purified by his suffering, the god counsels him to assault the fortress that the princess had advised him to climb. In Canto 23, Ratna-sēna takes Siddhguṭika (a pill by which a Yogi obtains enlightenment), and proceeds to the assault. The king,

Gandharvasen, father of Padmāvatī, sends messengers to Ratna-sēna to find out what he wants. Learning that it is his daughter, he orders Ratna-sēna slain.

Ratna-sēna sends the parrot with a letter to Padmāvatī, which she answers, confessing her love and commanding him to come quickly. In Canto 24, Ratna-sēna and his yogi followers scale the fortress. Gandharvasen captures Ratna-sēna, to the distress of Padmāvatī, who seeks the help of the parrot. In Canto 25, Ratna-sēna and the yogis are brought forth to be impaled. At the urging of Pārvatī, Mahadeo (Mahes) decides to intervene at this point. In the guise of a bard, he approaches Gandharvasen and informs him of the royal lineage of Ratna-sēna, but the king repulses the bard. Mahadeo rings the bell for battle, and all of Indra's gods appear. His monkey-general Hanuwant crushes the stake where Ratna-sēna is bound and sweeps the king's soldiers with his tail. Gandharvasen surrenders. Mahadeo enlightens the king as to the parrot's role in Ratna-sēna's pilgimage to Citaur, and the parrot, now accepted as a pandit, sings Ratna-sēna's praises. Gandharvasen consents to the wedding. Canto 26 describes in detail that wedding and the dower. Canto 27 is a detailed, sensuous, and erotic account of the wedding night. In Canto 28, Ratna-sēna retires to his own hall with his companions, to whom he distributes gifts, and in Canto 29, Padmāvatī assembles her companions, who sing the "song of the six seasons," in its traditional Sanskrit and Hindi form, as a setting for the love between the princess and Ratna-sēna.

In Canto 30, back home, Ratna-sēna's first wife, Nāgmatī, mourns the absence of her husband in a "song of the twelve months," which, in contrast to the "song of the seasons," is a song of unhappiness and lonesomeness. In Canto 31 she sends a bird with a message that Ratna-sēna's mother is blind with weeping for him and breathing her last. Ratna-sēna falls into a despair, and in Canto 32, the princess and her father, the king, approve his departure for Citaur. In Canto 33, on the homeward journey, accompanied by Padmāvatī, Ratna-sēna is beset by violent storms when Ocean, disguised as a mendicant, is rejected. The ships are broken to pieces. Ratna-sēna and the princess cling to two planks and are carried by the current in different directions.

In Canto 34, when the plank with Padmāvatī is washed ashore, she is revived by Lachhmi, daughter of Ocean, who upon hearing the princess's story goes to her father. Ocean tells her that he has Ratna-sēna on his beach and will bring him to Padmāvatī. Ratna-sēna is washed ashore at the foot of a peak and searches for Padmāvatī. Blaming his pride for his losses, he draws his scimitar to take his own life, but Ocean, in the form of a Brahman, stays his hand. Ocean then carries him to Padmāvatī. Lachhmi takes the form of Padmāvatī, but Ratna-sēna, finding her fragrance not that of the princess, is unconvinced. Lachhmi takes him to his real love, and there is a happy reunion. However, they remind her that if they return to Citaur without their wealth and their companions, they will be shamed. So Lachhmi goes to her father, who brings their companions back to life and gives them jewels, gold, and silver. He also gives them five special "jewels": ambrosia, a swan, a species of bird, a tiger cub, and the philosopher's stone, which is the source of gold. Mermen accompany them as far as Jagannath, where they buy rice with one of the jewels.

In Canto 35, Ratna-sēna and Padmāvatī return to Citaur with a triumphant entry. Ratna-sēna's first wife, Nāgmatī, awaits happily—until the arrival of Padmāvatī. Then she is overcome with jealousy, and averts her head when Ratna-sēna approaches her. He appeases her by reminding her that she is his first wedded wife, and they spend the night together. The next morning he returns to Padmāvatī, and declares that she is his dearest love. But Nāgmatī's happiness shows. In Canto 36 the contention between Nāgmatī and Padmāvatī comes to a head when they meet in the flower garden, each singing her own virtues. There is a struggle, broken up by the arrival of Ratna-sēna, who announces that they are both hues of his love, like Ganges and Jumna. Muhammed has decreed this relationship, so they should give up their contest and enjoy their bliss. Both women laugh. He takes them back to the palace, where golden couches have been spread and ambrosial meals brought in. He gives a golden palace to Nāgmatī and a silver palace to Padmāvatī. In Canto 37, Nāgmatī goves birth to a son, Nāgsen. Padmāvatī gives birth to another son, Kanwalsen. Astrologers predict both will be kings.

In Canto 38 a pandit, Raghava Chetan, incurs the disfavor of Ratna-sēna when his counsel is disliked. Ratna-sēna makes the unwise choice of banishing the pandit, a decision Padmāvatī does not like. She calls for Raghava. While he is there, she accidentally drops a golden bracelet. As it lands, there is a flash that dazes Raghava. When he comes to his senses, he embarks on a tirade against both Ratna-sēna and Padmāvatī. Her companions warn him that he has been unwise, so Raghava decides he should leave and go to the Turkish capital of Delhi, where Alauddin is sultan. There Raghava will describe the lotus (Padmāvatī), and when the sultan hears him, the sun (Ratna-sēna) will be darkened. He takes the fallen bracelet with him, hoping to sell it.

In Delhi (Canto 39), Raghava is brought to the sultan, whose informers have already told him about this mendicant Brahman. When Raghava appears, the flashing jeweled bracelet on his arm catches the attention of the sultan, who is curious why a mendicant would have such a costly jewel. Raghava describes the lady who "gave" it to him. The sultan is enthralled by the account and wants to know where this beauty is: He already has 1,600 "lotus women" from all the seven continents. If there is another, she is his. Such women, Raghava informs him, live in Singhala-dvipā. In Canto 40, Raghava boasts of expertise on women and proceeds to describe the different kinds: Hastinī (elephantlike) women, Sankhinī women (lionlike, couchlike), Chitrinī (women with various accomplishments), and the Padminī (lotuslike, perfect women [a classification from Indian lore]). Raghava tells the sultan of Padmāvatī, a Padminī who has "all the sixteen degrees and all the sixteen marks of beauty." In Canto 41, Raghava catalogs Padmāvatī's physical features. The sultan is so overcome that he loudly proclaims that he will "crush Citaur and seize the lady." Raghava encourages him, and adds the incentive of the five precious jewels that Ocean has given Ratna-sēna. The sultan sends Sarjā, "a mighty man of valour," with a letter to Ratna-sēna telling him to send the lotus lady to him. In Canto 42, Ratna-sēna reads the letter with anger, but Sarjā warns him that if the sultan attacks, the "world will be convulsed." Ratna-sēna offers to surrender his wealth, but not Padmāvatī. Alauddin assembles a mighty army and proceeds to Citaur.

Ratna-sēna is prepared. Alauddin draws near to Citaur. Ratna-sēna and the nobles watch from the battlements. He says, "One thing is clear: we must now die." All the kings and princes mount their horses. Ratna-sēna advances with music, before him the chariots and all the army. In Canto 43 the armies join battle. It is as if the sky rains blood and the earth mixes with it. The Turks surround the fortress and dig a mine. Their cannonballs smash the ramparts, but Ratna-sēna is not defeated in his heart. He prepares a dancing floor on the roof of the palace, bids his people dance, and while Alauddin assails the fortress, Ratna-sēna watches the dances. A shower of Turkish arrows are shot up high; one strikes a dancing girl. The dance stops. Ratna-sēna orders the preparation of funeral pyres, the men to make ready their swords, and the women to mark themselves with vermilion for the *Jauhar* (self-immolation). In Canto 44, Alauddin hears these orders and realizes that if there is a *Jauhar*, Padmāvatī will not come into his hands. He sends a message to Ratna-sēna that he will give up the siege and not take the lady, but he does want the five jewels given to Ratna-sēna by Ocean. Ratna-sēna acquiesces, and plans are made to receive the sultan at the palace.

In Canto 45 an elaborate banquet is prepared for Alauddin, but in Canto 46, two Rājput heroes, Gora and Badal, warn Ratna-sēna, and he is on his guard. After the banquet, the sultan plots to trick Padmāvatī so that he can see her in a mirror as she observes them from a lattice. When he sees her, Alauddin swoons. Pretending friendship, Alauddin departs (Canto 47), but as Ratna-sēna escorts him to the seventh gate, he seizes Ratna-sēna, takes him away, and threatens him with death. In Canto 48, Nāgmatī and Padmāvatī weep. In Canto 49, Devapal, prince of Khumbhalner and enemy of Ratna-sēna, plots with a Brahman woman who is skilled in spells to bring Padmāvatī to him. She is unsuccessful. In Canto 50, Padmāvatī calls an assembly of allies to release Ratna-sēna. Among them is a harlot whom Padmāvatī begs to take her to Alauddin disguised as a Yogini. Her friends caution against it. In Canto 51, Padmāvatī tells Gora and Badal that she plans to go to Ratna-sēna and share his imprisonment. When they also warn her, she asks them to go instead. In Cantos 52 and 53 they set forth pretending to accompany a wedding train with Padmāvatī, but with a blacksmith hidden in her litter. First Gora bribes Ratna-sēna's jailer to tell Alauddin that Padmāvatī has come to deliver the treasure-house keys to Ratna-sēna, and will then come to the sultan's palace. The sultan agrees.

At the prison, the blacksmith cuts Ratna-sēna's fetters. Badal takes the king away on horseback. Gora stays with his army, which is disguised as the wedding train, and faces the oncoming sultan's army. Sarjā impales Gora with his spear, but Badal reaches Citaur with the king. In Canto 54, Ratna-sēna and Padmāvatī are reunited. In Canto 55, learning of Devapal's conduct, Ratna-sēna confronts him, cuts off his head, and ties it to a thorn bush. Ratna-sēna returns (Canto 56), having been fatally wounded by Devapal's spear. He entrusts the fortress to Badal and dies on a bier. In Canto 57, Padmāvatī and Nāgmatī prepare for the *satī*. The funeral pyre is prepared, and they both lie down, caressing their dead husband. They are burned to ashes, but do not flinch.

Alauddin takes the fortress, comes to the place of assembly, throws a handful of ashes in the air, and says, "Earth is vanity." There is a charge. During the battle, Badal is slain. All the women commit *Jauhar,* and all the men perish in the battle. Alauddin demolishes the fortress. Thus Citaur becomes Islam.

"The Ṣūfī sages say the worlds are in man's body: The body is Citaur, the mind the king, the heart Singhala, the intellect the lotus lady. The spiritual guide is the parrot. Nāgmatī is the cares of this world, Raghava Chetan is Satan. The sultan Alauddin is illusion. Turkish, Arabic, Hindi—all the languages there are—illustrate that subject which is love." (TAP) (Kipling 1907; Payne n.d.; Sherriff 1944; Srivastava 1964)

See also Alauddin; Jāyasī; Ratna-sēna.

 # PALAMÁS, KOSTIS
(Or Koster)

Greek poet, author of two epics, *The Twelve Words of the Gypsy* (1907) and *The King's Flute* (1910). He was born in 1859 in Patras. Well-educated and a prolific writer, he produced 18 volumes of poetry, fiction, drama, translations, criticism, and articles. Palamás was inspired by ancient writers of Greece, writers of the Byzantine period, and those of the heroic era of 1821. He incorporated both folklore and the Romantic in his themes. He was honored as Greece's national poet, although he did not gain the international reputation his work deserved; he was often nominated for the Nobel Prize, but never received it. He died in 1943, at a time when Greece was occupied by the Nazis. His funeral sparked a spontaneous demonstration against tyranny. (Siepmann 1987)

 # PALMOTIĆ, JUNIJI

Ragusan (Dubrovnik) dramatist and poet, author of the religious epic *Kristijade* (ca. mid-17th c.) Palmotić was born in 1606. A devoted nationalist, he chose his drama subjects not from the classics, nor from Ariosto and Tasso, but from Ragusan history. His best-known drama, *Pavlimir,* describes the founding of Ragusa. His other great passion was Christianity. His religious epic *Kristijade* glorifies both the life of Christ and the church's struggle against the encroaching Turks. He died in 1657, hailed as one of the great poets of Dubrovnik's golden literary age. (Čiževskij 1971; Dvornik 1962)

 # PALUDAN-MÜLLER, FREDERIK

Danish poet, author of the lyrical epic *Danserinden* (The dancing girl, 1833) and a three-volume epic, *Adam Homo* (1841–1848). He was born in 1809 in

Kerteminde, on the island of Fyn, Denmark. His early epic, in the Byronic mode, gained him acclaim in the Romantic movement of the day; however, later he married, became more conservative, and recanted his Romantic leanings. His *Adam Homo* is autobiographical, considered one of the most important works in Danish literature. It tells the story of a man who seeks worldly success and loses his soul, saved only by the devotion of the spurned Alma. Henrik Ibsen is said to have modeled Peer Gynt after the character Adam. Paludan-Müller died in 1876 in Copenhagen, having become one of the leading Danish poets of all time. (Preminger 1979)

PAMPA
(Also Ādipampa, Jha, Nadyà, Oja, Ojha, Ovaja, and Upa-Dhayaya)

Indian Kannada poet (fl. 940), author of *Ādipurāṇa* and *Pampa-Bhārata*. He was born in South India into an orthodox Hindu family, but his father, Abhirāmadevarāya, converted to the Jaina faith, bringing his family with him. Pampa became devoted to his guru, Devendramuni, whom he praised in his writings. His poetry, written in the Kannada language, won him the patronage of King Arikāsari, as well as the title *ādikavi,* or "first of poets"—first to write in his native language rather than Sanskrit. He was an ascetic, eschewing wealth and giving away whatever he had. Pampa excelled in both sacred and secular epics. His greatest work, *Ādipurāṇa* (First scriptures), recounts the story of the Jaina hero Purudēva and his sons Bharata and Bāhubali, expounding upon Jaina teachings as well. The *Pampa-Bhārata,* called *Vikramārjuna Vijàya* (ca. 950), retells the great epic *Mahābhārata,* casting the poet's royal patron in the role of the hero Arjuna. For a synopsis of the *Mahābhārata,* see the *Encyclopedia of Traditional Epics.* (Thapar 1966)

PAN BALCER W BRAZYLJI

Polish epic poem (1910) by Maria Konopnicka (1842–1910). The poem, written in ottava rima, took the poet the last 20 years of her life to complete. The story is about the treatment of Polish peasants who migrated to Brazil, where they had to clear untouched, primeval forests. The hero, Mister Balcer, is a modest village blacksmith. (Miłosz 1969/1983)

PAN TADEUSZ

Polish epic (1834) by Adam Mickiewicz (1798–1855). The poem, in 12 books using the Polish alexandrine (13-syllable, 7-caesura, 6-line couplets), returns to the Lithuania of the poet's adolescence (1811/1812).

It begins with an invocation to Lithuania, whose sunrises, sunsets, serene skies, storms, and green countryside personify such grandeur that the lives of its common people take on importance. The poet says, "Lithuania, my country, you are like health:/how much you should be prized only he can learn/ who has lost you. Today your beauty in all its splendor/I see and describe, for I yearn for you." The characters are average people—albeit with peculiar hobbies—living in harmony with their surroundings. The poem is characterized by comic types and colloquial speech. Only one character, Father Robak, a monk, has a "Byronic" tragic past. The epic also gives a portrait of a gentry society in its last days. There is a half-ruined castle, a manor, a village of gentry farmers, tradesmen, and a Jewish innkeeper named Jankiel, skilled in playing the dulcimer. One person appearing from real life is Jakub Jasiński (1761–1794), called "a handsome and gloomy young man." The action occurs on the eve of the Napoleonic expedition against Moscow (1812). (Miłosz 1969/1983; Preminger 1974)

See also Mickiewicz, Adam.

 # *PAQUITA*

Portuguese epic poem (1866) by Paimundo de Bulhão Pato (1829–1912). Written over a number of years, the poem was received enthusiastically and compared by some to Byron's *Don Juan*. (Preminger 1974)

 # *PARADISE LOST*

English epic poem (1667, 1674) by John Milton (1608–1674). The poem was published in ten books in 1667; then in 1674, the year the poet died, he came out with a second edition organized into the 12 books with which most modern readers are familiar. In a note added in 1668, the poet explains that the poem is written in English heroic verse without rhyme, "Rhyme being no necessary Adjunct or true Ornament of Poem or good Verse, in longer Works especially, but the Invention of a barbarous Age, to set off wretched matter and lame Meter. . . ." The poem begins with a prayer in which the poet asks the creator of the world—who "Dove-like sat'st brooding on the vast Abyss/And mad'st it pregnant"—to serve as his Muse as he describes "man's first disobedience" and tries to "justify the ways of God to men." This prayer is sonorous and powerful, setting the tone for all that follows.

After the prayer Milton gives a foretaste of the whole story. He will tell why our "Grand Parents," lords of the world with only one minor restraint, chose to violate that restraint. The "infernal Serpent" it was; at this point Milton identifies Satan with the animal he used as his disguise in tricking Eve. He describes Satan's crime: rebellion—unsuccessful—against God, which resulted in his falling "nine Times the Space that measures Night and Day." The horrors of the fall and the new dwelling place, the "fiery Gulf" giving forth "Darkness visible," are mentioned, but the chief symbol of the fall is the fallen angel himself. He was a magnificent creature, almost indescribably impressive, but he is now wracked with pain and deep despair.

One evidence of Satan's great power is that legions of angelic creatures followed him in his hopeless war against God and fell with him. To one of his fallen followers Satan makes one of his most famous speeches, saying that their chief delight is to be found in doing ill, in perverting the ends of God in an attempt to grieve him. He ends the speech by saying "Better to reign in Hell than serve in Heaven." Book 1 concludes with a detailed catalog of creatures and places in Hell, many of them modeled on pagan idols and legends.

Book 2 starts with the famous conference in Hell that Antony Jay, author of *Management and Machiavelli*, used as a model for his description of shrewd manipulation of meetings. Satan knows what he wants to do, but he wants his chief henchmen to think they helped him decide to do it. He asks for advice, then calls first on Moloch to offer it. Moloch is the "fiercest spirit that fought in Heaven," and he urges open war. Belial, who looks like the distinguished man in a whiskey ad, "a fairer Creature lost not Heaven," stands up next and says that he would like that idea if he thought it had any chance of success, but since it doesn't, he recommends doing nothing. He counsels "ignoble Ease and peaceful Sloth." Mammon speaks next, making the most intelligent of the recommendations. He advises dismissing all thoughts of war and making the best of the situation at hand.

Finally, Beëlzebub stands. He is a formidable figure, "than whom, Satan except, none higher sat." With "grave/Aspect he rose, and in his Rising seem'd/a Pillar of State; deep on his Front engraven/Deliberation sat and public care. . . ." Milton completes the portrait by calling him "Majestic though in ruin." Beëlzebub proposes a plan subtly suggested to him by Satan, and naturally it is the plan that is adopted. He says that somewhere in the universe there is a new race called *Man* whom he proposes locating and seducing, thus gaining revenge on God.

Satan goes through the motions of trying to decide who will spy out this new world and set in motion some attack; in fact, he has long since decided to go himself. He makes his way through Hell and arrives at the gates, where we have an allegorical scene of great importance.

Before the brass, iron, and rock gates there sits on either side "a formidable shape." One is a woman to the waist, below that a monstrous, scorpionlike mass. Around her cry and bark and creep a horde of tiny creatures that continually climb into and out of her womb. The other is a shapeless Goblin: indistinguishable in member, joint, or limb. It is black and horrible, a "grisly terror."

Satan, the former angel who once made war on God, is not intimidated. He commands the shapeless monster to stand aside. The monster recognizes Satan and tries to send him back into the interior of Hell. Satan refuses to go, and battle seems likely, until the woman-creature cries out, "O Father, what intends thy hand . . ./Against thy only Son? What fury, O Son,/Possesses thee to bend that mortal Dart/against thy Father's head?"

The woman is Sin, born out of the head of Satan, who then "took joy" of her in secret and made her pregnant. The fruit of that pregnancy is the shapeless monster, Death. Upon being born, Death decided that he would rather rape his mother than kill her, so he did, and made her pregnant again, this time with the little creatures who crawl into and out of her womb. In other words, Sin, born out of the head of Satan, is attractive but "ends" in monstrosity, and as a result of Satan's incestuous love—read self-love—produces Death and more sins and little deaths.

Satan ends the standoff by promising to "recompense" his sordid offspring; Death lets him pass, and Sin gives him the keys to the gates of Hell, which she has in her keeping. Satan then stands on the brink of Hell and looks out through Chaos, then sets out through it to seek the new world of Man.

Book 3 depicts a conference in Heaven in which God the Father talks to God the Son. It is often remarked that Milton doesn't do nearly as well with Heaven as he does with Hell, nor with God as he does with Heaven; C. S. Lewis has responded that it is far easier to create a character who is much worse than you are than to create one who is infinitely better than you are. God and His Son look with pleasure down on Adam and Eve, but they also see Satan making his way toward them. God explains that although He knows what is going to happen, His foreknowledge does not interfere with Satan's freedom, or man's. He says a bit sadly that Adam will condemn all his progeny to death.

In the immensity of space, Satan searches for the tiny Earth. He finally finds the gleam of the sun, lands on it, disguises himself, and asks the guardian archangel Uriel for directions to Earth.

In Book 4, Satan reaches the Earth, bringing Hell with him. "Which way I fly is Hell; myself am Hell." This world, showing the awesome paradise created by his adversary, is almost frightening, but Satan reflects that he is now beyond hope, and "farewell Hope, and with Hope farewell Fear." He concludes by praying "Evil, be thou my Good." He stalks the area like a "prowling Wolf" and enters Paradise like a thief coming through a window. Through his eyes we see the beauties of Paradise.

Then among all the delightful creatures come "two of far nobler shape, erect and tall,/Godlike erect, with native Honour clad/In naked Majesty. . . ." The man is for contemplation and valor formed, the woman for softness and sweet, attractive grace. They are not only magnificent creatures physically, they are impressive in mental and moral stature as well. "So pass'd they naked on, nor shunn'd the sight/Of God or Angel; for they thought no ill:/So hand in hand they passed, the loveliest pair/That ever since in love's embraces met,/Adam the goodliest man of men since born/His sons; the fairest of her Daughters Eve."

Satan looks upon these people and realizes what he has lost. He determines that he will cause them to fall. Meanwhile, Adam is beginning to make love to Eve, while Satan looks on with envy at the pure delight in a coupling of godly and godlike people.

Off to the side Uriel, now concerned that he has given a stranger directions to Earth, visits the local guardian angel in charge, Gabriel. Warned, Gabriel divides his night watch into groups and begins to search for an intruder. Satan flees temporarily while Adam and Eve, who adore each other and everything about them, retire in a balmy evening.

In Book 5, Adam and Eve get their first hint of trouble in Paradise. Adam awakens in a beautiful dawn, looks over at Eve, and is surprised to see that she has had an "unquiet rest." He calls her, and she tells him about her dream: Someone whispers in her ear and rouses her, playing on her vanity by telling her of her beauty. She sees the disturber, who looks like one of the angels who guard the Earth but who poses some provocative questions. He gestures toward the tree of knowledge—the one from which Adam and Eve have been forbidden to eat, now even more beautiful than during the day—and asks why God forbids the gaining of knowledge. If man is not supposed to use the tree, why is it in the Garden? For the first time, apparently, Eve conceives the idea of being even happier than she already is. She knows that there is something wrong with this experience, and so does Adam. Still, he tries to cheer her up and get on with proper business. Eve, however, weeps a gentle tear from either eye.

In response to the couple's morning invocation, God sends Raphael to Earth to give them one more warning. He arrives about noon and joins Adam and Eve for lunch. Over the meal Raphael tells the couple a little about God and Heaven. Then, by way of warning them, he describes Satan's revolt and the war in Heaven.

Book 6 continues the description of the war in Heaven, which is won eventually by God the Son acting alone and sending the legions of Satan for a nine-day fall through Chaos to Hell.

Book 7 counterbalances the description of destruction in Heaven with a description of God's creation of a new universe containing the Earth. The story continues through the biblical creation story and the emergence of Adam and Eve.

In Book 8, Adam wants to prolong his visit with Raphael, and begins to ask questions about the nature of the universe, which Raphael answers inconclusively. Eve loses interest in this scientific discussion and excuses herself. Adam tells his and Eve's stories, then asks some philosophical questions, one of which has to do with Eve. Is it possible, he asks, that when God took the rib to make Eve, He took a little too much and so is responsible for Adam not always feeling completely in control of himself when he is around her? Raphael frowns and asserts that Nature is not at fault; man has the strength to control himself if he will exert it. This contention is worked into another warning against the test to come.

Book 9 is the center of the action. After a preface by Milton, Satan moves toward his prey, recognizing as he does that the revenge he gains will recoil on him. He finds the serpent asleep, enters his mouth, and takes over his body.

Preparing for the day's work, Eve suggests to Adam that they work separately, for when they work together they flirt too much and engage in too much casual conversation. Adam answers that they have no quota to fulfill. Then Eve's real problem begins to emerge: She doesn't like to feel that she has to be protected; she wants to feel that she can take care of herself. When Adam doesn't relent, she increases the intensity of her argument: "How are we happy, . . . in fear of harm?" Adam tries to explain, but when Eve refuses to yield to his urgings, he lets her go alone, saying "Go; for thy stay, not free, absents thee more." She goes, "like a Wood-Nymph. . . ."

The "Enemy of Mankind, enclos'd/In Serpent," an impressive, pleasing creature "with burnished Neck of verdant Gold," makes his approach and speaks to her. She is shocked. What can this mean? Language of man pronounced by tongue of beast? The tempter informs her that he was originally just a beast, but then he found this "goodly Tree . . ./Loaden with fruit of fairest colours mixt,/Ruddy and Gold. . . ." He ate of it and was immediately endowed with reason. Eve is skeptical: "Thy overpraising leaves in doubt/The virtue of that Fruit. . . ." Still, she is curious, and she lets the serpent lead her to the tree. When she sees it she knows that the demonstration has been in vain. This is the tree from which they cannot eat, lest they die.

The serpent points out that he has not died. He suggests that God might "praise/. . . your dauntless virtue" for daring to attempt what might lead to happier life and knowledge of good and evil. "If what is evil/Be real, why not known, since easier shunn'd?" He reasons that God cannot hurt her and be a just God."

Satan convinces the woman to eat. The eating scene is one of the most fascinating in Milton's work. Her rash hand reaches out to pluck the fruit, and she takes a bite. Earth feels the wound, and the serpent slinks back into the woods. The second bite is even more interesting. This lovely woman, a delight in her every feature and movement, a figure of almost inconceivable glory, having taken one bite, goes on to gorge herself "greedily . . . without restraint."

As C. S. Lewis points out, Eve's next act is murder. She debates the matter first. Now that she has knowledge, she has power; having been disturbed to think herself less than equal to her mate, she is now more than his equal, and perhaps it would be fun to stay that way. However, she is going to have to die, and if Adam doesn't eat he will not have to die. No doubt, then, God will send him another Eve, an unacceptable thought. She decides to induce him to eat; in effect, she will be deliberately giving him a lethal dose, an idea that does not bother her. She has not fallen quite so far as Satan, but she has fallen a long way.

Adam realizes quickly what has happened, and he is not convinced by Eve's "blithe story." He loves her, however, even in her fallen state, and he can't imagine living without her. "Against his better knowledge, not deceiv'd,/But fondly overcome with Female charm," he eats. Earth gives a second moan.

The fruit intoxicates them, and they have sexual intercourse that is mainly an exercise in lust, a disgusting contrast to the delightful scene of lovemaking of the day before. Feeling shame, they steal into the woods and fashion garments of fig leaves to cover their now-embarrassing nudity. The scene ends in an ugly argument about whose fault is the greater.

Book 10 begins with an address by God the Father to His assembled angels asserting that no decree of His was necessary to the fall of man, that man has fallen by the exercise of his own free will. God the Son offers to go down and "temper justice with mercy."

The Son has to call for Adam because Adam, "being naked," has hidden himself. When the Son asks for an explanation, Adam stumbles and tries to make excuses, blaming the crime on Eve and even hinting that God made her a bit too persuasive. God the Son answers this cur-like performance with what sounds much like real anger, asking Adam if he has resigned his manhood and suffered himself to be ruled by his woman. "Was shee [*sic*] thy God? . . ."

The Son then turns to Eve, who replies simply, "The Serpent beguil'd me and I did eat." Her reply is far more impressive than Adam's; the two responses taken together illustrate that whoever stands higher falls lower if he falls at all. The Son pronounces judgment, and the two humans prepare to leave Paradise. Meanwhile, Satan announces his empty victory to Sin and Death.

Books 11 and 12 concern a visit by the archangel Michael, who describes for Adam what the future of the world is going to be until the Flood, to the birth of the Son and beyond that. At the end Michael leads Adam and Eve out to the east of Eden. "Some natural tears they dropp'd, but wip'd them soon;/ The World was all before them, where to choose/Their place of rest, and Providence for their guide:/They hand in hand, with wandering steps and slow,/ Through Eden took their solitary way." (Lewis 1942; Milton/Ricks 1968)

See also Milton, John; *Paradise Regained.*

 # *PARADISE REGAINED*

English companion poem (1671) and sequel to *Paradise Lost* by John Milton (1608–1674). Consisting of four books in blank verse, it reviews the loss of the first Paradise, Eden, by Adam, then presents a second, different kind of Paradise, brought by Jesus the Messiah. It also contrasts the different nature of these two paradises: one without, one within. *Paradise Regained* is an account of Jesus's self-realization and self-discovery at the beginning of his ministry. He has just been made aware of his Messiahship and must find the direction he will take. At the same time, Satan learns of the appearance of this Son of God, a title *he* once had. Troubled by the potential threat to his past victory in the Garden of Eden, Satan decides to confront Jesus, take his measure, and try his powers on Jesus with a series of temptations. This God permits, He says, because it will prepare Jesus for his task as the Messiah.

Paradise Regained, in the form of a debate, deals with the use and misuse of power. Satan tries to make Jesus aware that the Messiahship can bring him power for self-gratification or for self-aggrandizement. Finally, Satan tempts Jesus with the means to establish a kingdom: a powerful national state. Jesus's rejection of this means reflects Milton's final disillusionment with his earlier Calvinist enthusiasm for the state as the means for renewal and perfectibility, a disillusionment evident as early as his *History of England.* This renewal, Milton now believed, is possible only in the inner man, and Jesus's Kingdom is an inner regeneration. *Paradise Regained* may thus be considered a meditation on the true nature of the Messiahship.

Whereas in *Paradise Lost* there is an epic sweep in language and imagery, *Paradise Regained* is brief. Its style is georgic, formal, and meditative; the imagery is more restrained.

Book One opens with a link to *Paradise Lost,* then jumps to the baptism of Jesus by John and the heavenly Voice declaring Jesus to be the fulfillment of the promise of a Messiah and the coming of the Kingdom. Aware of this, Satan, "the great Dictator," summons his Council to inform them that the "great Prophet" (John) has just announced the coming of the long-promised One. Satan reminds them that he "ruined" Adam, and says he will go to this Promised One and find a way to similar success with the Messiah. He proceeds to Jordan, "temptation and all guile."

Meanwhile, God's Council also meets, and Gabriel is reminded of his earlier mission to Mary with God's plan for the birth of a Perfect Man. Now, God announces, that promise is to be fulfilled, but Satan is about to renew his intrigues. God says that He permits this so as to prepare Jesus. Jesus will lay down the rudiments of his great warfare against Satan.

Jesus meditates how best he can begin his work as the Messiah. He recalls his boyhood—the visit to the Temple, learning from his mother about the events of his birth, and the teachings of the Prophets and the Law regarding the Messiah. He goes into the wilderness, where Satan approaches in the guise of an old man. He proceeds with the first temptation, working on Jesus's hunger after days without food, the temptation to exercise his powers as Son of God and turn the stones at his feet to bread. Seeing through Satan's disguise, Jesus affirms his faith in God's providence, then reviews Satan's past of unsuccessful intrigues against God. However, Jesus tells Satan, he will not forbid Satan's coming to him.

In Book Two, Milton reveals the atmosphere of doubt with which Jesus will have to contend, even among his followers. Andrew and Simon, missing Jesus for so long, begin to have doubts. They seek him everywhere, and end up back in Galilee, where they go to Mary, Jesus's mother. Hearing of her son's prolonged absence, she is also troubled and fears that the hopes given her are false. She finally decides to wait patiently.

In the meantime, Satan returns to his realm and recalls his Council. He confesses that he is now less confident and asks for assistance. Belial, the sensualist, and Asmodai, the Incubus, advise him to set amorous women in Jesus's eye and draw out his desires. Though Belial has been successful with men in the past, Satan answers that Jesus is too wise to succumb to such a temptation. However, Jesus hungers where no food is to be found, and Satan now knows what to do. So Satan departs, taking with him a chosen band of followers. Back with Jesus, they proceed to create a dream in which Jesus is brought a banquet prepared by angels, with Elijah and Daniel at the table with him. Awaking, Jesus climbs a nearby hill and looks out for signs of some habitation; seeing a

440

pleasant grove with singing birds, he descends. A well-dressed man suddenly appears before him and reminds him that others, like Elijah, were provided food by God. Why hasn't God provided Jesus with similar help? If Satan would now provide him with food, would he eat it? Jesus sees before him the banquet table with Elijah, richly provided, served by charming ladies to the accompaniment of sweet music. There can be no sin in satisfying hunger. Jesus answers that he himself has the power to produce a banquet and call angels as attendants. What is Satan's purpose? Satan replies that he knows Jesus has that power, but what is wrong with Satan's willingness to help? But since Jesus suspects his motives, he will withdraw the banquet. The scene disappears.

Satan reminds Jesus of the Messiah's great enterprise, but that Jesus's birth is lowly, in the home of an unknown carpenter. He has been bred in poverty. What means does he have to achieve that greatness to which he aspires? He needs money. Jesus answers that wealth without virtue, valor, and wisdom is impotent, and that men endowed with these qualities of character, even if lowly of birth, have risen to great deeds. He who reigns within himself and rules passions, desires, and fears is more than king. He must rule any anarchy within: This attracts the Soul and governs the inner man, the nobler part.

In Book Three, Satan is confounded and for a while mute. Then he collects his wits, and soothingly flatters Jesus, praising his wisdom and largeness of heart, but asks why Jesus keeps these virtues hidden. Why does he deprive the world of the fame and glory he deserves, a glory that came, with broad kingdoms, to such great men as Philip of Macedonia, Scipio, Pompey, Julius Caesar? Jesus answers that glory is transient, often at the whim of a confused and miscellaneous rabble impressed by vulgar things—a glory scarcely worth praise and admiration. True glory, says Jesus, is daring to be singularly good. The truly wise and intelligent are few, and rarely achieve glory. True glory is when God approves the just man and divulges him to God's angels, men like Job. Glory is false glory when attributed to things not glorious, such as conquest. It is achieved by other means, without ambition, not by war or violence. Besides, Jesus seeks not his own glory, but God's. Satan answers that Jesus should not despise glory. God himself requires glory. Jesus answers that glory is not God's prime end, that He accepts glory only to show forth His goodness and to communicate His nature to men freely, who render to Him their gratitude for His bounty.

At this, Satan is stricken with guilt for his own sinful appetite for glory, which resulted in his losing all. Then he thinks of another approach. True, he says, Jesus is not seeking glory, but he is born to bring a Kingdom to Man. He is the Messiah to sit upon David's throne, now in the hands of another power that will not easily part with it. Satan reminds Jesus of the burden his people, the Jews, carry under foreign rule, and of the hopes of the Prophets, which Jesus is committed to fulfill. Jesus's answer is that the prophecies will be fulfilled in due time. It is God's purpose that Jesus be first tried in a humble state and suffer tribulations, even violence, before his exaltation. But, Jesus asks, what concern is it of Satan when Jesus begins his Kingdom when it means Satan's fall and his destruction? Wracked by this reminder, Satan replies that it will come when it will come, but since there is no hope, what worse can he fear? All he can expect is the fire of Hell. Until then, however, he will willingly fly to the gentle brow of Jesus and hope that Jesus's reign, rather than aggravate Satan's evil state, will stand between Satan and God's anger (which Satan dreads even more than the fire of Hell) as a shelter, a cool interposition.

Satan asks why Jesus lingers in deep thought, detained from his great enterprise? He will transport Jesus, until now familiar only with provincial Galilean towns except for a short visit to Jerusalem, to where he can view the monarchies of the world. He sets Jesus atop a high mountain, where he can see Assyria, with its history of great empires and conquest of the Jews, and Parthia, with its mighty army and great conquests. Jesus cannot restore the kingdom of David, Satan tells him, unless he too uses similar means. Parthia and Rome are enemies, of equal strength. Satan can provide Jesus with the Parthian army whereby, by conquest or league against Rome, he can truly reinstall David's kingdom. Parthia is also the home of the lost tribes of Jews, who can be brought back into the kingdom. Jesus's answer is that resort to arms also involves policy, enmities, projects, leagues, the luggage of war: means plausible to the world but fragile instruments of human weakness, not strength. As for the Jewish kingdom, Satan had beguiled their earlier kingdoms, and they had then fallen into idolatries and heathenish crimes. If I free them, says Jesus, the Jews—unhumbled, unrepentant, unreformed—will only use that freedom to follow headlong into the same sins.

In Book Four, Satan stands perplexed and troubled at his lack of success. The rhetoric by which he beguiled Eve is useless against this man, and he does not know what to reply. He takes Jesus to the western side of the mountain and shows him Rome in all its splendor, to whom all nations pay obeisance. The emperor has no son, is old and retired to an island in the Bay of Naples. Jesus could, with Satan's help, expel this monster and ascend to his throne, not only ridding the world of a monster but also freeing Jesus's people. He would also have the power to bring his kingdom to all the world now under Rome. Jesus's answer is that Rome, although magnificent, is also the seat of gluttony, hollow compliments, lies, and flatteries. Why expel the brutish monster unless he also expels the devil who made him such? Let Conscience deal with the monster. Jesus has not been sent to deal with him, nor to free a people now vile and base, deservedly made vassal. What wise man would seek to free those by themselves enslaved?

Satan impudently accepts Jesus's rejection of his offers: He realizes they were too slight. So Satan now offers him *all* the kingdoms of the world, which have been given to Satan. However, there would be one condition: Jesus must recognize and worship him as his superior Lord, an easy condition. Jesus rejects the offer, which he endures because for the time being Satan has permission to tempt him. But only God is to be worshipped and served. The kingdoms of this world were not given to Satan but were only permitted to him. So Jesus tells Satan, "Get thee behind me!"

Satan, abashed with fear, asks Jesus not to be offended, that he has tried other Sons of God—Men and Angels—and now that he is confronted with One whose coming Satan has heard so much about, he is not to be blamed for trying this Son of a higher sort. Rather, Jesus is to be honored that Satan has given him such attention. But Satan will no longer attempt to advise Jesus. Satan now reviews Jesus's experience in the Temple and Jesus's mission to extend his mind over all the world, and that includes the Gentiles. This Jesus cannot do without a familiarity with their learning. Satan turns to the west and points out Athens, the center of great philosophers. Jesus must lend his ear to sage philosophy and ponder it, either in Athens or at home, until time matures him to a kingdom's "weight" of thought. Jesus answers that he is not as short on knowledge as Satan thinks, that he receives light from above, from God the fountain of knowledge. Even the wisest of the Greek philosophies falls short of true wisdom. However many books wise men read, if their reading brings not an equal spirit and judgment, they will remain uncertain and unsettled, shallow within themselves.

At a loss, Satan replies that since none of his offers pleases Jesus, why does Jesus stay in the world? He should go back to his wilderness as a hermit. Satan returns Jesus to the wilderness where, tired and hungry, Jesus lies down to rest. But his sleep is troubled by dreams full of violence brought him by Satan. Jesus awakens and walks into the bright sunny morning. Satan arrives and talks about the turbulence of the dream the night before, a reminder of the real turbulence in the affairs of men. Proceed your way, Satan says, and you will face dangers, adversities, and pain. Jesus walks on, but answers that the tribulations are not from God but sent by Satan himself, to terrify men to his will.

Swollen with rage, Satan again reviews the prophecies about the Messiah, the circumstances of Jesus's birth and baptism by John and the Voice from Heaven, and then adds that he, knowing all this, had come to find out for himself in what degree or meaning Jesus had been called Son of God, a position he, Satan, had once held. He had watched Jesus's entrance into the wilderness, had come to learn more about this One who was to be his adversary, and found him firm as a rock, wise and good. But he needs to know what it is about Jesus that makes him more than Man, so Satan will try one more test. Satan then catches up Jesus and flies with him through the air over the wilderness to Jerusalem and the Temple. He sets Jesus on the highest pinnacle and says to him, cast yourself down safely if you really are the Son of God. To this Jesus answers, tempt not the Lord thy God, and stands still. Smitten with amazement, Satan falls down to Hell, where his crew, expecting success, sinks into desperation and dismay. Straightaway a band of angels flies to Jesus, eases him to a green bank, and spreads before him a table of celestial food that refreshes him.

As the epic ends, an angelic choir sings praise for this "true image" of God, victor over Satan. Jesus has avenged Adam and regained the lost Paradise, fairer now for Adam and his sons. "Hail, Son of the Most High . . . now enter and begin to save mankind." Jesus, refreshed, is brought on his way, and "unobserv'd home to his Mother's house private return'd." (Fixler 1964; Frye 1965; Martz 1964; Nieman 1968; Tillyard 1938)

See also Milton, John; *Paradise Lost.*

PARAMANUCHIT
(Also Paramanujita Jinorasa)

Siamese prince-patriarch, author of the heroic epic *Taleng Phai* (19th c.). He was born in 1791 and very early entered the monastic service of the Siamese Buddhist church, serving as abbot of Watphra Jetubon, and eventually rising to the position of prince-patriarch of the church. Despite the cloistered and celibate life he led, he was a prolific and versatile writer with liberal ideas, composing both poetry and prose on a variety of patriotic, historical, and religious themes. His masterpiece is the *Taleng Phai*, depicting the sixteenth-century defeat of the Burmese by King Narescara of Ayutthaya, thus liberating his country from Burmese rule. He provided literary inscriptions in stone at Watphra Jetubon in the form of classical models of Siamese poetry. He died in 1852. (Dudley and Lang 1969)

See also Taleng Phai.

 # *PARTONOPIER UND MELIUR*

Middle High German romance-epic (ca. 2nd half 13th c.) by Konrad von Würzburg. The poem, consisting of more than 21,000 lines, is believed to be the second of Konrad's longer narrative poems, written in Basel. It is based on a French poem, *Partonopeus de Blois,* by Denis Piramus, which was translated for the poet by Heinruch Marschant.

In the introduction the poet names as his patrons Peter der Schaler and Arnotl Fuchs. The poem concerns young Count Partonopier of Blois who, losing his way while hunting, reaches the seashore where he boards a deserted ship anchored there. While he sleeps, the ship sails to a remote castle that also appears deserted. However, the young count finds elaborate meals prepared for him, and when he goes to bed he is joined by Princess Melius, who has used magic charms to bring him to the castle. She exacts a vow that he will not look upon her for three and one-half years.

After a year she gives him permission to return to Blois to visit his parents. While he is gone, his strong religious teachings—almost forgotten in the interim—cause him to wonder about the propriety of their love, and he begins to fear that she may be a daimon. On his return he shines a light on her and finds that she is a beautiful maiden. But for breaking his promise, she banishes him from her sight.

Partonopier roams the countryside, having many adventures, engaging in many jousts, but always pining for the lovely Melius. At length a grand tournament is held for her hand. Partonopier comes in disguise and wins the tournament and the hand of the princess.

The poet's stylistic virtuosity lifts the poem above other similar works of the period. (Garland and Garland 1986)

PARZIVAL

Middle High German epic poem (early 13th c.) by Wolfram von Eschenbach (ca. 1170–1220), who adapted it from the unfinished *Perceval* by Chrétien de Troyes. Nearly 25,000 lines long, the epic is one of the world's great narrative poems. It is believed to have been begun about 1200 and finished about 1210. It is divided into 16 chapters, or cantos.

The poem begins with the heroic Prince Gahmuret of Anjou, "the daring yet restrained." While in the East in the Kingdom of Zazamanc on knightly duties, he marries the "puissant" Moorish queen, Belacane ("although she was an infidel"). But he slips away when she is "twelve weeks gone with child," leaving her a letter relating the child's paternal heritage and saying, "Madam, you can still win me, if you will be baptized." She has a son, whom she names Feirefiz.

In Chapter 2, Gahmuret, whose cousin Kaylet is the king of Spain, strikes out for Toledo, but Kaylet has gone in search of tournaments. While Gahmuret roams looking for Kaylet, he comes to the land of Waleis, where Queen Herzeloyde has bidden a tournament. Gahmuret acquits himself well; he marries the queen, who also becomes with child. But he leaves again for the Orient before it is born, and he is killed there. The grieving widow gives birth to a son, named Parzival.

Between Chapters 2 and 3 is a section entitled "Wolfram's Apology," in which the poet introduces himself and indicates that he loves all women but one, "having found her unfaithful" and vowing, "my anger against her does not change."

Chapter 3 relates the boy Parzival's upbringing, shielded in the seclusion of the forest, in ignorance of the outside world. One day he sees two knights with a lady in seeming distress, followed soon by another knight so resplendent that the boy thinks he is a god. Parzival goes to his mother, demanding to be allowed to become a knight. She dresses him in "fool's clothing," hoping that he will be rejected by the world, advising him to "capture women's rings." As he leaves, she falls dead from grief. His first encounter is with Jeschute, wife of Duke Orilus of Lalander, whose ring he steals in his ignorance. When the duke returns, he is angry with his wife and tells her she will no longer share his bed. They pack up and set off to follow the boy thief. Parzival meets another woman, Sigune, holding a wounded knight, her dying husband. She recognizes Parzival, calls him cousin, and tells him that his name means "Pierce-through-the-heart." He goes off to avenge the knight's injury, but Sigune fears that he will be hurt, so she sends him in the wrong direction. He spends the night in the home of a fisherman, who directs him to King Arthur's court. On the way he meets the Red Knight Ither, who gives him a message of apology to deliver to Queen Ginover, on whom he spilled wine, and a challenge to anyone at court who would care to engage him. Parzival delivers the message and receives the king's scathing answer, which he delivers. The king also awards him Ither's armor, which Ither demands be returned. In the skirmish that follows, Parzival pierces Ither's eye with a javelin, killing him. It is *infra dig* to use missiles on one's enemies, or to be killed by missiles. Nevertheless, the boy is bathed and dressed like a knight, the Red Knight, although he is too uncouth as yet to be accepted at the Round Table. He travels on to the castle of Prince Gurnemanz de Graharz, who instructs him in knightly behavior and offers him his daughter Liaze for a wife. But Parzival is too young to care for women, and he asks permission to leave, thus insulting his host, who has lost three sons and had hoped that Parzival would become his son-in-law. But the youth promises, ". . . if ever I win fame as a knight such as would entitle me to sue for love, I shall ask you to give me Liaze. . . ."

In Chapter 4 he rides on to the land of Brobarz, ruled by Queen Cindwiramurs in her own right. He saves her from oppressors led by Clamide, winning both queen and kingdom and achieving knightly status.

In Chapter 5, Parzival leaves his wife behind and rides on to the Castle of the Gral. Taking Gurnemanz's advice not to ask questions too literally, he refrains from asking King Anfortas what ails him, a question that would have released the king from his suffering and cause Parzival to become the Gral King. Parzival leaves in disgrace. He meets Sigune again and learns that Anfortas is his mother's brother. She tells him that since he did not free Anfortas from his suffering, "knightly honour and esteem vanished with you at Munsalvaesche [the Gral Castle]! This is the last word you shall hear from me!" Parzival next meets Jeschut, who has been reduced to wearing rags, having been ill-treated by Orilus ever since Parzival stole her ring. Parzival challenges Orilus and bests him, forcing him to take his wife back, and Parzival returns her ring.

In Chapter 6, Parzival encounters the Round Table knights and acquits himself nobly. He returns to the Round Table as a knight. But Cundrie, the sorceress of the Gral, appears both at Arthur's court and to Parzival, cursing him for his failure to relieve his uncle's suffering. He leaves in disgrace, feeling betrayed even by God.

Chapters 7 and 8 digress to the knightly adventures of Gawain while Parzival wanders.

Chapter 9 is the pivotal chapter in the story, wherein Parzival is led to the hermit Trevrizent, who explains the Gral King's affliction and the Gral community. Parzival learns that the man he saw lying before the Gral was Titurel, his great-grandfather, who suffers from a laming disease, but he will never die because he gazes at the Gral so often. Trevrizent tells the contrite Parzival, "If you wish to make something fine and truly noble of your life, never vent your anger on women." And, "you must place your trust in the clergy." He absolves Parzival of his sins and restores his faith in God. It is the great turning point in Parzival's life.

Chapters 10–14 again digress into the adventures of Gawain. Among other exploits, from Schastel Marveile, Gawain gains the release of noble ladies imprisoned by the fiendish knight Clinschor, a castrated sorcerer.

In Chapter 15, Parzival meets his half-brother Feirez, whom he chooses to accompany him to the Gral Castle.

An anonymous knight, carved of stone in the thirteenth century, stands in the cathedral in Bamberg, Germany. The knight personifies the romantic themes of epics such as *Parzival* by Wolfram von Eschenbach, completed in about 1210.

In Chapter 16, Parzival returns to the Gral Castle and asks the question of his uncle, King Anfortas, "What ails thee?" thus releasing Anfortas from suffering the agony of grief. Parzival then becomes Gral King. He learns that Trevrizent is the brother of his mother and Anfortas, and thus his uncle as well. He is reunited with Cindwiramurs and his twin sons Kardeiz and Loherangrin. Feirez falls in love with Anfortas's sister Repanse de Schoye, is baptized, and marries her. They go on to establish Christianity in India, where Repanse gives birth to Prester John.

The poem ends with a brief account of Parzival's son Loherangrin, who becomes Knight of the Swan and marries the duchess of Brabant, extracting a vow from her that she never ask his identity. They have lovely children and are happy for many years before she asks his name. Then he sadly leaves her. (Wolfram von Eschenbach 1980)

 # *PASSIONSTANKAR*
(Thoughts on the passion)

Swedish religious epic (1728) by the Finn Jacob Frese, who is called Sweden's first significant subjective-emotional poet. The poem is steeped in Christian religiosity, emotional introspection, and pietism. (Preminger 1974)

 # *PATERSON*

American epic poem published in five volumes (1946–1958) by William Carlos Williams (1906–1963). The final poem consists of five books, with a sixth planned. The original version, published between 1946 and 1951, consisted of four books, but a fifth appeared in 1958. During the writing of the poem, in 1947, Williams said, "I am trying in *Paterson* to work out the problem of a new prosody. . . ." The poem has frequently been thought of not only as an answer to T. S. Eliot's *The Waste Land*, but also as an "anti-*Cantos*" (by Ezra Pound). In the poem Paterson is not only a New Jersey town near the poet's home but also the name of a symbolic man representing both the poet and the region. Williams commented that man himself is a city—beginning, seeking, achieving, and concluding his life in ways mirroring the life of a city. He chose Paterson because it has "a definite history associated with the beginnings of the U.S." In addition, it has a central feature, the Passaic Falls, about which the poet says in his introduction, "The noise of the Falls seemed to me to be a language which we were and are seeking, and my search . . . became to struggle to interpret and use this language." In the first four books the poem follows the course of the river, which the poet said seemed to resemble his own life, to the sea.

The preface to Book I introduces the theme of the beauty of language, from which modern man is separated. It begins with a question: "Rigor of beauty is the quest. But how will you find beauty when it is locked in the mind past all remonstrance?" and introduces the falls and Paterson.

Book I, "The Delineaments of the Giants," introduces the elemental character of Paterson, who lies on his right side in the valley under the falls: a giant eternally asleep, a spirit-place described with a Romantic voice. Then the voice changes to a clipped, less symbolic description of the landscape with bent, split, matted trees and houses with "blank faces." Interspersed in the free verse personifying Paterson are fragments of dialogue, portions of letters, news clippings, and brief passages of prose describing historical events connected with the falls or the city; for example, the finding in 1857 of mussels with pearls by a poor shoemaker and the tragic disappearance of a young bride into the cataract. The final portion of the first section, which is in prose, is entitled "THE GRRRREAT HISTORY of that old time Jersey Patriot N. F. PATERSON! (N for Noah; F for Faitoute; P for Short) 'Jersey Lightning' to the boys." It is the account of the building of a bridge across the chasm. As the bridge is being pulled across, a pin falls into the gorge. A man named Sam Patch dives in after it. This begins his career of diving into dangerous bodies of water. He is eventually killed diving into the Niagra River.

A number of disparate voices emerge. At the close of Section 2, Book I, the poet receives a letter from E. D. (Edward Dahlberg), accusing the poet of failure because he delineates between life and art and therefore cannot address the people's basic concerns. The voice of E. D. is a patriarchal, authoritative one, speaking from a developed tradition, a "red rose." The poet answers Dahlberg, at the opening of Book I, Section 3, claiming his new, undeveloped poetic voice, his "green rose," will bloom, will be "livid green" when E. D. is gone.

The point of view shifts to that of the narrator, who describes the poet, probing his ear with a hairpin while his imagination takes flight. From there, the voice is that of a tree, speaking from a rooted position, echoing that of Dahlberg. The poet then ponders the sequestered culture of tradition with its artificial standards, using as the standard of authority on beauty, for example, the collection of European heirlooms always withheld from the people that no one ever saw, used, or experienced.

Book II, "Sunday in the Park," describes Paterson, the man, climbing Garret Mountain Park in Paterson, New Jersey. Paterson is maimed by industrial "progress and wide socio-economic disparities." In the mind of Paterson (or the natural mind) there exists an "abiding but repressed" Native American culture "grounded" in the observance and understanding of experience. The poet calls this vision of desire the "first wife." That which works against this "generative" bent toward union reality is Hamiltonian capitalism, exploitative usury, aesthetic mediocrity, and ineffective education institutions dictated to by industrial and religious factions. As he walks, various incidents associated with the area are introduced in prose form. Interspersed are extracts of a letter from Marcia Nardi concerning her poetry and her search for employment. The poem is interrupted again by excerpts of a 1936 article from *The Prospector* describing an incident on Garret Mountain in 1880 when a property owner, William Dalzell, shot John Joseph Van Houten during a meeting of the German

Singing Societies. The angry singers converged on Dalzell's barn to bring him to justice, but he was rescued by William McNulty, dean of the Catholic Church, the highest prelate of the church in Paterson. Another article excerpt concerns a runaway animal, a mink, chased by officers into the cellar of a grocery store. The walker observes three "Colored girls . . ./their color flagrant." On the grass a white couple lie facing each other, "semi-roused." A letter from Florence Plarey to her neighbor Betty Stedman explains how the latter's dog got pregnant while Plarey was taking care of it.

The third section of Book II begins with an existential philosophical verse describing the descent from the mountain, from youth, from ego-involvement into buried memory, the descent "made of despairs/and without accomplishment." It is a descent both "endless and indestructible." The revelation, or awakening of psychic energies, that results from the descent restores to the poet new objectives, "unsuspected worlds," his awareness of a possible world.

The next sequence involves a dialogue with an inner voice that, like a Muse, sends him in to write. The sounds of the falls, of barking dogs, of speeding cars are heard under the May moon. Bathers must be out of the lake by 9:00 P.M.

There is a long excerpt from a letter from poet Marcia Nardi, in which she tells him, "You've never had to live . . . in any of the by-ways and dark underground passages where life so often has to be tested."

Book III, dated 1949 and entitled "The Library," is an indictment of the weakness in the American library tradition, borrowed from the Europeans. In Section 1 the poet enters the library where he hopes the "wind or ghost of a wind/in all books" will "lead the mind away." Four voices emerge. The first, "over his right shoulder/a vague outline," addressing "Beautiful thing," says, "The province of the poem is the world." The second is the narrative voice: "as his mind fades, joining the others, he/seeks to bring it back. . . ." The third, the book voice, says, "O Thalassa, Thalassa!/The lash and hiss of water. . . ." The last is the poet's voice: "Quit it. Quit this place. Go where all/mouths are rinsed: to the river for/an answer/for relief from 'meaning.'" The ghost voice tells the poet to "Give up/the poem. Give up the shilly-/shally of art."

In Section 2 the poet calls the library "pathetic," saying that it "contained/ perhaps, not one volume of distinction." About books, he says, "We read: not the flames/but the ruin left/by the conflagration."

In Section 3 the narrator says, "It is dangerous to leave written that which is badly written." There is great power in even a chance word which, "upon paper, may destroy the world." The poet is inundated with meaningless words going in every direction. A letter from Ezra Pound about a certain text urges, "Fer got sake don't so exaggerate/I never told you to *read* it./let erlone REread it." The texts cover them like mud, but not fertile mud. "Rather, a sort of muck, a detritus/. . . a pustular scum. . . ." At the end of Book III, the poet wants out of the library rhetoric: "I cannot stay here/to spend my life looking into the past:/the future's no answer. . . ."

Book IV (1951), entitled "The Run to the Sea," is a skewed modern-day pastoral idyll, marred by the excesses of usurious greed, lack of commitment leading to divorce, abandonment, abuse, and alienated refinement. It is "An

Idyl" of Corydon and Phyllis, in which Corydon, a lesbian poet, and Paterson vie for the affections of the dense but virtuous Phyllis. Corydon's poetry is a bad imitation of modern poets from Ezra Pound to Hart Crane, particularly of Crane's "The Tunnel," from his epic *The Bridge.* The implication is that modern poetry fails.

Book IV, Section 2, tells of Madame Curie, whose husband gave up his own work "to buttress her." It is a "dissonance/in the valence of Uranium" that led her to the discovery of radium. The poet extrapolates, "Dissonance/. . . leads to discovery." A note from Pound concerning local control of local purchasing power suggests that it is the difference between "squalor of spreading slums/and splendour of renaissance cities."

In Book IV, Section 3, as old man Paterson sleeps, the river twists and turns to where the ocean yawns. But the voice (from Book II) says, "The sea [representing time past, dream time] is not our home." Book IV contains a number of excerpts from letters from Allen Ginsberg. Early in Section 3, Williams discusses Virtue, describing it as "wholly/in the effort to be virtuous." He quotes an old friend: "Virtue . . ./is a stout old bird,/unpredictable. . . ." Thus, admitting that it is impossible for the modern poet to escape the dream of history, he assumes the mantle of a virtuoso poet. He concludes that a new prosody, a language capable of "meeting and winning" the reading public, will depend on the elimination of an economic and social system fostering "sequestered wealth" and on the redistribution of that wealth, as well as on the elimination of the exploitative mass-market mentality.

Book V, dedicated to Henri Toulouse-Lautrec, is a coda that reviews previous themes and synergizes a new code. Through transcendence by the human spirit, a New World comes about; it is the poet's function to bring artistic order out of industrial chaos. The poet returns to his original purpose: to work out the problem of a new prosody. To accomplish its role of leading society, letters from Josephine Herbert, Allen Ginsberg, and Gilbert Sorrentino seem to complement the poet's musings rather than inject irony, as do prose incursions in the rest of the poem. Paterson, he says, comes back to see what has happened to the old scenes "since Soupault gave him . . ./the Dadaist novel/to translate—/*The Last Night of Paris.*" He wonders what has happened to Paris since then, and what has happened to himself. The answer is: "A WORLD OF ART/THAT THROUGH THE YEARS HAS/*SURVIVED!*" He admits that, as the unicorn has no match, the artist has no peer, just as death has none. But what can't be fathomed is imagination: "It is through this hole/we escape."

Book V, Section 2, contains part of an interview of Williams with Mike Wallace in which the poet defines poetry as "words, rhythmically organized." The poem is a "complete little universe" and any poem that has worth "expressed the whole life of the poet."

Book V, Section 3, discusses the painting *The Adoration of the Kings* (1564) by Peter Brueghel the elder, who "painted/what he saw." The poet comments, "we have come in our time to the age of the shoddy. . . ." Paterson has grown older; he is approaching death, but "he is possessed by many poems." We can learn from poems that "an empty head tapped on/sounds hollow/in any

language!" We can know nothing, he ends, but "the dance, to dance to a measure/contrapuntally. . . ." (Williams 1992)
See also Williams, William Carlos.

 # PEDDANA

Indian Telegu poet (16th c.), author of *Manucaritra,* an epic based on an episode from the *Mārkandeya Purāṇa.* Peddana was chief poet at Vijayanagar king Kṛṣṇadēvarāya's court (r. 1509–1530). (Dudley and Lang 1969)
See also Manucaritra.

 # *PEDER PAARS*

Danish mock-epic (1719–1720) by Ludvig Holberg (1684–1754), a Dano-Norwegian who was influenced by Boileau's *Le Lutrin* and Cervantes's *Don Quixote.* The satire is both literary and social, the poet preferring the heroic lines of Homer and Vergil to express emotion. He attacks official dignitaries for their pedantry and pettiness. With this poem, Holberg became Danish literature's first spokesman for the middle class. (Preminger 1974)

 # PEDRO DE OÑA

Chilean poet, author of *Arauco domado* (Arauco tamed) (publ. 1596). The first writer born on Chilean soil, he was born about 1570 in Los Confines, Chile, in the area that formed the setting of Ercilla y Zuñiga's famous epic *La Araucana,* the first part of which appeared about the time of his birth. The second and third parts of the epic were published when he was 8 and 19, respectively. He was sent to Lima, Peru, to be educated at the University of San Marcos. The murder of his father by the Indians became the single event motivating many of his actions and writings. He joined the army, fighting in several battles against the Indians. His account of battles against Equadorian rebels was written in such malevolent terms that the Peruvian printer who published it had to flee to avoid incarceration. After only 120 of his 800 printed copies were sold, the manuscript was suppressed. Pedro de Oña was of a different mind about the events described in *La Araucana,* which glorified the Indian leaders. He was discouraged about attempting his own poem because of the high quality of Ercilla's work. He wrote, "Who would dare to sing of Arauco/after the superbly rich *Araucana?*" which he saw as "so refined and so perfectly developed." To compete with Ercilla's epic "would not be perfection but corruption." Still, he brought his own lyrical style to the material, which is Baroque and rich in metaphor, naming his version *Arauco domado*. Both poems used the same meter and eight-line stanza, but Ercilla's rhyme scheme is *abbaabcc*, whereas Pedro de Oña's is *abababcc*. His poem was meant to restore honor to the name and deeds of the marquis of Cañete, viceroy of Peru (1556–1560), García Hurtado de Mendoza, whom Ercilla's poem makes the villain. De Oño's was the first book in verse by a Hispanic-American writer. His writings were all historical; he wrote *Temblor de Lima en 1609* (Earthquake of Lima in 1609). When he was 65 he published another historical poem, *El vasauro* (1635). He also wrote *Ignatius of Cantabria* (1639), poems about St. Ignatius Loyola, a Jesuit who left the order and became a secular priest, that were meant to defend Spanish Catholicism against the heresies spreading throughout the rest of the world. Both Spain and Portugal outlawed the Jesuits.

Pedro de Oña, considered the second of Chile's epic poets after Ercilla y Zuñiga, died about 1643 in Lima. (Anderson-Imbert 1969; Jones 1966)

See also *Arauco domado.*

PEETRI KIRIKU KELLAD
(The bells of St. Peter's)

Estonian epic poem (20th c.) by Ivar Grünthal (b. 1924). The poem was written after World War II while the poet was in exile after Stalin sovietized Estonia. He wrote of war and of exile. Critics have said of his style that his "metrical virtuosity can be dazzling." His poetry has been called "erotically charged." (Preminger 1974; Rubulis 1970)

PEREGRINO INDIANO
(Pilgrim of the Indies)

Spanish epic poem (1599) by Antonio de Saavedra Guzmán (d. before 1570). The poem is a verse-chronicle of the military operations of Hernán Cortés from the time he left for Cuba (1504–1511) until his conquest of Mexico (1519–1521). The epic is enlivened by touches of love and romance. Early in the expedition to Mexico, as a peace offering the Tabascan Indians gave the Spaniards a group of women captives, among whom was a fetching, highly intelligent Indian princess, Malintzin, who spoke not only the Mayan of the coastal Indians, but also the Aztec of Montezuma, Nahuatl. She became Cortés's guide, interpreter (hence, the nickname Malinche, "The Tongue"), and mistress. She converted to Christianity and took the name Doña Marina, bearing Cortés a son, Martin. She was Cortés's liaison with Montezuma, employing such subtle psychology on the great Aztec leader that he actually became Cortés's prisoner voluntarily. (Anderson-Imbert 1969)

PÉREZ DE VILLAGRÁ, DON GASPAR

See Villagrá, Don Gaspar Pérez de.

PERSICA
(The Persians)

The name of at least two Greek epic poems of the fifth century B.C. One, by Samai poet Choerilus, is a verse chronicle, now lost, that probably related the Persian War as chronicled by Herodotus. It is known that the poem glorified the battle of Salamis during the Persian War, and it was so popular that the Athenians decreed that, along with Homer's epics, *Persica* should be recited at the Panathenaea, a festival held in mid-August honoring the city protectress, Athena (originally held every four years). The event often included a contest of poets.

The other *Persica* was by Timotheus of Miletus, who was in Athens at the time that the Milesian embassy was in Sparta protesting its involvement with Persia in a scheme that divided the city-states. Scholars believe Timotheus first exhibited the poem at the greater Panathenaea of 410 B.C. Its theme is the naval victory of Salamis in which the Athenians drove back the Cyprians. Themistocles prevailed upon Sparta and other Greek cities to enlarge their fleets and was responsible for the victory in 440 B.C. of their combined forces over the Persian ships of King Xerxes I. The poem contains subtle barbs against the Spartans, to whom the Milesian embassy was protesting against Persian diplomat Tissaphernes's friendship with Alcibiades, expelled from Sparta, and now adviser to Tissaphernes. At one point the poet has the Athenian naval hero Themistocles declare, "Ares is master! Hellas, at least, does not fear gold!" This refers to a treaty—already being violated—by which the Lacedaemonians were to be paid a subsidy. Themistocles was chiefly responsible for saving Greece from Persian subjection in 480 B.C. The battle account concludes with the triumphant setting up of the trophy and the cries of the "Paean," accompanied by a dancing chorus. The poem was wildly popular among the Athenians, who gave the poet their votes in the contest of poets. (Olmstead 1948)

PERUṄKATAI
(The great story)

Incomplete Indian epic of the period of the Pallavas, Hindu warrior kings (ca. 300–900), by an unknown Jaina author. The epic depicts Jaina kings with their ideals for nonviolence, salvation through sacrifice, and enjoyment of the good life. The poem contains depictions of the Indian countryside and mixes supernatural and natural themes. The narrative is told in an episodic manner with set descriptions of heroic, religious, and erotic elements. Later composers of epics drew on this and other Jaina epics for history and technique. (Thapar 1966)

PETER THE HERMIT
(Pierre l'Èrmite)

Historical person who appears in Tasso's *Gerusalemme liberata* (1581). He was born about 1050, probably in Amiens, and supposedly visited the Holy Land around 1093. Learning of Pope Urban's call for a crusade in 1095, he began traveling across France, picking up followers for the "People's Crusade."

They traveled to Constantinople and through Turkey. When he had troubles with discipline, he returned to Byzantine emperor Alexius I for help. While he was gone, the Turks annihilated most of his army. He joined the Crusaders from western Europe in Constantinople. On reaching Jerusalem, he was appointed almoner of the Christian army (1099). In July he led the entire army in solemn procession to the Mount of Olives, where he preached a sermon just before the attack on Jerusalem. After his return to Europe (1100), he founded and was appointed prior of the Augustinian monastery at Neufmoutier, where he died in 1115. (Runciman 1952)

PETRARCH
(Francesco Petrarca)

Italian scholar, humanist, and poet, author of the incomplete Latin epic *Africa* (begun in 1338 or 1339, pubished posthumously in 1386). He was born in 1304 in Arezzo, Italy, where his father, a lawyer, settled his family after being expelled from Florence two years previously. In 1312 the family moved to Avignon in the south of France, where the exiled Papal Court was established during the "Babylonian captivity." Petrarch studied at Carpentras, then went off to study law at Montpellier and Bologna. But he soon abandoned his studies for Latin and Greek literature. He had begun writing poems during his law-school days; his earliest extant poems are about the death of his mother (ca. 1318–1319).

After his father's death in 1326, Petrarch returned to Avignon and took minor clerical orders to qualify for religious benefices. In 1327 he fell in love with a woman he saw in church, now known only as Laura, whom he worshipped from afar for most of the rest of his life, writing a total of 366 poems to her until her death in 1348 of bubonic plague. The majority of these are sonnets, hailed by scholars as the most polished verses in Western literature.

As a poet and scholar, he soon became popular among aristocratic society, including popes and kings. In 1337 he purchased a "cottage" at Vaucluse

("Closed Valley") about 15 miles east of Avignon, where he retreated on occasions to fish and putter in his two gardens, alone except for two peasants and a dog. There, in about 1340, he began work on *Africa,* an epic poem about the Second Punic War. In 1341, in a ceremony revived from ancient times, he was crowned with the coveted laurel wreath, which he placed on the Apostle's tomb in St. Peter's Basilica as a gesture of his belief in a tie between Christianity and the classics.

He wrote many of his works, including *Africa,* in Latin, believing that fine literature must be written in that language. Although the epic was never completed, his Latin prose works gained wide success, among them *De viris illustribus* (On illustrious men), originally intended to be a collection of biographies of great Romans, later amended to include great men of all time, including Adam; and *Secretum,* an imaginary dialogue with St. Augustine (ca. 1342).

Two years after the death of his beloved Laura he returned to Rome and renounced all sensual pleasures. His work, long leaning toward the religious, now became increasingly ascetic. Soon tiring of the machinations of advancement within the church hierarchy, he left Rome in 1351 and settled in Vaucluse, where he worked on his Laura poems: *Rime in vita di Laura* (Poems during Laura's life) and *Rime in morte di Laura* (Poems after Laura's death). He also continued to work on the poems included in the *Epistolae metricae* (Sixty-six letters in Latin hexameter).

In 1353 he returned to Italy, settling in Milan and accepting the patronage of the Visconti family. He was a friend of Boccaccio, whom he persuaded to write in Latin. Petrarch himself translated the Griselda story of the *Decameron* into Latin, the version Chaucer used for his "Clerk's Tale." He was devoted to Cola di Rienzo's efforts to revive the Roman republic, a stand that cost him the friendship of Cardinal Colonna.

In 1361, to escape the encroaching plague, he moved to Padova, and in 1362 to Venice. He was presented a house, in return for which he would will his books to the government. His daughter Francesca joined him, and he continued to revise his lyrics and his other vernacular work, the *Trionfi,* which describes, in terza rima, "triumphs" of Love, Chastity, Fame, Death, Time, and Eternity.

In 1370, Pope Urban V called him to Rome to undertake a diplomatic mission, but at Ferrara he suffered a stroke. However, he continued to work; he was still working on the *Trionfe* when he died in 1374 at Arqua.

Petrarch's chief contribution was his insistence on the marrying of classical tradition and Christianity in one long continuity, thus inaugurating the Revival of Learning, ushering in the Renaissance. (Wilkins 1961)

 # PFAFFE AMIS, DER

Middle High German poem (ca. early 13th c.) of about 2,500 lines by Der Stricker. A satire on human folly, the poem depicts an English priest, Amis, who is harried by his bishop, whom he bests with his cleverness and superior intelligence. He then sets off in search of adventure, and through a series of a dozen exploits lives very well by his wits, using trickery and deception. Finally God puts a stop to his chicanery, and he enters a monastery, becoming its very proper and ethical abbott. (Garland and Garland 1986)

See also Stricker, Der.

PHARSALIA

(Also *Bellum civile*, or Civil war)

Latin epic poem (ca. A.D. 63) by Lucan (Marcus Annaeus Lucanus, A.D. 39–65). Unfinished at the time of the poet's forced suicide, the poem is an account in ten books of Julius Caesar's war against Pompey that ended the Roman Republic with the Battle of Pharsalus in 45 B.C. The poet intended to cover events up to Caesar's death in 44 B.C., but the poem breaks off abruptly while Caesar is in Alexandria, trapped in a "terrible ring of war." The extant poem covers the first two years of the civil war, from January 49 B.C. to the winter of 48–47 B.C., although the poet assumes the reader's knowledge of previous events, as well as those occurring two decades hence. It was written a century later, during the reign of Nero, to whom Lucan was opposed, and it was Lucan's activities in the conspiracy against Nero that condemned the poet to take his own life before the poem was completed.

The epic glorifies the old Roman republic and the heroism of Cato, Brutus, Pompey, and Caesar. Despite the fact that it is historically inaccurate in places, lacks a central heroic figure or even coherence and focus in places, and its style and meter have been called mediocre, the epic contains some noble passages and displays Lucan's talent for rhetoric and epigram. The lively battle descriptions and animated characters were probably responsible for the poem's being one of the first works printed after the printing press was invented. Before the year 1500, 23 editions of the poem had appeared. It became particularly popular during the Middle Ages when Christopher Marlowe translated the first book into blank verse (1600).

Book 1, "The Outbreak of the Civil War," consists of 696 lines and contains a flattering invocation to Nero—probably a necessity under the circumstances. According to Seneca, failure to flatter Nero adequately was taken as proof of ill-will. The poet expounds on the causes of the war, that "drove/a nation mad" and "shattered the world's/peace." He blames the war on the "three-way split of rule" between Crassus (b. 115 B.C.), Pompey (b. 106 B.C.), and their young ally Julius Caesar (b. 100 B.C.), the "First Triumvirate." To cement the alliance, Caesar's sister Julia is married to Pompey. But the alliance unravels with the deaths of both Crassus and Julia. When Caesar, at his provincial command in Gaul, is called to Rome—the senate having voted that both he and Pompey should give up their commands simultaneously—Caesar decides on war. He crosses the Rubicon River marking the border of his province saying, "I say goodbye to peace and so-called law. . . ." He marches in and takes nearby Rimini, makes a stirring speech to his forces, and gains support as he goes. He quickly takes Brundisium (Brindisi) and heads for Rome. Pompey, still in residence there, flees to the south of Italy.

Book 2, entitled "Pompey Abandons Italy," contains 736 lines. It begins with a section entitled "Knowledge of the Future No Kindness of the Gods," in which the poet requests, "Let fear still hope." A section entitled "Dismay in Rome: Atrocities of Marius and Sulla Recalled," relates that after defeating the Numidians (Libyans) and the Teutons and Cimbri (two invading German tribes), Marius, Caesar's uncle, goes into hiding (88 B.C.) when Sulla seizes Rome. He is eventually caught and brought in to be killed in revenge, but the Cimbrian soldier loses his nerve. Marius raises an army against Sulla and terrible carnage results, described by the poet in detail. A section entitled "Two True Patriots: Brutus Tyrannicide and Cato" describes, with much hyperbole, the virtues of Cato and his nephew Brutus. (This Brutus is not to be confused with Decimus Brutus Albinus, a loyal supporter of Caesar's who appears in Book 3. The latter is the Brutus in Shakespeare's *Julius Caesar* who joins the conspirators in betraying Caesar.) Brutus comes to Cato's door promising to follow neither Pompey nor Caesar, but Cato only. Noble Cato tells him, "Of all wrongs, Brutus, civil/war's the most profound." Nonetheless, he vows to defend Rome and fight in Pompey's ranks. A section entitled "Pompey Plans Resistance in Southern Italy" is self-explanatory, as is "Caesar's Descent from the North." At Corfinium, General Domitius Ahenobarbus tries to stop Caesar's sweep of Italy by destroying a bridge, but Caesar is too quick. He captures Domitius, then lets him go free. Pompey addresses his troops and retreats to Brindisi. To block his further retreat, Caesar, "tiger quick/to every act," dumps rocks into the harbor mouth and sets a mountain of logs atop them. Seeing the blockade, Pompey abandons Italy and flees to Greece.

Book 3, entitled "Caesar, Master of Rome, Extends the War to Gaul," contains 763 lines. It begins with Pompey's dream of his dead wife Julia, who tells him, "This civil war will make you mine at last." While Caesar returns to Rome, Pompey is amassing his forces in Greece. Caesar leaves the "walls of quaking Rome" and heads over the Alps toward Marseilles, putting it under siege on the way to Spain, to secure his empire to the west. Decimus Brutus takes a fleet down the Rhone and the Massaliotes are defeated at sea.

Book 4, "The War in Spain, Dalmatia, and Africa," contains 824 lines. In Spain, despite a flood, Caesar defeats Pompey's forces led by Petreius and Afranius. The poet digresses in a brief segment entitled "Simplicity of True Pleasure" before resuming the story of Caesar's conquests. Caesar sends Caius Antonius, younger brother of Mark Antony, to the Adriatic, where the boats run afoul of both the sea and the enemy. Caesar sends Curio to Libya, Africa, but he is defeated by Numidian king Juba and is slain.

Book 5, "Caesar Follows Pompey to Greece," contains 815 lines. Lentulus addresses the Senate of Rome, now in exile, and appoints Pompey sole commander. Appius Claudius Pulcher, the governing proconsul of Macedonia, including all of Greece, consults the oracle of Apollo at Delphi. She tells him in part, "Roman, spared a port/in world's collapse . . ./alone you'll keep long peace." Meanwhile, having conquered Spain, Caesar returns to Italy and makes himself consul (48 B.C.). We learn that Labienus, a trusted commander while Caesar was stationed in Gaul, deserted Caesar to join Pompey. Caesar sails from Brindisi across the Adriatic, bound for a confrontation with Pompey. Mark Antony sails for Greece and Pompey sends his new wife, Cornelia, to safety on Lesbos.

Book 6, "From Dyrrachium to Pharsalus," contains 830 lines. Caesar's forces under Magnus encircle Pompey's troops at the port of Dyrrachium (now Durrës in Albania), but Pompey manages to defeat them. When Caesar learns of the defeat he withdraws east to the Plain of Thessaly with Pompey in pursuit. Although the poet gives a description of the courageous centurion Scaeva's fight to the death against Pompey, in reality (by Caesar's account), he survived with 120 holes in his shield. In Thessaly, Pompey's son Sextus Pompey consults the witch Erictho, who performs a ghoulish necromancy, described in lurid detail, to foretell the destiny of his father's forces. She describes at great length what is to become of the various heroes. She ends, "O house/ill-starred! in the wide world you'll find no soil safer/than Pharsalus."

Book 7, "The Battle of Pharsalus," contains 873 lines. Before the battle, Pompey has a happy dream and is persuaded to risk battle. On 9 August 48 B.C., his army marches down from the hills and takes possession of the plain. Caesar and Pompey both address their troops. The poet interjects his own reflections on the cost of Pharsalus. The battle, in which the Pompeians are routed, is described in detail. Pompey himself is described in defeat, "the noble head unbowed by fate." Caesar is described in victory, when "shades and . . . the dungeons of hell/invade his sleep before Pompeius dies." The poet ends with a section entitled "Pharsalus Only One Act in a Tragedy of Civil War."

Book 8, "The Death of Pompey," deals with Pompey's flight to Lesbos and his reunion with his wife, Cornelia. Hoping to find men who will stand with him, he sets sail for Parthia, Libya, and Egypt. As scattered survivors of the battle rejoin him, he puts one of them ashore, King Deiotarus, ordering him to go east to Scythia to rally support. Pompey heads for Parthia, hopeful because "Parthia has no fear of Roman arms: they're bold/for war." Of Ptolemy XIII he says, "I put no faith in Egypt's/child-ruler." As for the Numidian king Juba, "The Moor disquiets/me: crafty, double-tongued, a tricky grandson of Carthage. . . ." But as he describes a liaison with Parthia, he hears his men muttering. Lentulus speaks for them: "Is . . . nothing left . . ./but grovelling to the Mede?" They sail on to Egypt, but from an outpost on shore the pharaoh's chamberlain, Pothinus, prepares to meet them with a company. This is the result of a meeting of the pharaoh with his advisers at which Acoreus, an old priest, speaks first to the boy-king: "The virtuous . . . are often victims/of their own ideals." He warns the Egyptians to "keep Nile free of Roman arms, lest Pompey's/base become the victor's plunder." The council approves the crime of assassination, as does the young pharaoh. Achillas is chosen for the deed and "equips a little boat with armed assassins" to meet Pompey. Pompey leaves his ship at their command, "preferring death/to show of fear." Achillas drives a sword into him and throws his headless body into the sea. The last segment describes his funeral rites.

Book 9, "Cato in Africa," contains 1,108 lines and begins as Pompey's immortal soul soars to heaven. Cato, Caesar's bitter enemy, delivers a magnificent panegyric on his fallen leader and vows to continue the war. The remnants of the army are assembled under the leadership of Cato; Pompey's father-in-law, Metellus Scipio; and Scipio's younger son, Craeus. Cato marches the troops through treacherous desert to Mauretania (North Africa). Much of the book is devoted to praising the heroic acts of Cato. Meantime, Caesar leaves Pharsalia and heads for Alexandria, where he is presented with Pompey's head. He pretends sorrow, knowing that "no mask but tears could hide the manifest joy / of his heart." The last segment is entitled "Arch-Hypocrisy of Caesar."

Book 10, "Caesar in Alexandria," consists of 548 lines. It describes his actions in Alexandria and his affair with Cleopatra. The troops of Achillas and Pothinus attack and put him under seige at the palace. At this point the poem breaks off. (Lucan 1989)

See also Lucan.

PHRA ABHAI MANI
(Also *Phra Aphaimani*)

Thai Romantic fantasy epic (ca. 1830) of great length, by Sunthọn Phu (or Bhu) (1786–1855), who as a child was a poetic prodigy. The imaginative poem contains a large number of cantos and is the best known of the poet's works. It was written after 1824, the year of the death of King Rama II, for whom Sunthọn Phu served as private secretary. His successor, King Rama III, a deeply religious man, disbanded the corps of writers, so the poem could be said to mark the end of court-directed literature. (Dudley and Lang 1969; Preminger 1974)

PHUTTALEUTLA
(Also Itsarasunthon or Rama II)

Siamese king (r. 1809–1824), poet, and dramatist, whose reign ushered in the golden age of Thai literature. He was born in 1768, the son of King Ramathibodi, or Rama I (Chaophraya Chakri, r. 1782–1809), former minister and army commander under Siamese king Taksin, who himself was a patron of literature, composing a Thai version of the Hindu epic *Rāmāyaṇa* and of the Naraian play *Inao*. Phuttaleutla came to power with the death of his father, assuming the title Rama II. He reversed the isolationist policy in effect since 1687, reinstating trade with foreign nations. He gathered a corps of writers in his court, among them Sunthọn Phu, his private secretary, a man of humble birth whose excellence in poetry gained him the post. Another light in the court was Prince Paramanuchit, author of the ode-epic *Taleng Phai* (Defeat of the Mons). Under Phuttaleutla's regime, women poets achieved prominence for the first time. Most notable among them was Khun Phum (1815–1880), who became a great supporter of poets.

Phuttaleutla, a gifted poet in his own right, contributed the dance-drama *Sankhong* and wrote the most famous version of the dance-drama *Inao*, as well as certain episodes of the *Rāmāyaṇa* (*Ramakien*). He participated with a corps of writers in recording the first *sepha*, teaching that, until then, had been transmitted orally from master to disciple. The work, consisting of 40,000 lines, is entitled *The Adventures of Khun Chang and Khun Phen*. Phuttaleutla died in 1824, closing an era on Thai court poetry, because his successor, Rama III, a deeply religious man, did not approve of secular writing. However, as a result of Phuttaleutla's fostering of women writers, Madam Khun Phum established a literary salon in her home that lasted for 40 years. (Dudley and Lang 1969; Preminger 1974)

 # PIERS PLOWMAN

(*The Vision of William Concerning Piers the Plowman*, or *Will's Vision of Piers the Plowman*)

English dream-vision allegory in unrhymed alliterative verse (ca. 1370–1387) containing passages of truly epic grandeur, attributed to William Langland. Some 53 manuscripts survive in three versions. The earliest, A-Text, is considered unfinished. The B-Text, a much longer revision of A, is the best known and the one discussed in this entry. The C-Text is a major revision of all but the final few sections. The poem is written in the "alliterative long line." It does not rhyme, and does not employ a set number of syllables per line or a regular pattern of alternating stressed and unstressed syllables. Each line contains four or more major stressed syllables, and a random number of unstressed syllables. Of the stressed words, at least the first three begin with the same sound. The poem consists of eight dreams told in some 7,303 lines divided into a prologue and 20 sections, which the poet labels "Passus," Latin for "step," as in steps along a pilgrimage or quest.

Within the dream-frame of the poem, the narrator, a dreamer named Will, sets out on a journey toward salvation, in search of Truth so as to learn how he can save his soul. The poem is divided into two unequal parts: *The Vision* (Dreams I and II) and *The Lives of Do-Well, Do-Better, and Do-Best* (Dreams II–VIII), with two dreams devoted to each of the three.

Prologue and Passus I–IV are concerned with the first dream, in which Will the Dreamer sees all the world spread out between two towers. Beginning with Passus I, Lady Holy Church teaches him its history and tells him the values necessary to deal with it: A Christian must practice not only charity and love, but also—and especially—truth. She explains the two towers, in one of which Truth dwells. The dungeon in the dale is the Castle of Care, whose captain is Wrong, father of falsehood. Will observes an attempt to marry Lady Meed (Reward) to False. This possible union is disrupted, and the matter is brought before the king, who suggests marrying her instead to Conscience. But Conscience refuses: "Before I wed such a wife, woe betide me!" Lady Meed and Conscience argue; Will observes her winking at men-of-law, and the people agree that Meed is "a cursed slut," while Meekness is a master. Reason steps in to say, "I shall render no mercy/While Meed maintains her mastery in the court of law." (IV.134–135)

Passus V–VII describe Dream II, in which Reason, preaching to the whole realm in a field, calls for society's repentance. One by one, the Seven Deadly Sins confess the results of their misspent lives. The people decide that they must find St. Truth, but the only person who knows where to find him is a lowly plowman named Piers. He argues that before he can lead the pilgrimage, he must plow his half-acre, and he organizes the people to help him. But they soon drop by the wayside, too lazy to work, claiming, "For we can't strain and sweat, such sickness afflicts us." Piers even calls upon Hunger to motivate the poeple, but to no avail. He takes pity on the slackers and sends Hunger away, but Hunger warns, "Comfort such at your own cost, . . ." (VI.219) advising him to "Go to Genesis" to read ". . . And labor for your livelihood, and so our Lord commanded." (VI.232,234) Hunger refuses to leave until he has dined and drunk his fill. So the poor people feed him until he falls asleep—temporarily. Truth sends Piers a pardon from punishment and from guilt—pardon "to pass through purgatory quickly," (VII.11) like kings and knights. When a priest tells Piers that the pardon only tells him to do well, he tears it up and vows to alter his life. The Dreamer, Will, wakes and also vows to rely on Do-Well.

In Dream III (Passus VIII–XII), dressed in the coarse russet of an ascetic, Will begins a search for Do-Well. He asks two friars whom he meets where both Do-Well and Do-Evil dwell, being quite certain that they do not dwell together. But one of the friars proposes to show him "How the steadiest man sins seven times a day." (VIII.27) The Dreamer lies down to sleep and has a dream in which he meets Thought, who tells him how to recognize not only Do-Well, but also Do-Better and Do-Best. Wit then describes the castle where Sir Do-Well dwells with Dame Anima (the Soul), his daughter Do-Better, and Do-Best, a bishop's peer. A cast of other characters is introduced. Wit's wife, Dame Study, gives her ideas on biblical history and morality, while Clergy and his wife, Scripture, offer even more rules. By this time, the Dreamer is so confused that he gives up trying to follow Do-Well and determines to follow Fortune instead. But finally Lewte (Justice) urges him to begin writing again. Scripture tells him, "Many men know many things and don't know themselves." (XI.3) Lewte's advice, "Be spare in your praise; be more spare in your blame," (XI.106) prompts Scripture to preach. The essence of her message is based on the gospel words "Many are called, but few are chosen." (Matthew 22:14) The Dreamer speaks with Roman emperor Trajan, a righteous pagan, and with Nature, Reason, and Imaginative, who explain the fate of the righteous heathen. Imaginative tells him to "Amend yourself while you may—you have been warned often. . . ." (XV.10)

In Dream IV (Passus XIII–XIV), Will the Dreamer and Conscience are invited to dine with Clergy and Scripture. Will meets a friar whom Conscience invites to join them, as well as Patience, who stands in the palace yard praying for food for a poor hermit. Patience and Dreamer are seated together at a side table. It is soon apparent that the friar is a hypocrite. They hear of new teachings of the almost forgotten Piers Plowman. When Clergy vows to stay behind and do his duty, Conscience and Dreamer leave with Patience. They meet a minstrel named Hawkin the Active Man.

In Dream V (Passus XV–XVII) the Dreamer meets Anima (Soul), who is distinguished by various names, according to his actions. He gives a long discourse on Charity, quoting St. Jerome: "It is sacrilege to give to the poor what is theirs/Likewise, to give to sinners is to sacrifice to devils. . . ." (XV.343) In a dream within a dream, Long Will the Dreamer meets Piers Plowman, who shows him his land to farm, plant, and weed, in the heart of which the Tree of Charity grows. Piers introduces him to Abraham-Faith, Moses-Hope, and the Good Samaritan–Charity (Christ).

In Dream VI, Passus XVIII, the Dreamer sees Christ's Passion, Crucifixion, and his Harrowing of Hell.

In Dream VII, Passus XIX, the Dreamer wakes, writes down his dream, and goes to Easter mass with his family. In the middle of mass, he falls asleep and sees the Descent of the Holy Ghost and the beginnings of the Christian Church, cultivated and tended by Piers Plowman. Piers builds a barn (Unity) into which Conscience gathers the community when Pride and his followers attack.

In Dream VIII, Passus XX, the Dreamer wakes with a heavy heart, not knowing where to eat or where to go. At noontime Need accosts him discourteously, calling him a fraud and reminding him that "he who was the world's creator was willfully needy,/. . . and none died poorer." (XX.49–50) Dreamer falls asleep again and sees the attack on the barn (Unity) by Antichrist. He meets and converses with Nature and finds himself suffering from the ailments of old age. He enters Unity and discovers it has been overrun by the enemy with the help of Friar Flatterer, who has enchanted the people with a drugged drink so that they dread no sin. Conscience vows to become a pilgrim to seek Piers the Plowman, "who might expunge Pride. . . ." Conscience cries for Grace until the Dreamer wakes. (Langland 1990)

 # POEMA DEL CID

See *Cid, Poema del.*

POLTAVA

Russian historical epic poem (1828, publ. 1829) by Alexandr Pushkin (1799–1837). The poem can be considered an extremely patriotic plea against the political rebellion threatening at the time. It grew out of the Byronic inspiration of the poet's years of exile in the south of Russia. It portrays in a new light the Cossack hetman Mazeppa, who joined Charles XII of Sweden and betrayed his loyalty to Peter I. In this version, not Peter but Mazeppa, living in the South and resembling a Byronic hero, becomes the immoral tyrant, while Peter is described in panegyric terms. (Bristol 1991)

 # POPE, ALEXANDER

English poet, author of the mock-epics *The Rape of the Lock* (1712, 1714) and *The Dunciad* (1728–1743), and the uncompleted epic *Brutus* (1744). Pope was born in 1688 in London into a wealthy Roman Catholic family that operated a linen-draper business. When Pope's father retired in 1700, the family moved to nearby Binfield in Windsor Forest. A serious childhood illness left Alexander Pope humpbacked, crippled, and short (four and one-half feet tall). He was constrained by his Roman Catholicism from gaining admittance to a university, but he taught himself Latin, Greek, French, and Italian. Before he was 25, he had earned the reputation as England's greatest living poet as well as the epithet "the wicked wasp of Twickenham" (his home). He had, in fact, written his first epic poem at age 15, *Alcander Prince of Rhodes,* which he decided to destroy. By the time he was 17, he had produced some important work. Written when he was only 23, his *Essay on Criticism* (1711), composed in heroic couplets and modeled on Horace's *Ars Poetica,* articulated an aesthetic for the poetry of his time: "Learn for ancient rules a just esteem/To copy nature is to copy them."

When he proposed a translation of the *Iliad,* a national campaign to finance the project resulted in subscriptions netting him 5,000 pounds, a veritable fortune at the time. After Pope completed the project (1720), he undertook with equal success a translation of the *Odyssey* (1726), following which he brought out an edition of Shakespeare.

Pope's special genius lay in his satiric verse, after the fashion of Dryden. He began *The Rape of the Lock* as a brilliant spoof of two cantos, but two years later augmented it into a mock-heroic parody on the artifices and foibles of aristocratic society. He wrote another mock-epic, *The Dunciad* (An epic of dunces) as a satire on all kinds of literary pedants and published it in various versions from 1728 to 1743.

In 1733 he turned from satire to philosophy with his *Essay on Man,* also written in couplets, which gives us at least two famous quotations: "Whatever is right, is right" and "The proper study of mankind is man." Pope is, in fact, responsible for giving the English language more familiar quotations than any poet except Shakespeare. His favorite meter was the ten-syllable iambic pentameter rhyming (heroic) couplet.

Pope, who had become the epitome of neoclassicists and the greatest English poet between Dryden and the Romantics, died in 1744 at Twickenham before completing a black verse epic, *Brutus*. (Mock 1969)
   See also The Dunciad; The Rape of the Lock.

POSTHOMERICA

See The Fall of Troy.

POTOCKI, WACŁAW

Polish poet, author of a vigorous historical epic, *Wojno chocimska* (The Chocim war, or The war of Khotim, 1670, publ. 1850). He was born in 1625 in Łużna, Poland, in an area that was a stronghold of Arianism and Calvinism. A talented natural poet, he had scant literary education but a keen interest in history. He married Catherine Morsztyn, a relative of the Arian poet Zbigniew Morsztyn. He became a country squire who composed voluminous verses (some 300,000 lines) for his own enjoyment. However, he was a careful student of history, as his epic attests: It is a historically accurate account of the 1621 defense of the city of Chocim by a force of only 65,000 Poles and Cossacks against an invading Turkish army of some 400,000. He finished the work in 1670. Another work of merit is a collection of epigrams entitled *Ogród fraszek* (Garden of rhymes), written over a period of 25 years (1670–1695). These poems give a vivid account of life among the gentry during a time of political and religious strife. None of his work was published in his lifetime. (*Wojno chocimska* was published in 1850; *Ogród fraszek* in 1907.)

He and his wife were Unitarians. When a decree banished all Unitarians from Poland, he converted to Catholicism, but his wife refused, and he feared for her safety for many years. He lost two sons, who died while serving in the army, and a daughter. He wrote almost until the end of his life, about 1696 or 1697. (Dvornik 1962; Miłosz 1969/1983)
   See also The War of Khotim.

POUND, EZRA LOOMIS

American poet, author of *The Cantos*. He was born in 1885 in Hailey, Idaho, to Isabel Weston and Homer Loomis Pound. His father worked for the Federal Land Office, and when Pound was about age two, the family moved east. In 1889, when the elder Pound was assigned to the U.S. Mint in Philadelphia, the family settled in Wyncote, Pennsylvania, where Ezra Pound grew to manhood.

American poet Ezra Pound in Paris, September 1923

For two years (1901–1903) he attended the University of Pennsylvania, where he met poet William Carlos Williams, a medical student who became his close friend. In 1905 he graduated from Hamilton College in Clinton, New York, with a degree in philosophy. He returned to the University of Pennsylvania for graduate studies. Also in 1905 he met the poet Hilda Doolittle, a student at Bryn Mawr, to whom he wrote a collection of poems later published as *Hilda's Book*. However, her father put an end to the affair. Pound received an M.A. degree in 1906, but quit in 1907 before finishing his doctoral studies, taking a teaching post at Wabash Presbyterian College in Crawfordsville, Indiana.

But after only one semester he left for Europe. In Venice, he self-published his first book of poems, *A lume spento* (1908). He went to England, where he fell in with a group of Imagists presided over by T. E. Hulme, and was accepted in the circle of William Butler Yeats. Ford Maddox Ford became a friend and published Pound's work in his *English Review*. Although Pound had been unable to find a publisher—or even an audience—in the United States, his work was greeted with more enthusiasm in England. In 1909 two collections of his poems appeared: *Personae* and *Exultations*. In 1910, *The Spirit of Romance*, a book based on lectures he had given in London the preceding year, was published. In 1912 he became the London correspondent for the Chicago-based magazine *Poetry, A Magazine of Verse*. In this position he became friends with beginning poets like Robert Frost and T. S. Eliot, as well as D. H. Lawrence. He became leader of the Imagist movement and delineated its guidelines, emphasizing direct, lean language and sharply defined images. In 1914 he edited the first anthology of Imagist poetry in *Des Imagistes.*

That same year he married Dorothy Shakespear, daughter of Olivia Shakespear, a friend of Yeats. He also began a collaboration with James Joyce that resulted in Joyce's obtaining financial assistance, culminating in the publishing of Joyce's *Portrait of the Artist as a Young Man* and *Ulysses*. Pound assisted many writers in finding publishers, including Eliot, Wyndham Lewis, his old friend William Carlos Williams, and Marianne Moore. Between 1913 and 1915 he began an ambitious work of his own that would be entitled *The Cantos.*

Although he continued to publish his own poetry, in 1915 he adapted and published the translations of Ernest Fenollosa (1853–1908) of the Chinese poet Li Po, under the title *Cathay*. This was followed by two volumes of Japanese Noh plays. In 1917 he published *Homage to Sextus Propertius*, his first major work, in the book *Quia Pauper Amavi*, which is a commentary of the British Empire of 1917. In 1920 he published another major work, *Hugh Selwyn Mauberley*, a commentary on the literary culture of England, decrying both war and commercialism, which he thought was detrimental to the arts.

The following year he moved to Paris, where he met Gertrude Stein, assisted Ernest Hemingway, and helped T. S. Eliot in editing *The Waste Land*. In 1924, Pound moved to Rapallo, Italy, remaining there for the next 20 years. In 1925 he published the first section of *The Cantos* and had a daughter, Maria, by Olga Rudge, an American violinist living in Europe, who gave the baby to an Italian peasant woman in the Tirol to rear. With Rudge's help, Pound brought a series of concerts to Rapallo, turning the public's attention to the seventeenth-century music of Antonio Vivaldi, all but forgotten by that time in his native Italy. The following year (1926) his wife Dorothy bore a son, Omar, who was reared by her family in England.

His publishing ventures continued at a steady pace. In 1927–1928 he edited his own literary magazine, *Exile*. In the 1930s he published several volumes of *The Cantos* (1930, 1934, 1937, 1940). He also published a book of his prose, *Make It New* (1934).

During World War II he made a number of broadcasts over Rome Radio in which he frequently condemned the United States for its policies against Fascist Italy. In 1945 he was arrested by U.S. occupying forces and forced to spend six months in a Pisan prison camp, charged with giving aid and comfort to the enemy. While there, he translated Confucius into English and wrote *The Pisan Cantos* (publ. 1948), considered the best section of *The Cantos*. He was returned to the United States to face charges of treason, but was pronounced insane and mentally unfit to stand trial. He was confined to St. Elizabeth's Hospital for the criminally insane in Washington, D.C., from 1946 to 1958, during which time he continued to write and publish *The Cantos*.

In 1949, still confined as insane, he was awarded the Bollingen Prize for the *Pisan Cantos*. In 1958 he was declared unfit to stand trial, and charges against him were dropped. He returned to Italy, where he died in Venice in 1972. (Kenner 1972)

See also The Cantos.

PRANG KOMPENI, HIKAJAT

Malaysian epic of the Atjehnese Holy War of 1873, which exists in manuscript form in the University Library at Leiden, Codex Ordinensis 8727b. The author wrote the poem during the war, adding new events as they occurred, but was killed before the war ended. It begins with a sultan's dream, which only the *oelama* (religious scholar) Teungkoe Koetakarang can interpret. He foresees in the dream the destruction of Atjeh by the Dutch. The king soon hands over his authority to the foremost of the territorial rulers, or *oelèbelang*. The poem depicts scenes of the homeless villagers of Atjeh searching for shelter following the Dutch invasion. The rest of the poem follows the deeds of various leaders, most of whom eventually die. (Siegel 1979)

PRAPANCA
(Also Prapañcha)

Javanese poet (fl. 14th c.), author of the vernacular epic poem *Nāgarakertāgama* (1365), the most important work of Old Javanese literature, which chronicles the kingdom of Java during the Majapahit empire of East Java, particularly the reign of King Hayam Wuruk (r. 1350–1389). The only information known about the author comes from the poem. He was the son of the Buddhist *adhyakṣa* (chaplain) and as such accompanied his father on his travels around the kingdom. Prapanca was a worshipper of King Kertanagara (r. 1268–1292) and may have begun his poem as an act of worship. He enjoyed the patronage of the powerful prime minister Gajah Mada and began composing his epic during the prime minister's time. However, Gajah Mada died before the epic was completed. The poem contains descriptions of the kingdom that provide valuable historical and sociological information about the period. (Dudley and Lang 1969)

See also Nāgarakertāgama.

PROMETHEUS DER DULDER
(Prometheus the Sufferer)

German-Swiss allegorical epic (1924) by Carl Spitteler (1845–1924). It is a recasting, in iambic hexameter, of his earlier work, *Prometheus und Epimetheus* (1880–1881). For a synopsis, see *Prometheus und Epimetheus.* (Highet 1976)

PROMETHEUS UND EPIMETHEUS
(Prometheus and Epimetheus)

German-Swiss allegorical epic (1880–1881) by Carl Spitteler (1845–1924). Published under the pen name of Carl Felix Tandem, the epic was originally printed as prose, but it contains a persistent iambic rhythm. A complex allegory, it was not a critical success.

Prometheus represents the human spirit rising to its rull grandeur, while Epimetheus represents it falling into the dull routine of habit and mediocrity.

The poem is based on the ancient myth of two brothers: Foresight and Hindsight; Vision and Repentance. One brother is wise, unselfish, long-suffering; the other is foolish, greedily taking the perfect Pandora with her dowry box of all the troubles of mankind.

The ruling angel offers a viceroyalty to Prometheus who refuses in order to keep his soul's independence. The angel offers it to Epimetheus, who accepts and becomes rich and powerful. However, he does not protect the angel's children—Myth, Hiero, and Messiah—from the evil Behemoth, so Prometheus, who has been exiled in poverty, is recalled. Prometheus saves the kingdom of the world, which henceforth will be ruled by the Messiah.

The epic was recast in 1924 in iambic hexameters with a new title, *Prometheus der Dulder* (Prometheus the Sufferer). (Highet 1976)

See also Prometheus der Dulder; Spitteler, Carl Friedrich Georg.

PROMETHIDENLOS

German epic (1885) by Gerhart Hauptmann (1862–1946). The poet's first work, it is considered "unoriginal." (Garland and Garland 1986)

See also Hauptmann, Gerhart.

 # PROSOPOPÉIA

Brazilian Portuguese epic (16th c.) by Portuguese-born Bento Teixeira Pinto (or just Bento Teixeira). It was the first Brazilian epic, although critics described it as "stumbling and underdeveloped pastiche" and said it was "without originality." One portion of note is the author's description of the Reef (Recife) of Pernambuco, from which the city of Recife takes its name. (Coutinho 1969; Putnam 1948/1971)

 # PṚTHVĪRĀJA-RĀSO
(Also *Pṛthvīrāj Rāsau, Pṛthvirāj, Prithvī Rāj*, or *Pṛithvirāj*)

Indian epic poem (12th c.) by Lahore poet Candbardaī (or Chand Bardaī). The poem is based on the life and feats of Pṛthvirāj III, twelfth-century Cauhān king, the last of that Hindi dynasty, whose kingdom of Delhi fell to Ghūrī Turks in 1192. The poet wrote the epic in Hindi, very soon after the events depicted took place. As his source he used material from the bardic tradition of the Rājput court, which also produced epics such as *Alhā* and *Gūgā*. (For a synopsis of both epics, see the *Encyclopedia of Traditional Epics*.) In an encounter against the Chandels earlier in his career, the historical Pṛthvīrāj triumphed over them, destroying them completely; however the battle so weakened him that he was unable to withstand the Muslim attack of Shahābuddīm Ghurī.

The king is remembered primarily for the Romantic epic (a Lochinvar story). Pṛthvīrāj's enemy, King Jaraccandra (or Jaichand) of Kanauj, has a daughter, Princess Sanyogita, whose time to marry arrives. As is the custom among princesses, a *svayamvara* is held, in which the eligible suitors from which she is to choose are assembled. The princess indicates her choice by placing a garland around the suitor's neck. As a deliberate insult, King Jaraccandra has not invited Pṛthvīrāj to the *svayamvara*, even though Sanyogita has her heart set on the gallant Cauhān king. To the puzzlement of those assembled at the *svayamvara*, the princess places the garland around a statue's neck. Pṛthvīrāj, who is hiding nearby, sweeps up the princess and rides away with her to his kingdom.

Māhil, prince of Mahoba (Parihār) before the Chandels take it over, persuades Pṛthvīrāj to demand the five flying horses of Mahoba because they are a threat to him. When the Banāphars refuse to relinquish the horses, they are banished, and they seek refuge in Kanauj with King Jaraccandra. At Māhil's insistence, Pṛthvīrāj marches on Mahoba and demands the surrender of Queen Malhanā, who is Māhil's sister. She asks for a grace period and sends her husband Parmāl's nephew to Kanauj to beg her sons Ālhā and Ūdal to come back home. When Pṛthvīrāj learns they are on the way, he sends his troops to the Betava River to prevent their return. A terrible battle ensues in which Pṛthvīrāj's troops are defeated and retreat to Delhi.

Pṛthvīrāj has a daughter named Belā and several sons, among them the arrogant Tāhar. The king has an army of 900,000 soldiers and 100 *sāmants* (vassals), among them the cruel Brahman general and adviser Chaunṛā. Princess Belā marries the Chandel prince Brahmā, but, because the Chandels are hierarchically below the Cauhāns, Pṛthvīrāj must oppose the marriage. He sends out his sons, one by one, to capture Brahmā, but each is defeated in turn. Finally, the king's son Tāhar conspires with Chaunṛā, who dresses like a woman, hides in the marriage litter that is to bear the bride to join her husband in Mahoba, and stabs Brahmā. But before he dies, Belā arrives. Brahmā tells her he will die in peace if someone will bring him Tāhar's head. Belā returns to Delhi, dons armor, and challenges her brother Tāhar, whom she kills. She presents his head to her dying husband and plans to immolate herself on his funeral pyre. Learning of his daughter's impending *satī*, Pṛthvīrāj rushes to the pyre and orders that it not be lit by anyone from Mahoba. Outraged at such a suggestion, the Mahobans attack, and a terrible battle ensues. During the conflict, Belā lets down her hair, which spontaneously ignites, lighting the fire and burning both bodies. (Blackburn 1989; Thapar 1966)

See also Candbardāi.

 # *PSALMODIA POLSKA*
(Polish psalmody)

Polish epic (1695) written by Wespazjan Kochowski (1633–1700). The *Psalmodia* consists of 36 psalms glorifying Poland as the savior of the world, ordained by God. The epic was inspired by King Jan III Sobieski's victory over the Turks in Vienna in 1683, at which battle the poet, as court historian, was present. The poet particularly admired King Sobieski, and describes the defeated Turks: "The rising sun saw their haughtiness; and the evening saw them badly smitten." He boasts, "The false prophet helped them not in that terror; nor did frequent ablutions purify the wicked of their sins." The Cossacks and Tartar forces defeated, the Christians begin to clear the battlefield: "Three days were not enough to gather booty. Not only were soldiers taking the abandoned riches, but also small children and the common mob." Of the pagan leaders, "Their crimson-vested overlords who would have said, 'Let us possess the Christian land,' have all perished. / Their vizir died in an unmanly way, strangled with a rope, and Jael soon drove a nail into the temple of that destroyer of the Lord's churches." The psalms prefigure the Romantic nationalistic movement of the nineteenth century. (Dvornik 1962; Miłosz 1969/1983)

 # PUCELLE, LA
(*La Pucelle d'Orléans*, The maid of Orleans)

The title of at least two French epics. The earlier is an unsuccessful French epic in 24 cantos about Jeanne d'Arc (Joan of Arc, 1412–1431) by Jean Chapelain (1595–1674). Written in classical style, the poem was a labor of more than two decades. The poet began work on it about 1636, but it was 20 years before the first 12 cantos appeared. The remaining 12 cantos were not published until 1882, over two centuries after his death. (Harvey and Heseltine 1959)

The more famous poem by that name is the French mock-heroic epic (published by the poet in 1756) by Voltaire (1694–1778). Voltaire began the poem, consisting of 21 cantos, in 1730, when guests of the duc de Richelieu suggested to the poet that he write the story of Jeanne d'Arc. The supernatural elements of the legend surrounding her inspired in the poet a burlesque treatment. Written in decasyllables rhymed at times in couplets and at other times in quatrains, the poem contained licentious and scandalous passages, which the poet delighted in reading to his friends.

The principal theme of the poem is the difficulty for Jeanne d'Arc to preserve her virginity, surrounded as she is by men, and thrown repeatedly into danger and temptation. She rides a winged donkey—modeled after Ariosto's hippogriff in *Orlando Furioso*. Like the ass in Apuleius's *Metamorphoses*, it falls in love with her, and speaks to her (having once been the talking ass belonging to the prophet Balaam). Although Jeanne is attracted to the donkey, with the aid of St. Louis she resists temptation.

From Canto II: When King Charles asks Jeanne if she is a "maid" (virgin), she answers in part: ". . . doctors sage, with spectacles on nose,/Who, versed in female mysteries can depose,/. . . clerks, apothecaries, matrons tried/Be called at once the matter to decide;/Let them all scrutinize and let them see." By this sage answer Charles knows that Jeanne must be "inspired and blessed with sweet virginity."

As late as 1753, Voltaire was reading from the rollicking poem for a gathering of literati hosted by the duke and duchess of Saxe-Gotha.

Originally, the poet had no intention of publishing the poem, written strictly for amusement—and added to by friends and enemies alike—because it ridiculed not only the heroic Jeanne d'Arc but also various creeds, rites, scandals, and dignitaries of the Catholic church. But in 1755 a scandalous version of the poem appeared in Basel, of which he disavowed authorship. Instead, he sent to Cardinal Richelieu, Madame de Pompadour, and various officials of the French government an expunged version of the poem, which he published in 1762.

In 1764, during the French Inquisition, buying or selling copies of the poem carried sentences ranging from pillory and flogging to nine years in the

Joan of Arc rides amid the confusion of battle before the walls of Orleans in 1429. She became a French national heroine, and several French poets, including Jean Chapelain and Voltaire, wrote of her exploits and subsequent martyrdom at the hands of her enemies.

galleys. When the Jesuit editor Guillaume François Berthier read the poem in 1757, he said of it, "Never has hell vomited up a more deadly plague. . . . The odor given off by these verses is enough to infect and corrupt every age and condition in society." (Durant and Durant 1965)

See also Voltaire.

 # THE PULKOV MERIDIAN

Russian epic poem (1943) by Vera Inber (1890–1972). The poem describes the blockade of Leningrad during World War II, depicting the common people rising to heroism. The poem gained great popularity in Russia. (Bristol 1991)

See also Inber, Vera.

 # PUNICA

Latin epic by Silius Italicus. It is the longest Latin poem, with 12,000 verses in 17 books. Written in classical hexameters, it deals with the Second Punic War between Carthage and Rome. Although the poet intended Scipio as the hero, Hannibal emerges as the central character. Much space is devoted to the six great battles of that war, with details that become monotonous and repulsive, but except for some digressions the narrative proceeds in orderly fashion. It also has vivid passages of more than carnage—drama, picturesque description, and genuine poetry.

In Book I the poet invokes the Muse to sing of the war by which "proud Carthage submitted to the rule of Rome." The war came after Rome began sending her fleets all over the world and aroused the fears of the Carthaginians. When Hannibal was a child, his father, Hamilcar, kindled in him a hatred for the Romans. Hamilcar had won allies in northern Africa and Spain, but he had been killed in a battle near the Pillars of Hercules. Hannibal proceeds to besiege Saguntum, a Greek city in Spain, a violation of a treaty with Italy, and Saguntum appeals to Rome. In an assembly of consuls, different views are expressed, so an embassy of senators—including Fabius, a descendant of Hercules, who founded Carthage—is sent to Hannibal.

In Book II, Hannibal dismisses the envoys and proceeds with the siege, but the Carthaginian senate listens to them, with a difference of opinion. Fabius declares war. Hannibal despoils those whose loyalty wavers, and returns to the siege. The goddess Loyalty is sent by Hercules, the city's founder, to encourage resistance, but Juno, his mother, does not want the war and sends a Fury to drive the people mad. Hannibal then takes the city.

In Book III, Bostar is sent to Africa to seek from Jupiter Ammon a good omen for Hannibal's enterprise. Hannibal goes to Gades (Cádiz) and views the famous temple of Hercules and the huge tides of the Atlantic Ocean. He sends his wife and infant son to Carthage, crosses the Pyrenees, and the Rhone and Druentia (Durance) rivers, and reaches the Alps. Hannibal crosses slowly; his men are terrified by the enormous cliffs. He persuades them to climb the heights, with rich promises, avoiding the path made by Hercules and forging a new one. The ascent is stiff with frozen ice, slippery with snow. When the snow thaws, it swallows men in avalanches. The wind strips the men of their shields and rolls them around and around. Finally, Hannibal pitches camp on the summit. Venus and Jupiter discuss the destiny of Rome, and Jupiter reassures her of Rome's coming greatness. Hannibal and his army slide down pathless slopes and reach Italy near Turin. Bostar brings back a welcome response from the oracle, which fills the army with a desire for instant battle.

In Book IV, Rome is alarmed at the news that Hannibal has reached Italy, but the Senate builds a defense with great courage and spirit. Hannibal's army is weary and stiff with the cold, but Hannibal points out that they are now on level ground and Rome is at their mercy. He courts the Gauls with bribes. Scipio returns to Rome from Marseilles. Both Hannibal and Scipio address their armies and prepare for battle. Suddenly a hawk appears in the sky and attacks a flock of doves dear to Venus. It kills 15 of them, and presses hard on the last dove, but an eagle from the east forces the hawk to flee. The dove flies to the Roman standards, pecks at the plume on the helmet of Scipio's son, then flies back into the sky. A Carthaginian seer warns Hannibal that this omen bodes ill for him. Bogus, however, says it is a good sign: The slaughter of the doves forecasts disaster for the Romans. Scipio is wounded in the battle but saved by his son, protected by Mars. Amazed, the Libyans and Spaniards give ground. Finding the level ground an advantage to Hannibal, Scipio withdraws to the Trebia River, where he is joined by an army under the consul Longus. Another battle ensues. Scipio withdraws to a fortified height. Meanwhile, Flaminius leads another army into Etruria. Hannibal rushes to meet him and encamps by Lake Trasimene, after crossing the Apennines. Senators come to him from Carthage with news that it is time for the annual sacrifice of a young child to Diana, and that Hanno, Hannibal's enemy, has demanded that this time the child be Hannibal's infant son. Hannibal refuses, but promises victims of war as sacrifices.

In Book V, Hannibal prepares a trap for the Romans, taking advantage of the frequent mist over the lake. The path around the lake narrows as it passes into a gorge, and Hannibal plans to hide there and surprise the Romans. Meanwhile, Flaminius foolishly disregards the warning of the soothsayer Corvinus and enourages his men to start fighting. The Carthaginians overwhelm the Romans, killing Flaminius. His followers stand over his body until it is covered with their corpses. Darknesss ends the slaughter.

In Book VI the Romans flee. One of the fugitives, Serranus, son of the famous Regulus, hero of the first Punic War, reaches the home of Marus, former squire of his father. Marus dresses Serranus's wounds, recalling the great conquests of Regulus as well as his captivity in Carthage. The news of the defeat reaches Rome. The Senate discusses plans as the Carthaginians approach, but an angry Jupiter hurls his thunderbolt until all Tuscany is lighted up, and a rift in the heavens appears right over the head of the Carthaginian army. Hannibal is turned away. Fabius, of noble birth, is chosen as dictator. He is wise, and a match for Hannibal. Hannibal now marches to Campania. As he goes through Liternum, on the temple walls he sees scenes of the First Punic War: a shattered Carthaginian fleet; his father, Hamilcar, fettered in a long row of prisoners; and Libyans raising their axes and begging for pardon. Angry, Hannibal orders them burned.

In Book VII, Fabius is "the one beacon-light in that dark hour." Hannibal is eager to know more about this man. Cilnius, one of the prisoners, tells him about Fabius's distinguished family history and character, predicting that he will be Hannibal's match. Back in Rome, Fabius brings discipline into the army but resists Hannibal's attempts to lure him into battle, so Hannibal goes to Apulia and tries unsuccessfully to provoke Fabius by pretending retreat. Finally, he returns to Campania and ravages the countryside. A perverse desire for battle grows strong in the Roman camp, but Fabius explains his policy of inaction, recalling the fatal rashness of Flaminius.

Hannibal tries to poison the minds of the Romans with a trick to make Fabius unpopular. As he ravages the countryside, he leaves untouched a small estate Fabius has inherited, to create the suspicion of a secret understanding with Fabius. Fabius sees through the trick, but he is too busy to fear jealousy. Instead he shuts in Hannibal so that his army is threatened with famine. Hannibal breaks out and camps on open ground.

A Carthaginian fleet lands at Caieta, land of the Laestrygonians, where the Nereids live. They are terrified, but calmed by the prophecy of Proteus that Carthage will be destroyed. In Rome, Minucius is eager to fight, and is given equal powers with Fabius and half the army. He rashly engages the enemy, but is rescued by Fabius. Fabius is now hailed as a savior by Minucius and the soldiers.

In Book VIII, Hannibal grows impatient and anxious, but Juno renews his hope of victory and his ambition by sending Anna, sister of Dido and now a nymph, who tells what happened to her after the death of Dido. She encourages Hannibal with her forecast of the Battle of Cannae. In Rome, Varro, an obscure, boastful orator who is liberal with his wealth, is elected consul and urges warfare. His fellow consul, Paulus, is afraid to oppose him, so they start for Apulia and Hannibal. When they reach Cannae, there is an evil omen. Javelins blaze up. Battlements fall. Mount Garganus collapses. Fire burns on the mountains. There is sudden darkness. A screech owl besets the camp. Bees swarm. Wild beasts burst into the camp. Men dream that the ghosts of Gauls break out of their graves.

In Book IX, Varro is eager to fight. Paulus tries to restrain him. A dying man writes a warning on his shield in his own blood: "Beware of battle!" The two armies draw up their lines, and the Battle of Cannae begins.

In Book X, Paulus distinguishes himself by bravery before he is killed. Without him, the courage of the Romans fails, and Hannibal, flushed with victory, plans to march on Rome the next day. However, Juno sends Sleep to stop him. Hannibal has unpeaceful dreams in which Jupiter threatens him with thunderbolts and warns him to stay: He "has gained enough glory." But Mago comes with the news that the remainder of the Roman army has surrendered during the night, and urges immediate attack. Among the Romans, Metellus, a defeatist, urges that the Romans abandon Italy, but Scipio threatens him and his followers with death. Rome is terrified. They have no fighting men left. They cannot trust their walls, and can rely only on their citadel. Then Fabius tells them there is no longer any reason for delay. He calms their anger at Varro, who returns to Rome, and Fabius and the senators quickly set their minds to the task ahead. They arm the young and bondsmen.

In Book XI many peoples of Italy revolt and join Hannibal's army. Even Capua, debased by wealth and luxury, is inclined to go over. One of their leaders, Pacuvius, urges that the Capuans demand of Rome an equal share in the office of consul, a demand he knows the Romans will never grant. Fabius and the senators indignantly refuse, so Capua—with one dissenter, Decius—also joins Hannibal. At a banquet, Pacuvius's son plots to assassinate Hannibal but is dissuaded by his father. Hannibal winters at Capua. Venus intervenes to enfeeble his army. Hannibal's brother Mago goes to Carthage to announce the victory, and makes a fierce attack on their enemy, Hanno, who answers by urging peace with Rome. However, the Carthaginians send reinforcements to Hannibal.

In Book XII, Hannibal's army has lost its vigor and momentum. Attacks on Parthenope (Naples), Cumae, and Puteoli fail. While his men labor, Hannibal visits the sights at Capua: the hot springs of Baiae, Lake Avernus, and other notable features. He goes to Nola, a colony from Cumae, but is driven off by Marcellus, who pursues and challenges him. However, as Hannibal turns to meet Marcellus, Juno intervenes to keep Hannibal "from rushing to his doom." A young Roman launches a spear that barely misses Hannibal, who rides off in haste. So accustomed to defeat, the Romans now take heart, and are encouraged by an oracle from Delphi. The consul Torquatus attacks Sardinia and defeats Hampsagoras, an ally of the Carthaginians. Hannibal sets fire to several cities, captures Tarentum, and returns to Capua, beleaguered by the Romans. Seeking a reputation for humanity, he stops en route to bury his Roman enemy Gracchus. Unable to enter Capua, Hannibal examines the city walls and surroundings, but is driven away by Fulvius. Two attempts at battle are stopped because of storms sent by Jupiter. A third attempt is prevented by Juno, following Jupiter's orders. The Romans rejoice.

In Book XIII, Hannibal withdraws to the river Tutia. The fear of Jupiter lingers in the minds of the soldiers, but they are willing to continue—with one dissenter, Dasius, a wealthy man but reluctant ally. He argues that Rome is impregnable so long as it contains the Palladium. Hannibal is discouraged and goes to Rhegium. The Romans capture Capua, but Scipio's father and uncle are killed in Spain. Scipio goes to Cumae, and with the help of Apollo's priestess descends into Hades to see them, as well as the ghosts of many famous men and women. At the end, he asks the Sibyl the fate of the Roman state. She answers that Hannibal's bones "shall not rest in his native land." He will suffer defeat and beg for his life. At the end he will swallow poison and "free the world at last from a long-enduring dread."

In Book XIV, Marcellus begins his campaign in Sicily, where a kindly ruler has died and been succeeded by a prince of unbridled passions. Right has disappeared, and wrong in every form is rife. When Hannibal proceeded against Rome, the new ruler determined to aid Hannibal, but was assassinated. All Sicily is now in turmoil. Marcellus arrives, takes Leontini, and blockades Syracuse. The two armies ready themselves. On the Sicilian side, Archimedes, a Greek, wears out the Romans with ingenious devices. A great Carthaginian fleet speeds to the aid of Syracuse. The Roman fleet meets them, light and maneuverable; the Carthaginian ships are huge and formidable. The Roman ships bombard their enemy's ships with burning pitch and set them on fire. The Romans would win except for the appearance of a plague that kills many of them, as well as Syracusians. Eventually the Romans capture the city.

In Book XV the Roman Senate faces the problem of helping the Spanish. Scipio is willing to go, but is dissuaded by his family. He is torn between Virtue and Pleasure, deciding in favor of Virtue. He sails a fleet to Tarraco, where his father's ghost tells him to take New Carthage (Cartagena), which he does. He next proceeds against Philip, king of Macedon. Back in Italy, Fabius takes Tarentum after bribing the Punic commander. Hannibal defeats the Romans in Apulia and kills Marcellus. In Spain, Scipio puts Hasdrubal to flight, and Hasdrubal crosses the Alps and joins the Carthaginians in Italy. Rome is alarmed. A consul marches against Hasdrubal in the Battle of the Metaurus, but Hasdrubal kills Hannibal's brother and displays his head to Hannibal.

In Book XVI, Hannibal retires behind ramparts in the land of the Brutii. In Spain, the Carthaginians are driven out. Mago, another of Hannibal's brothers, dies of his wounds aboard ship. In Italy the army of Hasdrubal is destroyed. In Africa, a Numidian prince joins Scipio. Together they arrange a treaty for the Numidian king to serve as peacemaker, but Scipio lacks the authority to accept this. He returns to Spain, then goes back to Rome, where he is elected consul. Despite opposition from Fabius, he gets permission to move directly against Carthage itself.

In Book XVII, arriving in Africa, Scipio warns the Numidian king not to break faith with Rome, but the king is the one hope of the Carthaginians and the chief menace to the Romans. The king is angered by the warning and threatens the Romans, who proceed to burn his camp and take him prisoner. Hasdrubal retreats to Carthage, and Hannibal is recalled from Italy, after a dream in which the ghosts of Paulus and other defeated Romans attack him with swords and drive him from Italy back across the Alps. He launches his ships, bound for Carthage, but has second thoughts and turns them back toward Italy, where a beleaguered Rome has enticed Scipio to return. But a dreadful storm smashes his ships, so Hannibal goes to Africa and rallies his soldiers. Jupiter and Juno discuss his fate. Jupiter grants Juno a reprieve for Carthage, but its days are numbered. The two armies meet at Zama in a bloody battle. The Carthaginians are in turmoil, the city is afire, and Scipio is impatient for victory and shouts defiance at Hannibal. Juno fears that Hannibal will hear it, and fashions "a shape in the likeness of Scipio" that approaches Hannibal and then, after an exchange, flees. In disguise Juno tricks Hannibal away from the battle to save his life. On a hill, Hannibal views the defeat of his army and joins a band of fugitives in the mountains. The war ends. Scipio has "gained glory to last for ages." He returns to Rome with a splendid triumphal procession. "Hail to thee, father and undefeated general! Rome tells no lie when she gives thee a divine origin and calls thee the son of the Thundergod!" (TAP) (Silius Italicus 1968)

See also Silius Italicus.

◆ PUSHKIN, ALEKSANDR SERGEYEVICH

Russia's greatest poet, author of the verse novel *Eugene Onegin* (1823–1831, publ. complete 1833); a mock-heroic folk epic, *Ruslan i Lyudmila* (1820); epic poems *Poltava* (1829, Engl. trans.) and *Medny vsadnik* (The bronze horseman, 1837); humorous epics *Graf Nulin* (Count Nulin, 1837); *Tazit*, or *Galub* (publ. posthumously 1837); *Domik v Kolomme* (A small house in Kolomna, 1833), as well as many other poems; many dramatic works, including *Boris Godunov* (1824/1825, publ. 1831, Engl. trans.); short stories; novels; and other prose. Pushkin was born in Moscow in 1799 to a well-to-do family: His father's family was one of the old boyar families, eclipsed by Peter the Great's new court aristocracy. His mother, a Gannibal, was a granddaughter of one Abraham Gannibal, or Hannibal, said to be an Abyssinian Negro prince bought as a slave from the Turkish court and adopted by Peter the Great and trained as an officer.

As was the custom in families of his class, Pushkin and his brother and sister were taught to read and speak French. He is described as being a clever but idle schoolboy. His nurse, Arina Rodionovna, a former serf, told him Russian folktales, which he incorporated into his writing at an early age. At the age of 12 he entered the Imperial Lyceum at Tsarskoye Selo, where he began his first major work, a mock-epic entitled *Ruslan i Lyudmila,* based on an old folktale and published in 1820.

In 1817, at the age of 18, he entered the service of the foreign office at St. Petersburg, where he enjoyed an active social life in both literary and political circles. Because of his political verses he was exiled from St. Petersburg to Yekaterinoslav, and later to the Crimea.

His experiences in the southern provinces provided inspiration for his "southern cycle" of Romantic narrative poems, after the fashion of Byron. In 1820 he was transferred to Kishinyov, and in 1823 to Odessa, where he had an affair with the wife of the governor general of the province. In 1823 he began work on his masterpiece, a novel in verse, *Yevgeny (Eugene) Onegin* (publ. 1833), on which he continued to work for eight years.

But Pushkin was soon in trouble again, when a letter was intercepted in which he wrote that he was "taking lessons in atheism." In 1824 he was expelled from the service and sent to his mother's estate at Mikhailovskoye. Outraged at their son's latest disgrace, his parents left for the capital, taking their younger two children with them. Pushkin spent two unhappy but highly

Russian author Aleksandr Sergeyevich Pushkin, 1799–1837, with his wife, Natalia Goncharova, at a court ball in St. Petersburg.

productive years alone on the estate, during which he wrote, among other works, the historical tragedy *Boris Godunov* (1821–1825).

Meanwhile Tsar Alexander died, and after the suppression of an uprising, the new tsar, Nicholas I, offered his patronage to Pushkin, whose writings had made him immensely popular. Pushkin returned from exile, much to the relief of his family.

In 1828 he met a dazzling 17-year-old beauty, Natalia Goncharova, whom he married three years later. By his own estimation, she was Woman Number 113 in his life. Despite the fact that she bore Pushkin five children, Natalia had caught the eye of the tsar as well as a young French émigré, Baron D'Anthès. Natalia's sister, who had come to live with them, fell in love with D'Anthès, and he entered into a courtship with her in order to be closer to Natalia. Gossip of the affair could not be ignored, and Pushkin sent D'Anthès's adopted father, the Dutch ambassador, an offensive letter. D'Anthès could do no less than challenge Pushkin on his father's behalf.

At the duel the following day, both men were wounded, D'Anthès only slightly. Pushkin died two days later (1837), having received a letter from the tsar exhorting him to die like a Christian and promising to care for his family. The tsar saw to it that Pushkin's debts were paid and that his widow received a pension. D'Anthès recovered and was sent back to France. He never expressed regret at having robbed Russia of its greatest poet. (Simmons [Ernest] 1964)

See also *The Bronze Horseman; Eugene Onegin; Graf Nulin; Poltava; Ruslan i Lyudmila.*

 # QUINTUS SMYRNAEUS
(Quintus of Smyrna)

Greek epic poet (fl ca. A.D. 375), author of *The Fall of Troy* (*Ta met' Homeron, Ton meth Omeron*, or *Posthomerica*), an epic sequel to Homer's *Iliad*. (For a synopsis of the *Iliad*, see the *Encyclopedia of Traditional Epics*.) Little is known about Quintus, and what is known comes from within the epic itself: his name, the period in which he lived (the fourth century A.D.), and his birthplace, Smyrna (Asia Minor)—near the site of the Trojan War. In ancient times, Smyrna (located in present-day western Turkey) was an important Greek city. By the poet's own account, as a boy he was tending sheep near Artemis's temple when he was inspired by the Muses to write. His work provides information about a period of Troy's history also covered in the lost epics *Little Iliad, Aethiopis*, and *Iliupersis*. His poem shows a familiarity with many natural features of this region in Asia Minor. (Bowder 1980; Quintus Smyrnaeus 1913)

See also The Fall of Troy.

RAGHUVAMŚA
(The line, or Dynasty of Raghu)

Indian Sanskrit epic poem (4th c.) by Kālidāsa (fl. A.D. 400), India's foremost classical dramatist and poet. His name has been associated with the court of King Vikramāditya, now thought to be the same as Chandra Gupta II (r. 375–413). The poem was written in honor of the house of Raghu and is his longest and best-known epic work. In 19 cantos it chronicles the kings of the Solar dynasty, among whom is Rāma, God incarnate, hero of the *Rāmāyaṇa*. The Solar dynasty also includes, among others, Kakustha ("standing on a hump"), Raghu ("fleet"), Daśaratha ("possessing ten chariots"), Rāma ("charming"), Kuśa, and Lava. For a synopsis of *Rāmāyaṇa,* see the *Encyclopedia of Traditional Epics.* (Dudley and Lang 1969; O'Flaherty 1975; Renou 1961)

RAJIĆ, JOVAN

Serbian poet, author of the epic *Boj zmaja s orlovi* (The battle of the dragon with the eagles). He was born in 1726, a southern Slav living under Ottoman Turkish rule. During his lifetime the seeds of revolution were spreading across Europe, causing unrest among the Serbs, who looked to Russia for protection. Rajić wrote a number of works, including his allegorical-historical epic, which is written in the artificial *rusko-slovenski* language popular with Serbian writers of the time. He died in 1801, three years too early to see the Serbian uprising for independence. (Preminger 1974)

 ## *RĀMCARITMĀNAS*
(Sacred lake of the acts of Rāma, or Mountain lake of Rāma's deeds, or The holy lake of the acts of Rāma)

Northern India religious epic poem written in Hindi (ca. 1574–ca. 1576/1577) by Tulsīdās (or Tulsī Dās) of Rājāpur (ca. 1523/1532/1543–1623). The poet freely utilized the ancient Sanskrit epic *Rāmāyana*, and more particularly the *Adhyātma-Rāmāyana*, a late medieval version that synthesizes the orthodox monotheistic doctrine with polytheistic Hindu mythology. *Rāmcaritmānas* is a lyrical epic in seven cantos in which Rāma is depicted as the supreme God who, out of love for humanity, incarnates himself as a fabulous hero. The popularity of the poem reaches far beyond the territory of the speakers of Hindī; in fact, it has been said that the poem is a bible for 100 million people. The poem has actually usurped the position of the original Sanskrit version among Hindī-speaking Indians. The oldest complete manuscript is dated 1647. It is written in Awadhi, an eastern Hindī dialect that Tulsīdās favored.

A detailed synopsis of the plot of *Rāmāyana* appears in the *Encyclopedia of Traditional Epics*. Briefly, the story is this: Rāma, rightful heir to the kingdom of Ayodhyā as eldest son of King Dasharatha, is deprived of the crown because of a boon granted by his father long before his birth to Rāma's stepmother, that her son be crowned king. Rāma voluntarily withdraws with his faithful wife Sītā to live for 14 years in the wilderness. Sages living a life of asceticism and penance seek Rāma's help against demons who have been bedeviling them. The demon king Rāvana kidnaps Sītā and holds her captive on the island of Sri Lanka, hoping to make her his consort. Rāma enlists the help of the monkey king Hanumān in rescuing her. After defeating Rāvana, Rāma is restored to his throne, where he sets a righteous example (even banishing Sītā because it is rumored that Rāvana may have violated her, making her impure).

In Canto 1 of *Rāmcaritmānas* the gist of the doctrine is contained in the sermon of the god Śiva (I:115 ff.), in which Śiva explains to his consort Pārvatī the complex nature of Rāma. Śiva calls him, among other things, "the Sun, the True Being, Consciousness, Bliss." Rāma is, furthermore, "the Fundamental Light, the Adorable." Although mortals experience both happiness and misery, knowledge and ignorance, conceit and pride, Rāma is "the Omnipresent Absolute, Supreme Bliss, Lord over all, and everlasting." Rāma is lord of Māyā (cosmic illusion): ". . . like the brilliance of an oyster shell, like the mirage in the rays of the sun, error is unreal and still none can ever escape it." But it is by favor of "that gracious Rāma" that such error is corrected.

Canto 2 contains a panegyric to Rāma in which he is called "guardian of the bounds of revelation" and "Lord of the Universe." His wife Jānakī (Sītā, adopted daughter of King Janaka) is Māyā, "which creates, preserves and destroys the world" at Rāma's pleasure. Rāma's brother and boon companion Lakṣmana is "the Serpent with [a] thousand hoods who supports the earth, sovereign of all things animate and inanimate." Rāma has taken a human form and come to earth "to destroy the army of demons."

Canto 6 contains the climactic battle scene in which Rāvana, the ten-headed demon king of Sri Lanka who kidnapped Sītā, is pitted against Rāma and his allies, the bears and the monkeys led by the monkey king Hanumān. After Rāvana is slain, his wife, Mandodarī, acknowledges Rāma's supremacy: "You deemed to be but mortal man Hari himself (Vishnu), come as a fire to burn the demon forest;/ . . . you refused to worship the Lord of all compassion, whom Śiva and Brahma and all the gods adore. . . ."

The epic is still staged annually during the Rām Līlā festival. (Dudley and Lang 1969; Hill 1952)

See also Tulsīdās.

RANGARĀYACARITRAMU

Indian religious epic (18th c.) by Diṭṭaakavi Nārāyaṇa Kavi, an eighteenth-century scholar. The poem, based on the Telegu folk epic *Bobbili Katha*, received attention from literary scholars of the day. (For more on the *Bobbili Katha* see the *Encyclopedia of Traditional Epics*.)

The Velama are land-owning peasants whose chief is Ranga Rao of the ruling Bobbili family. The main rival of the Bobbili is the chiefdom of Vijayanagar, a Kṣatriya clan. When a French commander, Bussy, arrives in the region, the Vijayanagar chief bribes his interpreters to convince Bussy that he should order Ranga Rao to vacate the Bobbili fort and move his clan southward. When the chief refuses to surrender his fort, the Vijayanagar and French attack. The Velama warriors defend the fort until they have all been slain. To avoid capture, their wives jump into a fire. (Blackburn and Ramanujan 1986)

RAPE OF PROSERPINE

Unfinished Latin epic poem (395–397) by Claudian (Claudius Claudianus, ca. 370–404). The poem, in three books of hexameters plus a brief elegiac introduction, is a descriptive poem with a theme taken from Greek myth, in which Persephone (Proserpine in Roman) is abducted by Pluto while she is out gathering flowers. He takes her to Hades and makes her his bride. Her mother, Demeter (Ceres), searches for her everywhere, threatening to destroy mankind if she is not found. Zeus (Jupiter or Jove in Roman) offers to release her if the girl has not eaten anything in Hades. But she has eaten some pomegranate seeds, so she is required to spend six months of each year in Hades. (Dudley and Lang 1969)

THE RAPE OF THE BUCKET
(*La Secchia Rapita*)

Italian mock-epic (1622) by Alessandro Tassoni (1565–1635). The poem is based on a historical incident that occurred in the early fourteenth century during an ongoing war between the cities of Modena and Bologna. The poem opens with the description of a raid on Bologna, in which the Modenese take the bucket from the Bologna town well. This did in fact occur, and the bucket remains in the cathedral at Modena to this day, despite many attempts by the Modenese to retrieve it. The poet peopled his epic, composed of 12 cantos, with Roman gods and goddesses, as well as many characters who were thinly disguised contemporaries.

The gods and goddesses are hardly venerable. Juno excuses herself from the council meeting to wash her hair. Jupiter arrives escorted by Mercury, who carries his hat and spectacles. Saturn, in a speech expressing his scorn for mankind, begins by breaking wind. At dusk the Chariot of Night crosses the Gibraltar Strait (Canto 10:1), while at dawn a blushing Aurora jumps out of the bed she has shared with Tithonus, hiding her nakedness with her shift (Canto 10:5).

The human characters are no more noble: the men of Modena are led by the Potta (short for Podesta, or Mayor). The people of Bologna are addressed as "breadbaskets full of broth." (Canto 1:12,23) Although the implements of war are often those of deadly destruction, at other places they are not: In Canto 3:77, a Bologna cook beans his opponent with a mortadella sausage-mixing pestle. (Highet 1962)

See also Tassoni, Alessandro.

 # *THE RAPE OF THE LOCK*

English mock-epic poem (1717) by Alexander Pope (1688–1744). The poem was published in stages, the last of which appeared in 1717. The poem was dedicated to Mrs. Arabella Fermor, to whom he addresses a letter saying, in part, ". . . all the passages . . . are as fabulous as the Vision at the beginning . . . (except the loss of your Hair, which I always mention with reverence)." He assures her that "the character of Belinda . . . resembles you in nothing but beauty." The "rape" was the taking without permission of a lock of a young woman's hair, and the poem, which alludes often to the *Iliad*, the *Aeneid*, and *Paradise Lost*, creates satire by treating the trivial in the language of the great. It has a war, but it is a war of the sexes; it has creatures of the air comparable to those in Milton, but these are Sylphs, the souls of dead coquettes; it has an underworld, a Cave of Spleen that symbolizes the inner nature of the society reflected and many of the people in it.

Canto 1 begins with questions reminiscent of Milton's intent to justify. Pope asks what could "compel a well-bred lord to assault a gentle belle?" and "what stranger cause, yet unexplored, could make a gentle belle reject a lord?" He continues with yet another question: "In tasks so bold can little men engage, and in soft bosoms dwells such mighty rage?"

Late in the morning, Belinda lies dreaming of a guardian Sylph, Ariel, who has warned her that, despite the protection of thousands of spirits guarding her beauty and virtue, something dreadful is to happen this day. Belinda's lapdog, Shock, leaps up on the bed and licks her face to awaken her. When she awakens the vision of the Sylph is gone, and as Belinda reads the love letters she has received, she forgets the warning. She goes to her cosmetic table to enhance her beauty. She and her maid, worshipping at the altar of her cosmetics table, and being assisted by the army of sylphs that surround them, put together an awesome beauty. Ariel has had her dreaming of beaux in fine clothes. The poet assures her that she is an important person, protected by the spirits of those who were once lovely ladies themselves. "Know further yet," the poet says, "whoever fair and chaste rejects mankind, is by some Sylph embraced . . . for spirits, freed from mortal laws, with ease assume what sexes and what shapes they please."

These sylphs guide young women and contrive worlds of glamor for them. Ariel warns her this morning to beware of all, but most beware of Man!

In Canto 2 the baron, Lord Petre, who admires her, offers a prayer asking for two locks of Belinda's hair. He builds an altar and makes a fiery sacrificial offering of "twelve vast French romances, . . . three garters, half a pair of gloves," plus all his former love trophies. The scene shifts to a pleasure boat going up the Thames to Hampton Court with Belinda and all her guardian sylphs aboard. Ariel warns the other sylphs to take extra precautions, assigning each a different part of her person. Will she "stain her honor or her new brocade?" Will she "lose her heart or her necklace . . . ? Will her lapdog Shock die? Belinda steps out beside the silver Thames wearing "on her white breast a sparkling cross." All eyes are on her, but she smiles on all alike, bestowing no particular favor on anyone.

Belinda has two locks of hair of which she is particularly proud. They hang in shining ringlets down the smooth ivory neck. The adventurous baron has admired these locks and wishes to win one of them. He meditates on how to get one, by force or fraud.

Canto 3 depicts the war scene. At Hampton Court, a bloody battle (of cards) takes place, Belinda taking on two adventurous gentlemen, one of them the baron. She wins, and her breast swells in conquest. But alas, Pope says, thoughtless mortals are "ever blind to fate, too soon dejected, and too soon elate." After the battle, coffee is served. As Belinda bends over her cup, the baron, his judgment presumably snapped by this great defeat, takes out his shears. He is poised to snip off a lock when a "wretched sylph" intervenes, and the shears cut the sylph in two. But it is soon reunited, and the hair is snipped: "the meeting points the sacred hair dissever from the fair head, forever and forever!" Whereupon, "flashed the living lightning from her eyes, and screams of horror rend the affrighted skies." Shrieks rise heavenward, louder even than when husbands or lapdogs die.

Ariel, weeping, has to leave Belinda in Canto 4, and is replaced by Umbriel, "a dusky, melancholy sprite" who hies down to the gloomy Cave of Spleen, returning to Hampton Court with a bag of Chagrin, which he breaks over Belinda's head. At once her fury bursts forth, and she curses the day that brought her to this wretched place and chastises the baron for not choosing "hairs less in sight."

She sends one of her beaux to demand the return of the lock, but the baron refuses. The canto ends with a sad note on the one remaining lock of the two that once gave new beauties to the snowy neck. "The sister lock now sits uncouth, alone, and in its fellow's fate foresees its own; uncurled it hangs, the fatal shears demands, and tempts once more thy sacrilegious hands."

Canto 5, the final section, begins with Clarissa advising Belinda to keep her good humor, noting that "she who scorns a man must die a maid." Belinda, however, hears nothing of this. She wants her hair back, and she and her sylphs and Umbriel and her social allies scatter "death" from their eyes, one beau dying in metaphor, another in song.

When the baron refuses entreaties to return the lock, Belinda gets physical, throwing snuff into his face, affecting his nose and eyes. "Restore the Lock!" she cries, but to no avail. During the ensuing battle, the lock disappears. The Muse has observed it rising upward and being transformed into a starry constellation. This new star will be sacred to lovers, and leaders of great nations will consult almanacs that chart its course. This is Belinda's only consolation; that, and the fact that her name is forever inscribed "'midst the stars." (Hibbard 1942)

See also Pope, Alexander.

RASI'L-GHULI

Swahili epic poem (ca. 18th c.) by an unknown author. The poem, containing 4,384 four-line stanzas with eight syllables per line, describes an expedition of vengeance undertaken by ʿAlī, Muḥammad's son-in-law, against the evil king Rasi'l-Ghuli. ʿAli defeats him and claims his country for Islam. (Knappert 1979)

RATNA-SĒNA
(Also Rana Ratan Singh, Ratna Singh, Ratansen, Bhimsi)

Hero of *Padmāvati*, by Jāyasī. He was *rána* (prince) of Chitor and a Rājput, the ruling dynasty and clan of Mewar. Besieged by Alauddin for five months, Ratna-sēna elicited the admiration of the enemy by forcing Alauddin to retreat to Delhi. Unlike the account in Jāyasī's epic, Ratna-sēna did not die in combat with the prince of Kumbhalner but survived for a number of years. Emboldened by a series of conquests in the meantime, Alauddin returned to Chitor; this time, despite a magnificent defense by the Rājputs, he defeated the Rājput army on 26 August 1303.

After this disaster, the entire population of Rājput women, led by Padmāvatī, proceeded to a pyre and the rite of *Jauhar*. Proud to the end, the princess gave orders that the entrance to the pyre be walled up so their ashes might remain inviolate. Animated by this heroic action, the army rushed out to give one final battle with the sultan's men, perishing to the last man. Among them was Bhimsi (Ratna-sēna). (Arshad 1967; Payne n.d.; Srivastava 1964; Waley 1927)

RAZGOVAR UGODNI
(Friendly story)

Croatian epic (1756) by Andrija Kacic Miosic, a Franciscan monk. He traveled extensively in Ottoman-occupied Slavic territory and imitated the local poetry in his epic, which was published in Venice. However, he ignored historical accuracy in presenting the region's past in both this epic and its companion, *Korablijica*. (Gazi 1973)

 # *REINEKE FUCHS*

German beast epic (publ. 1794) by Johann Wolfgang Goethe (1749–1832). Written in hexameters in 12 books, the poem is based on the fifteenth-century beast epic *Reinke de Vos* (variously known in earlier versions as *Roman de Renart*, twelfth-century French, and the fragmentary *Reinhart Fuchs*, ca. 1180, by Heinrich der Glîchezaere. The thirteenth-century Fleming Willem wrote a version, *Von den vos Reinaerde* (ca. 1250), from which the Dutch poem *Reinke de Vos* (1487), by Hinrek van Alkmaar, is derived. *Reinke de Vos,* printed at Lübeck in 1498, is also descended from the Dutch version.

The poem narrates the adventures of the wicked but resourceful Reynard the fox, twice arraigned for his many crimes, who outwits his enemies Ysegrin the wolf and Brun the bear by sheer deceit and brazen impudence. He becomes an honored citizen, praised by the lion king Nobel. The poem appeared in many editions, and from the sixteenth century was translated into High German. A 1752 edition, *Reineke Fuchs,* published by Johann Christoph Gottsched (1700–1766) inspired Goethe's version, which enhances the comic aspects of the story. To Goethe the tale seemed a parallel to the opportunistic and ruthless anti-French politics of his contemporary Germany. He wrote the poem in 1793 after returning from the 1792 campaign of Duke Karl August in the invasion of France by imperial troops, in which he was required to participate. The poem was published in 1794 in Goethe's *Neue Schriften* (Vol. 2). For more on the legend, see *Reynard the Fox* and *Roman de Renart* in the *Encyclopedia of Traditional Epics.* (Garland and Garland 1986)

See also Goethe, Johann Wolfgang von.

 # RENAISSANCE

A period of cultural "rebirth" in European history beginning in the early fourteenth, fifteenth, sixteenth, or early seventeenth century, depending on the country. Petrarch and Boccaccio are credited with ushering in the Italian Renaissance in the mid-fourteenth century. The period is characterized by a revival in learning of all sorts, of humanistic and classical studies disseminated, after the

Italian Giovanni Boccaccio (1313–1375) was a major figure in the early Renaissance, a period of cultural "rebirth" that began in the early fourteenth century in Europe and lasted for about 300 years.

mid-fifteenth century, through the art of printing. It is further characterized by a spirit of individualism and sophistication, and a thirst for knowledge through experience. An aspect of the Renaissance was the Reformation, a strong factor in Germany, less so in France and England, and of little significance in Italy. The Reformation, a religious movement in Christendom, resulted in the formation of various Protestant churches.

The epic enjoyed a revival as well, and Renaissance epics appeared in profusion. They are essentially a marriage between classical heroic epics and the medieval romances, characterized by love stories, color, and pageantry. The most widely read are Ariosto's *Orlando Furioso*, Tasso's *Gerusalemme Liberata*, Camões's *Os Lusíadas*, and Spenser's *Faerie Queene*. (Hornstein 1973)

 # *RENAUS*

French epic poem (ca. 12th c.) of some 18,000 lines by an anonymous author, who identifies the central character with St. Renault of Cologne. Renaus is the second of Count Aymon's four sons. He is a valiant and ferocious warrior, protected by God. In this original version, Charlemagne is hostile to Renaus, who in later poems becomes a paladin, cousin of Roland. When conspirators plot to slay Renaus, God performs a miracle to protect him. The poem introduces the character who becomes Renaud in the chanson de geste *Renaud de Montauban*, or *Les Quatre Fils Aymon* (late 12th or early 13th c.), one of the cycle of the *Doon de Mayence*. Renaus was Italianized as Rinaldo (or Ranaldo, or Rinaldi), who figures prominently in in Boiardo's *Orlando Innamorato* and Ariosto's *Orlando Furioso*. In Italy, the character of Rinaldi became so popular that *cantastorie* (oral performances) came to be called *Rinaldi*. A short story by Salvatore di Giacomo describes a *cantastorie* in Naples reciting exploits of Rinaldo at the end of the nineteenth century. During World War II, while Germany occupied Belgium (1940–1944), a dramatic version, *Les Quatre Fils Aymon*, which depicts resistance to authority, was performed "underground" because the occupying Nazis banned it. (Ariosto [Vol. 1] 1973; Harvey and Heseltine 1959)

 # REUTER, FRITZ

German poet, novelist, and dialect writer, author of the dialect verse epic *Hanne Nüte*, the short dialect epic poem *Kein Hüsung*, and the dialect verse narrative *De Reis nah Belligen* (1855). Reuter was born in 1810 in Stavenhagen, Mecklenburg. He studied law at Rostock University and at Jena, where he became a member of one of the unauthorized student corporations notorious for fostering subversive activities.

After an 1833 student attack on a Frankfort military guardhouse, Reuter (in Berlin at the time) was arrested by Prussian police and held for three years on suspicion before being condemned to death for treason. The sentence was commuted to 30 years in prison. His father worked tirelessly for his release, which was finally obtained from Frederick William IV in 1840. Unsuccessful in being readmitted to resume his studies, Reuter worked on the Mecklenburg estate until 1850, when he obtained a position as a tutor in Treptow. There he met and married Louise Kuntze in 1851.

He wrote two volumes of dialect verse, *Läuschen en Rimels* (1853 and 1858), that were well received. In 1855 he produced a verse narrative, *De Reis nah Belligen.* In 1856 he moved to Neubrandenburg, intending to continue to work as a tutor, but his success at dialect narrative convinced him to devote himself to writing. He wrote a short dialect epic about life as a serf, *Kein Hüsung.* Three comedies appeared in 1857 and 1858, all of which were produced on the stage. These were followed in 1859 by his first novel, *Ut de Franzosentid* (During the time of the French conquest), set in 1812 Mecklenburg during the Napoleonic Wars. This was followed in 1860 by the dialect verse epic *Hanne Nüte un de lütte Pudel.* The next year he produced a volume of short narratives, *Schurr-Murr.* In 1862 he wrote *Ut mine Festungstid* (During the time of my incarceration), a sometimes humorous autobiographical account of his fraudulent imprisonment. An autobiographical novel based on his years of working the land, *Ut mine Stromtid* (During my apprenticeship), his masterpiece, appeared in 1862–1864. Originally issued in three volumes from 1862 to 1864, the work follows the adventures of a comic hero, Entspektor Bräsig, a memorable character for which Reuter is chiefly known.

In 1863 he moved to Eisenach, where he lived and wrote for the rest of his life. His gift for dialect and the pervading sense of humor in his work make him one of Germany's most popular humorous writers. He died in 1874 in Eisenach. (Garland and Garland 1986)

 # RHIANUS
(Or Rhianos)

Greek poet and scholar, author of five epics, now lost. He was born on Crete about 275 B.C. Although he may have begun as a slave in charge of a wrestling school (*Suda*), he gained some education, probably at Alexandria. He is known to have written five epics, but only tiny fragments remain of *Archaica* and *Thessalica,* and only the contents are known of a third, *Messeniaca.* Pausanias used the latter work as a source. The emperor Tiberius is known to have appreciated his work. The poet wrote past the time when great "Homeric" epics were in vogue. Of the three great Hellenistic poets of his time—Callimachus, Theocritus, and Apollonius—only Apollonius attempted epics of a grand scale, and Rhianus followed his lead. Rhianus's only surviving works are epigrams in the Greek *Anthology,* a collection of about 4,000 poems (ca. 10th c. A.D.). (Bowder 1984)

RIBANJE I RIBARSKO PRIGOVARANJE
(Fishing and fishermen's talk)

Croatian idyllic epic (16th c.) by Petar Hektorović (1487–1572). The poem describes in a realistic manner a fishing expedition and the life of the fishermen on the island of Hvar.

The poet's graphic depictions of local life are sprinkled with philosophical musings about the virtues of subsistence existence: "While they were having lunch, I went to sit . . ./at the edge of the sea, and I was amazed/at how many people, simple to look at,/with shabby clothes, poor, still have enough./For among such people it is unusual for reason and good judgment to dwell and to adorn them./Virtue therefore dwells secretly among them/like gold that is covered by the earth. . . ."

To illustrate his point, the poet includes an example from the classical—Diogenes, "who had no property/and who lived in a bottomless barrel/but who was envied by King Alexander/since he saw in him a great gift of virtue. . . ."

The epic is one of the most original works of the period. Although Croatia was under Venetian domination at the time, the epic gives voice to the Turkish threat by including three epics (*Bugarštica*) on the popular hero of the Battle of Kosovo, Marko. An account of these (*The Battle of Kosovo, Marko Kraljević,* and *Janko the Duke*) can be found in the *Encyclopedia of Traditional Epics*. (Čiževskij 1971; Dvornik 1962; Gazi 1973)

RIME ROYAL

A septet (seven-line) stanza typically of iambic pentameter rhyming *ababbcc.* Geoffrey Chaucer used this stanza in his second masterpiece, *Troilus and Criseyde* (ca. 1385). The term "royal" became associated with the stanza in the fifteenth century after it was used by Scottish king James I in his poem *The Kingis Quair* (1423). (Turco 1986)

ROLANDSLIED DES PFAFFEN KONRAD

Early Middle High German poem (ca. 1170), a translation of the French *Chanson de Roland* (ca. 1100) by a priest, Konrad (of Regensburg?), for his patron Heinrich der Löwe (1129–1195), duke of Savoy, and his consort. Konrad produced a literal translation, first translating the poem into Latin and from there into German. The poem is based on the historical incidents surrounding Charlemagne's campaign into Spain to drive the infidels out of Christendom, which was disrupted by news of a Saxon revolt back home. As the paladins entered a narrow pass in the Pyrenees (778), many troops, including one

Hruodland (Roland), were ambushed by the Saracens and killed. Roland had been betrayed by Genelun (Ganelon), who convinced Charlemagne to assign Roland to the rear guard in the campaign. Filled with pride, Roland elects not to blow his horn to summon help until it is too late. But when Charlemagne does arrive, he wreaks terrible vengeance on the Saracens. The poem stresses Christian heroism, martyrdom, and patriotism. For more on *Chanson de Roland*, see the *Encyclopedia of Traditional Epics*. (Garland and Garland 1986)

 # ROMAN DE LA ROSE
(Romance of the rose)

French dream-allegory and satire in octosyllabic couplets (ca. 1235, 1280) by Guillaume de Lorris (fl. ca. 1st half 13th c.) and Jean de Meung (d. 1305).

The poem exerted great influence over poets of the fourteenth and fifteenth centuries particularly, thus giving rise to the popular saying that to understand the Middle Ages, one must read three books: Dante's *Divine Comedy*, Chaucer's *Canterbury Tales*, and *Romance of the Rose*.

The first portion of the poem, an elaborate allegory consisting of Guillaume de Lorris's 4,000 lines on "The Art of Love," is modeled on Ovid's but translated into the courtly chivalry of the times. The poet dreams that Oiseuse (Idleness) ushers him into an idyllic garden from which Avarice, Envy, Hypocrisy, Greed, and other evils are excluded. There he finds such persons as Déduit (Pleasure), Largesse (Bounty), Richesse (Opulence, Riches), Liesse (Merry-making), Doux Regard (Sweet Glances), and Cupidon, the God of Love. He accepts an invitation to join in a dance with Politesse (Courtesy), Venus (Love), Beauté (Beauty), Jeunesse (Youth), Franchise (Candor), Allégresse (Mirth), and Délices (Delight). He discovers in a fountain the reflection of a fascinating rosebud and wants to pick it. Cupidon pierces his heart with an arrow and instructs him on the code of courtly love, warning him of the sufferings involved. While Fair Welcome invites him to approach the rose, various others either encourage (Bel Accueil, Courtesy) or thwart him (Danger and Male Bouche, Slander). These represent various influences upon the lady-love's mind. Finally Reason dissuades him from continuing. Through Venus's and Pity's intervention, he is able to steal one kiss from Rose, but immediately Shame, Jealousy, and Slander prevent him from further contact. Walls are built around Rose and a duenna is set to guard her, while Fair Welcome is confined to a tower by Jealousy.

At this point Guillaume de Lorris's poem ends, probably cut short by his death. Some 50 years later, Jean de Meung added 18,000 lines to the poem. After hundreds of digressive passages given to social criticism, particularly against women, Faux Semblant (Hypocrisy, usually masquerading as a friar) overcomes Slander, and the duenna becomes sympathetic to the lovers' plight, as does Nature (who preaches that obedience to her laws is the touchstone to true nobility, true wealth, and true love). Venus goes on a rampage and drives away Shame, Fear, and Danger, and the Lover is allowed to pluck the Rose.

The poem influenced many French poets, as well as Boccaccio, Chaucer, and the author of *Sir Gawain and the Green Knight*. It was translated into Flemish and Italian as well as English.

In English, the *Romaunt of the Rose*, the translation and amplification of the de Lorris section with a small portion of the de Meung section, is attributed to Chaucer, but it was probably only partly written by him (the first 1,700 lines). (Harvey and Heseltine 1959)

ROMAN DE THÈBES

French epic poem (mid-12th c.) by an unknown author. Containing some 10,000 octosyllabic verses in rhyming couplets, the poem is one of the chief French epics dealing with subjects drawn from ancient Latin writers, called *Romans d'antiquité*. It relates the adventures of Oedipus, then of Eteocles and Polynices, and, following the account in Statius's *Thebaid*, the siege of Thebes, to which have been added various military encounters and a romantic element involving Antigone and Parthenopaeus. Toward the end, the hero Theseus interposes a halt until the mortally wounded aggressors fallen on the field can receive a proper burial. The poem ends with the city's destruction and Creon's death. (Harvey and Heseltine 1959)

ROMAN DE TROIE

French epic poem (ca. 1160) by Benoît de Sainte-Maure (fl. 12th c.). The poem, consisting of some 30,000 octosyllabic verses in rhyming couplets, is dedicated to Eleanor of Aquitaine and is one of the epics dealing with subjects drawn from ancient writers, called *Romans d'antiquité*. The poem was extremely popular, and over the years has been widely translated and imitated.

It depicts the legendary history of Troy from the time of the Argonauts to the death of Ulysses (Odysseus) following his return home. In this version Hector, not Achilles, becomes the hero in the Trojan War. The narrative is supposedly based on accounts by Trojan Dares Phrygus and Greek Dictys Cretensis, who each claimed to have fought in the war on opposite sides. The author portrays many aspects of his own feudal society in the Greek context. It is believed that the story of Troilus and Cressida (Briseida in this work) first appeared in this poem. (Harvey and Heseltine 1959)

ROMANTICISM

A cultural ethos or movement in literature and the arts originating in Europe toward the end of the eighteenth century and continuing to the first half of the nineteenth century. The antithesis of neoclassicism, it stressed emotions and imagination over Cartesian reason and intellect. Central to the original movement was the pantheistic vision. Jean Jacques Rousseau is considered the father of Romanticism, introducing in 1750 the idea that unspoiled nature is best and that what has been seen as "progress" is actually corruption of the natural state.

The Romantic movement developed later in the United States, where Poe, Longfellow, Emerson, Thoreau, and Whitman might be considered some of the best-known exemplifiers. The best-known German Romantics were Goethe, Heine, Schiller, and, later, Rilke. Blake, Wordsworth, Coleridge, Shelley, Byron, and Keats were but a few of the English Romantics. The movement spread to Poland, Italy, Russia, Spain, and Latin America as well.

Eschewing established poetic diction and forms, the poets used the vernacular of everyday people and experimented with various meters and stanzas, celebrating the submergence of the individual into the whole. (Riasanovsky 1992)

RONSARD, PIERRE DE

French poet (called the "prince of poets") and humanist, the pivotal figure in French Renaissance poetry, author of an unfinished epic, *La Franciade* (1572). He was born in 1524 in La Possonniere, France, the younger son of a noble family of the Vendômois. His father, a man of letters who had also served in Italy under Louis XII and François I, planned a diplomatic career for his son. Accordingly, in 1536 Ronsard became a page at court, visiting Scotland with both Queen Madeleine and Queen Marie de Guise. During a diplomatic assignment in Alsace in 1540, he contracted an illness that left him partially deaf, and he turned to a career in literature and scholarship. He became a member and subsequent leader of the *Pléiade,* a literary group formed to produce French poetry comparable to the best classical work. He perfected the 12-syllable or alexandrine line, establishing it as the classic medium for elegy, satire, and Romantic tragedy. His first collection, *Odes* (1550), was modeled after the work of Horace. *Les Amoures de Cassandre* (1552) are Petrarchan sonnet cycles in the Italian fashion, published with musical accompaniment. They were written for Cassandre Salviati, daughter of a Florentine banker living in France. The lady did not encourage him, but for him she was the epitome of ideal love.

He also wrote sonnets to an Angevin peasant girl known only as Marie, who died young.

Les Hymnes (1555/1556) are extended philosophical poems. He completed only four books of his epic *La Franciade,* which he intended to be the national epic. The poem relates the legend of the son of Hector of Troy, Francus, the legendary progenitor of the French kings. Modeled after Vergil's *Aeneid*, it was not written in the alexandrine in which Ronsard excelled, but in decasyllabic verse, reportedly at the request of Charles IX, but it was discontinued when the king died.

He did not find favor with Henry III and retired, although his output did not noticeably diminish. During his last years he wrote much court poetry and another collection of love sonnets, *Sonnets pour Hélène* (1578), for Hélène de Surgères, a maid of honor of Catherine de Medicis. The poems are written in a Platonic style, evincing a profound sense of melancholy over the close of his life. After a lengthy illness, he died in 1585 at a priory of Saint-Cosme near Tours, France. (Harvey and Heseltine 1959)

THE ROSE GARDEN

See Gulistān.

THE ROSSIAD

Russian patriotic epic (1779) by Mikhail Kheraskov (1733–1807). Kheraskov wrote the epic to fill a long-standing need for a national epic (the much older *Tale of Igor's Campaign* was not discovered until 1796). *The Rossiad*, written in alexandrine lines, relates the 1552 battle in which the Russians under Ivan the Terrible threw off the "Tatar yoke," defeating the khanate of Kazan. In the introduction the poet explains that he sees in the event the beginning of a centralized government in Russia. As Russia was just coming into the period of Enlightenment (1762–1790), the poet relates the history of the epic genre beginning with the *Iliad*. He credits Voltaire's *La Henriade* (1728) as his immediate inspiration. The poem appeared just before Catherine seized the Crimea, the last parcel held by the Golden Horde's descendants. It was an era of great anti-Turkish feeling; an era, as the poem says, "of Russia in ascent," as with the defeat of Kazan, "the start of peaceful years began," when peace "like a radiant dawn shone forth in Russian lands."

Canto I begins with the poet singing "of Mongol reign in dust and arrogance laid low," presenting the energetic young tsar Ivan as comparable to Peter I, while the Russian warriors are portrayed as heroic and chaste.

The epic borrows from the medieval romance, depicting chivalric incidents occurring at the court of Kazan. The khanate queen Sumbeka is protrayed in intimate love trysts. Folk figures make appearances in the epic, such as the evil sorcerer Kashchey. Magic spells are cast, and the Islamic forces are depicted as being clearly in league with Satan. But at the fall of Kazan, God comes to the Russians' aid.

In Canto XII a cataclysmic event occurs, when "at once the ties to hell were loosed, beneath the city." Mountains shake as the Lord moves the earth. "A gloomy crack appeared whence issued smoke and fire. . . ." The Lord is clearly on the side of Mother Russia, and the Turkish horde is laid low. (Bristol 1991)

See also Kheraskov, Mikhail.

RUDOLF VON EMS

Middle High German poet, author of six known epics, one now lost. The date of his birth, although unknown, was probably late in the twelfth century or at the turn of the century. He was a nobleman, a *ministeriale* in the retinue of the count of Montfort. "Ems" refers to Hohenems, in present-day western Austria between Bregenz and Feldkirch, the location of the Montfort castle. Rudolf belonged to the second generation of epic writers of the golden age of German medieval literature called *Blütezeit* (1180 to 1230). His earliest known epic, of almost 7,000 lines, *Der gute Gerhard,* was written about 1220, followed by *Barlaam und Josaphat,* about 16,000 lines (ca. 1223). His poem *Eustachius* is no longer extant. His next poem was probably *Willehalm von Orlens,* of almost 16,000 lines of rhyming couplets, written between 1235 and 1240. The remaining portion of *Alexander* contains more than 21,000 lines. His last work, an unfinished epic, is the 36,000-line *Weltchronik,* a historical chronicle that breaks off after the Hebrew kings.

Rudolf was a loyal patriot, accompanying King Konrad IV to Italy to defend Konrad's possessions against the papacy. He died about 1252 or 1253 while on the mission. (Garland and Garland 1986)

See also *Alexander; Barlaam und Josaphat; Gute Gerhard, Der; Willehalm von Orlens.*

 # RŪMĪ, JALAL UD-DĪN
(Jalāl ad-Dīn ar-Rūmī, or Jelaluddin Rumi, *Mawlānā,* "Our Master")

Persian mystic poet, author of the didactic epic *Masnavī-ye Ma'navi* (Spiritual couplets), which is called the "Persian Koran." He was born in 1207 in Balkh (now in Afghanistan), the son of a mystic whose ancestors were theologians and jurists. His father, Bāhā al-Dī Walad, a Ṣūfī, was a celebrated preacher, mystic, and writer who was forced to leave Balkh in 1218 to escape the approaching Mongol invasion. In 1228 the family settled near Konya in Anatolia ("Rūm," or "from Roman Anatolia," whence Rūmī comes), in present-day Turkey. Rūmī spent the rest of his life there, eventually succeeding to his father's professorship. Until the age of 37 he was apparently a conventional teacher living and writing under royal patronage. Using the writings of Rūmī and others, a Persian scholar has drawn the portrait of Rūmī as a thin man of sallow complexion who in earlier years wore a scholar's turban and a wide-sleeved gown. His eyes "flashed with a hypnotic brightness daunting to those who looked upon him." In demeanor he was "peaceful and tolerant towards men of all sects and creeds."

His whole way of life changed in 1244 when he wrote, "What I had thought of before as God, I met today as a person." He was referring to the wandering dervish Shams ad-Dīn (Sun of Religion) of Tabriz. Rūmī became his pupil and constant companion, neglecting his own family and disciples. After his meeting with Shams ad-Dīn, Rūmī changed his dress for a blue robe and a smoke-colored turban, and gave up the Islamic religious sciences. His poetry expressed a longing to be the Friend, the spiritual presence he recognized in Shams. Rūmī wrote a group of *ghazals* (lyric poems) called *Dīvān-i Shams-i Tabrīz*, signed with the name of his friend. In 1246, Shams ad-Dīn disappeared, forced to leave by Rūmī's followers. In bereavement, Rūmī wrote some 30,000 lines and many quatrains (*rubaiyat*) to his master. Because of Rūmī's devastation, his oldest son summoned the mystic back from Syria for a brief time. But in 1247, Shams disappeared completely, murdered by one of Rūmī's sons.

Later Rūmī met two more mystics and formed close relationships with both, seeing in each that close spiritual presence. The first, a goldsmith called Ṣalāḥ ad-Dīn Zarkūb, had a daughter who married Rūmī's eldest son. When this man died, Rūmī became attached to his scribe, Ḥusām ad-Dīn Chelebi, under whose tutelage he wrote his main work of nearly 26,000 couplets, the *Masnavī-ye Ma'navi*. Written in Persian in six books and incorporating fables, tales, and moral lessons, the poem reflects all aspects of thirteenth-century Ṣūfism. It is regarded by Persians as second only to Firdausi's *Shāh-Nāmah* as a Persian masterpiece. He also wrote nearly 2,000 quatrains and other poems.

During the last 30 years of his life he became an unfolding of that spiritual presence he had seen in others, a universal man. In one of his poems, he says, "I am neither Christian, nor Jew, nor Gabr (Zoroastrian), nor Moslem./ . . . My place is the Placeless, my trace is the Traceless;/ . . . One I seek, One I know . . . / If once in this world I win a moment with thee,/ . . . I will dance in triumph forever." The Persian scholar says that Rūmī was "never heard to utter one bitter reply." Rūmī died in Konya in 1273. After his death his followers founded the Ṣūfī order of Mowlavies (Whirling Dervishes). (Kritzeck 1964; Moyne and Barks 1984)

See also Masnavî-ye Ma'navî.

RUOLIEB

Incomplete Latin poem (ca. 1030/1050) by a monk of Tegernsee in Bavaria. A psychological tale of the Parzival type, the poem relates the story of Ruolieb, a youth born to the nobility, who ventures forth to seek his fortune and encounters various adventures, some involving magic. Some scholars regard it as a progenitor of the German novel. (Garland and Garland 1986)

RUSLAN I LYUDMILA
(Ruslan and Ludmila)

Russian mock-heroic folk epic (1820) by Aleksandr Pushkin (1799–1837). The poem was inspired by Ariosto's *Orlando Furioso*, Tasso's *Jerusalem Delivered*,

Voltaire's *La Pucelle,* and Bogdanovich's *Dushenka,* as well as various of the French ballets choreographer Charles Didelot brought to St. Petersburg.

It recaptures some of the medieval atmosphere of the old Russian *byliny,* or folk epics, which describe the exploits of popular if coarse heroes called *bogatyri.* In this case, Pushkin offers a spoof of knightly romance in relating the story, based on a folk tale, of Lyudmila and her three suitors. She is the daughter of Prince Vladimir, grand prince of Kiev. Vladimir anticipates a marriage between Lyudmila and one of her eligible suitors, chief of whom is Ruslan. Ruslan eventually wins her, but on her wedding night Lyudmila is kidnapped by the evil magician Chernomor. Ruslan undertakes a variety of exploits and adventures in order to rescue his bride. The parody veered far afield from literary norms of Pushkin's day and was savagely attacked by critics; however, it gained wide popularity and is now considered the masterpiece of Pushkin's youth. The poem established him as one of the distinguished young poets of the day. It became the subject of an opera (1842) by Mikhail Ivanovich Glinka. (Pushkin 1974)

 # RUSTAVELI, SHOTA
(Also Rusthaveli or Rust'haveli, Shot'ha)

Georgian poet, author of the national epic of Georgia, *Vephkhis Tgaosani* (also *Vep'khis-Tqaosani,* The man in the panther's skin, or The knight in the tiger skin, or The lord of the panther-skin, 12th c.). Rustaveli, considered Georgia's greatest poet, was born in 1172, a contemporary of Queen Thamar (ca. 1160–1212, r. 1184–1212), under whose reign sprang the golden age of Georgian literature. Rustaveli enjoyed the queen's patronage, and celebrated her in his verse. He is said to have studied in Athens, although nothing is known of his life. Unlike other poets of the time, he was attached to the queen's court and was thought to be in love with her. Because this epic was so popular with people of all classes, who memorized long passages of it, Rustaveli helped standardize the spoken language. He immortalized the Age of Chivalry in the history of Georgian feudalism. The poem remains today as a monument to Georgian medieval literature and, although Georgia is renowned for its latter-day poet-kings—e.g., King Theimuraz (1589–1663), King Ardil (1647–1715), King Vahktang (1675–1737), Sulkham Saba Orbeliani (ca. 1655–ca. 1725)—Rustaveli remains the most beloved poet of any Georgian age. He died in 1216 in Jerusalem while on a pilgrimage. (Dudley and Lang 1969; Rustaveli 1977; Suny 1988)

 SAAVEDRA GUZMÁN, ANTONIO DE

Mexican scholar (fl. 16th c.), author of *El Peregrino indiano* (The Indian pilgrim, or Pilgrim of the Indies, 1599). He was born in Mexico, son of one of the first colonists and great-grandson of the first count of Castelar, Don Juan Arias de Saavedra. He married a niece of Jorge de Alvarado, a captain in Cortés's army and brother of the conqueror Don Pedro de Alvarado. He devoted himself to the study of *belles lettres*, particularly of poetry and history, and to mastering the Nahuatlan language. He served as magistrate of Zacatecas and government inspector in Texcoco. He spent seven years collecting material for his epic about the military operations of Hernán Cortés.

Toward the end of the sixteenth century, he traveled to Spain. On the 70-day voyage, to the "rocking of the vessel," he composed his epic of 2,039 octaves. It begins with the expedition Cortés organized in Cuba and ends with the imprisonment of Cuauhtémoc. When he arrived in Madrid in 1599, he printed the poem, which had more historical than poetical merit. It is not known whether he returned to Mexico. One source gives his death as "before 1570," but it is likely that he simply was not heard from again in Mexico after that date. (Anderson-Imbert 1969; Peña 1968)

See also Peregrino indiano.

 SA'DĪ

(Pen name of Musharrif uddīn, or Moṣleḥ Od-dīn, or Musharrif al-Din bin Muslih)

Persian poet, philosopher, teacher, and Ṣūfī, author of the *Būstān* (The orchard, 1257) and the *Gulistān* (The rose garden, 1258). One of the greatest figures in classical Persian literature, he was born about 1184/1215 in Shīrāz, Persia. His father, whose name was apparently Ābdu'llāh, was descended from Ālī, son-in-law of Muḥammad, and died while Sa'dī was still a boy. During his lifetime, the father rose to no higher office than a minor position under the Dīwān. Sa'dī began his studies in Shīrāz, but as a young man he was sent to Baghdad, where he received an Islamic education at Nizâmiyya College (or Nezâmīyah), founded by the Persian statesman and writer Hasan bin 'Ali Nizâm al-Mulk. There he was a Fellow, companion of the great Ṣūfī sheikh Suhrawardi, and disciple of the teacher Gīlānī, with whom he made his first pilgrimage to Mecca. He was included in the great biographical collection of Jāmī. His affiliation was with the Naqshbandi ("Designers") School, the Path of Masters, a Ṣūfī order that set as its task the reformation of Ṣūfī teachings.

During the time of the Mongol invasion of Persia, he wandered abroad for 30 years to Egypt, Iraq, Syria, Anatolia, and Central Asia. His writings suggest that he also traveled to India during the reign of Uglamish (d. 1255). According to the *Gulistān*, on a visit to the Holy Land, Sa'dī left Damascus and was on his way to Jerusalem when he was captured by the Frankish Crusaders and put to work with a group of Jews in the trenches of the fortress of Tripoli until ransomed by "one of the principal men of Aleppo." The man took him to his home in Aleppo, where he married him to his daughter, with a dowry of 100 dīnārs. However, according to the poet, "the girl turned out of a bad temper, quarrelsome and unruly." She began to "give a loose to her tongue, and to disturb my happiness. . . ." The poet continues, "From a vixen wife protect us well,/ *Save us, O God! from the pains of hell*." (II.31) At other times during his travels, he was a renowned sheikh. He married a second time at Sanāa, the capital of Yaman, and in the *Būstān* bemoans the loss of his only son (IX.25).

He returned to Shīrāz in 1256 as an old man and began to publish his work, taking the pen name of Sa'dī. One of his best-known works, the *Būstān*, appeared in 1257. Written in epic meter, it is a didactic poem containing stories illustrating virtues, wisdom pertaining to every aspect of public and private life, and the practices of the dervishes. It was dedicated to the local ruler, Abū Bakr ibn Sa'd ibn Zangī. His *Gulistān*, published in 1258, is a combination of prose and verse dealing with human behavior in simple but elegant language. It is dedicated to the ruler deposed by the Muslims, Prince Sa'd ibn Abū Bakr. From these two men the poet took his pen name. He also wrote a number of lyric poems, collected in *Ghazalīyāt*, and odes, collected in *Qaṣā'īd*.

It is said of his work, "Each word of Sa'dī has seventy-two meanings."

Although he gained great renown, he eschewed wealth. When the prime minister of Hulaku Khān sent him a gift of 50,000 dīnārs, he used it to erect a house for travelers near Shīrāz.

He spent the last years of his life in retirement. He died in about 1292 at the age, according to tradition, of 107, having earned the reputation as the most popular Persian poet of all time, "the Nightingale of a Thousand Songs." (Kritzeck 1964; Sa'dī 1979; Siepmann 1987)

 # SAGA

Originally, a medieval Icelandic prose narrative, many of which were handed down from the oral tradition, dealing with Scandinavian kings or early settlers of Iceland. Some sagas not deriving from the oral tradition deal with individuals and circumstances of the author's time. The term has been used in modern times to refer to fiction dealing with several generations of a family. (Hornstein 1973)

 # SAINT-JUST, LOUIS-ANTOINE-LÉON DE

French revolutionary leader, author of a lengthy mock-epic, *Organt*. He was born in 1767 in Decize, France. His father died in 1777 when he was only ten. Saint-Just was a brash, good-looking young man. At the age of 21, disappointed in love, he left home for Paris, taking some of the family valuables. But his mother had him arrested and put in a reformatory. When he got out, he studied for the law. In 1789 he published anonymously the epic *Organt*, which ridiculed the political leaders of the day. It was largely ignored by the public; however, it was seized by authorities, and Saint-Just went into hiding. He became a lieutenant of Robespierre and was known as "the archangel of the Revolution." He was one of the chief orators of the Montagnards and a member of the *Comité de salut public*, active in overthrowing the Girondists and in instigating the Reign of Terror. Along with Robespierre, he was arrested in 1794 and guillotined. (Harvey and Heseltine 1959; Siepmann 1987)

See also Organt.

 # SANĀ'Ī
(Abū' l-Majd Majūd ibn Ādam, or Abū al-Majd Majdūd ibn Ādam)

Persian mystical poet (fl. 12th c.), author of *al-Ḥadīqat al-ḥaqīqah wa sharī'at aṭ-Ṭariqah* (The garden of truth and the law of practice). Little is known of his early days. He lived in Ghazna (modern-day Ghaznī, Afghanistan). As a young man he was poet at the Islamic court of a sultan of the Ghaznavid empire, taking the pen name of Sanā'ī.

After he experienced a spiritual conversion, he left the court and went to Merv to live a life of spiritual asceticism. His best-known work, dedicated to Sultan Bahrām Shāh (r. 1117–1157), is a philosophical work on Ṣūfism. He was the first poet to use the *maśnavī* (rhymed couplet), the *qaṣsīdah* (ode), and the *ghazal* (lyric) in expressing the philosophy of Ṣūfism.

As an old man, he returned to Ghazna to live out his days in retirement. He died there about 1131, having produced some 30,000 verses. (Dudley and Lang 1969)

 # *SATANIADA, LA*

Puerto Rican epic poem (19th c.) by Alejandro Tapia y Rivera (1826–1882). The work, consisting of 30 cantos in eight-line stanzas, is the most extensive poem in nineteenth-century Puerto Rico. A Romantic period poem, it exalts the past and rejoices in the landscape of the tropical paradise. (Preminger 1974)

 ## SAYYID ABDALLAH BIN ALI BIN NASIR

Swahili poet, author of the short epic poem *Wajiwaji wa Liyongo* (or *Takkmisa ya Liyongo,* Song of Liyongo) and the longer epic *Al Inkishafi* (Self-examination, early 19th c.). He was born about 1720/1730 in Lamu, Central East Africa. According to the poet himself, he was "Son of Ali, son of Nasir who has rank/A descendant from Mecca, from the stream of Tarim/The branch of Muhdar, Mutabli, and Hashim." (v. 27, *Liyongo*) Again, in the last stanza of the *Liyongo* poem, the poet promises to reveal his lineage: "It is Ali son of our lord Abubakar/Son of Salim from an honorable descent. . . ." (v. 25) According to the closing lines of the poem, he was Abdallah, a descendant of the prophet Muḥammad. Like at least four other leading poets, he was descended from Shaikh Abu Bakr bin Salim (b. 1584). A noted theologian and scholar, Sayyid Abdallah composed his *Wajiwaji wa Liyongo* around the life of the Swahili poet-hero Fumo Liyongo wa Baury, said by some to have lived as late as the seventeenth century, and about whom oral tradition abounds. The poem is written in the form of a dramatic monologue with the poet assuming the persona of Fumo Liyongo. His *utendi,* or epic, *Al-Inkishafi* is about the passing of the Arab city-states on the coast of East Africa and about the inevitability of death. Abdallah bin Nasir died in 1820. (Dudley and Lang 1969; Shariff [RAL] 1991)
    See also *Al-Inkishafi.*

 ## *SEJARAH MELAYU*
(Malay annals)

Malay literary chronicle (ca. 1535) written by an unknown author prior to 1536. It is believed that the original *Sejarah* was altered by Tun Seri Lanang (fl. 1611) in about 1612 by order of Sultan Abdullah Maayah Shah. Tun Seri Lanang was *Bendahara* (chief minister) of the former Muslim Malaccan sultanate then in Johore and was obviously educated and cosmopolitan. Copies of only the amended version survive. The *Sejarah,* considered the finest work ever written in the Malay language, gives a romanticized, lively chronicle of the Malaccan sultanate, beginning with ancestral myths prior to the founding (ca. 1400) of the Malaccan kingdom until it was defeated by the Portuguese (1511). The succinct and vivid style of the work has led it to be regarded as "classical" Malay. (Dudley and Lang 1969)

SELVINSKY, ILIA
(Real name: Karl)

Russian poet and playwright, author of the epic *The Ulialaev Uprising* (1927). He was born in 1899 in Crimea, the son of a furrier. He worked on the docks and in the circus, graduating from Moscow University. In 1924 he founded the constructivist literary school. His first book of lyrics, *Records,* appeared in 1926, and his most successful epic, a year later. He went to Kirghizia to teach fur farming. Later he traveled Europe and served in the army during World War II, during which he wrote of his experiences. After the war he wrote belated love lyrics. He died in 1968. (Bristol 1991)

See also The Ulialaev Uprising.

SHĀH-NĀMAH
(Also *Shāh-Nameh,* or Book [epic] of the kings)

Persian national epic (completed 1010) by Abu'l-Qāsim Ferdausi (or Ferdowsi) (ca. 935–ca. 1020), who spent some 35 years writing his epic. In scope the poem outranks all Western epics, with its over 55,000 couplets in 46–50 chapters (some versions are longer than others) covering a period of almost 4,000 years of Iranian history, from the legendary Kayûmars (3223 B.C.) to the fall of the Sassanian dynasty (A.D. 651). Written for Sultan Maḥmūd of Ghazna (997–1030), it is made up of two segments: the mythical first half and the "historical" second half. For the mythical half, the poet relied on a much older prose work, *Klavataynamak,* the versification of which had been begun by the poet Daqīqī (d. ca. 980), whose work Firdausi incorporated.

In the introduction, the world is created "out of nothing." The poet also describes how the poem came to be written. Chapter I, "The Reign of Keyūmars," tells of the primitive king who rules the world during the first 30 years. All creatures bow to him, and hence religion begins. In Chapter II, "The Reign of Hūshang," fire is discovered. After Hūshang, his son Tahmuras subjugates demons and becomes known as "Demon-binder." Chapter III, "The Reign of Jamshīd," tells of his son, the primal priest-king, who rules for 700 years. He builds a large underground palace to protect against a flood that will cover the earth. He constructs a magnificent throne upon which, in subsequent reigns, palaces are built. People see him sitting on his magnificent throne and begin worshipping him. He begins to believe in his own grandeur, and his hubris precipitates his fall and the world's cruel thousand-year subjection to the grotesque three-headed monster tyrant Ẓaḥḥāk, born with Arab blood in his veins. Chapter IV, "Farīdūn," tells of the birth of the hero Farīdūn, "beautiful as a slender cypress," who is summoned as king by Kāva the blacksmith, and makes war on Ẓaḥḥāk, chaining him in a cave in Mount Damāvand for 11,000 years, where he remains hanging, "his heart's blood pouring down on the earth." Farīdūn, the dragon king, divides the earth between his three sons, Iraj, Tur, and Salm. Iraj is murdered by his brothers, hence the long feud between Tur (Tutān) and Iran. Manuchehr, the son of Iraj, avenges his father's death, battling Tur. After a number of adventures, Manuchehr slays Salm and succeeds to the throne after Farīdūn's death. Among his courtiers is the mighty hero Sām, son of Narīmān.

Chapter V, "Zāl," tells of the birth and ascencion of Sām's son Zāl, who must be abandoned on an Indian mountain because he is albino. Years later, Sām dreams that his son is still alive. He consults the magi, who castigate him for abandoning him. He travels to India and finds his son, who was reared by a bird, the Simorgh. The bird loves Zāl like a son; she gives him a feather and tells him if he ever needs her help, to burn the feather and she will come immediately. Sām puts his son in charge of all his holdings.

On a trip to survey his lands, Zāl meets a Semite potentate, Mehrāb, a descendant of the cruel Ẓaḥḥāk. The two become friendly, and Zāl falls in love with Mehrāb's daughter, Rudābah. She, only hearing of his beauty, falls in love. The poet advises: "Refrain from describing masculine beauty when women are within earshot./In the heart of every female lurks a living devil./ . . . When desire enters a woman's heart, wisdom flies out the window."

Sām consults a magus, who reluctantly agrees to the wedding. But the shah, who hates Semites, orders Sām to burn Mehrāb's palace and kill him, his queen Sindokht, and his daughter. While Zāl pleads with the shah, the queen disguises herself as an Iranian warrior and takes much of Mehrāb's wealth to buy their safety from Sām. Impressed, he agrees to the marriage.

In Chapter VI, "Rostam," when it is time for the birth of their first child, Rudābah cannot deliver. As she lies near death, Zāl burns the feather of his bird-mother. The Simorgh appears and instructs him on how the arch-Mage (medicine man) should cut open her abdomen to bring the baby out. The newborn is exceedingly large and powerful, requiring the milk of 20 nurses. His mother, fully recovered from the ordeal, names him Rostam.

After the reign of Manuchehr ends, three shahs reign for short periods. Rostam has grown to young manhood when the third shah dies, and his father sends him on a mission to Mount Elbury to bring back the new shah, Kai-Kobad. Rostam is a giant of a man, and he chooses a giant of a horse, Rakhsh. The magnificent stallion remains with him always and saves his life on many occasions. Rostam brings back the new shah and then goes to war to drive away Afrāsiyāb, a pretender who has threatened several shahs. Kai-Kobad's reign of 100 years is followed by that of his son Kai-Kāvus, who does not prove to be the wisest of rulers.

Most of Rostam's heroic feats occur during Kai-Kāvus's reign. The king, on the advice of a demon disguised as a harpist, leads his warriors to conquer Māzindarān. But after a week of plundering, the shah is confronted by the White Demon, protector of the kingdom. In the storm that follows, Kai-Kāvus and his warriors are blinded, and 12,000 demons carry them away to a cave. Learning of their plight, Rostam sets off to rescue them, having many harrowing encounters along the way. He slays the White Demon and uses its blood to

A page from the fourteenth-century illustrated version of the Persian national epic *Shāh-Nāmah* by Abu'l-Qāsim Ferdausi depicts Ardashir, right, battling Bahman, son of Ardavān.

restore the sight of the shah and his warriors. Kai-Kāvus is restored to his throne, but soon he becomes restless and decides to launch a war against Yemen. When he has subdued the Yemenites, he decides to marry the king's daughter, Sudāba, who is perfectly agreeable. The Yemen king pretends to want to visit his daughter, but his plan is to capture the shah and bring his daughter home. Kāvus is captured, and Sudāba goes willingly with him into exile.

To rescue the shah this time, Rostam must wage war against the forces of Yemen, Berberistan, and Egypt, which he does with great courage and skill. Then on behalf of the shah, he leads his forces against Afrāsiyāb, the pretender who has plagued so many rulers. Rostam so intimidates the enemy troops that Afrāsiyāb deserts them and flees for his life. Meanwhile, another demon disguised as a youth convinces the restless shah that the proper place for his brilliance is in the sky. So the shah has his throne attached to four eagles and disappears into the blue. Again Rostam goes to the rescue, and when he finds Kai-Kāvus, he and the magi castigate him for his irresponsibility. The shah is genuinely chagrined and does penance for 40 days, promising to be more attentive to duty.

One day, while Rostam is napping on a hunting trip, Turkish nomads steal his horse. He thinks, "On foot, running, whither shall I go in my disgrace?" He searches, "his heart full of pain and grief, his body racked with torment and his spirit in agony." At the castle of Samangān, the king offers to help him find his horse. Princess Tahmina falls in love with Rostam and says she wants to give him the gift of a child. Rostam asks the king's permission to marry her that very night. The king agrees, and so long as Rostam remains in the province, he and Tahmina are husband and wife. But when the horse is found, he rides away forever, giving his bride an amulet for their unborn child.

The child is a boy, named Sohrāb by his mother, and he rapidly grows tall and powerful like his father. When Sohrāb learns he is the son of Rostam, he decides to travel to Iran, team up with his father, and defeat the hapless Kai-Kāvus so that Rostam can sit on the throne. Then the two, father and son, can go to Turān and defeat Afrāsiyāb so that Sohrāb can also have a throne. So goes his plan.

But Afrāsiyāb learns of the plan and instructs two of his henchmen to go along to make sure that father and son never recognize each other and will perhaps kill one another: "Perhaps the aged hero will find his death at the hands of this lion-man." The two henchmen are successful in preventing Sohrāb from learning the true identity of the man whom he challenges in battle. Through three days of bloodthirsty battles, Rostam and Sohrāb take turns besting one another. Finally, Rostam strikes the mortal blow. Only then, from the dying boy's lips, does Rostam learn that Sohrāb is his son: "Someone among the mighty and proud will carry to Rostam the tidings that Sohrāb is slain and overthrown in ignominy his one desire being only to find him." Heartbroken, Rostam builds a magnificent tomb for his son and mourns him for many months.

Chapter VII, "Siyāvosh," tells of Kai-Kāvus's son Siyāvosh. After a quarrel with his father over the affectionate Sudāba, Siyāvosh flees to the court of Afrāsiyāb, where he marries the king's daughter, Farangis. The Turanian king's brother, Garsevaz, becomes jealous of the favors Afrāsiyāb accords Siyāvosh and incites the king against the Iranian prince. He is seized and made to suffer a cruel death, but Pirān, chief of the army, comes to Farangis's rescue.

Chapter VIII, "Key Kosrow," tells of the birth of Farangis and Siyāvosh's son, who grows to manhood in Turān and is rescued by the Iranians. He feels the need to avenge his father's murder. After a great war and a long pursuit, Afrāsiyāb goes into hiding.

In Chapter IX, "Rostam and Akvān the Div," Rostam is summoned to save a herd of horses from what is thought to be an onager, but which in fact is Akvān the Demon (Div). Akvān hurls Rostam into the ocean, which is filled with monsters. Rostam slays them all, and he and his horse Rakhsh drive off Afrāsiyāb's horses and slay many of his guards.

Chapter X, a digression, is "The Adventure of Bizhan and Manizha," a romance inserted into the narrative.

In Chapter XI, "The Latter Days of Key Khosrow," Rostam and his troops continue the battle against Afrāsiyāb. King Khosrow dictates his last wishes to his warriors and nominates Lohrāsp as his successor. After bidding farewell to his family and his subjects, he leaves for the frontier of his realm, where he disappears in a snowstorm.

Chapter XII, "Lohrāsp and Goshtāsp," tells of the reigns of Lohrāsp and his son Goshtāsp, who becomes the lover and husband of Katāyum, daughter of the Caesar of Rum (Eastern Rome). Chapter XIII continues the story of Goshtāsp.

Chapter XIV, "Esfandiyār and Rostam," tells how Zoroaster introduces his new religion, supported by Goshtāsp's son Esfandiyār. He is kept from the throne long after his succession is due, and is eventually slain by Rostam, with the help of magic. Before he dies, Esfandiyār entrusts the education of his son Bahman to Rostam. Eventually Rostam and Goshtāsp become friends again. But Rostam is killed by the vile brother Saghād, although he manages to kill Saghād before he dies. In his turn, Farāmarz, Rostam's son, leads an army against the king of Zābol as vengeance for his father's death.

Chapters XV and XVI, "Goshtāsp Surrenders the Kingship to Bahman" and "The Story of Bahman Son of Esfandiyār," are self-explanatory. Bahman has a son, Sāsān, and a daughter, Homāy, called Chehrzād (Scheherezade). Because of her beauty, her father takes her as his wife, and when he is on his deathbed, be bequeaths his crown to her, until such time as their unborn son is of age. After Bahman dies, Sāsān leaves in shame and resentment.

Chapter XVII, "the Story of Dārāb," tells of the reign of Queen Homāy, who leaves her baby, Dārāb, in a casket on the Euphrates River. The babe is found and raised by a fuller and his wife. When he is grown, his identity is discovered and Homāy relinquishes her crown to her son. He marries Princess Nāhīd, who has a bad odor, so he returns her, although she is pregnant and soon bears a son. She names him Sekander (Alexander). In due course he becomes heir to the caesar's throne. Meanwhile, Dārāb remarries and has a son named Dārā, who succeeds him at the age of 12. (The names Dārāb and Dārā both represent Darius.)

Chapter XVIII, "The Reign of Dārā Son of Dārāb," is self-explanatory.

Chapter XIX, "The History of Sekander," and Chapter XX, "The Adventures of Sekander," tell the more or less mythical adventures of Alexander.

Chapter XXI, "Rule of the Ashkāni [Arsacid or Parthian] Kings," is a brief enumeration of the kings of the tribe of Ashk, including Ardavān.

Chapter XXII, "The Dynasty of Sāsān," begins the historical period of the poem, although it is interspersed with much that is legendary and romantic. Ardashir defeats Ardavān's son Bahman and marries Ardavān's daughter. He makes his capital at Fārs, and from there leads forays against the Kurds.

Chapter XXIII, "The Story of Haftvād and the Worm," is a digression relating a popular legend about a fabulous worm, from which the city of Kermān takes its name. After Haftvād is defeated, Ardashir ascends the throne.

Chapter XXIV, "The Reign of Ardashir," relates the king's reign, then gives a series of aphorisms and advice to a king on how to govern and keep his subjects contented.

Chapter XXV, "The Reign of Shāpur, Son of Ardashir. His War with the Romans," confuses Shāpur, son of Ormazd (Sapor II, A.D. 309–379), with Sapor I (A.D. 244–272). Also, Iran's two wars with Rome are confused in Ferdausi's account.

Chapter XXVI, "The Reign of Shāpur Zu'l Aktāf," explains that for a long period the throne is empty until a beautiful princess gives birth to a child, Shāpur. A large army led by Tā'ir sweeps through the land. Tā'ir hears of the king's beautiful aunt, Nusha, and comes to her palace, abducting and imprisoning her. She bears him a daughter, Māleka, who in time comes to love Shāpur. She betrays her father's fortress to Shāpur. Later, he goes to Rum, where he is cruelly maltreated until the caesar's wife helps him escape. The two travel together to Iran. Eventually, he manages to capture the caesar. A wise man and prophet, Māni, comes from China seeking converts, making the people doubt their own faith. At length Shāpur has him hanged at the gateway to the city. He asks his brother Ardashir to succeed him until his son, also named Shāpur, comes of age. Ardashir "the Beneficent" rules for 12 years, then relinquishes the throne to Shāpur, whose reign lasts 14 years. He is succeeded by Yazdegerd "the Sinner."

Chapter XXVII, "Yazdegerd the Sinner," tells of the birth and adventures of Yazdegerd's son Bahrām Gur, one of the favorite Persian heroes.

Following are annalistic accounts of the reigns of the kings following Bahrām, of which only the famine during the reign of Piruz is likely to hold the reader's attention. Only those chapters will be named:

Chapter XXVIII, "The Famine in the Reign of Piruz;" Chapter XXIX, "The Reign of Qobād;" Chapter XXX, "The Reign of Kasrā Nushirvān;" Chapter XXXI, "Bozorgmehr the Wise Vazir;" Chapter XXXII, "The Reign of Hormazd;" Chapter XXXIII, "Khosrow Parviz Comes to the Throne;" and Chapter XXXIV, "The Reign of Bahrām Chubina."

Chapter XXXV, a digression, is entitled "Ferdausi's Lament for the Death of his Son."

The chronicles continue, with several romantic episodes: Chapter XXXVI, "Bahrām Chubina in China;" Chapter XXXVII, "The Story of Gordiya, Sister of Bahrām;" Chapter XXXVIII, "The Romance of Khosrow Parviz and Shirin;" Chapter XXXIX, "Shiruy and Shirin, wife of Khosrow Parviz;" Chapter XL, "The Reign of Ardashir of Shiruy;" Chapter XLI, "The Reign of Gorāz Known as Farāyin;" Chapter XLII, "The Reign of Purān Dokht;" Chapter XLIII, "The Reign of Farrokh-Zād;" Chapter XLIV, "The Reign of Yazdegerd;" and Chapter XLV, "Mābuy Ascends the Throne."

The poem ends with material that was not originally in the story, continuing the tale from the time of the second reign of Khosrow II (590–628) to the overthrow of the Sassanian king Yazdgard (Yazdegerd) III in 651.

Chapter XLVI, "The Conclusion of the Shāh-Nāmah," is a brief section containing some dates purporting to give the poet's age at the time that he was finishing his work. (Levy 1967)

See also Firdausi, Abu'l Qasim; *Sohrāb and Rustum.*

THE SHAKING OF THE SKULLCAPS
(*Hazz al-Quḥūf*)

Egyptian mock-heroic epic (17th c.) by Yūsuf al-Shirbīnī (fl. 17th c.). First published in Cairo in 1857 as *Hazz al-Quḥūf fē sharḥ qaṣīd Abū Shādūf,* the poem is a vicious lampoon of the fellah, or peasant farmer, who is depicted as greedy and materialistic. Written in colloquial language, it is a parody of *al-sīra* (legendary biographies), specifically, the folk epic *Hilāliyya.* (For a synopsis of the *Hilāliyya,* see the *Encyclopedia of Traditional Epics.*) The poet uses the poetic formulas and rhythms of the folk poet (*shā'ir*) in telling the story in which the "hero" Abū Shādūf bemoans his fate. According to the poem, Nile Valley dirt farmers, in their dung-encrusted clothes, are to be despised: They do not trust each other, and few friendships exist; *Amān* (the pledge of security for refugees) is not honored, and they seldom offer hospitality; they are exploitative and power-hungry; they respect their oppressors and take every opportunity to repress others. The poem is followed by a mock-scholarly commentary in the literary idiom. (Connelly 1986)

See also Shirbīnī, Yūsuf al-.

SHATTAN, MERCHANT-PRINCE
(Cātaṉār, Càttaṉār, Càtaṉār, or Càttaṉ)

Indian poet and grain dealer of Madurai, author of *Manimekhalaï* (ca. 5th c. A.D.). He was one of the last members of the ancient Sangam, a famous academy of Madurai of Tamil poets that began hundreds of years before. He was the protégé of Chera king Senguttuvan (Ceṅkuṭṭuvaṉ, brother of Iḷaṅkō Aṭikaḷ, composer of *Cilappatikāram,* in which the king is mentioned as having reigned for more than 50 years and having made many great conquests for the kingdom of Chera (now Kerala, in South India). Shattan himself appears as a character in *Cilappatikāram*, where he is referred to as "the famed Tamil poet."

He was a friend of Prince Iḷaṅkō Aṭikaḷ (Ilangô Adigal), whose approval he received to continue the story of *Cilappatikāram* in his own epic, *Manimekhalaï*.

In order to write the epic, Shattan would also have had the approval of the great Buddhist priest of South India, Arvana Adigal, who appears as a character in the epic. (Parthasarathy 1993; Shattan 1989)

See also *Cilappatikāram; Manimēkhalaï.*

SHEIK BEDREDDEN, THE EPIC OF

See *The Epic of Sheik Bedredden.*

SHIRBĪNĪ, YŪSUF AL-

Egyptian critic and poet (17th c.), author of the mock-epic *Hazz al-Quhūf* (The shaking of the skullcaps). A Sạ'īdī, he was born and reared in a rural area but left home for Cairo and al-Azhar to follow the only path of upward mobility open to him. He entered the religious hierarchy of the *'ulamā* to become a religious sheikh. He looked with disdain on the peasant farmers with whom he was reared and wrote his epic to appeal to the literate urban audience of the upper classes. (Connelly 1986)

See also The Shaking of the Skullcaps.

SIEGE OF PARIS

Latin medieval scholastic epic by Benedictine French monk and scholar Saint Albon of Fleury (Abbo, ca. 945–1004), written in imitation of the Roman epic. (Preminger 1974)

SIGURD THE VOLSUNG
(*The Story of Sigurd the Volsung, and the Fall of the Niblungs*)

English epic (1877) by William Morris (1834–1896) written in four books of rhymed couplets. Purported to be a translation of the Icelandic folk epic *Völsunga Saga*, it carries Morris's own stamp and some original variations. (For a synposis of *Völsunga Saga*, see the *Encyclopedia of Traditional Epics*.) It is both a close rendering of the Norse story and an original Victorian epic, generally regarded as

Morris's greatest poetic achievement. It followed his acquaintance with Eríkr Magnusson, who introduced him to the Icelandic language and its literature. He and Magnusson made a prose translation of the *Völsunga Saga,* and in 1871 made a visit to Iceland. The landscape of that country would creep into some of the more vivid passages of *The Song of Sigurd.* In 1877 Morris published the epic, influenced also by the Gothic revivalism of the age, adding longer descriptions and passages of gifted lyrical intensity, introducing much more explicit emotion, and giving the story a tone of chivalrous honor and romantic love. Although it is set in the age of sagas, its values are those of Morris, including his Victorian socialism, which is revealed in Morris's description of Sigurd's awareness of social responsibility. Morris also discards the terse roughness of the original legend.

A central motif is the Norse god Odin, the ancestor of the Volsung family and the donor of Sigmund's sword. Odin wills the death of the aged Sigmund in his battle with the warriors of Lyngi in order to make way for the coming of Sigurd, assists Sigurd in his battle with the dragon Fafnir, and is present at the final battle of the Niblungs with Atli. It is primarily the story of the Volsungs: Sigurd's father, Sigmund; Sigurd and Brynhild; and finally, the destruction of the Volsungs by King Atli and the death of Sigurd's widow.

Book I, "Sigmund," describes Branstock, the "war-duke's weapon tree," towering over the Volsung throne. A messenger arrives from Siggeir, king of the Goths, proposing marriage to the king's daughter Signy. She and her father accept, but her brother Sigmund is displeased. The wedding feast is interrupted by the arrival of a "mighty man, one-eyed and seeming ancient, in a blue hood and gray cloak, with a battle-axe on his shoulder" (Odin). He plunges his sword into the Branstock, challenges anyone to pluck it out, and walks off. King Siggeir is unsuccessful, shaming his bride. His earls and all Volsung's men are also unsuccessful. Finally, Sigmund draws the sword. Siggeir asks Sigmund for it as a wedding gift; when he is refused, he is angered. However, he hides his feelings and invites Volsung and his sons to his home. Although Signy is Siggeir's bride, she distrusts him and begs her father and Sigmund not to go. Volsung answers that he cannot break his word.

When the Volsungs arrive, they are met with an armed attack, their king is killed, and his sons, except Sigmund, are taken captive and left fettered in the woods, where wolves kill them. With the help of his sister, Sigmund buries their brothers. She kisses him and returns to her lord, after urging Sigmund to return someday and avenge the deaths. Sigmund finds refuge in a cave.

After 10 years, Signy sends her son with a damsel into the wood to Sigmund, with instructions that Sigmund is to foster the boy. He tests the boy's courage, but the child panics, so Sigmund sends him back to Siggeir's father's hall. After another 10 years, Signy sends another son, Sinfiotli, to Sigmund. Sinfiotli passes Sigmund's tests and is accepted as his son to help him in planning the vengeance on Siggeir. When winter comes, the two go to Siggeir's palace and lurk near the wine storehouse until the feasters in the hall fall asleep. Two children discover them and warn the warriors, who attack, overwhelm, and hobble them.

Siggeir puts them in a pit with two chambers separated by a stone wall to await death. Signy steals to them and throws down a blade wrapped in wheat straw. The prisoners saw through the stone wall and the roof. They leap out, kill the night-watchman, and set the hall afire, killing Siggeir. Signy appears, kisses her son, and dies in the fire. Sigmund and Sinfiotli sail back to the land of the Volsungs, where Sigmund sits on the throne. Sinfiotli is poisoned by the sister of a warrior he has slain. Sigmund takes the boy's body in a white-sailed boat manned by "a mighty man, one-eyed, and seeming ancient," who wafts it over the water.

Sensing that his time is growing short, Sigmund woos Hiordis, the daughter of King Eylimi of the Islands. However, there is another suitor, King Lyngi, so Eylimi asks her to choose, and her choice is Sigmund. Eylimi tries to appease Lyngi, but he also warns Sigmund to bring warriors lest "ill betide." Sigmund sails to his wedding with many ships and warriors. As he returns home, he hears that a mighty army has landed on King Eylimi's coasts, so he returns to protect the Isle-King, brandishing the sword from the Branstock. Through the thick of the war-shafts appears "a mighty man, one-eyed and seeming ancient, in a gray kirtle and blue hood, bearing a battle-axe," who wades through the warriors and faces Sigmund. It is his will that Sigmund now die to make ready for Sigurd. Sigmund's sword falls in shards, the man vanishes, and Sigmund's foes fall on him. Lyngi departs. Hiordis creeps out of the thicket and finds Sigmund, not yet dead. He tells her that he has seen Odin, and heard his message: He has taken back the sword that he gave Sigmund, who is now going home to his kin, but she is to take the shards and keep them. A better one than Sigmund—Sigmund's son—will come, and for him the shards will be smithified. He will do what Sigmund has left undone. With that, Sigmund dies.

A ship with warriors approaches, so Hiordis flees back into the thicket and changes identities with her handmaiden. On the ship, King Elf, son of the Helper, sees the wreckage of a great battle and finds the body of what is surely a mighty lord. They find the women and the handmaiden, in the guise of Hiordis, informs them that the dead lord is Sigmund. They raise a mound like a throne, with the shields and banners of Sigurd's men, but are unable to find his sword to put in his hand. Hiordis, in the guise of the handmaiden, tells them that the shards of the sword must not be used but must go to Sigmund's queen. Elf then takes the women to his land.

Elf's old mother is curious as to why the handmaiden is dressed more richly and always gives wiser counsel than her mistress. She tells her son to take them unawares, and they trick the women into revealing their true identities. Elf tells Hiordis that he loves her, so she becomes his queen.

In Book II, "Regin," in the house of the Helper dwells a beardless man named Regin, short of stature, pinched and wan of visage, and very old. He fostered Elf in his youth, and before him the Helper, and his father's father. He knows the lore of all men, and is expert in all skills except the sword.

Before long, Hiordis gives birth to the last of the Volsungs. She tells him about Sigmund and the Volsungs, and then sends him to the Helper and his son, King Elf. Recalling the greatness of Sigmund, King Elf announces the birth of Sigmund's son, who is to be even greater. When Elf asks his name, a "man most ancient" arises and proposes the name of Sigurd. The boy grows in might and goodness. Regin reminds Elf that he fostered both the king's youth and the Helper's. Now he will foster Sigurd. The Helper distrusts Regin's talent for cunning, but Regin laughs and says that indeed he has taught the Helper his cunning, but he promises he will deal otherwise with Sigurd. If he cannot tutor Sigurd, what will he do? The king promises him he can live as he pleases, and when he is ready, die in peace. But Regin laughs. "Some day a beardless youth will slay me."

Regin begins to tutor Sigurd in everything except the craft of battle. Regin tells him of the deeds of past kings who have been bold and wise, and the lad desires to follow their example. Regin tells him that he should follow his Volsung fathers and roam afar, leaving these "peace-lovers and stay-at-homes." This angers Sigurd, who will not tolerate anything bad said against those who have reared him, but Regin appeases him and tells him to ask for a horse from King Gripir. King Elf agrees. Sigurd goes to old Gripir, who lives on a mountain crag, and Gripir offers Sigurd his choice of horses. On his way to the meadow, Sigurd is met by "a gray-clad man, one-eyed and seeming ancient," who points him to one special horse, Greyfell.

Back at Elf's hall, Regin tells Sigurd tales of his father, Sigmund, but reminds him that, unlike his father, he is so far "deedless." Sigurd asks what is the deed he is to do? Regin answers that Sigurd is to right a wrong too long endured: recover a treasure. Regin tells Sigurd his life story: He is of the race of dwarfs, son of Reidmar the Ancient and brother of Fafnir. When his father was old he gave Fafnir, the Serpent, a greedy heart, and to another brother, Otter, a snare and net and the longing to wander the wild woods and highways. To Regin, the youngest, he gave craftiness. All had the ability to change their appearance, even to take the forms of beasts, fowl, or fish.

As the years passed, Regin continues, three folk in the heavenly halls—Odin, Loki, and Hænir—came to earth, wandering until they came to a river where Otter, changed to a real otter, began to devour the fish. Loki saw Otter as an enemy and killed him. The three gods arrived at a great hall where they found Reidmar, who feasted them, then revealed that he was the father of the man they had just slain, and that he wanted revenge. Although Regin's brothers insisted on their deaths, Reidmar demanded that they give him the Gold of the Sea that the dwarf Andvari had hidden, and he loosed Loki to find it, in a desert in the uttermost part of the world, where a mighty water covered a wall of mountains. Loki arrived and bade Andvari to bring the gold to the surface. Andvari started to hurry away with a gold ring on his finger. Loki demanded the ring, which had hidden powers: To the wise, it was gold; to the foolish, it was the seed of woe and grief. When Loki brought the gold to Reidmar, Reidmar demanded the ring. As the gods were let go, Odin warned Reidmar of a disastrous fate. Regin asked his father to give him and Fafnir some of the treasure. Reidmar ignored their request. That night he died by the heaped-up gold. Fafnir declared himself king, and Regin fled to the land of King Elf. Since then, Regin has continued to long for his share of that gold and to resent Fafnir's kingship. Will Sigurd help him? Sigurd agrees, if Regin agrees to take upon himself the curse.

Sigurd goes to his mother and asks for the shards of his father's sword, and Regin welds them together into the Wrath. Sigurd and Regin ride to the mountains, passing through to the Glittering Heath. Before them appears "a mighty man, one-eyed and ancient-seeming," who asks them where they are going. The man praises Sigurd and tells him to find a pool where Fafnir goes when he is weary. Sigurd goes there and kills Fafnir, far off from the gold. Regin had disappeared some time earlier, but now comes forth and cries that Sigurd must atone for the deed. He tears out Fafnir's heart, and tells Sigurd to eat it. Immediately there is a change in him. Like the Dwarfs, Sigurd now understands the speech of the birds, and he sees into the heart of Regin. Eagles flying above warn him to kill Regin, who wants to be master of the world. Sigurd beheads Regin, then leaps upon Greyfell to seek out the gold on the edge of the heath. Beside the gold he finds the helmet of Aweing, a gold hauberk, and the ring of Andvari. He puts on the helmet and hauberk, and rides to the west.

He comes to a mountain, Hindfell, and a "shield-burg" with a wall of Odin's tiles. There he finds a sleeping woman, Brynhild, with whom he falls in love. When she awakens, she tells Sigurd that Odin has put a spell on her until she finds the fearless heart that she will wed. Now she has found him. Sigurd gives her Andvari's ring and she returns to Lymdale, her home, to await him.

In Book III, "Brynhild," Brynhild dwells in her sister's house, and Sigurd sets out to seek adventures to win the glory befitting one who is to wed Brynhild. He comes to the burg of the Niblungs, where he tells the king he is the son of Sigmund, that he has just slain the Serpent and got the ancient Gold, and now will take the sword "to the lords of evil." He joins the warriors of Giuki against tyrants, but his heart longs for Lymdale and Brynhild. Gudrun, the daughter of Giuki, sets her love on Sigurd, not knowing that his thoughts are on Brynhild. The queen, Grimhild, who is a witch-wife, plots how she can bind Sigurd to the Niblungs for the rest of his days, and gives him a witch-drink so that his love for Brynhild perishes. That night he sees Gudrun weeping in the doorway, knows she loves him, and offers to wed her.

When spring comes, Sigurd swears brotherhood with Gunnar and Hogni, Gudrun's older brothers. Giuki dies, and Gunnar succeeds him as king. Grimhild urges Gunnar to marry a wife from Lymdale—Brynhild, who waits for a man who will ride through the Wavering Fire. Sigurd agrees to go with Gunnar. Gunnar fails to ride through the fire. Hogni suggests that Sigurd exchange shapes with Gunnar: as Sigurd rides, the fire dies down. Brynhild now requires that the man she weds kill her other wooers, but when Sigurd insists she keep her earlier requirement, they share her bed, with the naked sword Gram between them. She gives him the Andvari ring. Sigurd and Gunnar resume their true identities and return home. Brynhild suspects that only Sigurd could have ridden through the flame, but her father tells her the matter of her wedding is settled, so she leaves her daughter by Sigurd, Aslaug, with him, and goes to the land of the Volsungs.

That night Gudrun notices the ring Sigurd brought back and asks him about it. He gives it to her. Brynhild is wedded to Gunnar. At the feast she suspects that the "fourth brother" is Sigurd and remembers their troth. Sigurd also suddenly remembers their oaths. They agree they must bear their sorrow alone. Gudrun now knows it was really Sigurd who rode through the fire, and broods on it. One day as Gudrun and Brynhild bathe in the river, Gudrun confirms to Brynhild that it was Sigurd who rode through the flame. Brynhild flees, cursing the house of the Niblungs. Gunnar, his mind poisoned by suspicions planted by Grimhild, accuses Brynhild of being in love with his foe. Sigurd admits to Brynhild that he gave the ring to Gudrun, and he realizes she knows the truth about the exchange of identities. They quarrel; she stalks off, he leaves her. She goes to Gunnar to get revenge. Gunnar remembers the oath of brotherhood he and Hogni made with Sigurd, but the youngest, Guttorm, was not party to the oath, so Grimhild gives a witch-drink to Guttorm, who stabs a sleeping Sigurd but is himself killed. Sigurd learns that this is Brynhild's doing. Outside in the hall, Brynhild laughs.

Gunnar tells the people to mourn: This is the day fore-ordered by Odin, but the house of Niblung shall stand. Gudrun curses all the Niblung house and flees. On the next day a pyre is raised. Brynhild asks her maids to bring her queenly raiment, then orders that the sword that had lain between her and Sigurd be brought. She plunges the sword into her breast and asks to be placed on the pyre. There is silence over the plain. "They are gone—the lovely, the mighty, the hope of the ancient earth."

In Book IV, "Gudrun," Gudrun arrives at the hall of Atli, king of the Outlands, where she is welcomed. Grimhild sends her a witch-drink so she does not remember and is reconciled to her brothers, and orders her to marry Atli, who plots to know where Sigurd's treasure is. Atli tricks Hogni into coming. A battle ensues in which Gudrun joins on the side of her brothers. They are seized, and Atli orders that Hogni's heart be cut out. Gunnar is placed in a snake pit, where he is bitten to death as he plays a harp given him by Gudrun; he hears the voice of Odin, and sees the doors of Valhalla. The next night, Gudrun sets fire to the hall with the treasures, goes to the chamber of Atli, and stabs him. She rushes to the sea, spreads out her arms, and leaps into the tide. The sea waves sweep over her.

"Ye have heard of Sigurd . . . how the foes of God he slew: . . . wakened Brynhild the Bright, and . . . shone in all men's sight. Ye have heard of Sigurd gone away. Now ye know the Need of the Niblungs and the end of broken troth, . . . the death of Kings and of kindreds and the Sorrow of Odin the Goth." (TAP) (Faulkner 1980; Noyes 1971; Thompson, 1967; Turner and Scott 1914)

See also Morris, William.

 # SILIUS ITALICUS

Latin epic poet, author of *Punica* (late 1st c. A.D.). He was born A.D. 101 at the time of the emperor Tiberius. Most of what is known of his life derives from a letter by his friend Pliny. Silius had two sons, one of them later a consul. Silius was himself a consul in the year A.D. 68, the year of Nero's death, and he won a distinguished reputation as proconsul, governing the province of Asia. There were hints of censurable conduct during Nero's reign, with suggestions of later atonement for indiscretions. Silius was famous as a pleader in the law courts. A rich man, he owned several fine country houses, which he filled with books, pictures, and statues. He was a great admirer of Vergil, collecting busts of that poet, and buying the site of his tomb, which had fallen into neglect, and restoring it. He observed Vergil's birthday, 15 October, with great ceremony. He also acquired the house that had belonged to Cicero, whom he highly respected as an orator. In retirement he had many visitors, with whom he liked to engage in literary conversations and to whom he would read extracts from his poems for their criticism. In these later years he composed his masterwork, the epic *Punica*. In failing health, he committed suicide by abstaining from food, dying in A.D. 101. (TAP) (Silius Italicus 1968)

See also Punica.

 # SIMONIDES OF CEOS

Greek epic poet, author of *Kingdom of Cambyses; Darius, Sea Fight with Xerxes;* and *Naval Battles of Artemesium and Salamis.* He was born about 556 B.C. at Iulis, Greece. He studied music and poetical composition on the island of Ceos, but left home as a young man to live in Athens. He has the distinction of being the first Greek poet to make a living from his writing, working on commission for fees. In addition to his epics, he wrote many epitaphs for the fallen heroes of the Great Persian War. He commemorated the dead at Thermopulae (480 B.C.) with "exquisite direcness." Hipparchus, the tyrant son of Pesistratus, invited Simonides to court. The poet valued the legends of the past, not for their religious content, but for intrinsic beauty. He depicted Danai and her baby with "grace and tenderness." His philosophy was that quickly changing circumstances ruled man's character, causing him to become evil in calamity. His epinician of 520 in honor of the victors in the Olympian games is the earliest recorded epinician ode. He may have been the originator of the form.

He died about 468 B.C. in Syracuse, Sicily. (Hammond [N. G. L.] 1959; Mitchell [Vol I] 1993; Olmstead 1948)

 # SIMONOV, KONSTANTIN

Contemporary Russian poet and novelist, author of the narrative poems *The Victor* (1937) and *Far Away in the East* (1941). Simonov was born in 1915 in Petrograd. His first attempt at long narrative poetry, *The Victor,* was written while he was still in school. It is an account of the tragic life of novelist Nikolay Ostrovsky, author of *How Steel Was Tempered* and the victim of a land mine in Poland. Simonov graduated from the Gorky Institute of Literature in 1938. The following year he became a correspondent, traveling to the far north, the Far East, and the Russian fronts during World War II. His first book of poems, *Road Poems,* came out of that experience, while he was in the Caucasus. His *Far Away in the East* was written to laud the tank personnel serving in battle in the desert's heat. He wrote four other narrative poems.

Simonov also wrote a collection of love poems, *With You and Without You* (1942) and several collections about his war years, most bearing the word "diary" in their titles. He also wrote four major novels about the war and several plays. Among his novels, *Days and Nights* (1944) is an account of the siege of Stalingrad.

After the war he served as secretary of the Union of Writers and edited the *Novyi mir* from 1946 to 1950 and again from 1954 to 1958; he also traveled extensively for many years. When he died in 1979, he had been the recipient of six Stalin Prizes, a Lenin Prize, and had been named Hero of Socialist Labor. (Bristol 1991)

 # SINUKE, THE STORY OF

Syrio-Egyptian epic (20th c. B.C., 12th dynasty) by an unknown author, possibly Sinuke himself. The story gives important insights into the political and social life of the early part of the twelfth dynasty (1991–1786 B.C.).

While Sinuke, a harem official for King Amenemhet I, is on an expedition to Libya (1962 B.C.), he learns of the king's assassination. He flees, either from fear or because of suspected complicity in the plot. His intention is to travel south, but while crossing the Nile, he is blown north and eventually finds himself in Palestine. After wandering through Palestine and Lebanon, he arrives in southern Syria, where a chieftain, preparing for a successor, adopts him and marries him to his eldest daughter. Sinuke defends his father-in-law's land, once slaying an enemy chief in hand-to-hand combat. He raises a family and becomes a patriarch on his own, entertaining emissaries to and from other countries, particularly Egypt.

When a new pharaoh, Sesostris I (r. 1971–1928 B.C.), invites him to return to Egypt, Sinuke accepts. The pharaoh welcomes him back and bestows gifts on him as a token of complete pardon for past "crimes." The epic stresses the king's clemency and accessibility. Sinuke remarries, and the pharaoh orders a fine tomb constructed for him. The poem becomes a panegyric for the new pharaoh, stressing his power and military prowess. (Encyclopedia Britannica 1983)

 # SKAGANIYE
(Tale, or Legend)

Medieval Russian epic (12th c.) by an anonymous author relating the exploits of Prince Boris and Prince Gleb, the sons of St. Vladimir, Grand Prince of Kiev, and his Bulgarian wife. Unlike the Byzantine work chronicling the life of a saint, the *Skaganiye* more nearly resembles a historical legend. During a struggle for power preceding Iaroslav the Wise's ascension to power in 1019, Boris and Gleb were murdered, allegedly by their eldest half brother, Sviatopolk ("the Damned"), who was himself assassinated. Iaroslav, another brother, then gained the throne. Boris and Gleb were elevated to sainthood as innocent victims of the civil war. Boris, in particular, preferred death to participating in the conflict. (Riasanovsky 1993)

SKANDA, BIRTH OF

See Kumārasaṃbhava.

SLÁVIE

Czech epic poem (1884) by Svatopluk Čech (1846–1908). In bombastic style, the poem celebrates the Czech national character, Slavic traits, and patriotic, democratic ideals. (Preminger 1974; Siepmann 1987)

SMIL FLAŠKA

See Flaška, Smil.

SMRT SMAIL-AGE ČENGIĆA
(The Death of Montenegro)

Croatian epic by Ivan Mažuranić (1814–1890). Written in the style of old folk epics, the poem vividly depicts the sufferings and privations of the people of Montenegro while under Turkish oppression. (Preminger 1974)

SMYRNAEUS, QUINTUS

See Quintus Smyrnaeus.

SOHRĀB AND RUSTUM

English epic "episode" (1853) by Matthew Arnold (1822–1888). This narrative poem of 892 lines, written in blank verse, is based on an episode from the great

Persian epic *Shāh-Nāmah,* in which Sohrāb, a young soldier in the force of Tartar chief Peran-Wisa, serving King Afrasiab, is seeking his Persian father, Rustum, whom he has never seen. But the famous warrior does not know he has a son. When the two meet on the battlefield, Sohrāb rushes forward and embraces Rustum's knees, asking, "Art thou not Rustum?" Full of hubris, Rustum believes that if he admits his identity, Sohrāb will shower him with gifts and go back to brag that he has met Rustum and left on equal terms. He denies his identity and challenges Sohrāb. After a fierce fight, Sohrāb lies dying in the sand. He tells Rustum, "The mighty Rustum shall avenge my death! / My father, whom I seek through all the world. . . ." When Rustum says, "The mighty Rustum never had a son," Sohrāb identifies his mother as the king's daughter, dwelling in Ader-baijan. Rustum recalls that the woman who had been awarded him as a wife had sent word to him that the baby had been "a puny girl" for fear that "Rustum should seek the boy to train him in arms." To prove his claim, Sohrāb tells him, "prick'd upon this arm I bear / that seal which Rustum to my mother gave." Too late Rustum realizes that he has killed his own son. As night falls, the Persians and Tartars go their separate ways, leaving Rustum sitting alone by Sohrāb's side. (Anderson and Buckler 1966)

See also *Shāh-Nāmah.*

SOMADEVA

Legendary Indian Sanskrit poet (11th c.), author of *Kathā-saritsāgara* (Ocean of rivers of stories, or The ocean of the streams of story, mid-11th c.) Somadeva was a Kashmiri Brahman (fl. 1070) of the Śaica sect (Śiva). For Queen Suryamati, at the behest of Kashmiri king Ananta, Somadeva committed to verse, in *Kathā-saritsāgara,* much of India's ancient folklore, borrowing from another Sanskrit work, *Bṛhat-katha* (Great tale) by Gunādhya. Somadeva's work is one of the three known Sanskrit versions of Gunādhya's lost work. The *Kathāsaritsāgara* is a "frame story" built around the adventures of Udayana, king of Vatsa, in which the principal story serves as a cadre to a large number of subsidiary stories. It is considered one of the treasures of Indian literature. (Dudley and Lang 1969; Lieber and Williams 1927; Runes 1961)

See also *Kathāsaritsāgara.*

THE SONG OF HIAWATHA

American long narrative poem (1855), called an "Indian Edda" by its author, Henry Wadsworth Longfellow (1807–1882). The poem is his most artistic work. According to the poet, the metrical form of the poem was inspired by the Finnish epic *Kalevala.* (For a synopsis of the *Kalevala,* see the *Encyclopedia of Traditional Epics.*)

The hero of the poem is founded on a legendary person of miraculous birth who is sent to the North American Indians "to help clear their rivers, forests, and fishing grounds, and to teach them the arts of peace." The poem is set among the Ojibways on the southern shore of Lake Superior. This location, which the poet based on the writings of Henry Schoolcraft, was erroneous. Hiawatha was an Iroquois, and the location should have been central New York.

Canto III tells how Hiawatha is reared by his grandmother, Nokomis (daughter of the Moon). He avenges his mother, Wenonah, against his father, West-Wind. Canto VII tells of "Hiawatha's Sailing," clearing the river for the people.

Canto X, entitled "Hiawatha's Wooing," tells of his "listless longing" for Minnehaha (Laughing Water), his winning her, and bringing her home to the lodge of old Nokomis. Canto XX, "The Famine," tells of the death of Minnehaha.

The poem enjoyed wide popularity, but since the poet's death its sentimental style has led to many parodies. (Snyder and Snyder 1935)

See also Longfellow, Henry Wadsworth.

 # SONG OF MYSELF

First section, comprising more than the first half of *Leaves of Grass* (1855) by American poet Walt Whitman (1819–1892), which he named *Song of Myself* in the 1881 edition. The poem is often considered Whitman's contribution to the American epic.

See also *Leaves of Grass*; Whitman, Walt.

 # THE SONG OF ROLAND
(*La Chanson de Roland*)

The earliest and greatest chanson de geste about Charlemagne, Roland, and the Battle of Roncesvals. For a synopsis of the poem, see the *Encyclopedia of Traditional Epics*.

 # SOUTHEY, ROBERT

English poet, author of several epics: *Joan of Arc, Madoc, The Curse of Kehama, Thalaba,* and *Roderick, the Last of the Goths.* He was born in 1774 in Bristol, England, the eldest surviving child of Robert Southey, a linen draper, and his wife, Margaret Hill. From the ages of two to six he lived in Bath with a rather imperious and pretentious maiden aunt who was fond of the theater, then in its heyday in Bath, and she frequently took young Robert. It soon dominated his imagination and vocabulary. At the age of three he was entered in his first school, a dame's school, where he remained until he returned to his parents' home and enrolled in another school kept by an old Baptist minister. But he was too terrified by both the master and the school bullies to learn much. He was removed at the end of the year and sent as as a day-boy to another school in Bristol, where he remained more content for four years, living at home during the school term, and with his aunt on holidays. When he was 14 he entered Westminster College, preparatory to Oxford University. At Westminster his work in routine classes was substandard, and he began reading on his own. He had already discovered English translations of Tasso's and Ariosto's epics, and he had gone on to Spenser, most of the pre-Romantic poets, a translation of Camões's *Os Lusiad,* Pope's *Homer,* Sidney's *Arcadia, Josephus,* and the *Arabian Nights.* Soon he began his own writing; at the age of nine he began a continuation of the epic *Orlando Furioso* in heroic couplets, but after reading Bysshe's *Art of Poetry* switched to blank verse. Before going to Westminster he had tried poems on Brutus the Trojan, the death of Richard III, and Egbert; tried his hand at translating Latin; and had written "a satirical description of English manners, as delivered by Omai, the Taheitan, to his countrymen on his return," his first recorded prose work. He also began a description of Stonehenge that impressed his master. At Westminster, Southey had to endure miseries from various tormentors, which he never forgot, but he also made lifelong friends. At Westminster he began to show signs of unruliness: participation in a raid on a private school, in the rebellion of November 1791 when the whole school decamped to see a fight and the students deserted the school to protest the floggings that followed; an interest in the French Revolution; and, finally, open expression of radical ideas. In 1788, a group of Westminster boys, attempting to compete with Etonian satire, established their own paper, *The Trifler,* to which Southey and his friends decided to add another paper, *The Flagellant.* Southey contributed an attack on corporal punishment under the pseudonym "Gualbertus." Discovered, he was expelled instantly. For a moment he weakened and wrote a letter of apology, an action that he quickly repented. A period of anger followed.

In the meantime, his father's business failed, and Southey set out to help his father, who by now had been imprisoned, not for his own indebtedness, but for a bill he had endorsed for a friend. Because of the family crisis and because Christ Church would not now accept him, Southey matriculated at the more liberal Balliol College. At Oxford he wrote thousands of blank verses, among them *Joan of Arc,* an epic poem reflecting a temporary enthusiasm for the French after the French Revolution, an enthusiam that died in his disillusionment with the movement. Leaving Oxford, he met Coleridge in June 1794, and a stormy friendship developed that continued through most of their lives. Coleridge soon sold Southey on his projected commune in Pennsylvania, which he called Pantisocracy, a project that involved capital—which they were never to raise—and a wife. On 14 November 1795, he married Edith Fricker.

Shortly thereafter, Southey began a series of wanderings that took him to Spain and Portugal, and he became intensely interested in their history, language,

English Romantic poet Robert Southey in an 1822 engraving

and culture. At this time (1799) he finished *Madoc,* begun in 1794. Shortly thereafter he translated the Spanish romances of chivalry—*Amadis of Gaul* (1802) and *Palmerin of England* (1807)—and the Spanish epic *The Chronicle of the Cid* (1808). During his lifetime he wrote several other epics, among them *Thalaba* (1800), *The Curse of Kehama* (1810–1812), and *Roderick, the Last of the Goths* (1814–1826). He also wrote histories of Brazil and the Peninsular War, and the life of King Arthur. In 1813 the poet laureateship was offered to Sir Walter Scott, who declined it for financial reasons and recommended Southey instead. Southey also hesitated because of the obligation it carried to write special birthday and New Year odes. A private understanding relieved him of this responsibility, and Southey accepted.

In his last years, Southey's mind began to fail, and he died at Keswick on 21 March 1843. (TAP) (Dowden n.d.; Haller 1966; Simmons [Jack] 1948)

See also *The Curse of Kehama; Don Roderick Madoc.*

 # SPENSER, EDMUND

English poet, author of the allegorical epic *The Faerie Queene* (1590, 1596). He was born about 1522 in London of middle-class parents. From about 1561 to 1569 he attended Merchant Taylors' School in London. He was well educated in classical studies, the humanities, English composition, and dramatic art. He studied at Cambridge for seven years, matriculating as a sizar at Pembroke Hall in 1569; he earned his M.A. degree in 1576.

In 1578 Spenser became secretary to John Young, bishop of Rochester. The following year he published, anonymously, a collection of 12 pastoral poems, *The Shepheardes Calender,* dedicated to Sir Philip Sidney. Later editions appeared in 1581, 1586, 1591, and 1597, earning him a respectable sum of money.

In 1580, Spenser went to Ireland as private secretary to the new lord deputy of Ireland, Lord Grey de Wilton. Ireland was to remain his home for most of the rest of his life. To justify Lord Grey's brutal devastation of Ireland, Spenser wrote *View of the Present State of Ireland* (ca. 1596, publ. 1633), in which he says that Lord Grey's savage military plunder was necessary to subdue the backward Irish. The castle of Kilcolman was confiscated and awarded to Spenser.

In 1589 his neighbor Sir Walter Raleigh visited him and read three books of Spenser's *The Faerie Queene* with enthusiasm. At Raleigh's urging, Spenser returned to London with him that fall, where the three books were published in 1590. The poem was dedicated to Empress Elizabeth, "the greatest Gloriana," heroine of the poem. It earned widespread acclaim and a pension from the queen of 50 pounds a year. But it did not earn him a government post in England, and it attracted no wealthy patron, so he disappointedly returned to Ireland. The following year in London, *Complaints* was published, which contained a bitter lament of his failure called *The Tears of the Muses* and a satire, *Mother Hubberds Tale. Dalphnaida* was also published in London that year.

In 1594 he married his longtime sweetheart, Elizabeth Boyle, to whom he had written some 89 sonnets (rhymed *abab bcbc cdcd ee*), published the following year as *The Amoretti*. Also published in 1595 was the *Epithalamion*, a song celebrating their marriage, which he wrote as a wedding gift. It is considered his finest poem. That same year saw the publication of *Colin Clouts come home againe*, a pastoral ecologue about his experiences at court.

In 1596 he returned to London to publish three more books of *The Faerie Queene*, also bringing out a second printing of books I and II, a second edition of *Daphnaida*, *Foure Hymnes* (two praising earthly love and beauty, two praising heavenly love and beauty), and the *Prothalamion*, a marriage poem honoring the double weddings of the daughters of the earl of Worcester.

In the summer of 1598, the Irish under Tyrone rebelled. Spenser's home, Kilcolman Castle, was pillaged and burned. Spenser, his wife, and four children fled first to Cork and then to London. During the ordeal one infant died. Exhausted and overwrought, Spenser died in January 1599, never having completed the intended 12 books of *The Faerie Queene*. Only six books, plus two cantos and two stanzas of the seventh, called *Cantos of Mutabilitie*, are extant.

Spenser is considered the greatest nondramatic poet of the Elizabethan age. The stanza he used for *The Faerie Queene* (eight lines of iambic pentameters followed by a ninth in iambic hexameter, rhymed *abab bcbcc*) is called the Spenserian stanza. (Spenser 1978)

See also *The Faerie Queene.*

 # SPENSERIAN STANZA

A rhymed stanza, with no set pattern, of nine lines: eight iambic pentameter lines followed by a ninth in iambic hexameter (alexandrine). The pattern, rhymed *abab bcbcc*, was created by Edmund Spenser for his *Faerie Queene*. The form has been used by other English and Scottish poets such as Percy Bysshe Shelley, John Keats, Alfred Tennyson, and Robert Burns. (Turco 1986)

 # SPITTELER, CARL FRIEDRICH GEORG
(Pen name Carl Felix Tandem)

German-Swiss poet, novelist, and essayist, author of modern Greek epics *Olympischer Frühling* (Olympian spring, 1910), *Prometheus und Epimetheus* (1880/1881), and *Prometheus der Dulder* (1824). He was born at Liestal near Basel in 1845, the son of a Swiss engineer. He studied law and theology at Basel and Heidelberg universities, but he abandoned religion as a career. At the age of 26, with the help of a friend of his father's, Colonel Sulzberger, he obtained a position as tutor in Russian Finland (1871), where he remained for eight years. He returned to Berne in 1879 as a schoolmaster, then went to Neuville in the same position.

In 1880/1881 Spitteler published his first work, a prose epic, *Prometheus und Epimetheus*, using a pen name, C. F. Tandem. The work was ignored by the critics and the public. In 1885 he took a position as journalist and literary editor for the *Neue Zürcher Zeitung*, becoming a contributor to a Munich literary fortnightly, *Der Kuntswort*, as well.

He received an inheritance that enabled him to devote all his time to writing, and he spent the rest of his life in Lucerne. In 1889 he published a volume of poems, *Schmetterlinge*. In 1900–1906 his epic *Der Olympische Frühling* appeared in four volumes. In 1906 he published an autobiographical novel, *Imago*. He revised the epic in 1910. In 1914 he wrote a short autobiographical study that impressed Sigmund Freud called *Meine frühesten Erlebnisse*, considered by many to be his best work. He was awarded the Nobel Prize for literature in 1919.

During the latter part of his life he devoted himself to writing a number of essays. In 1824 he wrote a new version of *Prometheus und Epimetheus*, this time in iambic hexameter. He titled the new version *Prometheus der Dulder* (Prometheus the Sufferer). He died in Lucerne that same year, almost unknown outside of Europe. (Garland and Garland 1986; Highet 1976)

 # STATIUS
(Full name: Publius Papinius Statius)

Roman poet, author of the epic poem *Thebaid* (ca. A.D. 90) and an incomplete epic poem, *Achilleid* (ca. A.D. 96). He was born about A.D. 45 in Neapolis (now Naples), descended from Greeks, and he himself spoke Greek. His father, a Neapolitan schoolteacher, had at one time been a poet and had gained success in poetry competitions in Greece. A poem from Statius's collection of five books of short poems, *Silvae*, indicates the poetic debt he owed his father.

Statius lived in Rome and was a court poet during the reign of the emperor Domitian (r. A.D. 81–96), from whom he received an award for poetry in A.D. 89 or 90. He married Claudia, a widow with one daughter, to whom he was devoted. He had no children of his own, but adopted at least one son, whose literary aptitude he encouraged, and whose death he mourns in the last poem of the *Silvae*. He also addressed an affectionate poem to Claudia (iii.5).

According to Statius in *Silvae* (xii.811), he labored 12 years on his epic *Thebaid*, which is about the war between Eteocles and Polynices, sons of Oedipus, for the throne of Thebes. Although the poem is considered to be second only to Vergil's *Aeneid* in Latin epics, Statius failed to win an award in the quinquennial Capitoline festival at Rome (probably its third, in A.D. 94) and was deeply depressed. In *Silvae* iii.5, in the form of a letter to his wife, he spoke of leaving Rome and retiring to Neapolis.

Thereafter he began a second epic, the *Achilleid*, which was meant to relate the whole story of Achilles's life. But at the time of his death, he had completed only one book and part of a second.

He died in A.D. 96, probably in Neapolis, having achieved the distinction of being one of the principal poets of Latin literature's Silver Age. (Howatson and Chilvers 1993; Statius 1992)

See also *Achilleid*; *Thebaid*.

STIERNHIELM, GEORG OLOFSON

Swedish poet, called the father of Swedish poetry, author of the allegorical epic *Hercules.* He was born in 1598 in Vika, Sweden, the son of a miner. A brilliant scholar, he studied at the University of Uppsala before traveling to Germany for studies at the universities of Greifswald, Wittenberg, and Helmstedt. At the age of 28 he returned to Sweden, where he eventually received a governmental appointment in Dorpat, or Tartu (now in Estonia), at that time under Swedish control. At the age of 33 he was raised to the nobility by King Gustavus II Adolphus. Following the king's death in 1632 and the ascension of his daughter Christina, Stiernhielm was frequently called from his home in Estonia to the Stockholm court by the queen, whose patronage encouraged the appearance of his first poetic works, as well as historical, philosophical, and philological works. Fiercely patriotic, he sought to purge the Swedish language—which he referred to as man's original tongue—of foreign words that had crept into popular usage. His epic *Hercules,* which greatly influenced the development of Swedish poetry, not only makes use of words from current Swedish vernacular, it revives old Swedish words long out of use. The poem was written about 1647 while he was still a resident of Estonia. In 1656, Russia invaded Estonia, and he fled to Stockholm, where he was to spend the rest of his life. Two years later, *Hercules,* a monumental poem in hexameters, was published, and its flawless execution, lofty ideals, and innovative use of language influenced the entire course of Swedish poetry. He died in Stockholm in 1672. (Preminger 1974)

THE STORY OF SINUKE

See Sinuke, The Story of.

STRASSBURG, GOTTFRIED VON

See Gottfried von Strassburg.

STRICKER, DER

Middle High German poet (fl. 1st half 13th c.), author of two epics: *Karl* (early 13th c.) and *Daniel vom blühenden Tal* (early 13th c.). A commoner by birth, Stricker was a native of Franconia, and he spent a great part of his life there. His principal genre is the *Schwank,* a humorous short story in verse form. Many of these shed light on the customs and conditions of life in the Middle Ages.

In addition to his epics and his *Schwank*, Der Stricker wrote *Der Pfaffe Amîs*, a satirical poem of about 2,500 lines in which an English priest, Amîs, outwits the inquisition of his bishop by deceit and superior intelligence. Der Stricker's epics are thought to be early works, *Karl* being the earlier. It is an adaptation of *Rolandslied* (Song of Roland, a synopsis of which can be found in the *Encyclopedia of Traditional Epics*). *Daniel vom blühenden Tal* is an Arthurian romance. (Garland and Garland 1986)

 # SÜLEYMAN, ÇELEBI
(Also Süleyman of Bursa)

Anatolian poet (15th c.), author of *Mevlūd-i Peygamberi* (or *Mevlüd-i Nebi*, or *Mevlid-i Şerif*, 1409). He was born in the fourteenth century in Bursa (now in Turkey), probably the son of Ahmed Paşa, a minister serving in the court of Ottoman sultan Murad I (r. 1360–1389). One of the most famous of Anatolian poets, Süleyman followed a religious career, becoming a leader of the orthodox Khalwaṭiya (Ṣūfi) dervish order. During the reign of Murad's successor, Bayezid I (r. 1389–1402), Süleyman was *imān* (priest) to the court. After Bayezid's death in 1402, Süleyman became *imān* of a prominent mosque in Bursa. While there, he wrote his great religious epic *Mevlūd-i Peygamberi*, celebrating the birth and life of the prophet Muḥammad. This work is his only surviving poem. He died in 1429 in Bursa. (Encyclopedia Britannica 1983)
See also Mevlūd-i Peygamberi.

 # SUNTHOṆ PHU
(Also Sunthorn Phu)

Thai poet and courtier, author of *Phra Abhai Mani* (*Phra Aphaimani*, 19th c.) He was born in 1786 of humble parents. As a youth the excellence of his poetry brought him to the attention of the poet-king Rama II (Phuttaleutla, r. 1809–1824), who called him to court, where he had assembled a large number of poets and dramatists. Sunthoṇ Phu rose to become the king's private secretary, in which capacity he assisted the king in the collaborative version of the Hindu epic *Rāmāyaṇa*. He also wrote several well-known *nirat*, or "separation poems."

When Rama II died in 1824, he was succeeded by Rama III. Being deeply religious, Rama III disbanded the corps of court dramatists and poets of his predecessor. After this period, Sunthoṇ Phu composed his most famous work, a long fantasy epic-romance of some 30,000 lines, *Phra Abhai Mani*, meant not for the court, but for the public. Sunthoṇ Phu died in 1855, the most accomplished poet of his day. (Dudley and Lang 1969; Preminger 1974)
See also Phra Abhai Mani; Phuttaleutla.

SURYAMAL MISRAMA

See Misrama, Suryamal.

SWENSKA FRIHETEN
(Swedish liberty)

Swedish epic poem (1742) by Olof von Dalin (1708–1763). The poem is written in alexandrines in the neoclassical style. It was considered very correct, but it was not particularly successful. (Brogan 1996)

SWIFA YA NGUVUMALI

See The Medicine Man.

SZIGETI VESZEDELEM
(The peril of Sziget)

Hungarian historical epic poem (1645/1646) by Hungarian statesman, general, and poet Count Miklós Zrínyi (or Nikola Zrinjski, or Zrinski). The poem, in 15 cantos, was the first epic poem in Hungarian literature and is still considered the finest. It depicts the siege of Szigetvár in 1566, in which Zrínyi's great-grandfather was the commander; he died defending the fortress against the Turkish armies of Sultan Suleiman II. The poet was influenced by the Baroque style prevalent in Rome and Austria at the time. Although the poem adheres to historical accuracy, it manages to convey the poet's political ideas through symbolism. (Dvornik 1962; Gazi 1973)

TA MET'HOMERON

See The Fall of Troy.

 ## *THE TALE OF IGOR'S CAMPAIGN*

Russian epic poem (1889) by Apollon Maikov (1821–1897). The poem is a modern version of the old Russian *Lay of the Host of Igor* (or *Tale of Igor's Campaign*). The old Russian epic, or *byliny*, was also translated into modern Russian in 1850 by Lev May (1822–1862). For more on the traditional epic, see the *Encyclopedia of Traditional Epics*. (Bristol 1991)

TALENG PHAI
(The defeat of the Mons)

Thai heroic epic (early 19th c.) by Prince Paramanuchit (1791–1852), prince-patriarch of the Siamese Buddhist Church. The epic celebrates the heroic struggle of Prince Naresvara (ca. 1555–1605; later King Naresuan, r. 1590–1605), of the old capital of Ayutthaya, to liberate the Siamese people from Burmese rule.

In the beginning, Prince Naresvara (real name Phra Naret), the son of vassal king Maha Dhammaraja, is himself made a Burmese vassal at the age of 16 and sent to govern Phitsanulok, where he is to drive out invading Cambodians. Having become a seasoned warrior when he is only 19, he turns on the Burmese overlords.

The poem describes a series of brilliant tactics by which three invading armies from Burma are defeated and driven out of the capital, reestablishing Siam's independence (1584–1587). The Cambodians are driven out as well. The poet depicts the Burmese as brave and worth opponents.

After Naresvara is crowned king (1590), he marches into Cambodia and captures its capital, Louek, making Cambodia Siam's vassal. The climax of the epic depicts the famous hand-to-hand combat with the Burmese crown prince

(1592) in which Naresvara kills the heir apparent. The king becomes a Thai national hero, known as the Black Prince. (Dudley and Lang 1969)

See also Paramanuchit.

TAMBUKA

See Herekali.

TANCRED

In *Gerusalemme liberata,* by Torquato Tasso, the character of Tancred is based on Tancrède of Hauteville, Norman lord of south Italy, who was one of the leaders of the First Crusade. He captured Tarsus from the Turks and came into conflict with a fellow Crusader, Baldwin of Boulogne. He played a prominent role in the capture of Jerusalem and received the title of Prince of Galilee. He was a prisoner of the Turks from 1101–1103. He served as regent of Antioch and Edessa from 1104 to 1108, later became Latin magnate of northern Syria, and was involved in continual warfare with the Turks and Byzantines until his death on 12 December 1112. His role in Tasso's *Gerusalemme liberata* is mostly imaginary. (Ostrogorsky 1969)

TASSO, BERNARDO

Italian poet, author of *Amadigi* (publ. 1560). Tasso was born in 1493 in Bergame, Italy. A distinguished man of letters, he served various noblemen throughout his career. In 1531 he introduced the first Horation odes to be published in Italy. While in the service of Ferrante Sanseverino, prince of Salerno, Tasso married Prozia de'Rossi (1536). The couple had several children, some of whom did not survive. His second surviving son, born in 1544, was Torquato, destined to be the greatest Italian poet of the late Renaissance.

In 1552, Bernardo went to Naples with the exiled Sanseverino. His wife died in 1556, leading to a lawsuit against him by her relatives. In 1557 he took his son to Pesaro and then to Urbino, where they joined the court of Duke Guidobaldo II. During these years Tasso wrote a great deal of lyric poetry, dedicating many to Isabella d'Este, and using the stanza for which he is known, called "the lyre": three 7-syllable and two 11-syllable lines.

Bernardo and Torquato later moved to Venice, and in 1560 he published his 100-canto epic called *Amadigi,* which the public found heavy and wooden in comparison with Ariosto's work. While in the service of Guglielmo Gonzaga, duke of Mantua, he was appointed governor of Ostiglia, where he remained until his death in 1569. He left unfinished an episode he planned to add to *Amadigi* to make it more palatable to the public. His son later reworked it, and in 1587 published it as *Floridante.* (Durant 1953/1981; Highet 1976; Siepmann 1987)

See also Amadigi; Floridante; Tasso, Torquato.

TASSO, TORQUATO

Italian poet, author of *Gerusalemme liberata* (1757, publ. 1581) and *Rinaldo* (1562). He was born in 1544 in Sorrento, Kingdom of Naples, the son of Bernardo Tasso, poet and courtier. After an unfortunate childhood, he joined his father in Rome in 1554 and later at the court of the duke of Urbino. He was educated with the duke's son, his imagination fired with stories of the Crusades, and affected by the attack of the Turks on Sorrento in 1558. In Venice in 1559 he began an epic in ottava rima, *Gerusalemme liberata,* about the First Crusade, but it was interrupted when he realized his lack of experience. Instead he turned to themes of chivalry, the result being *Rinaldo* (1562), an epic on one of Ariosto's heroes.

For the next few years he studied law, became deeply interested in Aristotle and literary art, and wrote lyrical poetry. In 1565 he entered the service of Luigi, Cardinal d'Este, and frequented the court at Ferrara. In 1570 he accompanied the cardinal to Paris, where he may have met Ronsard. During his residence in Ferrara he resumed work on *Gerusalemme liberata,* finishing it in 1575. Aware of its poetic novelty, Tasso went to Rome to arrange its revision in accordance with the formal rules laid down by Renaissance scholars, initiating long controversy on the epic's merits and comparing it to the work of Ariosto. The poem was finally published in 1581. Dissatisfied with this version, Tasso revised it periodically, finally publishing a drastically changed version in 1593

Italian Torquato Tasso, son of epic poet Bernardo Tasso, recites his own poem, published in 1581, *Gerusalemme liberata* (Jerusaleum delivered), about the Crusades.

under the title *Gerusalemme conquistata*. Critics and scholars, however, have traditionally preferred the 1581 edition.

In 1575, Tasso began to show signs of mental instability, and by 1579 his psychosis was so advanced that he was confined as a madman in the Hospital of St. Anna in Ferrara. In 1586 he was released through the intercession of Gonzaga, prince of Mantua, who took him into his court. He underwent a revival of creative inspiration. In November 1594 he went to Rome, where the pope granted him an annual pension and promised to make him poet laureate. However, Tasso became ill and was moved to the convent of San Onofrio, where he died on 25 April 1595.

He is generally recognized as the greatest Italian poet of the late Renaissance. (TAP) (Bowra 1961; Nash 1987; Nelson n.d.)

See also Floridante; Gerusalemme liberata; Tasso, Bernardo.

 # TASSONI, ALESSANDRO

Italian critic and poet, author of the mock-heroic epic *La secchia rapita* (The rape of the bucket, 1622). He was born in 1565 in Modena, Italy, and educated at the Universities of Bologna, Pisa, and Ferrara. In 1589, at the age of 24, he joined the Accademia della Crusca, and thereafter worked in the service of various cardinals in Rome. As a literary critic, he wrote a scathing attack on Petrarch and his school: *Considerazioni sopra le rime del Petrarca* (Observations on the poetry of Petrarch, 1609).

His best-known work is the satirical epic of 1622, *La secchia rapita,* based on the fourteenth-century feud between Modena and Bologna, during which the bucket from Bologna's town well was stolen by the Modenese, who have it to this day. His "epic," which depicts the various ploys the people take to retrieve their precious bucket, holds up well as comedic satire.

Tassoni died in 1635 in Modena. (Highet 1962, 1976)

 # *ṬAWQ AL-ḤAMĀMAH*
(The dove's necklace, or The ring of the dove)

Spanish-Arabic epic combining prose and poetry (11th c.) by Andalusian 'Ali ibn Ahmad Ibn Ḥazm (ca. 994–1064). The poem shows the influence of the idea of *Udhrah* love (*ḥubb 'udhrī*), in which the lover prefers death over achieving union with his beloved. The poet, an Islamic theologian, draws upon his own experiences of pure love in this poem, a treatise on the art of love. Apart from the poetry being a perfect example of highly developed Arabic *abab,* it is considered important for its frank treatment of romantic love. It is also an anthology of the author's own love poetry.

In one section the poet describes certain signs of love that "the intelligent man" can detect, such as "the brooding gaze," because "the eye is the wide gateway of the soul." It is the "scrutinizer of [the soul's] secrets." Even when the lover is supposedly speaking to someone else, he will direct his conversation to his beloved. Other signs are "that sudden confusion and excitement betrayed by the lover" when he unexpectedly comes upon his beloved unawares. All because of love, he asks, how often has the miser opened his purse-strings, the scowler ceased to frown, the coward leaped into the fray like a hero, the clod become sharp-witted, the boor become a gentleman, the "stinker transformed into the elegant dandy?"

He describes a strange kind of passion when a man falls in love simply by hearing the description of a person, without ever having seen her. However, the poet warns that such a love is "a tumbledown building without any foundations."

He admits, "Life holds no joy for me, and I do nothing but hang my head and feel utterly cast down, ever since I first tasted the bitterness from those I love."

He tells a personal story from his youth about loving a slave-girl "who happened to be a blonde." Since then he has never cared for brunettes. The same thing, he says, happened to his father, "and he remained faithful to his first preference until the term of his earthly life was done."

He names many beauties of nature, then says, "Not lovelier than any of these that union with the well-beloved, whose character is virtuous, and laudable her disposition, whose attributes are evenly matched in perfect beauty." It is such a miracle that "the mind reels before it, and the intellect stands abashed."

The work has been translated into many languages and distributed widely in the West. (Kritzeck 1964)

See also Ibn Ḥazam, ʿAli ibn Ahmad.

 # TEGNÉR, ESAIAS

Swedish poet, the most popular poet of his time in his native land, author of *Frithiofs saga* (1825). He was born in 1782 in Kyrkeried, Sweden. His father died when Esaias was nine, leaving the family destitute. However, at an early age the boy showed indications of being gifted, and he was admitted into the University of Lund, graduating in 1802. The following year he received an appointment at the university as a lecturer in aesthetics. His first collection of poetry, *Krigssäng för skänska lantvärnet*, appeared in 1808. By this time he was the leader of an intellectual circle of writers and thinkers.

In 1812 he was ordained as a minister and made professor with a chair of Greek. His second and third collections, *Säng till solen* and *Hjälten*, appeared in 1813. These were followed by two narrative poems, a religious idyll, *Nattvardsbarnen*, in 1820 (translated by Henry Wadsworth Longfellow as *The*

Children of the Lord's Supper in 1842), and *Axel* in 1822. He remained at the university until about 1824, when he became bishop of Växjö, a position he kept for life. The following year he published *Frithiofs saga,* his greatest achievement and one of the masterpieces of Scandinavian Romanticism.

Although he harks back to the "Gothic" Romantic ideal in his early work, his leanings became increasingly influenced by the classical era. During the latter years of his life, he abandoned the liberal stance that had guided his life and writings and became an ultraloyalist. By this time he was no longer writing, possibly due to a deteriorating mental state. He died in Östrabo, Sweden, in 1846, a few days before his sixty-fourth birthday. (Siepmann 1987)

See also *Fritiof'tager Arv.*

 # *TÉLÉMAQUE*

(*Suite du quatrième livre de l'Odysée d'Homère ou les Aventures de Télémaque, fils d'Ulysse,* Sequel to the fourth book of Homer's odyssey or the adventures of Telemachus, son of Ulysses)

French epic by François de Salignac de la Mothe-Fénelon (1651–1715), who called his work a "fabulous narrative in the form of a heroic poem . . . into which I incorporated the major lessons for a prince." It was obviously intended as a sequel to Homer's epic. Into it Fénelon incorporated his ideas on the achievement of man's ideal existence, the uses of adversity, true patriotism, the deceptive aspects of love, and his concept of a utopia.

Though written in prose, Fénelon described it as a poem; and it conforms to the subject matter, structure, and style of traditional epic poems. It is universally included in literary histories as one of the great epics, and one of the most popular. It consists of 24 books.

Book I describes the arrival of Telemachus on Calypso's island with Minerva in the guise of Mentor, after a shipwreck on his voyage to seek his father. Calypso, still bewailing Ulysses's departure, is overjoyed to see him and falls in love with him, offering him immortality. At her request he relates his voyage up to then.

In Book II, Telemachus gives an account of his captivity in Egypt and describes its government and the enslavement of Mentor and his exile to Ethiopia, and of himself as a shepherd. He tells of Termosiris, who initiates him into the cult for Apollo. Sesostris, the benevolent king, sends for him and promises him passage to Ithaca, but dies. Telemachus is confined as a prisoner by the new king, who is soon slain in a revolt by his subjects, aided by the Tyrians.

In Book III, Telemachus is freed by the Tyrians and taken by ship to Tyre in Phoenicia. On the way, Narbal, commander of the ship, tells him of the tyrannical nature of his king, Pygmalion. Pygmalion orders the death of Telemachus, who flees to Cyprus with the help of Astarbe, the king's mistress.

In Book IV, Telemachus sees the debauchery in Cyprus and is saved by the reappearance of Mentor. They go to Crete with Hasael, Mentor's new master.

In Book V they observe the courageous, healthy, and peace-loving inhabitants and learn about the late wise king, Minos, whose administration had been dedicated to the well-being of its citizens.

In Book VI, Telemachus tells how the Cretans decided to elect him king after he impressed them both in their athletic games and with his answers to the elders' questions on moral and political issues. He declined, and soon set sail with Mentor again for Ithaca. Venus, however, was angry that Telemachus despised her, and raised a storm, caused the shipwreck that brought them to Calypso's island.

In Book VII, Venus brings Cupid to her assistance against Telemachus. Mentor warns him, but Telemachus succumbs to the power of Venus, not with passion for Calypso but for one of her nymphs, Eucharis. To save Telemachus, Mentor reveals to Calypso Telemamachus's newfound love for the nymph. In a jealous rage, Calypso banishes Telemachus from her island. As he and Mentor prepare to sail, Cupid persuades the nymphs to burn his ship. Telemachus rejoices at the thought of having to stay, but Mentor pushes him into the sea to swim to a Phoenician ship nearby.

In Book VIII the commander of the Phoenician ship is Adoam, brother of the ship captain who had rescued him from Egypt. He promises to take Telemachus to Ithaca, tells them of the death of Pygmalion, and describes his visit to Betica, an ideal country with a marvelous climate and resources, where the inhabitants lead a peaceful and simple life.

In Book IX, Venus is incensed at Telemachus's success so far, and begs his destruction from Neptune. Unable by the Destinies to kill Telemachus, Neptune tricks the ship's pilot into believing he has arrived at Ithaca. Instead they land at Salentum, a kingdom recently established by Idomeneus, grandson of Minos, who welcomes them warmly. The priest is preparing a sacrifice to Jupiter for success in the oncoming war with the Manducians. He promises Idomeneus good fortune because of the presence of the two new guests.

In Book X, Idomeneus tells Mentor the reasons for his war against his neighbors, the Manducians. Some of their men have unknowingly violated a treaty, and in consequence the Manducians are preparing for war with them. Just then the Manducians appear at the Salentum gates. Mentor goes forth to propose conditions of peace.

In Book XI, Telemachus sees Mentor, is curious and follows him, and contributes to the conditions of peace agreed upon. Idomeneus accepts the conditions.

In Book XII, Nestor, a Manducian ally who has accompanied them, asks Idomeneus's help against his city's enemies, the Daunians. Idomeneus promises help, and Telemachus leaves at the head of a hundred noble Cretans. Mentor proceeds to show Idomeneus how to regulate and stimulate commerce by encouraging useful arts, banning the manufacture of luxury items, and promoting the development of agriculture. He suggests dividing the people into seven classes, ranking them by their different conditions.

In Book XIII, Idomeneus confesses to Mentor the intrigues of Protesilaus, an older man who deceived Idomeneus into believing Philocles was slandering the king, and persuaded him to exile Philocles to Samos.

In Book XIV, Mentor persuades Idomeneus to recall Philocles and give him a position of honor. The king's messengers find Philocles, now content with his poor and solitary life and not easily persuaded to return. But when he hears that it is the will of the gods, he comes back to Salentum, where he is received with marks of friendship by Idomeneus.

In Book XV, Telemachus joins the camp of Idomeneus's allies, where Philoctetes is suspicious of him because of his dislike of Telemachus's father, Ulysses. He reviews his past misfortunes, which he links to Ulysses: the death of his companion Hercules by the poisoned tunic, his punishment for revealing the secret of that death, the torments on the Island of Lemnos, Ulysses's pressure to make him return to the siege of Troy but his refusal to permit him to don the armor of the Atrides, his wounds in the war, and his healing by Esculapius. Although he still retains some aversion because of those sufferings, Philoctetes is forced, despite himself, to love the son who resembles the father. He finds in himself a tenderness toward both the son and father.

In Book XVI, Telemachus finds others antagonistic. Phalantus, the Lacedemonian general, and his brother Hippias despise Telemachus's youth. They quarrel over some Daunian prisoners, and Telemachus overcomes Hippias. Afterward, Telemachus bemoans his rashness, for which he would like to make amends. However, the camp is already divided over the quarrel. Adrastus, king of the Daunians, learns of the dissension and decides to take advantage of it. He marches on the allies to attack them unawares. He surprises a hundred of their ships, seizes them, and uses them to transport his own troops to the camp of the allies, which he sets on fire. He finds Hippias, slays him, and wounds Phalantus.

In Book XVII, Telemachus runs to the assistance of Phalantus, beats back the enemy, and is about to win a complete victory when a storm puts an end to the fighting. He personally performs the obsequies at Hippias's funeral.

In Book XVIII, Telemachus has a series of dreams that persuade him that his father, Ulysses, is dead. He decides to seek out the famous Cavern of Acherontia, the entrance to the Underworld. He arrives at the banks of the river Styx, where Charon takes him aboard his bark. He presents himself before Pluto, who is prepared to grant him permission to seek his father. He begins to traverse Tartarus, where he sees the torments inflicted upon the ungrateful, the perjured, the hypocritical, and especially the tyrannical, selfish, and negligent kings.

In Book XIX, Telemachus continues his journey through Tartarus, now entering the Elysian Fields, where he sees the rewards for good and just kings. He is recognized by his great-grandfather, Arcesius, who tells him that Ulysses is still alive, and that Telemachus will return to Ithaca and reign there after his father. Arcesius instructs Telemachus in the art of kingship. Telemachus departs and returns to the camp of the allies.

In Book XX, Telemachus is received back by the allied leaders. Adrastus has usurped the city of Venusium and has as much authority there as the inhabitants. A citizen of Venusium makes a secret agreement to open their gates to the allies, but Telemachus advises against fraudulent measures. In the battle that ensues, Telemachus finds Adrastus and kills him.

In Book XXI, now that Adrastus is dead, the Daunians offer peace and ask that they be permitted a king from their own ranks. Nestor, bemoaning the death of his son, absents himself from their assembly, where opinion is divided as to the terms of peace. One proposal is to divide the country and give the territory of Arpi to Telemachus, but Telemachus refuses and persuades the Daunians to choose Polydamas as their king. He convinces them to keep full possession of their lands but to give Arpi to Diomedes as an independent country of Greeks, confederate with the Daunians against any future enemy.

In Book XXII, Telemachus returns to Salentum and is surprised to find the country so fertile yet with so little magnificence. Mentor explains those things that will hinder a country from flourishing, and proposes the conduct and government of Idomeneus as a model for Telemachus. Telemachus reveals to Mentor his feelings for Antiope, daughter of Idomeneus. Mentor praises the choice and comments on Antiope's good qualities, adding that she is the gods' choice for Telemachus, but that for the present he should concentrate on returning to Ithaca and freeing Penelope from the persecution of her suitors.

In Book XXIII, Idomeneus is unhappy over the departure of Telemachus and devises means of preventing it. He proposes several knotty problems to Mentor, which he says he cannot solve without their help. Mentor offers solutions, but insists that Telemachus must return to Ithaca. Idomeneus then tries to stir up Telemachus's passion for Antiope by engaging them in a hunting match in which his daughter will participate. She is wounded by a wild boar, but Telemachus saves her. He is all the more reluctant to leave her and to bid Idomeneus farewell, but pressured by Mentor, he overcomes his weakness and leaves for Ithaca.

In Book XXIV, during their voyage, Telemachus comments on the art of government, including its difficulties. Among the problems is knowing Mankind, and employing the good without being deceived by the bad. After this conversation, their ship is becalmed, and they are forced to put in on a little island where Ulysses has just landed. They meet, and Telemachus speaks to his father but does not recognize him. However, when Ulysses goes onboard a ship, Telemachus feels a strange uneasiness he cannot explain. As the ship sails away, Telemachus meets an old man, who tells him that the stranger is a Cleomenes, a Phrygian who has been told by an oracle that he will become a king. However, if he grows up in his own country a dreadful plague will fall upon his people. So his parents took him to another land, where he was reared in private. When he was grown, he wandered in many lands, and now has no hope of ever returning to his country or of becoming its king. The story brings Telemachus to tears, and Mentor consoles him by revealing that the account was but a fiction concealing his father's return to Ithaca, that the stranger was Ulysses himself, and that Telemachus will soon be reunited with his father.

However, Mentor decides to make a further trial for Telemachus by delaying his departure with a sacrifice to Minerva. As soon as the sacrifice ends, the face of Mentor assumes a new form. The wrinkles disappear. His eyes turn a celestial blue and are filled with a celestial fire. He acquires a woman's face and rises into the air. A brilliant spear appears in her hand. Her voice is sweet and mild. Upon her helmet appears the owl, and upon her breast glitters the formidable Ígis. Telemachus recognizes that Mentor is really Minerva. Minerva proceeds to give Telemachus her last instructions. She has led him through shipwrecks, unknown countries, bloody wars, and all the evils that can try the heart of man. She has shown him examples of the true and the false maxims of government, and revealed that no man can govern wisely who has not suffered hardship or taken advantage of the sufferings resulting from his faults. Telemachus is now worthy to tread in his father's footsteps, so he is to go to Ithaca, where his father awaits him. He is to fight under his father, and obey him as if Telemachus were the lowliest of subjects, to whom he is to serve as an example. His father will procure Antiope as Telemachus's bride, and he will be happy with her. When he comes to reign, he is to place his whole glory in renewing the golden age: Hear everyone and trust but a few, taking care not to trust himself too much; not deceiving himself; loving his people; endeavoring to foresee all the consequences of any action he is about to take; avoiding luxury, pride, and profusion; placing his glory in simplicity; and letting virtue and good works be the marks of his person and of the palace. He should never forget that kings are not kings for their own glory but for the benefit of the people. Fear is the most valuable treasure of the heart of Man, to be accompanied by wisdom, justice, peace, joy, refined pleasure, true liberty, delicious plenty, and unblemished glory.

With these parting words, Minerva springs into the air, mantled with a cloud of gold and azure, and disappears. Telemachus stands amazed and transported. He falls prostrate on the ground, raises his hands to heaven. Then he wakes his companions and goes to Ithaca, where he finds his father at the house of the faithful Eumaeus. (TAP) (Davis 1979; Tillyard 1993)

See also Fénelon.

 # *TĒMPĀVAŅI*

Indian court epic (17th c.) by Father Beschi (fl. 17th c.). Written in the Tamil language in the style of the Hindu *Purāṇas*, the poem is a Christian epic on the life of St. Joseph. (For a discussion of the *Purāṇas*, see the *Encyclopedia of Traditional Epics*.) The poet, a European missionary who became a naturalized native teacher, is credited—along with another missionary, De Nobili—with inaugurating the modern Tamil poetry era. (Preminger 1974)

 # TENNYSON, LORD ALFRED

English poet, author of *Idylls of the King* (1859–1885), a cycle of narrative poems in 12 books based on the Arthurian legend. He was born in 1809 at Somersby,

Lincolnshire, the fourth of 12 children. A precocious lad, at the age of 12 he composed what he termed "an epic of 6,000 lines." His father, a rector, gave him a wide literary background. At the age of 16 Alfred attended Louth with his brothers Frederick and Charles, but left in 1820 and returned to the rectory. The solitary surroundings of the Lincolnshire countryside had a significant influence on his writings.

By 1824 his father had begun to drink heavily, disrupting family harmony and becoming increasingly careless about money. Two years later, the three brothers published a volume entitled *Poems by Two Brothers,* of which Alfred's work made up more than half and Charles Tennyson Turner's the rest.

After Tennyson had satisfied his father's stipulation that he be able to recite the odes of Horace by heart, he joined his brothers at Trinity College, Cambridge (1828). There he formed the greatest friendship of his life with Arthur H. Hallam, who took a romantic interest in his sister Emily. However, the elder Tennyson, fearing a precipitous attachment, forbade her corresponding with Hallam for a year.

In 1830, Alfred Tennyson won the chancellor's gold medal for his poem *Timbuctoo.* Tennyson and Hallam joined an exclusive group called the "Apostles," some of whom, in addition to pursuing intellectual interests, joined in the unsuccessful Spanish revolt against Ferdinand VII in 1830. That same year his collection *Poems, Chiefly Lyrical* was published.

In 1831 the elder Tennyson died, leaving a mountain of debts. Tennyson left Cambridge without receiving a degree, and the family existed on a grandfather's largesse.

Shortly after Hallam became engaged to Emily Tennyson, he died (1833), deeply grieving Tennyson. In memory of his friend, over the next 17 years he wrote 181 poems in *abba* lyric stanzas, which were published in 1850 as *In Memoriam.*

Three of his brothers—Edward, Charles, and Septimus—were suffering bouts of mental illness, while Tennyson was suffering not only the loss of his friend, but also setbacks in his romantic relationships and in his writing, which was not well received. However, in 1834 he published *The Two Voices,* which marked a turning point in his optimism.

In 1836, at the wedding of his brother Charles, Tennyson fell in love with Emily Sarah Sellwood, sister of the bride. The two corresponded for four years until the elder Sellwood, finding Tennyson too "loose" to be a proper suitor, forbade further correspondence.

In 1842 Tennyson published *Poems,* in two volumes, which, although not well received on the whole, earned the acclaim of Carlyle and Dickens, as well as of Sir Robert Peel, who awarded him a pension of 200 pounds.

In 1850 *In Memoriam* was published to critical and popular acclaim. Queen Victoria admired his work, and he was soon appointed poet laureate. That same year he was allowed to resume his friendship with Emily Sellwood. Two years later they were married, and Tennyson's life became stable and more secure. They moved to the Isle of Wight and raised their two sons, Hallam (b. 1852) and Lionel (b. 1854). In 1852 he published *Ode on the Death of the Duke of Wellington.*

In 1855 he published *Maud*, called a "monodrama," which, although poorly received, remained his favorite. His long planned *Idylls of the King*, based on the Arthurian legend, was first published in 1859 and was immediately popular. New *Idylls* were published in 1869, and the final version appeared in 1885. Other of his works include *Enoch Arden* (1864); poetic dramas *Queen Mary* (1875), *Harold* (1876), and *Becket* (1884); *Tiresias and Other Poems* (1885); *Demeter and Other Poems* (1889); *The Death of Oenone, Akbar's Dream, and Other Poems* (1892); and a play, *The Foresters* (1892).

In 1884, Tennyson was elevated to the peerage, although the Victorian style that made him so popular was soon to be devalued by a new breed of poet. He continued writing all his life, and in 1892, despite ill health, he corrected proofs on his last book. That year, while reading Shakespeare, he died at Aldworth. He received a public funeral in Westminster. Tennyson remains the leading poet of England's Victorian Age. (Tennyson 1961)

 # TERRAZAS, FRANCISCO DE

Mexican poet, author of the incomplete epic *Nuevo mundo y conquista* (New World and its conquest, ca. 1580). He was born about 1525 in Mexico, the first-born of the conquistador of the same name who came over with Cortés as his majordomo, and his native Indian wife. The elder Terrazas died in 1549 while he was serving as *alcalde ordinario* (justice of the peace) in Mexico City. The younger Terrazas had already gained a wide reputation as a poet of some learning by the early 1600s. According to Balthasar Dorantes de Carranza's (fl. 1600) *Brief Report of New Spain* (1604), Terrazas "wrote excellent poetry in the Tuscan, Latin, and Castilian languages." That he wrote in Tuscan would suggest either that he had traveled to Italy, or possibly that he had learned from the poet Gutierre de Cetina (lover of Countess Laura de Gonzaga), a guest in Mexico in 1546 with whom Terrazas is purported to have had intimate contact.

Only fragments of his work remain. His first known works were five sonnets in *Garlands of Varied Poetry*, compiled in Mexico in 1577. This old, incomplete manuscript contains 330 poems by 31 poets; prominent among them is Cetina, represented with 78 poems. Three of these sonnets also appear in Bartolomé José Gallardo's publication *Essay*. These poems show a definite influence of Cetina's style. Terrazas wrote courtly poetry in the Italian manner, rather than martial verse. Also attributed to him is a work entitled *Sea and Land*, cited in Muñoz Camargo's *History of Tlaxcala*, about the deeds of Cortés during his expedition to Honduras.

Miguel de Cervantes Saavedra (author of *Don Quixote*), wrote two octaves in his pastoral romance *La Galatea* (1583/1585) praising Americans, one of them Terrazas, who "has/A name known here and there./His genius has given a new Hippocrene/To his lucky native land."

Terrazas's epic poem *Nuevo mundo y conquista*, written in octaves, was left unfinished at his death; however, it was circulated among his contemporaries and inspired one poet, identified only as Arrázola, to write, "Francisco de Terrazas, solitary Phoenix,/The only one from pole to pole." Terrazas died in Mexico about 1600, the first native-born New World Spanish poet. (Anderson-Imbert 1969; Jones 1966; Peña 1968)

See also *The New World and Its Conquest.*

 # TERZA RIMA

An Italian rhyme scheme in which three-line, usually iambic pentameter, stanzas are connected by interlocking rhymes. The ending of the second line becomes the rhyme for the following stanza, as: *aba, bcb, cdc,* etc. The last stanza may be a couplet rhymed from the second line of the preceding triplet, as: *yzy zz,* or it may be a four-line stanza: *yzyz.* (Turco 1986)

 # *TESEIDA*
(*Teseida delle Nozze d'Emilia,* The book of Theseus)

Italian epic (ca. 1340/1342) in medieval Italian vernacular by Giovanni Boccaccio (1313–1375). The poem, in 12 books and over 15,000 lines of ottava rima, was written toward the end of the author's youthful sojourn in Naples. Drawing upon characters and events in Greek mythology, it represents an intermingling of the structure and trappings of the classical epic and lyric style proper for an audience that was both curial and bourgeois. It proposes to sing of valor in arms, and it was the poet's ambition to create a serious literary work of stature. It is also a charming love story that has served as a source for some of the world's literary masterpieces, by Chaucer and Shakespeare, among others.

Book One begins with the traditional invocation, in this case to the Nine Muses. It then deals with the provocation for Theseus's action against the Amazons. (For more on Theseus, see the *Encyclopedia of Traditional Epics.*) The Amazons have murdered their men and their queen, Hippolyta, has set up a strong kingdom banning all men, on pain of death. Any man forced by Fortune to land there has to leave some tribute as he leaves. Theseus, duke of Thebes, sets out to avenge her crimes. Hippolyta learns of his plan, rallies her women, arms them, and fortifies her harbors. Theseus arrives by ship and sends word to Hippolyta of his terms that she modify her policy, which she rejects vehemently. Theseus orders his men ashore, but they are prevented by fire and rocks thrown at them by the Amazons, which splinter their ships. Molten oil, pitch, and soap are poured on them. Theseus berates Mars for allowing women to discomfit him, and Minerva for siding with the women. Where they land they rout the women, pitch camp, and begin a siege. Hippolyta threatens Theseus, but discretion finally forces her to capitulate, and Theseus and his men are welcomed into the citadel.

The knights find willing brides among the Amazons, and Theseus weds Hippolyta. Among the wedding guests is one maiden whose loveliness surpasses that of all the others. When Theseus asks who she is, he is told she is Hippolyta's sister Emilia.

In Book Two, Peirithoüs, friend of Theseus, warns him in a vision to leave off his dalliance and return to Athens. Theseus sails for home with Hippolyta, Emilia, and his retinue. In Athens he is met by the widows of the hero-kings slain in the siege of Thebes. Creon has refused their burial. Theseus and his knights march against Creon, defeat him, and kill him. Theseus hands Thebes over to the widows, who proceed to burn the corpses. As the battlefield is looted, Arcites and Palaemon are found and brought to Theseus. He takes them to Athens as prisoners of war in his victory procession, then puts them in prison.

In Book Three, Arcites and Palaemon hear Emilia singing lightheartedly on her morning walk in the garden adjacent to their prison and fall in love with her. One morning the noble youth Peirithoüs comes to see Theseus, who mentions the two Thebans he holds in prison. Peirithoüs asks to see them. When he does, he recognizes Arcites as a friend, and persuades Theseus to free him. Theseus does, on the condition that Arcites leave Athens and never return under pain of death. Arcites leaves reluctantly, afraid he will never see Emilia again. He bids a sad farewell to Palaemon, who is also despondent because the weather has turned cold and Emilia no longer walks in the garden.

In Book Four, Arcites goes to Boethia and changes his name to Pentheus. He sees the ruins of Thebes, now deserted, and laments the losses. He goes to Maecena, where he enters the service of Menelaus, then to Aegina, where as a poor squire he serves Peleus. But unable to forget Emilia, he returns to Athens unrecognized and enters the service of Theseus. He becomes a favorite of the lord and enjoys the sight of Emilia, who recognizes him without his realizing it. Every night he goes to a grove to lament and express his love-longing, until Pamphilus, servant of the still-imprisoned Palaemon, hears him and recognizes him. He returns to Palaemon to tell him.

In Book Five, Palaemon is told of the return of Arcites, and plots to escape from prison by getting the guards drunk. He borrows armor and a horse, and goes to the grove where Arcites goes every night. He finds Arcites sleeping, wakens and embraces him, and they discuss their rivalry for Emilia. They decide, Arcites reluctantly, to settle the issue in a mortal combat. In the first charge, Palaemon is unhorsed and stunned, and Arcites grieves over his friend. He waits tearfully for Palaemon to recover consciousness. But Palaemon is still quarrelsome, and they resume the fight. Emilia happens by as she is out hunting with Theseus and a party. She calls for Theseus, who halts the fight and orders them to reveal their identities and why they are fighting. When they tell Theseus, he pardons them but orders a year's truce, after which each man, along with a hundred knights, will settle the dispute in a tournament. They all return to Athens, where the youths are cared for and given as many castles and possessions as they had before they were imprisoned.

In Book Six the two youths maintain a happy peace and renew their friendship, but Love still keeps them tightly in her bonds. They entertain lavishly, but although there is merriment and they enjoy themselves, they are restless for the day of decision. Each busies himself with preparations for the test, including finding huge, ferocious, spirited horses. These stallions are a new attraction for the Greeks and, as the day nears, for crowds of visitors as well, among them King Lycurgos of Nemea; King Peleus; Agamemnon; Menelaus: Castor and Pollux; Cephalus, the son of Hercules; Nestor, the king of Arcadia; Pirithoüs, the son of Ixion; Ulysses; Diomedes; Pygmalion; King Minos; and many others. Hippolyta receives them cheerfully and graciously. Arcites and Palaemon are not considered foolish; the visitors do not wonder that they do not want to yield. It is judged that the love of Emilia is more precious than to be lord of any realm. Not since the quarrel between Pallas and Neptune have so many people of noble station or such great gentility gathered.

In Book Seven, Theseus reminds the assembly of heroes that this is only a "game in honor of Mars," although settling the claims of Venus. His is a plea for reasonableness, against fratricidal shedding of blood. Arcites goes to the temple of Mars to pray for victory. Palaemon goes to the temple of Venus to pray for satisfaction of his love. Prayer to Mars finds Wrath, Fear, Betrayals, Discord, Difference, Threats, Cruel Design, Unhappy Valor, Death, and altars covered with blood. Mars gives signs that Arcites's prayer has been heard. Prayer to Venus finds Yearning, Voluptuousness, Elegance, Vain Delight, Boldness, Flattery, Pandering, Desires, Lust, and a temple with dancers. Venus departs to meet Mars to find a way to satisfy both petitions. Meanwhile, Emilia prays to Diana, but is given an ambiguous answer that she will be the bride of one of them.

When morning comes, the two youths are knighted by Theseus. They select coats of arms and devices for their banners, ride in a procession through the city, and enter the theater through separate portals. As the field waits, Arcites and Palaemon both see Emilia and are moved at the sight of her. Theseus announces the rules of combat. Each of the combatants encourages his men.

In Book Eight the watchers take sides. The mixed sounds arise of the arms, the horns, the tambourines, the trumpets, and the confused babble of different languages. The ranks charge one another without lances, and many of the horses collide, unseating their occupants, who mount their horses no more. The two principals meet, exchange blows, and fall. They remount and ride back to their men. In the encounter, many of the great nobles—Minos, Agamemnon, Nestor, Castor, Lycurgos, Peleus, Pollux, Ulysses, and others—clash. Everything is confused. Diomedes and Minos are captured. Peleus is carried out of the theater by a horse. After a while, some withdraw to pick up strength, among them Arcites, who raises his eyes and sees Emila, who smiles at him, renewing his strength, as it does Palaemon on the other side. After the first onslaught, the dust partly clears, enough that the action can be seen by the onlookers. Blood flows from horses and men, and every charger is so slimy with blood that no horseman can mount it again. Everyone has bloodstained weapons, bruised faces, shattered armor, and torn garments. Noting the skill of each combatant, Theseus can hardly restrain himself from joining the fray. He frequently weighs the battle and its outcome but cannot pass judgment, for fortunes continually change. Hippolyta watches attentively, praising the prowess on each side. If Theseus should desire, she is willing to join the battle too. Emilia is torn with conflicting emotions, feeling that she has been priced too high, that she will be hated for the hurt to the fighters. She is not sure which one she wants to win. Palaemon is almost killed by the man-eating horse of King Chromis, and Arcites, his ardor rekindled by Mars in the guise of Theseus, is declared the winner. Emilia is satisfied that the gods have given her the better man. Secretly she has already felt love for him. In high spirits Arcites advances, his sword held high, and rides around the field.

In Book Nine, Mars and Venus have watched, and now Venus turns to Mars and says that Arcites's prayer to Mars has been answered, but that Palaemon's to her is to be answered too. They have earlier agreed on a compromise. Arcites now has his victory, and Palaemon is to have the spoils. So Erinys, the Fury, emerges from her place in Dis and comes into the arena, standing in the way of the triumphant Arcites. His horse rears. He is thrown backward, and is crushed underneath the heavy saddle of his fallen mount. Many rush over to help him, disengaging him from the saddle only with difficulty. Emilia sees the accident and is afraid. They remove the armor from Arcites and wash his face. He recovers consciousness, but is unable to speak. Arcites's companions are disconsolate, and Palaemon, saddened, deeply mourns the injury to his friend. Theseus orders the theater emptied and has Arcites doctored. Arcites can finally speak, and he asks for Emilia. She comes, and he is consoled, asking to die in her arms. But Theseus will hear nothing about Arcites's dying, and has him placed in a triumphal chariot. Though still dazed, Arcites sits up, dressed in triumphal robes and crowned with laurel, and rides the countryside with Emilia at his side. They arrive at the palace, where Arcites is taken to a bed. Hippolyta comes to his side, with Emilia. Palaemon stands in mourning garb, but he is also saddened that he has lost what he desired. Theseus addresses the throng, consoling the defeated, and declaring that Palaemon is henceforth to be Emilia's prisoner. Palaemon's comrades leave, and he presents himself to Emilia. She sets him free with splendid gifts and advises him to find a bride elsewhere. She then weds the wounded Arcites before all the barons.

Book Ten describes the long, anguished dying of Arcites despite the best care of doctors. Arcites summons Theseus to dispose of his possessions and begs that Palaemon wed Emilia after his death. He has Palaemon summoned and tells him of this wish. Palamon is touched but answers that Emilia is Arcites's, and that Arcites will outlive him. But Arcites insists, and they weep together. Hippolyta enters with Emilia, and they ask why the weeping. When told, they try to give Arcites courage, and his spirits revive when he sees Emilia, yet he insists that he is near death and that he wishes Emilia to marry Palaemon. That is the will of the gods. Emilia sobs and they exchange their last kisses. After nine days, knowing the end is near, Arcites offers a sacrifice to Mercury, who transports the souls of men, and asks to be taken to Elysium. He laments the loss of his youthful strength, his hopes for fame and love, the play and pleasure with ladies and knights, and how everything will go on without him. As he dies, he opens his eyes toward Emilia and whispers "Farewell."

In Book Eleven the spirit of Arcites soars toward the eighth heaven and he looks back at Athens, laughing as he observes the vanity of humankind. He goes to the place that Mercury has chosen for him. In Athens, Emilia and Palaemon close Arcites's eyes, and the lamentation begins. Theseus orders the building of a pyre in the grove where Arcites made his complaints to Love. He has the body clothed and placed on a magnificent three-tiered bier made of the finest trees and covered with purple drapery sprinkled with gold and set over with flowers and perfumes. Grecian kings bear the body to the pyre, with weeping everywhere. Palaemon wears a robe of mourning, with neglected beard. Emilia weeps over the corpse. All the insignia of royalty are brought so as to render the full honors of Arcites's noble blood. Emilia lights the pyre, recalling that she had hoped instead to bear the bridal torch, then faints. Palaemon cuts off his beard and throws it on the pyre. At sunset the ashes are gathered and put reverently in an urn, wrapped in precious draperies, and placed temporarily in the temple of Mars. Funeral games are held.

Palaemon has a special temple built, storied with the adventures of Arcites, and he puts his friend's ashes there atop a marble column. Below he puts an epitaph.

In Book Twelve, Theseus declares an end to mourning and commands Paleamon to marry Emilia. Both object, but Theseus reminds them of Arcites's last wish. Life must go on, he says. He changes from mourning to a more cheerful garb. Palaemon is urged by several to consent. Emilia recalls her vow as an Amazon and pleads with Theseus to be allowed to serve Diana and die in Diana's temples. After Theseus accuses her of giving a lame excuse, she ceases her objection. When the day of the wedding arrives, Hippolyta adorns Emilia, and they proceed slowly toward the temple. They arrive at the temple of Venus, where they are received by the kings. They gather in a circle around the altar and invoke the aid of Hymen and of Juno. In the presence of all, Palaemon vows to take Emilia as his bride, and she makes a like promise. They return to the palace, where they enjoy feasting, music, and games. At night Palaemon and Emilia enter a rich chamber. The next morning Palaemon takes gifts to the temple of Cytherea, thanking her that he now possesses the beautiful Emilia, whom he has so loved and so long desired. Then he enters the rich hall where the feast has recommenced. It lasts several days, coming to an end after the fifteenth day. Each king takes leave of Theseus, the ladies, and Palaemon, and departs. Palaemon remains in great comfort, joy, and delight with his noble lady.

Boccaccio ends by praising the lady at whose instance his poem was composed, expressing expectations that, since it is the first to celebrate the deeds of Mars in the vernacular, he will receive the garlands and merited rewards due it. (TAP) (McCoy 1974)

See also Boccaccio, Giovanni; Hippolyta and Hippolytus.

THALABA

English epic poem (1801) by Robert Southey (1774–1843). The poem, in irregular verse, is a grandiose Romantic Oriental narrative about revenge. Set in Arabia, it contains some fine passages, but it lacks the poetic depth and vision to sustain reader interest and has not stood the test of time. (Grebanier 1949)

 # THEBAID
(*Thĕbăis*)

Latin epic poem (publ. ca. A.D. 90) by Publius Papinius Statius (ca. 45–ca. 96). The poem, about the war between Oedipus's sons for the throne of Thebes, is composed of 12 books of hexameters. It took the poet 12 years to write.

Book 1 begins with an introduction defining the theme: the expedition of the Seven against Thebes to help Polynices regain the throne from his brother Eteocles. Their father, Oedipus, imprisoned at Thebes, curses his sons and calls on the Fury Tisiphone to cause them to fight. The war is resolved by drawing lots. Polynices goes into exile to Argos until it is his turn to fight, while Jupiter makes plans to destroy Thebes in answer to Oedipus's prayer. Caught in a storm, Polynices seeks refuge at Adrastus's palace, where he meets and fights Tydeus, also seeking refuge. Adrastus invites them both inside, sure they are the sons-in-law foretold by an oracle. At a banquet he tells the story of Python and Coroebus.

In Book 2, Mercury, sent by Jupiter, carries Laius from the Underworld to Thebes, where Laius incites the sleeping Eteocles against his brother. Meanwhile, Adrastus promises his daughter Argia to Polynices and Deipyle to Tydeus. But Argia wears Harmonia's fatal necklace, the making of which is described. Tydeus is sent to Thebes to claim Polynices's right to the throne. Eteocles angrily rebuffs Tydeus and sends 50 men to kill him, but Tydeus slays all but Maeon, whom he sends back to Thebes with the news.

In Book 3, Maeon reports to Eteocles the slaying of all the men, then kills himself. The Thebans go to claim their dead. Tydeus returns to Argos to report his victory, but Adrastus consults two seers who foretell the deaths of the Argive leaders. Fired for battle by Mars, the populace ignores the oracles. Argia urges her father to fight.

Book 4 occurs three years later. Incited by Bellona, the leaders march to war: Adrastus, Polynices, Tydeus, Hippomedon, Capaneus, Amphiaraus, and the youth Parthenopaeus, whose mother, Atalanta, begs him not to go. Meanwhile, Eteocles consults the blind seer Tiresias and his daughter Manto, who summon Theban kings and queens from the Underworld, followed by the Argive leaders in tears. Tiresias thus predicts victory.

As the Argives reach Nemea, Bacchus commands the river gods to run dry, creating a great thirst among the Argives. They meet Hypsipyle, who takes them to the only river still flowing, the Langia.

In Book 5, as the Argives drink, Hypsipyle tells of her encounter with Jason, who married her and fathered her twins 20 years before, then abandoned her. While she speaks, her baby, Archemorus, is killed by a big snake. Capaneus kills the snake. The baby's father, Lycurgos, tries to kill Hypsipyle but is deterred by the Argives. Her twin sons, who have been searching for their mother, arrive and are reunited with her.

In Book 6 two great funeral pyres are built as Lycurgos grieves for his dead son. Crowds assemble for funeral games. Aided by Apollo, Amphiaraus bests Polynices in the chariot race. Parthenopaeus, after being cheated by Idas once, wins the foot race against him when it is run a second time. Hippomedon wins discus throwing; Capaneus bests Alcidamas at boxing; Tydeus beats Agylleus at wrestling. Adrastus performs an archery feat, the results of which suggest that only he will return from the war.

In Book 7, tricked by Mars into believing that the Thebans are about to attack, the Argives rush to arms. A messenger warns Eteocles of their approach. While the Argives camp near Thebes, Jocasta and her daughters enter camp and entreat Polynices to accompany them to see Eteocles. Tydeus convinces him not to go. Two tame tigers, incited by Fury to kill Amphiaraus's charioteer, are killed by Aconteus, causing the Thebans much grief. Jocasta flees back to Thebes. The battle begins. Apollo warns Amphiaraus that death is nigh. An earthquake causes a great crevice, into which Amphiaraus drives his chariot.

In Book 8, while Amphiaraus tries to explain to an incensed Pluto his sudden appearance in the Underworld, the Argives above are retreating, pursued by the Thebans until night falls. The next day a seer, Melampus, is chosen. The Thebans attack. Atys is brought in to die in Ismene's arms. Melanippus mortally wounds Tydeus and is himself wounded. As Tydeus lies dying, he calls for Melanippus's head, which he gloats over, then gnaws on it.

In Book 9, while Polynices mourns Tydeus's death, the Thebans, incensed at Tydeus's act, fight to sieze his body, which Hippomedon tries to defend. He kills Crenaeus, grandson of the river, which in revenge almost drowns Hippomedon until Juno urges Jupiter to intervene. Hippomedon crawls to the bank but dies of his wounds. Hypseus takes his sword and helmet but is slain by Capaneus.

Diana attempts to save the youth Parthenopaeus by entering the battlefield in disguise, but Mars orders her to leave. The lad dies in battle.

Book 10 takes place that night, when 30 Argive warriors slip into enemy camp and kill the sleeping Thebans. Hopleus and Dymas, squires of Parthenopaeus and Tydeus, rescue their masters' corpses, but are discovered and slain. By day, the Argives storm Theban walls and breach them. Tiresias prophesies that Menoeccus must die. Valor inspires Menoeccus to address his troops and then to sacrifice his life for his country, despite the efforts of his father, Creon, to dissuade him. Capaneus, scaling the fortress, challenges Jove and is killed by a lightning bolt.

In Book 11, following Capaneus's death, the Argives withdraw. Two Furies plot the fratricide of Eteocles and Polynices, who decides to challenge his brother to face-to-face mortal combat. The two kill each other. Oedipus, led by Antigone to the corpses of his sons, wants to kill himself, but she prevents it. Oedipus's wife, Jocasta, stabs herself, but their daughter Ismene stauches the flow of blood. Creon takes the throne of Thebes, banishing Oedipus to the nearby mountain of Cithaeron.

In Book 12, the Thebans give their dead splendid funeral pyres, but they forbid the Argives to be given burials. The Argive widows set out from Argos to claim their husbands' bodies. Warned that they will not be allowed to enter the battlefield, all but Argia set off for Athens to plead for Theseus's intervention. With Antigone's help, Argia sneaks onto the field and recovers Polynices's body. The two try to put the body on the still-smoldering pyre of Eteocles, but the pyre rejects Polynices's body and bursts into two flames. Guards seize the women and take them to Creon.

Meanwhile, the widows of Argive arrive in Athens and beseech the aid of Theseus, who is just home from his triumph over the Amazons. (For more on Theseus, see the *Encyclopedia of Traditional Epics*.) Theseus marches his army against the exhausted Thebans, who are quickly defeated. Theseus kills Creon, thundering to the Argive spirits, ". . . open wide/Hell's chaos and alert the avenging Furies!/See, Creon comes!"

At once the two armies join in mutual trust and Theseus is welcomed. The Argive women give their husbands grand funerals.

The poet's epilogue states that he worked "twelve long years" on the *Thebaid*, and he wonders if it will survive him. He does not try to match the *Aeneid*, he says, but he will be content to have his epic "follow from afar." (Statius 1992)

See also Statius.

 # *THEOGONY*
(Or Genealogy of the gods)

Greek didactic epic poem (ca. 8th c.) by Hesiod. The poem is probably earlier than *Works and Days*, also attributed to Hesiod. Both are probably of the Homeric period; however, whereas the *Iliad* and *Odyssey* are aimed at the Ionian aristocracy, Hesiod's work is written for the Boeotian peasantry. Although the poem consists of only 1,022 hexameter lines, as the surviving account of Greek gods and their genealogy it is of great importance in the study of early Greek religion.

The poem begins with a long introductory hymn of 115 lines to the Muses of Helicon, who "taught Hesiod to sing/. . . while he was shepherding his lambs." Thereafter the poet describes the beginning of the world, from primordial Chaos (Void). Next comes Gaia (Earth), described as "broad-bosomed"; Tartarus, deepest Underworld; and Eros (Love), who is the most beautiful of all the gods. Chaos produces both Nyx (Night) and Erebos (Darkness, another part of Underworld). These two mate to produce Day and Aither (Space).

Gaia produces Oranos (Uranus, Heaven) to be her equal, then makes hills as homes for the goddesses, and the sea. She mates with Oranos and produces Oceanus and 11 Titans: Koios, Kreius, Iapetos, Hyperion, Theia, Rhea, Themis,

Mnemosyne, Tethys, Phoebe, and Kronos. She bears the three one-eyed giants, Cyclopes (whose hearts are insolent). Their names are Brontēs (Thunderer), Steropēs (Lightner), and "proud-souled Argēs (Bright). Oranos and Gaia then bear the three "unspeakable" sons, each with 100 arms and 50 heads. They are Kottos, Gyes, and Briareus. Oranos hates them so much that he hides them inside Gaia. This causes her such discomfort that she plots with her clever young son Kronos to castrate his father with a saw-toothed scimitar. The blood drops on Gaia, who gives birth to the Furies, the Giants, and the Meliae (ash-tree nymphs). The genitals float out to sea, and from their foam grows Aphrodite. Oranos reproaches his sons, calling them Titans because they are insolent and did a deed for which later they will be punished.

Meanwhile, Night, without sleeping with any other god, produces Doom, Ker (a spirit of death), Death, Sleep, Dreams (the "whole tribe"), Blame, Distress, Herperides (the daughter who guards the tree with golden apples at the edge of Oceanus), the Destinies and Fates, Nemesis, Deceit and Love, Age, and Strife ("strong-willed"). Strife in turn gives birth to Work (called "wretched"), Forgetfulness, Famine, Pains, Battles, Fights, Murders, Killings, Quarrels, Lies, Stories, Disputes, Lawlessness and Ruin ("both allied"), and Oath.

Pontus (Sea) begets Nereus, the truthful; then Pontus and Gaias produce Thaumas, Phorkys, Ceto, and Eurybie ("with her heart of steel").

Nereus and Doris (daughter of Oceanus) produce 50 daughters (Nereids), whom the poet names. Thaumas and Electra (daughter of Oceanus) produce Iris (Rainbow) and the Harpies (Aēllo, "Storm Wind," and Okypete, "Swift Flying").

Ceto and Phorkys produce offspring, the youngest of which guards the golden apples in the Underground. Tethys and Oceanus bear a large number of offspring. Of their many daughters, Styx is deemed most important. Theia and Hyperion produce Helios (Sun), Selene (Moon), and Eos (Dawn).

Eurybie and Krios produce Astraios, Pallas, and Perses. Astraios and Eos produce the "winds/with mighty hearts": Zephyros, Notos, and Boreas. Eos also bears the Eosphoros and all other stars. Pallas and Styx produce Victory, Glory, Power, and Force. Phoebe and Koios produce Leto ("always mild and kind"), Olympus ("gentlest of all"), and Asterie, who becomes the bride of Perses and produces Hekate.

Forty-five lines are devoted to singing the praises of Hekate, who is able to give wealth, success, victory, fame, and glory. She is helpful in increasing herds of cattle, goats, and sheep. She is also a nurse.

At last, the Titan Rhea ("being forced by Kronos") produces the first generation of Olympian gods: Hestia, Demeter, Hera, Hades, Poseidon, and Zeus—all of whom, except Zeus, Kronos eats as soon as they are born. With the aid of her parents, Oranus and Gaia, Rhea saves Zeus by hiding the baby and offering Kronos a stone to swallow instead. Zeus later forces his father to vomit up his eaten children, restoring them to life.

Klymene ("lovely-ankled nymph") marries Iapetos and bears Atlas, Menoitios, Prometheus, and Epimetheus, who marries the first woman, created by Zeus as punishment for men. Her name is Pandora, and she brings

Greek poet Hesiod compiled *Theogony* late in the eighth century B.C. His work is an important source of information about the genealogy of the gods and goddesses of Greek mythology. Italian artist Andrea Mantegna represented a pantheon of the gods in his 1497 painting *Parnassus,* for the mountain in Greece considered home of the muses.

along a box of evils for men. Zeus casts Menoitios into Erebos, striking him with a thunderbolt because he is full of reckless pride. Atlas is forced "by hard necessity" to hold up the heavens. Prometheus deceives Zeus and is chained to a rock, where an eagle eats his liver.

War for supremacy breaks out between the Titans and the Olympians, led by Zeus, with his terrible displays of thunder and lightning. The Olympians are victorious, and the defeated Titans are thrown down to the punisher Tartarus, where they dwell in gloom in the Underworld.

After Zeus drives the Titans out of heaven, Gaia and Tartarus have a child, Typhoeus, a monster with 100 serpent heads. Zeus at once attacks him with thunderbolts, setting Aetna on fire in the process, and hurls the monster into Tartarus.

The gods choose Zeus to be their king. He proceeds to take a number of wives: Metis, conceiver of Athene; Themis, mother of the four Horae and the Fates; Eurynome, mother of the three Graces; Demeter, mother of Persephone; Mnemosyne, mother of the nine Muses; Leto, mother of Apollo and Artemis; and last, Hera, mother of Hēbē, Ares, and Eileithuia. Because Zeus swallowed Metis before she could give birth, he produces Athene from his own head.

Hera quarrels with Zeus and produces, without an "act of love," Hephaistos, the skilled craftsman. Poseidon and Amphirite produce Trāton, with human head and shoulders and a fish tail from the waist down. Ares and Cytherea bear Terror and Fear, then Cytherea bears Harmonia, who marries Cadmus.

Zeus has many illegitimate children. Atlas's daughter Maia bears Zeus "Glorious Hermes," who becomes herald to the gods. Cadmus's daughter Semele bears Zeus, "Glad Dionysus." Alcmene bears Zeus a son, Heracles the Strong.

The last part of the poem, dealing with the offspring of goddesses and mortal men, is not thought to be Hesiod's work. This section appears to have been added later to lead into the (ca. 6th c. B.C.) continuation of the poem entitled *Catalogue of Women*. This poem, in five books of hexameter lines, contained accounts of women who mated with gods and became the mothers of heroes. Only fragments of the latter work survive. (Wender 1973)

See also Hesiod.

 # TILL EULENSPIEGEL

(Full title: *Des grossen Kampffliegers, Landfahrers, Gauklers und Magiers Till Eulenspiegel Abenteuers, Streiche, Gaukeleun, Gesichte und Träm*, Concerning the Adventures, Pranks, Juggling, Visions and Dreams of the Great War Pilot, Land Driver, Juggler, Magician Till Eulenspiegel)

German epic poem (1928) by Gerhart Johann Robert Hauptmann (1862–1946). Written in hexameters and divided into 18 *abenteuer* ("adventures"), the poem is based on an old German tale popular in the sixteenth century, the oldest extant version being in High German and dated 1515. However, the original was probably written in Low German about 1480.

The poem relates a number of comic episodes by a practical joker, Till Eulenspiegel, who chooses as the targets of his pranks various members of the governing class such as priests and noblemen (although sometimes innskeepers and tradespeople) who are taken in by his guileless air as a "country bumpkin."

The historical Till Eulenspiegel who inspired the stories was a practical joker born at Kneitlingen in Brunswick, who died in 1350 at Mölln near Lauenburg. (Garland and Garland 1986)

See also Hauptmann, Gerhart.

 # TIMOTHEUS

Greek poet (fl. 5th c. B.C.), author of *Persica* (The Persians). He was born about 446 B.C. in Miletus. In 410 B.C., he was presumably in Athens for the Great Panathenaea of that year to exhibit his poem, which takes as its theme the naval victory of Salamis and the 480 B.C. Greek rout of the Persians. At the time, the poet was antagonistic to Sparta, and he makes subtle satirical barbs against them because of their growing friendship with the Persians and because a subsidy promised by the treaty had not been paid. His poem was performed in the contest of poets to a wildly enthusiastic audience. Timotheus easily won the vote of the Athenians. He died about 357 B.C.

English poet John Dryden refers to him in *Alexander's Feast*. (Olmstead 1948; Siepmann 1987)

See also Persica.

 # *TITUREL*

Middle High German unfinished epic by Sir Wolfram von Eschenbach (fl. ca. 1210). *Titurel* is the long-traditional title given to two fragments of the epic left in a manuscript also containing the complete *Parzival* by the same poet, presumably dating sometime between 1228 and 1236, the decade after Eschenbach's death. The title probably derives from the occurrence of that name in the opening line of the poem.

The subject of the poem is the love story of two young people, Schionatulander and Sigune, characters also found in Eschenbach's *Parzival*. It is written in long lines grouped in quatrains rhyming *aabb*; each line is broken by a caesura. In the first line of the quatrain, the first half of that line has three or four strong beats, followed in the second half by three strong beats. The second line has three or four strong beats in the first half, and five strong beats in the second half. The third line has five strong beats with no caesura. The last line has three or four strong beats in the first half, and five strong beats in the second half.

The First Fragment has 131 stanzas. The Second Fragment has 39 stanzas. There is an obvious time lapse and break in the story line between the two fragments.

Critics have lavishly praised this work, some finding it superior to Eschenbach's other two epics. There is an apparent time span between this same poet's *Parzival* and his *Willehalm*, and it has been theorized that he undertook *Titurel* at this time and abandoned it unfinished. It has also been theorized that the poet was working alternatively on *Titurel* and *Willehalm* in his last years and died before he could finish either one, but there are no signs of an aging writer in either work. Probably he interrupted his work on *Titurel* to begin work on *Willehalm* and never returned to *Titurel*.

In the first ten stanzas of the First Fragment, Titurel gives his speech of abdication from the Grail kingship because of advanced age. He hopes his young successors will maintain his knightly virtues. He recalls that his were the first human hands to receive the Grail from a host of angels. Of his children, Frimutel is to be given the Grail. In Stanzas 11 to 24 the poet lists the descendants of Titurel, ending with Sigune, whose mother died in childbirth.

In Stanzas 25 to 33, Sigune has an early playmate, Kondwiramurs, and then is removed to Kanvoleiz, capital of Waleis, to live with her mother's sister, Queen Herzeloyde. In Stanza 36, she grows to womanhood and begins to be haughty and frivolous but with womanly kindness.

In Stanzas 39 to 45 we are introduced to Schionatulander, the ward of the French queen Anphlise and grandson of Gurnemanz of Graharz (*q.v. Parzival*). Schionatulander is presented as a squire to Gahmuret when Gahmuret is knighted by Anphlise. The widowed Anphlise had offered Gahmuret a crown, scepter, and country if he would stay with her instead of marrying Herzeloyde, but a court of love had supported Herzeloyde's claim (*q.v. Parsifal*). Gahmuret takes the lad with him on his travels to heathendom and brings him back to Kanvoleiz in Waleis.

In Stanzas 46 to 57, Schionatulander and Sigune, both reared in the household of Gahmuret, fall in love although they are yet children, "still short of maturity" (Stanza 47) (he is probably age 13 or 14). They hide their love in secrecy and suffer torment in their hearts. But, by carrying secret messages between Anphlise and Gahmuret, the boy learns something about love procedures, so he summons up courage and approaches Sigune (Stanzas 57 to 73). In Stanza 72, he promises that when he is old enough (he is now probably 16) he will undertake those labors so that his service may win her later. She tells him she also loves him. This is the beginning of their love bond in words.

In Stanzas 74 to 82, Schionatulander leaves, with Gahmuret as his squire, on that knight's secret expedition to aid the baruch of Baldac. The queen gives Gahmuret her undershirt of white silk to wear into the mass jousting before Baldac. Gahmuret travels to Seville in Spain. In Stanzas 83 to 107, Schionatulander suffers the pangs of love. While the other young nobles are jousting and fighting, he avoids them. Gahmuret notices this. He too is disquieted by love and knows something about despondency, so he takes the young lover to a field off the highway, and asks the cause of his sadness. As a kinsman, Schionatulander should not keep secrets from him nor from the queen who reared him. The boy confesses his love for Sigune. Gahmuret tells him that noble love is granted according to rule. A brave man will win his love sooner than a wealthy coward. Gahmuret hails their love; he will enlist her aunt's help for Schionatulander.

In Stanzas 108 to 131, Sigune endures great distress. She has struggled long and hard to keep her feelings from her aunt, but the queen sees Sigune's suffering. Finally the young girl can no longer conceal them. The queen admits that she too has been sad, but hers is a different grief, for Gahmuret. She asks Sigune who is the object of her love. Sigune begins a long outpouring of her daydreams about her lover. Then she names Schionatulander as the one she loves. The queen is taken aback. Schionatulander is a rich prince of high rank, but not yet renowned enough. She exclaims that this must be the work of her archenemy and rival, the French queen Anphlise, from whom she had stolen Gahmuret. Anphlise must now be trying to lure both Schionatulander and Sigune away from her. She is sorry that Sigune is Schionatulander's *amie* when they are so young, but he will later surely rise in renown. She advises Sigune to grant him comforting joy but not let him bring sorrow upon her. Thus is love authorized. "How happy I am, my aunt," Sigune exclaims, "that I may now, with your permission, love Schionatulander before the eyes of the whole world."

A considerable time elapses between the two fragments, but Schionatulander is still a squire in the second fragment. In the meantime, according to *Parzival,* Gahmuret has died, and his squire has returned to Waleis. As the fragment begins, the two lovers are encamped in a summer woodland. They hear a hunting dog racing toward them, on the track of a wounded animal. Noted in knightly sports for his swiftness, Schionatulander jumps up and sets out in the direction of the barking. Along comes Duke Ehkunat's dog dragging its leash, which has slipped out of the prince's hands. As it breaks out of the underbrush onto the trail, its Arabian collar, studded with bright jewels, flashes in the sunlight. Schionatulander catches it and brings it to Sigune. The dog is not all that the prince catches. Grief lined with trouble lies ahead for him.

The leash is 12 fathoms long (almost 72 feet), made of ribbon silk in four colors—yellow, green, red, and brown—and clasped with rings of pearls. On the ribbon between the rings is some writing with the dog's name, Gardeviaz (Watchways), with mention of it as a love gift, and with a story about Clauditte, the young and now reigning queen, sister-in-law to Ilinot, son of King Arthur. It tells how she had summoned a court to choose her consort. Since her preference was le duc Ehkunat of Flowering Wildwood, uncle of Schionatulander, she has sent Ehkunat this letter, via the dog, to this wild wood. However, she intends to "watch her womanly way."

While Sigune reads this letter, Schionatulander angles for perch and trout with a feather-bait. Sigune unties the knot in the leash in order to read the writing better, and ties the leash to the tentpole. Gardeviaz strains at the rope, begging for food. She sends two attendants to get something for the dog to eat, but the leash cuts her hands and the dog escapes in pursuit of some quarry, dragging the tentcloth, which he has ripped off the holding pegs. Standing in the brook, Schionatulander hears the dog's barking, and, to his undoing, throws down his rod and runs after the dog, which eludes him. He returns, his legs badly scratched by the brambles, and goes into the tent to bathe them. He sees the bad cuts and burns on Sigune's hands, and she sees the cuts on his legs. They commiserate.

Now, the poet says, he must turn the story bitter. Sigune regrets the loss of the writing on the leash, and begs Schionatulander to get it back for her. He tries to dissuade her, arguing that he has not heard of many dog leashes with writing on them. Usually such writing is in books, which he has read, and he will read to her from them. The writing on the leash, he says, is of no concern to her. But she complains that she has not finished reading it, and there is an account of an adventure on it of which she must know the ending. She is even willing to give all the wealth she can get to have that writing. If his service is to seek her love, he should first get her that leash. He agrees. Even if she has to be won in combat, even if he loses his life, he will bring the leash back to her. She promises she will grant him all a girl should do for a "fair and noble friend," if he will fight for that leash. He agrees to seek it far and near, guided by her love. This is the beginning of much grief.

On this note, the fragment ends. In *Parzival* we learn that Schionatulander died, either in defense of Parzival's lands, or by Orilus in a joust, or as a result of his search for the hound's leash. The implication in this epic is that the latter is what happened. (TAP) (Wolfram von Eschenbach 1984)

See also *Parzival;* Wolfram von Eschenbach.

TOLDY TRILOGY
(Also *Toldi Trilogy*)

Hungarian epic trilogy consisting of *Toldi* (1847), *Toldi szerelme* (Toldi's love, 1848–1870), and *Toldi estéje* (Toldi's evening, 1954) by János Arany (1817–1882). The poet was inspired by a sixteenth-century verse chronicle, *Miklós Toldi*, by Péter Ilosvay-Selymes.

The first part of the story, set in the fourteenth century and written in a classical style but using the language of the people, relates the adventures of Toldi, a youth of great strength and physical prowess, in reaching the royal court. In the second part, Toldi suffers a tragic love affair. The poem touches on deep human concerns common to all. In the third part, Toldi contends with the king and finally dies. (Brogan 1996)

See also Arany, János.

TONGMYŎNG WANG P'YŌN
(The lay of King Tongmyŏng)

Brief Korean epic poem written by Yi Kyubo, who lived during the Kuryŏ dynasty (935–1392). The poem relates the heroic deeds of the legendary founder of the Koguryŏ kingdom (ca. 57 B.C.). The epic, whose plot derives from ancient legends, is written in an extravagant style in quatrains with five Chinese characters per line. The poet presumes knowledge of the legend, some of which is included here in parentheses.

It begins in the third year of Shen-ch'üeh of Han (59 B.C.), when Haemosu ("a true son of Heaven") comes down to Korea in a five-dragon chariot followed by a retinue of hundreds. While out hunting, he sees the River Earl's three beautiful daughters and loses his heart, "not from lust for the girls,/But from eager desire for an heir." When the maids flee into the river, he prepares a great palace and sets out wine for them. The three are lured inside, and when they are drunk, he captures the eldest, Willow Flower. The River Earl is furious and refuses to give Haemosu his daughter in marriage without proof that Haemosu is from God: "If you are God's own heir,/Prove your powers of transmogrification!" The River Earl changes into a carp, while the king turns into an otter and siezes it. The earl sprouts wings and becomes a pheasant, but the king becomes an eagle. The earl speeds away as a stag, pursued by the king, who becomes a wolf. The River Earl is convinced; a marriage contract is drawn and sealed with the drinking of much wine, leaving the king in a stupor.

The dragon chariot is made ready for the return trip to heaven, but by the time Haemosu wakes from his stupor, his bride is gone. He leaves for heaven alone, never to reappear.

The River Earl is furious and punishes his wayward daughter by stretching her lips three feet long and throwing her into the Ubal stream accompanied only by two maidservants. A fisherman sees the strange group and reports them to King Kŭmwa, who sets a trap and snares Willow Flower. Her huge lips must be trimmed three times before she can speak. The king then recognizes her as Haemosu's wife and gives her a palace to live in. The sun shines in her breast and in the year 58 B.C. she bears a child called Chumong ("able archer"). He is born from a "pottle-sized egg" that frightens all who see it. The king puts the egg in a horse corral, but the horses take care not to trample it. It is thrown down steep hills, but wild beasts protect it. The mother gets the egg and nurtures it until it is hatched. His first words are, "The flies are nibbling my eyes,/I cannot lie and sleep in peace." His mother makes him a bow and arrows, and he never misses a shot.

Chumong grows up, getting cleverer every day, until the crown prince, eldest of King Kŭmwa's seven sons, grows jealous. He tells his father, "If we do not act soon,/He will give trouble later." To test Chumong's intentions, the king sends him to tend horses. But Chumong thinks, "I had rather die than live like this." He would go south and found a nation but for his mother, whom he does not want to leave.

His mother urges him not to think about her. But she fears for his safety, since every knight needs a trusty stallion. So they go to the corral and find the finest horse. They stick a needle in his tongue so that he cannot eat. In a few days he wastes away. When the king sees the skinny horse, he gives him to Chumong, who takes the horse, removes the needle, and feeds the animal night and day. Chumong then selects three staunch friends and they all set out, pursued by the king's troops. When they reach the Ŏm with no way to cross, Chumong calls out to his ancestors, Haemosu and River Earl: "I have come here in flight from danger./Look on my pitiful orphaned heart." He strikes the water with his bow, and fishes and turtles band together to form a bridge over which they cross. Then the bridge melts away, leaving the king's troops stranded. Chumong chooses a site for his capital and becomes King Tongmyŏng ("Eastern Light").

Songyang, king of nearby Piryu, asks Tongmyŏng to be his vassal, making "rash demands," even though (in an archery contest to settle the matter) he, Songyang, cannot "hit the painted deer's navel." (In the legend, when Songyang claims he is the senior ruler because his palace is older, Tongmyŏng confuses him by constructing a palace of decaying wood. Seeing Tongmyŏng's "ancient pillars," Songyang returns home "biting his tongue.")

Tongmyŏng catches a deer, strings it up by the hind feet, and demands a flood to wash away Songyang's palace, saying, "I will not let you go/Till you help me vent my wrath." The deer's cries reach heaven, and a great deluge washes away Piryu. Tongmyŏng stakes his whip and draws a line where the waters should stop.

After Songyang is submerged, "thousands upon thousands" of carpenters are heard building a magnificent palace. Tongmyŏng rules there for 19 years until he rises to heaven (at the age of 40). (Lee 1981)

TRISTINO, GIOVAN GIORGIO
(Or Gian Giorgio, or Giangiorgio)

Italian poet and dramatist, author of *L'Italia liberata dai Goti* (Italy liberated from the Goths, 1547). He was born in 1478 in Vicenza, Italy, into a wealthy aristocratic family. He had the advantages of wide travel and of study in the various cultural centers of Italy before he settled down in Rome to take up a career as dramatist and poet. He wrote the first modern tragedy on Greek models, rather than Roman. His drama masterpiece, *Sofonisba*, in blank verse, was written in 1514/1515 and published in 1524, but it was not performed until 1562, long after his death. Trissino was the first Italian dramatist to use blank verse (*verso sciolto*) for Italian tragedy, which thereafter became the standard form.

In 1547, after 20 years of work, a "correct" Homeric epic appeared, the major work of his life: *L'Italia liberata dai Goti*. The poem describes the Byzantine liberation of Italy from the Goths in A.D. 535–555. Trissino was motivated to write the poem by his distaste for Ludovico's epic *Orlando Furioso*, which Trissino deemed unworthy of Italy. However, his own epic is generally regarded as a failure.

Trissino published a verse comedy in 1548, *I simillimi*, based on Plautus's *Menaechmi*. He also sponsored the young Vicenzan brick mason Andrea Palladio, educating him and giving him the name Palladio. Andrea Palladio went on to become a great architect and author of *Four Books of Architecture*, and almost single-handedly transformed Vicenza into an ancient Roman architectural model.

Trissino died in Rome in 1550. (Durant 1953/1981; Highet 1976; Siepmann 1987)
See also La Italia liberata da Gotti.

TRISTAN
(Or *Tristan und Isold*)

Middle High German Romantic epic (ca. 1210), unfinished, by Gottfried von Strassburg (d. ca. 1210). The source of the poem was the *Roman de Tristan* (mid-12th c.) by Thomas von Britanje, Anglo-Norman poet. Only fragments of the last part of Thomas's poem are extant, portions of the story Gottfried's poem does not reach. It breaks off at 19,000 lines, presumably at Gottfried's death.

The story begins with the account of Tristan's parents, Riwalin (ruler of Parmenie) and Blanchefleur (sister to the king of Cornwall), who meet in Britain while Riwalin is fighting in the defense of Cornwall. When Riwalin is wounded, Blanchefleur nurses him back to health. Riwalin takes her back to Parmenie as his bride. Soon, however, he is killed by the wicked duke Morgan. Heartbroken, Blanchefleur goes into labor and dies giving birth to Tristan. A faithful steward and his wife rear Tristan and give him a courtly education.

Later, Tristan is kidnapped by Norwegians, but he escapes during a storm at sea and makes his way to Cornwall, where he becomes a court hunter and earns the title Master of the Hunt. When his royal lineage comes to light, he becomes knight and vassal to his uncle, King Marke.

When Duke Morolt of Ireland comes to Cornwall demanding a tribute of maidens and youth or else a fight to the death, Tristan fights in King Marke's place and slays the duke. But Tristan sustains a wound that Morolt has told him only his sister, Queen Isold, can cure. Disguised as a beggar minstrel named Tantris, Tristan journeys to Ireland. After he is healed, he tutors the queen's daughter, Isold the Fair, in music and languages until his true identity is revealed. By this time the queen has grown fond of him. She forgives him for slaying her brother and allows him to return to Cornwall.

When Tristan tells King Marke of the younger Isold's beauty, some jealous noblemen, hoping to remove Tristan as the king's heir, suggest that Tristan return to Ireland to woo her as Marke's bride. On Tristan's arrival in Ireland, he slays a dragon that has long threatened the kingdom, earning the right to decide Isold's future.

During the return voyage, Isold's companion and cousin Brangäne fails to guard a love potion prepared for King Marke and Isold on their wedding night. Tristan and Isold accidentally drink the potion, which enslaves the two by love irrevocably. Bound by duty, tortured by desire, the two finally give in to love but keep their affair secret.

To deceive King Marke, Brangäne, a virgin, is substituted for Isold on the wedding night. The lovers continue to meet in secret until Marke learns of Tristan's treachery. The king tries to entrap them, but for a while they elude each attempt.

At length Marke exiles the lovers, but after he discovers them sleeping in a cave, separated by a sword, he relents and invites them to return. But the lovers continue their trysts, even though to be discovered will mean death. Finally Tristan is sent abroad, taking Isold's ring as a token of their fidelity.

Tristan performs knightly deeds in Germany, Champagne, and Arundel (Normandy). In Arundel, in gratitude for his valor, the duke awards him his daughter, Isold of the White Hands, as his bride. Drawn to the very name Isold, Tristan accepts.

The poem breaks off abruptly at this point. If it had continued, presuming that Gottfried intended to remain true to his source, Tristan would have received a wound by a poison spear, which only Isold the Fair could cure. Summoned from Cornwall but deceived by a wrong signal from Isold of the White Hands, Isold the Fair would arrive too late to save her lover. She too would die, of a broken heart. King Marke, learning of the magic love potion that bound them together, would forgive them and order them buried side by side.

Gottfried's poem inspired Richard Wagner's opera *Tristan und Isolde* (first performed 1865). (Garland and Garland 1986; Magill 1989)

See also Gottfried von Strassburg.

 # *TRISTRANT UND ISALDE*

Middle High German verse romance (ca. 1170) by Eilhart von Oberge (12th c.), the poem that introduced the story of Tristram and Iseult to German literature, although it derived elsewhere from one of the most frequently told tales of the Middle Ages. It is also the earliest complete text in any language. In turn, it had a marked influence on later versions, especially that by Gottfried von Strassburg. Except for some fragments, it was not preserved in its original form. The complete text came down in a revised version made in the twelfth century but preserved in a fifteenth-century manuscript of 9,524 lines and 21 sections.

Eilhart's version puts manly deeds before love, and is a mixture of courtly refinement and bathos. It employs rhetorical figures and a lively dialogue, often in alternate lines, or sometimes half-lines. His stylistic devices range from the sophisticated to conventional formulas. Eilhardt shows some originality in inventing a permanant abode for the lovers in the forest. In his world the ordinary rules of conduct do not apply.

After Section 1, a foreword to the epic, the next section (2) deals with the birth of Tristrant to Riwalin, king of Lohnois, and Blanchefleur, sister of King Mark of Cornwall; she dies shortly thereafter. Tristrant is taught the art of knighthood by the squire Kurneval. In Section 3, Tristrant is now ready to travel with Kurneval to the court of King Mark, where he is welcomed. In Section 4, an Irish giant, Morolt, demands tribute from King Mark, who is advised by his counselors to reject the demand. Morolt comes to Cornwall and issues an ultimatum: Either pay the tribute or there will be war. Tristrant challenges Morolt. Upon being questioned by Morolt, Tristrant reveals his credentials as a knight, and the challenge is accepted. They meet on a barren island, and Tristrant kills Morolt. However, he is seriously wounded from a poisoned spear and sails away alone. In Section 5, he lands in Ireland and is taken to the king, who cares for him. The king's daughter Isalde tends his wound with special herbs and heals him. Tristrant makes his way back to King Mark's castle in Cornwall.

In Section 6, King Mark decides to seek a bride so that he will have an heir. As he ponders where to find her, two swallows fly into the palace window,

Tristan and Isold, characters in a German Romantic epic completed in the mid-1100s, sail in a broad-beamed ship. The illustration is from the mid-fifteenth century.

dropping a long hair at the king's feet. It shines like the sun. The king announces that he will consider only the woman to whom the hair belongs. Remembering the golden-haired Isalde, Tristrant undertakes the search and leaves for Ireland. When he arrives, he encounters a dragon that has been ravaging Ireland, and kills it in a savage battle. For this deed, the king of Ireland had earlier promised the hand of his daughter. However, the lord high steward would have the king renege on this promise. The deceit of the steward is exposed. The Irish king agrees to the union of King Mark and his daughter.

In Section 7, Isalde's mother mixes a magic love potion, which she gives to Brangene, the maidservant, to administer to King Mark and Isalde just before their wedding night, after which she is to destroy the remainder. If drunk by anyone else, great misfortune will ensue. Aboard their ship for Cornwall, Tristrant wants to relieve Isalde's depression, and picks up the potion, thinking it a bottle of wine, and pours her a drink. After drinking, Isalde offers the remainder to Tristrant, who drinks it. Immediately a passion for each other engulfs them, and they surrender to it on the rest of their journey. Brangene discovers they have drunk the love potion, but does not tell them about it until she is moved by Isalde's tortured sense of guilt.

In Section 8, Isalde asks Brangene's silence. King Mark appoints Tristrant chamberlain to attend him on his wedding night. Faced with the fact that the king will discover that Isalde is no longer a maid, Tristant and Isalde plan to deceive him by substituting the virgin Brangene on the wedding night. Very reluctantly, Brangene agrees. Afterward, the hoodwinked king and Isalde live an apparently happy life together. But Isalde is afraid that Brangene, who is falling in love with the king after their night together, may reveal their secret to him, so she recruits two squires to lure Brangene into the forest to kill her. She changes her mind when she finds Brangene is willing to continue to help her.

In Section 9, Tristrant and Isalde continue their trysts in secret. Antret, a jealous baron, tells the king that Tristrant and Isalde are lovers. Angered, the king refuses to believe him, but the poison works on him. He calls in Tristrant, tells him what he has heard but does not believe, then requests that Tristrant go away. Tristrant hides in the forest, but the lovers continue their trysts in an orchard behind the castle. In the meantime, Antret brings in a dwarf who has the gift of uncovering secrets. He tells the king he can uncover any deceit being practiced by Isalde. They set up a listening post in a linden tree where they can watch the lovers, but both Tristrant and Isalde discover them. Thinking quickly, Isalde approaches Tristrant and, pretending surprise at his being there, asks why he wants to see her. Tristrant, also thinking quickly, answers that he only wants her to find out why the king hates him. The king softens, and on his return to the palace sends for Tristrant and brings him back to the court, once again in his good graces. But Antret persists in his accusation, and at the suggestion of the dwarf, the king plots a new trap: scattering flour beside the bed of Tristrant, whose footprints will reveal any excursion by him. Tristrant catches on and leaps over the flour, but he drips blood from a hunting wound, which gives him away. The king, in a rage, orders the death of both lovers.

In Section 10, Tristrant flees, jumping from the chapel window into the sea below. Kurneval is waiting, with a steed and a sword. They flee into the forest, but determine to rescue Isalde. In the meantime the leader of a band of lepers passing through persuades the king that a worse punishment than death would be banishment to a leper colony. The king agrees, but as Isalde is dragged away, Tristrant rushes out and carries her into the forest. He builds a hut from leafy branches, where they live happily. One day, Tristrant hears the baying of a dog. It is his old hunting dog Utant, who has tracked him by his scent.

In Section 11, the king learns where the lovers are and determines to find and kill them. In the meantime, a hermit, Ugrim, has persuaded them that they are sinning, so one day as they lie sleeping, Tristrant places a sword between them. Just then the king finds them, but is startled to see the sword between them. His anger leaves him, and after replacing Tristrant's sword with his, returns to his castle without waking the sleepers. When Tristrant and Isalde see the king's sword, they realize what has happened and begin to think. At the same time, the effect of the love potion begins to lose its effect. They find the hermit, and after talking to him they repent. Tristrant offers to return Isalde to the king, who accepts. Isalde is brought back, but Tristrant remains out of favor and banished.

In Section 12, Tristrant and Isalde part. He leaves his dog with her to remember him by, and she gives him a ring. He rides with Kurneval to Brittany and King Artus's (Alfred's) court, where he is welcomed. In a tournament he defeats the best knights, winning the friendship of Walwan (Gawain), who promises to reunite him and Isalde. Artus and Mark are friends, and there is to be a royal hunt nearby in the forest at Tintagel. Walwan delays the hunt so the lovers can meet.

In Section 13, Tristrant flees.

In Section 14, after traveling through a ravaged countryside, Tristrant arrives at Karahes, the realm of King Havelin. He is denied entrance to the capital city, which is suffering a famine. He learns that Riol, a vassal earl, has burned the land and is preparing to besiege the city. As the king's forces prepare a defense, Tristrant and Havelin enter into a binding friendship, and Tristrant is given supreme command of the forces. He marshals them into groups, and marches into a pitched battle, in which the enemy is badly defeated. Havelin then offers his daughter, Isalde of the White Hands, in marriage to Tristrant. Tristrant accepts and weds her, but the union is not consummated.

In Section 15, when Kehenis, son of Havelin, learns that the wedding has not been consummated, he wants to kill Tristrant, but refrains from any immediate action and only takes Tristrant to task. Tristrant then explains that there is a woman whom he loves dearly. He negotiates with Kehenis to return to Cornwall, but first to send Tristrant's friend Tinas there with a message. Tinas arrives at Mark's castle and arranges for a secret tryst with the first Isalde, the Golden-Haired Isalde, when the king is on a hunt. As an identifying sign he shows her the ring she gave Tristrant. Isalde comes—accompanied by Brangene, Gymele, and the chamberlain—and with the hound Tristrant left with her, who immediately recognizes Tristrant. Isalde is convinced, and the lovers embrace and kiss. In the meantime, Kehenis falls in love with Gymele but is rejected; embarrassed, he leaves the next day. Tristrant also prepares to leave the next day in high spirits, unaware that misfortune awaits him. His young squire, Pleherin, believes Tristrant is in flight from the kingdom and reports it to Isalde, causing her to quarrel with Tristrant. Tristrant justifies himself to Pleherin, but Isalde does not believe him. Tristrant departs in anger. The Golden-Haired Isalde regrets her conduct.

In Section 16, after the winter, the Golden-Haired Isalde sends her emissary Piloise to Tristrant, seeking a reconciliation on her behalf. Piloise arrives in Karahes and meets with Tristrant. He describes the mental anguish Isalde suffers for Tristrant's sake. Piloise presses so hard that Tristrant cannot resist. He forgives her and promises to see her again the following May. When May comes, Tristrant and Kurneval travel to Cornwall, disguised as pilgrims. Tristrant meets secretly with Isalde, and their love is rekindled. After Isalde leaves, Tristrant and Kurneval come across a tournament being held by King Mark, where Tristrant defeats all combatants. Suddenly, one of the knights spots Tristrant's scarlet coat underneath his pilgrim garb, and his true identity is discovered. Immediately, Tristrant and Kurneval dash for the forest, with the king's men in hard pursuit. They escape and proceed back home.

In Section 17, Nampetensis, a powerful earl in Karahes, has a beautiful wife, Gariole, of whom he is so jealous that he orders his men to watch her constantly. On one occasion, she sees Kehenis and falls madly in love with him, as does he with her. Nampetensis is especially suspicious of Kehenis, and on one of his frequent hunting trips, locks Gariole in his castle. However, with the help of Tristrant, who obtains a forged key for Kehenis, the two meet. Tristrant returns home to the news that his father is dead and the realm is without a monarch. Tristant turns over the responsibility to Kurneval, while he plans to return to the Golden-Haired Isalde.

In Section 18, Tristrant and Kurneval meet Tinas and ask him to carry a message to Isalde that they will see her in the orchard. But Antret discovers them and notifies the king, who takes measures to bar Tristrant. Tinas finds them and takes them into his care. They assume the guise of two foreign itinerants, but are again exposed by Antret and have to flee back to Karahes.

In Section 19, Tristrant is back in Karahes, where Riol is again ravaging the realm and the kingdom is caught in civil strife. Tristrant again saves Karahes. He takes a boat back to Cornwall, this time disguising himself as a jester. He goes to King Mark's castle, where he is not recognized, even by Isalde. He tells them he loves Isalde, and she, unaware of his identity, is insulted. But when he seems to know a great deal about her, she becomes suspicious and has him brought to her. She is still unconvinced until Tristrant shows her the ring she gave him. For three weeks they enjoy their love. Then Tristrant learns that Kehenis needs him, and he returns to Karahes.

In Section 20, Tristrant helps Kehenis arrange a meeting with Gariole while Nampetensis is away on a hunt, but upon his return the husband becomes aware of the tryst, traps Kehenis and Tristrant, and along with eight other men, engages them in combat. Nampetensis kills Kehenis. Tristrant slays four and wounds another of the enemy, and is himself badly wounded. Kehenis is buried.

In Section 21, Tristrant sends his steward with the ring given him by the Golden-Haired Isalde to ask her help in healing him. If she will come, the ship is to hoist a white flag. If not, a black flag. Isalde immediately sets out with medicines, and the steward's daughter is sent to the beach to watch for the ship. Under threats from Isalde of the White Hands, however, when the ship arrives, the steward's daughter conceals the fact from Tristrant. Tristrant's wife then goes to him and tells him that the flag is not white. He sinks back and dies. As is expected of her, his wife wails his death. But when the Golden-Haired Isalde comes, she approaches the bier and lies down beside Tristrant. As the bell tolls, it strikes deeply into her heart. "Now and forevermore," she cries. "Tristrant is dead!" Her cheeks pale. She can shed no tears. A terrible pressure arises in her breast, and she dies.

When King Mark learns all this, he goes to Karahes and brings the lovers back to Cornwall, burying them in the same grave. Out of Isalde's grows a rosebush, out of Tristant's a grapevine—the two closely intertwined. (TAP) (Holbrook 1970; Salmon 1967; Thomas 1978; Walshe 1962)

See also Eilhart von Oberge; *Tristan.*

 # TROILUS AND CRISEYDE

Middle English poem (ca. 1385) by Geoffrey Chaucer (ca. 1342–1400). The poem, of 3,239 lines in rime royal, is a retelling of Boccaccio's story, *Il Filostrato;* however, Chaucer treated the subject with more humor and employed more finely drawn characters. The poet borrowed and translated some 2,700 lines of Boccaccio's poem and expanded it to emphasize the irony and philosophical elements. The hero, Troilus, becomes more serious and profound in this version. Criseyde, a widow, is both aware of her dignified station and deeply, fearfully in love. Pandarus, Criseyde's uncle, is worldly and philosophical.

In Book I, containing 156 seven-line stanzas, Criseyde's father, Calkas, the Trojan prophet, has fled the Greeks, leaving her behind. Dressed in her brown silk widow's weeds, Criseyde falls on her knees before Hector, weeping and begging his compassion. Hector tells her to put her father's treason from her mind. He invites her to stay on in Troy as long as she pleases. So she remains in Troy, trying to uphold her honor.

Troilus, son of the king of Troy, sees her in the temple and is smitten by love, passion, and desire. He goes back to the palace and tries to learn the craft of love. Stanzas 58–60, entitled "The Song of Troilus," about his feelings of being in love, are taken from the eighty-eighth sonnet of Petrarch. Pandarus, Criseyde's uncle, offers to help Troilus win her.

In Book II, containing 251 stanzas, Pandarus convinces Criseyde that Troilus is literally dying of his love for her. He encourages the two to correspond and arranges for them to meet at a dinner party given by Troilus's brother Deiphebus

Geoffrey Chaucer, center, reads from *Troilus and Criseyde*, in a fifteenth-century illustration.

(or Deiphobus). At one point (Stanzas 217–218), he urges Troilus to feign a fever so as to fool his brother Deiphebus, but Troilus answers that there is no need to pretend, for he is indeed ill: love-sick (Stanza 219).

In Book III, containing 260 stanzas, Criseyde visits the ailing Troilus and gives him permission to love her only in the tradition of courtly love—a medieval code of behavior whereby the gallant knight performs noble deeds for the one he adores, but she remains chaste and unattainable.

At length Pandarus convinces her to allow Troilus to visit her in her bedchamber in his own house. One thing soon leads to another: Troilus goes from kneeling beside her bed to sitting on the bed to sharing it.

In Book IV, Calkas convinces the Greeks to bargain with King Priam for Criseyde, whom he regrets having left behind, in exchange for returning Prince Átenor, the Greeks' prisoner of war, to Troy. Although Hector protests, the exchange is made. The lovers bewail their separation, but Criseyde is to return ten days hence.

In Book V, containing 267 stanzas, Troilus labors to hide his grief, but after seeing Criseyde off, is "lost to joy for ever more." (Stanza 4) Meanwhile, Diomede, who leads her away by her horse's bridle, almost immediately begins a campaign to seduce her himself. On the tenth day, on which she has vowed to return to Troilus, she instead allows herself to be seduced by Diomede. He has convinced her that by now the Trojans are all in prison. Criseyde cries that she has "betrayed the gentlest and the best"; (Stanza 151) nevertheless, she does it, and she remains in Greece.

After waiting in vain for her at the gate, Troilus dreams of her betrayal, which his sister Cassandra, the prophetess, confirms. He writes Criseyde many letters, one of which she describes in her answer to him as "long, complaining." (Stanza 229) He refuses to believe the worst until he sees the brooch he gave Criseyde on Diomede's collar. Troilus rants and flings himself into battle, fighting Diomede in several encounters, but at length he is killed by Achilles.

The last 12 stanzas of the book, called the *Palinode,* follow Troilus out of this existence to view those who grieve for him. He is amused to watch them. He decries those acts of trying to satisfy blind desire and worldly vanities. He tells the reader to embrace, not a lover or a mistress, but Christ, who never betrays. The poem ends with a prayer (Stanza 267), the first three lines of which are taken from Dante's *Paradiso* (XIV 28–30), asking Jesu to "make us worthy to be thine."

Troilus and Criseyde is considered Chaucer's greatest poem. (Chaucer 1971) *See also* Chaucer, Geoffrey.

 # TROJANERKRIEG, DER

Middle High German romance-epic, left unfinished by Konrad von Würzburg (ca. 1225–1287). The last of the poet's three long verse narratives, this poem, about the Trojan War, runs more than 40,000 lines before breaking off abruptly. The poet was inspired by the long *Roman de Troye* by Benoit de Sainte More.

In the introduction, the poet names as his patron Dietrich von Basel an dem Orte. The poet devotes more than 23,000 lines to circumstances leading up to the preparations for the war. When Paris declares his love for Helen, her answer requires over 900 lines. The poem breaks off just before the death of Hector.

A lesser poet added some 9,000 lines to complete the poem, which became immensely popular. It spawned several imitations, among them *Der Göttweiger Trojanerkrieg* (ca. 1300), of more than 25,000 lines, by an unknown Swiss poet, and versions by both Hans Mair (fl. ca. 1390) and Heinrich von Braunschweig (fl. 1400). (Garland and Garland 1986)

See also Konrad von Würzburg.

 # TULSĪDĀS
(Tulsī Dās)

Indian religious poet, author of the epic *Rāmcaritmānas* (ca. 1576/1577), the greatest work of Hindī medieval literature. He was born at Rājāpur, Uttar Pradesh. A Brahman, at a young age he renounced the secular world and became a religious adherent. He lived most of his adult life at Vārānasi (Benares).

In 1574 Tulsīdās began his famous epic, based on the Sanskrit *Rāmāyana*, in the Eastern Hindī dialect of Awadi, probably completing it in 1576 or 1577. This work has become a Hindu "Bible" for the Hindī-speaking area of western and northern India. (For a synopsis of the *Rāmāyana*, see the *Encyclopedia of Traditional Epics*.)

Other works attributed to him are an abbreviated version of the story of Rāmā called *Baravai rāmāyan; Krsna gitāvalī,* a cycle of 61 songs honoring Krsna; verses of Rāmā emphasizing Rāmā's heroism, called *Kavittāvalī;* verses emphasizing Rāmā's gentle nature, called *Gitāvalī;* a collection of speeches in verse, *Vinay pattrikā,* addressed primarily to Rāmā and his consort Sītā; and others.

Tulsīdās died in Vārānasi in 1623, but he remains a dominant voice in religious poetry in modern India. (Dudley and Lang 1969; Embree 1988; Renou 1961)

See also Rāmcaritmānas.

 # TVARDOVSKY, ALEKSANDR

Russian poet, author of several epics, most notably the comic *Vasily Terkin* (1942–1945). He was born in 1910 into a peasant family in a village near Smolensk. During the period of collectivization, his father was killed as a *kulak.* Tvardovsky began writing poetry to strengthen the morale of the people in their hardships.

In the 1930s he became a journalist in Smolensk. His first successful epic was *The Road to Socialism* (1931); his next was *The Land of Muravia* (1934–1936).

Russian poet Aleksandr Tvardovsky, April 1961

The latter poem, written in imitation of an ancient *byliny*, marks Tvardovsky's revival of the genre of the comic epic.

He attended the Moscow Institute of Philosophy, Literature, and History, graduating in 1939. Thereafter he became a war correspondent, reporting first on the Finnish campaign of 1940 and on World War II from 1941 to 1945. During this time he wrote a number of poems, all set from Smolensk south to the Ukraine along the Dnieper. *Vasily Terkin* (1942–1945), a comic epic about a simple soldier, was possibly the most popular literary work of the entire war. During the same period he also wrote a more morose epic about those left behind, *A House by the Road* (1942–1946).

After the war, Tvardovsky journeyed on the Trans-Siberian Railroad in an attempt to portray the array of Soviet people across the country's vast area. The result was *Distance beyond Distance* (1950–1960).

Along the way he garnered four Stalin Prizes and the Lenin Prize (1951). He edited the prestigious magazine *Novyi mir* (New world) from 1950 to 1954, and again from 1958 to 1970.

His last epic, *Terkin in the Other World* (1963) is a satire in which conditions in the Soviet Union are compared to those in Hell. He also wrote poems in memory of his mother and of Lenin. He wrote a poem, published abroad in 1969, in which he revealed for the first time his father's fate.

He died in 1971, having brought the magazine he edited until shortly before his death to a level of international prominence. (Bristol 1991)

See also *The Land of Muravia; Vasily Terkin.*

 # THE TWELVE

Russian epic (1918) by Aleksandr Blok (1880-1921), who is considered by some to be this century's greatest Russian poet. The poem, which celebrates the so-called October Revolution, was written in two days in January 1918 and is acclaimed as the poet's masterpiece.

Blok uses the cadences of popular urban songs of the day, in particular, the *chastushka*, or factory song. The setting is Petrograd (St. Petersburg), where the streets are hung with red banners and the only signs of the city's gluttonous past are a fat priest and a starving dog. The "Twelve" refers to the twelve "sinful" breakaway Red Guards (Bolsheviks), later likened to the Twelve Apostles, as the revolutionaries sought to see the hand of God in the Revolution, which Blok interpreted as a millennial event.

The central event around which the narrative revolves is the accidental shooting by a Red Guard named Peter of his former lover, a beautiful prostitute—Blok's embodiment of Divine Wisdom—because she has been tempted by the material goods offered by counterrevolutionaries.

In the early days of the overthrow, the Revolution was seen as a sequel to the revolution begun by Christ. At the end of the poem, during a snowstorm, a shadowy figure emerges and leads the revolutionaries, while Red soldiers shoot at him. It is Jesus Christ: "Soft his step above the snowstorm,/Pearly-hued his snowy dusting,/White the roses of his crown—/Jesus Christ walks ahead."

However, Blok's enthusiasm for the Revolution was soon to turn to disappointment, and he died three years later after a winter famine. (Hayward 1983/ 1984; Bristol 1991)

 ## THE TWELVE WORDS OF THE GYPSY
(*O dodecalogos tou gyftou,* or The dodecalogue of the gypsy)

Greek lyrical epic poem (1907) by Kostis (Koster) Palamás (1859–1943). The philosophical poem, considered Palamás's masterpiece, combines ancient and modern Greek traditions to express the aspirations and dreams of the Greek people. The hero of the poem is an ancient Gypsy musician who initially symbolizes freedom and art, and embodies the struggle between the ideal and the real. Gradually, in the course of the "Lays," he matures into the Greek patriot, and finally into the Hellene, teacher and citizen of the world. (Palamás 1964)

See also Palamás, Kostis.

THE ULIALAEV UPRISING

Russian epic poem (1927) by Ilia (Karl) Selvinsky (1899–1968). The poem describes the fortunes of a *kulak,* Ulialaev, who seizes the estate of its pre-Revolutionary owner, taking the owner's wife for his own. Later Ulialaev is defeated in an anarchist rebellion by the Red Army. He is shot and decapitated, and his wife is brutally murdered, her body dragged by a horse. The Red Army commander impales her head on a spear.

In the 1950s the epic had to undergo a rewriting. In the new version, Lenin becomes the hero. (Bristol 1991)

See also Selvinsky, Ilia.

ULRICH VON ETZENBACH
(Also Ulrich von Eschenbach)

Bohemian poet (fl. 13th c.), author of the Middle High German epic *Alexandreis* (ca. 1287), one version of the epic romance *Wilhelm von Wenden* (ca. 1290), and probably one version of the epic poem *Herzog Ernst.* A commoner, he nevertheless received a good education and became active at the courts of both Ottokar II (r. 1253–1278) and his successor Wenzel II (r. 1278–1305). Ulrich began his *Alexandreis* in about 1271 with the intention of honoring King Ottokar, but it was not completed until long after Ottokar's death. He wrote *Wilhelm von Wenden* in honor of King Wenzel and his consort, Queen Guta. Scholars believe that he also wrote a version of *Herzog Ernst.*

A Bulgarian version of *Alexandreis,* a fragment of more than 3,300 lines representing about half the original work, was probably influenced by Ulrich's version. (Čiževskij 1971; Garland and Garland 1986)

See also Alexandreis.

URUGUAI

(*O Uruguai*, The Uruguay)

Portuguese Brazilian epic poem (1769) by José Basílio da Gama (1740–1795), described as the best, "most nearly perfect poem" produced in the colonial period. This Romantic historical epic is written in blank verse, in the *academie-Arcadian* lyrical style of the *mineira* school in which academically trained poets from the Minas region "revolted" in an attempt to form a truly nationalistic style separate from Portugal's. It represents, in other words, a break from the style of Camões, Portugal's national poet, author of *Os Lusíadas*.

It relates the story of the Seven Missions Wars, uprisings of the Guaraní Indians of Uruguay incited by the Jesuit missionaries to revolt against provisions of a 1750 treaty. The revolts were met by a combined force of Portuguese and Spanish troops.

These Jesuit padres had settled their converts in *aldeas* (villages), where they were taught under the priests' protection, which was necessary because the Indians were preyed upon by slave traders and plantation owners wanting cheap labor. The Jesuits were the first to protest their treatment and make an attempt to protect them.

However, the king of Spain presented his father-in-law, the king of Portugal, with a gift: the seven villages, which he wanted vacated immediately by the Guaraní for whom they were home. Canto I describes the arrival of the Portuguese, "from far around the purple canopy," bringing their wealth: "The captains come to the merry, laden board;/Their weighty cares are exiled, banished all,/As they pour the wines of Europe in cups of gold. . . ."

The poem depicts the Portuguese and Spanish soldiers' perilous expedition through uncharted wilds, fording the overflowing rivers, passing the great plantations where "the patient earth/Shows its plow-torn bosom. . . ." They arrive at a mountaintop and view for the first time the idyllic villages below: "A broad expanse of fields carved here and there/With tremulous rivulets—how very bright/The fountains and how crystalline the lakes. . . ." (Canto IV) The poem depicts, for the first time, Indian life. The soldiers drive the Indians from their homes, but at night the Indians sneak back. When the fortresses are burned, Jesuits claim it is an act of God. In the battle of Cabaté Hill, 1,500 Guaraní are slain. The missions are razed, and three years later (1759) the Jesuits are expelled and the missions secularized. From the wreckage of San Luis Gonzaga, one of the villages, the Indians send a letter to the governor of Buenos Aires decrying the custom of "every man for himself" instead of the Indian way of "helping one another."

However, the poem is "stubbornly anti-clerical," despite the fact that the poet was a Jesuit, fleeing to Portugal with the other ousted Jesuits. Once there, he was imprisoned and sentenced to exile in Angola, saving himself only by writing a poem in honor of the marriage of the daughter of the marquis of Pombal, minister of the realm. Basílio da Gama's anti-Jesuit tone was probably necessary under the circumstances. Despite the fact that—or perhaps because—it was written by a poet in exile, the poem evinces a new spirit of patriotism and nationalism and the appearance of the Indian character, marking the work as a forerunner of an independent Brazilian poetics. (Basílio da Gama 1977; Coutinho 1969; Putnam 1948/1971)

See also Basílio da Gama, José.

 ## VALENTIN UND NAMELOS

Middle Low German epic poem (mid-15th c.) by an unknown author. The poem, of some 2,600 lines, is a translation from the Flemish, but the original poem was French. It relates the story of twins who are abandoned to die in the wilderness. One of them, Valentin, is brought up as a knight; the other, Namelos, becomes a wild man, living in the forest. After various adventures, each twin marries the woman of his choice. The poem is closely akin to *Valentine and Orson* and to a Volksbuch translated from the French by Wilhelm Ziely of Berne called *Valentin und Orsus* (publ. 1511). (Garland and Garland 1986)
   See also *Valentine and Orson.*

 ## VALENTINE AND ORSON
(Also *Valentin und Orsus*)

Medieval epic of French origin in which Orson, the wild man living in the forest, is captured by hunters and made to live in civilized society. He is educated and taught the doctrines of Christianity. He becomes an exceptional knight, but after performing many chivalrous deeds, he elects to return to the forest to devote himself to knowing God. He returns as an ascetic to his former home, where the sacred and profane are now seen as one. (Bernheimer 1952)
   See also *Valentin und Namelos.*

 ## VALERIUS FLACCUS
(Gaius Valerius Flaccus Setinus Balbus)

Latin poet (fl. 1st c. A.D.), author of an unfinished epic, *Argonautica*. Little is known about his life. His only extant work was begun 15 or 20 years prior to his death, which is believed to have been about A.D. 90/95. In Quintillian's *Institutio oratorio* (probably prior to A.D. 96), the author mourns the death of

Valerius Flaccus. Valerius's work shows a familiarity with the writings of Ovid, Apollonius of Rhodes, and Vergil. His *Argonautica* was lost until 1417, when Italian humanist Paggio discovered four and one-half books of it at St. Gall. It was finally published in 1474. (Bowder 1980)

 # VALMIKI

Legendary author of the *Rāmāyaṇa*. For a synopsis of the *Rāmāyaṇa*, see the *Encyclopedia of Traditional Epics*. (Jackson 1994)

 # VAN DEN VONDEL, JOOST

Dutch poet and dramatist, author of the epic *Johannes de Boelgezandt* (John the Baptist), often called the greatest poet and dramatist the Netherlands has produced. He was born in 1587 in Cologne. He was a self-educated man—he taught himself French—with a deep commitment to morality and to the Counter-Reformation movement. Early in his career he wrote a political allegory entitled *Palamedes* which attacked the strict Calvinists. Also early in his career he aroused the wrath of Amsterdam Protestants with a historical drama, *Gijsbrecht van Aemstel,* which presented Catholic ritual in a favorable light. Another play of the period was *Maagden* (The Maidens), the protrayal of a saint's legend.

In 1564 he wrote *Lucifer,* a drama written in alexandrine couplets, the first of three Baroque masterpieces he was to produce. *Jephta,* a Sophoclean drama in alexandrine couplets, followed five years later. *Adam in Ballingschap* (Adam in Banishment), a drama in pentameter couplets and the second of his trilogy of Baroque masterpieces, appeared in 1663. The third in the trilogy was *Noah,* which appeared in 1667. The choruses of these last works are among his highest achievements.

In 1641 van den Vondel entered the Roman Catholic Church, a courageous act at a time when Catholicism had become an unpopular minority. He died in Amsterdam in 1679. (Preminger 1974)

 # *VAN DEN VOS REINAERDE*
(Reynard the fox)

Dutch beast epic (ca. early 13th c.) by an unknown author. An irreverent and witty parody of society, the poem is considered one of the genre's best. (Brogan 1996)

See also *Reineke Fuchs.*

VASILY TERKIN

Russian comic epic (1942–1945) by Aleksandr Tvardovsky (1910–1971). The epic depicts the adventures of a simple soldier, an ordinary villager from the area of Smolensk. Terkin does everything to excess: drinking, eating, smoking, even sleeping, but under fire he must learn to lie flat and still on the ground. His paternalistic commander is a man of modest means as well, but when combat brings the troop near his home, he invites the whole unit to dinner. Afterward, the commander stays up all night chopping wood for his hard-working wife, left at home alone with all the chores.

Terkin becomes a resourceful warrior, at one point fighting a German soldier in hand-to-hand combat. When Terkin is wounded, lying "on a bed of snow" freezing, he faces Death with defiance: "Then go on. Your scythe take with you./I will live to fight today." He wants to participate in victory celebrations: "Let me promenade a little/With the living on that day!/Let me tap at just one window/In the land where I was born!" He and his comrades triumph and occupy Berlin. (Bristol 1991)

 VAZETJE SIGETA GRADA
(The fall of the city of Szigeth)

Croatian epic by Dalmatian poet Brno Karnarutic (fl. 17th c.), a captain in the Venetian cavalry. His epic tells the heroic deeds of Count Nikola Zrínjski, commander of the fortress Szigetvár, who lost his life in 1566 defending it against the Turk Suleiman II. Zrínjski's great-grandson also wrote an epic about him. (Dvornik 1962; Gazi 1973)

See also Karnarutic, Brno; Zrínjski, Count Miklos.

 VEGA, LOPE DE

See Lope de Vega.

 VERGIL
(Also Virgil; full name: Publius Vergilius Maro)

Latin poet, author of the *Aeneid*, the *Ecologues*, and the *Georgics*. He was born in 70 B.C. on the family estate near Mantua in northern Italy. Although educated for a career in public life at schools in Cremona, Milan, and Rome, his delicate health and retiring temperament and nature made him unfit for such an

A Russian soldier waves the Soviet Union's hammer and sickle flag from the Reichstag to mark the May 1945 fall of the Nazi capital of Berlin. Aleksandr Tvardovsky wrote *Vasily Terkin*, a comic epic whose hero wants to celebrate such a victory, and does.

occupation in the bustle of a city like Rome. He was modest and retiring, much preferring the solitude of country life, so after his university years he returned to his family's farm and a bucolic life more suited to the writing of poetry. However, following the civil war battle of Philippi in 42 B.C. when Mark Antony and Octavian defeated Brutus and Cassius, destroying the Roman Republic, the family lands were confiscated for returning veterans. Vergil's *Ecologues,* ten pastoral poems composed between 42 and 37 B.C., give only vague clues as to what transpired. Some scholars point to certain passages as indicating that Augustus (Octavian) restored his lands after a personal appeal was made.

By the time Octavian (the future Augustus) defeated Mark Antony at the battle of Actium (31 B.C.), Vergil had already gained a reputation in literary circles at court with the future emperor's chief minister Maecenas, a literary patron. Despite his shy and retiring nature, Vergil gained the notice of wealthy people in high places who rewarded him with their patronage. He was much liked and esteemed by such luminaries as Horace. He was awarded an estate in southern Italy and the financial means allowing him to write.

At the time, Emperor Augustus was attempting to restore the Italian agricultural industry, devastated by the war. Maecenas urged Vergil to write a poem on agriculture, which he did. However, the *Georgics* (Poem on agriculture), which took the poet seven years to polish to perfection, is not merely a didactic guide to farming. Although patterned after Hesiod's *Works and Days,* it is a superb philosophical paean to the land, to work, to nature, to all life and its mysteries. The section entitled "Praises of Italy" (III.136–176) is still the most revered.

To celebrate the Pax Romana and glorify the establishment of the Roman Empire under Augustus, Vergil had long worked on a national epic, begun when he was 40—the year after the battle of Actium, the first year of Augustus's reign. He envisioned a patriotic work (the *Aeneid*) dealing with the mythical Roman past, and 11 years later (19 B.C.), he still had not finished his final version, which he reckoned would require three more years. That year he planned a visit to Greece and Asia Minor, the setting of parts of his epic. At Athens he met Augustus and joined his retinue for a return trip to Rome. But at Megara he became ill and his condition worsened on the voyage to such a state that he feared he might die before finishing his epic. If that should happen, he requested that the emperor burn the *Aeneid.* He died shortly after the ship arrived in Italy and was buried near Naples. Augustus refused to honor the poet's dying wish and published the poem, with minor revisions, two years later. (Dickenson 1961)

See also Aeneid.

 # *VEP'KHIS-IQAOSANI*

See The Knight in the Panther's Skin

VIKRAMĀRJUNA VIJĀYA
(Also *Pampa-Bhārata*)

South Indian epic (ca. 950) by Jaina poet Pampa. The epic, written in a smooth combination of Sanskrit and Kannada, retells the Hindu epic *Mahābhārata*, casting the poet's royal patron Arikēsarī in the mold of the hero Arjuna. The epic is noted for its deeply moving passages, for its well-drawn characterizations and colorful depictions of South Indian landscapes and the Kannada court of Arikēsarī. For a synopsis of the *Mahābhārata*, see *Encyclopedia of Traditional Epics*. (Encyclopedia Britannica 1983; Jackson 1994)

VILLA RICA

Brazilian heroic epic poem (18th c.) by Cláudio Manoel da Costa (d. 1789), a member of the so-called "School of Minas" poets, or the "Minas Conspiracy." The poet, in fact, wrote *Obras Poéticas* (1768), which marked the beginning of the Minas School. His epic was written in honor of his native Minas; however, critic Silvio Romero (fl. 19th c.) called the epic "vulgar, prosaic, harsh, futile." Along with many other poets, da Costa was arrested in 1789 and put in prison, where he committed suicide. (Coutinho 1969; Putnam 1948/1971)

VILLAGRÁ, GASPAR PÉREZ DE

Spanish poet and historian (fl. 1610), author of the epic poem, *Historia de la nueva Mexico* (History of New Mexico, 1610). The poet accompanied the 1599 expedition led by Vicente de Zaldívar against a pueblo of Acoma Indians. While the general led a band of eleven up one side of the mesa, on the other side, protected by an eighteen-foot-deep chasm, Spaniards placed a beam across the gorge over which they meant to cross. When only 13 men had crossed, the beam was pulled away. The poet Pérez de Villagrá leapt the gorge and replaced the beam, allowing the others to cross and surprise the Indians from behind. He recounted the escapade in his epic. (Hammond 1927)

VIRA SATSAĪ

Indian historical epic (20th c.) by Suryamal Misrama (1872-1952). The poem, written in couplets in the Rajasthani language, relates the exploits of various Indian historical heroes. This epic, along with Misrama's *Vamsa Bhaskara*, mark the beginning of modern Rajasthani literature. (*Encyclopedia Britannica* 1983)

VITEZOVIC, PAVAO RITTER

Croatian poet, author of the epic *Odiljenje sigetsko*, published in Linz in 1684. He was born in 1652 and earned early renown with his poetry, written at times in Latin and at other times in Croatian. Passionate about the fate of his country, he also wrote political treatises, notably *Croatia rediviva*, published in Zagreb in 1703, and *Bosnia captiva*, published in Trnava in 1712. He died in 1713. (Gazi 1973)

 # VOLSUNGS

According to Norse legend, the name of a royal family descended from Volsung. He was born to King Rerir when, after praying to Odin for a son, his mother was made pregnant after eating an apple sent her by Frigg, consort of Odin. He was also the grandson of Sigi, son of Odin, who became the protecting genius of the Volsungs. The son of Volsung was Sigmund, and his grandson was Sigurd, heroes of the *Völsunga saga*. (For a synopsis of *Völsunga saga*, see the *Encyclopedia of Traditional Epics*.) The legends were probably derived from the wars between the Burgundians and the Huns in the fifth century A.D. A distinguishing feature of Volsung's palace was that it was built around a living tree beside Volsung's throne, probably derived from the Norse custom of such a tree being sacred to Thor and a symbol of good fortune. The family died out after the death of Sigurd's daughter Swanhild. She was killed by her jealous husband, King Jomunrek, trampled to death by horses. (Davidson 1964; Evans 1970; Turville-Petre 1964)

 # VOLTAIRE

Pen name of François-Marie Arouet, French dramatist, poet, historian, author of romances. He was born in Paris in 1694. His father was a notary; his mother, who died when he was seven, was apparently socially well-connected. At the age of ten he was sent to the Jesuit Collège Louis-le-Grand. At the age of 17 he left school to pursue a literary career over his father's opposition.

To appease his father, he made an attempt to read for the law but was too disinterested to complete it. By the age of 20, he was already well known for his writing. But he was soon accused of libel for writing some satirical poems at the expense of powerful people, and in May 1716 he was sent away from Paris. When he returned in 1717, he was imprisoned in the Bastille for 11 months. Once released, he was soon exiled again.

When his father died, he received a small fortune, and later he received a pension as well. But he could not seem to stay out of trouble: he had a quarrel with a Paris nobleman, was threatened with a duel, and imprisoned again.

It was during one of his stays in the Bastille that he added "de Voltaire" to his name.

When he was released, he was exiled to England, where he spent three years. There he became an admirer of the British political system. He became acquainted with the Walpoles, the dramatist Congreve, and with Alexander Pope.

Soon after his return to France, Voltaire was invited to take up residence at Potsdam at the court of Frederick the Great of Prussia. Once there, he tried to influence the emperor's policies. He amassed a huge fortune by a series of clever speculations, but after three years he was asked to leave the country.

He returned to France only to be rebuffed, so he took semi-exile in Les Délices, Switzerland. Later he moved to Fernay, still on Lake Geneva but inside the French border. There he gained the reputation as a champion of social justice for the oppressed. During his lifetime he produced some 70 volumes of literature, including dramas, of which *Zaïre* and *Mérope* are the best known; philosophical tales, the most famous of which are *Zadig* (1748) and *Candide* (1759); history, such as his *Siècle de Louis XIV*; epic poems such as *La Henriade* and the mock-epic *La Pucelle*; and his personal correspondence.

He made a triumphal return to Paris in 1778 for the production of his *Irene*, but he died that same year. During the French Revolution his body was disinterred and borne by honor guard to the ruins of the Bastille, then buried at the Pantheon. (Hibbard 1942)

See also Henriade, La; Pucelle, La.

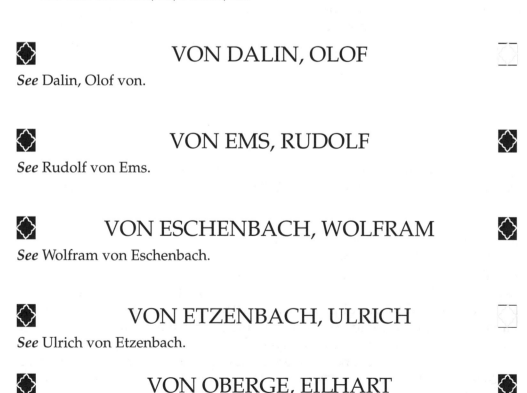

VON DALIN, OLOF

See Dalin, Olof von.

VON EMS, RUDOLF

See Rudolf von Ems.

VON ESCHENBACH, WOLFRAM

See Wolfram von Eschenbach.

VON ETZENBACH, ULRICH

See Ulrich von Etzenbach.

VON OBERGE, EILHART

See Eilhart von Oberge.

VON STRASSBURG, GOTTFRIED

See Gottfried von Strassburg.

VON WÜRZBURG, KONRAD

See Konrad von Würtzburg.

VÖRÖSMARTY, MIHÁLY

Hungarian poet, author of the epic poem *Zalán futasa* (The flight of Zalán, 1825). Born in 1800 in Nyék, Hungary, to an impoverished family of the nobility, he had to begin supporting himself at the age of 15. He tutored students while still a student himself, and eventually studied law. Vörösmarty became a leading figure in Hungarian literary circles, producing works in every genre. He was the first Hungarian to make a (meager) living from literature. In addition to his ten-canto epic, written in hexameters, he wrote a verse play, *Csongor and Tünde* (1830), and lyrics. In 1843 he married Laura Csajághy and addressed at least two of his poems to her: "Dream" and "To a Dreamer." He expressed his devastation over the failure of Hungary's war of independence (1848–1849) in his poem "The Old Gypsy." Thereafter he became a member of Parliament, but soon had to go into hiding with his three children. He died in 1855 in Pest. (Brogan 1996)

VUČIĆEVIĆ, J. BUNIĆ-
(Also J. Bunić-Vučićevic)

Croatian poet, author of the epic *Magdalene Repentant,* a work on a religious theme. Born in 1594, he is known chiefly as a lyric poet, specializing in *versus rapportati*, where the last line repeats the content of the poem. His poems were often on religious themes. He died in 1658. (Čiževskij 1971)

VYĀSA
(Also Kṛṣṇa Dvaipayāna, or Bādarāyana)

Indian sage (ca. 5th c. B.C.?), traditional composer of the Sanskrit epic *Mahābhārata*. In the beginning of the epic it says, "For three years Vyāsa composed the *Mahābhārata* in his mind, and when it was finished, he summoned Ganesha to be his scribe." For a synopsis of the epic, see the *Encyclopedia of Traditional Epics*. (Buck 1973)

 WAJIWAJI WA LIYONGO

(Also *Takhmis ya Liyongo,* Poem of Liyongo)

Swahili epic poem (ca. late 18th/early 19th c.) by Sayyid Abdallah bin Ali bin Nasir (or Ali bin Nasr, ca. 1720/1730–1810/1820). The poem is based on traditional songs concerning the legendary Swahili poet-hero Liyongo Fumo. The so-called *Liyongo Epic* upon which the Liyongo legend rests is considered a "lost epic"; only a fragment remains. For more on the tradition, see *Liongo Fumo* and *Liyongo* in the *Encyclopedia of Traditional Epics.* (Dudley and Lang 1969)

See also Sayyid Abdallah bin Ali bin Nasir.

 # WALCOTT, DEREK ALTON

West Indian poet and playwright, author of *Omeros.* One of twins, he was born in 1930 in Castries, St. Lucia, to Warwick and Alix Walcott, a Methodist family on a Catholic island. Both his grandmothers were descendants of slaves; his grandfathers were English and Dutch. He was isolated not only because of his religion, but also because of his mixed heritage. At the age of 18 (1948) he wrote a notable sonnet about a fire that had all but destroyed Castries. The University of West Indies was founded that year, and he attended in 1950. He received a B.A. in 1953 at the University of West Indies in Kingston, Jamaica. In 1954 he married Faye Moston. The couple had one son. Walcott's twin brother Roderick became a playwright.

In 1958 he arrived in New York on a theater fellowship sponsored by the Rockefeller Foundation. In 1959 his marriage ended, and he returned to Port of Spain, Trinidad, where he founded the Trinidad Theater Workshop. While he composed his plays and poetry, he taught on St. Lucia, Grenada, and Jamaica.

In 1962 a collection of his poems, *In a Green Night,* was published. That same year he married Margaret Ruth Maillard. The couple had two daughters and later divorced. In 1964 his *Selected Poems* appeared; the next year *The Castaway and Other Poems* was published, followed by *The Gulf and Other Poems* in 1969.

West Indian Derek Alton Walcott at an 8 October 1992 press conference at Boston University

In 1971 his play *The Dream on Monkey Mountain* won an Obie award as the best foreign play of 1971. Other works of the period include the autobiographical poem *Another Life* (1973), *Sea Grapes* (1976), and *The Star-Apple Kingdom* (1979). He completed a Litt.D. degree in 1972. In the early 1970s he began serving as a visiting lecturer at U.S. universities: Yale, Rutgers, Harvard, and Princeton. He married Norline Metivier, but has since divorced.

In 1980 he was poet-in-residence at Hollins College in Roanoke, Virginia, and visiting professor at Columbia (1981), Harvard (1982), and Boston University (1985). In 1981 *The Fortunate Traveller* appeared, followed by *Midsummer* (1984), *Collected Poems* (1986), *The Arkansas Testament* (1987), and the epic *Omeros* (1990). In 1992 he was awarded the Nobel Prize for Literature. It is one of many awards he has received in his career.

Since 1992 he has been teaching at Boston University. Part of the year he lives in Brookline, Massachusetts, returning to Trinidad for the rest. (Anderson [Jervis] 1991; Crystal 1994; Marquis 1996)

See also Omeros.

 # WALTHARIUS

Latin heroic poem (ca. 9th or 10th c.) sometimes attributed to a Swiss monk, Ekkehard I the Elder of St. Gall (d. 973), with corrections attributed to Ekkehard IV

(980–1069). Consisting of 1,456 hexameter lines, the poem is related to the Anglo-Saxon alliterative verse fragments by the same name, although they may not predate it. (For a discussion of the Anglo-Saxon *Waltharius,* or *Waldhere,* see the *Encyclopedia of Traditional Epics.*) It is believed to be founded on a lost German lay.

It relates the story of three kings, Frankish Gibicho, Burgundian Heriricus, and Aquitaine's Alphere, who pay tribute to Attila the Hun and provide him hostages. Gibicho gives his loyal vassal Hagano, Heriricus gives his daughter Hiltgunt, and Alphere gives his son Walther with the Strong Hand (Waltharius mance fortis). As children, Waltharius and Hiltgunt are betrothed. The Huns educate the three as befits their station.

When Gibicho dies, his son Guntharius succeeds him. Word reaches Hagano that Guntharius does not plan to continue paying tribute, so he flees back to the Frankish kingdom. Worried that Waltharius may leave also, Attila makes plans for him to marry a Hunnish princess. Waltharius and his betrothed, Hiltgunt, escape, bearing their treasure with them.

When they reach the Rhine, word of their presence—and their treasure—reaches Guntharius. He decides to pursue them for their treasure even though his vassal Hagano has no wish to attack his friend. The troops attack the couple near Worms.

Waltharius positions himself in a narrow passageway at the end of a ravine and engages 11 of Guntharius's men in combat, one by one. After killing them all, he and Hiltgunt continue their journey, but when they reach the plain, they are attacked by Guntharius and by Hagano, who by now feels bound by fealty to his master to join in the fight. All three men are wounded, but Waltharius is able to drag himself away. He and Hiltgunt continue their journey to Aquitaine, where they live happily ever after.

The poem has been called the first chivalric epic, in that it recasts the Teutonic tale in the language of Vergil and of Prudentius (d. ca. 405), creator of the Christian ode and Christian allegory. (Dickens 1915; Garland and Garland 1986; Preminger 1974)

 # THE WAR OF KHOTIM
(*Wojna chocimska,* also *The Chocim War*)

Polish historical epic (1670, publ. 1850) by Wacław Potocki (1635–1696). The poem is a vivid depiction of the 1621 battle when a Polish and Cossack army of 65,000 men successfully resisted the assaults on the city of Khotim (Chocim) by a Turkish army some 400,000 strong. Factual descriptions in the poem are taken from the diary of a soldier who participated in the battle. These are interlaced with satirical and moralistic digressions about the nature of society. The poem, which in many ways resembles a medieval chivalric chronicle, uses rich colloquial language. The poem was not published during the poet's lifetime. (Miłosz 1969/1983)

See also Potocki, Wacław.

WESTERN STAR

American epic, incomplete, by Stephen Vincent Benét (1898–1943). The poet began the poem in 1934, about the western migration of the American pioneers. It was to be perhaps four or five books long. However, only the first book, of some 200 pages, including the invocation and prelude, was completed at the time of his death. It was awarded a posthumous Pulitzer Prize in 1944.

The invocation celebrates those pioneers who tamed rivers and earth and now lie buried under the hills: "I fill the hollow darkness with their names," the poet says.

The prelude, in five sections, depicts Conestoga wagons creaking across the prairie, music twanging from banjo and frying pan, travelers moving west toward an invisible coast.

Book One, consisting of some 4,600 lines, begins with a "wind over England" bringing news of "golden Virginia": a fair, fresh land, an "earthly Paradise" that attracts gamblers, hungry lords, men with "little beards" and "reckless eyes," and poor, restless, striving, broken knights. In London, young Dickon Heron, youngest of ten children, apprenticed since age 13 to a mercer, Master Gregory Knapp, slips out at night from his garret cot to go to the waterfront, until Knapp puts bars on the window. Still, Dickon vows to find a way out, wondering if the stars shine brightly on the ocean.

Meanwhile, Matthew Laynard, journeyman carpenter, and his Puritan wife, Rose, have a new baby whom they name Humility, while a poet makes up poems about a Virginia he has never seen. The little secretary at "The Company" politely rejects the poem.

Wealthy merchant Sir Thomas Smyth, governor of the India Company, sits before his maps and plans the voyages and the men who will lead them: John Smith, Wingfield, Kendall, George Percy, Kit Newport, Bartholomew Gosnold. Across town, Sir Walter Raleigh, imprisoned in the Tower of London by King James I, wishes for ships so he can return to the Guianas in South America to look for gold.

George Percy, eighth son of Northumberland, listens while John Smith fills him with tales of his past adventures, and dreams of seeking "a phantom fortune in the West."

On an errand to pick up a parcel for his master, Dickon Heron stops to watch the three ships set sail: the *Discovery,* the *Hope,* and the *Godspeed.* When they are gone, he realizes the parcel has been trodden upon and knows he will surely be punished. But what does that matter? He has seen them sail!

There are 144 Englishmen who set out on a five-months' voyage "to settle Mars." They land in Virginia in April. The poet describes the passengers and their futures. They are not all young men: Wingfield is 46, a patrician like Percy. He will be president of Virginia before he is killed. Newport, 41, will live ten years and die on his ship, the *Hope,* off the coast of Java. Ratcliffe, "who will take the reins/when Wingfield drops them," will be hated for trying to build a governor's palace and will be killed while trading with the Indians. Sickly John

Martin will live 20 years despite his ill health, always bickering with the councils and burgesses. Robert Hume, the minister who will lose everything in the Jamestown fire, will never complain.

The band settles upriver and are raising a fort when the Indians attack, killing one boy and injuring 17 men. In June, after the fort and a few thatched cabins have been built, the ships leave.

By August the men are dying. George Percy writes down their names as they die: William Brewster, gentleman, dies on the tenth day, "of a worm"; John Asbie on the sixth, "of flux;" George Fowler on the ninth, "of a swelling." On the fourteenth, three: Jeremy Alicock, Francis Midwinter, and Edward Marrish—and so on.

By mid-September half of them are dead. No one governs; it is anarchy. Then for no reason the Indians come, smiling, bringing corn.

John Smith, "step-child of Ulysses," goes exploring. He meets an Indian princess, Pocahontas, who saves his life. Later she will marry John Rolfe, become a Christian, and be presented to the queen as Rebecca Rolfe. Captain Smith will always believe that this is a good country.

Meanwhile, in June 1608, Newport returns from his second voyage to America, his arrival in America having saved John Smith from hanging. (Kendall has been shot for treason and Wingfield has been deposed.) Raleigh still paces in his cell. Tired of harrassment, the Puritans flee to Amsterdam. Dickon Heron has grown an inch, the poet has written a play, the earl of Northumberland speaks proudly of his brother George (Percy), but the dowager countess only wishes he would come home. The carpenter Matthey Lanyard has lost both his wife Rose and their new baby son, leaving him to raise their small daughter, Humility, alone.

By September 1608 some 70-odd artisans and laborers set sail for the New World. One man brings his wife and her serving girl, who will later have the first wedding in Virginia—to John Laydon, laborer.

In 1609, Champlain is in Quebec; Henrik Hudson, looking for the Northwest Passage, finds instead Hudson's River and Hudson's Bay. People are coming to the New World "like bees to the clover-field," only to starve or freeze or die of pestilence.

In London, Sir Thomas Smyth, treasurer of the new Company, sends out broadsides and pamphlets soliciting subscriptions to parcels of land in the New World. The news reaches the carpenter Matthew Lanyard, who has enlisted the help of Katharine, his late wife's sister, in rearing his daughter Humility. He does not want her to grow up like the neighboring "Billington brats," screaming in the gutters of London.

A knight, Sir Gilbert Hay, offers to let Dickon Heron hire on as his servant. Dickon does not trust him, but he wants to get to Virginia at any price. He leaves, knowing he could hang for leaving, realizing the news will grieve his parents. Sir Gilbert treats him cruelly aboard ship, but Dickon thinks, "Some day I shall be my own man." He listens to the men planning on becoming rich planters and having many Indian wives and children. Dickon feels the "small tick-tock in his veins" that says, "To be my own man. To be my own man."

As they approach land, longboats set out to meet them, which they imagine will be "crammed with gold." But they are full of hungry gray-faced men fleeing the land, where they have been forced to eat their own dead to survive. Sir Gilbert realizes that instead of gold, they will find only fever and death.

The Puritans tell their story of leaving London and then leaving Amsterdam to settle in Leyden (Leiden), where they are still outsiders. They try to be good neighbors. They are industrious, quiet, and humble.

In England the carpenter Matthew Lanyard has married his sister-in-law Katharine, who is a stern religious taskmaster to his daughter Humility. But now Katharine carries his son. She hopes to learn to love Humility.

Dickon Heron has now been in Virginia three years. He has been granted three acres, on which he is growing tobacco. Sir Gilbert is dead, as are 150 others. Dickon waits for the supply ship and Jimmy Crews to bring him a plow. But instead Jimmy Crews brings two people: his friend Jack Blount and Jack's sister Alice.

Two months later, Jack has died and the sister, having no one else, marries Dickon. Alice is like a pippin: both sweet and tart. They marry on the very day that Jack is buried: "For life is simple, stripped to the bone,/And the hearth must be swept and the seed be sown."

The Englishmen resolve to be Englishmen wherever they may be. They do not know that they will not be English again. New ships go back and forth. People come: "duty" boys, poor children, 100 maids "guaranteed pure" and priced at 150 pounds of tobacco each, idlers and hangers-on who get in the way of the king's party at the races and cause him to complain, convicts, indentured servants, free men who are younger sons of gentry "with good names" but no inheritance. But "the contented and the portly" stay behind in England.

The Company eventually splits, then declares bankruptcy. The Crown must take over the colony, where John Rolfe has made tobacco king.

The Puritans, who have lived in Leyden for 11 years, must leave. William Bradford and the soldier Captain Miles Standish are going. In London, Matthew Lanyard, his daughter Humility, his wife Katharine, and their sons Elias and Martin plan to join the Leyden travelers to the New World. Mother Billington, son Jacky, his wife Ellen, and the grandchildren are going.

They make two false starts aboard the *Speedwell,* which leaks. Finally, on 16 September they set sail aboard the *Mayflower,* "the Trudging Housewife," with Christopher Jones as master. Of the 131 aboard, only 35 are from the Leyden church. The rest are from London and Southampton. There are 38 grown men, including Brewster and Carver, in their fifties, to the young bachelors, among them John Alden; 18 married women, three pregnant; 20 boys; 11 girls, seven of whom are parish waifs from London; nine servants; five hired men, including two sailors; and a spaniel and a mastiff. They sail in cramped quarters for 65 days. During the journey, one boy, the servant of Doctor Fuller, dies, as do four or five crewmen. One woman named Elizabeth Hopkins gives birth to a son named Oceanus.

On 19 November they sight Cape Cod, but the currents are running fast, and Captain Jones works his ship back into deep water. They drop anchor on the sixty-seventh day in Provincetown Harbor—not Plymouth Rock—and Captain Standish leads 16 men ashore. They see five or six Indian natives with a dog, who all run away. They find an abandoned house and corn buried nearby. They camp out overnight. The next morning, they take the corn and a deer trap back to the ship.

Humility, Katharine, Martin, and Elias wait on the boat for the sight of Matthew Lanyard, who is one of the exploring party, grateful when they see that he is safe.

Susanna White bears her child Peregrine, a wanderer, in the abandoned house. As winter approaches, they know they must find refuge and plant. An exploring party staves off an Indian attack with nobody hurt on either side. They rest on the Sabbath, and the next day they come to Plymouth. They decide that this is the ideal place to settle, and hurry back to tell the others. But they are met with bad news: William Bradford's wife Dorothy has drowned, falling—or jumping—off the *Mayflower*. Bradford, who will go on to rule the colony for many years, writes nothing of this in his journal.

At last they get the *Mayflower* to Plymouth, where Mary Allerton has a stillborn child. As they face winter, these city-bred people fight both scurvy and the New England weather. Once, their common house catches fire, but the flames do not reach the powder. Two men chasing a deer with the mastiff get lost and are caught in a snowstorm, but somehow they survive.

Martin Lanyard, three years old, dies in the late winter. Matthew thinks of their daughter Devoted, left behind in England, who loves her little brother so. Katharine Lanyard knows she must not question God. Humility tries to comfort Elias, who has bad dreams and is afraid to die.

Rose Standish dies, but her husband Miles, William Brewster, and five other men stay sound and nurse the sick. When the sickness passes, there are four women left from the original 18. Four households are completely wiped out, four spared completely—one is the Billingtons, one the Brewsters. All but six children have been saved.

New France grows, New Netherlands begins. The colonies grow, as do Indian problems. And the first slaves are brought to the new land.

Dickon has become a successful planter whom they address as Captain Heron, from Heron's Bend. He recalls that he came for "a lump of gold," but he will die like a squire, with his sons around him. One day he is attacked and killed in his field by Indians. His wife Alice tells the neighbors that they must all get to the fort—nine miles away—by dark. They fill the boat with the living and dead, and as the shallop sets off, they see the fires of their burning homes.

The years pass. Humility Lanyard marries Henry Shenton, the butcher's son, who found God in jail. There are dozens who plant and fail, plant and succeed. There is another house at Heron's Bend. Dickon's sons are now "tall boys with gipsy eyes." Dickon's widow Alice has married Jeremy Crews.

Matthew Lanyard walks through the settlement, thinking of the thousands who are coming, knowing that it is a good thing. As he passes the gallows, old Joan Billington asks him to cut her son Jack down. He tells her Jack was a murderer, tried in court for killing John Newcomen in cold blood. Matthew tries to pray but cannot, at first. "And yet, I know we came in love," he tries to remind himself.

Katharine Lanyard has no sympathy for the Billington woman. She believes that Humility's husband, Henry Shenton, is wicked. Her only son Elias is following after her. She cuts a cutworm in two, and so she would do to any who knows not God.

Henry Shenton explains to Humility that they must leave the settlement. He is not content with some of Bradford's "points of grace." He wants to go where he can have religious freedom, even though their children are small. Humility readily agrees to go. She cannot foresee the future, with Henry twice on trial, twice being driven out—while Katharine Lanyard looks on, "bitter and grim"—to the safety of Rhode Island. They set out, dreaming of a world where none will be whipped or bound, but will live like brothers, "though not yet."

The west wind blows in the faces of Dickon's sons. They look to the west and see a sharp star. (Benét 1943)

See also Benét, Stephen Vincent.

 # WHITMAN, WALT
(Walter)

American poet, author of *Leaves of Grass* (1855/1892). He was born in 1819 at West Hills, Long Island, of Dutch and English heritage. His father, Walter Whitman, was a farmer/carpenter/contractor who gave up farming in 1823 and moved the family to Brooklyn. The younger Whitman was educated in the Brooklyn public schools until he was 12. In 1830 he became a printer's apprentice, and in 1835, at the age of 16, he became a journeyman printer, working in New York.

The following year he began teaching, boarding in the homes of his country pupils on Long Island. In 1842, at the age of 23, he wrote his only novel, a temperance book entitled *Franklin Evans.*

He worked on a number of newspapers and edited several: the *Aurora, The Long Islander, The Evening Tattler, The Brooklyn Daily Eagle, The Brooklyn Weekly Freeman.* He also worked as a carpenter in his father's business. In 1849 he took an extended journey through the north, southern Canada, and the south, working aboard the *Crescent* out of New Orleans, returning by way of the Mississippi and Ohio Rivers.

In 1855 he published the first edition of *Leaves of Grass,* a collection of 12 untitled poems to be read as one work, the longest of which would later be titled *Song of Myself.* Considered radical in both thought and expression, the poems formed a trilogy celebrating body, democracy, and religion. His aim was to transcend traditional epics. Both Emerson and Thoreau early recognized his genius, although many critics attacked his work as immoral. Even Emerson cooled as Whitman continued to emphasize body over soul.

Whitman lived for more than ten years in Washington, D.C. (1862–1873). He worked as a war nurse in a hospital during the Civil War (when his brother George was wounded at Fredericksburg in 1862, Whitman went there to act as nurse), and in 1865 he was a clerk in the U.S. Department of Interior. However, he was discharged after only four months because the secretary of state considered *Leaves of Grass* indecent. Afterward he obtained a post in the office of the U.S. attorney general.

Over the years he continued to revise and enlarge *Leaves of Grass*. In 1867 a fourth edition was published.

In 1873 he suffered a stroke and, partially paralyzed, he returned to his brother's home in Camden, New Jersey, to be with his dying mother. Eventually, in 1884, he realized enough from a Philadelphia edition of *Leaves of Grass* to buy a house in Camden.

Among his other works are *Drum-Taps* (1865); *Democratic Vistas* (1871); *Passage to India* (1871); *Specimen Days* (1875), containing his autobiographical narrative *Memoranda during the War* (1882); and *November Boughs* (1888).

He died in 1892 in Camden, but his reputation continued to grow. More than any other poet, he transformed modern American poetry with his disregard for meter, substituting the line for the rhythmical unit. (Hibbard 1942)

See also Leaves of Grass.

 # WIELAND, CHRISTOPH MARTIN

German novelist, playwright, and poet, author of the epic *Der geprüfte Abraham* (1753) and the epic verse romance *Oberon* (1780), considered his best work. The son of a Pietist Protestant parson, he was born in the small Imperial market town of Biberach, Germany, in 1733. Study at Halle was a family tradition, and the precocious young boy was already writing poetry at the age of 11. Soon after, he began writing Latin verses and then composed an epic poem on the destruction of Jerusalem. He later matriculated as a student at the University of Erfurt, a training school for future administrators of the Electorate of Mainz, where he came under the influence of Cervantes's *Don Quixote*. He had an adolescent love affair with Sophie von Gutermann because she was more polished than most girls he knew. Though she soon tired of him, they remained friends for the rest of their lives.

Wieland moved on to the University of Tübingen to study law, which he quickly found boring and abandoned. He returned to the writing of poetry, modeled on the pre-Romantics. An epic poem on a German national hero attracted some attention. In 1753 he was invited to come to Zurich, the gathering place of young poets rebelling against the current neoclassical fashion. Here he was exposed to a wider range of poetic techniques. When he was 24 he moved to Berne, eager to stand on his own feet. While he was in Switzerland, his engagement with Sophie von Gutermann was broken off. Later he became betrothed to Julie von Bondeli of Berne.

In 1758 he tried his hand at writing plays, winning some recognition, and in 1760 he was invited back to Biberach. He was elected a senator. In 1763 his engagement to Julie von Bondeli was broken off because of his love affair with Christine Hagel in Biberach. In 1764 he was appointed town clerk, in effect minister of the interior of a small urban republic, a position that gave him time to write. In 1765 he married Dorothea von Hillenbrand and had a number of children. He became a frequent guest at the palace of an imperial lord. Wieland did his best work in these years, largely in the neoclassical mold. He finally turned to the writing of novels; his first was published in two volumes in 1764; his second, also in two volumes, was published in 1766/1767.

In 1769 he accepted the Chair of Philosophy at the University of Erfurt—a mistake. His colleagues were offended by his literary successes, and he was dismissed. A didactic, picaresque novel of his attracted the attention of important nobles, and he was invited to Weimar, where he won the attention and then the friendship of Goethe and even influenced him. In 1780 his *Oberon* won the admiration of the upcoming generation of Romantics, although essentially Wieland was a neoclassicist. Wieland never earned a great fortune, receiving only scant help from the Weimar rulers.

During this last period of Wieland's life, John Quincy Adams was U.S. minister to Prussia (1798–1801), and while he was there, he learned of Wieland. Adams acquired a set of Wieland's works in 1799 and almost immediately began abstracting, canto by canto, then translating *Oberon* (1799–1801). He revised it painstakingly for another year. A mutual friend sent a copy of Adams's translation of the first canto to Wieland himself, who praised it for its fidelity.

His old age was serene, and he died in Weimar on 20 January 1813. (TAP) (Adams 1940; Van Abbé 1961)

See also Neoclassicism; *Oberon.*

 # WILLEHALM

Middle High German epic poem by Wolfram von Eschenbach (ca. 1170–ca. 1220), composed in medieval German between 1221 and 1226. It is a reworking of the Old French poem of *Aliscans,* written some 30 years earlier by an unknown northern Frenchman. The French work in turn retells the story of "William," itself derived from legends about an actual person named William, a first cousin of the emperor Charlemagne. It relates how Willehalm (William), march count of Provence, after being defeated by "heathens" (Moors), returns to rout them on the same battlefield. Part of Wolfram's plan was to connect this story with that of Roland, and for this purpose he drew upon both the French and German Roland poems. The poem was preserved in a number of manuscripts. It is written in units, *dreissiger*—sets of 30 lines each, four stresses to a line, 14,001 lines in all, grouped into ten books. The story seems to end abruptly, and in the Middle Ages a later poem with the same characters was read as the sequel. Whether Wolfram intended an additional book is open to dispute.

At the time of the poem's composition, Europe was still involved in the Crusades, but east-west politics were in a snarl, complicated by the emergence of the Mongols into the hostilities, and conflicts within Christian and Muslim ranks. Wolfram's epic displays a more sympathetic attitude, viewing the Muslims not as the demi-ogres and brutes of the Old French poems, but as gentlemen misled by a false religion.

Critical opinion of this poem has been highly favorable. It was carefully preserved for 300 years and widely read, and it has been the source for later literature and operas.

Book I (sets 1 to 57) begins with an invocation of the Holy Trinity, a reference to baptism as the criterion for separating Christians from heathens, and a second prayer to Sir Saint Willehalm. It mentions the poet's recently completed *Parzival*, and the French source for this poem, recently brought to the Thuringian court by visiting minstrels. The next lines introduce his principal characters: the seven sons of Le Comte Heimrich of Narbonne—Guillaume (Willehalm), Bertram, Buov, young Heimrich, Arnalt, Bernart, and Gibert—who were left no patrimony and told to win wealth by themselves. The poem gives the gist of the story situation: Willehalm has wooed and carried off Arabel, daughter of the heathen king Terramer of Córdoba and wife of King Tibalt. She has been converted and baptized as a Christian, taking the name of Giburc; and Tibalt has incited Terramer to warfare against Willehalm.

In the rest of Book I, the battle begins. The Christian knight Vivianz, mortally wounded, continues to fight. With dwindling forces, Willehalm fights desperately, slaying some of the chief kings of the heathen, but finally he is forced to flee.

In Book II (sets 58 to 105), as Willehalm retreats he finds his wounded nephew Vivianz still alive and hears his deathbed confession. He lifts the body onto his horse and heads for the mountains. Along the way, he is intercepted by 15 kings, each carrying a dead kinsman or lord off the battlefield. Ehmereiz, his stepson (Giburic's son by Tibalt), recognizes him and charges against him for "dishonoring" Giburc, but Willehalm spares him, killing seven others while the rest flee. On his way home there are more battles in which more heathens are slain, but Willehalm's horse Puzzat is killed and Willehalm takes over Volatin, the horse of one of his victims, and the dead man's armor. At the gates of Orange, the queen arrives, and seeing Willehalm with a strange shield and horse, mistakes him for one of the heathen. A plunder group of the heathen army arrives herding 500 captive Christians. Willehalm forces them to flee. He convinces the queen of his identity by a scar on his nose. They retire to their home and spend the night together.

In Book III (sets 106 to 161), the heathen army besieges Orange, and Willehalm goes to Orleans. Unrecognized, he is engaged in a joust by his brother. After Arnalt is unhorsed, he recognizes his brother. Willehalm rides on to Etampes, where he leaves his shield at an abbey as payment for lodging. Arriving at French king Louis's courtyard in Munleum, where many distinguished nobles are gathering for a festival, Willehalm is at first ignored and abused. The king hears about him, but the queen, Willehalm's sister, argues that

Willehalm has caused the French woe with his campaigns and is there looking for a new army. She gives orders to lock him out. A merchant from the city, however, invites him into his home.

Later, Willehalm confronts the king, who has Willehalm's father at his side and four of his brothers close by. The brothers spring forward to embrace him, and the king welcomes him after wrenching the crown off the head of the queen. But her daughter Alice intervenes on her behalf, and Willehalm forgives her.

In Book IV (sets 162 to 214), the queen persists in her opposition, and Willehalm is still angered. The quarrel is finally made up, and the queen now intercedes on his behalf, supported by Willehalm's father and brothers, who advocate assistance to Willehalm. During the activities, Rennewart, the kitchen scullion, comes in and awkwardly spills a bucket of water. The butt of jokes, the scullion seizes one of his tormentors and swings him across the room. Impressed, Willehalm intervenes. The lad tells his story: He is a Muslim from Mecca sold into slavery, who has now turned to Christ and is willing to join Willehalm's expedition. The king starts for Orleans, with the queen and Willehalm. They arrive at the monastery where Willehalm has left his shield, but it has burned, leaving no trace of the shield. Willehalm tells how he won the Saracen accoutrement.

Hosts join the king on his way to Orleans, and in Orleans he prepares for battle. Meanwhile, Willehalm's father and brothers are taking separate routes toward Orange.

In Book V (sets 215 to 268), Giburc defends her Christian baptism to her father, Terramer, as she stands on the battlements of Orange and he stands below, gloomy and angry. The battle begins, and the city is set on fire. Willehalm and Rennewart arrive. The king and Giburc watch from a tower as other Christian armies approach to help. Young Heimrich, Willehalm's brother, arrives with the king of Tandaras. All gather at the palace to dine with the ladies, who are dressed in their finest apparel. Old Heimrich praises Willehalm for his action against Terramer and approves of his winning Giburc away from Tibalt. Giburc expresses grief at the loss not only of the Christian princes but also of her Muslim kinsmen, although her heart belongs to Willehalm. Old Heimrich asks her which of the heathen nobles bore her the greatest hatred. She answers that all did except for her son Ehmereiz, who had power against her but did not exercise it.

In Book VI (sets 269 to 313), Rennewart comes to the palace carrying his club and is introduced to Old Heimrich. He sits at the table, but his manners are crude. A group of young squires knock over his club, which is leaning against the wall. Rennewart jumps to his feet, picks up the club, and swings it. The lads scatter. That night, as all are asleep, Rennewart bustles about and seeks out the kitchen, where he lies down.

We now learn how he was seized as a baby for ransom and kept as a slave under the care of King Louis of Rome, who wanted him to be baptized, but he had held out against it. He grew up hating his father, Terramer, for not ransoming him—unfairly, because the father did not know he was there. In the morning, while he still sleeps in the kitchen, the cook takes an ember and singes off Rennewart's beard. Rennewart seizes him and tosses him into the fire, then pours out his anger at the treatment he has endured over the years, when he is after all of royal lineage. The queen has already guessed that he is of her family, but he tells her to keep it a secret. She offers to outfit him for the coming battle. After mass, Willehalm gives his charge to his allies, and they set out.

In Book VII (sets 314 to 361), Rennewart sends back to retrieve his club. They ascend a hill and find Terramer encamped betweeen the hills and the sea. Many of the allies are dismayed at such a flood of heathen and turn back toward France, but Willehalm stands fast. When Rennewart sees the fugitives, who have met some resistance at a defile, he storms toward them swinging his club. The fugitives try to bribe him to join them. Rennewart gives them a choice between his club or passage through a dangerous swamp. They join Rennewart. The news reaches Terramer that the Christians are approaching, and he encourages his army on behalf of all the gods of heathendom. They are to lay waste Orange and Paris, and then go on to Rome, putting to death those who wish to live by Jesus's help.

The Christians arrive. Terramer orders that his gods be erected on tall poles and arrayed with gold ornaments. He marshals his ten armies, led by ten heathen kings, with diatribes against his daughter, who has disgraced them, and the "baptized" followers of "Jesus the sorcerer." The fighting breaks out.

In Book VIII (362 to 402), each of the nine heathen troops and Terramer's own tenth troop enters the battle, one after the other, wave after wave against the Christians.

In Book IX (sets 403 to 450), the poet begins with an invocation to Giburc, "holy lady," then returns to the fighting. Impelled by spurs, Terramer and his tenth troop come at a dead run, leaving the chariots with their lofty gods stranded behind. Six banners of the Christians are isolated and split up, but they rally to one another by sighting other banners and following their battle cries. Old Heimrich, wearing a corselet with crosses on front and back, clashes with Cernubilê, king of Amirafel, and slays him. Bernart of Brubant, Willehalm's brother, is attacked by Cliboris, young king of Tanamark, who flaps his wings like a dragon and wears a boat on his helmet, with jewels that flash when Cliboris wags his head. Cliboris is slain. Young Heimrich kills the son of another king. Rennewart liberates eight captives imprisoned in the heathen ships. Halzebier, heathen king of Falfundê, attacks them and kills one captive, but is in turn slain.

With a somewhat dilapidated club, Rennewart comes to the aid of Gerart. His club shatters in the combat. The Saracens flee toward the seashore; some plunge into the waters, and some into the swamp. Terramer retreats to the ships, and Rennewart sees him. Father and son face each other, but nothing happens. Terramer waits, impassive and unflinching. Rennewart withdraws, then goes back to the fighting, slaying heathen after heathen. The wounded Terramer boards his escape ship. Christian victory is proclaimed and booty is taken. The victors feast on the enemy's food supplies. The poet comments that

Jesus gave the Christians the victory and Giburc to Willehalm. However, he asks himself, was it a sin to slaughter the unbaptized like cattle? His answer is yes, for they too are God's handiwork.

In Book X (sets 451 to 467), the wounded are cared for, and the Christian princes prepare to depart with their vassals. Willehalm seeks his friend Rennewart and cannot find him, and laments the loss. He praises Rennewart's role: He has redeemed Willehalm's kinsmen, brought back the Frenchmen when they were deserting, fought the enemy, and upheld the honor of baptism. His brother Bernart comes and scolds him for such immoderate sorrow. It is "womanish." Great trouble demands gallant courage. Willehalm and six other strong men of such high birth must be lords over countries. Lands and the treasures of land cannot be won except by blood and sword blades. He too grieves for Rennewart, and they will seek him by hill and valley, but they must also depart this field where so many corpses lie. If Rennewart has been captured, they have 20 or more high kings important enough that they can be exchanged for him. Willehalm must go home and give an account of the battle. To protect their country on their return, he must have hostages. They begin to collect highborn heathen prisoners for this purpose. Among them is King Matribleiz of Scandinavia, but when the captives are brought before Old Heimrich, Matribleiz is set free to gather up the 23 dead kings slain in the first battle and any others, and arrange for taking them back to their own countries for burial. For this purpose, Willehalm provides an escort through Christian territory.

Willehalm begins to magnify his lamentation. Such conduct, the wise Gibert tells him, does not befit a man whom God has provided with a victorious army.

The text breaks off here; apparently the poem is incomplete. A minority of scholars, however, suggest that Rennewart perished in the battle, and point out that since the epic begins with the invasion by the heathens and ends with their withdrawal, it is complete. (TAP) (Passage 1977)

See also Parzival; Wolfram von Eschenbach.

 # *WILLEHALM VON ORLENS*

Middle High German epic (ca. 1235–1240) by Rudolf von Ems (d. 1252/1253). The poem was written at the behest of Count Johannes von Ravensburg, who wanted a translation of a lost French work. Konrad von Winterstetten recommended Rudolf von Ems for the assignment. The resultant poem, of almost 16,000 lines, was widely popular, as evidenced by the fact that 76 copies of the manuscript exist; it is also the subject of frescos painted about 1400 in the castle of Runkelstein in South Tyrol.

It tells the story of Willehalm, orphaned when his knight father is killed by Jofrit (Godfroi) von Bouillon. Jofrit adopts Willehalm and takes him to be reared at the English court, where Willehalm falls in love with the king's daughter Amalie. When the king announces that a political marriage has been arranged for his daughter, Willehalm attempts to elope with her but is apprehended and

American poet William Carlos Williams rehearses with actors for the 1949 New York premiere of his play *Dream of Love*.

wounded. The king pardons him, with the stipulation that he go abroad and take a vow of silence until Amalie releases him from it. Willehalm keeps his vow, conducting himself at all times with decorum, performing many chivalrous deeds. Finally Amalie releases him from his vow, and the two are married. (Garland and Garland 1986)

See also Rudolf von Ems.

 # WILLIAMS, WILLIAM CARLOS

American poet, author of *Paterson* (1946/1948/1950/1951/1958, complete edition 1963). He was born in 1883 in Rutherford, New Jersey. He received an M.D. degree from the University of Pennsylvania in 1906, did graduate work in pediatrics in Leipzig, and returned to Rutherford in 1910 to set up practice, raise a family—his sons are William Eric and Paul H. Williams—and write poetry. He became a friend of Ezra Pound and was influenced by his school of imagism.

Among his volumes of verse were *The Tempers* (1913), *Al Que Quirer!* (1917), *Kora in Hell* (1920), *Sour Grapes* (1921), *Collected Poems* (1934), *Later Collected*

Poems (1950), *Collected Earlier Poems* (1951), *Pictures from Brueghel and Other Poems* (1963, for which he was posthumously awarded the Pulitzer Prize), and his five-volume epic *Paterson,* published separately in 1946, 1948, 1950, 1951, and 1958, with a complete edition appearing in 1963. He also wrote novels, short stories, and plays.

In his search for "a redeeming language," Williams eschewed traditional rhyme and meter and developed the "variable foot" to express idiomatic speech patterns. His poetry and his theories as set forth in *Selected Essays* (1954), *Selected Letters* (1951), and *Autobiography of William Carlos Williams* (1951) exerted a great influence over twentieth-century American poetry, such that he became this century's most widely imitated poet. He died in 1963 in Rutherford, New Jersey. (Williams 1967; Williams 1992)

See also Paterson.

 # WIS AND RAMIN

(Also *Vis va Ramin* or *Visramiani,* The story of the loves of Vis and Ramin)

Persian romance epic (11th c.) by Fakhr al-Din Gorgani (or Gurgani, fl. 1054); also a Georgian prose version of the twelfth century traditionally ascribed to Sargis Tmogveli, a feudal magnate from the Tamaran period. It is a parallel to the Irish story of Diarmaid and Grainne, or Tristam and Iseult; however, it has not been established that the Persian poem is derived from the Tristan story. It has been theorized that the same theme might have developed due to certain parallels in the sociological and ideological development in the two regions. The Persian version dates back to an Iranian romance of Parthian times.

The meeting of the two is described as electric. When Ramin sees Vis, "it was as if lightning shown forth from a cloud, or suddenly the sun arose; and at her appearing the heart of Ramin was taken captive." At one look, his soul is "reft from him." The fire of love burns his brain. "From his love such a tree came forth, whose fruit was roaming in the field and madness." He falls from his horse in a faint and lies unconscious for a long time.

Ramin becomes lovesick: "He wept without ceasing." His sickness bears a similarity to Orlando's in *Orlando Furioso:* "He roamed about like a madman like a wild ass and a wild goat he avoided men." (Brogan 1996; Morrison 1972)

See also Tristan.

 # WOLFRAM VON ESCHENBACH

Middle High German poet, author of three epic poems, *Parzival* (late 12th/ early 13th c.), *Willehalm,* and *Titurel,* as well as eight surviving lyric poems. He was born ca. 1170 of noble parentage. He lived at Eschenbach, which is probably the present-day village by that name located near Ansbach. Although his parents were of high birth, Wolfram was poor and had to depend upon the patronage of Landgraf Hermann of Thuringia. In his writings he stated that he was unlettered; however, evidence suggests that he was not. According to his writings, he chose as his profession that of a knight, but history suggests that his true profession was that of a poet.

His poetry was widely read and, in some arenas, acclaimed; although Gottfried von Strassburg is thought to have had Wolfram in mind when he wrote some scathing criticism.

Early in the 1200s Wolfram wrote the epic *Parzival*. The following epic, *Willehalm*, was never finished. A third, *Titurel*, exists only in two fragments.

Wolfram died ca. 1226. He appears as a character in Richard Wagner's *Tannhäuser*. (Wolfram von Eschenbach/ Passage 1984; Garland and Garland 1986)

See also Parzival; Titurel; Willehalm.

 YAMEN

(Also Yama)

In early Vedic literature, Yamen (Yama) rules with his sister-wife Yami in a sort of Valhalla for fallen warriors, where they enjoy all sorts of carnal pleasures. Later, when Brahman gods enter the picture, Yamen becomes the Hindu god of the dead, king of the underworld, grim and harsh ruler over the south, and one of the guardians of the months. In his grim aspect, he appears in Southey's *The Curse of Kehama*. (Colum 1930; Koster 1964; Sykes 1993)

 YUSUF AND ZULEIKA

(*Yūsof o Zalīkhā*, or *Yūsuf u Zulaikhā*, or *Zulaykha*)

The name of more than one Persian epic. One epic (ca. mid-12th c.), by an unknown author, was sometimes erroneously attributed to Firdausi, who died in 1020. The poem is based on the Koranic version of the love of Joseph and Potiphar's wife (known as Zulaykha in Islamic tradition), a popular subject in Persian literature. The biblical version of the story is found in Genesis 39:7–23. The Koranic version is to be found in 12.30–31. Persian poets have treated the tale as a tragic love story, portraying Zuleika as having irresistible beauty.

Rūmī (1207–1273), in his *Masnavī-ye Ma'navi* (Book VI:4020–4043), writes of Joseph and Zuleika in his poem *The Phrasing Must Change*. He describes Zuleika's love: "Zuleika let *every*thing be the name of Joseph, from celery seed/ to aloes-wood. She loved him so much, she concealed his name/in many different phrases, the inner meanings/known only to her. . . ." (Book VI:4020–4043)

The most celebrated version of the work is by Jāmī (Nū al-Dīn 'Abd al-Rahmān Jāmī, 1414–1492), the last great classical figure in Persia's golden age of literature. Jāmī based his *masnavī* version on the Koranic account, and in this excerpt he describes how Zulaikha's reputation is sullied: "The women of Memphis, who heard the tale first,/The whispered slander received and nursed./Then, attacking Zulaikha for right and wrong,/Their uttered reproaches were loud and long: 'Heedless of honour and name she gave/The love of her heart to the Hebrew slave. . . .'"

Potiphar's wife pursues Joseph in a Byzantine codex from the sixth century. The biblical version, told in Genesis, is similar to Persian epics with the same theme, in which Joseph is Yūsuf and Potiphar's wife is known as Zulaikha.

Hearing the slander, Zulaikha invites the women of Memphis to a banquet, ending the feast with an orange and knife at each place. She asks the dames if they would like to see her "Hebrew boy." They vow not to cut into their oranges until they see him for themselves. She sends him a message: "Come, free-waving cypress, come forth to us./Let us worship the ground which thy dear feet press. . . ."

But Yūsuf does not come, so she hurries to his house, kneels at his feet, and tells him, "For thee have I forfeited all: my name/Through thee has been made a reproach and shame." She begs him: "Yet let not the women of Memphis see/That I am so hated and scorned by thee."

Yūsuf's heart softens, and he allows himself to be decked out in gay bejeweled garb. The poet describes Yūsuf's appearance at great length, from the "scented locks of his curling hair" to "so dainty a waist" to his "shadow-like" walk in shoes fastened with rubies and pearls, then says, "Too weak were my tongue if it tried to express/The charm of his wonderful loveliness." They go back to the party where "The women of Memphis beheld him, and took/From that garden of glory the rose of a look./One glance at his beauty o'erpowered each soul/And drew from their fingers the reins of control." The women slash themselves terribly while trying to cut their oranges. "Of those who wounded their hands, a part/Lost reason and patience, and mind and heart. . . ." (Ralph T. H. Griffith, trans.) Some flee madly, aflame with love. (Kritzeck 1964; Moyne and Barks 1984; Siepmann 1987)

See also Jāmī, Nūr al-Dīn 'Abd al-Rahmān; Rūmī, Jalal ud-Dīn.

 ## ZADONSHCHINA

Russian military epic (14th c.) on the same subject covered in *The Tale of Igor's Campaign* (12th c.). This version records a victory of the Russians over the Mongols, rather than a defeat. Some claim that the Igor epic is an eighteenth-century forgery adapted from *Zadonshchina*; however, most scholars believe *Zadonshchina* to be the later tale, although the two are obviously related. A twentieth-century poet, Marina Tsvetaeva (1892–1941), echoes both epics in her collection of poems *The Swans' Stand* (1922), in which she imagines the hardships of battle, praises the heroes, and grieves for the fallen. (Bristol 1991)

 ## ZALÁN FUTÁSA

Hungarian epic poem (1835) by Mihály Vörösmarty (1800–1855). (Bristol 1991)
  See also Vörösmarty, Mihály.

 ## ZRÍNJSKI, COUNT MIKLÓS
(Or Zrínyi, Nikola)

Hungarian poet, statesman, and general, author of the epic *Szigeti Veszedelem* (1645/1646). He was born in 1620 in Csákvár, Hungary, into a wealthy and aristocratic family of the oldest Croatian nobility. Three years after his birth the family converted to Catholicism. He was educated by Jesuits who, with their Baroque style of literature, influenced him in his own style.

Zrínjski wrote essays on military and political science. He was particularly interested in the Turkish invasion of Suleiman II in 1566 during which his great-grandfather, Count Nikola Zrínjski, commanded the forces at the fortress Szigetvár. The count lost his life while leading his garrison in an attempted sortie. In 1645–1646 he composed an epic poem on the event, entitled *Szegeti Veszedelem*, the first epic poem written in the Hungarian language, and still considered the finest.

In 1647, Zrínjski became viceroy of Croatia and his goal was to drive the Turks out of Hungary. He became the outstanding military leader of the seventeenth century. In 1664 he organized an anti-Hapsburg organization, known as the Zrínjski Conspiracy, with hopes of returning his country to home rule. However, that year he was killed by a wild boar. He died in Csáktornya in 1644.

His second in command was his brother Petar, also an outstanding military leader and Croatian poet and writer in his own right.

Count Nikola Zrínjski's exploits were also celebrated in a seventeenth-century Croatian epic, *Vazetje Sigeta grada* (The fall of the city of Szigeth), by Brno Karnarutic. (Dvornik 1962; Gazi 1973)

See also *Vazetje Sigeta Grada.*

 # ZUKOFSKY, LOUIS

American poet, author of the epic poem *"A,"* begun in 1928, completed in 1974. He was born in 1904 in New York City to Chana and Pinchos Zukofsky, Yiddish-speaking immigrants. Louis was the first child in the family to be born in the United States. He grew up in the Jewish Quarter of New York's Lower East Side. Anxious to please his mother, Zukofsky became an excellent student at the public school. When he was four, he began going with his older brother to a Yiddish theater, the Thalia, on the Bowery. By the age of nine, he had seen "a good deal of Shakespeare, Ibsen, Strindberg and Tolstoy performed—all in Yiddish." At the age of 11 he won a prize in English class for reading all of Shakespeare's plays and answering questions about them.

He attended Columbia University, where he was among the wide circle of friends of Mortimer Adler, who later remembered him as "pale and frail." His professor, Mark Van Doren, in a 1927 article "Jewish Students I Have Known," described him as "a pale and subtle poet" with a "painfully inarticulate soul." While at Columbia, Zukofsky became interested in literature and Marxism. He joined the Boar's Head Society, whose editors took turns editing and writing for a periodical, *Morningside.* In 1924 he received his M.A. in English.

Soon after leaving Columbia he wrote "Poem Beginning 'The,' " a poem in six movements that he said was "a direct reply" to Eliot's *The Waste Land.* He sent the poem to Ezra Pound, knowing that Pound was encouraging, promoting, and publishing new talent. The result was a friendship that lasted until Pound's death. Pound also was responsible for putting him in touch with William Carlos Williams, Basil Bunting, and Carl Rakosi.

In 1928 he began a more comprehensive work, which he called the "poem of a life": *"A."* He was to work on this poem, consisting of 147 poems divided into 24 parts, or movements, for almost 50 years, completing it in 1974, just four years before he died.

In 1931, through Pound's efforts, Harriet Monroe invited Zukofsky to edit an issue of *Poetry* (Chicago), but his own poetry was not published in book form until 1965.

In 1939 he married the composer-musician Celia Thaew. Their son Paul, a child prodigy, was born in 1943. Paul Zukofsky eventually became a concert violinist.

He spent many years teaching at Brooklyn Polytech, once noting in a letter to Pound that he could not teach at Columbia because he was Jewish. Pound's anti-Semitism was a source of conflict for Zukofsky. After World War II, he broke free of the influence of Pound's style and developed a style uniquely his own.

Besides his epic poem, his published works include *All: The Collected Short Poems, 1923–64* (1971); *Autobiography* (1970); *55 Poems; Prepositions*, a collection of criticism (1967); and *A Test of Poetry*, a would-be textbook (1938, publ. 1948, 1964) He also wrote a novel, *Little*, published in 1970. Two monumental works undertaken late in life were a long critical essay, *Bottom: On Shakespeare* (begun in 1947, finished in 1963), and *Catullus*, a translation in collaboration with his wife Celia.

Zukofsky died in 1978, never having achieved the recognition to which his work entitled him. (Ahearn 1983; Perelman 1994; Zukofsky 1970)

See also "A."

BIBLIOGRAPHY

Books

Abdalla bin Ali, Sayyid. *Al-Inkishafi*. James de Vere Allen, trans. Nairobi: East African Literary Bureau, 1977.

Adams, John Quincy. *Oberon. A Poetical Romance in Twelve Books Translated from the German of Wieland (1799–1801)*. A. B. Faust, intro. New York: F. S. Crofts, 1940.

Ahearn, Barry. *Zukofsky's "A." An Introduction*. Berkeley: University of California Press, 1983.

Allen, J. W. T., trans. *The Customs of the Swahili People: The Desturi Za Waswahili of Mtoro bin Mwinyi Bakari*. Berkeley: University of California Press, 1981.

Aly, Lucile F. *John G. Neihardt*. Boise, ID: Boise State University Press, 1976.

Anderson, George K., and William E. Buckler. *The Literature of England in 2 Volumes*. Glenview, IL: Scott Foresman, 1966.

Anderson-Imbert, E. *Spanish-American Literature, A History in 2 Volumes*. Detroit, MI: Wayne State University Press, 1969.

Arberry, A. J., trans. *Tales from the Masnavi*. London: Allen & Unwin, 1961.

Ariosto, Ludovico. *Cinque Canti*. Alexander Sheers and David Quint, trans. Berkeley: University of California Press, 1996.

———. *Orlando Furioso. In 2 Volumes*. Barbara Reynolds, trans. Harmondsworth, Middlesex: Penguin Books, 1973 (Vol. 1) and 1977 (Vol. 2).

Arnold, Edwin. *The Light of Asia or The Great Renunciation*. New York: A. L. Burt, n.d.

Arshad, Mohammed. *An Advanced History of Muslim Rule in Indo-Pakistan*. Decca: Ideal Publications, 1967.

Atkinson, William C., trans. *Luis Voz de Camões, The Luciads*. Harmondsworth, Middlesex: Penguin Books, 1952.

Attar, Farid ud-Din. *The Conference of the Birds.* Afkham Darbandi and Dick Davis, trans. Harmondsworth, Middlesex: Penguin Books, 1984.

————. *Muslim Saints and Mystics. Episodes from the Tadhkirat al-Auliya' (Memorial of the Saints).* A. J. Arberry, trans. London: Arkana, 1966/1990.

Barber, R. W. *Arthur of Albion: An Introduction to Arthurian Literature and Legends of England.* London: Cambridge University Press, 1961.

Barlow, Joel. *The Works of Joel Barlow.* Vol. II: *Poetry.* William K. Bottorff and Arthur L. Ford, eds. Gainesville, FL: Scholars' Facsimiles and Reprints, 1970.

Basílio da Gama, José. *The Uruguay.* Sir Richard Burton, trans. Frederick G. H. García and Edward Stanton, eds. Berkeley: University of California Press, 1977.

Beazley, Mitchell, ed. *The Illustrated Biographical Dictionary.* Douglas Harvey and Don E. Fehrenbacher, cons. eds. New York: Dorset Press, 1985.

Beck, Warren A. *New Mexico. A History of Four Centuries.* Norman: University of Oklahoma Press, 1962.

Benét, Stephen Vincent. *Western Star.* New York: Farrar & Rinehart, 1943.

Bernheimer, Richard. *Wild Men of the Middle Ages.* Cambridge: Harvard University Press, 1952.

Bernstein, Michael. *The Tale of the Tribe: Ezra Pound and the Modern Verse Epic.* Princeton, NJ: Princeton University Press, 1980.

Blackburn, Stuart H., and A. K. Ramanujan, eds. *Another Harmony, New Essays on the Folklore of India.* Berkeley: University of California Press, 1986.

Blackburn, Stuart H., et al., eds. *Oral Epics in India.* Berkeley: University of California Press, 1989.

Blair, Walter, and Franklin J. Meine. *Mike Fink, King of the Mississippi Boatmen.* Westport, CT: Greenwood Press, 1933.

Blake, William. *Poems and Prophecies.* New York: Everyman's Library, Alfred A. Knopf, 1991.

Block, Haskell M., and Robert G. Shedd, eds. *Masters of Modern Drama.* New York: Random House, 1962.

Bly, Robert, ed. *Neruda and Vallejo. Selected Poems.* Robert Bly, Joseph Knoepfle, and James Wright, trans. Boston: Beacon Press, 1971.

Boiardo, Matteo Mario. *Orlando Innamorato.* Charles Stanley Ross, trans. Berkeley: University of California Press, 1989, 1995.

Botkin, B. A., ed. *A Treasury of Western Folklore.* New York and Avenel, NJ: Wings Books, 1975.

Bowder, Diana, ed. *Who Was Who in the Greek World.* New York: Washington Square Press, 1984.

————. *Who Was Who in the Roman World.* New York: Washington Square Press, 1980.

Bowra, C. M. *From Virgil to Milton.* London: Macmillan, 1961.

Branca, Vittore. *Boccaccio. The Man and His Works.* Richard Monges, trans. New York: New York University Press, 1976.

Briggs, Katharine. *The Vanishing People. Fairy Lore and Legends.* New York: Pantheon Books, 1978.

Bristol, Evelyn. *A History of Russian Poetry.* New York, Oxford: Oxford University Press, 1991.

Brogan, T. V. F., ed. *The Princeton Handbook of Multicultural Poetries.* Princeton, NJ: Princeton University Press, 1996.

Brotherston, Gordon, ed. *Latin American Poetry.* Cambridge: Cambridge University Press, 1975.

Browne, Edward Granville. *Literary History of Persia.* Vol. 2: *From Firdausi to Sa'di.* Cambridge: Harvard University Press, 1983.

Brundage, Burr Cartwright. *A Rain of Darts. The Mexican Aztecs.* Austin: University of Texas Press, 1972.

Brunetière, Ferdinand. *Manual of the History of French Literature.* Ralph Derechef, trans. New York: Haskell House Publishers Ltd., 1970.

Brunner, Edward. *Splendid Failure: Hart Crane and the Making of the Bridge.* Urbana: University of Illinois Press, 1985.

Buck, William. *Mahabharata.* Berkeley: University of California Press, 1973.

————. *Ramayana.* Berkeley: University of California Press, 1976.

Bullfinch, Thomas. *Bullfinch's Mythology.* New York: Thomas Y. Crowell, 1970.

Burgess, Glyn S., and Anne Cobby, trans. *The Pilgrimage to Charlemagne and Aucassin and Nicolette.* New York: Garland, 1989.

Burnett, Paula, ed. *The Penguin Book of Caribbean Verse in English.* Harmondsworth, Middlesex: Penguin Books, 1986.

Chaucer, Geoffrey. *The Canterbury Tales.* Donald R. Howard, ed. Harmondsworth, Middlesex: Penguin Books, 1969.

————. *Troilus and Criseyde.* Nevill Coghill, trans. Harmondsworth, Middlesex: Penguin Books, 1971.

Chrétien de Troyes. *The Complete Romances.* David Straines, trans. Bloomington: Indiana University Press, 1990.

Christenson, Paul. *Charles Olson: Call Him Ishmael.* Austin: University of Texas Press, 1979.

Čiževskij, Dmitrij. *Comparative History of Slavic Literatures.* Richard Noel Porter and Martin P. Rice, trans. Serge A. Zenkousky, ed. Nashville, TN: Vanderbilt University Press, 1971.

Clauss, James J. *The Best of the Argonauts.* Berkeley: University of California Press, 1993.

Colum, Patrick (Padraic). *Myths of the World.* New York: Universal Library, Grosset and Dunlap, 1930.

Connelly, Bridget. *Arab Folk Epic and Identity.* Berkeley: University of California Press, 1986.

Cortés, Hernán. *Five Letters, 1519–1526.* J. Bayard Morris, trans. New York: Robert M. McBride, 1929.

Coutinho, Afrânio. *An Introduction to Literature in Brazil.* Gregory Rabasso, trans. New York: Columbia University Press, 1969.

Cox, George C. *An American Epic.* Francestown, NH: Golden Quill Press, 1975.

Crane, Hart. *The Complete Poems and Selected Letters and Prose of Hart Crane.* Brom Weber, ed. New York: Anchor Books, Doubleday, 1933, 1966.

Crystal, David. *Cambridge Biographical Dictionary.* Cambridge: Cambridge University Press, 1994.

Curnow, A., comp. *The Penguin Book of New Zealand Verse.* Harmondsworth, Middlesex: Penguin Books, 1960.

Dante Alighieri. *The Divine Comedy. Cantica 1: Hell (L'Inferno).* Dorothy L. Sayers, trans. Harmondsworth, Middlesex: Penguin Books, 1949/1979.

———. *The Divine Comedy. Paradiso.* Allen Mandelbaum, trans. New York: Bantam Books, 1986.

———. *The Divine Comedy. Purgatorio.* Allen Mandelbaum, trans. New York: Bantam Books, 1982/1984.

Davidson, H. R. Ellis. *Gods and Myths of Northern Europe.* Baltimore and Harmondsworth, Middlesex: Penguin Books, 1964.

Davis, James Herbert. *Fénelon.* Boston: Twayne, 1979.

Deutsch, Babette. *Poetry Handbook.* New York: HarperCollins, 1974.

Dickens, Bruce, ed. *Runic and Heroic Poems of the Old Teutonic Peoples.* Cambridge: Cambridge University Press, 1915.

Dickinson, Patric, trans. *Vergil, The Aeneid.* New York: Mentor Books, 1961.

Douglas, Archibald A. H. "Foreword" to *The Bruce. An Epic Poem Written around the Year A.D. 1375 by John Barbour, Archdeacon of Aberdeen.* Glasgow: William MacLellan, 1964.

Dowden, Edward. *Southey.* New York and London: Harper, n.d.

Dryden, John. *A Selection of His Finest Works.* Keith Walker, ed. Oxford: Oxford University Press, 1994,

Dryden, John, trans. *The Works of Virgil in English.* Vol. 5: *Ecologues, Georgics.* Berkeley: University of California Press, 1979.

Dudley, D. R., and D. M. Lang, eds. *The Penguin Companion to Literature: Classical and Byzantine, Oriental and African Literature.* Harmondsworth, Middlesex: Penguin Books, 1969.

Dundas, Judith. *The Spider and the Bee: The Artistry of Spenser's Faerie Queene.* Urbana: University of Illinois Press, 1985.

Durant, Will. *The Story of Civilization.* Part V: *The Renaissance.* New York: M. J. F. Books, 1953; renewed 1981.

Durant, Will, and Ariel Durant. *The Story of Civilization.* Part IX: *The Age of Voltaire.* New York: Simon & Schuster, 1965.

Dvornik, Francis. *The Slavs in European History and Civilization.* New Brunswick, NJ: Rutgers University Press, 1962.

Elton, Oliver. *A Survey of English Literature 1830–1880.* London: Edward Arnold, 1920.

Embree, Ainslie T., ed. *Sources of Indian Tradition.* Vol. 1: *From the Beginning to 1800.* New York: Columbia University Press, 1988.

Encyclopedia Britannica. 15th ed. Chicago: Encyclopedia Britannica, Inc. 1983.

*Encyclopedia of Traditional Epic*s by Guida M. Jackson. Santa Barbara, CA: ABC-CLIO, 1994.

Ercilla, Alonso de. *The Araucaniad.* P. T. Manchester and C. N. Lancaster, trans. Nashville, TN: Vanderbilt University Press, 1945.

Erdoes, Richard, and Alfonso Ortiz, eds. *American Indian Myths and Legends.* New York: Pantheon Books, 1984.

Evans, Bergen. *Dictionary of Mythology. Mainly Classical.* Lincoln, NE: Centennial Press, 1970.

Falk, Signe Lenea. *Archibald MacLeish.* New York: Twayne, 1965.

Faulkner, Peter. *Against the Age. An Introduction to William Morris.* London: Allen & Unwin, 1980.

Faust, A. B. *Oberon. A Poetical Romance in Twelve Books. Translated from the German of Wieland (1799–1801) by John Quincy Adams.* New York: F. S. Crofts, 1940.

Fixler, Michael. *Milton and the Kingdom of God.* Evanston, IL: Northwestern University Press, 1964.

Fleming, Margaret. *Teaching the Epic.* Urbana, IL: National Council of Teachers of English, 1974.

Ford, Arthur L. *Joel Barlow.* New York: Twayne, 1971.

Frye, Northrop. *Fearful Symmetry. A Study of William Blake.* Princeton, NJ: Princeton University Press, 1947.

———. *The Return of Eden.* Toronto: University of Toronto Press, 1965.

Garcilaso de la Vega, El Inca. *Royal Commentaries of the Incas and General History of Peru.* Harold V. Livermore, trans. Austin: University of Texas Press, 1966.

Garland, Henry, and Mary Garland. *The Oxford Companion to German Literature.* 2nd ed. Oxford: Oxford University Press, 1986.

Gazi, Stephen. *A History of Croatia.* New York: Philosophical Library, 1973.

Gibbon, Edward. *The Decline and Fall of the Roman Empire in Three Volumes.* New York: The Modern Library/Random House, n.d.

Gillis, M. M., trans. *The Argonautica of Apollonius Rhodius.* Cambridge: Cambridge University Press, 1928.

Goethe, Johann Wolfgang von. *The Collected Works.* Vol. 8: *Verse Plays and Epic.* Cyrus Hamlin and Frank Ryder, eds. Princeton, NJ: Princeton University Press, 1995.

Goodrich, Norma Lorre. *The Medieval Myths.* New York: NAL/Mentor Books, 1961.

Grant, Richard B. *The Perilous Quest. Image, Myth, and Prophecy in the Narratives of Victor Hugo.* Durham, NC: Duke University Press, 1968.

Grebanier, Bernard D., et al., comps. *English Literature and Its Backgrounds.* Vol II. *From The Forerunners of Romanticism to the Present.* New York: Holt, Rinehart, & Winston, 1949.

Haller, William. *The Early Life of Robert Southey. 1773–1803.* New York: Octagon Books, 1966.

Hamilton, Edith. *Mythology.* New York: New American Library, 1940.

Hammond, George P. *Don Juan de Oñate and the Founding of New Mexico.* Santa Fe: University of New Mexico Press, 1927.

Hammond, N. G. L. *A History of Greece to 322 B.C.* Oxford: Oxford University Press, 1959.

Hanning, Robert, and Joan Ferrante, trans. *The Laís of Maríe de France.* Durham, NC: Labyrinth Press, 1978.

Harrison, Robert Pogue. *Forests. The Shadow of Civilization.* Chicago: University of Chicago Press, 1992.

Hartmann von Aue. *Erec.* Michael Resler, trans. Philadelphia: University of Pennsylvania Press, 1987.

Harvey, Sir Paul, and J. E. Heseltine, comps. *The Oxford Companion to French Literature*. Oxford: Oxford University Press, 1959.

Hatto, A. T., trans. *The Nibelungenlied*. Harmondsworth, Middlesex: Penguin Books, 1969.

Hawkridge, Emma. *Indian Gods and Kings*. Freeport, NY: Books for Libraries Press, 1968.

Hayes, Francis. *Lope de Vega*. New York: Twayne, 1967.

Hayward, Max. *Writers in Russia: 1917–1978*. New York and Orlando: Harcourt Brace Jovanovich, Publishers, 1983/1984.

Heale, Elizabeth. *The Faerie Queene. A Reader's Guide*. Cambridge: Cambridge University Press, 1987.

Heine, Heinrich. *Prose and Poetry*. Intro by Ernest Rhep. London: J. M. Dent, 1966.

Hernández, José. *The Gaucho Martín Fierro*. Frank G. Carrino, Alberto J. Sarlos, and Norman Mangouni, trans. Albany: State University of New York Press, 1936, 1974.

Hibbard, Addison, ed. *Writers of the Western World*. Cambridge: Riverside Press, 1942.

Hichens, William, and Mbarak bin Hinawy, trans. *Al-Inkishagi: The Soul's Awakening*. Nairobi: Oxford University Press, 1972.

Highet, Gilbert. *The Anatomy of Satire*. Princeton, NJ: Princeton University Press, 1962.

———. *The Classical Tradition. Greek and Roman Influence on Western Literature*. Oxford and New York: Oxford University Press, 1976.

Hikmet, Nazim. *The Epic of Sheik Bedreddin and Other Poems*. Randy Blasing and Mutlu Konuk, trans. New York: Persea Books, 1977.

Hubert, Henri. *The Greatness and Decline of the Celts*. M. R. Dobie, trans. New York: Arno Press, 1980.

———. *Human Landscapes*. Randy Blasing and Mutlu Konuk, trans. New York: Persea Books, 1982.

Hill, W. Douglas, P., trans. *The Holy Lake of the Acts of Rama. An English Translation of Tulsī Dās's Rāmacaritamānasa*. London: Oxford University Press, 1952.

Holbrook, Sara. *Sir Tristan of All Time*. New York: Farrar, Straus & Giroux, 1970.

Hornstein, Lillian Herlands, et al., eds., *The Reader's Companion to World Literature*. New York: Mentor Books, 1973.

Howatson, M. C., and Ian Chilvers, eds. *The Concise Oxford Companion to Classical Literature*. Oxford: Oxford University Press, 1993.

Hugo, Victor. *La Légende des Siècles.* G. F. Bridge, trans. Oxford: Clarendon Press, 1907.

Hulpach, Vladimir, Emanuel Frynta, and Václav Cibula. *Heroes of Folk Tale and Legend.* London: Paul Hamlyn, 1970.

Jackson, Guida M. *Encyclopedia of Traditional Epics.* Santa Barbara, CA: ABC-CLIO, 1994.

Jinasena. *Mahāpurāṇa.* P. Jain, trans. Banares, India: Chowkhamba Sanskrit Series Office, Government Sanskrit Library, 1951.

Johnston, Charles, trans. *Narrative Poems by Alexander Pushkin and by Mikhail Lermontov.* New York: Random House, 1983.

Jones, Willis Knapp, ed. *Spanish-American Literature in Translation in 2 Volumes.* New York: Frederick Ungar, 1966.

Jordan, Hoover H. *Bolt Upright. The Life of Thomas Moore.* Salzburg, Austria: Institut für Englishe Sprache und Literatur, Universität Salzburg, 1975.

Josephson, Matthew. *Victor Hugo.* Garden City, NY: Doubleday Doran, 1942.

Kālidāsa. *Kumārasambhava.* With commentary of Mallinātha (1–8) and Sitārāma (9–17). Bombay: Nirnayasagara Press, 1955.

Kazantzakís, Helen. *Nikos Kazantzakís: A Biography.* Berkeley, CA: Creative Arts Book Co., 1968.

Kazantzakís, Nikos. *The Odyssey, A Modern Sequel.* Kimon Friar, trans. New York: Simon & Schuster, 1958.

Kenner, Hugh. *The Pound Era.* Berkeley: University of California Press, 1972.

Ker, W. P. *The Art of Poetry.* Freeport, NY: Books for Libraries Press, 1967.

———. *Epic and Romance.* New York: Macmillan, 1980.

Kingsley, James, ed. *The Poems of John Dryden.* Oxford: Oxford University Press, 1958.

Kipling, Rudyard. *From Sea to Sea. Letters of Travel.* New York: Doubleday Pages, 1907.

Klaniczay, Tíbor, and H. H. Remak, eds. *A History of Hungarian Literature.* New York: Harper & Row, 1986.

Knappert, Jan. *Epic Poetry in Swahili and Other African Languages.* Leiden: J. Brill, 1983.

———. *Four Centuries of Swahili Verse.* London: Heinemann, 1979.

Koster, Joseph, ed. *Putnam Concise Mythological Dictionary.* New York: Capricorn Books, 1964.

Kritzeck, James, ed. *An Anthology of Islamic Literature.* New York: Penguin Books, 1964.

Kunitz, Stanley, and Howard Haycroft, comps. *British Authors of the Nineteenth Century.* New York: H. W. Wilson, 1936.

Kuntsman, H. *Denkmäler der alttschechischen Literatur von ihren Anfängen bis zur Hussitenbewegung.* Berlin: University of Berlin, 1955.

Langland, William. *Piers Plowman.* E. Talbot Donaldson, trans. New York: W. W. Norton, 1990.

Laylor, Chi Chi. *Kingdon of the Leopand, An Epic of Old Benin.* Spring, TX: Counterpoint/Touchstone Press, 1995.

Lee, Peter H., ed. *Anthology of Korean Literature from Early Times to the Nineteenth Century.* Honolulu: University of Hawaii Press, 1981.

Leonard, Irving A. *Books of the Brave.* Berkeley: University of California Press, 1967.

Levy, Reuben, trans. *The Epic of Kings. Shāh-Nāma.* Chicago: University of Chicago Press, 1967.

Lewis, C. S. *The Allegory of Love. A Study in Medieval Tradition.* Oxford: Oxford University Press, 1936.

———. *A Preface to Paradise Lost.* Oxford: Oxford University Press, 1942.

Lewis, Oscar, comp. *The Autobiography of the West.* New York: Henry Holt, 1958.

Lieber, J., and M. M. Williams, eds. *Great Stories of All Nations.* New York: Coward-McCann, Inc., 1927.

Lienhardt, P., trans. *The Medicine Man of Hazani bin Ismail.* Oxford: Oxford University Press, 1968.

Longfellow, Henry Wadsworth. *Evangeline.* New York: Thomas Y. Crowell, 1893.

Lucan. *Pharsalia. The Civil War.* Douglas Little, trans. Dunedin, New Zealand: University of Otago Press, 1989.

McCoy, Bernadette Marie, trans. *The Book of Theseus. Teseida delle Nozze d'Emilia by Giovanni Boccaccio.* New York: Medieval Text Association, 1974.

Mackail, J. W. *The Life of William Morris.* New York and London: Benjamin Bloom, 1968.

Magill, Frank N., ed. *Magill's Survey of World Literature.* New York and London: Marshall Cavendish, 1993.

———. *Masterpieces of Latino Literature.* New York: HarperCollins, 1994.

———. *Masterpieces of World Literature.* New York: HarperCollins, 1989.

Marquis Who's Who in the World. 13th ed. New Providence, NJ: Reed Reference Publishing, 1995.

Martz, Louis L. *The Paradise Within.* New Haven, CT, and London: Yale University Press, 1964.

Matarasso, P. M., trans. *The Quest of the Holy Grail*. Harmondsworth, Middlesex: Penguin Classics, 1969.

Mavrogordato, John. *The Erotokoritos*. London: Oxford University Press, 1929.

Meister, Michael W., ed. *Discourses on Śiva*. Philadelphia: University of Pennsylvania Press, 1984.

Merwin, W. S., trans. *Poem of El Cid*. New York: NAL/Mentor, 1962.

Miller, Barbara Stoler, trans. *Love Song of the Dark Lord: Jayadeva's Gitagovinda*. New York: Columbia University Press, 1977.

Miłosz, Czeslaw. *The History of Polish Literature*. Berkeley: University of California Press, 1969/1983.

Milton, John. *Paradise Lost and Paradise Regained*. Christopher Ricks, ed. New York: Signet Classic/Penguin, 1968.

Mitchell, Stephen. *Anatolia, Land, Men, and Gods in Asia Minor. Vol. I: The Celts in Anatolia and the Impact of Roman Rule*. Oxford: Clarendon Press, 1993.

Mock, Maynard. *Alexander Pope: A Life*. New York: W. W. Norton, 1969.

Mooney, James. *The Ghost-Dance Religion and the Sioux Outbreak of 1890*. Chicago and London: University of Chicago Press, 1965.

Morrison, George, trans. *Vis and Ramin*. New York: Columbia University Press, 1972.

Moyne, John, and Coleman Barks, trans. *Open Secret. Versions of Rumi*. Putney, VT: Threshold Books, 1984.

Mozley, J. H., trans. *Statius. Complete Works*. Cambridge: Loeb Classical Library, 1928.

Murphy, S. J., and G. Ronald, trans. *The Heliand: The Saxon Gospel*. New York and Oxford: Oxford University Press, 1992.

Musa, Mark, trans. *Dante's Vita Nuova*. Bloomington: Indiana University Press, 1973.

Myers, Alan, ed. trans., and Joseph Brodsky, foreword and biog. notes. *An Age Ago. A Selection of Nineteenth Century Russian Poetry*. New York: Farrar, Straus, & Giroux, 1988.

Nash, Ralph, trans. *Jerusalem Delivered. Torquato Tasso*. Detroit: Wayne State University Press, 1987.

Nelson, John Charles, trans. *Torquato Tasso. Jerusalem Delivered*. New York: Capricorn Books, n.d.

Neruda, Pablo. *Canto General*. Jack Schmitt, trans. Berkeley: University of California Press, 1991.

Nizāmī. *Haft Paykar*. Julia Scott Meisami, trans. Oxford and New York: Oxford University Press, 1995.

Nonnos. *Dionysiaca.* H. J. Rose, trans. Cambridge, MA: Loeb Classical Library, Harvard University Press, 1962.

Noyes, Alfred. *William Morris.* New York: Benjamin Bloom, 1971.

O'Flaherty, Wendy Doniger, trans. *Hindu Myths.* Harmondsworth, Middlesex: Penguin Books, 1975.

Olmstead, A. T. *History of the Persian Empire.* Chicago: University of Chicago Press, 1948.

Olson, Charles. *The Maximus Poems.* George F. Butterick, ed. Berkeley: University of California Press, 1983.

Oña, Pedro de. *Arauco domado.* C. N. Lancaster and P. T. Manchester, trans. Albuquerque: University of New Mexico Press, 1948.

Ostrogorsky, George. *History of the Byzantine State.* Rev. ed. New Brunswick, NJ: Rutgers University Press, 1969.

Padgett, Ron, ed. *Handbook of Poetic Forms.* New York: Teachers and Writers Collaborative, 1987.

Palamás, Kostis. *Twelve Words of the Gypsy.* Frederic Will, trans. Lincoln: University of Nebraska Press, 1964.

Parthasarathy, R. trans. *The Tale of an Anklet. The Cilappatikāram of Iḷankō Aṭikaḷ.* New York: Columbia University Press, 1993.

Passage, Charles E. *The Middle High German Poem of Willehalm by Wolfram of Eschenbach.* New York: Frederick Ungar, 1977.

Payne, C. H. *Tod's Annals of Rajasthan. The Annals of Mewar.* London: Routledge & Sons, n.d.

Peña, Carlos González. *History of Mexican Literature.* Gusta Barfield Nance and Florene Johnson Dunstan, trans. Dallas, TX: Southern Methodist University Press, 1968.

Perelman, Bob. *The Trouble with Genius. Reading Pound, Joyce, Stein, and Zukofsky.* Berkeley: University of California Press, 1994.

Pope, Alexander. *The Twickenham Edition of the Poems of Alexander Pope in 11 Volumes.* John Butt, ed. New Haven, CT: Yale University Press, 1939/1967.

Pound, Ezra. *The Cantos.* New York: New Directions, 1970/1991.

Preminger, Alex, et al., eds. *Princeton Encyclopedia of Poetry and Poetics.* Princeton, NJ: Princeton University Press, 1974.

Pushkin, Aleksandr. *The Bronze Horseman.* D. M. Thomas, trans. New York: Viking Press, 1982.

———. *Eugene Onegin.* Charles Johnston, trans. John Bayley, intro. Harmondsworth, Middlesex: Penguin Books, 1979.

———. *Ruslan and Liudmila.* Walter Arndt, trans. Ann Arbor, MI: Ardis, 1974.

Putnam, Samuel. *Marvelous Journey. A Survey of Four Centuries of Brazilian Writing.* New York: Octagon Books, 1948/1971.

Quintus Smyrnaeus. *The Fall of Troy.* Arthur S. Way, trans. Cambridge: Harvard University Press, 1913.

Quirino, Carlos. "Preface" to Mabini's Version. *Florante at Laura.* Manila: National Heroes Commission, 1964.

Raby, F. J. E. *A History of Christian-Latin Poetry from the Beginning to the Close of the Middle Ages.* Oxford: Oxford University Press, 1953.

———. *A History of Secular Latin Poetry in the Middle Ages. 2 vols.* Oxford: Oxford University Press, 1934.

Rennert, Hugo Albert. *The Life of Lope de Vega.* New York: G. E. Stechert, 1937.

Renou, Louis, ed. *Hinduism.* New York: George Braziller, 1961.

Riasanovsky, Nicholas V. *The Emergence of Romanticism.* New York and Oxford: Oxford University Press, 1992.

———. *A History of Russia.* 5th ed. New York and Oxford: Oxford University Press, 1993.

Richardson, Joanna. *Victor Hugo.* New York: St. Martin's Press, 1976.

Rioseco, Arturo Torres, and Juan B. Rael, comps. *Antología escolar de la poesía mexicana.* Guadalajara, Mexico: Editorial Gráfica, 1960.

Rubulis, Aleksis. *Baltic Literature. A Survey of Finnish, Estonian, Latvian, and Lithuanian Literature.* Notre Dame: University of Notre Dame Press, 1970.

Runciman, Steven. *A History of the Crusades.* 3 vols. Vol. II: *The Kingdom of Jerusalem and the Frankish East, 1100–1187.* New York and Cambridge: Cambridge University Press, 1952.

Runes, Dagobert D., comp. *Treasury of World Literature.* New York: Philosophical Library, 1961.

Rustaveli (Rostaveli), Shota. *The Knight in the Panther's Skin.* Venera Urushadze, trans. Tbilisi: Sabchota Sakartvelo, 1968.

———. *The Lord of the Panther-Skin.* R. H. Stevenson, trans. Albany: State University of New York Press, 1977.

Rutherford, Ward. *Celtic Mythology.* Wellingborough, England: Aquarian Press, 1987.

Saʻdī. *The Rose Garden.* Edward B. Eastwick, trans. London: Octagon Press, 1979.

Salmon, Paul. *Literature in Medieval Germany.* New York: Barnes & Noble, 1967.

Serafini-Sauli, Judith Powers. *Giovanni Boccaccio.* Boston: Twayne, 1982.

Shattan, Merchant-Prince. *Manimekhalaï.* Alain Daniélou, trans. New York: New Directions, 1989.

Sherriff, A. G., ed. *Padmāvatī*. Calcutta: Royal Asiatic Society of Bengal, 1944.

Siegel, James, *Shadow and Sound. The Historical Thought of the Sumatran People.* Chicago: University of Chicago Press, 1979.

Siepmann, Katherine Baker, ed. *Benét's Reader's Encyclopedia.* New York: HarperCollins, 1987.

Silius Italicus. *Punica.* J. D. Duff, trans. Cambridge: Harvard University Press, 1968.

Simmons, Ernest J. *Pushkin.* New York: Vintage Books, 1964.

Simmons, Jack. *Southey.* New Haven, CT: Yale University Press, 1948.

Snyder, Franklyn B., and Edward D. Snyder, eds. *A Book of American Literature.* New York: Macmillan, 1935.

Southey, Robert. *The Poems of Robert Southey.* Maurice H. Fitzgerald, ed. London: Oxford University Press, 1909.

Spenser, Edmund. *The Faerie Queene.* Thomas P. Roche, Jr., ed. Harmondsworth, Middlesex: Penguin Books, 1978.

Srivastava, Ashirbadilal. *The History of India* (1000 A.D.–1707 A.D.). Jaipur, Agra, Indore: Shiva Lal Agarwala, 1964.

Statius. *Complete Works in 2 Volumes.* J. H. Mozley, trans. Cambridge: Loeb Classical Library, 1928.

———. *Thebaid.* A. D. Melville, trans. D. W. T. Vessey, intro. Oxford: Oxford University Press, 1992.

Stone, Brian, trans. *Sir Gawain and the Green Knight.* Harmondsworth, Middlesex: Penguin Books, 1959/1974.

Strong, L. A. G. *The Minstrel Boy. A Portrait of Tom Moore.* New York: Alfred A. Knopf, 1937.

Stroud, Parry. *Stephen Vincent Benét.* New York: Twayne, 1962.

Subido, Tarrosa, ed. *Mabini's Version of "Florante at Laura."* Manila: National Heroes Commission, 1964.

Suetonius. *Lives of the Caesars, Lives of Illustrious Men, Grammarians and Rhetoricians and Poets.* Vol. 2. J. C. Rolfe, trans. Cambridge: Loeb Classical Library, Harvard University Press, 1981.

Suny, Ronald Grigor. *The Making of the Georgian Nation.* Bloomington: Indiana University Press, 1988.

Swinburne, Algernon Charles. *A Study of Victor Hugo.* London: Chatto & Windus, n.d.

Sykes, Egerton, *Who's Who in Non-Classical Mythology.* New York: Oxford University Press, 1993.

Tasso, Torquato. *Jerusalem Delivered*. John Charles Nelson, trans. New York: Capricorn Books, n.d.

Tennyson, Lord Alfred. *Idylls of the King*. Harmondsworth, Middlesex: Penguin Books, 1961.

Thapar, Romila. *A History of India*. Vol. 1: *From the Discovery of India to 1526*. Harmondsworth, Middlesex: Penguin Books, 1966/1987.

Thomas, J. W. *Eilhart von Oberg's Tristrant*. Lincoln and London: University of Nebraska Press, 1978.

Thompson, Paul, ed. *The Works of William Morris*. New York: Viking Press, 1967.

Tillyard, E. M. W. *The English Epic and Its Background*. New York: Barnes & Noble, 1993.

———. *The Miltonic Setting, Past and Present*. Cambridge: Cambridge University Press, 1938.

Torres-Rioseco, Arturo, and Juan B. Rael. *Antologia escolar de la poesía mexicana*. Guadalajara, Mexico: Editorial Gráfica, 1960.

Trypanis, C. A. *Greek Poetry. From Homer to Seferis*. Chicago: University of Chicago Press, 1981.

Tulsīdās. *Rāmacaritamāmasa*. Yādava Shamkara Jāmadāra, ed. Poona, India: Vadyakapatrikā Press, 1913.

Turco, Lewis. *The New Book of Forms. A Handbook of Poetics*. Hanover, NH: University of New England, 1986.

Turner, Winifred, and Helen Scott. *The Story of Sigurd the Volsung*. London: Longmans, Green, 1914.

Turville-Petre, E. O. G. *Myth and Religion of the North. The Religion of Ancient Scandinavia*. Westport, CT: Greenwood Press, 1964.

Untermeyer, Louis. *Heinrich Heine: Paradox and Poet*. Vol. I: *The Life*. New York: Harcourt, Brace, 1937.

Van Abbé, Derek Maurice. *Cristoph Martin Wieland (1733–1813). A Literary Biography*. London: George G. Harrap, 1961.

Van Buitenen, J. A. B., trans. *Tales of Ancient India*. Chicago: University of Chicago Press, 1959.

Voltaire. *Works*. 44 Volumes in 22. New York, 1927.

Walcott, Derek. *Omeros*. New York: Noonday Press; Farrar, Straus & Giroux, 1990.

Waley, Adolf. *A Pageant of India*. London: Constable, 1927.

Walker, Hugh. *The Literature of the Victorian Era*. Cambridge: Cambridge University Press, 1931.

Walker, Jeffrey. *Bardic Ethos and the American Epic Poem: Whitman, Pound, Crane, Williams, Olson.* Baton Rouge: Louisiana State University Press, 1989.

Walshe, M. O'C. *Medieval German Literature. A Survey.* Cambridge: Harvard University Press, 1962.

Watts, A. E., trans. *The Metamorphoses of Ovid, An English Version.* San Francisco: North Point Press, 1980.

Wender, Dorothea, trans. and intro. *Hesiod and Theogonis.* Harmondsworth, Middlesex: Penguin Books, 1973.

Whitman, Walt. *Leaves of Grass, the First (1835) Edition.* New York: Penguin Books USA, 1959.

Whitney, Blair. *John G. Neihardt.* Boston: Twayne, 1976.

Wilkins, Ernest H. *Life of Petrarch.* Cambridge: Harvard University Press, 1961.

Williams, William Carlos. *The Autobiography of William Carlos Williams.* New York: New Directions, 1967.

———. *Paterson.* New York: New Directions, 1992.

Wolfram von Eschenbach. *Parzival.* A. T. Hatto, trans. Harmondsworth, Middlesex: Penguin Books, 1980.

———. *Titurel.* Charles E. Passage, trans. New York: Frederick Ungar, 1984.

Woodress, James. *A Yankee's Odyssey. The Life of Joel Barlow.* New York: Greenwood Press, 1958.

Wright, F. A. *A History of Later Greek Literature from the Death of Alexander in 323 B.C. to the Death of Justinian in 565 A.D.* New York: Macmillan, 1932.

Wright, W. C. *A Short History of Greek Literature from Homer to Julian.* New York: American Book Co., 1907.

Yohannan, John D., ed. *A Treasury of Asian Literature.* New York: NAL/ Mentor/Day, 1956/1958.

Zimmerman, J. E. *Dictionary of Classical Mythology.* New York: Harper & Row, 1961.

Zukofsky, Louis. *"A."* Berkeley: University of California Press, 1978.

———. *Autobiography.* New York: Grossman, 1970.

Journals

Research in African Literatures. Vol. 7 (Spring). University of Texas Press, 1976.

Research in African Literatures. Vol. 22, no. 2. Indiana University Press, with Ohio State University, 1991.

Research in African Literatures. Vol. 22, no. 4. Indiana University Press, with Ohio State University, 1991.

Articles

Anderson, Jervis. "Derek Walcott's Odyssey." *New Yorker* (21 December 1991): 71–79.

Gírard, Albert S. "Structure and Values in Three Swahili Epics." *RAL* 7 (1976): 7–22.

Jeffrey, Francis. "Review of *The Curse of Kehama.*" *Edinburgh Review* 17 (February 1811): 429–265.

Nieman, Lawrence J. "The Nature of the Temptations in *Paradise Regained Books I and II.*" *University Review*—Kansas City 34 (1968): 133–138.

Savage, D. S. "The Americanization of Hart Crane." *Horizon* 5 (May 1942).

Scott, Walter. "Review of *The Curse of Kehama.*" *Quarterly Review* 5 (1811): 40–61.

Shariff, Ibrahim Noor. "The Liyongo Conundrum: Reexamining the Historicity of Swahilis' National Poet-Hero." *RAL* 22:2 (1991): 153–167.

Westley, David. "A Bibliography of African Epic." *RAL* 22:4 (1991): 99–115.

ILLUSTRATION CREDITS

218   Bettmann Archive.

226   Francois Dubois d'Amiens. Museum Arland, Geneva. Bettmann Archive.

239   Corbis-Bettmann.

256   *Capture of John Brown in the Engine-house.* Corbis-Bettmann.

269   Herat, 1494. Or. 6810, f 106v, Oriental and India Office, British Library.

285   Parvati, Consort of Siva, Founders Society Purchase, Sarah Bacon Hill Fund (41.81), Detroit Institute of Arts.

301   Krefeld, early fifteenth century. Corbis-Bettmann.

313   UPI/Bettmann.

319   Engraving after a painting by Galgado. Corbis-Bettmann.

325   UPI/Bettmann.

361   Theodor de Bry KB+1590 [America] Frankfort, 1590, Part V, plate VII. New York Public Library.

371   Bettmann Archive.

447   Foto Marburg/Art Resource, New York.

466   UPI/Bettmann.

473   Illustration by Frank Schoonover. Bettmann Archive.

480   Painting by P. Ulyanov. Bettmann Archive.

492   Andrea del Castagno. Former Convent of Saint Apollonia. S. Apollonia, Florence; Alinari/Art Resource, New York.

509   *Ardashir Battling Bahman, Son of Ardavan.* Detroit Institute of Arts 35.54.

526   Painting by T. Phillips; engraving by S.W. Reynolds, 1822. Corbis-Bettmann.

535   *Tasso at the Court of Ferrara.* Corbis-Bettmann.

554   Louvre. Scala/Art Resource, New York.

570   Ms 61 fr. The Master and Fellows of Corpus Christi College, Cambridge.

564   Museum Conde, Chantilly, France; Giraudon/Art Resource.

572   UPI/Corbis-Bettmann.

582   Photograph by V. Grebnev, APN. Sovfoto/Eastfoto.

590   Reuters/Bettmann.

603   UPI/Bettmann Newsphotos.

608   Vienna Genesis, Byzantium, sixth century, cod. theol. graec, 31, f. 16r. Picture Archive, Austrian National Library, Vienna.

INDEX

Note: Page numbers in **boldface** denote major entry headings.

Ref PN 56 .E65 J33 1996b

Jackson-Laufer, Guida M.

Encyclopedia of literary
epics